California
Real Estate
Law

Fifth Edition

William H Pivar
Robert J. Bruss

Dearborn™
Real Estate Education

This publication is designed to provide accurate and authoritative information in regard to the subject matter covered. It is sold with the understanding that the publisher is not engaged in rendering legal, accounting, or other professional service. If legal advice or other expert assistance is required, the services of a competent professional person should be sought.

Senior Vice President and General Manager: Roy Lipner
Publisher and Director of Distance Learning: Evan M. Butterfield
Managing Editor, Print Products: Louise Benzer
Development Editor: Christopher Oler
Editorial Production Manager: Bryan Samolinski
Senior Typesetter: Janet Schroeder
Creative Director: Lucy Jenkins

Published by Dearborn™ Real Estate Education,
a division of Dearborn Financial Publishing, Inc.®
A Kaplan Professional Company
30 South Wacker Drive
Chicago, Illinois 60606-7481
(312) 836-4400
www.dearbornRE.com

Printed in the United States of America.
  05   10   9   8   7   6   5

Library of Congress Cataloging-in-Publication Data

Pivar, William H. and Robert S. Bruss
    California real estate law / William H. Pivar, Robert J. Bruss. - 5th ed.
      p.cm.
    Includes index.
    ISBN 0-7931-60804
    1. Vendors and purchasers-California. 2. Real estate business-
    Law and legislation-California. 3. Real property-California. I. Title.

KFC169.P58 2003
346.79404'3 21-dc21   99-045983

CONTENTS

ABOUT THE AUTHORS

William H. Pivar

From 1971 to 1994, William Pivar served as Real Estate Coordinator and Professor of Business Education at the College of the Desert, Palm Desert, California. Prior to choosing an academic career, he practiced as a private, corporate, and government attorney specializing in real property.

Pivar is author of more than 30 textbooks and numerous articles and has served as an Arbitrator for the Federal Mediation and Conciliation Service. He holds a bachelor's degree and a law degree from the University of Wisconsin.

His other publications include *Real Estate Ethics, Real Estate Exam Guide, Classified Secrets, Power Real Estate Listing, Power Real Estate Selling, Power Real Estate Negotiation, Power Real Estate Letters,* and *California Real Estate Practice,* all published by Real Estate Education Company®

Robert J. Bruss

For more than 28 years, Robert Bruss has written the weekly syndicated "Real Estate Mailbag" question-and-answer newspaper column, the "Real Estate Notebook" feature on real estate trends, "Real Estate Law and You" articles about new court decisions affecting real estate, and "Real Estate Book Review" features. The Chicago Tribune Media Services Syndicate distributes these features to several hundred newspapers nationwide each week. Many of these recent articles can now be found at www.robert-bruss.com.

Bruss also publishes two monthly real estate newsletters, *The Robert Bruss California Real Estate Law Newsletter* and *The Robert Bruss National Real Estate Newsletter.* He is the author of the books *The Smart Investor's Guide to Real Estate* and *The California Foreclosure Book: How to Earn Big Profits in California Foreclosure and Distressed Properties.*

Originally from Minneapolis, Bruss graduated from Northwestern University School of Business in Evanston, Illinois. He received his Juris Doctor degree from the University of California's Hastings College of the Law in San Francisco. He is a California real estate attorney and licensed real estate broker as well as a lifetime member of the National Association of Real Estate Editors. Bruss teaches Real Estate Law at the College of San Mateo and has taught real estate courses for the University of Southern California's College of Continuing Education.

INTRODUCTION

■ ABOUT THE TEXT

This book is an introduction to the vast body of law that governs real estate transactions in California. It will not, however, qualify you to give legal advice, which would be the unauthorized practice of law. Rather, it will help you recognize situations in which legal counsel should be sought and help you understand rights and obligations under the law. Only by understanding these rights and obligations can you professionally serve and protect the interests of your clients as well as the public.

To aid students and instructors of legal aspects of real estate, the book has been organized to parallel the student guide and the instructor's guide published by the California Community College chancellor's office.

Perhaps the most useful of the pedagogical features in this text are the many **Case Examples** and **Discussion Cases** presented throughout. Case Examples are the author's synopses of actual cases, including the facts, the court's decisions, and some of the reasons for their decisions. These learning aids directly relate to the topics they appear with, illustrating key principles of the discussion.

End-of-chapter Discussion Cases also summarize actual court cases and are relevant to the preceding chapter. However, instead of presenting their final decisions, they pose a question to the reader, prompting individual consideration or classroom discussion. The case results and a short analysis can be found at the Dearborn Financial Publishing Web site at www.dearbornRE.com (click Instructor Resources link, then scroll down to the link entitled **California Real Estate Law 5th Edition**). This link will provide you with the table of contents and case answers to the class discussion chapters for the appropriate text chapters.

The link entitled **California Real Estate Law Cases "Student Resource"** will also provide you with details of cases merely referenced in the text as well as appropriate updated new cases by appropriate chapter.

Each of the 15 chapters of this text opens with a list of **key terms,** alerting readers to important vocabulary words that will be discussed in that chapter. These terms appear in boldface the first time they are introduced in the chapter discussions and are then briefly defined in a **Glossary** that appears at the end of the book.

Every chapter also ends with a **Chapter Quiz,** consisting of multiple-choice questions similar in form, content, and difficulty level to questions found on the California Real Estate Brokers' Examination.

Legal citations are included for both the Case Examples and the Discussion Questions. You might wish to look up cases at one of your county's law libraries. Law libraries that are open to the public generally are located in the buildings housing superior courts.

■ THE FIFTH EDITION

This is the Fifth Edition of **California Real Estate Law,** first published in 1987. In each new edition, we have updated the text with new relevant cases and updates to the discussions spurred by developments in the real estate field and by changes in our laws. We also carefully incorporated the input of many instructors and students concerning ways in which we could better meet their needs.

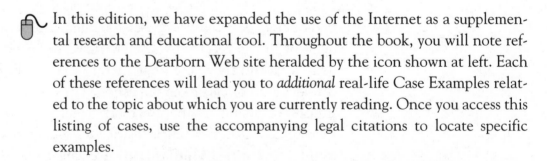 In this edition, we have expanded the use of the Internet as a supplemental research and educational tool. Throughout the book, you will note references to the Dearborn Web site heralded by the icon shown at left. Each of these references will lead you to *additional* real-life Case Examples related to the topic about which you are currently reading. Once you access this listing of cases, use the accompanying legal citations to locate specific examples.

From time to time, we will add *brand new* Case Examples related to this fifth edition of *California Real Estate Law* at www.dearbornRE.com as well. These will be divided by text chapter topic for easier reference. Be sure to check the site periodically, not only as you complete your course but throughout your professional career. These ever-changing case studies will help you stay sharp and up-to-date on recent court decisions affecting California's real estate law.

On the following pages, we also offer guidance on using various search engines to access the massive database that is the Internet. We also list 40 useful Web sites you can use to further broaden your legal research capabilities.

■ LEGAL CITATIONS

A legal citation has three parts: volume, particular set of books, and page. The letter **C.** stands for **California Reports**, which are cases from the California Supreme Court. **C.A.** refers to **California Appellate Reports** from the California appellate courts. Most of the citations listed are from these two sets of law books.

Because of the sheer number of volumes, books have gone into new series, so **2d** means **second series**. A citation 19 C.A. 3d. 468 would mean **Volume 19** of the **3rd Series** of **California Appellate Reports,** and the case cited would be on **page 468**.

Besides separate state reporters of appellate and supreme court cases, there are regional reporter series covering state Supreme Court cases from a number of states. Examples are the **Atlantic Reporter,** shown by the letter **A,** and the **Pacific Reporter**, shown by **P.** California cases are in the Pacific Reporter.

Federal district court cases are reported in **The Federal Supplement** series and are shown as **F. Supp.** Federal appellate court cases are reported in the **Federal Reporter,** shown as **F.,** or **Second Series**, shown as **F. 2d.**

U.S. Supreme Court cases are found in **United States Reports**, indicated by **U.S.,** or **Lawyers Edition Second Series**, shown as <u>**L.Ed.2d.**</u>

The majority of statutes relating to activities in real estate are contained in one inexpensive volume entitled **Real Estate Law**, which is published by the California Department of Real Estate and is available through many college bookstores or directly from the Department of Real Estate.

Laws are not static. Besides annual changes in the statutes that create new law, court decisions can change duties and responsibilities under existing statutes. The changing nature of laws requires that a real estate agent keep current with these changes through professional papers and magazines, seminars, and continuing education. It is hoped that this book will be just one step in your continuing program of professional training.

■ USING THE INTERNET

The Internet can be an important tool for the real estate professional. It has applications toward all aspects of real estate, including the law, and its usefulness can be expected to increase significantly in the future.

Search engines are Internet sites that enable a computer user to find information by typing a word or combination of words. They search what is currently 800 million pages containing 6 trillion characters. The growth of the database has resulted in searches that cover just a fraction of the available data. The average search engine covers only about one-sixth of Internet pages.

Assume you wanted information about a tenant's right to claim constructive eviction in order to be released from lease obligations. Using a search engine such as hotbot.com, if you searched Californiarealestatelaw you would find thousands of references, too many to make a meaningful search. If you used Californiarealestatelaw/landlord/tenant you would reduce the number of sites to several hundred. Defining your interest by using California real estate law/constructive eviction would reduce your search to a manageable number of matches. Use of additional search engines would give you a number of additional sites. Some additional search engines are Northernlight, excite, snap, altavista, infoseek, microsoft, google, yahoo, and dialer.

The following Internet sites will help meet your legal research needs:

www.callaw.com

A daily briefing on California law and California courts.

www.calrealestatelaw.com

This site, which has an annual fee of $24.95, provides online legal update service including case summaries, laws, current issues, etc.

www.car.org

California Association of **REALTORS**® Web site, real estate legal news, proposed laws, CAR opinions, lots more.

www.ceres.ca.gov

This information site developed by the California Resource Agency includes a database containing California environmental law and links to federal law.

www.dre.ca.gov

California real estate salesperson and broker license status, how to get a real estate license, and lots of other valuable material.

www.epa.gov

The Environmental Protection Agency site provides information on programs and laws.

www.fairhousing.com

The site of the National Fair Housing Advocate offers information on housing discrimination issues.

www.fanniemae.com

This site of the Federal National Mortgage Association (now renamed Fannie Mae) includes information on FNMA-owned properties, FNMA services, and mortgage-backed securities.

www.fastsearch.com/law

The Web's premier law and legal research page. Court decisions, state laws, newspapers, law school libraries—this site is great!

www.fedstats.gov

Access is provided to statistics prepared by various federal agencies.

www.fema.gov

This site provides information on FEMA programs including National Flood Insurance.

www.findlaw.com

Lots of links to cases, statutes, lawyers, law schools, subjects, directories, U.S. Supreme Court opinions since 1893, and endless resources. One of the best Web sites. www.findlaw.com/cacases is devoted to California cases.

www.freddiemac.com

This is the site of the Federal Home Loan Mortgage Corporation (now renamed Freddie Mac). Includes information on mortgage-backed securities and services.

www.ftb.ca.gov/forms/index.htm

California state income tax forms back to 1994.

www.ginniemae.com

Site of the Government National Mortgage Association (now renamed Ginnie Mae), this site includes information on mortgage-backed securities and GNMA services.

www.gksoft.com/govt/en/

Through this database you can link to any U.S. government agency.

www.hud.gov

This site offers information on HUD programs.

www.inman.com

Most complete source of up-to-the-minute real estate news. This site is linked to www.bobbruss.com, which includes a featured weekly real estate article.

www.ired.com

A must! Directory of 25,000 real estate Web sites. *International Real Estate Digest*. Click on Law and Legal. This real estate directory offers links to bulletin boards on a wide range of subjects.

www.irs.ustreas.gov/prod/forms_pubs/inidex.html

Federal income tax forms back to 1992.

www.law.cornell.edu/topics/

Lots of information on federal and state mortgage law and court decisions.

www.lawforum.net

This site can help you locate law firms in your area with real estate specialties.

www.lawnewsnetwork.com

Up-to-date legal news from the *National Law Journal*.

www.leginfo.ca.gov

This State of California Web site includes an index of all of California's statutory law. Search by key word.

www.ss.ca.gov

Secretary of State site for information on the Uniform Commercial Code, tax liens, limited partnerships, and limited liability company and corporate records.

www.boe.ca.gov

Board of Equalization site for sales tax registrations.

http://secure.dre.ca.gov/publicasp/pplinfo.asp

Information site as to real estate licensing.

www.courtinfo.ca.gov/opinions

California Supreme Court and appellate court listings.

www.martindale.com

Directory of lawyers, who's who in American law. Click on lawyers.com to locate a nearby real estate attorney.

www.napalaw.com

This site provides updates, alerts, and new case laws. It also links to other applicable sites.

www.nareb@aol.org

The National Association of Real Estate Brokers site offers research information as well as educational and certification programs.

www.nolo.com

Great self-help law center, even lawyer jokes. Click on the legal encyclopedia for great real estate law information.

www.nsc.org

The National Safety Council site offers information on environmental hazards (lead poisoning).

www.realtimes.com

Real estate consumer and industry news presented in a lively format. Late developments on legal aspects from a consumer view.

www.realtor.com

Lots of information for real estate agents, home buyers and sellers, legal questions and answers, and much more. One of the most complete real estate Web sites.

www.relibrary.com

Click the legal and professional page. Lots of forms, articles, case histories, and legal journals in the legal library.

www.reprofile.com

Commercial real estate news, real estate legislation, real estate law, and tracking of proposed California statutes.

www.va.gov

The information site on VA programs.

www.westlaw.com

More than 10,000 databases of statutes, cases, and public records; some material is free, other material is fee based.

Note: While the Internet is an extremely valuable tool for obtaining information, do not confuse information with legal advice. For the applicability of information to specific situations, you should consider obtaining the services of an attorney.

Members of the California Association of **REALTORS®** (CAR) can obtain advice from CAR's legal staff by calling (213) 739-8282 (Monday through Friday, 9 A.M. to 6 P.M.).

CAR members can be provided late-breaking legal information by e-mail through REALEGALTM, a broadcast e-mail service.

ACKNOWEDGMENTS

The authors wish to acknowledge the many attorneys, educators, and other professionals who have responded to our user survey, as well as the following reviewers who contributed so much thought and effort to our book:

Steven Johnson
Old Republic Title Company
Redwood City

Paul Hammann
First American Title Company
Santa Ana

Michael Bury
Butte Community College

Michael Botello
El Camino College

Bruce Gold
Orange Coast College

Ignacio Gonzalez
Mendocino Community College

James Lawson
The Real Estate School
Woodland

Marc B. Robinson
Hartmann & Robinson LLP
Stockton

John Smylie
Palomar Community College

We would also like to recognize those who helped with past editions of California Real Estate Law.

David J. Deka, J.D.
Dearborn/Anthony Schools

Ed Estes, Jr.
Palomar College

Michael C. Glazer
Ivy Tech State College

Bruce Gold
Orange Coast College

Gerald Haight
Modesto Junior College

Don Kalal
California Broker's Institute

Robert R. Keeling
Sacramento City College

Alan R. Klofkorn
Irvine Valley College

Meldy Langager
Diablo Valley College

James F. Miller, Esq.
University of Southern California

Michael A. Olden
Diablo Valley College

Robert J. Pacheco
Crofton Hills College

Bobra G. Tahan
Dearborn/Anthony Schools

Joe Wood
Evergreen Valley College

Dat Yen
Glendale College,
Los Angeles City College

Frank Zotter, Jr.
Chief Deputy County Counsel,
County of Mendocino

FIGURE 1.1

The Thirteen Federal
Judicial Circuits

CHAPTER ONE

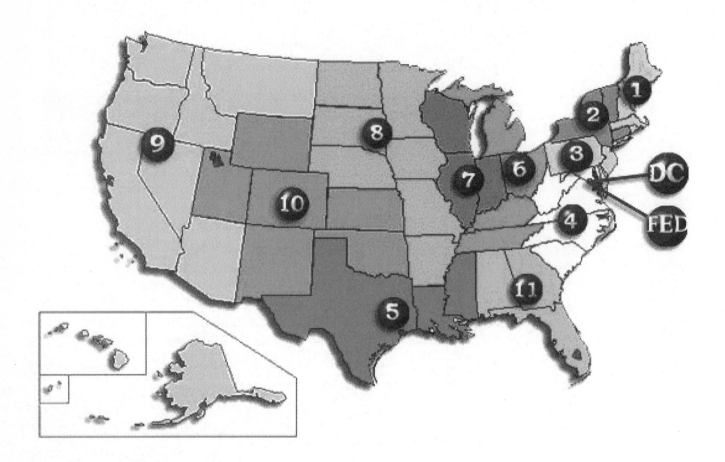

SOURCES OF LAW AND THE JUDICIAL SYSTEM

■ KEY TERMS

administrative agency   Department of Real   quiet title
arbitration   Estate   reformation
civil law   exemplary damages   rescission
common law   foreclosure   specific performance
compensatory damages   injunction   stare decisis
constitutional law   mediation   statutory law
declaratory relief action   nominal damages

■ DEFINITION OF LAW

Law is the body of principles governing our conduct that can be enforced
through our judicial system. Laws serve various purposes, such as protecting the health, safety, morals, and general welfare of the citizens; protecting the state; protecting property; and achieving equity or justice. Every
civilization has realized the necessity for laws, for without the guidance of
laws there would be chaos.

The law is not static. It reflects the views of our society, and as our views change, so do our laws. Because law is in a constant state of evolution, it is not always possible to predict the outcome of a dispute. A slight difference in facts can affect the outcome, as can current trends in opinion and even the philosophy of the court where a case is being heard. Courts will often differ regarding interpretations of the law and rights under the law.

■ INFLUENCES ON OUR LEGAL SYSTEM

English Influence

Most of the basic precepts of our real estate law as well as our legal vocabulary have evolved from English common law. Establishment of a centralized court system at the time of the Norman Conquest (A.D. 1066) made precedent, or previous decisions, the basis for judging disputes. This reliance on previous decisions is known as **stare decisis**. Thereafter a body of judge-made law developed. While judges already had been able to differentiate among situations, reliance on previous decisions gave the legal system stability, because laws were now more likely to be changed by slight degree than by radical departure from the past. The precepts developed by the courts became known as the **common law**.

The rigid system imposed on the courts by previous decisions often, however, resulted in injustice. In addition, the courts of common law had to wait until a wrong had been committed to make a decision. People would petition the king for special relief, which at times would be granted. This led to the establishment of a second court system, known as *courts of equity* (chancellory court), which could offer remedies based on what was just and equitable rather than solely on the decisions of the past.

Because of the large number of court decisions, attorneys seldom have a problem finding precedent for conflicting views. State courts rely most heavily on the most recent decisions of higher courts within their own state system. They also consider court decisions from other states, especially sister states and states with similar laws, as well as cases decided through the federal court system. Previous decisions of particular courts, and even particular justices, can influence decisions.

Case decisions might differ among California or federal courts. Conflicts of law can exist until they are clarified by a higher court. For example, a U.S. Supreme Court decision would clarify conflicts between two U.S. courts of appeals decisions. Federal district courts place the greatest emphasis on appellate decisions of their own appellate circuit (the court of appeals that would rule on any appeal from that court). Similarly, California superior courts place the greatest emphasis on appellate decisions of their own appellate court.

Often the decisions of an individual state's courts exhibit a particular trend that characterizes that court system over the years. California courts have been leaders in favoring consumer rights. Throughout this book, the case studies indicate our courts' contribution to expanding consumer protection.

Roman Influence

In the United States we follow the Roman system of Civil law. **Civil law** refers to laws enacted by legislative bodies and codified as statutes. Our courts interpret the laws. We have merged the functions of the English common-law courts and the courts of equity into a single system in which judges may follow previous decisions but are not bound to them and have both legal and equitable remedies at their disposal. Case law really serves to define and at times modify our statutes. It aids in defining the law under specific fact situations.

Spanish Influence

The Treaty of Guadalupe Hidalgo (1848) ended the Mexican War, resulting in California's becoming part of the United States. Under this treaty the United States agreed to recognize the property rights of Mexican citizens. This agreement represented more than just recognizing title to property, however. It also made California a community property state. Mexico had adopted from Spain the concept of community property, in which property acquired during marriage is owned equally by husband and wife. (See Chapter 8 for details on community property rights.)

■ CONSTITUTIONAL AND STATUTORY LAW

All levels of government (federal, state, and local) enact legislation affecting real property. Law set forth in federal or state constitutions, or **constitutional law**, is distinguished from law based on enacted statutes, or **statutory law**.

Figure 1.2 illustrates the sources of California real estate law.

Federal

U.S. Constitution. The original 13 states granted power to our federal government through the U.S. Constitution. The states reserved to themselves all powers not granted to the federal government. The Constitution is the supreme law of the land, and all legislation enacted at any level must conform to it.

Parts of the Constitution of particular importance to real estate law include the following amendments.

First Amendment (Rights of Free Speech). This amendment protects the right to place For Sale signs on property as well as to advertise real estate.

FIGURE 1.2

Sources of California
Real Estate Law

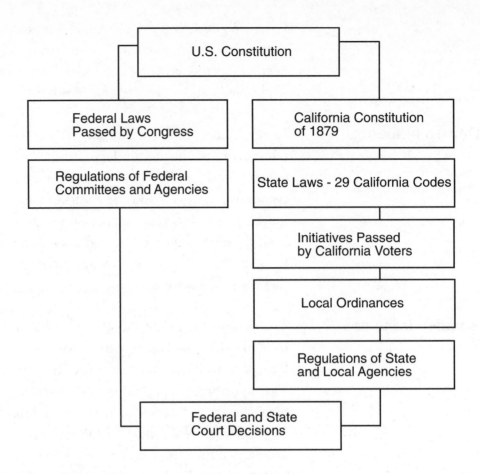

Case Study

The case of *Greater Baltimore Board of REALTORS® v. Baltimore County* (1990) 752 F. Supp. 193 involved a county statute barring real estate agents from door-to-door or telephone solicitations for listings. The county claimed the law was necessary to stop blockbusting. The court held that the First Amendment of the U.S. Constitution protects commercial speech from unwarranted governmental regulation. Although the purpose of the law was allegedly to prevent blockbusting, the prohibition was too broad to serve its intended purpose and was therefore an unconstitutional prohibition of commercial free speech.

Case Study

The case of *Robins v. Pruneyard Shopping Center* (1979) 23 C.3d 899 involved a plaintiff who had set up a card table in a corner of a courtyard at a shopping center to collect petition signatures. The activity violated policies of the shopping center, and the plaintiff was required to leave. The California Supreme Court held that the speech and petition provisions of the California State Constitution protect speech and petitioning reasonably exercised, even in privately owned shopping centers. The court noted that

(continued on next page)

shopping centers have supplanted the town square as a meeting place where free speech can be exercised. The court held that where rights of individual property owners conflict with the interests of society, individual interests must be subordinated. However, reasonable rules can be imposed by the shopping center.

Fourth Amendment (Security from Unwarranted Search and Seizure). This amendment protects private property from unreasonable searches and seizures. Search warrants will be issued only on the basis of probable cause.

Fifth Amendment (Rights of Accused). This amendment states that an accused shall not "be deprived of life, liberty, or property, without due process of law." Before property can be taken away from its owner, that person must be given his or her day in court. The Fifth Amendment also prohibits the taking of private property for public use without just compensation and in effect gives the government the power to condemn private property for public use upon payment of just compensation (called the *power of eminent domain*). The Fourteenth Amendment makes the Fifth Amendment applicable to the states.

Tenth Amendment (Powers Reserved for States). This amendment allows the states all powers not delegated to the federal government or prohibited to the states. The states are empowered to enact legislation under this amendment. (The U.S. Constitution determines when the states do not have authority.)

Thirteenth Amendment (Abolishment of Slavery). This amendment has been held to be the basis for the Civil Rights Act of 1968.

Fourteenth Amendment (Equal Protection). This amendment makes the Fifth Amendment applicable to the states. It also provided the basis for our antidiscrimination laws.

Case Study

In the case of *Bank of Stockton v. Church of Soldiers of the Cross of Christ* (1996) 44 C.A.4th 1623, the bank obtained an injunction against the Church of Soldiers of the Cross of Christ from soliciting donations from bank customers at the bank entrance on bank property.

(continued on next page)

> The court of appeal ruled that church members could not solicit on the property because it was a modest retail business and not a public place required to allow free speech. The court held that the bank did not have to show interference with its operation to prohibit free speech on the property. The court held that the First Amendment would apply to public forums such as large supermarkets and shopping centers.

Treaties. Federal treaties with other governments and with Native American tribes have affected both the ownership of real property and the rights to use property. For example, treaties that gave Indian tribes special sovereignty over reservation lands have exempted the lands from local land-use control. As previously noted, the Treaty of Guadalupe Hidalgo recognized the property rights of Mexican citizens in the United States. This agreement had a particularly strong impact in California and is the basis of our community property laws.**Federal Statutes.** A number of federal statutes directly affect real property transactions. Federal statutes are diverse, ranging from antidiscrimination measures to consumer and debtor protection. Examples of federal legislation include

- Federal Housing Act, 12 U.S. Code §1701 et seq.;
- Real Estate Settlement Procedures Act, 12 U.S. Code §2601 et seq.;
- Truth-in-Lending Act, 15 U.S. Code §1601 et seq.;
- Equal Credit Opportunity Act, 15 U.S. Code §1691 et seq.;
- Fair Credit Reporting Act, 15 U.S. Code §1681 et seq.;
- Federal Bankruptcy Act, 11 U.S. Code;
- Civil Rights Act of 1968, 18 U.S. Code §241 et seq.;
- Civil Rights Act of 1866, C. 31, 14 Stat. 27;
- Interstate Land Sales Full Disclosure Act, 15 U.S. Code §1701 et seq.;
- Financial Institutions Reform, Recovery and Enforcement Act of 1989 (FIRREA) 18 U.S. Code §1014; and
- Foreign Investment in Real Property Tax Act (FIRPTA), I.R.C. 13455 et seq.

Federal Administrative Agencies. Administrative agencies make rules and regulations to implement our federal laws. While these rules and regulations are not law, they have the force and effect of law. The Department of Housing and Urban Development (HUD) is responsible for enforcing civil rights laws, the Interstate Land Sales Act, and numerous other federal laws. The Federal Trade Commission (FTC) enforces the Truth-in-Lending Act. The Federal Housing Administration (FHA) is involved with real estate loans and subsidized housing. The Environmental Protection Agency (EPA) makes rules and regulations protecting our environment.

Administrative agencies have the power to prohibit action and to impose fines for violations. Each agency conducts its investigation, prosecution, and decision making in administrative hearings. Unlike the courts, the agency is not bound by legal principles of evidence and even can make decisions prior to a hearing.

The right to an attorney supplied by the government or to a jury trial does not apply before an administrative agency. Decisions of administrative agencies can be appealed to the courts, provided all administrative appeals have been exhausted. Courts will overturn administrative agency decisions only if they are found to be arbitrary or capricious.

California

Constitution. While the California State Constitution is the supreme law of California, it is subordinate to the U.S. Constitution. In the event of any conflict, the federal Constitution takes precedence.

California Statutes. The Civil Code contains the fundamental principles of California real estate law, including ownership rights. Additional statutes related to real estate are scattered throughout California's various legal codes, including the Business and Professions Code, Code of Civil Procedure, Corporations Code, Financial Code, Government Code, Labor Code, Penal Code, and Public Resources Code.

Real estate licensing is covered in Sections 1000 through 10581 of the Business and Professions Code. The regulation of real estate licensees is covered in Sections 11000 through 11030 of the Business and Professions Code. The primary purpose of these statutes is to protect the public by regulating those engaged in the real estate business.

California has incorporated English common law in the Civil Code: "The common law of England, so far as it is not repugnant to or inconsistent with the Constitution of the United States, or the constitution or laws of this state, is the rule of decision in all the courts of this state." (Civil Code Section 22.2). In 1939, the California Supreme Court held that where the codes and other statutes are silent, the common law will govern (*In re Patterson's Estate*, 34 C.A.2d 305).

Uniform Codes. Because of a need for conformity in the statutes of various states, the National Conference of Commissioners on Uniform State Laws drafted recommended statutes for adoption by the states. The

Uniform Commercial Code is one of those statutes. Areas covered by the Uniform Commercial Code of particular interest to real estate licensees include the definition of personal property, security interests in personal property, what constitutes a fixture, negotiable instruments, laws governing commercial property, the Bulk Sales Act, and the Statute of Frauds for personal property. There is, however, no uniform code for real property laws, which vary significantly among the states.

State Administrative Agencies. The Office of Real Estate Appraisers in the Business, Transportation, and Housing Agency regulates the licensing and certification of California appraisers. The Department of Corporations regulates California real estate syndicates, franchise sales, and independent escrow agents. The Department of Health is concerned with safety and health standards, including water quality and waste disposal. Other state agencies also have regulations that affect the real estate business and transactions in real property.

Department of Real Estate. The **Department of Real Estate**, which is also included in the Business, Transportation, and Housing Agency, is the primary state agency to administer California real estate law. The department was created by legislative act in 1917 and provided the first law in the United States for the licensing and regulation of real estate agents. These laws became a model for legislation in many other states.

Discipline Procedures. The real estate commissioner, appointed by the governor, is the chief executive officer of the department. The commissioner presides over meetings of the Real Estate Advisory Commission. The commissioner determines administrative policy and enforces the provisions of the real estate law in a manner that provides maximum protection for the purchasers of real property and those persons dealing with real estate licensees.

The real estate commissioner can issue regulations to aid in the administration and enforcement of the law. These regulations, formally known as the *Regulations of the Real Estate Commissioner*, are set forth in Title 10 of the California Code of Regulations starting with Section 2705 and have the force and effect of the law.

When adopting regulations, administrative agencies must follow the procedures set forth in the California Administrative Procedure Act, which include public hearings. To be upheld by the court, administrative regulations must be reasonably necessary to carry out statutes and must not conflict with or exceed the scope of statutes. Individuals have the right to petition the Department of Real Estate to adopt or repeal a regulation. Courts will generally overrule an administrative regulation only if it was enacted without authority, proper procedures were not followed, or the regulation is arbitrary, capricious, or otherwise unreasonable.

The Administrative Procedure Act authorizes the commissioner to hold formal hearings to determine issues involving a licensee, license applicant, or subdivider. After a hearing, the commissioner may suspend, revoke, or deny a license or halt sales in a subdivision. (See Figure 1.3.) A corporation may be disciplined for the action of a corporate broker who was acting on behalf of the corporation.

Actions of the real estate commissioner can be appealed to the courts. The California Supreme Court has held that power to regulate cannot be the arbitrary power to grant or refuse a license. In *Riley v. Chambers* (1919) 181 C. 589, the supreme court held: "While the right to engage in a lawful and useful occupation cannot be taken away under the guise of regulation, such an occupation may be subjected to regulation in the public interest even though such regulation involves in some degree a limitation upon the exercise of the right regulated."

The real estate commissioner does not have the authority to settle commission disputes. These matters are determined through a court of law; through the state labor commissioner, Department of Industrial Relations (for employer-employee disputes); or by arbitration if agreed to by the parties.

City and County Ordinances. Under their police power, cities and counties can enact legislation concerning the use of real property to protect health, safety, morals, and general welfare. Such measures include local building codes, health ordinances, police and fire ordinances, and zoning.

City and County Administrative Agencies. Local agencies also make decisions that affect real property. By law every city and county is charged with the development of a general plan. Local planning agencies not only develop planning but also hear and decide on requests for rezoning. Community redevelopment agencies carry out redevelopment at a local level.

FIGURE 1.3

**License Discipline
Hearing Procedure**

The following is reprinted from the *California DRE Real Estate Bulletin*, summer 1990:

Disciplinary hearings are conducted under the Administrative Procedure Act (Government Code Sections 11500-11528) and are presided over by an administrative law judge who is employed by a state agency independent of the Department of Real Estate. The hearings are conducted in a manner similar to court trials without a jury. At the hearing, the department has the burden of proving the charges contained in the accusation and usually does so by calling witnesses and presenting documents in evidence. The department is represented by its own attorneys at the hearing, and the respondent may be represented by his or her attorney or may proceed without an attorney. There is no provision of law which allows the respondent to be represented by an attorney at state expense similar to the public defender in criminal cases. The respondent has the right to object to evidence offered by the department and to cross-examine witnesses called by the department. The respondent also has the right to present evidence and to call witnesses to testify on his or her behalf.

The document which initiates the process to determine whether a licensee should be formally disciplined is known as an accusation. The accusation sets forth in ordinary and concise language the acts or omissions with which the licensee (referred to as the respondent) is charged.

After the accusation has been filed as a formal document with the department, it must be served on the respondent. Service is effected by personal delivery or by certified mail to the respondent's last known business, residence or mailing address on file with the department. After being served, the respondent has 15 days to file a notice of defense with the department. The notice of defense serves two functions: first, as a formal denial of the charges in the accusation and secondly, as a request for a hearing. A failure to file a notice of defense allows the department to proceed to disciplinary action (usually a license revocation) without hearing.

After a notice of defense is filed, the department asks the Office of Administrative Hearings to schedule a hearing. Depending on the length of time required, the hearing will generally be held from two months to 12 months from the date the notice of defense is filed. The respondent has the right under the discovery provisions of the law to examine evidence in the department's investigative file and to be told the names and addresses of witnesses who may be called.

After the hearing is concluded, the administrative law judge prepares a proposed decision which is sent to the real estate commissioner. The commissioner has three options: adopt the proposed decision as his/her own, reduce the penalty or reject the decision. If rejected, the commissioner must obtain a complete transcript and record of the hearing and issue a decision based on review of the transcript and exhibits.

If an adverse decision is issued by the commissioner, the respondent may petition the commissioner for reconsideration or may seek judicial review of the decision in Superior Court. After the decision becomes final, the respondent may petition the commissioner for reinstatement of a license one year after the effective date of the decision.

This brief overview of the process is provided to give you a greater understanding of what takes place in license disciplinary actions. As you can see, the law provides a number of rights to a respondent in a disciplinary action to insure that a fair hearing has been held.

Those interested in learning more about Administrative Procedure Act hearings should refer to Section 11500 et seq. of the Government Code.

■ COURT STRUCTURE

Federal Courts

Because much of our real estate law is based on appellate judicial decisions, it is important to have a basic knowledge of our federal and state court systems. The appellate process provides judicial guidance in the form of interpretation and clarification to ensure uniformity in the application of our laws.

District Courts. District courts are courts of original jurisdiction. Of the 98 federal district courts, four of them are in California (Northern, Southern, Eastern, and Central districts). Besides hearing matters relating to federal law, they accept cases in which plaintiff and defendant are residents of different states (diversity of citizenship) if the case involves a claim of more than $75,000.

Court of Appeals. These courts are limited to hearing appeals from federal district courts. The United States has 13 appeal courts. California is in the Ninth Circuit. (See Figure 1.1 at the opening of the chapter.)

U.S. Supreme Court. The U.S. Supreme Court is the highest court in the land. The nine justices are appointed by the president with approval of the U.S. Senate and serve for life. The U.S. Supreme Court can hear appeals from the highest state court if a federal statute, treaty, or constitutional issue is involved. It also hears appeals from the federal courts of appeals.

The Supreme Court is able to hear only a small percentage of the appeals brought to it. Therefore it tries to choose cases involving important issues. If the Supreme Court refuses to hear an appeal, the lower court decision stands.

The Supreme Court has the power of judicial review of the legislative branch. This power is, however, not set forth in the U.S. Constitution.

Case Study

In *Marbury v. Madison* (1803) 1 Cranch 137, the Supreme Court indicated the legislative branch must take notice of the Constitution. The court declared that an act of Congress that is repugnant to the Constitution of the United States cannot become a law, and it is the province of the judiciary to declare when a law is in conflict with the Constitution.

Special Courts. A number of special federal courts, including the tax court, court of military appeals, customs court, and court of claims, have very limited jurisdiction.

Figure 1.4 shows the basic structures of the state and federal court systems.

California Courts

Small Claims Courts. The small claims court is a branch of the superior court. A small claims court commissioner, temporary judge, or judge may preside. Cases are limited to matters involving $5,000 or less. They originally were intended to be consumer courts, but today they are often used by creditors against consumers. Small claims courts follow a relatively informal procedure, with the parties pleading and defending their own cases; attorney representation is not allowed. A plaintiff (party bringing the action) who loses a case may not appeal, but a defendant (party being sued) who loses may appeal the decision to the superior court, Appellate Division.

Superior Courts. As of July 1998, judges in each county were allowed to vote if they wanted their county to combine its municipal and superior courts. By 2001, every California county had opted for court unification.

FIGURE 1.4

State and Federal Court Systems

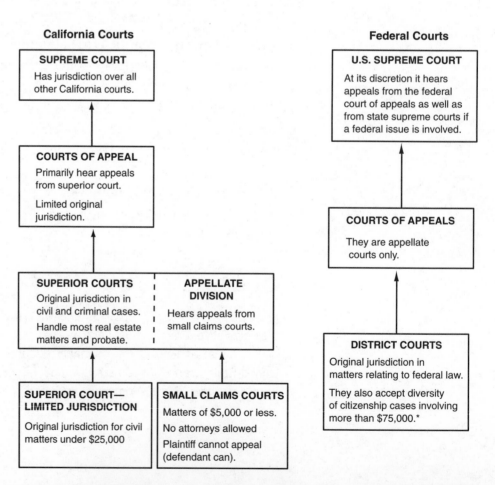

*Note that there are several U.S. courts of limited jurisdiction such as tax court, court of claims, customs court, and bankruptcy court.

What were formerly municipal courts became Limited Jurisdiction Superior Courts that handle civil matters under $25,000 as well as minor criminal matters (misdemeanors). General Jurisdiction Superior Courts have original jurisdiction in civil cases in excess of $25,000, felonies, probate, marriage dissolution, mortgage foreclosures, quiet title actions (actions to clear real estate titles), and most real estate disputes. Civil cases involving less than $25,000 are known as limited civil cases, including unlawful detainer evictions. Every California county has a superior court.

Superior Court, Appellate Division. Each Superior Court has an Appellate Division. It can adjudicate Small Claims Court appeals brought by defendants (plaintiffs who lose in Small Claims Court have no right of appeal). The Appellate Division also hears appeals of unlawful detainer evictions and limited civil cases involving less than $25,000.

California Courts of Appeal. These courts have very limited original jurisdiction and hear primarily appeals from the superior courts. There are six courts of appeal in California: Fresno, Los Angeles, San Diego, San Francisco, San Jose, and Sacramento. Each court of appeal consists of several panels, each composed of a presiding justice plus two associate justices.

California Supreme Court. Consisting of a chief justice and six associate justices, the California Supreme Court has discretionary appellate jurisdiction over all other California courts. If the California Supreme Court declines to accept a case, then the decision of the lesser court stands. The supreme court can decertify decisions of a court of appeal, which means that while a decision stands, it cannot be cited as a precedent for future decisions.

Additional information about California's court system can be researched at www.courtinfo.ca.gov.

■ LAWSUIT PROCEDURE

This book uses the case study method as a primary teaching tool. Because most real estate cases are civil matters adjudicated between the parties, rather than criminal matters (where the defendant is charged by the state with a criminal offense), understanding lawsuit procedure will enhance your understanding of the cases to be studied.

A civil lawsuit begins when a plaintiff files a complaint in court. The complaint describes the claim and requests relief. A copy of the complaint, as well as a summons to respond, is then served on the defendant.

The defendant then has the option of

- answering the complaint, denying or admitting the allegations;
- filing a complaint of his or her own (a countersuit) against the plaintiff or against a third party, making the third party part of the action; or
- requesting dismissal based on, among other reasons, lack of jurisdiction; res judicata (a prior judgment on the issue between the parties); the facts, if true, not stating a cause of action (demur); the statute of limitations (the plaintiff waited too long to begin action); or the party bringing the action has no standing to sue.

During the pretrial period a discovery process might take place (there is no discovery in small claims cases). During discovery, parties will subpoena witnesses to provide sworn testimony and may also use written interrogatories (questions presented in writing). Parties are also allowed access to records.

Most cases are settled prior to trial. If the lawsuit goes to trial, the trial begins with opening statements by the plaintiff and defendant. The plaintiff then brings forth witnesses. The plaintiff's examination of witnesses is called a *direct examination*. After the plaintiff's examination, the defendant has the right to examine the witness (called a *cross-examination*). The plaintiff may then question the witness—redirect examination—and the defendant then has an opportunity to re-cross-examine. Next the defendant has the right to produce witnesses, and the examination process is repeated. Finally the parties make their closing statements.

If there is a jury, the court will direct questions of fact to the jury. For example: "Did the plaintiff give the defendant a $2,000 cash deposit?" "What is the amount of monetary damages sustained by the plaintiff?" Unless appealed, the decision of the court trial is binding on the parties.

■ JUDICIAL REMEDIES

The English common-law remedies or legal remedies were primarily monetary damages. Remedies developed by the chancellory courts were known as *equitable remedies*. The equity courts did not generally award monetary damages; their remedies were based on conscience or what was right. As previously stated, U.S. courts are not limited to legal remedies and can award equitable remedies to right a wrong.

Monetary Remedies (Damages)

Compensatory Damages. **Compensatory damages** are money damages to cover the loss for the injury sustained. The court also can assess a party with court costs when provided for by contract or by statute. Attorney's fees also may be recoverable.

For example, if a seller forged a termite inspection report that indicated no infestation or damage and, after the sale, the purchaser discovered serious infestation and damage, a court might award the buyer actual costs to correct the problem (compensatory damages) plus exemplary or punitive damages to punish the seller for willful and outrageous conduct.

Exemplary Damages. **Exemplary** (or punitive) **damages** go beyond actual compensation for an injury. They are awarded to punish the wrong-doer for an action that was aggravated by its willful nature, malice, fraud, or wanton and wicked conduct.

For example, if a seller breached a contract to sell a house for $150,000 so as to sell the house to another buyer for $200,000, the court might award exemplary damages, in addition to the compensatory damages, for this wrongful and willful breach of contract.

Nominal Damages. **Nominal damages** are monetary damages in a token sum such as $1. They are awarded to show a defendant was in the wrong but no substantial damage to person, property, or reputation occurred. An example would be a trespass where a person crossed the land of another without permission or right but caused no damage.

■ EQUITABLE REMEDIES

Specific Performance. The court can force a person to perform as agreed. **Specific performance** is an equitable remedy usually awarded where money damages are inadequate. Because every parcel of real property is considered unique, specific performance is a proper remedy for breach of a real property sales agreement. While the remedy of specific performance is readily available to purchasers, courts rarely force buyers to buy because money damages are ascertainable. A seller who consequently sells to another buyer for less money usually will receive damages amounting to the difference in the sales prices. (For an exception, see *BD Inns v. Pooley*, cited in Chapter 5, where the buyer was forced to complete the sale.)

Specific performance is not available for personal services. That is, the court will not require one person to work for another, because that would violate the Thirteenth Amendment to the U.S. Constitution.

Specific performance will not be granted if the court does not deem the consideration adequate.

Rescission. Rescission is the mutual release of the parties to a contract. The contract is set aside, and the consideration that was given is returned. This equitable remedy would be used when promises were made because of a mutual mistake or when the contract became impossible to perform or the performance of the contract, while legal when the contract was made, became illegal because of a change in the law.

Reformation. Through **reformation**, the courts rewrite a contract to read as it was intended to read by the parties rather than as stated. For example, a court would likely reform a lease that described the wrong premises when it was clear from the evidence which premises were intended to be leased.

Injunction. Using an **injunction** as an equitable remedy, courts will order a party to cease and desist from an activity such as a trespass or a nuisance.

Foreclosure. **Foreclosure** is an *action in rem*, an action against property, rather than an *action in personam*, which is an action directed against a specific person, such as an action for damages. A foreclosure action seeks to terminate a person's interest in property. Foreclosure actions would be brought by lienholders such as a lender or a holder of a mechanic's lien. Foreclosure is discussed in detail in Chapter 10.

Quiet Title. **Quiet title** is a legal action to determine the ownership or rights in real property. It can be used to wipe out claims against a property to provide an owner with a marketable title as well as to clear any cloud on a title (such as a misspelled name on a deed).

Declaratory Relief Action. Under common law, a party had to wait until rights had been violated to obtain a legal interpretation of the rights involved. Now, however, a unique equitable remedy is available. Called a **declaratory relief action**, it can be brought to have the court determine rights *before* an invasion of rights has occurred. A declaratory relief action may be used in conjunction with the demand for other relief such as an injunction.

■ NONJUDICIAL REMEDIES

In addition to judicial remedies, nonjudicial remedies of arbitration and mediation are available to disputing parties.

Arbitration

Arbitration is a process for resolution of disputes. Many contracts call for mandatory arbitration, and the courts generally will enforce these agreements. The contracts usually provide for the choosing of the arbitrator and may state that the rules of the American Arbitration Association apply. In some cases, nonbinding arbitration can be ordered by the courts. Also, parties can agree to voluntary arbitration, in which the arbitrator serves much as a judge in hearing a case but is not bound by the legal rules of evidence or normal court formalities.

The principal benefits of arbitration are that it is faster and less expensive than court action. Appeals are not allowed in cases of binding arbitration.

Mediation

Mediation is a process in which a neutral third party (mediator) works with the parties in a dispute to help them reach a satisfactory solution. The mediator suggests solutions and alternatives and might confer with the parties separately as well as together. The mediation process is not binding on the parties.

■ SUMMARY

We are governed by a system of laws enacted by our representatives that are enforceable through our legal system. Our laws range from the U.S. Constitution, which is the supreme law of the land, to local ordinances. The basic precepts of much of our real estate law as well as a great deal of our legal vocabulary come from English common law. The common law, however, was judge-made law rather than the statutory law that governs our conduct. The common law was built up over generations by legal precedent.

In addition to the law courts, England also developed separate courts of equity. Courts in the United States combine the equity functions of the English equity courts with those of the common-law courts.

We have parallel federal and state court systems that provide for appeals from trial court decisions. The appellate systems provide greater uniformity in our courts.

To effectuate justice, our court system has a wide variety of remedies available to it. These include the remedies available to the English common-law courts as well as the courts of equity. An injured party can request a remedy that best meets his or her specific needs.

 The authors will be posting new cases concerning the Sources of Law and the Judicial System on the Internet at **www.dearbornRE.com**.

■ DISCUSSION TOPICS

The maxims of jurisprudence (fundamental principles of law) were developed in English common law. California has enacted these maxims into its Civil Code. Rather than being inflexible rules, they are aids to the just application of statutory law. The maxims do not nullify specific statutes.

The majority of the maxims are included below, along with the Civil Code citation. Consider the meaning and purpose of each of these maxims as it relates to real property law.

Civ. Code §3510 When the reason of a rule ceases, so should the rule itself.

Civ. Code §3511 Where the reason is the same, the rule should be the same.

Civ. Code §3512 One must not change his or her purpose to the injury of another.

Civ. Code §3513 Anyone may waive the advantage of a law intended solely for his or her benefit, but a law established for a public reason cannot be contradicted.

Civ. Code §3514 One must use his or her own rights so as not to infringe on the rights of others.

Civ. Code §3515 One who consents to an act is not wronged by it.

Civ. Code §3516 Acquiescence in error takes away the right of objecting to it.

Civ. Code §3517 No one can take advantage of his or her own wrong.

Civ. Code §3518 One who has fraudulently dispossessed himself of a thing may be treated as if he still had possession.

Civ. Code §3519 One who can and does not forbid what is done on his or her behalf is deemed to have bidden it.

Civ. Code §3520 No one should suffer by the acts of another.

Civ. Code §3521 One who takes the benefit must bear the burden.

Civ. Code §3522 One who grants a thing is presumed to grant also whatever is essential to its use.

Civ. Code §3523 For every wrong there is a remedy.

Civ. Code §3524 Between those who are equally in the right or equally in the wrong, the law does not interpose.

Civ. Code §3525 Between rights otherwise equal, the earliest is preferred.

Civ. Code §3526 No person is responsible for what no person can control.

Civ. Code §3527 The law helps the vigilant before those who sleep on their rights.

Civ. Code §3528 The law respects form less than substance.

Civ. Code §3529 That which ought to have been done is to be regarded as done, in favor of the one to whom, and against the one from whom, performance is due.

Civ. Code §3530 What does not appear to exist is to be regarded as if it did not exist.

Civ. Code §3531 The law never requires impossibilities.

Civ. Code §3532 The law neither does nor requires idle acts.

Civ. Code §3533 The law disregards trifles.

Civ. Code §3534 Particular expressions qualify those that are general.

Civ. Code §3535 Contemporaneous exposition is in general the best.

Civ. Code §3536 The greater contains the less.

Civ. Code §3537 Superfluity does not vitiate.

Civ. Code §3538 That is certain which can be made certain.

Civ. Code §3539 Time does not confirm a void act.

Civ. Code §3540 The incident follows the principal and not the principal the incident.

Civ. Code §3541 An interpretation that gives effect is preferred to one that makes void.

Civ. Code §3542 Interpretation must be reasonable.

Civ. Code §3543 Where one of two innocent persons must suffer by the act of a third, the person by whose negligence it happened must be the sufferer.

Civ. Code §3545 Private transactions are fair and regular.

Civ. Code §3546 Things happen according to the ordinary course of nature and the ordinary habits of life.

Civ. Code §3547 A thing continues to exist as long as is usual with things of that nature.

Civ. Code §3548 The law has been obeyed.

Check the Web site for the meaning and purpose of the Maxims of Jurisprudence.

■ DISCUSSION CASES

1. A homebuyer who was not satisfied with the workmanship in her new home posted signs saying, "I bought a $200,000 fixer-upper," "My house leaks and no one gives a damn," and "We moved to Paradise Hills but we live in hell." At various times, up to 20 other homeowners posted similar signs. The developer sued, alleging that the statements were made with intent to injure the developer's sales activity. The developer did not allege that the statements made were false. **Was the homeowner acting within her rights?**

   Paradise Hills Associates v. Procel (1991) 235 C.A.3d 1528

2. A man was prohibited from distributing religious tracts in the parking lot of a shopping center. **Were his constitutional rights violated?**

   Savage v. Trammell Crow Co., Inc. (1990) 223 C.A.3d 1562

3. Antiabortion activists protested in the parking lot of a medical center. They handed out material and prayed aloud. An agent of the landlord sought injunctive relief to prohibit the activities of the protestors. **Should it be granted?**

   Allred v. Harris (1993) 14 C.A.4th 1386

4. Golden Gateway Center includes a retail center plus 1,254 residential rental units. Building management prohibits door-to-door solicitations and leafleting within the buildings. The center sought to enjoin the tenant association from distributing newsletters. The association cross-complained for injunctive and declaratory relief. The San Francisco Superior Court ruled in favor of the tenant association. The building owner appealed. **Should the Superior Court ruling be upheld?**

Golden Gateway Center v. Golden Gateway Tenants Association
(1999) 73 C.A.4th 908

5. A city ordinance prohibited homeowners from displaying signs on their property except resident identification, for sale and warning signs. The city refused to permit a homeowner to place a sign on her front lawn opposing the Persian Gulf War. **Is the restriction on signs justified?**

City of Ladue v. Gilleo (1994) 114 S Ct 2038

6. **When there is a binding arbitration agreement and the arbitrator has clearly made an erroneous decision, will the courts set it aside?**

Moore v. First Bank of San Luis Obispo (1998) 68 C.A.4th 768

The court decisions for the above cases can be found on our website at **www.dearbornRE.com.** Click on the **"Instructor Resources"** link, then scroll down the page until you find the link titled "California Real Estate Law 5th Edition."

■ CHAPTER QUIZ

1. Most of California real estate law originally came from

   a. Spanish law.
   b. English common law.
   c. Mexican law.
   d. the commissioner's regulations.

2. Reliance on previous decisions is best described as

   a. common law.
   b. equity.
   c. stare decisis.
   d. civil law.

3. Our system of *statutes* in California could best be described as

    a. civil law.
    b. equity.
    c. stare decisis.
    d. constitutional law.

4. The Equal Credit Opportunity Act is best described as

    a. stare decisis.
    b. civil law.
    c. common law.
    d. constitutional law.

5. The power of eminent domain is based in which amendment to the U.S. Constitution?

    a. The First Amendment
    b. The Fifth Amendment
    c. The Thirteenth Amendment
    d. The Fourteenth Amendment

6. In an administrative hearing, a person would have the right to

    a. a jury.
    b. an attorney furnished by the government if he or she could not afford one.
    c. Both a and b
    d. Neither a nor b

7. Laws governing ownership rights are set forth in

    a. state statutes.
    b. federal statutes.
    c. local ordinances.
    d. the English common law.

8. The regulation of real estate licensees is covered in the

    a. Administrative Code.
    b. Civil Code.
    c. Corporation Code.
    d. Business and Professions Code

9. There is no uniform code for

    a. personal property.
    b. real property.
    c. commercial paper.
    d. All of the above

10. The commissioner's regulations

    a. have the force and effect of law.
    b. are known as the real estate law.
    c. are included in the Business and Professions Code.
    d. None of the above

11. In adopting regulations, an administrative agency must provide for

    a. alternative remedies.
    b. a public hearing.
    c. arbitration of disputes.
    d. All of the above

12. The real estate commissioner conducts hearings in accordance with the

    a. Administrative Procedure Act.
    b. Business and Professions Code.
    c. Labor Code.
    d. Public Resources Code.

13. Decisions of the Department of Real Estate

    a. are binding and final.
    b. may be appealed to the courts.
    c. must be made unanimously by the commission.
    d. must be concurred with by a majority of the commission.

14. The document that initiates the process to determine whether a licensee should be formally disciplined is known as a(n)

    a. quiet title action.
    b. accusation.
    c. summons and complaint.
    d. declaratory relief action.

15. The court that has original jurisdiction in claims of more than $25,000 is the

    a. justice court.
    b. small claims court.
    c. superior court.
    d. court of appeal.

16. Most real estate disputes are adjudicated in

    a. federal courts.
    b. municipal courts.
    c. superior courts.
    d. the supreme court.

17. Most lawsuits involving real estate matters can be described as

    a. criminal proceedings.
    b. administrative agency actions.
    c. common law actions.
    d. civil actions.

18. Which of the following statements about lawsuits is *incorrect?*

    a. The defendant commences the action with a complaint.
    b. A direct examination of a witness is followed by a cross-examination.
    c. Most lawsuits are settled before trial.
    d. If there is a jury, the jury determines questions of fact.

19. Money awarded to an injured person for damages received is called

    a. exemplary damages.   c. compensatory damages.
    b. nominal damages.   d. specific performance.

20. Equitable remedies include all of the following except

    a. monetary damages.   c. reformation.
    b. rescission.   d. specific performance.

21. The remedy in which a person is ordered to cease and desist from an activity is known as

    a. reformation.   c. specific performance.
    b. an injunction.   d. None of the above

22. A legal action to determine ownership rights in real property would be

    a. an injunction.   c. reformation.
    b. a declaratory relief action.   d. a quiet title action.

23. Which of the following is *not* an advantage of voluntary arbitration?

    a. Savings in money   c. Right to appeal
    b. Savings in time.   d. None of the above

24. The process whereby a third person works to resolve a problem but cannot impose a decision on the parties is known as

    a. arbitration.   c. mediation.
    b. declaratory relief.   d. quiet title.

25. Mediation could be described as

    a. empowering a third person to make a decision for you.
    b. a judicial process.
    c. Both a and b
    d. Neither a nor b

CHAPTER TWO

LAW OF AGENCY

■ KEY TERMS

agency	equal dignities rule	implied authority
agency coupled with	estoppel	ostensible agency
an interest	express agency	power of attorney
agent	express authority	principal
attorney-in-fact	fiduciary duty	ratification
customary authority	general agent	respondent superior
dual agency	implied agency	special agent

■ AGENTS AND AGENCY DEFINED

Section 2295 of the California Civil Code states, "An **agent** is one who acts for or represents another, called the **principal**, in dealings with third persons. Such representation is called an **agency**." Therefore, an agent is one who acts for or represents another.

Because an agent represents a principal, payment to the agent is generally considered payment to the principal. In the same manner, notifying the agent of a fact is the same as notifying the principal. The legal relationship of an agency requires free consent of both the agent and the principal. Courts will not force an agency relationship on parties against their will, nor will they generally require the continuance of an agency if either party wants to end it. Therefore, the principal or the agent can generally end an agency relationship at any time. A party who does so, however, might be liable for damages if terminating the agency breaks a contractual promise.

Those who can perform an act themselves can legally appoint someone to act as their agent to perform the act.

Civil Code Section 2296 states, "Any person having the capacity to contract may appoint an agent and any person may be an agent." A person who wishes to appoint an agent must have both the legal and mental capacity to do so. Legal capacity involves age and/or legal restrictions on contracting, while mental capacity is defined by state of mind. (Legal and mental capacity are covered in detail in Chapter 5.) A principal who lacks the capacity to perform an act or become contractually bound cannot appoint an agent to perform the act or to contractually bind himself or herself.

■ TYPES OF AGENTS

General Agent

A **general agent** has the authority to perform all necessary acts for the principal within a specified area. For example, a property manager who has authority to rent or lease, collect rents, hire and fire personnel, and make repairs and/or improvements would likely be a general agent of the property owner.

Special Agent

While a general agent has broad powers to act for his or her principal, a **special agent** is limited to those acts specifically set forth in the agency agreement. For example, a real estate licensee is normally a special agent of an owner with authority to locate a buyer for a property. (The real estate agent normally has no power to sell the owner's property or contractually bind the owner.)

Power of Attorney

A **power of attorney** is a written agreement whereby a principal appoints an agent to act in his or her place, known as an *attorney-in-fact*. An **attorney-in-fact** should not be confused with an attorney-at-law. Powers of attorney are normally given for specific purposes such as to sign a deed when the owner is not available; this is an example of a specific power of attorney. A general power of attorney conveys broad powers to the attorney-in-fact to operate in the place of the principal and to contractually bind the principal within the specified area of the agency. The statutory power of attorney form is found in Civil Code Section 2450.

■ HOW AGENCIES ARE CREATED

Express Agency

An **express agency** is an agency created by a specific agreement, either written or verbal. Most agencies are express agencies. Listings are the written agency agreements used to authorize an agent to procure buyers or lessees or to locate property for purchase or lease.

Implied Agency

Most agencies are express agencies created by a written or verbal agreement. An **implied agency** is not the result of a stated agreement but is created by the actions of the parties. For example, if a broker's actions reasonably lead another person to believe that the broker is representing the person as his or her agent, an implied agency could be formed, and the broker could have all of the duties of an agent toward that principal.

Ostensible Agency

California Civil Code Section 2298 states, "An agency is either actual or ostensible." If one person causes others to believe that another person is his or her agent when that is not true, the courts can declare the principal bound due to the existence of an apparent or **ostensible agency**. Section 2300 of the Civil Code states: "An agency is ostensible when the principal intentionally, or by want of ordinary care, causes a third person to believe another to be his agent who is not really employed by him." For example, assume a real estate agent took a prospective tenant to a property owner's place of business and asked the owner of the property for the key to show the property. Assume the owner complied in the presence of the prospective tenant. A court may declare that the owner's actions (or inaction) resulted in the prospective tenant's reasonably believing that an agency existed. The owner could therefore be liable to the tenant for actions of the ostensible agent.

Case Study

The case of *Kaplan v. Coldwell Banker* (1997) 59 C.A.4th 741 indicates that there could be an ostensible agency between the franchisor and franchisee. A superior court judge, Kaplan, was the plaintiff. Kaplan purchased a lemon grove from a Coldwell Banker franchise broker. After discovering misrepresentations that were made, Kaplan sued the agents and brokers involved as well as the franchisor under respondeat superior and ostensible agency theories. The court of appeal originally ruled that the franchisor could not be held liable on either theory. But on a rehearing, the court of appeal reversed, sending the case back for trial on the ostensible agency theory. The court indicated that the franchisor might be held liable

(continued on next page)

as an ostensible agent if the injured party can prove (1) a reasonable belief in the agent's (franchisee's) authority, (2) the belief is generated by some act or neglect of the principal (the franchisor), and (3) the person relying on the agent's apparent authority was not negligent. While the court indicated they were not declaring large real estate franchise companies to be fair game, that appears to be the effect of this decision.

Agency by Estoppel

When an ostensible agency is created and a third person reasonably acts to their detriment based on the belief of the existence of the agency, the person who allowed the ostensible agency to exist would be estopped (barred) from denying the existence of the agency. For example, assume an out-of-town owner informed a broker that the owner's cousin had the authority to give a listing on the owner's property. The broker, acting on this assertion, listed and then procured a buyer for the owner's property. The owner would be estopped from denying the existence of the agency because his other words led the broker to act to the broker's detriment. The agency created is called an *agency by estoppel*. The doctrine of **estoppel** is one of equity to achieve justice. (See *Phillippe v. Shappel Indus. Inc.*, Chapter 5.)

Agency by Ratification

By accepting the benefits of an agreement made by an unauthorized agent or by an agent who has exceeded his or her authority, a principal can form an agency by **ratification**.

If a principal had the authority to permit the unauthorized act at the time of the act, the principal has the authority to ratify or approve the act after it has been made. A principal cannot ratify part of an indivisible agreement; the entire agreement must be ratified.

After knowing of the unauthorized act, the principal can ratify the act by words or actions that indicate he or she intends to be bound by said act. The principal can also ratify through silence or the failure to repudiate an unauthorized act after receiving knowledge of it. For example, an owner who accepts the rents under a lease entered into by his or her unauthorized agent could be ratifying all of the provisions of the lease.

A principal can void his or her ratification if the ratification was made with imperfect knowledge of the material facts of the transaction (Civil Code Section 2314). In the preceding case, assume that in ratifying the tenancy the owner believed the unauthorized agent had entered into a month-to-month tenancy. Upon discovering the tenancy was actually for 20 years, the owner could rescind the ratification.

Dual Agency

A **dual agency** exists when an agent represents two principals who are negotiating with each other and thus have conflicting interests. Any conduct that reasonably leads a buyer to believe that a seller's agent is representing both buyer and seller might create a dual agency.

Because agents often serve as confidants and advisers to purchasers, purchasers easily could be led to believe that the agent is representing them. To avoid the possibility of a court determination that a dual agency exists, a broker must make certain that buyers fully understand that the broker might not be their representative.

While some purchase agreements state that the broker is the representative of the seller, not the buyer, this probably would not be enough to avoid a determination of dual agency if the agent's conduct has led a buyer to believe he or she was being represented.

Because of misunderstandings by buyers and sellers as to whom the agent represents and what the agency duties are, California now requires the agent to provide written disclosure to the parties for the sale, purchase, exchange, or lease of one to four residential units and mobile homes (Civil Code Section 2375). The listing agent can elect to be either a seller's agent or a dual agent representing both seller and buyer. Because he or she has specific duties to the seller, the listing agent cannot elect to be solely a buyer's agent. The selling agent who locates a buyer, however, can elect to be a seller's agent, a buyer's agent, or a dual agent.

California Association of REALTORS® (CAR) Forms AD-11 and AC-6 indicate the agency duties and confirm the relationship of the parties. Figure 2.1 is the disclosure statement (Form AD-11) that explains the agent's responsibility as seller's agent, buyer's agent, or dual agent representing both seller and buyer. Figure 2.2 is Form AC-6, the confirmation of the particular agency relationship chosen. Many California residential purchase forms also include agency confirmation.

Case Study

In the case of *Huijers v. De Marrais* (1993) 11 C.A.4th 676, a real estate agent failed to provide the owner with a copy of the residential agency disclosure form at the time the listing was taken. The court of appeal ruled that the listing agent's failure to provide the disclosure (as required by Civil Code Section 2373, etc.) at the time of listing relieved the sellers of any duty to pay a sales commission.

FIGURE 2.1

Agency Disclosure Form

DISCLOSURE REGARDING REAL ESTATE AGENCY RELATIONSHIPS
(As required by the Civil Code)
(C.A.R. Form AD-11, Revised 10/01)

CALIFORNIA ASSOCIATION OF REALTORS®

When you enter into a discussion with a real estate agent regarding a real estate transaction, you should from the outset understand what type of agency relationship or representation you wish to have with the agent in the transaction.

SELLER'S AGENT
A Seller's agent under a listing agreement with the Seller acts as the agent for the Seller only. A Seller's agent or a subagent of that agent has the following affirmative obligations:
To the Seller:
   A Fiduciary duty of utmost care, integrity, honesty, and loyalty in dealings with the Seller.
To the Buyer and the Seller:
   (a) Diligent exercise of reasonable skill and care in performance of the agent's duties.
   (b) A duty of honest and fair dealing and good faith.
   (c) A duty to disclose all facts known to the agent materially affecting the value or desirability of the property that are not known to, or within the diligent attention and observation of, the parties.

An agent is not obligated to reveal to either party any confidential information obtained from the other party that does not involve the affirmative duties set forth above.

BUYER'S AGENT
A selling agent can, with a Buyer's consent, agree to act as agent for the Buyer only. In these situations, the agent is not the Seller's agent, even if by agreement the agent may receive compensation for services rendered, either in full or in part from the Seller. An agent acting only for a Buyer has the following affirmative obligations:
To the Buyer:
   A fiduciary duty of utmost care, integrity, honesty, and loyalty in dealings with the Buyer.
To the Buyer and the Seller:
   (a) Diligent exercise of reasonable skill and care in performance of the agent's duties.
   (b) A duty of honest and fair dealing and good faith.
   (c) A duty to disclose all facts known to the agent materially affecting the value or desirability of the property that are not known to, or within the diligent attention and observation of, the parties.

An agent is not obligated to reveal to either party any confidential information obtained from the other party that does not involve the affirmative duties set forth above.

AGENT REPRESENTING BOTH SELLER AND BUYER
A real estate agent, either acting directly or through one or more associate licensees, can legally be the agent of both the Seller and the Buyer in a transaction, but only with the knowledge and consent of both the Seller and the Buyer.

In a dual agency situation, the agent has the following affirmative obligations to both the Seller and the Buyer:
   (a) A fiduciary duty of utmost care, integrity, honesty and loyalty in the dealings with either the Seller or the Buyer.
   (b) Other duties to the Seller and the Buyer as stated above in their respective sections.

In representing both Seller and Buyer, the agent may not, without the express permission of the respective party, disclose to the other party that the Seller will accept a price less than the listing price or that the Buyer will pay a price greater than the price offered.

The above duties of the agent in a real estate transaction do not relieve a Seller or Buyer from the responsibility to protect his or her own interests. You should carefully read all agreements to assure that they adequately express your understanding of the transaction. A real estate agent is a person qualified to advise about real estate. If legal or tax advice is desired, consult a competent professional.

Throughout your real property transaction you may receive more than one disclosure form, depending upon the number of agents assisting in the transaction. The law requires each agent with whom you have more than a casual relationship to present you with this disclosure form. You should read its contents each time it is presented to you, considering the relationship between you and the real estate agent in your specific transaction.

This disclosure form includes the provisions of Sections 2079.13 to 2079.24, inclusive, of the Civil Code set forth on the reverse hereof. Read it carefully.

I/WE ACKNOWLEDGE RECEIPT OF A COPY OF THIS DISCLOSURE.

BUYER/SELLER _____ Date _____ Time _____ AM/PM

BUYER/SELLER _____ Date _____ Time _____ AM/PM

AGENT _____ By _____ Date _____
          (Please Print)   (Associate-Licensee or Broker Signature)

THIS FORM SHALL BE PROVIDED AND ACKNOWLEDGED AS FOLLOWS (Civil Code §2079.14):
•When the listing brokerage company also represents the Buyer, the Listing Agent shall give one AD-11 form to the Seller and one to the Buyer.
•When Buyer and Seller are represented by different brokerage companies, then the Listing Agent shall give one AD-11 form to the Seller and the Buyer's Agent shall give one AD-11 form to the Buyer and one AD-11 form to the Seller.

SEE REVERSE SIDE FOR FURTHER INFORMATION

The copyright laws of the United States (Title 17 U.S. Code) forbid the unauthorized reproduction of this form, or any portion thereof, by photocopy machine or any other means, including facsimile or computerized formats. Copyright © 1991-2001, CALIFORNIA ASSOCIATION OF REALTORS®, INC. ALL RIGHTS RESERVED.

THIS FORM HAS BEEN APPROVED BY THE CALIFORNIA ASSOCIATION OF REALTORS® (C.A.R.). NO REPRESENTATION IS MADE AS TO THE LEGAL VALIDITY OR ADEQUACY OF ANY PROVISION IN ANY SPECIFIC TRANSACTION. A REAL ESTATE BROKER IS THE PERSON QUALIFIED TO ADVISE ON REAL ESTATE TRANSACTIONS. IF YOU DESIRE LEGAL OR TAX ADVICE, CONSULT AN APPROPRIATE PROFESSIONAL.

This form is available for use by the entire real estate industry. It is not intended to identify the user as a REALTOR®. REALTOR® is a registered collective membership mark which may be used only by members of the NATIONAL ASSOCIATION OF REALTORS® who subscribe to its Code of Ethics.

Published and Distributed by:
REAL ESTATE BUSINESS SERVICES, INC.
a subsidiary of the CALIFORNIA ASSOCIATION OF REALTORS®
525 South Virgil Avenue, Los Angeles, California 90020

Reviewed by _____
Broker or Designee _____ Date _____

EQUAL HOUSING OPPORTUNITY

AD-11 REVISED 10/01 (PAGE 1 OF 1)   Print Date

DISCLOSURE REGARDING REAL ESTATE AGENCY RELATIONSHIPS (AD-11 PAGE 1 OF 1)

FIGURE 2.2

**Confirmation of Real Estate
Agency Relationships**

CALIFORNIA
ASSOCIATION
OF REALTORS®

CONFIRMATION REAL ESTATE AGENCY RELATIONSHIPS
(As required by the Civil Code)

Subject Property Address _____

The following agency relationship(s) is/are hereby confirmed for this transaction:

LISTING AGENT: _____   SELLING AGENT: _____
  is the agent of (check one):   (if not the same as Listing Agent)
  ❏ the Seller exclusively; or   is the agent of (check one):
  ❏ both the Buyer and Seller   ❏ the Buyer exclusively; or
                                            ❏ the Seller exclusively; or
                                            ❏ both the Buyer and Seller

I/WE ACKNOWLEDGE RECEIPT OF A COPY OF THIS CONFIRMATION.

Seller _____ Date _____   Buyer _____ Date _____

Seller _____ Date _____   Buyer _____ Date _____

Listing Agent _____ By _____ Date _____
                (Please Print)   (Associate Licensee or Broker-Signature)

Selling Agent _____ By _____ Date _____
                (Please Print)   (Associate Licensee or Broker-Signature)

A REAL ESTATE BROKER IS QUALIFIED TO ADVISE ON REAL ESTATE. IF YOU DESIRE LEGAL ADVICE, CONSULT YOUR ATTORNEY.

This form is available for use by the entire real estate industry. It is not intended to identify the user as a REALTOR®. REALTOR® is a registered collective membership mark which may be used only by members of the NATIONAL ASSOCIATION OF REALTORS® who subscribe to its Code of Ethics.

The copyright laws of the United States (17 U.S. Code) forbid the unauthorized reproduction of this form by any means, including facsimile or computerized formats. Copyright © 1987-1997, CALIFORNIA ASSOCIATION OF REALTORS®

REBS INC   Published and Distributed by:
REAL ESTATE BUSINESS SERVICES, INC.
a subsidiary of the CALIFORNIA ASSOCIATION OF REALTORS®
525 South Virgil Avenue, Los Angeles, California 90020

Page _____ of _____ Pages.

OFFICE USE ONLY
Reviewed by Broker
or Designee _____
Date _____

EQUAL HOUSING
OPPORTUNITY

CONFIRMATION REAL ESTATE AGENCY RELATIONSHIPS (AC-6 PAGE 1 OF 1) REVISED 1987

Reprinted with permission, California Associaton of REALTORS®. Endorsement not implied.

Case Study

The case of *Brown v. FSR Brokerage, Inc.* (1998) 62 C.A. 4th 766, involved a situation where an agent from Fred Sands Realty listed Brown's home for $2,695,000. The seller's agent verbally informed Brown that he was Brown's exclusive agent. The agent told Brown that unless the price were reduced to $2.4 million, he would lose a prospective buyer. (During the negotiation process, the agent had told the seller how much the buyer was willing to offer and also told the buyer how little the seller was willing to accept, but eventually advised the seller not to accept less than a full-price offer.) While no written offer was presented to Brown, the agent said it was time to go to escrow. Brown signed, but failed to read the agency confirmation stating that the agent was a dual agent.

The superior court ruled that the agency had been properly confirmed. The court of appeal reversed, holding that a dual agency must be disclosed as soon as practical. The agency was represented as being a seller's agent, and the agent misrepresented whom he was representing until the confirmation. The court also pointed out that the agent breached duties by revealing to each party the position of the other party.

While compensation is an indication of an agency relationship, an agent need not receive consideration for an agency relationship to exist.

In the case of *McPhetridge v. Smith* (1929) 101 C.A.122, the court held: "A gratuitous agent upon entering into the performance of the agency is, in common with all other agents, bound to exercise the utmost good faith in dealing with his principal." Doing someone a favor could result in liability if a licensee breaches an agency duty. The fact that the buyer does not directly pay the broker does not mean that the broker is not the buyer's agent.

A broker who acts for more than one party to a transaction without the knowledge and consent of all parties involved would be subject to disciplinary action. An undisclosed dual agency also would be grounds for rescission of the contract as well as forfeiture of rights to compensation.

Note: A number of states provide for designated agency where agency within an office is divided. The listing agent would be the seller's agent, and the selling agent (within the same office) would be the buyer's agent. This creates opposing adversaries within the same office and is not currently authorized in California.

Case Study

L. Byron Culver & Assoc. v. Jaoudi Industrial & Trading Corporation
(1991) 1 C.A.4d 300 involved a broker who had been locating suitable
property for Del Rayo for several years. The broker obtained Del Rayo's
permission to initiate negotiations to acquire property owned by Jaoudi. A
salesperson for the broker then obtained a one-time listing for the property that provided for a 3 percent sales commission. The salesperson
then brought in an offer from Del Rayo for $1,750,000. Jaoudi inquired if
the broker Culver and Del Rayo were associated in any way. The salesperson denied any association. Jaoudi later instructed the escrow not to
pay Culver any commission. The court of appeal, in affirming a superior
court decision denying compensation, stated: "An agent has a fiduciary
duty to his principal to disclose all information in the agent's possession
relevant to the subject matter of the agency," and in a real estate agency
the penalty for failure to disclose a dual agency at the time of the transaction is forfeiture of the real estate sales commission. The court of
appeal noted that the fact that the agent acted fairly and honorably to both
principals did not affect the forfeiture of commission. Jaoudi believed the
agent was acting solely as his agent, but the inevitable conclusion is that
Culver represented both the buyer and the seller.

■ PROOF OF AGENCY

The burden of proving the existence of an agency relationship is on the person who seeks to benefit by the existence of the agency. Persons seeking such
benefit might include an agent seeking compensation from a principal or a
principal who wishes to prove that a person was in fact his or her agent to
establish the existence of agency duties. A third person might wish to prove
that the person he or she contracted with was actually an agent so as to hold
a principal liable. As an example, rather than bring a lawsuit against a defendant with little money and no insurance, an injured party might assert that
the person who caused the injury was an agent. In this way the injured party
might be able to sue a principal who has money and/or insurance.

■ AUTHORITY OF AGENTS

Express Authority

Agents have the stated authority given to them in the agency agreement
(either verbal or written). This is known as **express authority**.

A person cannot verbally authorize an agent to perform an act that is required to be in writing. According to the **equal dignities rule**, if the statute of frauds requires the act to be in writing, the agency agreements, such as listings and sales contracts, must be in writing to be legally enforceable. (The statute of frauds is covered in Chapter 5.)

Civil Code Section 1624 states that no contract for the sale of real property can be enforced unless signed by the person against whom enforcement is sought. Therefore, a document signed by a real estate agent "as per phone conversation" would be unenforceable.

Implied Authority

Agents also have **implied authority** to perform the acts reasonably necessary to accomplish the purpose of the agency. For example, a managing agent with the power to enter into commercial leases has the implied authority to engage an attorney to draft a lease.

Customary Authority

Customary authority is authority implied by the agent's position. A person dealing with an agent could assume that the agent has the authority customary for such an agency. A general manager of a real estate office would have the customary authority to order stationery and place advertisements.

Secret limitations on the agent's authority that are not known by persons dealing with the agent do not limit the agent's customary authority. Assume a real estate agent was the rental and management agent for a commercial building. The agency agreement required all leases for more than 18 months to be signed by the owner. If a tenant received a lease for two years signed by the agent without any knowledge of the limitations on the agent's authority, the tenant could rely on the customary authority of such an agent. (Of course, the agent could be liable to the owner for exceeding his or her authority.)

A third person should not rely on an agent's claim to have greater than customary authority. If, for example, a leasing agent indicates she has authority to give the prospective tenant an option to purchase the property as part of the lease, the prospective tenant has a duty to ascertain whether the agent actually has this authority.

In the normal real estate brokerage situation the real estate listing agent has express authority (set forth in a listing) to seek buyers for the property of a principal. The broker usually has no express or implied authority to obligate the principal contractually.

Delegation of Agent's Authority

Unless expressly authorized by the principal, an agent has no authority to delegate agency duties, with the exception of

- purely mechanical acts, such as erecting signs, maintaining buildings, and making repairs;
- acts the agent cannot lawfully perform, such as functions requiring an attorney; and
- acts that commonly are delegated, such as the closing function (delegated to an escrow firm).

Unless a listing authorizes an agent to work with subagents, a broker does not have the authority to cooperate with other agents or to disseminate listing information through a multiple-listing service.

■ DUTIES OF AN AGENT

Fiduciary Duty

An agent has a duty of trust and must protect his or her principal's interests. Under this **fiduciary duty**, the agent must act in a manner that is consistent with the best interests of his or her principal. The agent may not obtain any advantage over the principal by misrepresentation, duress, or adverse pressure.

 For an example of a breach of fiduciary duty case, see *Mitchell v. Gould* (1928) 90 C.A. 647. Where the principal wanted a short-term lease, but the broker got tenant to offer a long-term lease. The broker lost his commission.

The agent must account for all funds received or disbursed on behalf of the principal. Making a secret profit would be a breach of the agent's fiduciary duty. The agent's only benefits must be those agreed to by the principal.

A dual agency in which the agent is employed by contract with a seller to sell a property and is also undertaking to assist the buyer to purchase that property presents a peculiar and touchy question of duty. An agent may not act for more than one party in a transaction without the knowledge or consent of all the parties thereto (Business and Professions Code Section 10176[d]). In a dual agency situation the agent has an affirmative obligation to both the seller and the buyer as follows:

- A fiduciary duty of utmost care, integrity, and loyalty in any dealings with either the buyer or the seller
- A duty to exercise diligent, reasonable skill and care in the performance of the agent's duties
- A duty of honesty, fair dealings, and good faith

■ A duty to disclose all facts that the agent knows or should know to affect the value or desirability of the property

Full Disclosure

Notice to an agent is considered to be notice to the principal. Therefore, the agent has a duty to inform the principal of any facts that would be likely to influence the principal in making a decision. Unless expressly instructed by the owner not to present such an offer, or unless the offer is patently frivolous, every offer received, whether verbal or written, must be communicated promptly to the principal. For example, offers must be presented even if received after the principal has accepted an offer and is contractually bound. The principal may wish to breach the existing contract, suffer the damages, and accept the new offer. The best rule for agents is to present all offers to the seller and let the seller decide to accept, reject, or counteroffer.

Full disclosure extends to warning the principal about any dangers or financial problems to be considered, as well as to accurately conveying information about value. An agent who has an option to purchase coupled with a listing has a duty to inform the owner of any offers the agent has prior to exercising the purchase option. Negligence of an agent alone is not enough to make the agent liable; there must be damages.

Due Care

An agent must exercise reasonable or due care in carrying out the duties of the agency. Real estate agents' duties are based on their having the higher knowledge and skills required of a real estate licensee.

Case Study

The case of *Furla v. Jon Douglas Co.* (1998) 65 C.A. 4th 1069 involved a listing broker who had stated that a house was approximately 5,500 square feet but qualified it with "information deemed reliable but not guaranteed." The listing agent had received this information from the owner's daughter who said it came from the architectural plans. During negotiations with the seller and the buyer's agent, Furla, the buyer, said, "OK! 5,500 square feet. I'll pay $170 a square foot." The offer was accepted.

When the buyer later decided to sell, an agent told him "a knowledgeable REALTOR® would easily recognize that the residence is substantially less than 5,500 square feet." Furla hired an appraiser. who said it was 4,615 square feet. Another appraiser measured it at 4,437 square feet. Furla then sued the listing agent for negligent misrepresentation.While the superior court granted summary judgment for the listing broker, the court of appeals reversed, holding that there are genuine issues of material fact

(continued on next page)

regarding whether the listing agent had the reasonable basis to report the house as 5,500 square feet and if the buyer relied on this representation. The court of appeals emphasized that the square-feet estimate was not merely inaccurate; it was "grossly inaccurate," by more than 20 percent. The court remanded the issues to a jury.

Note: The selling broker was not sued, probably because the purchase contract strongly recommended that the buyer obtain independent inspections. It also stated that the buyer's agent, Fred Sands REALTOR®, made no representations as to the size of the structure.

Loyalty

The agent cannot, without permission, disclose to third parties any confidential facts about the principal or agency that would not be in the principal's best interests. This duty continues even after the agency has terminated.

A dual agent cannot disclose to one principal information received in confidence from the other principal, such as that the seller will accept less or the buyer will pay more.

Honesty

The agent must not only fully disclose all material facts to his or her principal but must do so in a fair and honest manner so as not to prejudice the judgment of the principal. The agency duty of fairness and honesty extends to all persons with which the agent is dealing.

Integrity

An agent's moral conduct in his or her dealings must be beyond reproach. The agent should strive to eliminate even the appearance of conflict of interest. Others should be able to rely on the agent's word.

An agent cannot compete with his or her principal. For example, a buyer's agent may not submit his or her own higher offer when submitting an offer from the buyer.

Case Study

The case of *Field v. Century 21 Klowden-Forness Realty* (1998) 63 C.A.4th 18, involved buyers who sued their buyer agent for negligent representation. The agent failed to recommend inspection of the septic system for code compliance, did not advise buyers to check for a room addition building permit,

(continued on next page)

and did not alert buyers to obvious physical defects. The agent also failed to check the preliminary title report to determine the scope of the easement revealed by the seller's Transfer Disclosure Statement. The easement gave the Otay Water District the right to flood part of the property. The superior court held that the agent breached her fiduciary duty to the buyers.

The court of appeal affirmed and pointed out that the broker's fiduciary duty to clients requires the highest good faith.

The court differentiated between the statutory duty, that is, a nonfiduciary duty mandated after *Easton v. Strassburger* (1984) 152 C.A.3d 90, and the common-law fiduciary duty of an agent that demands the highest good faith and undivided service and loyalty. The court indicated this duty may encompass the duty to research, investigate, and counsel.

The court's decision was that the case was not barred by the two-year statute of limitations. The three-year statute of limitations (from date of discovery of the breach) applies to the breach of fiduciary duties.

Obedience

An agent has a duty to obey the **lawful** instructions of the principal (illegal instructions, such as not to show a home to a member of a minority group, must not be followed). An agent who fails to obey instructions or exceeds the authority granted could be held liable for resulting damages.

Agent's Duty to Third Persons

An agent has a duty of honest and fair dealings with others. The principal and agent could be held liable for the agent's misrepresentation, fraud, or failure to disclose to a third party detrimental information that the agent knew or should have known.

■ LIABILITY OF AGENTS

Agents are personally liable for their torts and crimes even when committed at the direction of the principal. (A **tort** is a civil wrong or violation of a duty.) Civil wrongs that are torts include libel, slander, trespass, assault, negligent injury to others, etc. Some torts such as assault or trespass can also be crimes. The principal also could be liable.

An agent who does not disclose to third parties that he or she is acting in an agency capacity can be held personally liable by the third party, even when the principal has directed the agent to maintain secrecy. A principal might, for example, direct an agent or agents not to reveal the agency when the purpose of the agency is to buy up parcels needed for a development (assemblage).

A third party who suffers injury because of a breach of contract can seek recovery from either the agent or the principal, but not both. The secret agent would, of course, have the right to be reimbursed by the principal for losses suffered if the agent was acting properly within the scope of the agency.

Section 2336 of the Civil Code provides that "One who deals with an agent without knowing or having reason to believe that the agent acts as such in the transaction, may set off against any claim of the principal arising out of the same, all claims which he might have set off against the agent before notice of the agency."

A person who claims to be an agent without having authority would be liable for his or her acts. Section 2342 of the Civil Code states: "One who assumes to act as an agent thereby warrants to all who deal with him in that capacity that he has the authority which he assumes."

Agents who violate their agency duties can be held liable to their principal for resulting damages.

While an agent normally must obey the instructions of his or her principal, at times, such as emergencies, obeying those instructions would not be in the best interests of the principal. For example, it could be in the principal's best interests for a managing agent to exceed limitations on expenditures to protect a property from flood damage when the agent is unable to contact the principal. Civil Code Section 2320 provides for this type of situation: "An agent has power to disobey instructions in dealing with the subject of the agency, in cases where it is clearly for the interest of his principal that he should do so, and there is no time to communicate with the principal."

■ LIABILITY OF PRINCIPALS

The doctrine of **respondeat superior** is that a master is liable for the actions of his or her servants or employees. The principal is therefore liable for the acts or omissions of his or her real estate agent acting within the scope of the real estate agency. This liability extends to subagents and includes liability for negligence and misrepresentation. The principal bears the risk of loss of the buyer's deposit caused by the negligence or fraud of the agent.

Case Study

A basement apartment was advertised as "ideal for two men." A woman was refused the rental, and the unit was rented to two men. A jury determined that the property manager had discriminated against the woman because of her gender. The jury failed to award damages against the owner, who had directed the manager in writing not to discriminate.

The 4th U.S. Circuit Court of Appeal, however, held the owner liable. It was pointed out that an owner cannot shirk a duty to pay taxes or meet safety standards simply because the owner gave someone else responsibility. The duty to comply with the law rests on the owner. *Walker v. Crigler* (1992) 976 F.2d 900.

The principal can be held liable for the misrepresentation of his or her agent even when the misrepresentation is made without the principal's knowledge. Unless the agent's actions are directed by the principal, however, the principal will not be held criminally liable for crimes of the agent, though the principal could be civilly liable for damages.

For an example of an agent fraud case see *Ach v. Finkelstein* (1968) 264 C.A.2d 667.

The principal is not liable to third parties who know or should know from the agent's actions that the agent is exceeding his or her authority. Where the agent's actions are clearly inconsistent with the best interests of the principal, third parties should realize that the agent is exceeding the authority granted.

If an agent exceeded his or her authority in appointing a subagent, then the subagent would be the agent of the broker and not of the principal. In such a case, the principal would not be liable for actions of the subagent (Civil Code 2350).

If the agent suffers a personal loss because he or she followed the instructions of the principal, the principal will be obligated to the agent for that loss.

The principal has a duty to deal in good faith with his or her agent. The principal is liable to the agent for compensation as agreed to by their agency.

The principal could be liable for acts of an agent after termination of the agency if third parties dealing with the agent do not know of the termination and the former agent continues to act as if a valid agency continues.

Of course, the former agent would be liable to the principal for damages suffered by his or her wrongful actions.

■ BREACH OF AGENCY

Either the principal or the agent might breach the agency. If the principal wrongfully terminates the agency agreement, the agent is entitled to damages. Listing contracts customarily provide for a full commission should the principal wrongfully terminate. The agent generally cannot, however, force the owner to continue the agency, because an agency requires the consent of the parties.

Because the agent's interest is the commission, the agent cannot force the owner to accept an offer in conformance with the listing (specific performance). However, if an owner rejects a purchase offer that meets the exact terms of the listing, the agent is entitled to a full sales commission.

Exceeding the authority granted, breaching agency duties, and wrongfully renouncing the agency are examples of agents' breaches. Should the agent breach the agency, the agent is liable in damages to the principal. The agent also could be liable for punitive damages for breach of duty if the courts determine that the act was of such a willful and outrageous nature that the agent should be punished.

■ TERMINATION OF AGENCY

An agency agreement may be ended in a number of ways:

1. *Expiration of its term.* An agency automatically ends with the expiration of its stated term.
2. *Extinction of the subject matter.* The destruction of the property automatically terminates a listing or management agency agreement in the absence of any agreement to the contrary. In other words, impossibility terminates the agency. For example, if an agent were employed to find a tenant for a property, the destruction of that property would terminate the agency.
3. *Death.* Because an agency is a personal relationship, death of either the principal or the agent terminates the agency. If either the principal or the agent is a corporation, the death of corporate officers would not terminate the agency because a corporation is considered a separate legal entity.

4. *Renunciation*. Because an agency requires consent of the parties, either the principal or the agent can renounce the agency. As stated earlier, if a party wrongfully breaches the agency, that party could be liable for damages.

5. *Incapacity of agent or principal*. If the agent is no longer capable of acting as an agent or the principal becomes mentally incapacitated, the agency terminates. An agent who loses his or her license would be incapable of performance, so the agency would terminate.

6. *Agreement of the parties*. The principal and the agent can mutually agree to terminate their agency.

7. *Full performance*. Satisfactory completion of the object of the agency terminates the agency.

8. *Bankruptcy*. The trustee in a bankruptcy can terminate an agency or allow it to continue. If the bankruptcy of an agent impairs the agent's ability to perform, the principal can terminate the agency.

Agency Coupled with an Interest

In an **agency coupled with an interest** the agent has an interest in the subject matter of the agency. That is, the agency is created to benefit the agent or a third party. For example, an agent might advance a principal money to stop a foreclosure under an agreement to obtain a listing. The agent then has an interest in the property.

Section 2356 of the Civil Code states that an agency coupled with an interest cannot be terminated by death or incapacity of the principal or by the unilateral act of the principal.

Case Study

In the case of *Pacific Landmark Hotel, Ltd. v. Marriott Hotels, Inc.* (1993) 19 C.A. 4th 615, the owner of a San Diego hotel had signed a 50-year management contract with Marriott Hotels, Inc., for a management fee plus 30 percent of the cash flow. At the time of the agreement, Marriott subsidiary corporations made trust deed loans of $23 million to the hotel. The owner filed a lawsuit against Marriott Hotels, Inc., and various subsidiaries seeking damages for breach of contract, as well as for cancellation of the management contract. Marriott refused to give up management, claiming an agency coupled with an interest. The San Diego Superior Court denied a preliminary injunction terminating the agency because the agency was coupled with an interest.

The court of appeal reversed, and ruled as a matter of law that the loans were made by other Marriott corporations so Marriott Hotels, Inc., had no interest. Therefore, the agency could be terminated, as there was no agency coupled with an interest in the property. (Each corporation was a separate legal entity.)

■ SUMMARY

An agency relationship is a legal relationship whereby a principal (which in real estate is normally the owner) appoints an agent (the broker) to act on his or her behalf.

Agents can be given broad powers or limited powers. In real estate the agent customarily has the limited power to obtain a buyer.

Agencies can be created in several ways. While most agencies are formed by express agreements, an agency can be implied by the actions of the parties or created by estoppel or ratification. In real estate the agency is created by the listing or management agreement.

To prevent misunderstandings about whether the agent is the buyer's agent, the seller's agent, or a dual agent, California requires that an agent provide written disclosure to buyers and sellers for the sale, purchase, or exchange of one to four residential units or mobile homes and for leases that exceed one year.

The agent has duties based on the good faith and trust required in an agency relationship. These duties include

- fiduciary responsibility–the agent has a duty of trust and must act in the best interests of his or her principal;
- full disclosure–the agent must disclose to the principal all facts that would be likely to influence the principal's decisions;
- due care–an agent not only must use reasonable care in carrying out the agency but also must use the special knowledge and skills that the agent possesses;
- loyalty–an agent's primary duty is to his or her principal. The agent cannot act in a self-serving manner to the detriment of the principal or in any manner not in the principal's best interests; and
- obedience–an agent has a duty to obey the legal instructions of his or her principal.

The duties of agents go beyond obligations to the principal. The agent has a duty of honest, good-faith dealings with all parties. An agent who breaches his or her duties can be held personally liable.

The principal is liable for acts of the agent within the scope of the agency. The principal has the duty of good-faith dealing with his or her agent.

Besides the express authority given to the agent by the principal, the agent has implied power to do those acts that are reasonably necessary to carry out the purpose of the agency.

Agencies can be terminated by expiration of the term, destruction of the subject property, death, renunciation by or agreement of the parties, incapacity of agent or principal, or bankruptcy.

■ DISCUSSION CASES

1. A property was listed for sale at $100,000. An offer for $90,000 was accepted, but the sale failed because the prospective buyer could not obtain financing. A real estate agent later informed a prospect that the property could be purchased for less than its listed price. **What, if any, are the problems in this scenario?**

2. A broker helped the seller determine the list price for a net listing. The broker subsequently sold the property to his daughter and son-in-law without informing the seller of his relationship with the buyers. Should the fact that it was a net listing and the seller got what he or she wanted affect the agency duty? **In this case, what were the duties of the broker?**

   Sierra Pacific Industries v. Carter (1980) 104 C.A. 3d 579

3. A broker represented to the owner that an offer of $300 per acre was a fair price. The broker knew that a very similar tract of land had been sold for $400 per acre but failed to inform the seller of this sale. **What has the broker done wrong, and what would be the appropriate remedy?**

   Moore v. Turner (1952) 137 WV 299, 71 S.E.2d 342

4. A mortgage broker failed to inform the principal that the mortgage broker was going to receive a fee from the lender. In fact, the mortgage broker affirmatively denied he would receive any lender compensation. The mortgage broker did, however, receive such a fee. **Discuss the wrongs and remedy.**

   Spraltin v. Hawn (1967) 156 S.E.2d 402

5. Several brokers were engaged in a property exchange. It became apparent that to provide cash for the commissions, a property that an owner wanted $100,000 for would have to be sold for a higher price. A buyer was induced to pay $115,000 for the property. She was told that the price was firm. After the close of escrow she learned that the owner had wanted only $100,000 for the property. **What are the buyer's rights?**

Crogan v. Metz (1956) 47 C.2d 398

6. The plaintiff agreed to list property at $15,900 based on the defendant broker's advice. Both the owner and the broker knew that the property eventually would be condemned for a highway. Prior to actually listing the property, the broker opened an escrow with his name as the buyer. After listing the property, the broker told the owner he was advertising it, but no effort actually was made to do so. The broker indicated to the owner that he had a purported buyer at less than list price. Eventually a transaction was closed at a price of $13,000. The broker did not reveal that the buyer was a friend who was applying for a salesperson's license under the broker. The offer accepted provided for title to be in the name of the purchaser or a party to be named later. The owner signed a deed in blank. The broker inserted the names of his wife and himself. Revenue stamps were affixed to indicate a sales price of $40,000, which the broker later claimed he had paid. The broker wanted $100,000 from the state for the property. **What are the problem areas that would concern the parties in a lawsuit?**

Smith v. Zak (1971) 20 C.A.3d 785

7. A purchaser declined to complete the 10 percent deposit as required and indicated willingness to forfeit the deposit that had been made. The owners were told that the broker would be participating in the purchase. Not disclosed were the facts that the original purchaser had declined to complete the deposit and that the balance was to be paid by the broker. The broker also failed to inform the owner that his participation amounted to a seven-eighths interest. **Was the broker's disclosure adequate?**

Bate v. Marsteler (1959) 175 C.A. 2d 573

8. Alldis, a real estate broker, while acting as an agent for the owners, failed to disclose that Mrs. Alldis was the purchaser. The property was resold at a profit. **What are the seller's rights?**

Adams v. Herman (1951) 106 C.A.2d 92

9. The defendants listed a residential property for sale. They received an offer less than the list price and persuaded the plaintiffs to accept it. They informed the plaintiffs that the purchaser intended to live in the property, although they knew the purchasers were investors who intended to resell it. After the sale the defendants obtained a listing on the property and resold it at a profit. **Have the defendants breached an agency duty?**

   Jorgensen v. Beach 'N' Bay Realty Inc. (1981) 125 C.A.3d 155

10. The plaintiff sellers accepted a promissory note secured by a first trust deed on property other than what was being sold. The sellers' agent represented to the plaintiffs that the security was adequate and the maker was financially responsible. The encumbered property was actually inadequate security for the note, and the maker was in shaky financial condition. The trust deed for $12,000 was created by the defendant by conveying the property on August 15 (day of sale) to the Fullmers. On August 15 the Fullmers then reconveyed the property to Schmidt. It appears these conveyances had the sole purpose of creating paper to be used for the purchase. **In what ways did the agent breach his duties?**

    Banville v. Schmidt (1974) 37 C.A.3d 92

11. A real estate agent used the key in a multiple-listing lockbox to show a home. While the listing indicated the house was occupied, the agent discovered it to be unfurnished except for some stereos and television sets in cabinets and closets. The agent contacted the police, who searched the house. In addition to stolen property, they discovered drugs. **Was the agent's action proper?**

    People v. Jaquez (1984) 163 C.A.3d 918

12. An appraisal by a professional appraiser showed a property value of $610,000 for a home. While the appraisal indicated the appraiser had studied the property, he had not done so. The appraisal had been prepared by an employee of the appraiser. The appraisal misstated the number of bedrooms, baths, skylights, and fireplaces as well as the total square feet. It also failed to point out that construction work was still in progress. Based on the appraisal, the plaintiff made a $200,000 loan secured by a second trust deed on the property. When the borrower defaulted, the lender sued the appraiser. **Is the appraiser liable?**

    Foggy v. Ralph F. Clark & Assoc. Inc. (1987) 192 C.A.3d 1204

13. A licensed real estate salesperson, working as a loan agent, submitted a loan package to his real estate broker. The broker rejected it. Nevertheless, the salesperson submitted the package to a mortgage lender. The borrower had never authorized the loan and her signature was forged on the application. The true value of the property was only $480,000 but the $600,000 loan application showed an $800,000 purchase price. The loan was funded. The broker was sued for loss suffered by the mortgage lender based on respondeat superior, negligent supervision, and equitable indemnity. The broker argued that when the salesperson committed the fraudulent acts, he was not acting within the scope of his agency. **Do you agree?**

Inter Mountain Mortgage, Inc. v. Salimen (2000) 78 C.A.4th 1434

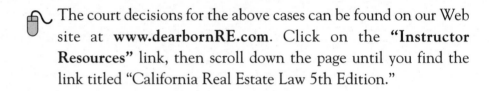 The court decisions for the above cases can be found on our Web site at **www.dearbornRE.com**. Click on the **"Instructor Resources"** link, then scroll down the page until you find the link titled "California Real Estate Law 5th Edition."

■ CHAPTER QUIZ

1. A legal agency requires that

    a. the agent have the capacity to contract.
    b. consideration flow from the principal to the agent.
    c. all of the agency duties be stated in writing.
    d. the parties consent to the agency.

2. An agency relationship could be created by all of the following *except*

    a. court order.
    b. verbal agreement.
    c. implication.
    d. ratification.

3. The relationship that exists between a broker and an owner under a listing is most likely a(n)

    a. employer-employee relationship.
    b. special agency.
    c. universal agency.
    d. general agency.

4. An agency created by a principal who intentionally, or by want of ordinary care, causes a third person to believe another to be his or her agent who is not really employed by him or her would be a(n)

   a. express agency.
   b. power of attorney.
   c. ostensible agency.
   d. special agency.

5. You made a statement that induced a person to act in reliance on that statement. The legal principle that now prevents you from asserting facts that are contrary to your previous declaration is known as

   a. estoppel.
   b. ratification.
   c. respondeat superior.
   d. laches.

6. Broker Thomas, who was not your agent, told prospective tenants that he was your agent to lease your property. Thomas leased your property and you accepted the rent from the tenant. You cannot now deny the agency because of

   a. ratification.
   b. interest coupled with the agency.
   c. waiver.
   d. estoppel.

7. A management agent, who had no authority to sign leases, entered into a three-year lease for the owner. After learning of the lease, the owner accepted rent from the tenant. The lease would be judged valid based on the legal principle of

   a. waiver.
   b. the equal dignities rule.
   c. ratification.
   d. rescission.

8. A selling agent can represent

   a. the buyer only.
   b. both buyer and seller.
   c. the seller only.
   d. Any of the above

9. A real estate agency disclosure form is *not* required to be given to the buyer and seller of a(n)

   a. single-family home.
   b. condominium apartment unit.
   c. triplex.
   d. office building.

10. An agent failed to give an owner a copy of the agency disclosure form at the time the residential listing was taken. The most likely consequence for the agent will be

    a. a fine and/or prison.
    b. inability to collect a commission should a sale be made.
    c. automatic revocation of the agent's license.
    d. no action, because disclosure is required only upon sale.

11. Which of the following is *not* a requirement of an agency relationship?

    a. Compensation to the agent
    b. Contractual capacity of principal
    c. Loyalty of agent to principal
    d. Full disclosure by agent to principal

12. The equal dignities rule concerns

    a. discriminating practices.
    b. the requirement that certain agency agreements be in writing.
    c. ratification of unauthorized acts.
    d. the implied authority of an agent standing in the shoes of the principal.

13. Which of the following is correct as to agencies?

    a. To be valid, an agency requires consideration.
    b. An agent who exceeds his or her authority will always be personally liable.
    c. All agency duties must be expressly agreed to.
    d. Some agency duties are implied.

14. A seller's agent, in selling a home, must

    a. be compensated by the seller.
    b. disclose the agency representation to both buyer and seller.
    c. Both a and b
    d. Neither a nor b

15. A fiduciary relationship exists between a

    a. a broker and his or her principal.
    b. a seller and buyer.
    c. Both a and b
    d. Neither a nor b

16. A seller's listing agent is required to

    a. reveal confidential information received from the other party.
    b. disclose to a buyer all material facts known affecting value.
    c. Both a and b
    d. Neither a nor b

17. A dual agent must

    a. tell the buyer that the seller will accept less.
    b. tell the seller that the buyer will pay more.
    c. receive compensation from both buyer and seller.
    d. None of the above

18. Agents could be held personally liable if they

    a. claimed to be acting as a principal.
    b. made false representations upon the direction of their principal.
    c. exceeded their authority.
    d. All of the above

19. An agent exceeds a secret limitation in the agency agreement while dealing with a third party. Which of the following would be correct?

    a. The agent could be personally liable to the principal.
    b. The third party could hold the principal liable for the agent's action.
    c. Both a and b
    d. Neither a nor b

20. Which of the following is a true statement about real estate agents' liability?

    a. An agent will always be liable for disobeying a principal's instructions.
    b. An agent will not be liable for a tort committed at the direction of the principal.
    c. The principal will never be liable for acts of the agent after termination of the agency.
    d. An agent can be held liable for a tort committed by the agent during the agency.

21. When an agent commits a tort while carrying out agency duties, the

    a. principal has no liability for the tort.
    b. principal would not be liable if the principal told the agent not to commit any torts.
    c. agent is exonerated from liability for the tort because the act was committed in an agency capacity.
    d. agent would be personally liable for the tort.

22. When broker Clyde died, he had 36 exclusive listings. The executor of his estate, who was also a broker, wanted to continue the business until it could be sold. The executor must

    a. notify the owners that he or she has taken over the duties of broker Clyde.
    b. obtain Department of Real Estate approval for the substitution.
    c. renegotiate all listings.
    d. record his or her authority.

23. All of the following events would terminate an agency *except*

    a. the death of a corporate officer of the agent's principal.
    b. agreement of the parties.
    c. renunciation by the principal.
    d. extinction of the subject matter.

24. An agency for a stated period of time would be terminated prior to the expiration date by all of the following *except*

    a. termination by the principal without cause.
    b. termination by the agent.
    c. refusal of the principal to accept an offer.
    d. destruction of the subject matter of the agency.

25. A principal cannot unilaterally terminate an agency when

    a. the agency is a written agreement.
    b. the agency is coupled with an interest.
    c. the principal has received benefits from the agency.
    d. consideration is due the agent.

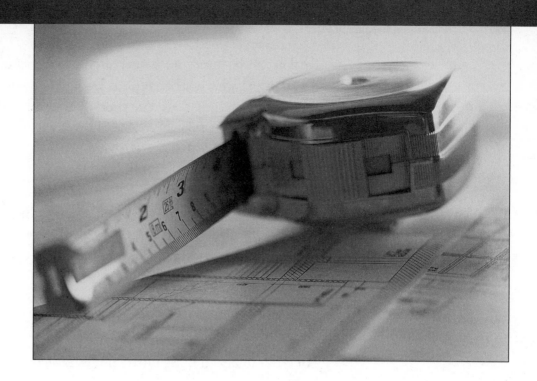

3

DUTIES AND RESPONSIBILITIES OF LICENSEES

■ KEY TERMS

"as is"	latent defect	secret profit
blind ad	Megan's Law	subagent
employee	misrepresentation	subordination clause
ethics	net listing	Transfer Disclosure
finder's fee	option listing	Statement
fraud	patent defect	
independent	puffing	
contractor	rent skimming	

■ LAW AND ETHICS

Laws set the minimum standards of acceptable human behavior. **Ethics** go far beyond the law and determine not if an action is legal but whether it is right or just.

Real estate licensees no longer simply can rely on the letter of the law in determining whether behavior is legal. They also must ask themselves if it is ethical. The time-tested method to determine if an action is ethical is to apply the golden rule. If you would not wish to be treated in a particular manner, you know it is not ethical.

Ethics in fact precede the law. Actions that formerly were legal but unethical are now often illegal as well. Court decisions have been applying the precepts of ethics to activities in real estate and determining that legal duties exist where no duties formerly were recognized. Licensees who pursue an unethical course of action run the risk of having a court determine that they have breached a duty and are liable for the resulting damages, even though such action had been considered legal in the past.

For a full understanding of the duties of licensees, the relationship among licensees must be examined.

■ SALESPERSON STATUS

Employee vs. Independent Contractor

The salesperson working for a broker is usually regarded as an **employee** of the broker. The broker, not the salesperson, is really the principal's agent.

An **independent contractor** is one who is engaged to perform a duty but is not under the direct control of the principal. An independent contractor is accountable only for results. Control is the determining factor when considering employee versus independent contractor status. An independent contractor is reimbursed for results and is not subject to control and direction regarding how those results are achieved.

Most real estate brokers use contracts that specify the salesperson is an independent contractor rather than an employee. They take this measure to avoid withholding income taxes and contributing to Social Security. The Internal Revenue Service will treat the real estate salesperson as an independent contractor if the following three criteria are met:

1. The salesperson is licensed as a real estate agent.
2. Reimbursement is based solely on sales, not on hours worked.
3. There is a written contract that specifies the salesperson shall be treated as an independent contractor for tax purposes.

The IRS treatment of a real estate salesperson as an independent contractor applies only to income tax withholding and Social Security contributions. It does not apply to broker liability.

Brokers will often use independent contractors in an attempt to avoid liability for acts of agents or employees. Despite independent contractor agreements, real estate salespersons are considered employees as to liability for torts (wrongful acts). The broker is liable for the torts of his or her employees within the scope of their employment. Likewise, independent contractor agreements do not appear to protect brokers from injury claims by salespersons under workers' compensation. Brokers, therefore, should obtain workers' compensation coverage.

Case Study

The case of *Barry v. Raskov* (1991) 232 C.A.3d 447 involved an investor who was induced to put $55,000 into a $175,000 second mortgage on a property subject to a first trust deed of $100,000. The broker's appraiser indicated a property value of $400,000. The loan broker earned a $30,000 commission on the transaction. After default, another appraisal set the value of the property at $98,000.

The court held Raskov (the loan broker) liable for the torts of the appraiser. The court held that the fact that the appraiser may have been an independent contractor did not protect Raskov, as Section 10232.5 of the Business and Professions Code requires the broker to give potential lenders a statement of the estimated fair value of the property. This duty cannot be delegated.

Note: The court refused to award punitive damages because it did not feel the evidence of fraud was clear and convincing.

Grubb & Ellis Company v. Spengler (1983) 143 C.A.3d 890, indicates that real estate salespersons are not entitled to minimum wages or unemployment compensation.

Section 10177(h) of the Business and Professions Code requires that brokers supervise their salespeople. Exercise of supervision precludes an independent contractor relationship. Therefore, a salesperson is an employee of his or her broker regardless of what the contract with the broker claims the relationship to be [*Payne v. White House Properties Inc.* (1980) 112 C.A.3d 465].

Formerly, the broker had a duty to review contracts prepared by salespersons within five days. This has been replaced by a "reasonable supervision policy."

A salesperson who has a commission dispute with his or her broker could, as an employee, take the dispute to the state labor commissioner in the Department of Industrial Relations.

While a salesperson can only be compensated by his or her own broker, a salesperson can be compensated directly from an escrow company if the broker issues specific instructions on a case-by-case basis for such direct payment.

Because a broker can be held liable for the torts of his or her salespeople within the scope of employment (the doctrine of respondeat superior), the broker should ascertain that all salespersons carry and maintain adequate automobile insurance coverage. In addition, brokers should consider maintaining a high-limit general liability policy as well as an errors and omissions policy (malpractice) that covers the broker and all employees for negligence but not for intentional acts such as misrepresentation.

Due to their potential liability, many brokers astutely check references and past employers of prospective salespeople. A salesperson who places his or her own interests above honesty to all parties could mean financial ruin for his or her broker.

Franchisees

A franchise is a right to operate under a common name and marketing plan. Many large real estate firms are franchises.

Franchisees ordinarily are independent contractors, and the franchisor is not liable for the wrongful acts of the franchisee. If, however, the actions of the franchisor and franchisee are such that third parties could assume that the franchisee is an agent, the franchisor could be held liable for the acts of the franchisee. The franchisor should therefore make certain that advertising clearly reveals that the franchisee is an independent operator. (See *Kaplan v. Coldwell Banker*, Chapter 2.)

■ AGENT'S DUTIES TO THE PRINCIPAL

An agent's primary responsibility is to the principal, ordinarily the owner of property listed for sale or lease (although the principal could be the buyer alone or both buyer and seller under a dual agency).

In listing property, the agent has a duty to ascertain the value of the property. An agent could be held liable for suggesting a sales price that was too low and could not be justified by acceptable appraisal methods. Even if the owners suggest a sales price, the agent, as a real estate specialist, has a duty to provide the owner with a supported opinion of value. An agent could not knowingly arrange a sale of the principal's property at an amount significantly less than market value and escape liability with the defense that the owner set the price and did not ask the agent what the property was worth.

An agent must protect his or her principal. Sharp operators often seek to trade property of dubious value or to get sellers to accept offers that are not what they appear to be and are not in the sellers' best interests. The owner must be warned about offers with **subordination clauses.** Subordination clauses allow later loans to take priority over seller financing and endanger the seller's security in the property. They allow the purchaser to wipe out the seller's security interest by placing priority liens against the property. The owner also must be warned about exchanges involving trust deeds on other properties and about any transaction in which the purchaser will end up receiving cash.

Another fraudulent activity is **rent skimming,** where a purchaser takes possession with little if any down payment, but promising the seller to be "cashed out" in a short period of time. Usually the false promise involves the close of a nonexistent escrow. The buyer then rents the property, keeping rent receipts and making no payments. The definition of rent skimming has now been expanded to include collecting rents and deposits for property not owned or controlled by the landlord (protection for tenants) [Civil Code Section 890].

Case Study

The case of *People v. Lapcheske* (1999) 73 C.A.4th 571 involved a defendant who was convicted by the San Bernardino Superior Court of rent skimming, conspiracy to commit trespass, and grand theft. The defendant took over properties believed to be abandoned and rented them to tenants. He claimed, as an adverse possessor, he could not be guilty of rent skimming.

The court of appeal reversed the grand theft conviction but affirmed the other convictions. As an adverse possessor he had a legal right to collect rents so there was no grand theft. However, collecting rent without paying the existing mortgage is rent skimming.

Note: If Lapcheske had personally occupied the premises, he would not have been guilty of rent skimming.

In general the agent must caution the seller about any transaction in which the seller's interests are in any way endangered.

The agent must protect the principal from the fraud of others. In exchange situations the broker should make no representation about value that has not been appraised adequately, and the agent should provide the basis for the appraisal. The agent should suggest that expert help be obtained for situations beyond the agent's ability.

Case Study

In the case of *Schoenberg v. Romike Properties* (1967) 251 C.A.2d 154, a real estate agent induced the plaintiffs to part with valuable property in exchange for worthless security. The defendants told the owner that the buyer's security was better than taking security on the property sold. The agent failed to inform the owner that no investigation of the value of the security taken was made and that the agent had no knowledge of its true value. The agent had accepted an appraisal made for the owner that set value at ten times the real value. The court held that the plaintiffs had a right to rely on the defendants' statements and had no duty to make an independent investigation. The defendants' actions were held to be, at the very least, culpable negligence, and the buyer's fraud was held not to excuse that negligence.

The agent has a duty to reveal all pertinent information. For example, in a transaction where the seller is financing the buyer, the fact that the buyer borrowed the down payment could be pertinent. The agent should not make statements about the creditworthiness of the buyer unless such statements can be supported by fact. As protection from later owner claims of credit misrepresentation, the agent should arrange for a credit report on the purchaser to be obtained.

An agent must disclose all offers, including verbal offers. The agent must keep the principal informed on all matters likely to influence decision making. Included would be offers received after an offer has been accepted, right up to the close of escrow. However, acceptance of a second offer after a first offer has already been accepted should be conditioned on the seller's release from the first offer. Such a second offer is called a *backup offer*.

If acceptance of an offer is not in the principal's best interests, the agent must be careful not to encourage its acceptance. An agent could be liable for abusive pressure on a principal. Present case law does not indicate that an agent has an affirmative duty to recommend rejection of offers the agent believes to be unreasonable. However, because of the fiduciary relationship between the agent and the principal, a future decision about this duty is conceivable.

The agent cannot make a **secret profit**. The agent works for the principal and is entitled only to the compensation agreed on. The fact that the principal received a good price and was treated fairly is immaterial. The principal is entitled to any secret profit the agent receives. As an example, if the agent were in fact the purchaser through secret control of a corporation that purchased the property, the agent would have to give up the profit made on the subsequent resale. In addition, the agent would have to return any commission received, because the agent breached his or her fiduciary duty.

If a buyer intends to relist the property or another property with the agent, the agent has a duty to reveal the fact that the owner's acceptance of an offer would put the agent in a position of being able to earn another commission.

The agent has a duty of confidentiality. The seller's agent could be held liable for revealing to a purchaser without the owner's authorization information that weakens the principal's bargaining ability. The agent's duty of confidentiality continues even after the expiration of the agency. An agent who later uses confidential information obtained through the agency relationship to the detriment of the former principal is breaching his or her fiduciary duty.

An agent could be liable for negligence in drafting an agreement and should consider this potential liability before attempting to draft any agreement or make major modifications to a printed contract. Obtaining professional legal assistance should be considered. An agent must avoid the unauthorized practice of law. An agent's duty does not extend to giving tax advice to buyers and sellers.

Case Study

The case of *Carleton v. Tortosa* (1993) 14 C.A.4th 745 concerned an experienced investor, Carleton, who listed property for sale. Carleton asked the agent how many days he had to reinvest the sale proceeds. The agent told the owner to "ask your tax person." Carleton was unable to reach his accountant, but the accountant's assistant told Carleton that he had 45 days. After the sale Carleton learned he owed approximately $34,000 in taxes. Carleton sued the agent for professional negligence in failing to recognized a tax-deferred exchange situation. The court of appeal emphasized that a real estate agent has no duty to give tax advice. The listing statement, "A real estate agent is a person qualified to advise about real estate. If legal or tax advice is desired, consult a competent professional," strengthened the agent's defense.

Note: If the agent had given tax advice, she could have been found negligent and liable for damages.

Net Listings

Under a **net listing** the agent's commission is all money received for a property over a net amount set in the listing. Illegal in a number of other states, net listings are legal in California. However, serious conflict-of-interest problems can arise. The broker is no longer working simply to consummate a sale but wants a sale at as much over the listing price as possible. In setting the net price, the agent's best interest thus is served by as low a price as possible. That is contrary to the principal's best interests.

Prior to or at the time of acceptance of an offer on a net listing the broker must disclose to the principal the amount of commission to be received [Business and Professions Code Section 10176(g)]. If the licensee makes an extraordinary profit from a net listing, the owner may claim that the agent, in helping to set the list price, was acting in a self-serving manner and therefore breached his or her duties of financial trust. A net listing could very well be an invitation to a lawsuit.

Option Listings

In an **option listing** the broker takes a listing combined with an option to purchase. This places the broker in the dual role of agent and principal. To exercise the option, the agent would have to reveal all offers received. This probably extends to oral offers as well as written ones.

Section 10176(h) of the Business and Professions Code requires the agent to reveal fully, in writing, the amount of profit and to obtain the principal's written consent to the amount of profit. The withholding of approval could prevent the exercise of the option.

In a combined listing-option agreement the broker also should make certain that the owner understands that the exercise of the option is at the broker's discretion. The listing-option agreement is not a guaranteed sales agreement in which the broker agrees to purchase in the event a buyer is not found.

Agent as Buyer

When a licensee is acting as a principal, the agent should inform the buyers and sellers that he or she, while a licensed real estate agent, is dealing as a principal and not in an agency capacity.

Full disclosure could extend beyond revealing that the purchaser is an agent and is associated with the listing firm to revealing the motives or intentions of the purchaser. If the agent intends to purchase the property for resale, the agent should disclose not only that fact but also what the agent hopes to obtain and any possible purchasers then known to the agent. If the agent intends to do work on the property to make the property more valuable, the agent should disclose these intentions.

Many firms will not allow any of their salespeople or brokers to purchase office listings because they feel that the firm and purchaser also could be buying litigation. Because the agent has the duty to represent the owner and the owner's best interests, the principal should have the opportunity to use the expertise of the agent to the principal's advantage and not have the principal's property used by the agent in a self-serving manner. In purchasing an office listing, the agent appears to be putting self-interest above the interests of a client, which violates the agent's fiduciary duties. Courts are likely to determine that an agent was acting in a self-serving manner rather than protecting the interests of the principal if there is evidence that the purchase price was substantially below market value.

If the agent helped set the list price and purchased at the list price or less and then sold at a profit, a court very likely would determine that the agent purposely set the price too low. Action such as this could result in not only compensatory damages but punitive damages as well.

Even if the owner set the list price, the agent would have a duty of financial trust to inform the owner of the property's value. If the agent accomplished a rapid resale at a profit, the courts would be more likely to determine that the agent breached his or her duty of full disclosure. The courts could determine that the agent made a secret profit, which would then have to be turned over to the principal.

When property is purchased by an agent and resold at a profit, the courts are likely to burden the agent with proving that full disclosure has been made. As a means of protection the agent should prepare a complete disclosure of all material facts, including his or her intentions, and have it signed by the sellers prior to the purchase agreement.

Even with full disclosure, courts could determine that undue influence was used to obtain an agreement based on the principal-agent relationship of trust. Additional protection against such claims would require that the seller obtain independent legal counsel and that the seller's attorney also receive all disclosures.

Disclosures also should be made when the purchaser is related to the agent by blood or marriage or connected by a strong business or social relationship. If an appearance of impropriety exists, courts are likely to determine that a duty was breached.

Even if an agent prevails in a lawsuit, a suit by a client can damage a firm's reputation and be costly in time and money.

Case Study

In the case of *In re Estate of De Harte* (1961) 196 C.A.2d 452, a broker neglected to inform the administrator of an estate that the purchaser was his mother. Seventeen days after the sale was approved for $9,600, the purchaser entered into an agreement to sell the property for $11,900. The agreement was arranged by the broker. The court held that the good-faith duties of an agent preclude the agent from taking an adverse position. The court considered this sale a fraud on the court and the administrator. The sale and the prior confirmation of the broker's commission were vacated by the court.

■ AGENT'S DUTIES TO BUYERS

In the past, what an agent did not know could not hurt the agent. Agents did not want to be aware of detrimental information about a property so they would have no duty of disclosure.

The *Easton* Case

Now, not only must an agent disclose detrimental facts known about a property but the case of *Easton v. Strassburger* (1984) 152 C.A.3d 90 determined that the agent also has an *affirmative duty* to find out material facts. A broker's duty of disclosure applies to facts that should be known as well as known facts. In this case a home was sold for $170,000 through a broker. After the sale the property suffered extreme damage in a landslide. The cost to repair was estimated at $213,000.

The court held that the duties of the real estate broker include "the affirmative duty to conduct a reasonably competent and diligent inspection of the residential property listed for sale and to disclose to prospective purchasers all facts materially affecting the value of the property that such an investigation would reveal."

In this case a reasonable inspection would have revealed the problem because testimony indicated that

- a listing agent had seen netting on a hill used to repair a prior landslide;
- at least one agent knew the house was built on filled land; and
- the floor of the guesthouse was known not to be level.

The court in the *Easton* case indicated that its decision did not necessarily apply to commercial transactions, in which buyers are likely to be more sophisticated. (This was later confirmed in the *Smith v. Rickard* case referenced on page 62, which refused to extend *Easton* to commercial property.)

The California Supreme Court declined to hear the *Easton* case, which makes the decision an authority for the duties of licensees.

California Civil Code Section 2079 et seq. was passed to codify, clarify and modify the duties imposed by the *Easton* decision. According to the *Department of Real Estate Bulletin* the impact of the bill can be summarized as follows:

- It [the bill] mandates only a reasonably competent visual inspection of the property. The decision in *Easton* does not clearly indicate the type of inspection required.
- The duty to make the visual inspection is limited to residential real property of one to four units. The duty in *Easton* was limited to residential property.
- It defines the standard of care owed by a broker to a prospective purchaser as the degree of care a reasonably prudent real estate licensee would exercise and is measured by the degree of knowledge through education, experience, and examination required to obtain a real estate license under California law. *Easton* did not clearly define the measure of the standard of care owed by a broker to the buyer.
- It would apply the duty only to a broker who has entered into a written contract with the seller to find or obtain a buyer and to a broker who acts in cooperation with such a (listing) broker to find and obtain a buyer. *Easton* did not limit its application to brokers with written contracts, nor did it impose a duty on cooperating brokers.
- It provides that the duty of inspection does not include or involve areas that are reasonably and normally inaccessible to such inspection or to inspection of common areas in common-interest subdivisions if the seller or broker supplies the prospective buyer with the documents and information specified in Civil Code Section 1360. *Easton* did not address the issue of the scope of the inspection.
- It established a two-year statute of limitations that runs from the date of recordation, close of escrow, or occupancy, whichever occurs first.
- It provides that the buyer or prospective buyer has a duty to exercise reasonable care to protect himself or herself, including knowledge of adverse facts that are known to or within the diligent attention and observation of the buyer or prospective buyer. *Easton* stated that a buyer has a duty to make a reasonable inspection but did not limit its application to cases where the facts were not known but determinable by a diligent inspection or observation by the buyer.
- Although not directly related to the duties imposed under *Easton*, the bill provides that no professional liability insurer may exclude under its policy coverage for liability arising as a result of a breach of the duty established by the bill and the *Easton* decision.

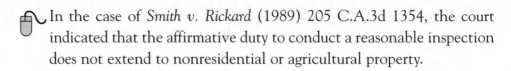 In the case of *Smith v. Rickard* (1989) 205 C.A.3d 1354, the court indicated that the affirmative duty to conduct a reasonable inspection does not extend to nonresidential or agricultural property.

Oral and Written Disclosures

The duty of a seller to disclose relevant facts concerning the property for sale can be found in California statutes, case law, and real estate law.

Section 1102 of the Civil Code requires that a seller of one to four residential units provide a written disclosure of known property defects to a purchaser. To comply with this disclosure requirement the California Association of REALTORS® has developed the Real Estate **Transfer Disclosure Statement**.

Shown in Figure 3.1, this form requires sellers to disclose defects that are known to them. The seller certifies that the information given is true and correct to the seller's knowledge. Defects are not limited to the physical aspects of the property but also include items such as zoning violations and nuisances in the area. The seller's agent and cooperating agent (if applicable) also execute this disclosure statement, indicating the existence of defects based on a reasonably competent and diligent visual inspection of the accessible areas of the property. The form also advises the purchasers that they may wish to obtain professional advice or their own inspection of the property.

The disclosure of known facts includes any negative fact that would be likely to influence a purchaser's decision. The presence of minority group members in the area is not considered a detrimental fact and should not be revealed. In fact, providing such information to a buyer likely would be considered steering, which would be a violation of the Civil Rights Act of 1968.

The transferor of one to four residential units built before January 1, 1960, must give a buyer a booklet entitled *Homeowner Guide to Earthquake Safety* prior to the transfer and disclose any known deficiencies such as absence of anchor bolts, unreinforced masonry walls, unanchored water heater, etc. The seller or his agent must also complete a Natural Hazards Disclosure Statement that indicates if the property is in a special flood hazard area, an area of potential flooding, a very high fire hazard severity zone, a wildlife area which may contain substantial fire risks and hazards, an earthquake fault zone, or a seismic hazard zone.

It is in the best interests of the seller as well as the buyer for the seller to disclose all potential problems of the property. Revealing possible problem areas not only alerts the buyers but also protects the seller against later claims of misrepresentation.

FIGURE 3.1

**Real Estate Transfer
Disclosure Statement**

CALIFORNIA
ASSOCIATION
OF REALTORS®

REAL ESTATE TRANSFER DISCLOSURE STATEMENT
(CALIFORNIA CIVIL CODE 1102, ET SEQ)
(C.A.R. Form TDS, Revised 10/01)

THIS DISCLOSURE STATEMENT CONCERNS THE REAL PROPERTY SITUATED IN THE CITY OF _____
_____, COUNTY OF _____, STATE OF CALIFORNIA,
DESCRIBED AS _____.
THIS STATEMENT IS A DISCLOSURE OF THE CONDITION OF THE ABOVE DESCRIBED PROPERTY IN COMPLIANCE
WITH SECTION 1102 OF THE CIVIL CODE AS OF (date) _____. IT IS NOT A WARRANTY OF ANY
KIND BY THE SELLER(S) OR ANY AGENT(S) REPRESENTING ANY PRINCIPAL(S) IN THIS TRANSACTION, AND IS
NOT A SUBSTITUTE FOR ANY INSPECTIONS OR WARRANTIES THE PRINCIPAL(S) MAY WISH TO OBTAIN.

I. COORDINATION WITH OTHER DISCLOSURE FORMS

This Real Estate Transfer Disclosure Statement is made pursuant to Section 1102 of the Civil Code. Other statutes require disclosures, depending upon the details of the particular real estate transaction (for example: special study zone and purchase-money liens on residential property).

Substituted Disclosures: The following disclosures have or will be made in connection with this real estate transfer, and are intended to satisfy the disclosure obligations on this form, where the subject matter is the same:

☐ Inspection reports completed pursuant to the contract of sale or receipt for deposit.

☐ Additional inspection reports or disclosures: _____

II. SELLER'S INFORMATION

The Seller discloses the following information with the knowledge that even though this is not a warranty, prospective Buyers may rely on this information in deciding whether and on what terms to purchase the subject property. Seller hereby authorizes any agent(s) representing any principal(s) in this transaction to provide a copy of this statement to any person or entity in connection with any actual or anticipated sale of the property.

THE FOLLOWING ARE REPRESENTATIONS MADE BY THE SELLER(S) AND ARE NOT THE REPRESENTATIONS OF THE AGENT(S), IF ANY. THIS INFORMATION IS A DISCLOSURE AND IS NOT INTENDED TO BE PART OF ANY CONTRACT BETWEEN THE BUYER AND SELLER.

Seller ☐ is ☐ is not occupying the property.

A. The subject property has the items checked below (read across)

☐ Range ☐ Oven ☐ Microwave
☐ Dishwasher ☐ Trash Compactor ☐ Garbage Disposal
☐ Washer/Dryer Hookups ☐ Rain Gutters
☐ Burglar Alarms ☐ Smoke Detector(s) ☐ Fire Alarm
☐ T.V. Antenna ☐ Satellite Dish ☐ Intercom
☐ Central Heating ☐ Central Air Conditioning ☐ Evaporator Cooler(s)
☐ Wall/Window Air Conditioning ☐ Sprinklers ☐ Public Sewer System
☐ Septic Tank ☐ Sump Pump ☐ Water Softener
☐ Patio/Decking ☐ Built-in Barbecue ☐ Gazebo
☐ Sauna
☐ Hot Tub ☐ Locking Safety Cover* ☐ Pool ☐ Child Resistant Barrier* ☐ Spa ☐ Locking Safety Cover*
☐ Security Gate(s) ☐ Automatic Garage Door Opener(s)* ☐ Number Remote Controls ____
Garage: ☐ Attached ☐ Not Attached ☐ Carport
Pool/Spa Heater: ☐ Gas ☐ Solar ☐ Electric
Water Heater: ☐ Gas ☐ Water Heater Anchored, Braced, or Strapped*
Water Supply: ☐ City ☐ Well ☐ Private Utility or
Gas Supply: ☐ Utility ☐ Bottled Other _____
☐ Window Screens ☐ Window Security Bars ☐ Quick Release Mechanism on Bedroom Windows*

Exhaust Fan(s) in _____ 220 Volt Wiring in _____ Fireplace(s) in _____
☐ Gas Starter _____ ☐ Roof(s): Type: _____ Age: _____ (approx.)
☐ Other: _____
Are there, to the best of your (Seller's) knowledge, any of the above that are not in operating condition? ☐ Yes ☐ No. If yes, then describe. (Attach additional sheets if necessary): _____

(*see footnote on page 2)

The copyright laws of the United States (Title 17 U.S. Code) forbid the unauthorized reproduction of this form, or any portion thereof, by photocopy machine or any other means, including facsimile or computerized formats. Copyright © 1991-2001, CALIFORNIA ASSOCIATION OF REALTORS®, INC. ALL RIGHTS RESERVED.

TDS-11 REVISED 10/01 (PAGE 1 OF 3) Print Date

Buyer and Seller acknowledge receipt of a copy of this page.
Buyer's Initials (_____)(_____)
Seller's Initials (_____)(_____)
Reviewed by
Broker or Designee _____ Date _____

EQUAL HOUSING OPPORTUNITY

REAL ESTATE TRANSFER DISCLOSURE STATEMENT (TDS-11 PAGE 1 OF 3)

Reprinted with permission, California Associaton of REALTORS®. Endorsement not implied.

FIGURE 3.1 (continued)

**Real Estate Transfer
Disclosure Statement**

Property Address: _____ Date: _____

B. Are you (Seller) aware of any significant defects/malfunctions in any of the following? ☐ Yes ☐ No. If yes, check appropriate space(s) below.

☐ Interior Walls ☐ Ceilings ☐ Floors ☐ Exterior Walls ☐ Insulation ☐ Roof(s ☐ Windows ☐ Doors ☐ Foundation ☐ Slab(s)
☐ Driveways ☐ Sidewalks ☐ Walls/Fences ☐ Electrical Systems ☐ Plumbing/Sewers/Septics ☐ Other Structural Components
(Describe:_____
_____)
If any of the above is checked, explain. (Attach additional sheets if necessary):_____
_____
_____

*This garage door opener or child resistant pool barrier may not be in compliance with the safety standards relating to automatic reversing devices as set forth in Chapter 12.5 (commencing with Section 19890) of Part 3 of Division 13 of, or with the pool safety standards of Article 2.5 (commencing with Section 115920) of Chapter 5 of Part 10 of Division 104 of, the Health and Safety Code. The water heater may not be anchored, braced, or strapped in accordance with Section 19211 of the Health and Safety Code. Window security bars may not have quick release mechanisms in compliance with the 1995 Edition of the California Building Standards Code.

C. Are you (Seller) aware of any of the following:
1. Substances, materials, or products which may be an environmental hazard such as, but not limited to, asbestos, formaldehyde, radon gas, lead-based paint, mold, fuel or chemical storage tanks, and contaminated soil or water on the subject property . . . . ☐ Yes ☐ No
2. Features of the property shared in common with adjoining landowners, such as walls, fences, and driveways, whose use or responsibility for maintenance may have an effect on the subject property . . . . ☐ Yes ☐ No
3. Any encroachments, easements or similar matters that may affect your interest in the subject property . . . . ☐ Yes ☐ No
4. Room additions, structural modifications, or other alterations or repairs made without necessary permits . . . . ☐ Yes ☐ No
5. Room additions, structural modifications, or other alterations or repairs not in compliance with building codes . . . . . . ☐ Yes ☐ No
6. Fill (compacted or otherwise) on the property or any portion thereof . . . . ☐ Yes ☐ No
7. Any settling from any cause, or slippage, sliding, or other soil problems . . . . ☐ Yes ☐ No
8. Flooding, drainage or grading problems . . . . ☐ Yes ☐ No
9. Major damage to the property or any of the structures from fire, earthquake, floods, or landslides . . . . ☐ Yes ☐ No
10. Any zoning violations, nonconforming uses, violations of "setback" requirements . . . . ☐ Yes ☐ No
11. Neighborhood noise problems or other nuisances . . . . ☐ Yes ☐ No
12. CC&R's or other deed restrictions or obligations . . . . ☐ Yes ☐ No
13. Homeowners' Association which has any authority over the subject property . . . . ☐ Yes ☐ No
14. Any "common area" (facilities such as pools, tennis courts, walkways, or other areas co-owned in undivided interest with others) . . . . ☐ Yes ☐ No
15. Any notices of abatement or citations against the property . . . . ☐ Yes ☐ No
16. Any lawsuits by or against the seller threatening to or affecting this real property, including any lawsuits alleging a defect or deficiency in this real property or "common areas" (facilities such as pools, tennis courts, walkways, or other areas, co-owned in undivided interest with others) . . . . ☐ Yes ☐ No

If the answer to any of these is yes, explain. (Attach additional sheets if necessary): _____
_____
_____

Seller certifies that the information herein is true and correct to the best of the Seller's knowledge as of the date signed by the Seller.

Seller_____ Date _____

Seller_____ Date _____

TDS-11 REVISED 10/01 (PAGE 2 OF 3) Print Date

Buyer and Seller acknowledge receipt of a copy of this page.
Buyer's Initials (_____)(_____)
Seller's Initials (_____)(_____)

Reviewed by _____
Broker or Designee _____ Date _____

EQUAL HOUSING OPPORTUNITY

REAL ESTATE TRANSFER DISCLOSURE STATEMENT (TDS-11 PAGE 2 OF 3)

FIGURE 3.1 (continued)

**Real Estate Transfer
Disclosure Statement**

Property Address: _____ Date: _____

III. AGENT'S INSPECTION DISCLOSURE
(To be completed only if the Seller is represented by an agent in this transaction.)

THE UNDERSIGNED, BASED ON THE ABOVE INQUIRY OF THE SELLER(S) AS TO THE CONDITION OF THE PROPERTY AND BASED ON A REASONABLY COMPETENT AND DILIGENT VISUAL INSPECTION OF THE ACCESSIBLE AREAS OF THE PROPERTY IN CONJUNCTION WITH THAT INQUIRY, STATES THE FOLLOWING:

☐ Agent notes no items for disclosure.
☐ Agent notes the following items: _____
_____
_____
_____

Agent (Broker Representing Seller) _____ By _____ Date _____
(Please Print)   (Associate-License or Broker Signature)

IV. AGENT'S INSPECTION DISCLOSURE
(To be completed only if the agent who has obtained the offer is other than the agent above.)

THE UNDERSIGNED, BASED ON A REASONABLY COMPETENT AND DILIGENT VISUAL INSPECTION OF THE ACCESSIBLE AREAS OF THE PROPERTY, STATES THE FOLLOWING:

☐ Agent notes no items for disclosure.
☐ Agent notes the following items: _____
_____
_____

Agent (Broker Obtaining the Offer) _____ By _____ Date _____
(Please Print)   (Associate-License or Broker Signature)

V. BUYER(S) AND SELLER(S) MAY WISH TO OBTAIN PROFESSIONAL ADVICE AND/OR INSPECTIONS OF THE PROPERTY AND TO PROVIDE FOR APPROPRIATE PROVISIONS IN A CONTRACT BETWEEN BUYER AND SELLER(S) WITH RESPECT TO ANY ADVICE/INSPECTIONS/DEFECTS.

I/WE ACKNOWLEDGE RECEIPT OF A COPY OF THIS STATEMENT.

Seller _____ Date _____   Buyer _____ Date _____

Seller _____ Date _____   Buyer _____ Date _____

Agent (Broker Representing Seller) _____ By _____ Date _____
(Associate-License or Broker Signature)

Agent (Broker Obtaining the Offer) _____ By _____ Date _____
(Associate-License or Broker Signature)

SECTION 1102.3 OF THE CIVIL CODE PROVIDES A BUYER WITH THE RIGHT TO RESCIND A PURCHASE CONTRACT FOR AT LEAST THREE DAYS AFTER THE DELIVERY OF THIS DISCLOSURE IF DELIVERY OCCURS AFTER THE SIGNING OF AN OFFER TO PURCHASE. IF YOU WISH TO RESCIND THE CONTRACT, YOU MUST ACT WITHIN THE PRESCRIBED PERIOD.

A REAL ESTATE BROKER IS QUALIFIED TO ADVISE ON REAL ESTATE. IF YOU DESIRE LEGAL ADVICE, CONSULT YOUR ATTORNEY.

TDS-11 REVISED 10/01 (PAGE 3 OF 3) Print Date

REAL ESTATE TRANSFER DISCLOSURE STATEMENT (TDS-11 PAGE 3 OF 3)

Case Study

In the case of *Geernaent v. Mitchell* (1995) 31 C.A.4th 601, a seller indicated that there were no foundation problems and modifications made were to code. True facts were apparently concealed in order to make the sale. The house was sold and then resold. The buyer sued the original owner for misrepresentation. The trial court held that homeowners could not sue a prior owner for alleged fraudulent misrepresentations because the misrepresentations were not made directly to the plaintiffs.

But the appeals court held that a seller can be liable to subsequent buyers for misrepresentations made to previous buyers even if there is no privity of contract. The court pointed out that the plaintiff still had the burden of showing that defendants could reasonably expect subsequent purchasers to rely on their misrepresentation.

After three years, an agent need not disclose the cause of death of a prior occupant from any cause. Civil Code 1710.2 states "No cause of action arises against an owner of real property or his or her agent, or any agent of a transferee for failure to disclose the occurrence of an occupant's death upon the real estate or the manner of death where the death has occurred more than three years prior to the date the transferee offers to purchase...." Civil Code Section 1710.2 does not actually require disclosing a death on the premises within the three years before the sale. However, many agents feel that such disclosure is implied by the statute and they should disclose death by murder or suicide within three years of the sale.

Case Study

The case of *Reed v. King* (1983) 145 C.A.3d 261 involved a sale in which the agent did not inform the purchaser that five murders had been committed in the house ten years earlier. The agent was held to have breached the duty of disclosure because the fact of the murders could have been expected to disturb a purchaser and could materially affect a property's value. The rule of the *Reed v. King* case has, however, now been modified by Civil Code Section 1710.2.

What facts need to be disclosed is an issue that is always evolving. For example, in recent years the prevalence of AIDS (acquired immunodeficiency syndrome) in the United States has created a new dilemma for real estate agents. Should a broker reveal that a tenant or owner had AIDS or suspected AIDS? The risk of slander if the agent were mistaken and the question of whether the presence of AIDS is a material fact requiring disclosure have been discussed at length within the real estate and legal professions. The situation was resolved by Civil Code Section 1710.2, which provides that neither the owner nor the agent shall be liable to the transferee for failing to disclose that an occupant was afflicted with or died of AIDS.

Opinion 95-907 of the California Attorney General indicates that an agent need not disclose the nearby location of a licensed care facility servicing six or fewer people (a larger facility would likely require disclosure).

Megan's Law concerns the registration of sex offenders and making information regarding sex offenders available to the public. Civil Code Section 2079.10(a) now requires that every lease or rental agreement for residential real property and every contract for the sale of one to four residential units must include a specific notice informing consumers of the available public information regarding registered sex offenders at local police and sheriff offices.

If an agent knows that a contemplated use is not allowed or is unlikely to be allowed because of zoning or other restrictions, the agent has an affirmative duty to tell the buyer.

Agents may not use blind ads to attract buyers. A **blind ad** is one that fails to indicate that the advertiser is an agent and not a principal. (See Figure 4.1 on page 97 for advertising requirements.)

Inducing the purchase of a particular property by giving false comparables could subject an agent to damages for fraud. Agents have been known to show overpriced listings to make the property they hope to sell appear to be a bargain. Courts conceivably could treat this practice as a fraudulent representation of value.

Case Study

A broker neglected to inform a purchaser that there was a due-on-sale clause in a second trust deed being assumed. This clause required that the loan be repaid in full should the property be sold. The property subsequently was lost by foreclosure of the second trust deed. The court held that even though the agent might have believed the loan was assumable despite the due-on-sale clause, the agent breached a duty to inform the purchaser about the clause. The court awarded damages amounting to

(continued on next page)

the difference between the purchase price and encumbrances (purchaser's equity) as well as expenses incurred to prevent foreclosure [*Pepitone v. Russo* (1997) 64 C.A.3d 685].

Case Study

The case of *Jue v. Smiser* (1994) 23 C.A. 4th 312 involved a late disclosure. Buyers contracted to buy a home represented to have been designed by renowned architect Julia Morgan. The name Julia Morgan added to the prestige value of the property. Apparently, the sellers had some doubt as to that representation because three days before the close of escrow, the sellers asked the buyers to sign a document acknowledging that there were no plans available that verified the architect. The buyers refused to sign but went through with the purchase. Then discovering the house was not designed by Julia Morgan, the buyers then sued the sellers and their broker for misrepresentation. The trial court held that there was no reliance on the misrepresentation because of the disclosure prior to the closing of escrow.

The court of appeal reversed the trial court, holding that it is not necessary that there be continuing reliance until the contract is executed.

Note: While full disclosure of detrimental facts learned is required prior to closing, the disclosure might not be enough to avoid liability. In a case such as this, the last-minute disclosure could place buyers in a position where they would have to complete the purchase or be homeless.

Case Study

The case of *Salahutin v. Valley of Calif. Inc.* (1994) 24 C.A.4th 555 involved buyers who in 1979 told a real estate agent that they wanted to buy a home that could eventually be divided into two lots (for each of their children). The agent found a home listed by another agent and the MLS listing said "1 Acre+."

The agent knew that the Hillsborough property had to be at least 1 acre to allow a future lot split. In 1989, the buyers discovered that the lot contained only .998 acres so it could not be split. The value of the parcel was $175,000 less than it would have been if a split were possible. The court held that the selling broker had a fiduciary duty either to investigate the

(continued on next page)

size of the lot or to tell the buyer he had not done so, as size was of significant importance to the buyers.

Constructive fraud can occur when the broker is merely an innocent conduit of misinformation. The court applied damages based on value at time of discovery of the fraud rather than at time of purchase. (The buyers paid only $274,000 in 1979, but it would have been worth $1,100,000 in 1989 if it could have been subdivided.)

Note: If any representation by the owner or listing broker is of importance to a buyer, the selling broker should either check it out or disclose to the buyer that it is the representation of another, which he or she has not verified

An agent cannot avoid full disclosure by using words such as **"as is"** in the sale of residential property. "As is" means the property is being sold in its present condition and the seller will not pay for any repairs. Courts generally have held that "as is" applies only to specific named items or to obvious defects that would be seen by a buyer (**patent defects**). Courts have held that "as is" does not protect an agent from known **latent defects**–those that would be unlikely to be disclosed by an inspection. Exceptions include probate, tax, and foreclosure sales where the sale may be "as is."

Mobile Home Transfers A mobile home transfer disclosure statement, similar to the one- to four-unit residential transfer disclosure statement, is required upon transfer of a personal property mobile home or manufactured home. The agents are also required to make a visual inspection.

The Real Estate Transfer Disclosure Statement is not required for business and income property. In the sale of income property or business opportunities, reliance by the buyer on false information likely could result in a lawsuit involving the broker. The broker, whenever possible, should attempt to verify figures from the owner's income tax returns and/or sales tax reports. The broker should never report income and expense figures as fact but should state that they come only from the owner and should note if and how they were verified.

An agent who showed a prospective buyer only a few units in an apartment complex probably would be implying that they were representative of all of the units. If in fact the units shown were only the few updated units, the broker's action might be considered fraud even though specific representations were not made.

The case of *Ford v. Cournale* (1974) 36 C.A.3d 172 held that providing income data based on 100 percent occupancy was misrepresentation for which the broker could be held liable.

The Unsophisticated Buyer

Court decisions seem to indicate that an agent has greater duties when dealing with an unsophisticated party than when dealing with a sophisticated party. With an unsophisticated buyer the agent should ascertain that the purchaser fully understands the effect of balloon payments, points, and other matters that might not be obvious to such a buyer.

If an unsophisticated buyer requested property tax information, the agent probably would have the duty to explain that past property taxes are not indicative of what property taxes will be in the future because the property will be reassessed upon sale.

Agents should avoid discouraging prospective buyers from obtaining professional help such as an attorney or a fee appraiser and should take care not to convey a false sense of urgency. Such actions would adversely affect a broker's defense in a lawsuit involving a breach of duty or fraud.

Fraud, Misrepresentation and Puffing

Fraud is intentional deceit to induce a party to act to his or her detriment. Courts might award punitive as well as compensatory damages for an agent's fraud. In addition, fraud could result in criminal prosecution.

Case Study

The federal court in *U.S. v. Mayberry* (1990) 913 F.2d 719 upheld the criminal conviction of a broker. The broker arranged for his clients to purchase property and caused them to provide HUD with false information so they could obtain federally insured mortgages. The representations included that they had made larger down payments than they actually had and that they had personally paid all settlement costs.

Misrepresentation is the unintentional misstatement of a material fact. Misrepresentation could result in civil damages to compensate the injured party as well as other contractual remedies.

There is some question about the broker's liability to a buyer when repeating false information provided by the owner. If the broker knew or should have known the information was false, the broker likely would be liable. It is not known if the *Easton* decision would extend to a duty to check facts provided by an owner. As minimum protection, when supplying facts that have not been verified, a broker should indicate the source of the facts and that they have not been verified.

Puffing is considered sales talk and is a statement of opinion, such as "You will be happy in this house" or "I consider this home to be an exceptional value." There can be a fine line between allowable puffing and misrepresentation or fraud. If an agent were to represent nearly worthless desert property as "a sound investment," a court might determine such a statement to be fraud or misrepresentation rather than mere puffing.

Referral Fees

When someone is moving from the area, brokers often will recommend that he or she see a particular broker in the new area. The prospective buyer reasonably could believe that the broker is acting as a gratuitous agent in recommending someone who can best meet his or her needs. This often is not the case; the broker may in fact be recommending that the buyer see a particular broker because that broker will give the agent part of any commission upon any resulting sale. A case could be made that this fee is a secret profit being made by the presumed gratuitous agent of the buyer. If the courts agreed to this supposition, the buyer would be entitled to the secret profit paid to the agent. Brokers could protect themselves by making full disclosure of any financial arrangements they have with the recommended firm.

A real estate licensee may not offer premium gifts or anything of value to a purchaser or lender as an inducement to make a loan or buy a promissory note or sales contract. However, the restriction has been removed as to prospective borrowers. (Business and Professions Code Section 10236.1)

■ DUTIES TO OTHER BROKERS

A broker has no legal duty to cooperate with other brokers; however, brokers customarily cooperate with one another because doing so is in their best interests. The various associations serving the real estate business have codes of ethics and rules that help set standards for professional conduct. These are not laws, though statutes cover some of the same areas. The penalties for breaching these rules generally are fines or expulsion from the organization. If the exclusion of a broker from an organization would have a detrimental economic effect on that broker's business, then exclusion can be effected only for good cause.

The largest association of brokers is the National Association of REALTORS® (NAR). The state organization of NAR is the California Association of REALTORS® (CAR). The word REALTOR® is a trademark word, and it is a violation of the law for a person who is not a member of the NAR to use the REALTORS® designation. The same is true for Realtist, which denotes a member of the National Association of Real Estate Brokers.

The National Association of REALTORS® encourages arbitration of broker disputes, but brokers can sue one another in court.

To work with **subagents**, the broker must have the specific approval of the principal. If the listing authorizes subbrokers (subagents), an agency is created between the seller and the subbroker. The seller is liable to third persons for the subbroker's actions, and the subbroker has a fiduciary responsibility to the owner. (Listings that authorize the listing agent to make the property available to a multiple-listing service really authorize the creation of subagents.)

If a subbroker is appointed properly, the original agent is not responsible to third parties for the acts of the subbroker. If an agent appoints a subbroker without authority to do so, the subbroker is the agent of the listing broker and not of the principal.

A broker could be held liable to another broker if the first broker indicated that he or she had an exclusive-right-to-sell listing and the other broker obtained a buyer only to find there was no listing.

Multiple-listing services may not exclude listings that are not exclusive-right-to-sell listings. Such action would be an unreasonable restraint of trade, as would agreements setting minimum commissions among brokers.

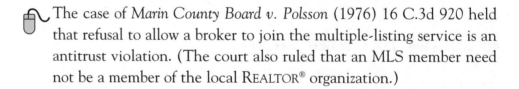 The case of *Marin County Board v. Polsson* (1976) 16 C.3d 920 held that refusal to allow a broker to join the multiple-listing service is an antitrust violation. (The court also ruled that an MLS member need not be a member of the local REALTOR® organization.)

Sherman Antitrust Act of 1890

The Sherman Antitrust Act was enacted to prevent businesses from conspiring to control prices and/or competition. Penalties for violations include fines, damages, court costs, and up to three years' imprisonment.

Antitrust violations include the following:

1. Price-Fixing. It would be illegal for a group of brokers to agree on minimum commissions that they would charge.
2. Market Allocation. Agreements of firms to divide a marketplace geographically or by type of service would be a violation, as it would tend to reduce or eliminate competition.
3. Group Boycotting. Firms may not agree to refuse to do business

with a firm or individual. As an example, it would be a violation of the act for two or more firms to agree not to allow another firm to show their listings.

4. Tie-in Agreements. Agreements that require a business to buy additional goods or services in order to get the goods or services desired would be illegal. An example of a tie-in agreement would be the requirement that the buyer agree to keep the property insured through a firm controlled by the broker as a condition of submitting the buyer's offer.

The Cartwright Act is California's antitrust act that prohibits agreements restraining trade.

■ FEES TO NONLICENSEES

A licensee can pay a referral fee or **finder's fee** to a nonlicensee for an introduction. The introduction must, however, be the extent of the finder's involvement; the nonlicensee cannot quote prices, show property, or perform any duty for which a license is required. A broker may not compensate an unlicensed finder who performs any act for which a license is required (Business and Professions Code Section 10137).

Case Study

Tenzer, a director of Superscope, was asked to find a buyer for property owned by the corporation. The president orally agreed to a 10 percent finder's fee, and Tenzer produced a buyer who purchased the property for $16 million. The corporation refused to pay Tenzer a finder's fee. After a summary judgment in favor of Superscope, the case was appealed to the California Supreme Court.

The court held that a finder without a written agreement may recover if the principal is estopped from pleading the statute of frauds.

The court held that if Tenzer was not otherwise obligated to reveal the names of the prospective purchaser and did so upon the verbal promise of a finder's fee, then Superscope would be estopped from raising the defense of the statute of frauds. While licensed brokers cannot get around the statute of frauds by claiming estoppel, Tenzer was not licensed. The supreme court indicated that the trial court should determine if Tenzer was a mere finder or participated in sale negotiations. If he participated, he would have had to have been licensed to collect a fee. The court also indicated that Tenzer could recover based on fraud if Superscope's president never intended to pay him.

(continued on next page)

Because the plaintiff's claim was based on equity, the court held that the plaintiff must show that the agreement was fair [*Tenzer v. Superscope, Inc.* (1985) 39 C.3d 18].

Case Study

The case of *Preach v. Rainbow* (1993) 12 C.A.4th 1441 involved a lease negotiation with Home Club. Broker Preach contacted attorney Singer, who knew McNulty, president of Home Club. Preach agreed to pay Singer 33 percent of any commission received if Singer could convince McNulty to lease a property owned by Monter Rainbow. Singer negotiated the lease between Home Club and Monter Rainbow. Monter Rainbow refused to pay Preach the $300,000 commission due in the lease because Preach had engaged a nonlicensee for negotiation activities. It claimed that Singer was not protected as a "finder" because he actively engaged in the negotiations.

The court remanded the case for trial on the issues of whether a joint venture existed between Preach and Singer, whether Singer performed negotiations for which a broker's license was required, and whether Preach knew of Singer's unlawful activities. The court held that if any of these were found to exist, then no leasing commission would be payable to Preach because Singer was performing acts requiring a real estate broker's license.

■ DUTY OF BUYERS

While sellers have a duty of disclosure, buyers have no corresponding duty to disclose material facts that they are aware of, such as why they are buying.

Case Study

The case of *Nussbaum v. Weeks* (1989) 214 C.A.3d 1589 involved a purchase of the plaintiff's land by the general manager of the water district. The sellers sued the buyer for failure to disclose the probability that the water district would increase the availability of water to the land purchased. The court of appeal, in reversing a superior court decision, held that a property buyer has no duty to disclose material facts to a seller and that the buyer had no special duty as general manager of the water district to explain that the board of directors might vote to increase water supplies.

■ SUMMARY

In Chapter 2 you learned about agency rights and duties. This chapter expands the framework established by Chapter 2.

While our laws set the minimum standard of acceptable conduct, ethics go beyond the law to what *should* be. Understanding ethics is important to the real estate licensee because ethics precede the law. What apparently was legal but unethical at the time of an action might later be determined to have been illegal by our courts. Licensees who use the law alone as a standard of conduct could find themselves facing great future liability.

Employment contracts between brokers and salespersons often specify that the salesperson is an independent contractor. The reason for this type of contract is to avoid withholding tax and Social Security contributions by the broker. The Department of Real Estate, however, regards a salesperson to be an employee of the broker. The broker is liable for the wrongful acts of the salesperson within the scope of employment.

The agent's primary duty is to his or her principal. The agent's conduct must be governed by what is in the best interests of the principal. The agent not only must be honest with the principal but must also protect the principal from the dishonest conduct of others. The agent also must be particularly careful to protect the principal's interests when the agent has an interest as well, such as in the case of a net listing, an option listing, or when the agent is also a buyer.

The agent's duty to buyers is much more than simply revealing anything detrimental about a property that the agent is aware of. The agent has an affirmative duty to conduct a reasonably competent and diligent inspection of residential property and to disclose to prospective purchasers all facts materially affecting the value of the property that such an investigation reveals. The seller of one to four residential units also has a duty to disclose known defects to a buyer. Both the seller and the broker must execute the Real Estate Transfer Disclosure Statement.

Neither the principal nor the agent can avoid liability by selling property "as is." "As is" applies only to obvious defects and offers no protection to agents and/or owners from hidden defects that they knew of but failed to disclose.

Although brokers have no legal duty to cooperate with other brokers, they should be aware of the liabilities and responsibilities imposed by subagency.

Buyers do not have the duty to disclose that falls on sellers.

■ DISCUSSION CASES

1. The sellers' broker obtained one termite report, which indicated $971 worth of work was required. A second report indicating termite infestation, dry rot, and fungus estimated correction costs of $1,155. The broker did not disclose the second report to the buyers but provided for paying the buyers the cost of doing the work discovered on the first report. The buyers discovered the extensive dry rot and termite infestation when they moved in. **What is the liability of the broker?**

   Godfrey v. Steinpress (1982) 128 C.A.3d 154

2. A broker did not wish to belong to a board of REALTORS® or pay a multiple-listing service fee. The board had an initial fee plus a monthly fee that was the same for all users. The broker wished to use the services on a book-by-book basis when needed, because he conducted business on a statewide basis and could not afford the regular fees. **Was the board's refusal to provide individual access fees for the broker a restraint on trade?**

   Feldman v. Sacramento Board of REALTORS®
   (1981) 119 C.A.3d 739

3. A multiple-listing service refused to accept any listings but exclusive-right-to-sell listings. **Was the action of the multiple-listing service proper?**

   People v. National Association of REALTORS® (1981)
   120 C.A.3d 459

4. The defendant, a real estate salesman, failed to recommend a title search when the plaintiffs leased a chicken ranch with an option to purchase. The defendant, without actual knowledge, represented that one trust deed against the property existed and that the payments included interest. In fact there was a second trust deed and the payments on the first trust deed did not include the interest. The plaintiffs indicated that had they known of the condition of the title, they would not have entered into the lease agreement. **What problems does this case present?**

   Wilson v. Hisey (1957) 147 C.A.2d 433

5. A broker fraudulently represented to the purchaser that he was the agent of a property owner. He quoted a price of $1,000 more per acre than was being asked for a   72-acre-plus parcel. The broker presented his own offer of $4,000 per acre to the owner after he had

induced the purchaser to make an offer of $5,000 per acre. **What is the broker's liability, and to whom, if anyone, would he be liable?**

Ward v. Taggart (1959) 51 C.2d 736

6. Sutherland transferred and sold his house to a relocation company. In the Transfer Disclosure Statement he answered "No" as to any neighborhood noise problems or other nuisances. Shapiro purchased the home and immediately discovered loud disturbances from the family next door (arguments and late night music). Shapiro learned that the Sutherlands had called the police a number of times about the arguments and late music. Shapiro asked for a rescission of the sale. The Sutherlands said that they had no contractual relationship with Shapiro. **Are the Sutherlands liable to Shapiro?**

Shapiro v. Sutherland (1998) 60 C.A.4th 666

7. A broker who was not an attorney advised a husband and wife about the kind of document they should execute to secure a loan. **Was the broker's advice proper?**

People v. Sipper (1943) 61 C.A.2d 844

8. While viewing a property, a prospective tenant thought she was entering a closet and fell down basement stairs behind an inward-swinging door. The stairs had no landing or handrail. **What is the liability of the agent?**

Merrill v. Buck (1962) 58 C.2d 552

9. While the plaintiff did not read the written agreement, the plaintiff asked the loan broker about the loan terms and received misleading and incomplete information. Late charges also were made that could not be justified. **What duties, if any, has the loan broker breached?**

Wyatt v. Union Mortgage Company (1979) 24 C.3d 773

10. A private individual brought suit against a board of REALTORS® because he was denied access to its multiple-listing service. He claimed that refusing him the ability to list his house with the service forced him to deal through a broker, which violated the antitrust laws. **Was his complaint valid?**

Derish v. San Mateo-Burlingame Board (1982) 136 C.A.3d 534

11. Carter, a broker, sold a net listing to his daughter and received a $5,000 commission. The seller had agreed to the list price based on

the broker's recommendations. **What are the problems involved in this case?**

Sierra Pacific Industries v. Carter (1980) 104 C.A.3d 579

12. A multiple-listing service provided that disputes among members over commissions be submitted to an arbitration procedure and that members who refused to arbitrate could be expelled. Bernstein refused to arbitrate and was expelled from the service. **Was expulsion proper?**

United Multiple Listing Service v. Bernstein (1982)
134 C.A.3d 486

13. A broker purchased a house listed by another broker. The purchasing broker indicated that he was a broker and would share in the commission. He also indicated that he was purchasing the house as his residence. The broker opened a second escrow because he had a purchaser for the house. **Did the purchasing broker do anything wrong?**

Gray v. Fox (1984) 151 C.A.3d 482

14. Traweek Investment Co. promoted and managed a limited partnership. Three months after buying a building for $4 million (including 6 percent commission to Traweek), the company placed the building on the market for $5.7 million. Ballou, a broker, produced an offer for $5.4 million. While Ballou had been promised a 6 percent commission, Traweek indicated that Ballou would have to agree to a $100,000 commission, claiming that was all that could be paid because the general partners had guaranteed returns that had to be met. Later Ballou agreed to a further reduction to $50,000 based on Traweek's assertion that no other commissions were being paid. Ballou later discovered Traweek received $222,000 in commission for the sale. **What are Ballou's rights?**

Ballou v. Masters Props. No. 6 (1987) 189 C.A.3d 65

15. A neighbor operated a tree-trimming business from his home, engaged in noisy activities, poured motor oil on his roof, and had a cabana not in conformance with the subdivision restrictions. Five families sued to abate alleged nuisances. **Does a seller have a duty to disclose these facts to a buyer?**

Alexander v. McKnight (1992) 7 C.A.4th 973

16. A buyer received a seller-disclosure that a house was in a floodplain. It did not disclose that a city ordinance prohibited enlarging such homes or rebuilding them if they were destroyed. **Was the disclosure adequate?**

Sweat v. Hollister (1995) 37 C.A.4th 603

17. A broker suggested to a seller that a lead paint test be made because the home was built in 1860. The test was positive. While the seller completed the lead paint disclosure form that referenced the report, the report was not given to the buyer. The broker, acting as a dual agent, verbally advised the buyers of the lead paint and the existence of the report but the broker was not able to get the report from the sellers. However, it was provided at closing.

    A written disclosure of known lead-based paint is required by the Residential Lead-Base Paint Hazards Reduction Act of 1992 and must be signed by the buyer. The act calls for treble damages when a person "knowingly" violates the statute. **Was the broker's verbal disclosure adequate?**

Smith v. Coldwell Banker Real Estate Services (2000)
122 F. Supp 2d 267

18. Cal Fed acquired a condominium unit through its nonjudicial trustee's foreclosure sale. Assilzadeh, a tenant in another unit, made a purchase offer through Fred Sands Realty who disclosed it was acting as a dual agent. The seller's counteroffer stated, "Buyer to be aware that property was acquired through foreclosure and Seller is exempt from providing a property disclosure statement...No warranties expressed or implied are included in this sale. Subject property is being sold in its present 'As Is' condition. Buyer will satisfy himself-herself as to the condition of said property, and their requirement regarding permitted and nonpermitted areas of the subject property." During escrow, Assilzadeh signed an amendment to the purchase contract which said "Buyer hereby acknowledges that there has been no representation by the Seller regarding the condition of the property....Buyer is hereby granted the right to inspect the Property or to obtain inspection reports from qualified experts at his own expense...If such reports reveal any latent defects which are unacceptable to Buyer...neither Buyer nor Seller shall have any further liability to the other." The dual agent verbally informed Assilzadeh of the homeowner's association lawsuit against the developer and its recent settlement for $5.1 million.

    Assilzadeh inspected the condo with her son, Amin. She also hired a professional inspector. After escrow closed, Assilzadeh bought marble flooring. But the homeowner's association said she could not install it because of structural defects affecting the load capabilities of the high-rise building. She sued Cal Fed, Fred Sands Realty, and the sales agent for rescission and restitution, as well as fraudulent concealment, negligence, and breach of fiduciary duty against FSR and the agent. **Were adequate disclosures made by the agent?**

Assilzadeh v. California Federal Bank (2000) 82 C.A. 4th 399

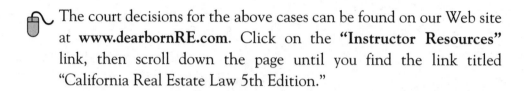 The court decisions for the above cases can be found on our Web site at **www.dearbornRE.com**. Click on the **"Instructor Resources"** link, then scroll down the page until you find the link titled "California Real Estate Law 5th Edition."

■ CHAPTER QUIZ

1. Ethics would best be described as

   a. obeying the law.
   b. doing what is right.
   c. an agency duty.
   d. treating all people the same.

2. In selling listings of another broker, a real estate salesperson is directly responsible to

   a. his or her broker.
   b. the owner.
   c. the listing broker.
   d. the multiple-listing service.

3. Which of the following is *not* an IRS requirement for a real estate salesperson to be treated as an independent contractor so that the employing broker can avoid withholding taxes and Social Security contributions?

   a. That the salesperson have a valid California real estate license
   b. That reimbursement be based solely on sales and not on hours worked
   c. That there be a written contract that the salesperson will be treated as an independent contractor for tax purposes
   d. That the salesperson work without supervision

4. A broker would most likely be responsible to salespersons for

   a. unemployment compensation.
   b. minimum wages.
   c. workers' compensation.
   d. All of the above

5. Commission disputes between a broker and salespeople would likely be referred to the

   a. state labor commissioner.   c. agency review board.
   b. court of appeal.   d. real estate commissioner.

6. A nonlicensee may properly be paid a finder's fee if he or she

   a. participated in negotiations.
   b. introduced the parties.
   c. obtained the offer to purchase.
   d. had a signed agreement to act as an agent of a broker.

7. In presenting two identical offers requiring seller financing to an owner, which act of the broker would be wrong?

   a. Mentioning that one buyer had only recently been hired after a long period of unemployment
   b. Mentioning that one buyer was black
   c. Mentioning that one buyer had substantially greater income
   d. Mentioning that one buyer had not given truthful credit information

8. A prospective buyer knows that the owner is considering accepting an offer from another party. He asks you, the broker, the amount of the offer so that he can exceed it. You should

   a. tell him, because it is in the owner's best interests.
   b. tell him, because you must reveal all known facts to a buyer.
   c. notify the owner of the request.
   d. refuse to tell him or to accept any offer unless the present offer is rejected.

9. A seller's broker may *not* inform a prospective purchaser that

   a. the owner will accept less than the list price.
   b. the present use of the structure does not conform to zoning.
   c. there are material defects in the improvements.
   d. the building is on filled land.

10. An agent need not disclose to an owner that he or she has received an offer when

   a. the owner has already accepted another offer.
   b. the offer is verbal.
   c. escrow has already closed.
   d. the offer is less than the listing price.

11. Which of the following is a true statement regarding net listings?

    a. They are illegal in California.
    b. The broker must disclose the amount of commission to be received.
    c. The broker's best interests would be served by setting as high a net price as possible.
    d. None of the above.

12. Which of the following is a *false* statement regarding option listings?

    a. If a property fails to sell, the broker must exercise the purchase option.
    b. Prior to exercising the option, the broker must reveal all offers received.
    c. The broker must reveal the amount of profit, if any, to the owner to exercise the option.
    d. The owner must consent in writing to the agent's profit should the option be exercised.

13. A broker sold an apartment building to a syndicate of which the broker was a member without informing the seller of this interest. Before closing, the owner discovers the broker's interest and refuses to sell. Which of the following probably would result from a suit to collect a commission?

    a. The broker's license would be revoked.
    b. The broker would get the commission.
    c. No commission would be paid.
    d. The buyer would obtain specific performance.

14. During the term of an escrow a listing broker discovered that an addition to the building had been made without a building permit and that the addition was in violation of the building code. The broker should notify

    a. the buyer only.
    b. the seller only.
    c. both the buyer and the seller.
    d. neither, because the broker obtained this knowledge after the contract was entered into.

15. An owner told his broker about serious problems with the well on the owner's property, but the broker neglected to inform the purchaser. In a lawsuit by the buyer a court would likely find

    a. the broker alone to be liable.
    b. the owner alone to be liable.
    c. the broker and owner to be liable.
    d. None of the above

16. Which of the following is a true statement about required disclosures to residential buyers?

    a. There is a two-year statute of limitations on disclosure.
    b. The buyer also has a duty to exercise reasonable care.
    c. The duty of inspection is limited to one to four residential units.
    d. All of the above

17. The *Easton* decision about required disclosures does *not* apply to

    a. single-family residences.
    b. defects that would be discovered by a reasonably competent inspection.
    c. nonresidential property.
    d. patent defects.

18. An agent would most likely have to inform a prospective purchaser about the

    a. triple murder in the home six months earlier.
    b. race of the previous occupants.
    c. former owner's having died of AIDS five years ago.
    d. present owner's having AIDS.

19. Which of the following is an example of blind advertising?

    a. Failure to advertise a location
    b. Failure to indicate that the advertiser is an agent
    c. Failure to include the name of the agent
    d. Failure to include the price

20. In selling a commercial property, an agent's duty to the buyer includes

    a. informing the buyer of the results of a reasonably competent and diligent visual inspection.
    b. informing the buyer that the zoning is not appropriate for the intended use.
    c. telling the buyer the reason the seller is selling.
    d. providing the buyer a disclosure statement regarding agency relationships.

21. A broker told prospective purchasers, "You will love living in this neighborhood." After experiencing problems with their new neighbors, they sued the broker for this false statement. A court would likely determine the statement was

    a. criminal fraud.
    b. misrepresentation.
    c. puffing.
    d. None of the above

22. A listing broker is *not* ordinarily responsible for wrongful acts committed in the course of a sale by

    a. his employees.
    b. his salespersons having independent contractor contracts.
    c. other brokers acting as subagents.
    d. None of the above

23. An agent may pay a fee to an unlicensed party who

    a. shows property.
    b. negotiates sale or lease terms.
    c. takes a deposit from a buyer.
    d. introduces the buyer to the broker.

24. Which of the following is true of the buyer's duties?

    a. Buyers have the same disclosure duties as sellers.
    b. Buyers are required to complete a disclosure statement only for residential purchases.
    c. Buyers are subject to *Easton* liability for nondisclosure.
    d. Buyers have no duty to disclose material facts to the seller.

25. Buyers must disclose to sellers

    a. any information they have of which the seller is unaware.
    b. the purpose of their purchase.
    c. other purchases they have made.
    d. None of the above

CHAPTER FOUR

REGULATION OF LICENSEES

■ KEY TERMS

advance fee
Americans with
  Disabilities Act
Article 5
Article 7
blockbusting
Bulk Sales Act
Civil Rights Act
  of 1866
Civil Rights Act of
  1968

Fair Housing
  Amendment Act
  of 1988
Franchise Investment
  Law
MOG broker
Real Estate Advisory
  Commission
redlining
restricted license

Rumford Act
send-out slip
sexual harassment
steering
Unruh Civil Rights
  Act

■ THE DEPARTMENT OF REAL ESTATE

The purpose of the real estate law is to ensure, as far as possible, that real estate brokers and salespeople will be honest, truthful, and of good reputation. *Brown v. Gordon* (1966) 240 C.A.2d 659.

The real estate commissioner is the chief executive of the Department of Real Estate. The primary responsibility of the real estate commissioner, who is appointed by the governor, is to enforce the real estate law in such a manner that purchasers of real estate and those persons dealing with real estate licensees are afforded maximum protection. The commissioner appoints a ten-person **Real Estate Advisory Commission** composed of six real estate brokers and four public members. The commissioner must call at least four meetings of the commission each year. The commission consults and makes recommendations to the commissioner about the function and policies of the department and about how the department can best serve the people of the state while recognizing the legitimate needs of the real estate industry.

The commissioner has full authority to control the issuance, suspension, and revocation of real estate licenses. The commissioner also has the authority to adopt or repeal rules and regulations necessary to enforce the real estate law. As mentioned in Chapter 1, these rules and regulations have the force and effect of law.

The real estate commissioner may bring an action in the name of the people of California in the superior court against persons the commissioner believes to be in violation of the real estate law. (The California attorney general is the legal adviser to the real estate commissioner.) In that action the commissioner may ask the court to enjoin any further violations of the law. The commissioner may include in any action a claim for restitution in the names of persons injured (Business and Professions Code Section 10081). Any criminal action against a licensee for a wrongful act is brought by the district attorney in the county where the offense took place, not by the commissioner.

If the commissioner believes, from satisfactory evidence, that trust funds are not being accounted for properly or are in danger, the commissioner may ask the superior court for an injunction. If the commissioner has conducted an audit that indicates a conversion of funds in excess of $10,000, the court may order the broker to refrain from further exercising the privileges of his or her real estate license. After a hearing, the court may appoint a receiver.

Before revoking, suspending, or denying any real estate license, the commissioner must hold a hearing in accordance with the Administrative Procedure Act.

■ ACTIVITIES REQUIRING A LICENSE

A real estate broker is a person who, for compensation or the expectation of compensation, does one or more of the following acts for others:

- Sells or offers to sell, buys or offers to buy, solicits prospective sellers or purchasers of, solicits or obtains listings of, or negotiates the purchase, sale, or exchange of real property or a business opportunity [Business and Professions Code 10131(a)];

- Leases or rents or offers to lease or rent, or places for rent, or solicits listings of places for rent, or solicits for prospective tenants, or negotiates the sale, purchase, or exchange of leases on real property or on a business opportunity, or collects rents from real property or improvements thereon or from business opportunities [Business and Professions Code Section 10131(b)];

- Assists or offers to assist in filing an application for the purchase or lease of or in locating or entering upon lands owned by the state or federal government [Business and Professions Code Section 10131(c)];

- Solicits borrowers or lenders for or negotiates loans or collects payments or performs services for borrowers or lenders or note owners in connection with loans secured directly or collaterally by liens on real property or on a business opportunity [Business and Professions Code Section 10131(d)];

- Sells or offers to sell, buys or offers to buy, or exchanges or offers to exchange a real property sales contract or a promissory note secured directly or collaterally by a lien on real property or on a business opportunity and performs services for the holders thereof [Business and Professions Code Section 10131(e)];

- Collects an **advance fee** in connection with promoting the sale, lease or exchange of real property or of a business opportunity or to arrange a loan thereon (Business and Professions Code Section 10131.2);

- Issues, sells, exchanges, negotiates, or solicits sellers or purchasers of securities specified in Section 25206 of the Corporations Code (shares in real estate syndicates). These syndicate interests also may be sold by broker/dealers licensed by the commissioner of corporations (Business and Professions Code Section 10131.3);

- Buys and sells or offers to buy and sell, negotiate for, or solicit purchasers or sellers of mobile homes. Dealers licensed by the Department of Housing and Community Development are also authorized to sell mobile homes (Business and Professions Code Section 10131.6).

■ WHEN LICENSING IS NOT REQUIRED

Exempt from real estate licensure are

- those dealing in their own property as principals, except those buying, selling, or exchanging eight or more notes per year secured by deeds of trust or sales contracts and those dealing in real property security transactions (the exemption applies only to those dealing in guaranteed notes);

- officers dealing for a corporation in corporation property for which they receive no special compensation;

- those dealing under an executed power of attorney;

- attorneys-at-law rendering services while acting as attorneys-at-law;

- those operating under court order (receivers, trustees in bankruptcy, executors of estates, etc.);

- trustees selling under a power of sale in a trust deed;

- banks, trust companies, savings associations, industrial loan companies, pension trusts, credit unions, insurance companies, or their employees;

- lenders making loans insured by an agency of the federal government or for which such a commitment has been made;

- nonprofit agricultural cooperatives engaged in lending and marketing;

- persons licensed as personal property brokers, consumer finance lenders, or commercial finance lenders, while acting in that capacity;

- cemetery authorities and their agents;

- those who make real estate loan collections for the owners, provided they collect $40,000 or less from ten or fewer loans in one year or they are corporations licensed as escrows;

- stenographers, bookkeepers, receptionists, and other clerical help carrying out normal clerical duties;

- resident managers of apartment complexes (Business and Professions Code Section 10131.01 has expanded the resident manager exception to include employees of a property management firm retained to manage a residential apartment building—potentially including nonresident employees—working under the supervision of a licensed broker or salesperson. Also exempt are persons renting transient accommodations.);

- condominium association managers who do not rent or sell units; and

- finders who receive a fee for introducing the parties.

Case Study

A power of attorney cannot be used to circumvent licensing requirements. In *Sheetz v. Edmonds* (1988) 201 C.A.3d 1432, the court of appeal upheld the real estate commissioner's order to Sheetz to stop managing 23 properties. Sheetz, who was not licensed as a broker, performed management services for compensation and claimed to be exempt from Business and Professions Code Section 10133 because she held a power of attorney from the owner. The exemption was judged to apply

(continued on next page)

only to a particular or isolated transaction and cannot be used as a substitute for a broker's license. The court considered the fact that the owner was a close friend of Sheetz's to be irrelevant.

■ LICENSE REQUIREMENTS

Applicable sections of the California Business and Professions Code as well as regulations of the real estate commissioner dealing with licensing requirements can be found in the Real Estate Law volume published by the Department of Real Estate.

Salesperson's License   To qualify for a salesperson's license, the applicant must

- provide proof of U.S. citizenship or legal presence in the United States (The Federal Personal Responsibility and Work Opportunity Act denies public benefits, including professional licenses, to illegal immigrants.);
- be at least 18 years of age;
- take and pass the real estate examination for salespersons;
- be fingerprinted;
- have an employing broker at the time the license is issued (broker affiliation is not required to sit for the examination);
- apply for a license within one year after passing the salesperson's examination;
- have completed the college-level course in real estate principles; and
- be honest and truthful (Conviction of a felony or crime involving moral turpitude may result in denial of license.);
- pay the applicable fee.

Note: U.S. citizenship is not required for either the salesperson or the broker license; however, proof of legal presence in the U.S. must be shown, such as a U.S. birth certificate, U.S. passport, or resident alien card.

Broker's License   An applicant for a broker's license must:

- provide proof of U.S. citizenship or legal presence in the United States (The Federal Personal Responsibility and Work Opportunity Act denies public benefits, including professional licenses, to illegal immigrants.);
- be at least 18 years of age;

- have two years' experience or the equivalent as a real estate salesperson within the prior five-year period or a valid four-year college degree;
- have successfully completed college-level courses in real estate practice, legal aspects of real estate, real estate finance, real estate appraisal, and accounting or real estate economics;
- have successfully completed three college-level courses selected from real estate office administration, advanced legal aspects of real estate, advanced real estate appraisal, advanced real estate finance, real estate principles, business law, mortgage loan brokering and lending, property management, and escrows;
- pass the broker's examination;
- be fingerprinted;
- be honest and truthful (Conviction of a felony or crime involving moral turpitude may result in denial of license.); and
- pay the applicable fee.

Partnership Licenses

While there is no specific partnership license, a broker can be a partner with a salesperson in a real estate brokerage business. However, every partner through whom the partnership acts must be a licensed real estate broker. A broker may be a partner with a nonlicensee in business activities where real estate licenses are not required.

Corporation Licenses

A real estate sales corporation must have one real estate broker who has a corporation officer license. The broker also can have a separate individual license.

A salesperson can be an officer and a stockholder of a corporation. The salesperson can be a majority stockholder only if the responsible corporate broker is also an officer and director of the corporation.

Nonresident Licensees

A new license will be issued to a nonresident of California only if California residents can obtain licenses in the applicant's state. Nonresidents holding California real estate licenses must agree that they can be sued in California courts. Legal service to institute a lawsuit may be made on the Secretary of State if by using reasonable diligence, process cannot be personally served on the licensee in California.

■ LICENSE RENEWALS

The original real estate license and each renewal are in effect for four years. There is no examination for license renewal, but new salespersons must complete two three-credit college-level real estate courses within 18 months of licensing, one of which must be Real Estate Practice, or their license will automatically be suspended. They must also complete three-hour courses in real estate ethics, agency relationships, fair housing, and trust fund handling (a total of 12 clock hours) prior to their first renewal. Prior to the second renewal, brokers and salespersons must complete 45 hours of continuing education, including 18 hours of consumer protection and a six-hour survey course of the four courses taken for the first renewal. Broker requirements differ in that the first renewal requires 45 hours, including the four mandated courses as well as 18 hours of consumer protection courses.

The Department of Real Estate can withhold issuance or renewal of a real estate license of a party who has been placed on a certified list of persons who are delinquent in child or family support payments. The DRE can issue a temporary license for a period of 150 days during which period the licensee must comply with required payments.

■ GROUNDS FOR DISCIPLINARY ACTION

All real estate licensees are subject to disciplinary proceedings by the real estate commissioner for

- making a substantial misrepresentation;
- making a false promise likely to influence, persuade, or induce;
- engaging in a continued and flagrant course of misrepresentation or making false promises;
- acting for more than one party to a transaction without the knowledge and consent of all the parties;
- commingling with his or her own money or property the money or property of others entrusted to the agent's care;
- claiming or receiving a fee for any exclusive listing that does not include a definite termination date;
- making a secret profit;
- exercising an option coupled with a listing where the licensee failed to reveal the amount of profit and obtain the consent of the owner for the amount of profit;
- engaging in any conduct that constitutes fraud or dishonest dealing;
- obtaining the agreement of a prospective purchaser that the purchaser will deal only through the agent with regard to a particular property (send-out slip) without the written authorization of the owner;
- procuring or attempting to procure a real estate license by fraud, misrepresentation, or deceit or by a material misstatement of fact in an application for a license, license renewal, or license reinstatement

(within 90 days after issuance the commissioner can suspend a license so obtained, without a hearing);

■ entering a plea of guilty or nolo contendere to, or being found guilty of, a felony or crime involving moral turpitude if the time for appeal has passed;

■ knowingly aiding in the publication or circulation of a material false statement concerning the licensee's business or any business opportunity, land, or subdivision;

■ willfully disregarding any provision of the real estate law;

■ using the term REALTOR®, Realtist, or any trade name or insignia when not entitled to such use;

■ performing any action that would have warranted the denial of a license;

■ demonstrating negligence or incompetence in performing any act requiring a real estate license;

■ failing to exercise reasonable supervision over the acts of salespersons;

■ using their employment by a government agency in such a way as to violate the confidentiality of the access provided;

■ violating any terms, conditions, or limitations of a restricted license;

■ inducing the listing of residential property because of increase in crime, decline of quality in the schools, or loss of value caused by the entry or prospective entry into the community of persons of another race, color, religion, ancestry, or national origin (blockbusting);

■ violating any provision of the Franchise Investment Law (discussed later in this chapter);

■ violating any provision of the Corporations Code; and

■ failing, as agent for the buyer, to disclose any direct or indirect ownership in the property being purchased.

To revoke or suspend a license, the Department of Real Estate must show "convincing proof to a reasonable certainty," not proof beyond a reasonable doubt [*Realty Projects Inc. v. Smith* (1973) 32 C.A.3d 204].

Case Study

In *Madrid v. Department of Real Estate* (1984) 152 C.A.3d 454, an applicant for a real estate license neglected to disclose an out-of-state conviction five years earlier for bingo fraud but did disclose a 20-year-old conviction for contracting without a license. The plaintiff claimed to have forgotten about the conviction and claimed license revocation was improper. While failure to disclose a minor matter could be excused, the court held this to be a major matter and a recent conviction that was omitted knowingly. Because knowledge of the conviction would have justified denial of license, revocation of the plaintiff's license was held to be proper.

Statute of Limitations

Disciplinary action must be brought within three years of the wrongful act except in the case of fraud, where it is three years after the act or one year after discovery, whichever comes later, but in no event later than ten years from the wrongful act (Business and Professions Code Section 10101).

Criminal Liability

The grounds for disciplinary action also are considered a misdemeanor subject to criminal prosecution (Business and Professions Code Section 10185).

Restricted Licenses

Probationary or restricted real estate licenses may be granted by the commissioner after a license has been revoked, suspended, or denied subsequent to a hearing.

The **restricted license** can be restricted to a period of time, to the type or area of activity, or to employment by a particular broker (salesperson). The commissioner can require detailed reports of each transaction, a surety bond, other conditions, or a combination of conditions.

The restricted licensee has no automatic right to renewal. The commissioner can suspend a restricted license for a violation prior to a formal hearing; however, revocation requires a hearing.

As a condition of issuance of a regular license the commissioner can require that the continuing education requirements be met.

Education, Research and Recovery Allocation

Twenty percent of license fees go into a special fund that in turn is divided into two separate accounts. Twelve percent of all fees go into a recovery account that provides restitution to members of the public who suffer a loss because of a wrongful act of a real estate licensee. Eight percent of all fees go into the Education and Research Account.

An aggrieved party who obtains an uncollectible judgment against a licensee because of fraud, misrepresentation, deceit, or conversion of trust funds can apply to the DRE for recovery from the fund. The fund will pay only if the wrongful act required a real estate license.

Case Study

The case of *Yergen v. Department of Real Estate* (2000) 77 C.A. 4th 959 involved a claim against the fund arising out of a lawsuit against brokers alleging breach of fiduciary duty, fraud, deceit, negligent misrepresentation, negligent and intentional infliction of emotional distress, and fraudulent conveyance. The parties agreed to a settlement. In addition to other

(continued on next page)

payments by defendants and insurers, REM, a licensed real estate corporation, agreed to pay $50,000 for professional negligence and breach of duty. When REM failed to pay, a stipulated judgment was entered against REM. The plaintiffs applied to the California Department of Real Estate recovery fund.The Los Angeles Superior Court denied payment, which was affirmed by the court of appeal. The court ruled that the plaintiffs did not have a valid judgment for fraud, so they were not entitled to recovery from the fund. A judgment for fraud, misrepresentation or deceit with intent to defraud, or conversion of trust funds is a mandatory prerequisite to payment from the recovery fund.

The plaintiff had agreed that the payment was for professional negligence and breach of duty.

Up to a maximum of $20,000 will be paid to any one claimant because of any one transaction, regardless of the number of persons injured or the number of licensees involved [Business and Professions Code Section 10471(b)].

No more than $100,000 will be paid out for multiple claims against one licensee [Business and Professions Code Section 10474(c)].

Should the fund pay a claim because of a licensee, the licensee's license automatically will be suspended. No reinstatement will be made until the fund has been repaid, including prevailing interest. A discharge in bankruptcy will not relieve a person from the repayment requirements for reinstatement. Repayment to the fund will not nullify or modify any other disciplinary action that is brought because of the licensee's actions.

An illegal alien is not entitled to compensation from the recovery account.

Case Study

The case of *Direnfield v. Stabile* (1988) 198 C.A.3d 126 involved an unemployed licensed real estate salesman who arranged loans in which Direnfield was the lender. While previously employed by a broker, Stabile had arranged other loans for Direnfield. The loans he arranged while unemployed were for 30 percent interest. Two years later the borrowers sued Direnfield for usury because the loans were not made through a real estate broker. A settlement allowed Direnfield only the return of principal. Direnfield sued Stabile for failing to disclose that he was not employed by a broker. Stabile could not pay the judgment granted, so Direnfield requested payment from the recovery fund.

(continued on next page)

The court of appeal held that the recovery fund can be required to pay for an action of an unemployed salesperson because the salesperson's license was not terminated while the salesperson was unemployed. (Direnfield was limited to interest at the statutory rate [7 percent], not the 30 percent rate of the loan.)

■ MORTGAGE BROKERS

Mortgage loan brokers make or arrange loans for compensation. The mortgage loan broker is thus a middleman, matching borrowers and lenders. The mortgage loan broker has the duty of fair dealing to both lenders and borrowers.

Business and Professions Code Section 10131(d) requires that a person who solicits borrowers and lenders, makes loans, or performs services for borrowers and lenders when such loans are secured by real property be licensed as a real estate broker and be subject to the regulations of the real estate commissioner. While an owner normally can sell his or her own property without a license, an owner who engages in eight or more trust deed transactions within one year must have a broker's license.

The license requirements apply to the sale, exchange, and servicing of existing loans as well as to arranging new loans [Business and Professions Code Section 10131(e)].

Persons who make loan collections on ten or fewer loans and do not negotiate loans need not be licensed as brokers. A person who collects on more than ten loans or collects an amount exceeding $40,000 per year must either have a broker's license or apply to the real estate commissioner for an exemption. To obtain the exemption, the person must agree to comply with the provisions of the real estate law and the commissioner's regulations and must post a bond or other security to protect client funds.

Article 5 of the real estate law (Business and Professions Code Sections 10230–10236.1) governs transactions in trust deeds and real property sales contracts. The provisions of Article 5 do not apply to one to four residential unit sales involving seller carryback financing. The provisions of Article 5 also do not apply when the broker has a direct or an indirect monetary interest as a party to the transaction [Business and Professions Code Section 10230(a)].

Article 5 provisions include the following:

- Brokers cannot accept funds from prospective real property lenders unless the broker has a specific loan arranged for the funds (Business and Professions Code Section 10231).
- In servicing a real property loan, the broker cannot retain funds for more than 25 days unless there is a written agreement with the purchaser or lender, in which case the interest must be paid on the funds retained.
- A real estate broker is prohibited from advertising or giving gifts or premiums to prospective purchasers or lenders as an inducement for making a loan (Business and Professions Code Section 10236.1).
- Any real estate licensee who undertakes to service a loan must have a written authorization from the purchaser or lender of the loan (Business and Professions Code Section 10233).
- If a broker who is servicing a loan remits funds other than the funds of the obligor (the broker advances the funds), then within ten days of such payment the broker must notify the holder of the loan as to the source of the funds and the reason for making the advance (Business and Professions Code Section 10233.1).
- If the broker is going to benefit directly or indirectly by the loan, other than commission or fees, the broker must notify the Department of Real Estate and lender or purchaser of the facts (Business and Professions Code Section 10231.2).
- The mortgage broker who places a loan must deliver copies of any deed of trust to the investor or lender and to the borrower.
- Real estate licensees who negotiate loans secured by real property must have the instruments recorded prior to the disbursement of funds unless the lender authorizes prior release, in which case within ten days of the release of funds the broker must either record the trust deed or deliver it to the lender with a written recommendation that it be recorded immediately.
- If the licensee arranges an assignment of an existing trust deed or sales contract, he or she must have the assignment recorded within ten working days after close of escrow or deliver the trust deed or sales contract to the purchaser with the written recommendation that it be recorded immediately (Business and Professions Code Section 10234).

Advertising a specific yield greater than the rate stated on the note is misleading advertising unless the ad also includes the actual interest rates and purchase discount.

Advertising

Mortgage loan brokers must include their license number in their advertising soliciting borrowers or investors. They must also include a telephone number, established by the DRE, to enable consumers to check on the

TABLE 4.1	**Required Information for Ads**	**Soliciting for Borrowers**	**Soliciting for Investors (Lenders)**	**All Other Broker Advertising**
Advertising Requirements	Phrasing	CA Dept. of Real Estate—Real Estate Broker; or Real Estate Broker—CA Dept. of Real Estate	Broker, agent, REALTOR®, loan correspondent, or abbreviations bro., agt., or other similar terms or abbreviations	Broker, agent, REALTOR®, or abbreviations bro., agt., or other similar terms or abbreviations
	Identification Number	8-digit broker license ID	8-digit broker license ID	N/A
	Telephone Number	DRE "license information" telephone number: (916) 227-0931		N/A

broker's licensed status. The advertising requirements for loan and investor solicitation, as well as for other broker ads, are set forth in Figure 4.1.

Costs and Charges

Article 7 of the real estate law (Business and Professions Code Sections 10240–10248.3) covers loan broker maximum costs and commissions as well as loan payment requirements. This article applies only to regulated loans (first trust deeds of less than $30,000 and second trust deeds of less than $20,000). Larger loans have no upper limit on costs and fees.

Mortgage Broker Costs for Regulated Loans

Maximum $700

5% of the loan

Minimum $390

Loan broker costs for a regulated loan (first loans of less than $30,000 and second loans of less than $20,000) cannot exceed actual costs and expenses and are limited to 5 percent of the loan or $390, whichever is greater, but in no event more than $700. As examples, for a loan of $2,000 the costs can be up to $390 (5 percent or $390, whichever is greater); for a $19,000 loan the costs cannot exceed $700 (5 percent is $950, but the maximum that can be charged is $700). Examples of costs are appraisal fees, escrow charges, title insurance, notary fees, and credit report charges.

Mortgage Broker Commissions for Regulated Loans

		2 Yrs.	3 Yrs.
First Trust Deeds		5%	10%
Second Trust Deeds	5%	10%	15%

The loan broker commission for negotiating a regulated loan also is limited. For first trust deeds up to three years the maximum commission is 5 percent of the amount borrowed; for three years or more it is 10 percent. For second trust deeds up to two years the maximum commission is 5 percent; for more than two years but less than three years it is 10 percent; for three years or more it is 15 percent.

If a broker charges more than the maximum allowable fees or costs, the borrower may recover three times the excess fees or costs charged (Business and Professions Code Section 10246).

The broker may not enter into an exclusive agreement with a prospective borrower to procure a loan that ties up the borrower for more than 45 days (Business and Professions Code Section 10243).

The licensee may not condition the granting of a loan on the purchase of credit group life or disability insurance.

Late Charges

Late charges after ten days may not exceed 10 percent of the installment due, with a minimum late charge of $5. (For loans not made through loan brokers the late charge generally is limited to 6 percent.) Late charges may not be pyramided.

Prepayment Fees

For loans on owner-occupied single-family dwellings the loans may be prepaid at any time, but prepayments within seven years may be subject to prepayment penalties. (For residential loans made by other than loan brokers prepayment penalties may not be imposed after five years.) Prepayment penalties may not exceed six months' interest. Up to 20 percent of the loan always can be prepaid in any 12-month year without penalty (Business and Professions Code Section 10242.6).

When loans are made without consideration of borrowers' ability to pay (predatory lending), prepayment penalties are limited to the first 36 months.

Loans made by loan brokers must have substantially equal payments.

Balloon payments (payments greater than twice the amount of the smallest payment) may not be imposed on a loan secured by an owner-occupied dwelling if the loan is for six years or less.

Case Study

The case of *Carboni v. Arrospide* (1991) 2 C.A.4th 76 involved a $4,000 broker loan bearing interest at 200 percent that was originally due in three

(continued on next page)

months. Additional advances were made by the broker totaling $99,346, all at the 200 percent rate. By the time of trial for judicial foreclosure and deficiency judgment, accumulated interest was nearly $390,000. The trial court wrote, "While in regard to short-term loans of 90 days or so, as was anticipated here, interest at the rate of 200 percent per annum may or may not shock the conscience of the court, interest at that rate for one and one-half years does." The trial court set the interest at 24 percent. The Court of Appeal affirmed, explaining that Civil Code Section 1670.5 allows a court to refuse to enforce an unconscionable contract or to modify it to avoid an unconscionable result.

Usury laws (laws setting the maximum interest rates that can be charged) do not apply to loans made or arranged by loan brokers. Even though loans made by real estate brokers may be exempt from usury limits, they are not necessarily without limits.

If the broker uses his or her own funds wholly or in part for the loan, the broker must notify the borrower prior to the close of escrow (Business and Professions Code Section 10241.2).

Every loan broker who negotiates a loan to be secured by real estate must deliver to the borrower a statement in writing containing all of the cost information as well as loan terms. This statement must be delivered within three business days after receipt of a completed written loan application or before the borrower becomes obligated, whichever is earlier. The broker must keep a copy of the statement, signed by the borrower, for three years.

Disclosures

Article 7 requires that a real estate broker who makes or arranges a mortgage loan of any kind or in any amount is to present a Mortgage Loan Disclosure Statement to the borrower within three days of receipt of a completed loan application. The borrower's signature on the disclosure must be obtained prior to the time that the borrower becomes obligated to make the loan. The disclosure requires that specific important features of the loan be set forth.

Brokers who arrange loans must provide the purchaser with a Lender/Purchaser Disclosure Statement providing information regarding the loan and a statement of the property's fair market value, as determined by an appraisal, as well as a copy of the appraisal. The lender or purchaser must also be given a copy of the loan application and credit report, and the option of purchasing a title policy.

■ REAL PROPERTY SYNDICATES

The Department of Corporations has jurisdiction over both corporate and noncorporate syndicates. Broker/dealers licensed by the Department of Corporations can sell syndicate interests.

The Department of Corporations has transferred control of noncorporate syndicates having 100 or fewer investors to the Department of Real Estate. Real estate brokers are exempt from licensing requirements of the Corporations Code when selling these interests.

A real estate broker's violation of the Corporations Code can be the basis of disciplinary action by the real estate commissioner.

■ MINERAL, OIL, AND GAS BROKERS

New mineral, oil, and gas (MOG) licenses have not been issued since 1993. However, existing MOG licenses may be renewed every four years for the life of the holder. However, a person holding a real estate broker's license can engage in MOG transactions without additional licensing or qualifications. Anyone engaged in a MOG transaction without holding a valid MOG or real estate license could be fined up to $500 and/or face imprisonment for up to six months. Grounds for revocation or suspension of MOG licenses are similar to the grounds for revocation or suspension of real estate licenses, and are set forth in Section 10561 of the Business and Professions Code.

The permits and licenses once necessary to handle MOG transactions are no longer required. This special licensing was initially established due to past sales abuses. Investors were sold parcels in oil and gas subdivisions that were touted as great investments offering fantastic potential. However, in some cases, the parcels sold had remote if any possibility of containing oil or gas products. Eventually, a number of promoters were convicted of grand theft, and approximately 600 real estate salespersons and brokers had their licenses revoked. The licensing and activities of **MOG brokers** have now been placed under the Department of Real Estate.

■ ESCROW AGENT

The regulation of escrows is covered in Division 6 of the California Financial Code and requires that escrow agents be licensed by the commissioner of corporations.

Among those exempted are real estate brokers licensed by the real estate commissioner while performing acts in the course of or incidental to real estate transactions in which the brokers are principals or acting as agents in performing acts for which a real estate license is required [Financial Code Section 17006(d)].

The Department of Corporations has interpreted this exemption to be personal to the broker. The broker cannot set up an association with other brokers to conduct escrows or contract out the escrow services. The broker cannot advertise escrow services without making it clear that the services are only incidental to real estate transactions.

Escrows are covered in detail in Chapter 14.

■ MOBILE HOME SALES

Mobile homes are factory-built housing units that are transported to a site on their own chassis. They are usually set up on a permanent foundation and connected to utilities.

Once considered only temporary homes or for travel, mobile homes have become used as principal residences or stationary vacation homes. Their relatively low cost has resulted in growing numbers of mobile home parks in some communities. They make up a significant portion of single-family housing priced under $100,000.

Since July 1975, real estate licensees have been granted limited rights to act as agents in the sale of mobile homes. They can list and sell these mobile homes in rental spaces as well as with the land. Salespeople sometimes specialize in mobile home sales in particular, while some specialize in specific mobile home parks. In so acting, they are subject to these limitations:

- The mobile home must be in place. It must be able to remain on its rented lot. If the mobile home is sold with a lot, the lot must be zoned properly so the home can remain.
- Real estate licensees cannot advertise that no down payment is required for a mobile home when in fact secondary financing will be used to finance the down payment.
- Real estate licensees must withdraw all advertising of a mobile home for sale within 48 hours after receipt of notice that the mobile home is no longer available for sale, lease, or financing.
- A real estate broker who is not also licensed as a mobile home dealer may not have an office where two or more mobile homes are displayed and offered for sale. (There is a separate license for mobile home sales.)

- A real estate licensee is prohibited from prorating license or title fees unless the buyer and the seller agree to the proration or the licensee was required to pay the fees to avoid penalties for late payment.

- A licensee may not represent that the mobile home can be transported over California highways unless it meets all physical requirements for such transport. The licensee must reveal any material facts pertaining to the equipment requirements.

- The licensee must have all transfer papers delivered. Mobile homes must be registered annually with the Department of Housing and Community Development (HCD). Formerly, registration was required with the Department of Motor Vehicles. Exceptions to the annual registration are mobile homes sold new on or after July 1, 1980, mobile homes affixed to a permanent foundation, and mobile homes sold prior to July 1, 1980, that have become more than 120 days delinquent in the payment of license fees.

  Mobile homes not subject to annual registration are registered only at the time of title transfer. These homes are on local property tax rolls.

  Not later than ten calendar days after the sale of a used mobile home that is subject to registration, the broker must supply written notice of the transfer to the Department of Housing and Community Development. For details on transferring title and registering a mobile home, see Section 18100.5 et seq. of the Health and Safety Code. The Department of Housing and Community Development has a toll-free number for mobile home transfer information: 1 (800) 452-8356.

- Real estate licensees cannot include any added license or transfer fee if such a fee is not due to the state.

Exceptions to the limitations set forth are mobile homes attached to a permanent foundation so as to have become real property. The four prerequisites for a mobile home to become real property are

1. obtaining a building permit;
2. placing the mobile home on a permanent foundation;
3. obtaining a certificate of occupancy; and
4. recording a document reflecting that the mobile home has been affixed to a foundation.

Section 10177.2 of the Business and Professions Code provides for the discipline of a licensee who

- used a fictitious name in the registration of a mobile home or knowingly concealed any fact in the registration or otherwise committed fraud in the registration application;
- failed to provide for the delivery of a properly endorsed certificate of ownership or certificate of title from the seller to the buyer;
- knowingly participated in the acquisition or sale of a stolen mobile home;
- submitted a bad check to the Department of Housing and Community Development; or
- violated other provisions of the California codes.

There is a Manufactured Home Recovery Fund similar to the real estate recovery fund. After receiving a final judgment against a dealer or salesperson for failure to honor warranties, fraud, or willful misrepresentation, a claimant can receive a maximum of $75,000 from the fund.

■ ADVANCE FEE RENTAL AGENTS

There is a separate license available to operate a prepaid rental listing service (PRLS). No examination is required for a two-year PRLS license. Licensed real estate brokers are exempt from this requirement (Business and Professions Code Section 10167 et seq.).

Licensees must provide a prospective tenant with a DRE-approved written contract that describes the services to be provided and the prospective tenant's needs.

If the licensee fails to provide a list of at least three rental properties to the prospective tenant within five days, the advance fee must be refunded in full.

The licensee must refund within ten days of request any amount more than $50 in charges if the prospective tenant does not obtain a rental through the licensee and demands a return within ten days of expiration of the contract. The right to refund must be set forth in boldface type (Business and Professions Code Section 10167.10). For example, if a prospective tenant paid a $100 advance fee and qualified for a refund, $50 would be refunded to the prospective tenant.

The licensee must not knowingly refer a property to a prospective tenant where

- the property does not exist or is not available for occupancy;
- the property has been described by the licensee in a false, misleading or deceptive manner;

- the licensee has not confirmed the availability of the property during the four-day period preceding the referral (however, it is not a violation to refer property when availability was not confirmed from five to seven days after the last confirmation if the licensee has made a good-faith effort to confirm availability); or
- the licensee has not obtained written or oral permission to list the property from the owner or agent.

■ BUSINESS OPPORTUNITY BROKERS

A business opportunity broker sells or leases an existing business enterprise, including its goodwill. While real estate might be included with a business opportunity sale, generally all that is sold is personal property. At one time separate licensing was available to those engaged in the sale or lease of business opportunities. Since 1966, however, a real estate license has been required to engage in such transactions.

In business opportunity sales, more than in any other transaction, buyers tend to rely on the broker's expertise. The danger of dual agency is always present. The broker must make his or her status clear to the prospective buyer.

For protection, the broker should not repeat the owner's verbal statements about gross or net income but should instead ask for copies of the seller's federal tax returns and state sales tax returns and get the seller's permission to disclose the information to prospective purchasers. Even then the broker must indicate to prospective purchasers that the information was supplied by the owner and that the broker does not warrant its authenticity. The broker could still be liable if a court determined the broker should have doubted the information provided by the owner.

The broker must make sure that the purchaser is protected. Some of the items for consideration are

- transferability of leases;
- obtaining of necessary licenses and permits;
- compliance with the Bulk Sales Act;
- compliance with the fictitious name requirements (Business and Professions Code Section 17900 et seq.);
- obtaining a clearance receipt from the Board of Equalization certifying that prior sales tax has been paid so that the purchaser is not liable for the unpaid sales taxes (under *successor liability* the purchaser of a business is liable for sales taxes collected but not remitted to the state by the prior owner of the business);

- complete agreement as to terms consistent with such a sale, such as covenant not to compete; and
- obtaining agreement on apportionment of the sales price for tax purposes.

Failure to protect the purchaser might be considered negligence on the part of the broker and subject the broker to damages and/or disciplinary action.

Bulk Sales Act

The Bulk Sales Act (Commercial Code Sections 6101–6111) is of particular interest to brokers engaged in the sale of business opportunities. A bulk sale is a sale not in the course of the seller's ordinary business. The sale of the seller's business or a substantial part of the materials, supplies, merchandise, or other inventory would be a bulk sale. The Bulk Sales Act is intended to give notice to the creditors of the seller so that they can protect their interests.

Compliance with the act requires

- recording of a notice of sale at least 12 business days before the sale is to be consummated;
- publication of a notice in a newspaper of general circulation within the judicial district in which the property is located at least 12 business days prior to the sale; and
- sending of a registered or certified letter to the county tax collector at least 12 business days prior to the sale.

Such notice must include

- the statement that a bulk transfer is to be made;
- the name and address of the transferor and transferee and all other business names and addresses used by the transferor within three years, as far as known by the transferee;
- the location and general description of the property to be transferred;
- the place and date on which the bulk transfer is to be consummated; and
- the name and address of the person with whom claims may be filed and the last date for filing claims.

If the sale is to be made by auction, notice that the sale is to be made by auction must be given, including the name of the auctioneer and the time and place of the auction.

If the bulk sales notice provides for an escrow, the buyer must deposit the full purchase price with the escrow holder.

When statutory notices are not complied with, the sale is fraudulent and void with regard to those creditors who hold claims based on transactions prior to the bulk transfer.

In the case of an auction the responsibility for notices rests on the auctioneer. Failure to comply does not render an auction sale fraudulent and void, but the auctioneer is held personally liable to the transferor's creditors up to the reasonable value of the assets sold.

Franchise Sales

A franchise is a contract by which a business operator (franchisee) is granted, for some payment, the right to engage in a business of marketing goods or services under a plan or system prescribed by the seller of the franchise (franchisor) and associated with the franchisor's name, trademark, logo, advertising, or other commercial symbol. Agreements between petroleum companies and distributors and retailers to use brand identification or lease agreements allowing the sale of products under a trade identification are examples of franchises.

Because of the advantages of national advertising and training programs, a tremendous growth in real estate franchises has occurred.

Franchise sales are regulated by the **Franchise Investment Law**, which requires disclosure from the franchisor to the franchisee. The California corporations commissioner controls sales, and franchise offerings must be registered with the corporation commissioner prior to sale. Exempt from registration are franchises with a net worth of $5 million or more that have had a minimum of 25 franchises in operation during the five years prior to the sale. Most major real estate franchises therefore would be exempt from registration.

Required disclosures must be set forth in an offering prospectus, which must be delivered to a prospective purchaser at least ten business days prior to a binding franchise agreement or the receipt of any consideration, whichever comes first.

The disclosure requirements enable prospective franchisees to make a decision based on a full understanding of the duties and rights of the franchisor and franchisee. The purpose of the law is to protect against fraud or the likelihood that the franchisor's promises will not be met.

Three groups of people are authorized to sell franchises:

1. The person identified in the application for offering (the franchisor or agent)
2. A person licensed by the Department of Real Estate as a broker or salesperson
3. A person licensed by the commissioner of corporations as a broker/dealer

■ APPRAISERS

Title XI, Real Estate Appraisal Reform Amendment of the Federal Financial Institutions Reform, Recovery and Enforcement Act (FIRREA) of 1989, requires that appraisers be licensed or certified by the state for real estate transactions involving federal financial and public policy interests. This covers loans made by practically all of our financial institutions.

Every state must enact legislation to provide for certification, which is consistent with criteria established by the Appraisal Foundation, a private non-profit corporation. Certification must be in residential and general categories (general includes income as well as residential property). An examination is required without exception. For federally related transactions that do not require a certified appraiser, the appraiser must be licensed. The criteria for licensing must be consistent with Title XI. Every state must set minimum appraiser standards, even for appraisals that are not federally related.

Business and Professions Code Sections 11300–11421 enact the Real Estate Appraisers Licensing and Certification Law (California). The Office of Real Estate Appraisers within the Business, Transportation and Housing Agency administers and enforces the law. The law also created a Real Estate Appraisers Regulation Fund, which includes a Recovery Account similar to the Real Estate Recovery Account.

The law prohibits any licensed or certified appraiser from making an appraisal where the appraised value affects the appraiser's compensation.

■ FAIR HOUSING

Fair housing laws mandate that real estate licensees deal with buyers, sellers, lessors, and lessees in a nondiscriminatory manner. Besides the legal penalties of our various fair housing laws, violations of fair housing legislation may be the basis of disciplinary action by the Department of Real Estate.

Federal and state fair housing legislation overlaps. A single act can violate more than one fair housing act.

Federal Laws

Civil Rights Act of 1866. The Civil Rights Act of 1866 (C. 31, 14 Stat. 27) gave citizens of all races the same rights enjoyed by white citizens to inherit, purchase, lease, sell, or hold real and personal property. This act covered only race.

For many years the act was ineffective because of the narrow court interpretation that it did not apply to private property. The Supreme Court really nullified the effect of this act.

Under the act an aggrieved party may sue in federal court for damages, obtain an injunction to prohibit the sale to another, or obtain an order forcing the owner to sell.

Case Study

In *Jones v. Mayer* (1968) 392 U.S. 409, the U.S. Supreme Court held the act to be valid under the Thirteenth Amendment. In this case an owner refused to sell his own house because of race. The court determined that the act prohibits all racial discrimination (both public and private) in the sale or rental of property.

Federal Fair Housing Act. This act, Title VIII of the **Civil Rights Act of 1968** (U.S. Code, Title 18, 241 et seq.), provides that no one can refuse to sell or rent to another because of race, color, sex, religion, or national origin, and no real estate licensee can do so regardless of his or her principal's direction. The **Fair Housing Amendment Act of 1988** has now extended federal protection against housing discrimination to handicapped persons and those with "familial status." *Familial status* refers to those under the age of 18 living with a parent or guardian, those in the process of settling legal custody issues, and any pregnant person. Exempt from discrimination on the basis of age are communities having at least 80 percent of the units occupied by at least one person 55 years of age or older. Also exempt are housing units intended for and solely occupied by persons 62 years of age or older.

Case Study

The case of *Taylor v. Rancho Santa Barbara* (2000) 206 F.3d 932 involved a buyer of a mobile home who was refused a rental agreement because he was less than 55 years of age. The plaintiff challenged the

(continued on next page)

constitutionality of amendments to the Fair Housing Act that eliminated the requirement that senior citizens housing provide special services and facilities for seniors. He also challenged California Mobile Home Residency Law (MRL) that authorizes age restrictions complying with Federal Law. The basis of the plaintiff's action was a violation of the Fourteenth Amendment Equal Protection Clause as well as the Fifth Amendment's Due Process Clause. The U.S. District Court, for failure to state a claim, dismissed the case and the court of appeals affirmed that neither the federal nor California laws violate the Constitution. Age-restrictive apartments and mobile home communities are an exception to antidiscrimination statutes based on family status. The court pointed out the rational basis of these laws was to provide inexpensive housing for retirees on fixed incomes.

Even if an apartment complex has a family section, designation of an area as *all-adult* is prohibited. Steering prospective tenants toward a particular area in an apartment complex and away from another area would also violate the act.

Apartments can have rules for children's use of facilities when there is a nondiscriminatory reason for the difference in rules. The act does not prohibit owners from setting maximum occupancy of units as long as the rule is enforced without discrimination (unreasonably limited occupancy rules are likely to be unenforceable).

Handicapped refers to both mentally and physically handicapped persons. AIDS is considered a handicap under the act, so landlords and sellers cannot discriminate against a person with HIV. The law specifically prohibits discrimination against Seeing Eye dogs and support animals.

The landlord must make reasonable adjustment to rules, policies, practices, or services to afford a handicapped person the equal opportunity to enjoy a unit.

The act requires that a landlord allow a handicapped person to make reasonable modification to the premises, at the tenant's expense, if necessary for the tenant's full use and enjoyment of the premises. The landlord can insist on restoration of the premises at the end of the tenancy if the premises would be undesirable for able-bodied persons.

The landlord also must allow the tenant, at the tenant's expense, to make reasonable alterations to the common area that are necessary for the tenant's use of that area. However, the tenant does not have to restore the common area at the end of the tenancy.

For four or more new rental units built after March 13, 1991, the act specifies structural requirements for handicapped access.

Discrimination under the act includes charging families higher security fees, requiring additional fees for handicapped persons who modify their units, and, possibly, selective use of advertising media as well as the models used for advertising.

The Civil Rights Act of 1968 prohibits

- discrimination by brokers toward clients and customers;
- refusal to show, rent, or sell through false representation that a property is not available;
- discrimination in access to multiple-listing services;
- **steering,** that is, directing people of different races, religions, etc., away from or toward a particular area;
- discriminatory advertising–prohibited even when related to those activities exempt from the act;
- retaliatory acts against those making fair housing complaints and intimidation to discourage complaints;
- discriminatory sale or loan terms;
- **blockbusting,** that is, inducing panic selling by representing that prices will drop because of the entrance or possible entrance of minority groups;
- **redlining,** that is, refusal to loan or insure within an area [*Harrison v. Heinzroth Mortgage Co.* (1977) 430 F. Supp. 893].

Exempted from the act are

- religious groups, which can discriminate in providing nonprofit housing, provided that the religion is open to all, regardless of race, sex, or national origin;
- private clubs, which can discriminate or give preference to members when selling or leasing housing for noncommercial purposes;
- owners of single-family homes, who can discriminate when selling or renting without an agent, provided they do not own more than three such homes and are not in the business*; and
- owners of one to four residential units who occupy a unit, who can discriminate when renting without an agent.

---

*These exceptions to the Civil Rights Act of 1968 are still violations of the Civil Rights Act of 1866 as far as racial discrimination is concerned.

The Federal Fair Housing Act is enforced by the Department of Housing and Urban Development (HUD). While HUD can initiate complaints on its own, the aggrieved party may take either of two courses:

1. He or she may bring a complaint to HUD within one year of the discriminatory action. A hearing on the complaint would be held before an administrative law judge, who can assess civil penalties from $10,000 to $50,000, as well as actual damage and compensation for humiliation suffered because of discriminatory practices.
2. He or she may bring a civil action in state or federal district court within two years after the occurrence. In this case the court could award
   - actual damages plus punitive damages, court costs, and attorney fees; and
   - a permanent or temporary injunction or restraining order.

Failure of a broker to post in the broker's place of business the equal housing opportunity poster shown in Figure 4.2 can shift the burden onto the broker to prove an act was not discriminatory should a complaint be made.

Case Study

In the case of *Pfaff v. U.S. Dept. of Housing and Urban Renewal* (1996) 88 F.3rd 739, a family of five was denied a 1,200-square-foot, two-bedroom rental because the owner felt that four persons was the maximum based on size and that the property lacked a basement or a backyard. HUD alleged violations of Title VIII of the Civil Rights Act of 1968, in that there was discrimination based on family size.

An administrative law judge ruled there was prima facie discrimination because the owner had not shown a business necessity for a numerical occupancy requirement, and awarded $4,212.61 in compensatory damages and $20,000 in emotional distress damages plus an $8,000 civil penalty. The court of appeal reversed, stating that the landlord did not have to rebut any prima facie case against them and did not have to prove a compelling business necessity to justify numerical occupancy guidelines, as HUD has no current occupancy guidelines. The owners' numerical restriction was not unreasonable to prevent dilapidation of their little house. The court held that "HUD's actions were well outside the tenets of good or acceptable government."

While the government was arbitrary in the previous case, the following case involved a landlord who appeared to be arbitrary in a similar situation.

Case Study

In the case of *Fair Housing Council of Orange County Inc., v. Ayres* (1994) 855 F. Supp. 315, a landlord had an occupancy restriction of two persons per unit. It was alleged to have a disparate impact on families with children and was therefore discriminatory as to familial status. Families with children were denied rental if there were more than two persons in the household. Couples who had children while tenants were forced to leave.

The court indicated that this was a prima facie case of discrimination, therefore the defendant had a burden to show legitimate nondiscriminatory justification for the restriction. The defendant failed to show such a reason. The defendant indicated that the purpose was to protect the units against excessive wear and tear. The court pointed out that this purpose could have been accomplished with higher security deposits, greater care in tenant selection, and more frequent inspections to protect the premises.

Case Study

The case of *Gilligan v. Jamco Development Corporation* (1997) 108 F.3d 246 involved a family who received federal aid to families with dependent children. In applying for a rental they were denied because the income source was AFDC. The defendant never inquired as to the amount of income the Gilligans were receiving nor did the defendant tell the Gilligans the monthly rent. Instead, they were told that Verduga Gardens is not a "welfare building" and they were refused the right to inspect a unit.

The court held that prospective tenants must be allowed to inspect as well as apply for residential units and to refuse to accept a rental application from an AFDC or welfare recipient is illegal discrimination. While a review of their finances might reveal that they are unqualified to rent, their status as AFDC recipients does not make them unqualified to apply.

Case Study

The case of *Beliveau v. Caras* (1995) 873 F.Supp.1393 involved an action brought to federal court based on a claim of **sexual harassment**.

A female tenant alleged she was sexually harassed by a resident manager. Among other things, the manager allegedly stared at her when she was lying by the pool in her swimsuit and made off-color flirtatious remarks. It was alleged that while making faucet repairs, the manager put his arm around her and told her she was an attractive woman and that he would like to keep her company. He made remarks about her breasts and

(continued on next page)

grabbed her buttock when she walked away. In an action to dismiss, the court held that she had shown a good cause of action.

The court pointed out that discrimination may be based on a sexual harassment case. Offensive touching, if proved, would support a sexual harassment claim. If the manager was found to have sexually harassed the tenant, the owner of the property could be held liable under the doctrine of respondeat superior.

Note: This case could open a floodgate of allegations by tenants. To avoid false allegations, landlords and property managers should be careful about being alone with a tenant in an apartment.

This case has been remanded to the U.S. District Court for rehearing

Case Study

The case of *Meyer v. Holley* (2003) 123 S. CT. 824 involved a mixed-race couple, the Holleys, who contacted Triad Realty salesperson Grove Crank regarding homes in the $100,000 to $150,000 range located in the Twentynine Palms, California area. They were allegedly shown four homes, all priced above $150,000. Later, the couple found a home on their own that Triad had listed for $145,000. They placed a $145,000 offer with a $5,000 deposit to hold the home for six months, when they expected to close on the sale of their existing home. Their sales agent was told by Crank that a $5,000 deposit was not sufficient to hold the home, but the Holleys declined to increase their purchase offer. Their offer was never presented to the builder.

When the builder later learned of the offer and contacted Triad, Crank allegedly told him he did not want to "deal with those [racial epithet]" and called them a "salt and pepper team." The builder eventually sold his house for $20,000 less than the Holleys had offered. Both the builder and the Holleys sued Crank and Triad for violation of state and federal fair housing laws. The U.S. district court ruled Crank's discriminating acts could be imputed to Triad but not personally to Triad's broker, David Meyer. The Ninth U.S. Circuit Court of Appeals reversed, ruling Meyer, the designated officer-broker of Triad Corporation, can be held vicariously liable for violations of the Fair Housing Act by its licensed salesperson.

However, the U.S. Supreme Court reversed the Court of Appeals, ruling 9-0. "It is well established that traditional vicarious liability rules ordinarily make principals or employers vicariously liable for acts of their employees in the scope of their authority or employment. And in the absence of special circumstances it is the corporation, not its owner or officer, who is the principal or employer, and thus subject to vicarious liability for torts committed by its employees or agents." The court ruled there is nothing in the federal Fair Housing Act to extend strict tort vicarious liability rules to cor-

(continued on next page)

FIGURE 4.1

Equal Housing
Opportunity Poster

U.S. Department of Housing and Urban Development

**EQUAL HOUSING
OPPORTUNITY**

We Do Business in Accordance With the Federal Fair Housing Law
(The Fair Housing Amendments Act of 1988)

It is Illegal to Discriminate Against Any Person Because of Race, Color, Religion, Sex, Handicap, Familial Status, or National Origin

- In the sale or rental of housing or residential lots
- In advertising the sale or rental of housing
- In the financing of housing

- In the provision of real estate brokerage services
- In the appraisal of housing
- Blockbusting is also illegal

Anyone who feels he or she has been discriminated against may file a complaint of housing discrimination with the:
1-800-424-8590 (Toll Free)
1-800-424-8529 (TDD)

**U.S. Department of Housing and Urban Development
Assistant Secretary for Fair Housing and Equal Opportunity
Washington, D.C. 20410**

Previous editions are obsolete

form **HUD-928.1** (3-89)

porate officers for the acts of their employees or independent contractors. Broker Meyer cannot be individually held vicariously liable, but the corporation can be found vicariously liable, the court ruled.

Americans with Disabilities Act (ADA). The Americans with Disabilities Act prohibits discrimination in a place of public accommodation based on an individual's physical or mental disabilities. The law also prohibits employers having 15 or more employees from discriminating against handicapped employees. Employers must alter the workplace to provide reasonable accommodations for disabled employees, unless it creates an undue hardship to the business.

Case Study

The case of *Long v. Coast Resorts Inc.* (2002) 267 F.3d 918 involved the Orleans Hotel and Casino in Las Vegas. The hotel was built in 1997, well after the enactment of the Americans with Disabilities Act. There were 819 bathroom doors 28 inches wide, but ADA requires a 32-inch width for new construction. In addition, the casino bar areas were not accessible for handicapped individuals.

The Court of Appeals ruled that the hotel must modify 819 of its rooms to expand the bathroom doors as well as make the casino bar areas accessible.

Note: While architects should understand ADA requirements and building inspectors should check plans for ADA compliance, they don't always do so. In this case, it was a costly oversight.

A "place of public accommodation" refers to a facility with a nonresidential, commercial use (stores, offices, etc.). Owners and operators of commercial facilities, including property managers and lessees, must make the facilities accessible to the extent readily achievable. "Readily achievable" is defined as easily accomplished without a great deal of expense and is based on the relationship of the costs involved to the total property value, as well as the financial abilities of the person(s) involved. Under the ADA, new construction must be readily accessible and usable by handi-capped persons as well, unless it is structurally impractical to do so.

The ADA may be enforced by an action by the U.S. Attorney or through a civil action by a private citizen. Penalties include $50,000 in civil penalties for the first violation, and $100,000 for each subsequent violation, including compensatory damages and attorney's fees.

State Laws

Unruh Civil Rights Act. "All persons within the jurisdiction of this state are free and equal, and no matter what their race, color, religion, ancestry or national origin are entitled to the full and equal accommodations, advantages, facilities, or services in all business establishments of every kind whatsoever" (Civil Code Section 51). Because real estate brokerage is a business, discrimination against clients or customers by a broker is a violation of the **Unruh Civil Rights Act.** The Unruh Act is enforced through civil action for damages. Each person discriminated against is entitled to actual damages suffered plus $250 for every offense. Thus a family of four discriminated against through a wrongful refusal to rent on two separate occasions could accumulate $2,000 in punitive damages plus actual damages. Persons who suffer any violence or intimidation can be awarded a civil penalty of $25,000 plus attorney fees.

The California Supreme Court held that the anti-discrimination provisions of the Unruh Civil Rights Act are not confined only to the limited category of protective classes but rather protect all persons from any arbitrary discrimination by a business establishment [*Marina Point, Ltd., v. Wolfson* (1982) 30 C.3d 721]. Thus the act was extended to cover age discrimination; it has also been extended to include blindness and other physical disabilities.

Case Study

In the case of *Hubert v. Williams* (1982) 133 C.A.3d Supp. 1, a quadriplegic was evicted because his 24-hour-a-day attendant was an alleged lesbian and the quadriplegic associated with homosexuals. The Unruh Act was held also to extend to discrimination based on sexual preference. The court held that if homosexuals are protected, then persons who associate with this protected group also should be protected.

The small claims court has jurisdiction in cases involving the Unruh Act where damages do not exceed $5,000.

Case Study

In the case of *Botosan v. Paul McNally Realty* (2000) 216 F.3d 827 involved a paraplegic who claimed ADA and Unruh Act violations because a Realty World Office lacked handicapped parking so he was precluded

(continued on next page)

from patronizing the office. Before filing suit, the plaintiff did not notify any-local authorities as to the alleged violations. The district court awarded Botosan $1,000 minimum statutory Unruh Act damages. The court of appeals affirmed, ruling that prior notification of local authorities is not required, damages need not be proven, nor can an owner avoid liability by transferring compliance responsibility under a lease provision.

Note: This case points out that owners and tenants must take the Americans with Disabilities Act seriously and comply because some people might be looking to profit by failure to do so.

California Fair Employment and Housing Act (Rumford Act). The California Fair Employment and Housing Act (Government Code Section 12900 et seq.) prohibits discrimination because of race, color, religion, sex, marital status, national origin, or ancestry in supplying housing accommodations. The Rumford Act has been expanded to include all housing, including single-family residences. The only exception is renting to a roomer or boarder in a single-family house with no more than one roomer or boarder.

Complaints under the act are brought within 60 days of the discriminatory action to the Department of Fair Employment and Housing. The filing of such a complaint does not preclude the injured party from commencing an action under any other law.

The Department of Fair Employment and Housing will investigate and can order the owner to

- sell or rent the unit to the complainant, or
- offer to the complainant the next available unit, or
- pay civil damages up to $10,000 ($25,000 if there has been a prior violation).

A constitutional amendment was enacted that barred the state from interfering with an owner's right to sell or lease his or her property. This amendment, which would have had the effect of repealing the Rumford Act, was held to violate the equal protection clause of the Fourteenth Amendment to the U.S. Constitution.

Case Study

The case of *Smith v. Fair Employment & Housing Commission* (1996) 12

(continued on next page)

C.4th 1143 involved a landlord who refused to rent to an unmarried couple based on her religious convictions that to do so would be to condone sin.

The couple filed a complaint with the California Fair Employment and Housing Commission alleging violation of the Unruh Act as well as California's Fair Employment and Housing Act. While an administrative law judge ruled in favor of the couple and awarded damages, the decision was appealed to the court of appeals, where it was reversed.

The California Supreme Court reversed the court of appeals and pointed out that neither federal nor state law allows an exemption to a landlord for discrimination because of a personal contrary religious belief.

Business and Professions Code. Section 125.6 of California's Business and Professions Code provides that "every person who holds a license under the provisions of this code is subject to disciplinary action . . . if, because of the applicant's race, color, sex, religion, ancestry, physical handicap, marital status or national origin, he or she refuses to perform the licensed activity or aids or incites the refusal to perform such licensed activity by another licensee . . . or makes any discrimination or restriction in the performance of the licensed activity." The code would appear to cover any discriminatory practice committed while acting as a licensee.

■ SUMMARY

The purpose of the real estate law is to protect the public. The Department of Real Estate administers the licensing of brokers and salespersons as well as the regulation of their activities. This chapter sets forth the activities requiring licensure as well as those activities exempt from the real estate licensing requirements.

After a hearing, in accordance with the Administrative Procedure Act, licenses can be revoked, suspended, or denied for a number of specified violations. After a license has been revoked, suspended, or denied, the real estate commissioner has the power to grant a restricted license, which is probationary in nature.

If a member of the public is injured because of his or her dealings with a real estate licensee for an activity for which licensing is required, and the injured party obtains a judgment against the licensee that is uncollectible, the injured party can apply to the Department of Real Estate for reimbursement. The injured party can collect up to $20,000 from the recovery account.

Besides the listing and sale of real property, licensing allows the broker to engage in a number of specialized activities, including these:

- Mortgage broker: These brokers solicit borrowers and lenders for loans secured by real estate, and their activities are strictly regulated.
- Real property syndicate security dealer: A real estate broker is exempt from the licensing requirements of the Corporations Code and may sell both corporate and noncorporate syndicate interests.
- Mineral, oil, and gas broker: While MOG licenses are no longer being issued, a real estate licensee can engage in MOG transactions without additional licensing and without permits.
- Escrow agent: A real estate broker can act as an escrow agent in those transactions in which he or she represented either the buyer or seller or in which the broker was a principal to the transaction.
- Mobile home sales: With specified restrictions a real estate licensee can engage in the sale of mobile homes.
- Advance fee rental agent: While there is a separate rental agent license, a real estate broker is exempt from the licensing requirement and may engage in a prepaid rental listing service.
- Business opportunity broker: A real estate licensee can engage in the sale of business opportunities.
- Franchise sales: A real estate licensee is authorized to sell franchise opportunities.

Real estate licensees must comply with all federal and state fair housing laws. These include the following:

- Civil Rights Act of 1866: Citizens of all races shall have the same rights as enjoyed by white citizens to inherit, purchase, lease, sell, or hold real and personal property.
- Civil Rights Act of 1968 (Federal Fair Housing Act): This act prohibits discrimination in housing based on race, color, sex, religion, or national origin. A 1988 amendment extended its coverage to the handicapped and children.
- Unruh Civil Rights Act: This act prohibits discrimination by a business on the basis of race, color, religion, ancestry, national origin, age, sex, and sexual preference.
- Fair Employment and Housing Act (Rumford Act): This act prohibits discrimination based on race, color, religion, sex, marital status, national origin, or ancestry.
- Business and Professions Code: Provides for commissioner disciplinary action against licensees for discriminatory practices.

Because of overlapping coverage, a civil rights violation is likely to be a violation of several acts.

■ DISCUSSION CASES

1. The plaintiff negotiated a lease and an option to extend the lease. The defendant agreed to pay the plaintiff $7,500 if the option was exercised. Prior to the expiration of the lease period and after the broker's license had lapsed, the lessor and lessee agreed to a new option, and a new lease was entered into at terms different from those originally specified. **Is the former broker entitled to $7,500?**

   Cline v. Yamaga (1979) 97 C.A.3d 239

2. Katz, a broker, purchased a building that he knew had code violations and was subject to an order to demolish an illegal room. Katz advertised the property as a "fixer upper" that would be sold "as is." Katz asked the buyer's broker if he knew there were code violations. The buyer's broker mentioned he had noticed some. Katz did not inform the buyer's broker of all of the violations or of the city order to demolish the room. The purchaser later discovered the violations. Katz offered to rescind the sale but refused to pay for work already performed by the purchaser. **Was the Department of Real Estate justified in revoking Katz's license?**

   Katz v. Department of Real Estate (1979) 96 C.A.3d 895

3. During a marriage that lasted two months and was subsequently annulled because of fraud, a wife invested in a joint venture with her husband. The wife was defrauded in the joint venture and subsequently obtained a judgment against her former husband, who was a real estate broker. The judgment was uncollectible against the broker. **Is the former wife entitled to compensation from the Recovery Account?**

   Powers v. Fox (1979) 96 C.A.3d 440

4. A broker represented that he was the agent, not the owner, of a house he actually owned. He also indicated that a drainage system would be installed. The drainage system was never installed, and the purchaser obtained a judgment against the broker. **Is the purchaser entitled to collection from the recovery account?**

    Robinson v. Murphy (1979) 96 C.A.3d 763

5. The recovery account, in determining what to pay, used a setoff of tax benefits received by an investor against the loss. **Was this action proper?**

    Froid v. Fox (1982) 132 C.A.3d 832

6. A mortgage loan broker charged escrow fees based on the maximum allowed by law. **Was this action proper?**

    Pacific Plan of California v. Kinder (1978) 84 C.A.3d 215

7. A landlord had a minimum income policy for rentals. The requirement was a gross income at least three times greater than the rent. The plaintiff claimed that the policy arbitrarily discriminated against persons with lower incomes regardless of their actual ability to pay and that it discriminated against women because of disparate earnings. **Does this income test violate the Unruh Act?**

    Harris v. Capital Growth Investors XIV (1991) 52 C.3d 1142

8. The real estate commissioner denied a license on the grounds that the applicant had been convicted of distributing cocaine. **Was the action of the real estate commissioner proper?**

    Brandt v. Fox (1979) 90 C.A.3d 737

9. The plaintiff was arrested after landing an airplane containing between 800 and 1,000 pounds of marijuana. He pleaded guilty to possession for the purpose of sale. **Was the commissioner's action to revoke the plaintiff's license proper?**

    Golde v. Fox (1979) 98 C.A.3d 167

10. Pieri pleaded guilty to obtaining unemployment benefits by fraud. He was placed on probation, and the charge was dismissed at the end of the probationary period. Pieri's application for a broker's license three years later was denied because of a conviction for a crime involving moral turpitude. **Was the commissioner's action proper?**

    Pieri v. Fox (1979) 96 C.A.3d 802

11. A landlord had a policy allowing two adults and two children to occupy an apartment only if the second child was born after the family had taken possession. **Is the landlord's policy proper?**

    Smith v. Ring Bros. Management Corp. (1986) 183 C.A.3d 649

12. A real estate salesman falsely represented himself as a real estate broker to induce the plaintiff to invest in short-term loans secured by trust deeds. The salesperson took the money but did not invest in the trust deeds. After a judgment that could not be collected, the plaintiff asked for reimbursement from the recovery account. The commissioner took the position that the defendant was not licensed as a broker and so could not engage in the transactions; therefore the account should not be liable. **Do you agree?**

    Vinci v. Edmonds (1986) 185 C.A.3d 1251

13. **Is a creditor who has obtained a judgment entitled to recover from the recovery account when the broker's debt was discharged in bankruptcy?**

    Armenta v. Edmonds (1988) 201 C.A.3d 464

14. The town of Huntington, New York, has about 200,000 residents, of which 95 percent are white and less than 4 percent are black. A private developer sought to change the zoning from single-family housing to multifamily rental to build a project fostering integration. The town refused to rezone. **Does the town's action violate the Civil Rights Act of 1968?**

    Town of Huntington v. Huntington Branch, NAACP (1989)
    488 U.S. 15

15. A mobile home park charged a per diem guest fee as well as a parking fee for a home health-care aide required for an infant with respiratory problems. **Is there any problem as to these fees?**

    U.S. v. California Mobile Home Park Management Co. (1994)
    29 F.3d 1413

16. The real estate commissioner automatically suspended the license of a broker who failed to reimburse the recovery fund. The broker alleged that due process was violated because he did not have a hearing. **Is the broker correct?**

    Rodriguez v. Calif. Dept. of Real Estate (1997) 51 C.A.4th 1289

17. A title insurer paid a lender's claim after a mortgage broker embezzled the funds that were to pay off existing trust deeds. The title insurer then sued the broker and obtained a judgment that could not be collected. The title insurer then filed a claim with the California Department of Real Estate Recovery Fund. **Does the title insurer have a valid claim against the recovery fund?**

Stewart Title Guaranty Co. v. Park (2001) 250 F.3d 1249

18. Using a business visitor pass, Jankey frequently visited the Twentieth Century Fox film and production lot in Los Angeles. Because he was confined to a wheelchair, he was unable to access the commissary, studio store, or automatic teller machine. Jankey alleged violation of the Americans With Disabilities Act. **Was the act violated as to Jankey?**

Jankey v. Twentieth Century Fox Film Corporation (2000) 212 F.3d 1159

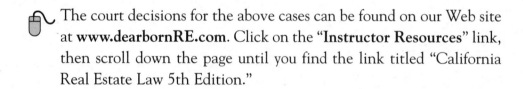 The court decisions for the above cases can be found on our Web site at **www.dearbornRE.com**. Click on the "**Instructor Resources**" link, then scroll down the page until you find the link titled "California Real Estate Law 5th Edition."

■ CHAPTER QUIZ

1. A person would most likely contact the real estate commissioner to

   a. resolve a salesperson-broker commission dispute.
   b. report fraud of a licensee.
   c. obtain an opinion of the legality of a course of action.
   d. arbitrate disputes between brokers.

2. Which of the following persons would require a real estate license?

   a. An attorney-in-fact selling property of another
   b. An attorney-at-law taking a listing
   c. A paid administrator of an estate selling the decedent's property
   d. None of the above

3. A broker for a corporation who also wants to conduct a separate brokerage business must

   a. sell his or her corporate stock.
   b. obtain a separate broker's license.
   c. operate through another licensee.
   d. return the corporate license to the commissioner.

4. A nonresident who wishes to obtain a California real estate license must

   a. first establish California residency.
   b. consent to process service on the secretary of state if the prospective licensee cannot be located within the state.
   c. also be licensed in his or her state of residency.
   d. be 21 years of age.

5. A three-hour course in ethics is required to be taken

   a. prior to taking the real estate broker examination.
   b. within 18 months of obtaining a salesperson's license.
   c. prior to a salesperson's first license renewal.
   d. for license renewals but only after the first renewal for salespersons.

6. Which of the following is *not* sufficient cause for the revocation of a real estate license?

   a. Commingling with the licensee's own money or property the property or money of others received and held by the licensee
   b. Acting for more than one party in a transaction
   c. Making a substantial misrepresentation
   d. Making any false promises of a character likely to influence, persuade, or induce

7. Which of the following is *not* grounds for disciplinary action by the real estate commissioner?

   a. Failure of an agent to disclose an ownership interest in property being sold
   b. Failure to exercise reasonable supervision over the acts of salespersons
   c. Violation of the Franchise Investment Law
   d. Revealing to a buyer problems that make the property unsuited to his purpose

8. Broker Thomas, who was a member of the city planning commission, told his friend broker Jones that an area was to be rezoned from agricultural use to commercial use. Broker Thomas did not receive any consideration for this information. Broker Jones purchased several parcels in the area and made a profit when the zoning was changed. Which broker has placed his license in jeopardy?

   a. Thomas
   b. Jones
   c. Both a and b
   d. Neither a nor b

9. The maximum amount a person can obtain from a licensee after obtaining a judgment against the licensee for a fraudulent act is

   a. $20,000.
   b. $20,000 for each offense.
   c. $100,000.
   d. the amount of the judgment.

10. Which of the following activities requires a real estate license?

    a. Being the resident manager of an apartment building
    b. Selling more than eight parcels of one's own real estate in one year
    c. Subdividing one's own property
    d. Acting as a mortgage loan broker

11. A $5,000 fee that a broker charged for negotiating a three-year second trust deed for $20,000 is

    a. usurious.
    b. voidable.
    c. illegal.
    d. legal.

12. A broker's loan statement is prepared for the benefit of the

    a. broker.
    b. Department of Real Estate.
    c. lender.
    d. borrower.

13. In advertising a mobile home a broker used "no down payment" in the ads because he had arranged a separate loan to cover the down payment. The advertising was

    a. proper, because there was 100 percent financing.
    b. expressly prohibited by law.
    c. unethical but not illegal.
    d. proper if all loan terms were included in the ad.

14. In selling mobile homes a real estate broker may *not*

    a. have an office where six model homes are displayed.
    b. advertise "no down payment" if the payment is to be borrowed.
    c. fail to withdraw advertising within 48 hours of receipt of notice of non-availability.
    d. All of the above

15. After collecting an advance rental fee of $75, you are unable to provide your client with a rental that suits her. When she requests a refund, upon expiration of her rental contract you must return

    a. nothing if you provided a list of at least three rentals.
    b. $50.
    c. $25.
    d. $40.

16. Which of the following is *not* required to be included in the notice required under the Bulk Sales Act?

    a. Name of seller
    b. Date and place of sale
    c. Sales price and terms
    d. All of the above

17. In cases of noncompliance with the Bulk Sales Act the party likely to be most adversely affected would be the

    a. seller.
    b. purchaser.
    c. creditors of the seller.
    d. Franchise Tax Board.

18. As a licensee dealing with people of other races you should

    a. suggest that they could be better served by dealing with agents of their own race.
    b. be frank and honest in explaining the problems of locating in areas having few people of their race.
    c. be proper and helpful even though you would prefer they seek help elsewhere.
    d. be completely "color-blind" regarding race.

19. The federal case that upheld fair housing was

    a. *Jones v. Mayer.*
    b. *Brown v. Board of Education.*
    c. *Shelley v. Kraemer.*
    d. *Wellenkamp v. Bank of America.*

20. A nonprofit women's organization intends to develop housing for members. It will limit rentals to women and will give preference to unmarried mothers. This action would likely be a violation of the

    a. Civil Rights Act of 1866.
    b. Civil Rights Act of 1968.
    c. Rumford Act.
    d. Both b and c

21. The Civil Rights Act of 1968, as amended, does *not* prohibit

    a. sex discrimination.
    b. age discrimination.
    c. housing reserved for the elderly.
    d. discrimination against handicapped persons.

22. A broker takes listings in an area where property values are going down because of a changing neighborhood, and there is a mass exodus of whites. Which of the following actions by the broker would be a violation of fair housing laws?

    a. Advertising "Sell your property fast before you lose equity"
    b. Offering whites a lower commission rate to sell their property
    c. Both a and b
    d. Neither a nor b

23. Which of the following is an example of steering?

    a. Directing whites away from mixed-race areas
    b. Advertising properties in black areas only in newspapers aimed at black readers
    c. Both a and b
    d. Neither a nor b

24. Refusal to make a mortgage loan within a designated area is known as

    a. steering.
    b. redlining.
    c. blockbusting.
    d. None of the above

25. For a broker's violation of the Civil Rights Act of 1968 the courts would *not*

    a. issue a restraining order.
    b. award actual damages.
    c. award punitive damages.
    d. revoke or suspend the broker's license.

CHAPTER FIVE

LAW OF CONTRACTS

■ KEY TERMS

accord and satisfaction	illusory contract	quasi contract
bilateral contract	implied contract	right of first refusal
breach of contract	laches	statute of frauds
commercial frustration	liquidated damages	time is of the essence
devisible contract	menace	undue influence
duress	misrepresentation	unilateral contract
emancipated minor	novation	waiver
express contract	option	
fraud	parol evidence rule	

■ TYPES OF CONTRACTS

A contract is an agreement between two or more parties to do or not to do something. Valid contracts are generally enforceable under the law.

Express vs. Implied

Contracts are either express or implied. An **express contract** is an agreement stated in words. The terms of the agreement may be set forth either orally or in writing. An agreement whereby a buyer agrees to buy and a seller agrees to sell a property at an agreed-on price and terms would be an express contract. Later in this chapter you will learn why most real estate contracts must be express contracts.

An **implied contract** is an agreement that, while not specifically stated, is understood by the parties. Section 1621 of the Civil Code states, "An implied contract is one, the existence and terms of which are manifested by conduct." For example, assume that you ask a pest control firm to make a termite inspection of a property. While you never agreed to pay a particular amount, or even any amount, for the termite inspection, a reasonable person would understand that the pest control firm will expect to be paid for its services. The party ordering the report should expect to be charged for the work, and the party performing the work should expect to be paid. Therefore, an implied contract to pay the reasonable value of the services rendered exists.

Quasi Contract

In a **quasi contract** no real contractual intent exists. The law implies the existence of a contract. The law often will imply a contract when one party benefited but did not really consent to any agreement. For example, suppose by mistake your neighbor paid the real estate taxes on your property. You would be obligated, as a matter of equity or fairness, in a quasi contract to reimburse your neighbor for the amount of taxes paid for your benefit.

Bilateral v. Unilateral

Contracts may be bilateral or unilateral agreements. A **bilateral contract** is an agreement in which a mutual exchange of promises occurs—a promise for a promise. If a pest control firm offered to provide a termite inspection for a property at a stated price and you agreed to have it performed at the price stated, you would have formed a bilateral contract. This is an example of an express (stated) bilateral contract.

Offers to purchase real estate, when accepted, form bilateral contracts. The buyer, who is usually the offeror, agrees to buy at a specified price and terms, and the seller, usually the offeree, agrees to sell at that price and those terms.

Exclusive-right-to-sell listings are bilateral contracts. The owners promise to pay a fee to the broker if the broker obtains a ready, willing, and able buyer according to the terms of the listing or any other terms the sellers are willing to accept. In exchange, the broker promises to use diligence to obtain a buyer.

A **unilateral contract** is a promise for an act; one party makes a promise to induce another party to act. The second party (offeree) is not bound to act, but if the offeree accepts the offer by performing the requested act, a binding contract is formed. For example, suppose you offered to pay a painter $800 if he would repair the stucco on your garage and paint the exterior with two coats of paint. The painter would not be obligated to perform, because you cannot bind another party to a contract without that party's assent. However, if the painter were to repair the stucco and paint the garage as requested, he would have accepted your offer by his performance and would be entitled to be paid as agreed.

An open (nonexclusive) listing is a unilateral contract. Under an open listing an owner promises to pay a broker should the broker succeed in procuring a buyer. The broker is under no obligation to use diligence to look for a buyer, but if the broker does procure a buyer, he or she would, by performance, be accepting the offer. If the listing required that a broker use due diligence to seek a buyer, it would be a bilateral contract (promise for a promise) and not an open listing (promise for an act).

Executory v. Executed   A contract is either executory or executed. An executory contract is one that has not yet been fully performed. An agreement between a buyer and seller for the sale of land would be executory until escrow was closed. The agreement would be executory until title was transferred and the consideration was paid.

An executed contract is one in which everything that was required to be performed has been performed. After escrow closes on a sales agreement, the contract becomes an executed one. (Do not confuse an executed contract with the execution of a document, which is the signing of the document.)

■ ESSENTIALS OF A VALID CONTRACT

For a valid contract to exist, four elements are necessary:

1. Competent parties
2. Mutual consent
3. Legal purpose
4. Consideration

Valid contracts generally are enforceable. Exceptions are contracts outlawed by the statute of limitations or discharged in bankruptcy, which while valid agreements are nevertheless unenforceable.

Competent Parties   A minor is anyone under the age of 18. Contracts for the purchase or sale of real property entered into by minors are void. A void contract is the same as having no agreement at all because the agreement does not bind either of the parties to it. (See page 140 for more information on void contracts.) A minor can contract only for necessities–items required for support, such as food and clothing.

Contracts by minors for other than necessities are subject to disaffirmance (annulment) by the minor within a reasonable time after reaching the age of 18. In California, only the former minor has this right to disaffirm and not the person with whom the minor contracted. A minor who lied about his or her age is not prevented from disaffirming the contract. Therefore, parties who deal with individuals who could be minors have a duty to ascertain the status of the person they are dealing with.

After reaching the age of 18, a person can ratify contracts made as a minor so that the contracts no longer can be disaffirmed. After the age of 18, any action indicating that the person intended to be bound–payment on a property, repairing, altering, renting, or offering the property for sale–would be a ratification.

An **emancipated minor** is an exception to the general rule that minors cannot contract for other than necessities. Emancipated minors can contract as adults and cannot disaffirm their contracts. Minors can be emancipated if they

- are married or unmarried (widowed or divorced);
- enter military service on active duty; or
- receive a declaration of emancipation from the court (Civil Code Section 62).

If a broker arranges a sale to a minor and the minor later disaffirms the purchase agreement, the minor could be entitled to the return of consideration paid to the seller. The broker could be liable to the seller for the damages suffered.

A person adjudged insane cannot contract. Any contract entered into would be void. The same holds true for persons not adjudged insane but who are wholly without understanding. Both minors and incompetents can, however, convey, mortgage, lease, or acquire real property following a superior court order obtained through appropriate guardianship or conservatorship proceedings.

A person who is of unsound mind but not wholly without understanding and who has not been adjudged insane can void his or her contracts. These contracts are valid unless voided. After regaining his or her sanity, a person can ratify or disaffirm a contract made while of unsound mind.

A person of unsound mind who has not been adjudged insane and who has lucid periods could enter into a binding contract during a lucid period.

A person who is under the influence of alcohol and/or drugs and as a result is wholly without understanding cannot contract. However, merely being under the influence of alcohol and/or drugs generally is not sufficient by itself to void a contract.

Persons sentenced to imprisonment in state prisons are deprived of their civil rights to the extent necessary for the security of the institution in which they are confined and for the reasonable protection of the public. Convicts do not forfeit their property. They may acquire property by gift, inheritance, or will under certain conditions, and they may convey their property or acquire property through conveyance. The Department of Corrections may restrict conveyances made for business purposes.

Aliens have contractual capacity in California.

Mutual Consent

An offer and acceptance that indicate a meeting of the minds on a definite and certain agreement usually are considered evidence of mutual consent.

The Offer. The offer must be a clear and definite offer made with the intent that when it is accepted, there will be a binding agreement.

A letter of intent is a nonbinding expression of interest. Even though definite terms may be expressed, it is not an offer. Breach of a letter of intent would not entitle the other party to damages.

Acceptance. A contract is formed when the offeree (person to whom a definite and certain offer is made) accepts the offer of the offeror (person making the offer). An offer can specify the manner of acceptance, but if no form for acceptance is specified, the offer can be accepted in any reasonable manner.

In the case of *Hofer v. Young* (1995) 38 C.A.4th 52, the court held that a FAX is "a reasonable and increasingly common means of modern communication." While acceptance may be by FAX, unless the offer prescribes the means of acceptance, records should be kept to prove that the FAX was sent as well as the time it was received.

Professional Publishing Corporation's 2001 Standard Residential Purchase Agreement provides that a document is to be considered delivered at the time the FAX is transmitted, provided a transmission report is generated reflecting the accurate transmission of the document.

Acceptance is possible by e-mail, as e-mail is "a reasonable and increasingly common means of modern communication." Pads are available that allow signatures to be electronically attached to documents. A problem with the technology is that electronic signatures can be easily forged.

At an auction the persons who are bidding are the offerors. They make their bids to the auctioneer, who is the offeree. The auctioneer does not have to accept any offer unless the auction is being conducted *without reserve*, which means the seller has agreed in advance that the highest bid will be accepted. A bidder at a real estate auction that is not held "without reserve" should realize that the high bid does not mean the bidder has made a purchase unless the bid is accepted.

Acceptance takes place when the offeree notifies the offeror or the offeror's agent of the acceptance. Communicating acceptance to a third party who is not an agent of the offeror is not an acceptance. At an auction the fall of the auctioneer's hammer signifies acceptance and is considered notification to the bidder. The act of mailing a written acceptance constitutes notification (effective upon posting, Civil Code 1583). Because it might become necessary to prove mailing, a postal receipt is desirable.

Case Study

In the case of *Gibbs v. American Savings* (1990) 217 C.A.3d 1372, the buyers gave their acceptance of a seller's counteroffer to a company mail clerk at 10:00 A.M. The mail clerk failed to take it promptly to the post office. At 11:00 A.M. the seller called to revoke the counteroffer. The buyers sued the seller for damages and specific performance. The court held that a contract would have been formed if the acceptance had been deposited in the U.S. mail beyond the buyers' further control, but in this case a contract had not been formed because the acceptance had not been mailed.

The acceptance must be made by the offeree. A third person who has knowledge of an offer to sell cannot, by acceptance, form a binding contract, because the offer was not made to that party.

Silence to an offer generally is regarded as neither acceptance nor rejection. Even if an offer states, "Failure to reply within ten days will be considered acceptance," failure to reply will not in fact be acceptance of the offer. Only if the parties by their prior dealings have established silence as acceptance might silence be construed as acceptance.

Intent to enter into a contract must be present. Acceptance of an offer obviously made in jest will not form a binding agreement.

Newspaper advertisements of real estate are not offers to sell; they are merely invitations to negotiate. A buyer's acceptance does not form a binding contract because newspaper advertisements are really announcements that the property is being placed on the market. Therefore, a buyer cannot accept an "offer" made in an ad. Similarly, providing information to a multiple-listing service is an invitation to negotiate only and not an offer to sell.

If an offer fails to state how long it will remain open for acceptance, it can be accepted within a reasonable period of time. Even if the offer does state a period for acceptance, courts often will allow acceptance after that period unless the offer indicates that time is critical, usually accomplished by including the words **"time is of the essence."**

Although several cases have held that a "time is of the essence" clause does not always make time essential in a contract [*Nash v. Superior Court* (1978) 86 C.A.3d 690], these decisions have applied to contractual performance and not to the period for acceptance of an offer.

Counteroffer. An acceptance that varies from the offer is not an acceptance but a counteroffer. A counteroffer is, in fact, a rejection of the original offer. Assume an offer calls for a 90-day escrow. An acceptance that states, "Accepted provided the escrow period be 30 days," represents a material change in the offer. The offeror really is making a counteroffer and rejecting the original offer. After such rejection the offeree no longer can form a binding contract by later accepting the original offer.

In a counteroffer the offeree becomes the new offeror. The original offeror is now the offeree and can accept the counteroffer and form a binding contract, reject it, or make a new counteroffer.

A request for a change in the proposed contract that does not condition the acceptance is not a counteroffer. For example, in an accepted offer that has the notation "It would be appreciated if escrow could be closed before December 30th," the acceptance forms a binding contract, because acceptance is not conditioned on this request. That is, the offeror is not bound to the December 30th date.

Case Study

The case of *Roth v. Malson* (1998) 67 C.A.4th 552 involved an acreage parcel that was listed for sale at $47,600. A buyer offered $41,650 cash and a close of escrow within 30 days of acceptance. The seller made a counteroffer of $44,000. The buyer signed and dated the counter to counteroffer portion of the counteroffer form and wrote, "Price to be $44,000 as above. Escrow to close on or before December 6, 1995. All cash."

(continued on next page)

> Subsequently, the seller notified the buyer that the property was being withdrawn from the market. The buyer then sued for specific performance. The superior court granted judgment for seller Malson, concluding that no sale contract was ever formed.
>
> The court of appeal affirmed since Roth, the buyer, failed to accept the counteroffer. Civil Code 1585 requires that an acceptance must be "absolute and unqualified." The buyer changed the close of escrow from "within 30 days of acceptance" to "on or before December 6th." This was a counter to the seller's counteroffer requiring the seller's acceptance.

Revocation. Prior to notification of acceptance, an offeror can withdraw the offer. This generally is true even if the offeror promised to keep the offer open for a specified period of time. Unless consideration is given to keep an offer open (this would be an option), the offer generally can be revoked. One exception is that the offeror can no longer revoke the offer after performance has started on a unilateral contract.

Case Study

The case of *Ersa Grae Corp. v. Fluor Corp.* (1991) 1 C.A.4th 613 involved a firm that had negotiated simultaneously with two different buyers. It communicated to its broker that it was withdrawing the counteroffer it had made to one of the buyers. However, the broker did not communicate the revocation to the buyer. The court found that while the property owner had communicated revocation of its counteroffer to the broker before the counteroffer was accepted, the broker was not acting as the buyer's agent and had not communicated the revocation to the buyer. Accordingly, the buyer's acceptance of the seller's counteroffer constituted a contract. The seller sold the same property twice and was liable to Ersa Grae Corp. for nondelivery damages.

Revocation must be made to the offeree or the offeree's agent to be effective.

Revocation takes place upon receipt, so contrary to an acceptance, mailing a revocation has no effect until it is received. Assume a revocation was mailed on the first of the month, and the offeree mailed an acceptance on the third of the month. The revocation was received on the fourth of the month, and the acceptance was received on the fifth of the month. A valid contract would result because acceptance took place on the third (upon mailing), and the revocation had no effect because it was not effective (received) until after the offer was accepted.

When an offeror dies or becomes mentally incapacitated prior to acceptance, the offer is dead, and a later acceptance will not form a binding contract. When the offeror is a corporation, the death of the officer making the offer will not affect the offer, because the corporation is a separate legal entity and does not die with the death of its officers.

Unless a contract calls for personal services, death or mental incapacity after acceptance will not affect a contract. The contract will bind the heirs or estates.

The destruction of the subject matter terminates an offer. If a house is destroyed by fire prior to acceptance of an offer, acceptance by the seller after the destruction will not form a binding contract.

When the acceptor fails to fulfill a condition precedent to acceptance, such as verifying gross or net income within a stated period of time, the offer is revoked.

Definiteness. An agreement must be definite. An agreement to buy "the house on Third Street" probably would be definite enough if the seller owned only one house on Third Street. However, if the seller owned several houses on Third Street, the agreement might not be binding.

Agreement to buy a property at "a price to be agreed on" would not be binding, because it would lack definitiveness. An agreement to buy real estate at a price to be determined by a definite formula would be binding, even though the exact price is not known at the time the agreement is entered into. For example, an agreement to buy at the average appraisal price of three named appraisers could be binding.

The case of *Goodyear Rubber Corporation v. Munoz* (1985) 170 C.A.3d 919 held that an option to buy at "fair market value" was valid. However, the case of *ETCO Corporation v. Hauer* (1984) 161 C.A.3d 1154 held that a lease at a rent to be mutually agreed upon rendered the option unenforceable.

When a purchase is subject to the purchaser's or seller's later decision about whether to complete the transaction, the contract is an **illusory contract**, and neither party is bound. "I will pay you $100,000 for the lot if I decide to buy it" is not an agreement. Prospective tenants often sign letters of intent that indicate they will seriously negotiate with the owner for space. While letters of intent from quality tenants might influence a construction lender, they are not valid contracts. Again, these are illusory contracts and are agreements only that the parties will attempt to agree.

"Subject to" provisions do not make a contract illusory. Offers are frequently written subject to zoning changes, appraisals, financing, and other contingencies.

Requirements that work is to be performed to a person's satisfaction have been held to mean that dissatisfaction must be exercised in good faith and not merely to break the agreement.

For a contract to be valid the parties not only must be identified but also must exist. Parties may use fictitious names or pseudonyms, but they must be real people or business entities. An agreement by an entity that does not exist, such as a nonexistent corporation, would not be enforceable. However, the parties can agree that a party will be designated later to perform or to receive performance, as in naming a designee to receive the deed.

The manner and time of payment do not have to be specified in the contract. Payment in cash at the time of closing is implied unless specified otherwise. When a closing date is not specified in an agreement, a closing within a reasonable period of time is implied. Similarly, in the absence of a stated time for possession to be given to the buyer, it is implied that possession will transfer upon close of escrow.

Also implied is that the seller will convey marketable title and that any work to be performed will be performed in a workmanlike manner.

Mistakes. A contract can be voided on the basis of a bilateral mistake as to fact. For example, if both buyer and seller believed that a trust deed was assumable but discovered that it was not after the sales agreement had been signed, the buyer would be able to void the agreement because of the mutual mistake.

A unilateral mistake, in contrast, will not be the basis for voiding a contract. In the preceding example, if only the purchaser believed that the loan was assumable and the seller was unaware of the buyer's intent to assume the loan and had done nothing to warrant the buyer's belief, the contract would be enforceable.

Case Study

In the case of *Levy v. Wolff* (1956) 46 C.2d 367, a buyer paid $16,500 for a parcel of land that both the buyer and seller believed to be subject to a valid lease. Subsequent to the sale the tenant brought an action that resulted in a court determination that the lease "had never been binding or in force." The court held that the mutual mistake as to fact would allow rescission. In this case the purchaser wanted to keep the land, so the court allowed the purchaser to recover damages (the difference between the value of the land with the lease and the value without the lease).

A party who realizes that the other party is mistaken cannot take advantage and hold the mistaken party. This is an exception to the rule that a unilateral mistake is not grounds to void a contract.

Legal Purpose

If parties enter into a contract in violation of the law, they generally cannot ask for enforcement of the agreement. A lease of premises for a specified illegal purpose, for example, could not be enforced by the lessor or lessee.

Neither party can enforce an illegal executory contract. If executed, either party can rescind the agreement because of its illegal purpose.

A change in the law that results in an agreement becoming illegal voids a contract. It also revokes an unaccepted offer.

If an illegality is minor or not related directly to the agreement, the courts ordinarily will allow enforcement. For example, a masonry contractor who builds a proper block wall with building permits and in accordance with the contractual specifications will not be barred from collecting the value of his work because a business permit in the community where the wall was constructed has expired or because he paid a laborer less than minimum wage.

Where the law was intended to protect a party from a wrongdoer, the law cannot be used to protect the wrongdoer. A broker who sold an unregistered real property security would be liable to the purchaser for any misrepresentations even though the sale violated the law, because the registration requirement was intended to protect purchasers of securities, not sellers.

When one party is less guilty than the other, the less guilty party might be able to recover. This is especially true if the other person has a greater knowledge of the law and represents the agreement as being legal.

If a contract is composed of several **devisible contracts**, the illegality of one part will not void the balance of the agreement. For example, assume a lease agreement covered several properties with separate rents. If one of the leases provided for a percentage of the gross from a specified illegal activity, that portion would be unenforceable, but the rest of the contract could be enforceable.

When an agreement is subject to two interpretations, one that is lawful and another that is illegal, in the absence of other evidence as to intent, the court will determine that the agreement should be given the legal interpretation.

Contracts that unreasonably restrain a person from engaging in business are against public policy and are unenforceable. In the sale of a barbershop an agreement that the seller never will open another barbershop anywhere would be unenforceable because it is too severe a restraint. An agreement that the seller would not open another shop within a five-mile radius of the shop for a period of three years, however, probably would be considered reasonable and therefore enforceable.

An agreement between a real estate salesperson and a broker that the salesperson would never become a broker or never would work for any other broker would not only be against public policy but would likely be in violation of antitrust legislation.

Consideration

Consideration is anything of value given in exchange for a promise or performance of another. Consideration could be forbearance from acting as well as a promise to act. For example, a creditor's agreeing not to start foreclosure for 90 days, when the creditor was entitled to foreclose, would be consideration for the transfer of other property.

A promise unsupported by consideration generally is considered unenforceable. It is merely a promise to make a gift. While an enforceable promise requires consideration, an executed transfer requires no consideration. Such a transfer is a completed gift.

The reason that an offeror can withdraw an offer anytime prior to acceptance is that an offer is unsupported by consideration. On the other hand, the presence of consideration requires that the offeror keep the offer open. In an option the optionor receives consideration from the optionee so that the offer cannot be withdrawn.

Courts ordinarily will not get involved in evaluating the adequacy of consideration. The courts will, however, consider the amount of consideration when a party claims fraud, undue influence, or a mutual mistake as to a material fact. If a court determines that a contract is so unfair as to be unconscionable, the court may refuse to enforce it and allow the injured party to rescind the agreement or provide the injured party with other appropriate relief.

In cases involving specific performance, adequacy of consideration is essential. Without fair consideration, specific performance cannot be enforced (Civil Code Section 3391). (Specific performance, as stated in Chapter 1, is an equitable remedy. Therefore, unless the consideration is fair, this equitable remedy will be denied.)

A third party can enforce a contract even when that third party did not pay consideration: "A contract made expressly for the benefit of a third party, may be enforced by him at any time before the parties thereto rescind it" (Civil Code Section 1559). For example, Alfred agreed to build a shed for Baker. Assume that Alfred then paid Charley to build the shed. If Charley failed to perform, then Baker, who is a third-party beneficiary of the contract between Alfred and Charley, could enforce the contract.

Past consideration cannot be used as consideration to enforce a present promise in excess of the promisor's duty. For example, a past gift given freely will not be consideration for a new promise, because the promisor was under no obligation or duty to act, forbear to act, or make any promise.

The promise to honor an existing obligation or to pay a just debt also is not consideration for a new promise. However, an agreement to pay a debt before it is due or after it was uncollectible or discharged in bankruptcy will be consideration for a new promise.

A contract does not need to cite the consideration. However, when a contract does recite a consideration, the consideration is presumed to have been given. This presumption can, however, be rebutted by evidence to the contrary.

■ VOID AND VOIDABLE CONTRACTS

A void contract is one that never had any legal existence or effect. A void contract cannot be enforced. It is treated as if it was never made. A contract that lacks one of the four required contractual elements is void.

A voidable contract is a valid contract unless or until voided. What this means is that a wronged party has the right or election to void the contract or let it stand as an enforceable agreement against the wrongdoer.

Fraud

Fraud is an intentional misrepresentation of fact by words, conduct, or concealment that is intended to deceive another to act to his or her detriment and that does in fact so deceive the other party. Making false statements without knowing whether they are true also could be considered fraud.

To make a contract voidable, the fraud must have been material; that is, it must induce a party to contract. When one party knows that the other party is lying, fraud does not exist, because the party lied to did not rely on the false statements in contracting.

A statement made in a contract that the parties are not relying on any oral statements or promises does not relieve the parties of responsibility for fraud.

Only the injured party can cancel the contract for fraud. Failure to void the contract within a reasonable period of time after learning of the fraud could be regarded as affirmation of the agreement.

A seller can be liable for failure to disclose the buyer's fraud to a third party.

Case Study

The case of *U.S. v. Cloud* (1989) 872 F.2d 846 involved the sale of the Cal-Neva Lodge by Cloud. The sales price was $17 million. At a preclosing conference, Cloud discovered that the escrow agreement indicated a $27.5 million price and showed $7.5 million had been paid outside of escrow. The figures had been inflated so that the buyer could obtain a $20 million loan.

Cloud did not tell the escrow officers of the fraud but did insist that the escrow instructions reflect he was netting only $17 million from the loan. The lender eventually lost more than $24.5 million because of this loan. Cloud appealed his conviction for bank fraud and conspiracy. The Court of Appeal upheld the conviction because Cloud knew that the sales price was inflated and that he had not received money outside of escrow. His amendment to the escrow instructions did not exonerate him. In fact it indicated that he fully understood and knowingly agreed to be part of a fraudulent scheme that was a conspiracy.

Misrepresentation

Misrepresentation is a civil wrong that differs from criminal fraud in that it is not intentional. While there are no criminal penalties for misrepresentation it, like criminal fraud, makes a contract voidable and may induce civil damages.

A person who honestly believed that his or her false assertions of fact were true but had no reasonable grounds for this belief will have committed the tort of negligent misrepresentation.

Duress and Menace

Duress generally is regarded as force. The wrongful confinement of a person or detention of property is duress. **Menace** is the threat of (1) confinement of a person, (2) detention of property, or (3) injury to the person, property, or character of another. A contract made under duress or menace makes the contract voidable at the election of the injured party.

Undue Influence

Undue influence is improper persuasion based on the relationship of the parties whereby a person really is not acting under his or her own free will. An example might be a nephew's persuading an elderly uncle to transfer property to him for a token consideration. Contracts entered into because of undue influence are voidable.

■ OPTIONS TO CONTRACT

An **option** is a contract to make a contract. The optionor (the owner) gives the optionee (potential purchaser or lessee) the right to buy or lease the property during a stated period of time for a specified price and terms.

An option is a contract and as such requires consideration be given to the optionor. The consideration must actually change hands. Reciting "in consideration of $1 and other good and valuable consideration" is not sufficient.

If the option to buy is part of a lease agreement, part of the rent would suffice as consideration for the option. Because consideration is present, the optionor cannot revoke the option after it has been given. However, if the purchase price were not adequate, a court would not grant the optionee the remedy of specific performance. (Further discussion of options is included in Chapter 6.)

Right of First Refusal

A **right of first refusal** differs from an option in that the prospective buyer is not given the absolute right to purchase but only the right to match an offer from a third party. A right generally is given to buy only if the owner decides to sell. Before the owner can sell, the owner must offer the property to the holder of the right of first refusal at the price and terms that the owner wishes to accept from a buyer. The holder of the right of first refusal loses that right if he or she does not meet the price and terms of the offer within a certain period of time.

A tenant with a right of first refusal might have difficulty exercising that right when consideration offered by another buyer is other than cash.

Case Study

In the case of *Ellis v. Chevron U.S.A., Inc.* (1988) 201 C.A.3d 132, Chevron's lease gave it the right of first refusal as to lease proposals

(continued on next page)

made by third parties when its own lease expired. Ellis, the owner, received a lease offer of $3,000 a month; the lessee was to construct a new building on the site, acquire the adjacent site and give Ellis the right to buy the adjacent site at the end of the lease.

Chevron offered to meet the rent but took the position that it had no need for a new building or the adjacent site and so these provisions should not be included. The Court of Appeal held that Chevron's right of first refusal was set forth in a lease it had prepared, and therefore any ambiguities should be resolved against Chevron. Chevron claimed that an implied covenant of good faith and fair dealings restricted the term of offers that Ellis could entertain. The court, however, held that as long as a landlord solicited reasonable offers the covenant was not breached.

■ INTERPRETATION OF CONTRACTS

Courts ordinarily will try to interpret contracts in accordance with the intent of the parties. Words will be given the general meaning they hold within the trade or profession involved.

In the event of an ambiguity the courts generally will resolve the ambiguity against the party drafting the instrument if it was not drafted as a mutual effort.

Case Study

The case of *Wilson v. Gentile* (1992) 8 C.A.4th 759 involved a lease option that provided for the exercise of the option "within thirty (30) days prior to the expiration of this option." Seven days prior to the expiration of the option, the optionee notified the optionor in writing of the exercise of the option. The optionor claimed the language required that the option be exercised at least 30 days prior to lease expiration. The court of appeal ruled that while the optionor may have had another intent, there was no ambiguity. The clause had to be interpreted in accordance with its plain meaning. The wording meant that there was a beginning date and an ending date to exercise the option.

Note: The optionor sued the real estate broker who drafted the clause. If the owner intended that the option be exercised only up to a specified date (30 days prior to the expiration of the lease), that should have been stated clearly. Precise drafting of legal instruments can be critical. This case points out the need for legal review.

If printed numerals differ from the words, the words generally will govern. So if a contract provided for monthly payments of "Four hundred dollars ($40.00)," the monthly payment will be $400.

In an ambiguity involving something added in typewriting to a printed form, the typewritten addition governs. If the ambiguity involves a hand-written portion, handwriting takes precedence over the printed or typed portions because it more clearly indicates intent.

Typographical errors ordinarily can be disregarded. See the case of *Gutzie Assocs. v. Switer* (1989) 215 C.A.3d 1636.

If conflicting agreements are present, the last one in time generally governs because it indicates the final intent of the parties. For example, if a purchase agreement and later signed escrow instructions differ, the escrow instructions generally will govern. Because they were signed later, they more clearly indicate the final intent of the parties.

■ DISCHARGE OF CONTRACTS

Impossibility of Performance

A party is excused from performance because of impossibility. For example, a property manager who has a long-term contract to manage a structure that is now being taken by the city under eminent domain will be excused from performing for the remainder of the term.

Commercial Frustration

Performance will be excused in cases where the court determines **commercial frustration** is present. That is, performance is not impossible but has become impractical because of an unforeseen occurrence. The nonoccurrence of the event or act actually was an implied condition of the contract. The doctrine of commercial frustration does not apply to situations in which the event reasonably could have been foreseen.

An example of commercial frustration would be a lease that allowed the premises to be used only for the sale of new automobiles. If a war resulted in new automobiles not being available, the courts probably would allow the lessee out of the lease because of commercial frustration.

Unconscionable Contracts

Courts will refuse to enforce contracts that are so grossly unfair that they offend public conscience. As an example, assume a property was in danger because of a flood, and the person owning the only available pump wanted $1,000 per hour for the use of the pump when $50 a day was the normal rental. Even though a property owner agreed to the charge, a court would likely refuse to enforce the agreement as written.

A contract that does not allow a person to modify the agreement (take it or leave it) is considered a contract of adhesion. An example of such a contract would be a standard loan agreement used by all banks. If such a contract takes unreasonable advantage of the party who did not prepare it, courts will refuse to enforce the provision against that party.

Case Study

In *Carboni v. Arrospide* (1992) 2 C.A.4th 76, the court refused to enforce a promissory note secured by a deed of trust at a 200 percent interest rate, which the court found to be unconscionable. However, the court did allow interest at 24 percent. The loan was exempt from California usury limits because Carboni was a real estate broker.

Breach of Contract

Most contracts end with performance according to their terms. However, some contracts are breached. A **breach of contract** is a failure to perform a contractual provision as agreed.

A party does not have to wait to start legal action until an actual breach has occurred if there has been an anticipatory breach. Examples of anticipatory breach are

- renunciation of the agreement by the other party;
- an act that would make performance impossible, such as the seller conveying title to another prior to a scheduled close of escrow.

Often parties will look for ways to get out of contracts that are disadvantageous. If they disavow the contract by treating an action of the other party as a contractual breach when it was not such a breach, they might be guilty of breaching the contract themselves.

Accord and Satisfaction

Accord and satisfaction is an agreement to accept something different from (usually less than) what a contract provides for in satisfaction of the obligation.

When a debt is in dispute, based on factors such as the condition of the property or the quality of repairs made, the parties can agree to accept a lesser sum. For example, if a debt is in dispute and a check is tendered with a statement that it is in full satisfaction of the debt, endorsing and cashing the check will be considered full satisfaction of the debt. However, Civil Code Section 1526 says the creditor may cross out the words "payment in full" on a check and cash it without agreeing to accord and satisfaction of a disputed amount or debt.

Novation

A **novation** is an agreement to substitute. Usually it is the substitution of one party for another party under the contract. The prior party, in that case, would be relieved of all obligations under the contract.

Tender

A **tender** is an offer to perform. A party might refuse a proper tender in the mistaken belief that the tender was improper. As an example, a party might refuse $4,000 to discharge a debt with the mistaken belief that $4,400 was due. The refusal of full payment under a contract does not excuse the debt, but it does prevent future interest from accumulating until the party agrees to accept the proper tender.

If a person's performance is a condition precedent or a concurrent condition for the performance of the other party, the first party must make a tender of his or her performance to hold the other party in default.

Tender is not required to hold another party in default if tender of performance would be an idle act. For example, if a seller under a purchase contract sells the property to another, the buyer does not have to tender the purchase price, because the seller is no longer capable of making a conveyance.

Doctrine of Substantial Performance

Substantial performance allows recovery when an unintentional breach has occurred and the noncompliance is not related to substantial matters. Normally the doctrine of substantial performance involves construction contracts, where a different or less expensive material than was specified was used but the different material did not endanger the structure. In such a case the court normally will say that the contract price should be reduced by the difference in value of the structure as built and the value the structure would have had if the contract had been strictly complied with.

■ CONTRACTUAL REMEDIES

The judicial remedies discussed in Chapter 1 apply to breach of contract.

Monetary Damages

Compensatory Damages. Compensatory damages are awarded to make the injured party whole. They are financial compensation for the loss suffered.

When a real estate purchase contract is breached, the measure of monetary damages would be the difference between the contract price and the property's fair market value at the time of the contract breach. [*Reese v. Wong* (2001), 93 C.A.4th 51.]

If a service or construction contract were breached, the measure of damages would be the additional reasonable costs incurred for the work in excess of the original contract price.

An injured party has a duty to keep damages at a minimum or to mitigate them. For example, if a lessee breaches a lease, the lessor has a duty to use reasonable efforts to rerent the premises.

Case Study

The case of *Erlich v. Menezes* (1999) 21 C.4th 543 involved a "dream home" built on an ocean view lot. Two months after occupancy, rain saturated the bedrooms and left three inches of water in the living room. Nearly every window leaked. The garage ceiling liquefied and fell in chunks. Structural engineers found serious construction errors. The Erlichs sued the builder Menezes. The San Luis Obispo County Superior Court awarded them $406,700 cost of repairs, $100,000 for emotional distress, and $50,000 for physical pain and suffering. The court of appeal affirmed the award.

The California Supreme Court affirmed as to the cost of repair but reversed the award for emotional distress. The court held that negligent breach of contract is not sufficient alone to support a tort action. To find the builder liable for emotional distress, the breach of contract must be accompanied by fraud or the party must realize the breach will cause serious harm in the form of anguish, etc.

Note: Damages for defective construction are limited to repair costs, lost use and/or relocation expenses, or the diminution in value.

Punitive or Exemplary Damages. These damages are awarded in addition to compensatory damages to punish the wrongdoer. They are awarded by courts for intentional and outrageous acts. Excessive punitive damages will not be upheld by the courts.

Case Study

In the case of *Storage Services v. C.R. Oosterbann et al.* (1989) 214 C.A.3d 498, the trial court had awarded $75,000 in punitive damages against an agent because of fraud. This was at least one-third of the agent's net worth and more than the agent's annual gross income. The court pointed out that generally punitive damage awards exceeding 10 percent of a defendant's net worth have been considered excessive. The court ordered a new trial on the damages unless the plaintiff agreed to a reduced award of $20,000.

Nominal Damages. Nominal damages are a token sum, such as $1 or $10, awarded for a breach where no real compensatory damages were warranted.

Liquidated Damages. Liquidated damages are agreed to at the time of contracting. Typically, purchase agreements call for the forfeiture of the down payment as liquidated damages in the event the buyer defaults. Construction contracts often have a per-day charge as liquidated damages in the event of a delay in completion.

Since July 1, 1978, liquidated damages on residential purchase agreements of one to four units where the buyer intends to occupy a unit have been limited by law. The liquidated damages to be forfeited if the buyer defaults cannot exceed 3 percent of the sales price or the actual deposit amount, whichever is less if both parties so agreed in the contract.

Liquidated damages for commercial property and for more than four residential units are not subject to these limitations. They are allowed so long as they are reasonable and reflect what possible damages could be anticipated if a breach of the contract were to occur. If, however, the damages are unreasonably high, the court will consider them a penalty and will not enforce the damages.

Waiver of Damages

In a contract a person cannot waive his or her rights to hold another personally liable for damages for fraud, willful acts, or violations of the law, either willful or negligent (Civil Code Section 1668). Nevertheless, some contracts still contain such waivers of this type, apparently based on the reasoning that if people do not think they have any rights they will not seek to enforce them.

Case Study

In the case of *Salton Bay Marina v. Imperial Irr. Dist.* (1985) 172 C.A.3d 914, the plaintiffs had a written agreement with the irrigation district that shielded the irrigation district from liability and gave the district the right to flood the plaintiffs' property. According to Civil Code Section 1668, contracts affecting public interest that purport to exempt a party from liability for negligence are against public policy and void. The court held that the flooding agreements were contracts affecting the public interest that attempted to exempt the district from its own negligence. The agreement was therefore against public policy and void.

Equitable Remedies

Specific Performance.   Specific performance forces a party to perform as agreed and is awarded only when compensating damages are inadequate.

Because land is a unique commodity, specific performance will be enforced for the sale or lease of land, agreements to convey easements, and lease assignments. Specific performance would be most likely to be granted to buyers or lessees when there is a compelling need for a particular property. Property sellers normally resell and sue for consequential damages from the defaulting first buyer rather than seek specific performance; however, sellers may be granted specific performance.

Case Study

The case of *B D Inns v. Pooley* (1990) 218 C.A.3d 289 involved an agreement by Pooley to buy an 840-unit motel built by B D Inns for $6,825,000. The court held that, while B D Inns could have sued for monetary damages, it still had a legal remedy of specific performance to which it was entitled.

Because specific performance is an equitable remedy, it will not be granted if

- there has not been adequate consideration;
- it is not just and reasonable;
- the agreement was obtained by unfair practices; or
- the agreement was entered into under a misapprehension (Civil Code Section 3391).

Case Study

In the case of *Gilbert v. Mercer* (1960) 179 C.A.2d 29, an owner agreed to sell 65 acres of land for $325. Before the title was transferred, the prospective purchaser gave a listing on the property for $3,750 and received an offer for $3,500. The court refused to grant the buyer specific performance. The court held that there was sufficient evidence that the consideration was not adequate and that in an action for specific performance the plaintiff must plead and prove adequacy of consideration.

Reformation.   In asking for the equitable remedy of reformation, a party is requesting that the contract be modified to reflect what was intended by the parties. Reformation will be granted only when there was a complete understanding between the parties that was not properly reflected because of fraud or a mutual mistake in drafting the contract, such as a typographical error in a legal description in a deed that provides a transfer of property other than what was intended to be conveyed.

Injunction. An injunction is a remedy in equity that orders a party to cease an activity such as trespass. Prohibiting an action prevents future harm. Courts may order a permanent injunction or simply a temporary restraining order. As an example, a court might order a person to cease an activity that is in violation of a deed restriction.

Declaratory Relief. The remedy of declaratory relief results in a court order determining the rights and duties of the parties. This remedy can be sought before actual damages occur.

Rescission. Rescission is a retroactive cancellation or annulment of a contract. Cancellation terminates future obligations, but rescission returns parties to their position prior to contracting. The basis for rescission can be fraud, mutual mistake of fact, impossibility of performance, undue influence, or lack of contractual capacity.

Statutes provide for rescission in a number of specific cases, including the following:

- Time-share purchasers in California have 72 hours after contracting to rescind their contracts.
- Purchasers in undivided interest subdivisions have a right of rescission within three days of executing the contract.
- Civil Code Section 1689.6, dealing with home solicitation sales, provides a three-business-day right of rescission.
- Civil Code Sections 1695.13–1695.14 provide for rescission within two years on home equity sales where a buyer of one to four residential units took unconscionable advantage of an owner in foreclosure.
- Section 66499.32 of the Government Code allows buyers to rescind within one year of discovery that a parcel was wrongfully divided according to the Subdivision Map Act.
- The Interstate Land Full Disclosure Sales Act, 15 U.S. Code Section 1703(b), gives purchasers the right to rescind within seven days after signing for purchase of undeveloped land covered by the act.
- According to the Truth-in-Lending Act, 15 U.S. Code Section 1635(a), buyers may rescind up until midnight on the third business day following a transaction that places a lien on the borrower's residence. The rescission rights do not apply to purchase money primary loans or to loans in which a state agency is the lender.

For a minor breach, courts ordinarily will allow only compensatory damages, not rescission.

Waiver. Waiver is the act of giving up a right. A party to a contract can waive a breach and accept the performance as received. A party also can waive any contractual condition that was for his or her sole benefit. For example, if a contract required a termite report prior to closing, the purchaser could waive the noncompliance because the report was for the purchaser's sole benefit.

■ ASSIGNMENT OF CONTRACT

In an **assignment of a contract** the assignor transfers his or her interest in the contract to a third-person assignee. In an assignment the assignee becomes primarily liable under the contract, while the assignor retains secondary liability should the assignee default on required performance (to avoid this contingent liability, see "Novation" earlier in the chapter). The assignee takes all of the rights and duties of the assignor.

In the absence of an agreement to the contrary, all or part of the performance under a contract can be assigned to another. The nature of some contracts, however, precludes their assignment. When a person contracts for another person's skill, such as an architect's services, the architect generally cannot assign the contract to another. If an agreement required taking an unsecured personal note, the person giving the note would not be able to assign that function to another. Because an agency agreement is considered personal in nature, agencies generally cannot be assigned.

Delegation of Duties

The obligations under a contract can be delegated to another when they are not personal services and are standardized in nature. Unlike an assignment, the person obligated under the contract retains full liability for the performance of the duties, although the person to whom the duties have been delegated can also be held liable.

■ STATUTE OF FRAUDS

The **statute of frauds** comes from English common law and was designed to prevent people from committing fraud by claiming to have orally agreed to purchase the land of another person. Because land was considered the basis of all wealth, it was determined that agreements concerning land were too important to be verbal. The California Statute of Frauds (Civil Code Section 1624) requires the following agreements to be in writing:

- Contracts for the transfer of real property or any interest therein
- Real property leases for more than one year (a verbal lease for six months therefore could be valid)
- Contracts that cannot be performed within one year (an agreement for a six-month lease starting in seven months would have to be in writing because it could not be performed within one year of the agreement)
- Sales of personal property for more than $500
- Contracts by executors or administrators of estates
- Agreements to answer to the debt or default of another
- Listing agreements for the sale or lease of real property for more than one year [Civil Code Section 1624(5)]

The statute of frauds applies significantly to executory contracts because contracts that fail to comply are unenforceable. After a contract has been fully performed (executed contract), however, the statute of frauds cannot be raised.

The statute of frauds does not require a formal contract, but a note or letter memorandum or a series of notes and memorandums must show a complete agreement. A telegram, for example, can satisfy the statute of frauds.

The agreement need not be signed by all the parties. It need be signed only by the party who is sought to be bound to the agreement or by that person's agent. The signature on the document need not be handwritten as long as it was intended as a signature. For example, if it could be shown that a person used a rubber stamp to sign an agreement, the rubber stamp signature would satisfy the statute of frauds.

Case Study

In *Seck v. Foulkes* (1972) 25 C.A.3d 556, the memorandum in Figure 5.1 was written on the back of the broker's business card and was initialed by the owner.

The court held that the memorandum need not be a complete contract, provided it showed authority to act. The other terms may be shown by parol (verbal) evidence. In this case parol evidence indicated that "Sitten" referred to the seller's attorney, to whom the offer was to be presented. '310 M/L' referred to the parcel size, 310 acres, more or less. The agreement was entered into on 3/24/65 and was to terminate on 10/1/65. The court determined in this case that the writing was sufficient to satisfy the statute of frauds.

FIGURE 5.1

The "Sitten" Memorandum

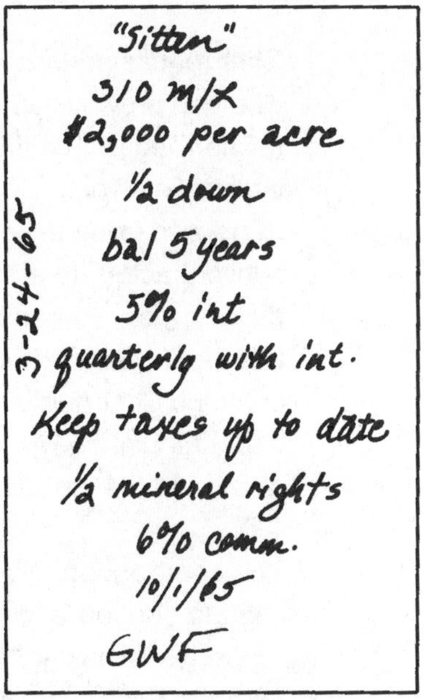

"Sitten"

310 m/x

$2,000 per acre

½ down

bal 5 years

5% int

quarterly with int.

Keep taxes up to date

½ mineral rights

6% comm.

10/1/65

GWF

3-24-65

Case Study

The case of *Phillippe v. Shapell Indus. Inc.* (1987) 43 C.3d 1247 involved an oral promise to pay a commission. Prince, the director of land acquisitions for Shapell, orally agreed to pay Phillippe, a licensed real estate broker, a commission for land found by Phillippe that was acquired by Shapell. Phillippe showed a parcel of land to Shapell that was rejected because of zoning. When the zoning was amended a year later, Shapell purchased the parcel for $2.7 million.

While the trial court awarded Phillippe $125,000 in commission, the California Supreme Court reversed the judgment. Civil Code Section 1624(d) requires that a broker employment agreement be in writing. The fact that Shapell was itself a broker does not alter the statute (this was not an agreement between brokers to split a commission). The court stated that, except for a few narrow exceptions, a broker may not assert estoppel as a defense against the statute of frauds. While the broker had been promised a commission, Phillippe knew the rules and was not entitled to any commission due to a lack of a written sales commission agreement.

Case Study

The case of *ARYA Group, Inc. v. Cher* (2000), 77 C.A.4th 610 involved a partially completed verbal construction contract. The entertainer, Cher, negotiated with the ARYA Group, Inc., to design and build a house on her Malibu property for $4,217,529 with progress payments. The contract was delivered to Cher and, despite her promise to do so, the contract was never signed by Cher and delivered to the contractor. The contractor was induced to begin work and did receive some progress payments.

(continued on next page)

Cher requested that ARYA meet with Janet Bussell of Tuft Design Group, who had previously worked with Cher on a speculative residential project. It was alleged that the purpose of the meetings was to obtain proprietary information from ARYA. Cher then terminated the "verbal" contract with ARYA and failed to pay $415,169.41 due to ARYA. Cher contacted ARYA's subcontractors to induce them to work directly with her and had ARYA's building permits transferred to her name. It was alleged that Cher never intended to sign the contract with ARYA. ARYA sued Cher for breach of contract. Cher demurred on the grounds that the Statute of Frauds (B&PC 7164) required a written contract. The Los Angeles County Superior Court dismissed the lawsuit because ARYA did not have a signed contract.

The court of appeals reversed, ruling that ARYA's allegations were sufficient to support a claim of unjust enrichment. While the court noted that "generally speaking" a contract made in violation of a regulatory statute is void, the rule is not inflexible. The court noted that Cher is a highly sophisticated homeowner with previous involvement in residential construction projects and that legal representatives assisted Cher in negotiating the construction agreement. The court pointed out substantial work had been completed and Cher would be unjustly enriched if she were not required to compensate ARYA. The court distinguished this case from *Phillipe v. Shapell Indus. Inc.* because construction is tangible and the benefit is apparent, while a broker's services are intangible. The court noted that if failure to pay the contractor would not have resulted in unjust enrichment, then the contractor would not have been entitled to collect.

Parol Evidence Rule

The **parol evidence rule** provides that verbal extrinsic evidence may not be introduced to modify a written document that is complete on its face. While parol evidence cannot be used to modify a clearly written contract, it is admissible to show a later verbal modification of the written contract.

Parol evidence also can be used to clarify an ambiguity; to show fraud, undue influence, or a mutual mistake of fact; or to show that the instrument was represented to be other than a contract.

Estoppel

The **doctrine of estoppel** or promissory estoppel means that a person may not assert a right when that person's previous statements, actions, or silence caused another party to act to his or her detriment. For example, assume that a verbal agreement had been made for the sale of a lot and the purchaser, with the knowledge of the seller, made extensive improvements to the lot. The seller would be estopped (prevented) from raising the defense of the statute of frauds, because the seller's statement caused the purchaser to act to his detriment.

■ STATUTE OF LIMITATIONS

If an action is not brought within a prescribed period of time, it becomes barred by the **statute of limitations.** Thus a contract may be valid but unenforceable. A person who ignores his or her rights can lose them through the passage of time.

In California, the statute of limitations provides the following time periods:

- 90 days–actions by former tenants to recover belongings left in furnished quarters
- Two years–personal injury
- Two years–actions based on verbal contracts
- Three years–actions for damages due to trespass
- Three years–attachment lien
- Three years from date of discovery–actions for relief under a contract based on fraud or mistake
- Three years–replevin actions (to recover goods wrongfully held by another)
- Three years–disciplinary actions against a real estate licensee (if the action is based on fraud, the time period is three years or one year after discovery of fraud, whichever is later)
- Four years–most actions based on written contracts (the statute of limitations for contracts runs from the time the agreement was breached, not from the date of the agreement)
- Five years–actions for recovery of real property and the profits from the property
- Five years–to challenge a void or voidable deed or other document (20 years if the claimant is a minor or insane)
- Ten years–actions based on judgments and latent defects in real property
- Code of Civil Procedure §323–unless otherwise stated the statute of limitations is four years

If a partial payment is made and accepted on a debt, the statute of limitations period on the debt would start again from the date of the partial payment.

■ LACHES

Laches is preventing a person from asserting a right or claim when his or her delay in asserting that right causes or results in disadvantage, injury, injustice, detriment, or prejudice to the defendant in a lawsuit. For example, a person could be estopped by laches from having an encroachment removed if he or she were aware of the construction and waited until it was completed to demand its removal. To grant the landowner his or her rights would not be equitable, based on the delay in bringing action. (Unlike the statute of limitations, laches is considered an equitable defense.)

■ SEALS

Seals–marks or impressions–were required on certain contracts in England to authenticate the execution of a document. Their use grew out of a period when most individuals were illiterate and had to make their "mark."

States that require seals accept a simple "(Seal)" or "L.S.," which stands for "Locus Sigilli" (the place of the seal).

California does not require seals on any documents, but if a corporation that has a seal uses it on a document, it is presumed that the person(s) signing did so with corporate authority.

■ JUDGMENTS

When a court adjudicates a dispute, the final order of the court is a judgment. Unless the order is appealed to a higher court, the judgment is enforceable. Most judgments are for a monetary payment.

Recording an abstract of a monetary judgment creates a lien on all of the debtor's property in the county where it is recorded. A judgment lien is good for ten years and may be renewed. Judgment liens for child or spousal support remain enforceable until paid in full without the necessity of renewal.

If the debtor fails to pay after a judgment has been entered, the creditor can get a writ of execution whereby the sheriff seizes and sells assets of the debtor to satisfy the debt. (Judgments will be covered in greater detail in Chapter 11.)

Attorneys often tell clients that there are three necessities for a successful lawsuit. There must be (1) a wrongful act or omission that (2) has resulted in a loss or injury to the plaintiff and (3) the defendant must have assets or insurance coverage. Without number 1, the defendant has no liability. Without number 2, there are no damages to be compensated. Without number 3, time and money would be expended to gain an uncollectible judgment.

■ SUMMARY

Contracts are either express (stated) or implied, bilateral (promise for a promise) or unilateral (promise for an act), executory (not yet fully performed) or executed (fully performed).

Contracts that meet all contractual requirements are valid contracts; contracts that do not are void. Voidable contracts are valid unless voided by the injured party.

A contract can be disaffirmed by minors within a reasonable period after reaching the age of 18 or by persons lacking mental capacities to contract but not declared incompetent.

Other reasons for voiding a contract include

- fraud,
- misrepresentation,
- duress and menace, and
- undue influence.

Options to contract are agreements whereby one party has the right to contract. A right of first refusal is a first right to purchase should a seller decide to sell to another.

Courts ordinarily will try to interpret contracts in accordance with the intent of the parties.

Excuses for nonperformance include impossibility of performance and commercial frustration.

A breach of a contract is a failure to perform a contractual provision as agreed.

A party can waive a breach by the other party or waive any contractual condition that is for his or her sole benefit.

Parties can agree to accept something other than what was agreed to. This is known as *accord and satisfaction*. A novation is an agreement to substitute one party for another under the contract and relieves the original party of all obligations under the contract.

A tender is an offer to perform a contract.

The doctrine of substantial performance excuses a minor unintentional breach of a contract. While the breach would not be a basis for terminating the agreement, the contract price would be reduced to reflect the difference in performance.

Contractual remedies for a breach of contract are monetary or equitable.

Monetary remedies include compensatory damages, punitive or exemplary damages, and nominal damages, as well as liquidated damages.

Equitable remedies include specific performance, reformation, injunction, declaratory relief, and rescission.

Contracts that do not by their terms prohibit assignment and are not personal in nature can be assigned. Under an assignment, the assignee becomes primarily liable under the contract. Obligations under a contract can be delegated to another. Unlike an assignment, the person obligated retains full liability for the contractual performance.

The statute of frauds requires certain contracts, including contracts for the transfer of real property and leases for more than one year, to be in writing.

Parol or verbal evidence cannot be used to show that a contract that appears complete upon its face means other than what it says. Parol evidence can be used to show fraud or to clarify an ambiguity.

Persons can be estopped from raising the defense of the statute of frauds if, by their words or actions, they caused another to act to his or her detriment.

The statute of limitations deals with statutory limitations on bringing legal action.

Laches is an equitable defense that prevents a party from asserting a claim if his or her unreasonable delay in bringing action worked to the prejudice of the other party.

A judgment is the final order of a court. When recorded, an abstract of judgment becomes a judgment lien on all of the debtor's property in the county where the judgment is recorded.

■ DISCUSSION CASES

1. A notation on a check stated, "Down payment on Lot 16 of Berwyn Heights. Full Price to be $4,000." The check was endorsed by the payee. **In the absence of any other written document, has the statute of frauds been complied with?**

2. In the sale of four lots the escrow inadvertently left out the necessary reservation of a right-of-way from one of the lots. A subsequent holder requests reformation. **Will it be granted?**

    Shupe v. Nelson (1967) 254 C.A.2d 693

3. The plaintiff acted as a rental agent and informed the owner that he would like to represent him in selling the property. No written agreement was drawn up, although several offers were submitted. The plaintiff received an offer for $100,000 and requested authorization to sell. The owner sent a telegram to the plaintiff stating, "This will confirm that I will sell 608 South Bay Front Balboa Island for $100,000 cash. This offer good until noon 1-19-60. Chas. P. Hansen." The owner subsequently refused to sign a standard form deposit receipt providing for a 5 percent commission. **Is the plaintiff broker entitled to a commission?**

    Franklin v. Hansen (1963) 59 C.2d 570

4. A purchase agreement provided for $20,000 in liquidated damages should the buyer resell the property to an uncle of the seller. After purchase the buyer resold to the seller's uncle. The purchaser claimed that the prohibition against resale to the uncle was an unreasonable restraint on alienation (conveyance). **Do you agree?**

    Zlotoff v. Tucker (1984) 154 C.A.3d 988

5. A purchaser of a property was given the preemptive right to purchase an adjoining parcel for $10,000. The owner subsequently sold the lot for $22,000 without offering it to the holder of the preemptive right to purchase. Was there a valid right to purchase? **If so, what would the damages be?**

    Mercer v. Lemmens (1964) 230 C.A.2d 167

6. The lessee leased premises for a restaurant. The greater portion of the premises (on the second floor) had not been used for 14 years. The lease specified that the premises were taken "as is." After

entering into the lease, the lessee discovered that extensive and expensive work had to be done inside and outside the premises to meet the building codes. Because of basic structural weaknesses in the building, the second floor could not support a restaurant operation. **Is the lessee liable under the lease?**

William v. Puccinelli (1965) 236 C.A.2d 512

7. The lessor's real estate agent notified the lessee that the lessor was willing to terminate the written lease four months prior to its expiration if the lessee would agree to vacate at that time. The real estate agent had been the lessor's agent in negotiating the original lease and in all dealings with the lessee. The tenant vacated as agreed. The landlord then sought to hold the lessee liable under the written lease. **What are the lessee's rights?**

Kelley v. R. F. Jones Co. (1969) 272 C.A.2d 113

8. The defendants gave the broker an unsigned typewritten document entitled "Re Beverly Wilshire Hotel." It included a description of the hotel, the price of $2,000,000, and the commission that the hotel would pay. After extensive work by the plaintiff the defendants gave the plaintiff a carbon copy on a hotel letterhead that included a description of the property and the sale terms. This copy indicated a price of $2,250,000 and provided for a broker's commission of 5 percent on $50,000 and 2½ percent on the balance. This memo also was unsigned. Testimony was given that the broker protested that the price was being raised, which would make the sale more difficult, and that the commission was being lowered. A verbal agreement was made to a $57,500 commission, and an unsigned note later was given indicating a $57,500 commission. The plaintiff was the procuring cause of the sale, and the defendants refused to pay a commission. **What are the rights of the broker?**

Marks v. Walter G. McCarty Corp. (1949) 33 C.2d 814

9. A lessee of a property authorized repairs, and the owner of the property failed to post a notice of nonresponsibility, which would have protected him against mechanics' liens. In an action to foreclose on a mechanic's lien the owner raised the fact that he was under the age of 18. **Is this a good defense?**

Burnand v. Irigoyen (1947) 30 C.2d 861

10. A deposit receipt provided that the payment terms were to be arranged after new financing was obtained. **Was there an enforceable contract?**

Burgess v. Rodom (1953) 121 C.A.2d 71

11. The vice president of a bank told both buyers and sellers that the bank would make a $40 million loan to the purchasers of 11 acres on Wilshire Boulevard in Los Angeles. Based on the oral promise, the buyer and seller agreed to a sales contract of $1 million down, $2 million in 30 days, and $7 million in 50 days. While the bank covered the first two payments, it rejected the loan application five days prior to the $7 million becoming due, which caused the purchasers to default. **Is the bank liable for breach of its oral agreement to make the loan?**

Landes Constr. Co. v. Royal Bank (1987) 833 F.2d 1365

12. A lender agreed to provide financing if the borrower's parents would provide security. The parents agreed to execute a trust deed on property in Sebastopol that they owned with their son. The lender's cover letter referred to the Sebastopol property, but the trust deed prepared by the lender described the parents' residence in Petaluma. **After the son defaulted, what are the rights of the parties?**

Balistreri v. Nevada Livestock Prod. Credit Ass'n (1989) 214 C.A.3d 635

13. An arbitration clause in a purchase contract was initialed by the buyer but not the seller. The clause stated "buyer, seller and agent agree that such controversy shall be settled by final binding arbitration . . ." **Is arbitration mandatory?**

Marcus Millichap Real Estate Investment Brokerage Co. v. Hock Investment Co. (1998) 68 C.A.4th 83

14. A husband, who had a stroke, made an oral promise to his wife that if she would care for him at home, so he didn't end up in a nursing home, he would leave her specified property. The wife performed her part of the agreement but discovered, upon his death, that the property was willed to his daughter. **Does the wife have rights as to the property?**

Borelli v. Brusseau (1993) 12 C.A.4th 647

The court decisions for the above cases can be found on our Web site at **www.dearbornRE.com.** Click on the **"Instructor Resources"** link, then scroll down the page until you find the link titled "California Real Estate Law 5th Edition."

■ CHAPTER QUIZ

1. A written contract whereby the seller agrees to convey at an agreed price at a definite time in the future and the buyer agrees to buy at said time and price would be a(n)

   a. executory, express, bilateral contract.
   b. executed, implied, unilateral contract.
   c. valid, express, unilateral contract.
   d. enforceable, bilateral, executed contract.

2. When a person, while not of sound mind but not declared insane or wholly without understanding, contracts to buy real property, the contract likely is

   a. void.   c. illegal.
   b. voidable.   d. valid.

3. Mutuality in a contract would ordinarily be indicated by

   a. consideration.   c. execution.
   b. offer and acceptance.   d. waiver.

4. An offer would *not* be terminated by

   a. revocation by the offeror.
   b. a counteroffer.
   c. request for an extension for acceptance by the offeree.
   d. the death of the offeror.

5. In which of the following situations can an offer *not* be withdrawn?

   a. When the seller has not yet had an opportunity to accept it
   b. When the stated period for which it would remain open has not expired
   c. When notification of acceptance has been made
   d. When the deposit has not been forfeited

6. Which of the following is true regarding acceptance and/or revocation of an offer?

    a. Revocation takes place upon receipt.
    b. Acceptance takes place upon mailing.
    c. Both a and b
    d. Neither a nor b

7. Albert gave his friend Baker a deed to a property, which Baker recorded. A year later Albert and Baker had a dispute. Albert demanded the return of the property because Baker had not given any consideration for the property transfer. Assuming there was no consideration, which of the following is correct?

    a. Albert can obtain revocation because of lack of consideration.
    b. The agreement is void because of lack of consideration.
    c. Albert is entitled to the fair market value of the property conveyed.
    d. Baker can keep the property, which was a completed gift.

8. Which of the following is(are) an example(s) of fraud?

    a. A promise made by one who did not intend to keep it
    b. A false statement of fact by one who does not know if it is fact or not
    c. The act of hiding a defect so another party will not know of it
    d. All of the above

9. Albert knew that Keith was lying about the property's income, but Albert nevertheless completed the purchase. When Albert changed his mind, Albert could

    a. void the contract.
    b. collect damages for the fraud.
    c. Either a or b
    d. Neither a nor b

10. Which of the following is a false statement regarding options?

    a. Consideration is necessary for a valid option.
    b. The optionee has the option to exercise or refrain from exercising the option.
    c. The optionor can revoke the option by returning the consideration.
    d. Options can be assigned unless personal in nature or prohibited by the option terms.

11. Which of the following describes how a court will interpret an ambiguous contract?

    a. Words take precedence over numerals.
    b. Parol evidence can be admitted to show intent.
    c. Handwritten takes precedence over typed.
    d. All of the above

12. An agreement whereby one party to a contract is discharged and another party becomes obligated is a(n)

    a. accord and satisfaction.
    b. reformation.
    c. novation.
    d. rescission.

13. Which of the following is *not* an equitable remedy?

    a. Reformation
    b. Compensatory damages
    c. Rescission
    d. Specific performance

14. Forfeiture of agreed damages in a contract is known as

    a. mitigated damages.
    b. liquidated damages.
    c. subordination.
    d. punitive damages.

15. Liquidated damages on a duplex that the buyer intended to occupy called for the forfeiture of a $10,000 deposit on a $100,000 purchase price. After the buyer's default, the seller must return

    a. the entire deposit.
    b. $7,000.
    c. $23,000.
    d. nothing.

16. The fact that every parcel of real estate is unique is the reason for the remedy of

    a. specific performance.   c. reformation.
    b. injunction.   d. punitive damages.

17. When, after close of escrow, the purchaser discovered that the seller's broker had materially misrepresented the income, the purchaser could

    a. sue for rescission.
    b. accept the property as is.
    c. sue the seller and the broker for damages.
    d. Any of the above

18. Which of the following is true regarding the difference between waiver and rescission?

    a. Waiver leaves the parties as they are.
    b. Rescission puts the parties back the way they were.
    c. Both a and b
    d. Neither a nor b

19. Which of the following is *not* a requirement of every valid contract?

    a. Consideration   c. Writing
    b. Meeting of the minds   d. Legal purpose

20. A verbal real estate lease for six months starting in six months is

    a. valid.   c. voidable.
    b. void.   d. illegal.

21. After Albert agreed verbally to sell to Smith, Smith made extensive improvements to the property with the knowledge of Albert. Albert now refuses to sell because the sales agreement was verbal. What will be the result?

    a. Albert does not have to sell, based on the statute of frauds.
    b. Albert must sell, because of the doctrine of estoppel.
    c. Albert must sell, because of laches.
    d. Albert's only remedy is compensatory damages.

22. The passage of time can make a valid contract

    a. invalid.   c. unenforceable.
    b. illegal.   d. voidable.

23. In California the statute of limitations for verbal contracts is

    a. two years.   c. four years.
    b. three years.   d. ten years.

24. Losing a right because of failure to assert it in a timely manner is known as

    a. rescission.   c. estoppel.
    b. laches.   d. specific performance.

25. Which of the following is (are) true about judgments?

    a. They are good for ten years.
    b. They can be renewed.
    c. When recorded, they create a general lien in the county of recordation.
    d. All of the above

CHAPTER SIX

REAL ESTATE CONTRACTS

■ KEY TERMS

advance fee addendum
burden of proof
buyer listing
cooperating broker fee
  agreement
exclusive-agency listing

exclusive authorization
  and right-to-sell
  listing
hold harmless clause
interim occupancy
  agreement

loan broker listing
no deal–no commission
open listing
privity of contract
procuring cause
safety clause

■ LISTINGS

A listing is an agency contract whereby a principal (usually the property owner) appoints an agent (a real estate broker) to perform some task. Customarily the principal gives the agent a listing to procure a buyer or lessee for specified property, but listings also can be created for the purpose of locating property for a buyer or obtaining financing.

An agent who is to procure a buyer generally is not given the power to obligate the principal contractually. The agent solicits offers; the principal accepts or rejects them.

To be enforceable, listing agreements for real estate must be in writing [Civil Code Section 1624(5)].

The case of *Franklin v. Hansen* (1963) 59 C.2d 570 makes it clear that a broker cannot enforce a verbal commission agreement.

Because listings are contracts, they require all the elements of a valid contract to be enforceable: mutual consent (for an exclusive listing, discussed later in this chapter), consideration, legal purpose, and competent parties.

Listings must be specific about the subject matter of the agency. They also should be specific about price and terms, if any. If no price is specified, the principal will not be obligated to the agent if the principal refuses an offer at a fair price. If no terms are specified, the principal can refuse a full-price offer if not for cash, and the principal will not be obligated to any commission.

Listings usually authorize an agent to place a For Sale sign on the property. Without such authorization the agent does not have the right to place a sign.

An agent is not entitled to compensation if not provided for in the listing agreement. Authorizing an agent to procure a buyer does not imply that the owner will pay a fee if the agent is successful.

Unless the listing authorizes the agent to accept a deposit, the agent will have to take deposits as the agent of the buyer.

Hold harmless clauses customarily are included in listings. The owner agrees to hold the agent harmless and indemnify the agent for losses in the event the owner fails to provide a disclosure or fails to provide correct information. Such a clause probably would not entitle the broker to recover a loss if he or she knew or should have known an owner was mistaken.

Like most contracts, listings usually provide that in the event of legal action the prevailing party will be entitled to legal fees.

Unless a listing authorizes an agent to employ subagents, the agent has no authority to do so. An agency is a personal relationship that requires consent, and the principal is responsible for the acts of the agent within the scope of the agency. The agent therefore has no authority to expand the liability of the principal to acts of subagents without the express authority of the principal. The listing form in Figure 6.1 provides that the agent can employ subagents.

The listing agreement is between the principal and the agent and cannot be enforced by third parties. For example, a prospective buyer could not force an owner to accept an offer at a property's listed price because no **privity of contract** (contractual relationship) exists between the owner and the prospective buyer. The agent, however, might be entitled to a commission. An exception would be refusal of the owner to accept an offer on the terms of the listing because of unlawful discrimination (see the discussion of fair housing in Chapter 4).

If the consummation of a sale is prevented by the default of the agent's principal or by the principal's inability to convey marketable title, the sales agent will be entitled to a commission because the agent fully performed as required by the agency.

The **burden of proof** of performance is on the agent. To collect a commission, the agent must show full compliance with the agent's obligations according to the contract or the principal's wrongful breach of obligations.

The rate or amount of commission may not be preprinted in a listing contract for the sale of a building with one to four residential units. This includes mobile homes. The agreement also must contain the following statement in ten-point **boldface type:** "Notice: The amount or rate of real estate commissions is not fixed by law. They are set by each Broker individually and may be negotiable between Seller and Broker." You will find this notice on the sample listing agreement (Figure 6.1).

A commission customarily is earned under a valid listing upon the execution of a valid purchase agreement unless conditions remain to be fulfilled. The commission normally is paid upon close of escrow, which could be some time after it is earned.

If a listing requires consummation of the sale, the sale must be consummated for the broker to earn a commission (**no deal-no commission**). If in such a case the buyer breaches the contract and the owner does not pursue legal remedies for the breach, the broker gets nothing.

If the owner breaches the agreement, the broker is entitled to a commission because the principal's action violated the implied condition of good-faith dealings. Similarly, if the buyer's obligation was conditional and the seller prevented the satisfaction of the conditions, the broker would be entitled to his or her commission.

FIGURE 6.1

**Exclusive Authorization and
Right to Sell**

CALIFORNIA ASSOCIATION OF REALTORS®

RESIDENTIAL LISTING AGREEMENT
(Exclusive Authorization and Right to Sell)
(C.A.R. Form LA, Revised 10/01)

1. **EXCLUSIVE RIGHT TO SELL:** _____ ("Seller")
hereby employs and grants _____ ("Broker")
beginning (date) _____ and ending at 11:59 P.M. on (date) _____ ("Listing Period")
the exclusive and irrevocable right to sell or exchange the real property in the City of _____,
County of _____, California, described as: _____
_____ ("Property").

2. **ITEMS EXCLUDED AND INCLUDED:** Unless otherwise specified in a real estate purchase agreement, all fixtures and fittings that
are attached to the Property are included, and personal property items are excluded, from the purchase price.
ADDITIONAL ITEMS EXCLUDED: _____.
ADDITIONAL ITEMS INCLUDED: _____
Seller intends that the above items be excluded or included in offering the Property for sale, but understands that: **(i)** the purchase
agreement supersedes any intention expressed above and will ultimately determine which items are excluded and included in the
sale; and **(ii)** Broker is not responsible for and does not guarantee that the above exclusions and/or inclusions will be in the purchase
agreement.

3. **LISTING PRICE AND TERMS:**
   A. The listing price shall be: _____
   _____ Dollars ($ _____).
   B. Additional Terms: _____
   _____

4. **COMPENSATION TO BROKER:**
   **Notice: The amount or rate of real estate commissions is not fixed by law. They are set by each Broker
   individually and may be negotiable between Seller and Broker (real estate commissions include all
   compensation and fees to Broker).**
   A. Seller agrees to pay to Broker as compensation for services irrespective of agency relationship(s), either ☐ _____ percent
   of the listing price (or if a purchase agreement is entered into, of the purchase price), or ☐ $ _____,
   AND (if checked) ☐ an administrative/transaction fee of $ _____, as follows:
      (1) If Broker, Seller, cooperating broker, or any other person procures a buyer(s) who offers to purchase the Property on the
      above price and terms, or on any price and terms acceptable to Seller during the Listing Period, or any extension.
      (2) If Seller, within _____ calendar days after the end of the Listing Period or any extension, enters into a contract to sell,
      convey, lease or otherwise transfer the Property to anyone ("Prospective Buyer") or that person's related entity: **(i)** who
      physically entered and was shown the Property during the Listing Period or any extension by Broker or a cooperating broker,
      or **(ii)** for whom Broker or any cooperating broker submitted to Seller a signed, written offer to acquire, lease, exchange or
      obtain an option on the Property. Seller, however, shall have no obligation to Broker under paragraph 4A(2) unless, not later
      than **3 calendar days** after the end of the Listing Period or any extension, Broker has given Seller a written notice of the
      names of such Prospective Buyers.
      (3) If, without Broker's prior written consent, the Property is withdrawn from sale, conveyed, leased, rented, otherwise
      transferred, or made unmarketable by a voluntary act of Seller during the Listing Period, or any extension.
   B. If completion of the sale is prevented by a party to the transaction other than Seller, then compensation due under paragraph
   4A shall be payable only if and when Seller collects damages by suit, arbitration, settlement, or otherwise, and then in an
   amount equal to the lesser of one-half of the damages recovered or the above compensation, after first deducting title and
   escrow expenses and the expenses of collection, if any.
   C. In addition, Seller agrees to pay Broker: _____.
   D. **(1)** Broker is authorized to cooperate and compensate brokers participating through the multiple listing service(s) ("MLS"):
   (i) in any manner, **OR (ii)** (if checked) Broker shall offer MLS brokers: either ☐ _____ percent of the purchase price, or
   ☐ $ _____.
      (2) Broker is authorized to cooperate and compensate brokers operating outside the MLS in any manner.
   E. Seller hereby irrevocably assigns to Broker the above compensation from Seller's funds and proceeds in escrow. Broker may
   submit this listing agreement, as instructions to compensate Broker pursuant to paragraph 4A, to any escrow regarding the
   Property involving Seller and a buyer, Prospective Buyer or other transferee.
   F. **(1)** Seller represents that Seller has not previously entered into a listing agreement with another broker regarding the Property,
   unless specified as follows: _____
      (2) Seller warrants that Seller has no obligation to pay compensation to any other broker regarding the Property unless the
      Property is transferred to any of the following individuals or entities: _____
      _____
      (3) If the Property is sold to anyone listed above during the time Seller is obligated to compensate another broker: **(i)** Broker is
      not entitled to compensation under this agreement; and **(ii)** Broker is not obligated to represent Seller in such transaction.

Seller acknowledges receipt of a copy of this page.

Seller's Initials (_____)(_____)

EQUAL HOUSING OPPORTUNITY

LA-11 REVISED 10/01 (PAGE 1 OF 3) Print Date

Reviewed by _____
Broker or Designee _____ Date _____

RESIDENTIAL LISTING AGREEMENT-EXCLUSIVE (LA-11 PAGE 1 OF 3)

Reprinted with permission, California Association of REALTORS®. Endorsement not implied.

FIGURE 6.1 (continued)

**Exclusive Authorization and
Right to Sell**

Property Address: _____   Date: _____

5. **OWNERSHIP, TITLE AND AUTHORITY:** Seller warrants that: **(i)** Seller is the owner of the Property; **(ii)** no other persons or entities have title to the Property; and **(iii)** Seller has the authority to both execute this agreement and sell the Property. Exceptions to ownership, title and authority are as follows: _____.

6. **MULTIPLE LISTING SERVICE:** Information about this listing will (or ☐ will not) be provided to the MLS of Broker's selection. All terms of the transaction, including financing, if applicable, will be provided to the selected MLS for publication, dissemination and use by persons and entities on terms approved by the MLS. Seller authorizes Broker to comply with all applicable MLS rules. MLS rules allow MLS data to be made available by the MLS to additional Internet sites unless Broker gives the MLS instructions to the contrary.

7. **SELLER REPRESENTATIONS:** Seller represents that, unless otherwise specified in writing, Seller is unaware of: **(i)** any Notice of Default recorded against the Property; **(ii)** any delinquent amounts due under any loan secured by, or other obligation affecting, the Property; **(iii)** any bankruptcy, insolvency or similar proceeding affecting the Property; **(iv)** any litigation, arbitration, administrative action, government investigation, or other pending or threatened action that affects or may affect the Property or Seller's ability to transfer it; and **(v)** any current, pending or proposed special assessments affecting the Property. Seller shall promptly notify Broker in writing if Seller becomes aware of any of these items during the Listing Period or any extension thereof.

8. **BROKER'S AND SELLER'S DUTIES:** Broker agrees to exercise reasonable effort and due diligence to achieve the purposes of this agreement. Unless Seller gives Broker written instructions to the contrary, Broker is authorized to order reports and disclosures, as appropriate or necessary, and advertise and market the Property in any method and any medium, including the Internet, selected by Broker, and, to the extent permitted by these media, including MLS, control the dissemination of the information submitted to any medium. Seller agrees to consider offers presented by Broker, and to act in good faith to accomplish the sale of the Property by, among others things, making the Property available for showing at reasonable times and referring to Broker all inquiries of any party interested in the Property. Seller is responsible for determining at what price to list and sell the Property. **Seller further agrees to indemnify, defend and hold Broker harmless from all claims, disputes, litigation, judgments and attorney fees arising from any incorrect information supplied by Seller, or from any material facts that Seller knows but fails to disclose.**

9. **DEPOSIT:** Broker is authorized to accept and hold on Seller's behalf any deposits to be applied toward the purchase price.

10. **AGENCY RELATIONSHIPS:**
    A. **Disclosure:** If the Property includes residential property with one-to-four dwelling units, Seller shall receive a "Disclosure Regarding Agency Relationships" form prior to entering into this agreement.
    B. **Seller Representation:** Broker shall represent Seller in any resulting transaction, except as specified in paragraph 4F.
    C. **Possible Dual Agency With Buyer:** Depending upon the circumstances, it may be necessary or appropriate for Broker to act as an agent for both Seller and buyer, exchange party, or one or more additional parties ("Buyer"). Broker shall, as soon as practicable, disclose to Seller any election to act as a dual agent representing both Seller and Buyer. If a Buyer is procured directly by Broker or an associate licensee in Broker's firm, Seller hereby consents to Broker acting as a dual agent for Seller and such Buyer. In the event of an exchange, Seller hereby consents to Broker collecting compensation from additional parties for services rendered, provided there is disclosure to all parties of such agency and compensation. Seller understands and agrees that: **(i)** Broker, without the prior written consent of Seller, will not disclose to Buyer that Seller is willing to sell the Property at a price less than the listing price; **(ii)** Broker, without the prior written consent of Buyer, will not disclose to Seller the Buyer is willing to pay a price greater than the offered price; and **(iii)** except for (i) and (ii) above, a dual agent is obligated to disclose known facts materially affecting the value or desirability of the Property to both parties.
    D. **Other Sellers:** Seller understands that Broker may have or obtain listings on other properties, and that potential buyers may consider, make offers on, or purchase through Broker, property the same as or similar to Seller's Property. Seller consents to Broker's representation of sellers and buyers of other properties before, during, and after the end of this agreement.
    E. **Confirmation:** If the Property includes residential property with one-to-four dwelling units, Broker shall confirm the agency relationship described above, or as modified, in writing, prior to or concurrent with Seller's execution of a purchase agreement.

11. **SECURITY AND INSURANCE:** Broker is not responsible for loss of or damage to personal or real property or person, whether attributable to use of a keysafe/lockbox, a showing of the Property, or otherwise. Third parties, including but not limited to, appraisers, inspectors, brokers and prospective buyers, may have access to, and take videos and photographs of, the interior of the Property. Seller agrees: **(i)** to take reasonable precautions to safeguard and protect valuables that might be accessible during showings of the Property; and **(ii)** to obtain insurance to protect against these risks. Broker does not maintain insurance to protect Seller.

12. **KEYSAFE/LOCKBOX:** A keysafe/lockbox is designed to hold a key to the Property to permit access to the Property by Broker, cooperating brokers, MLS participants, their authorized licensees and representatives, authorized inspectors, and accompanied prospective buyers. Broker, cooperating brokers, MLS and Associations/Boards of REALTORS® are **not** insurers against injury, theft, loss, vandalism, or damage attributed to the use of a keysafe/lockbox. Seller does (or if checked ☐ does not) authorize Broker to install a keysafe/lockbox. If Seller does not occupy the Property, Seller shall be responsible for obtaining occupant(s)' written permission for use of a keysafe/lockbox.

13. **SIGN:** Seller does (or if checked ☐ does not) authorize Broker to install a FOR SALE/SOLD sign on the Property.

14. **EQUAL HOUSING OPPORTUNITY:** The Property is offered in compliance with federal, state, and local anti-discrimination laws.

15. **ATTORNEY FEES:** In any action, proceeding, or arbitration between Seller and Broker regarding the obligation to pay compensation under this agreement, the prevailing Seller or Broker shall be entitled to reasonable attorney fees and costs, except as provided in paragraph 19A.

16. **ADDITIONAL TERMS:** _____
_____
_____

17. **MANAGEMENT APPROVAL:** If an associate licensee in Broker's office (salesperson or broker-associate) enters into this agreement on Broker's behalf, and Broker or Manager does not approve of its terms, Broker or Manager has the right to cancel this agreement, in writing, within 5 days after its execution.

18. **SUCCESSORS AND ASSIGNS:** This agreement shall be binding upon Seller and Seller's successors and assigns.

LA-11 REVISED 10/01 (PAGE 2 OF 3)   Print Date

Seller acknowledges receipt of a copy of this page.
Seller's Initials (_____)(_____)
Reviewed by
Broker or Designee _____ Date _____

EQUAL HOUSING OPPORTUNITY

RESIDENTIAL LISTING AGREEMENT-EXCLUSIVE (LA-11 PAGE 2 OF 3)

FIGURE 6.1 (continued)

**Exclusive Authorization and
Right to Sell**

Property Address: _____   Date: _____

19. DISPUTE RESOLUTION:

   A.   MEDIATION: Seller and Broker agree to mediate any dispute or claim arising between them out of this agreement, or any resulting transaction, before resorting to arbitration or court action, subject to paragraph 19B(2) below. Paragraph 19B(2) below applies whether or not the arbitration provision is initialed. Mediation fees, if any, shall be divided equally among the parties involved. If, for any dispute or claim to which this paragraph applies, any party commences an action without first attempting to resolve the matter through mediation, or refuses to mediate after a request has been made, then that party shall not be entitled to recover attorney fees, even if they would otherwise be available to that party in any such action. THIS MEDIATION PROVISION APPLIES WHETHER OR NOT THE ARBITRATION PROVISION IS INITIALED.

   B.   ARBITRATION OF DISPUTES: (1) Seller and Broker agree that any dispute or claim in Law or equity arising between them regarding the obligation to pay compensation under this agreement, which is not settled through mediation, shall be decided by neutral, binding arbitration, including and subject to paragraph 19B(2) below. The arbitrator shall be a retired judge or justice, or an attorney with at least five years of residential real estate law experience, unless the parties mutually agree to a different arbitrator, who shall render an award in accordance with substantive California Law. In all other respects, the arbitration shall be conducted in accordance with Part III, Title 9 of the California Code of Civil Procedure. Judgment upon the award of the arbitrator(s) may be entered in any court having jurisdiction. The parties shall have the right to discovery in accordance with Code of Civil Procedure §1283.05.
   (2) EXCLUSIONS FROM MEDIATION AND ARBITRATION: The following matters are excluded from mediation and arbitration hereunder: **(i)** a judicial or non-judicial foreclosure or other action or proceeding to enforce a deed of trust, mortgage, or installment land sale contract as defined in Civil Code §2985; **(ii)** an unlawful detainer action; **(iii)** the filing or enforcement of a mechanic's lien; **(iv)** any matter that is within the jurisdiction of a probate, small claims, or bankruptcy court; and **(v)** an action for bodily injury or wrongful death, or for any right of action to which Code of Civil Procedure §337.1 or §337.15 applies. The filing of a court action to enable the recording of a notice of pending action, for order of attachment, receivership, injunction, or other provisional remedies, shall not constitute a violation of the mediation and arbitration provisions.
   "**NOTICE: BY INITIALING IN THE SPACE BELOW YOU ARE AGREEING TO HAVE ANY DISPUTE ARISING OUT OF THE MATTERS INCLUDED IN THE 'ARBITRATION OF DISPUTES' PROVISION DECIDED BY NEUTRAL ARBITRATION AS PROVIDED BY CALIFORNIA LAW AND YOU ARE GIVING UP ANY RIGHTS YOU MIGHT POSSESS TO HAVE THE DISPUTE LITIGATED IN A COURT OR JURY TRIAL. BY INITIALING IN THE SPACE BELOW YOU ARE GIVING UP YOUR JUDICIAL RIGHTS TO DISCOVERY AND APPEAL, UNLESS THOSE RIGHTS ARE SPECIFICALLY INCLUDED IN THE 'ARBITRATION OF DISPUTES' PROVISION. IF YOU REFUSE TO SUBMIT TO ARBITRATION AFTER AGREEING TO THIS PROVISION, YOU MAY BE COMPELLED TO ARBITRATE UNDER THE AUTHORITY OF THE CALIFORNIA CODE OF CIVIL PROCEDURE. YOUR AGREEMENT TO THIS ARBITRATION PROVISION IS VOLUNTARY.**"
   "**WE HAVE READ AND UNDERSTAND THE FOREGOING AND AGREE TO SUBMIT DISPUTES ARISING OUT OF THE MATTERS INCLUDED IN THE 'ARBITRATION OF DISPUTES' PROVISION TO NEUTRAL ARBITRATION.**"

   Seller's Initials _____/_____   Broker's Initials _____/_____

20. ENTIRE CONTRACT: All prior discussions, negotiations, and agreements between the parties concerning the subject matter of this agreement are superseded by this agreement, which constitutes the entire contract and a complete and exclusive expression of their agreement, and may not be contradicted by evidence of any prior agreement or contemporaneous oral agreement. If any provision of this agreement is held to be ineffective or invalid, the remaining provisions will nevertheless be given full force and effect. This agreement and any supplement, addendum, or modification, including any photocopy or facsimile, may be executed in counterparts.

By signing below, Seller acknowledges that Seller has read, understands, accepts and has received a copy of this agreement.

Seller _____   Date _____

Address _____ City _____ State _____ Zip _____

Telephone _____ Fax _____ E-mail _____

Seller _____   Date _____

Address _____ City _____ State _____ Zip _____

Telephone _____ Fax _____ E-mail _____

Real Estate Broker (Firm) _____

By (Agent) _____   Date _____

Address _____ City _____ State _____ Zip _____

Telephone _____ Fax _____ E-mail _____

Published and Distributed by:
REAL ESTATE BUSINESS SERVICES, INC.
a subsidiary of the CALIFORNIA ASSOCIATION OF REALTORS®
525 South Virgil Avenue, Los Angeles, California 90020

Reviewed by _____

Broker or Designee _____ Date _____

EQUAL HOUSING OPPORTUNITY

LA-11 REVISED 10/01 (PAGE 3 OF 3)   Print Date

RESIDENTIAL LISTING AGREEMENT-EXCLUSIVE (LA-11 PAGE 3 OF 3)

Case Study

The case of *R.J. Kuhl Corp. v. Sullivan* (1993) 13 C.A.4th 1589 involved a buyer's agent who entered into negotiations for a purchase. The buyer's agent contract called for a commission if a sale was consummated. The negotiations failed and a third party purchased the property. The third party gave the broker's client (Sullivan) an option to buy the property and also agreed to share in paying any commission that the buyer might owe.

The broker sued Sullivan and the third party for breach of contract, failure to pay a commission, and interference and conspiring to interfere with a contractual relationship.

The court held that Sullivan's obligation was subject to the covenant of good faith and fair dealing. The client benefited from the broker's services and profited unfairly. Even though the sale was never consummated, the breach of the covenant of good faith and fair dealing excused the consummation of the sale as a condition of payment.

Exclusive Listings

Most listings are exclusive listings, in which the owner makes the agent his or her exclusive agent to procure a buyer and agrees to pay a commission should the agent succeed. The agent promises to use due diligence in procuring a buyer. As mentioned in Chapter 5, this mutual exchange of promises makes exclusive listings bilateral contracts.

Case Study

In the case of *City of Turlock v. Paul M. Zagaris Inc.* (1989) 209 C.A.3d 189, a real estate contract signed only by the buyer and seller acknowledged that the seller owed the broker a 6 percent sales commission to be paid as the price was received. This was the sole agreement on commission. Because the city acquired the property by condemnation, escrow never closed. The broker asserted his commission in the condemnation action, alleging "vested contractual rights." The court of appeal held that the broker's right was contingent on the escrow closing, so the broker lost his rights when the escrow failed to close.

Exclusive listings must be signed by the owner. While the signature of one spouse alone on any listing is sufficient to obligate the community property to a commission, both spouses must sign the deed to sell community property. A spouse who has signed the listing will be less likely to refuse to convey; therefore, the signatures of both spouses are desirable.

Agents are required to give a copy of an exclusive listing to the owners at the time they sign. Failure to do so does not void the listing, but it does subject the agent to disciplinary action. Listings normally include a statement above the principal's signature that the principal acknowledges having received a copy of the listing. This acknowledgment serves as protection against later claims by principals that they did not receive a copy as required. (Notice the statement above the signature space in Figure 6.1.)

Exclusive listings must have a definite termination date. Stating that the listing shall expire within a stated period after a notice is given to terminate is not enough. In the absence of a definite termination date the listing can be terminated by the owner without notice, provided the owner has not benefited from the listing by a sale. The absence of a termination date on an exclusive listing also subjects the agent to disciplinary action that could include suspension or revocation of his or her license.

Exclusive listings generally provide that if the seller cancels the listing, leases or rents the property without the approval of the agent, or otherwise adversely affects its marketability, the agent is entitled to his or her commission.

While owners usually cannot cancel an exclusive listing without obligation, courts have held that an owner properly may cancel an exclusive listing if the agent has failed in his or her duty to use good-faith efforts to procure a buyer.

There are two types of exclusive listings: exclusive-right-to-sell listings and exclusive-agency listings.

Exclusive Authorization and Right-To-Sell Listing.   With an **exclusive authorization and right-to-sell listing** the owner agrees to pay a commission to an agent if the agent, any other agent, or the owner procures a buyer in accordance with the price and terms of the listing or for any other price or terms that the owner accepts. The broker will not be entitled to a commission if the buyer located lacks the financial ability to complete the purchase, because the broker has failed to procure a ready, willing, and able buyer.

Because the listing agent earns a commission no matter who sells the property, this is the most desirable listing for brokers.

Case Study

In *Nystrom v. First National Bank of Fresno* (1978) 81 C.A.3d 759, a 90-day exclusive listing was not to be effective until a deed was

(continued on next page)

acquired at a forthcoming trustee's sale. In an action to collect a commission where a sale was consummated by another broker, the court held that while the beginning date was uncertain, the listing did have a definite date for termination.

Exclusive-right-to-sell listings frequently contain a **safety clause**. This clause customarily provides that the owner is obligated to pay a commission if a sale is made within a stated period after expiration of the listing to any person the agent negotiated with and whose name was furnished in writing to the owner within three days after the expiration of the listing. Sometimes these clauses provide that in the event another listing is entered into, the owner no longer is obligated under the safety clause. Without such an exception, an owner could be obligated to pay more than one commission. Notice the safety clause, paragraph 4.A.2, in the listing agreement (Figure 6.1). Often the rules of a local board of REALTORS® have the effect of a safety clause on subsequent listings.

Paragraph 12 covers keybox authorization, and the owner is advised to obtain appropriate insurance coverage. If an agent recommends a keybox without any warnings to the owner, conceivably the agent could be held liable for any resulting loss.

Paragraph 19-B provides that by initialing, the parties agree to arbitration of any disputes arising from the agreement (mandatory arbitration).

Exclusive-Agency Listing.   Under an exclusive-agency listing the named broker is the exclusive agent for the owner, and if the listing broker or any other agent procures a purchaser in accordance with the terms of the listing, or any other price and terms the owner might agree to, the agent has earned a commission. The owner can, however, sell the property by himself or herself without any obligation to pay a commission.

Exclusive-agency listings usually are entered into when an owner might have one or more prospective buyers. A better arrangement, however, would be to write an exclusive-right-to-sell listing that excludes named individuals for a set period of time. This would encourage the seller's prospects to buy if they are serious buyers. After the expiration of the stated period of time the exception would be removed.

Exclusive-agency listings usually require that the owner notify the agent of any sale and identify the purchasers. They usually also prohibit the owner from offering the property at a lower price than that offered by the agent.

Under an exclusive-agency listing the owner might be encouraged to subvert the agent's efforts. Problems arise as to who really was the procuring cause of a sale when the agent had contact with the owner's buyer (procuring cause is discussed further below). Because of the possible problems of exclusive-agency listings, many brokers refuse to accept them.

Open Listings

Open listings are nonexclusive listings; they may be offered to one or more brokers. The broker who earns the commission is the first agent to bring the owner an offer that meets the terms of the listing or that the owner accepts. A sale under one open listing automatically cancels all other open listings. The principal has no duty to notify the agents under other open listings of the sale.

An open listing may be simply a note or memorandum that describes the property and states the price wanted and that a stated commission will be paid. The agent need not sign the open listing, but it must be signed by the principal (property owner).

The open listing is really a unilateral contract. The agent makes no promise to use diligence to obtain a buyer. By procuring a buyer the agent accepts the owner's promise to pay a commission.

Unlike exclusive listings, open listings need not have a definite termination date. An owner generally can cancel the open listing at any time without obligation but cannot cancel an open listing to avoid paying a commission and then accept the benefits of the agent's efforts by consummating a sale to a buyer procured by the agent. An owner who cancels an open listing in good faith is not obligated to the agent simply because a sale later was made to a buyer whom the agent had contacted.

Open listings often lead to disagreements between owners and agents as well as among agents over who was the procuring cause of a sale. The California Association of REALTORS® (CAR) provides an open listing form NEA-14. An advantage of a formal listing is the broker protection of the safety clause.

Procuring Cause

The agent who is the procuring cause of a sale is that agent who initiated an uninterrupted series of events that led to the sale. Under open listings and exclusive-agency listings an agent who was the procuring cause of the sale is entitled to a commission.

If a break in the chain of events occurred, such as failure to contact a prospective buyer for several months or failure to obtain financing, the original agent who failed for lack of diligence or effort generally would not be considered the procuring cause. Simply telling a person about a property or giving a buyer a list in which a property is included would not qualify an agent as a procuring cause.

> ## Case Study
> In the case of *Coldwell Banker and Co. v. Pepper Tree Office Center Assocs.* (1980) 106 C.A.3d 272, the plaintiff had an exclusive-agency listing. The court held that submitting a one-page brochure and forwarding floor plans to the broker of a prospective tenant did not reasonably constitute procuring cause.

The agent who claims that he or she was the procuring cause has the burden of proof. When the broker's efforts led directly to the buyer and seller getting together, the courts generally will consider the broker to have been the procuring cause.

Procuring cause problems often arise when a prospective buyer fails to inform an agent that he or she has already been exposed to a particular property by another agent. An agent who discovers after a sale that the buyer had previous contact with another agent should have the buyer make a written statement about the nature of the contact and the dates, as well as the reason the buyer did not continue to negotiate with the original agent. If this statement shows that another agent might have a reasonable claim to being the procuring cause, the selling agent should consider negotiating a fair settlement.

An owner who has given multiple open listings may assume, unless notified otherwise, that the broker presenting the offer is the procuring cause.

The safety clause in a listing appears only to require that the agent introduced the buyer to the property. This is much less than the requirement under procuring cause. Therefore, a broker could be in a better position claiming notification under the safety clause than making a claim as to procuring cause. A prior offer made by the ultimate purchaser has been held to satisfy the notification requirements of the safety clause.

Verbal Listings

While listings of real property are required to be in writing to be enforceable, one exception may exist. If, after a listing expires, the owner encourages the broker to continue to work on the sale of the property, the owner may have waived his or her rights to claim the statute of frauds as a defense against paying a commission. The doctrine of estoppel might apply.

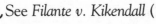 See *Filante v. Kikendall* (1955) 134 C.A.2d 695 for an example.

Buyer Listings

As discussed earlier, the agent can represent the buyer only rather than the seller. **Buyer listings**, like listings from owners, can be exclusive: the broker has the sole right to locate property for a buyer. In a buyer exclusive-agency listing the buyer can locate property for himself or herself, but the broker is the exclusive agent. In an open buyer listing the broker is given nonexclusive authorization to locate property.

Like a seller's listing, a buyer's listing, to be enforceable, must be in writing and signed to satisfy the statute of frauds. An oral agreement by a buyer to pay a commission is unenforceable.

Like a seller's listing, a buyer's listing must authorize the broker to cooperate with other brokers so that the broker may work with subagents. The terms in the buyer's listing are very similar to those found in the usual listings given by owners. One difference is the fee structure. Buyers' listings for residential property generally provide that the buyer will pay the agent's commission if the seller or selling agent does not pay or share a commission with the buyer's agent. Buyers' listings frequently provide a fee for obtaining an option to purchase and another fee when exercised. Buyers' listings sometimes include an hourly fee as well as an advance against expenses.

Net Listings

Net listings refer to the commission payment only and provide that all money received over a stated or net amount shall be the agent's commission. They are illegal in many states because they create a serious conflict of interest. The agent under a net listing really is dealing more as a principal than as an agent. The agent is closer to being an optionee (with an option to buy) than a representative of the owner.

Even though net listings are legal in California, agents should be aware that the seller is likely to allege fraud or misrepresentation should the sales price result in a commission that is greater than customary.

A net listing does not relieve the broker from informing the owner of offers at or less than the list price. When an owner accepts such an offer, the broker is not entitled to a commission.

The agent must disclose the amount of his or her net commission prior to or at the time the principal commits to the transaction. Failure to do so could be grounds for disciplinary action.

Because of the ethical problems involved with net listings, a net listing form has not been included in this chapter.

Other Listing Forms

Advance Fee Addendum.   The growth of professionalism in real estate has led to a growing acceptance of advance fees. While more common in buyer listings, they also are gaining acceptance in seller listings, especially listings involving larger residential, commercial, or industrial property where a great deal of professional effort will be required prior to a sale.

The **advance fee addendum** usually sets forth specific activities that the agent is to be compensated for as well as an hourly rate (or set rate) for the compensation. The agreement is very similar to an agreement that an attorney makes with his or her client.

The Department of Real Estate requires approval of all advance fee forms (approval does not extend to photocopies of approved forms). Any additions or deletions to an approved form must be submitted to the Department of Real Estate at least 10 days prior to entering into an agreement. Failure to do so could result in disciplinary action.

Advance fees must be placed in the broker's trust account until they are earned.

Advance Costs.   Advance costs differ from advance fees in that they are paid to the agent to cover cash outlays in carrying out the agency. They are not intended to cover brokerage fees or general overhead expenses.

Monies collected to cover advance costs must be treated as trust money and must be placed in the broker's trust account. The trust fund remains the property of the principal until disbursed by the agent for the principal.

The broker must provide the principal with a quarterly accounting of all disbursements, and any remaining funds must be returned to the principal at the expiration of the agreement along with a final accounting.

Listing Modification.   While it is possible for a broker and a principal to enter into a new listing agreement that by its terms supersedes an existing listing, it is far simpler to enter a simple modification. The California Association of REALTORS® form MT is used as an all-purpose listing modification form.

Loan Broker Listing Agreement.   A mortgage loan broker represents a borrower, as his or her agent, to obtain a loan. The agency agreement setting forth the rights and obligations of the parties is known as a **loan broker listing agreement.**

Loan brokers' commissions and costs on regulated loans are limited by law (see Chapter 4). Loan brokers' listings cannot exceed 45 days when seeking a residential loan of $2,000 or less.

A loan broker listing agreement generally allows the broker to work with subagents, provides a safety clause pertaining to loans made after the expiration of the listing, and contains other provisions that are similar to those found in exclusive-right-to-sell listings.

Seller's Net.   Often sellers do not understand the effect of escrow costs, prorations, prepayment penalties, title insurance costs, seller's points, and other matters. Surprises can result in sellers refusing to sell, filing a complaint against the agent, and even suing the agent.

California Association of REALTORS® form ESP shows estimated seller's proceeds. It can be used at the time a listing is taken, when an offer is received, or in preparing a counteroffer. The more open an agent is in his or her dealings, the less chance the agent has of being sued by a party to a transaction.

■ OPTIONS

As pointed out in Chapter 5, an option is a contract to make a contract. The option must clearly show the price if the option is exercised. (The price can be determined by a formula; however, it cannot be ambiguous.) Time is considered to be of the essence in options in that the option *must* be exercised within the period provided.

Generally, option-to-purchase forms provide for the method of exercising the option, include any agreed-on sales terms, and contain provisions for escrow and delivery of title as well as for brokerage fees. The form in Figure 6.2 protects the broker during any extensions to the option as well as for a safety period of one year after the expiration of the option or extensions thereto. Some option forms provide for option extensions upon the payment of additional consideration.

An owner cannot avoid a commission by giving an option during the listing period that is to be exercised after the listing expires.

See *Anthony v. Enzler* (1976) 61 C.A. 3d 872 on our Web site for an example of a court decision regarding this.

As discussed in Chapter 3, in California an agent with a listing may also obtain an option to purchase the property. However, because the broker is

FIGURE 6.2

Standard Option to Purchase Form

STANDARD OPTION TO PURCHASE
Irrevocable Right-to-Buy

DATE:_____, 19_____, at _____, California.

Option Money: Optionor herewith receives from Optionee option money in the amount of $_____ evidenced by ☐ cash, ☐ check, or ☐ _____, given in consideration for this option to purchase.

Real Property Description:

Address: _____

_____

Legal Description: _____

Option Period: Optionor hereby grants to Optionee the irrevocable option to purchase the Optionor's rights, title and interest in the property on the terms stated, for a period commencing with the acceptance of this option and expiring _____/_____/_____.

Exercise of Option: Optionee may exercise this option during the option period by:

1. Preparing and signing escrow instructions, identical in provisions to those attached as Exhibit 'A'; and
2. Depositing cash in escrow of $_____; and
3. Delivering a certified copy of the signed escrow instructions to Optionor, within the option period, in person or by certified mail.

Escrow Contract: In the event this option is exercised, the transaction shall be escrowed with:

_____

Escrow shall close within_____days after exercise of option.

Delivery of Title: Within_____days after exercise, Optionor shall place all documents and instruments into escrow necessary to close within the escrow period.

Additional Consideration: As further consideration for this option and at Optionee's expense, Optionee to obtain and deliver up to Optionor the following checked studies and reports:

☐ Property survey report by licensed California surveyors.
☐ Application for a parcel map or waiver.
☐ Application for a conditional use permit.
☐ Land use study.   ☐ Architectural plans and specifications.
☐ Soil engineer's report.   ☐ Zoning ordinance request.
☐ Off-site improvement plans.   ☐ On-site engineering plans.

Brokerage Fee: Optionor agrees to pay a brokerage fee of _____ of the selling price IF:

1. This option is exercised;
2. Within one year after expiration of option period and any extension or renewal, Optionor enters into an agreement to sell, lease or exchange with Optionee, or their assigns; or
3. Optionor wrongfully prevents the exercise of this option.

To Broker:_____

Address:_____

_____ Phone (____)_____

Sale Terms: Price of $_____ payable as noted below:

1. ☐ All cash.
2. Cash down payment in the amount of $_____.
3. Assume a trust deed note with a balance of $_____. Interest not to exceed _____%, ☐ VIR, payable approximately $_____ monthly over the loan's remaining life, impounds being $_____ monthly.
   3.1 Loan balance differences to be adjusted in _____.
4. Assume a trust deed note with a balance of $_____. Interest not to exceed _____%, payable approximately $_____ monthly, due and payable _____.
5. A NOTE for the balance of the purchase price in the amount of $_____ to be executed by Buyer in favor of Seller and secured by a trust deed on the property being purchased, payable $_____ monthly or more, starting one month after closing, including interest at ____% from closing, due and payable _____ years after closing.
   5.1 This note and trust deed to contain provisions to be provided by Optionor for:
      ☐ due-on-sale, ☐ prepayment penalty,
      ☐ late charges
   5.2 ☐ The attached Carryback Disclosure Statement is an addendum to this agreement (mandatory on four or less residential units).
   5.3 Buyer to provide a Request for Notice of Delinquency to senior encumbrancers.

General Provisions (items left blank or unchecked, not applicable):

1. ☐ See addendum for additional provisions.
2. ☐ See attached Seller's Improvement (transfer) Disclosure.
3. Buyer has inspected the property and improvements.
4. ☐ This property is located in Special Studies Zone and a geologic report may be required prior to issuance of any building permit for construction, additions or alterations to the property or its improvements.
5. Possession of the property to be delivered on: ☐ close of escrow, or ☐ see attached Occupancy Agreement.
6. Both parties reserve their rights to assign and agree to cooperate in effecting an Internal Revenue Code 1031 exchange prior to close of escrow, on either party's written notice.
7. In any legal action between Optionee and Optionor arising out of this agreement, the prevailing party shall be entitled to reasonable attorney's fees and costs.

Expiration of Option: This offer to sell shall be deemed expired if not accepted by exercise during the option period. This option contract shall automatically expire/terminate on _____/_____/_____.

I hereby grant this option and agree to perform under its terms.

Date:_____, 19 _____
Optionor's Name:_____
Address: _____
_____ Phone (___)_____
Optionor's Signature:_____

Broker's Approval:_____ ___/___/___

I hereby accept this option and agree to perform under its terms.

Date:_____, 19 _____
Optionee's Name:_____
Address: _____
_____ Phone (___)_____
Optionee's Signature:_____

Broker's Approval:_____ ___/___/___

FORM 161   12-89   ©1989 first tuesday, P.O. BOX 20068, RIVERSIDE, CA 92516 (909) 781-7300

Reprinted from First Tuesday, P.O. Box 20688, Riverside CA 92516, telephone (909) 781-7300

dealing as an agent under the listing and as a principal under the option, a serious conflict of interest arises. As stated earlier, before the option can be exercised the agent must disclose fully if he or she has an offer and the amount of the offer and his or her profit. The agent also must obtain the owner's written consent after said disclosure to exercise the option.

Because of the serious ethical questions raised by options combined with listings, the authors strongly advise against the use of these agreements.

Case Study

The case of *Rattray v. Scudder* (1946) 28 C.2d 214 involved a listing-option agreement. The broker located a buyer but indicated to the owner that he was unable to find one. He then negotiated a lower purchase price for himself. The court held that a broker, when pursuing his own interests, cannot ignore those of his principal. The broker cannot be allowed to enjoy the fruits of an advantage taken under a fiduciary relationship.

■ BROKER'S FORMS

Finder's Fee

An agent may not pay a commission to an unlicensed party for any act that requires a real estate license. Finders' fees, however (discussed in Chapter 3), are legal. They are not paid for an act requiring a real estate license; they are paid for a referral to a buyer, seller, borrower, or lender. Sharing part of a sales commission with an unlicensed person nevertheless is illegal.

Verbal agreements made with brokers have been enforced on the theory that the broker does not need the protection of the statute of frauds. For the protection of both the broker and the finder a written agreement should be prepared.

Generally in finder's fee agreements the finder agrees not to participate in or conduct negotiations with prospective clients or to solicit loans on behalf of prospective clients.

Cooperating Broker Agreements

Agreements between brokers to split commissions are not required by the statute of frauds to be in writing. They deal in dollars and not real estate.

To avoid misunderstandings, brokers may enter into written agreements setting forth the commission split. Some **cooperating broker fee agreements** require that the nonlisting broker identify prospective buyers so that the listing broker can notify the owner of these prospective purchasers (to be protected under the safety clause of the listing). Brokers seldom use these agreements, however, because generally both listing and selling brokers are members of a trade group, such as a multiple-listing service, that enforces commission split agreements.

■ REAL ESTATE PURCHASE CONTRACT

The California Association of Realtors® (CAR) has prepared several real estate purchase contract forms. We have included a Residential Purchase

Agreement and Joint Escrow Instructions as Figure 6.3. This form provides for most contingencies and avoids the necessity of agent-drafted provisions that might not clearly reflect the intentions of the parties. The form also serves as escrow instructions. Included here are comments on the paragraphs to aid in your understanding of the purpose and applications of the provisions of this contract.

Paragraph 1: Defines the form as an offer from offeror, describes property, sets purchase price, and specifies closing time.

Paragraph 2: Provides for financing as a contingency of the purchase, buyer's deposit and deposit increase, the terms of the loan that the offer is contingent upon, and a contingency that the appraisal will at least equal sale price, and by checking the appropriate block, the offer can be made without a financing contingency.

Paragraph 3: Indicates if buyer intends property as principal residence (see Paragraph 16).

Paragraph 4: Indicates who is responsible for which costs.

Paragraph 5: The requirements of the Transfer Disclosure Statement, Natural Hazard Disclosures, Subsequent Disclosures, and Mello-Roos Notice are set forth.

Paragraph 6: Additional required disclosure are set forth, which include "Megan's Law" disclosure as to the availability of information of known sex offenders in the community from the local police or sheriff's office.

Paragraph 7: Sets forth that the property is sold in its present condition, it will be maintained, and personal property and trash will be removed by close of escrow. The paragraph reiterates that the seller will disclose known material facts and defects. The seller's right to inspect and request for repairs is also set forth. If the seller refuses or is unable to make repairs, the buyer has cancellation rights. The buyer is strongly advised to conduct an inspection, as the seller may not be aware of all problems.

Paragraph 8: Provides that fixtures and fittings shall remain with the property (free of liens) as well as additional items to be included with the sale or items to be excluded from the sale.

Paragraph 9: Sets forth buyer's rights to conduct inspections and tests.

Paragraph 10: Provides that seller repairs shall comply with applicable law and be performed in a skillful manner, but there is no limit to cost.

FIGURE 6.3

Residential Purchase Agreement and Joint Escrow Instructions (and receipt for deposit)

CALIFORNIA ASSOCIATION OF REALTORS®

**RESIDENTIAL PURCHASE AGREEMENT
AND JOINT ESCROW INSTRUCTIONS
(AND RECEIPT FOR DEPOSIT)**
For Use With Single Family Residential Property — Attached or Detached

Date _____, at _____, California.

1. **OFFER:**
   A. **THIS IS AN OFFER FROM** _____ ("Buyer"),
   B. **THE REAL PROPERTY TO BE ACQUIRED** is described as _____
   _____, Assessor's Parcel No. _____, situated in
   _____, County of_____, California, ("Property").
   C. **THE PURCHASE PRICE** offered is _____
   _____ Dollars $ _____
   D. **CLOSE OF ESCROW** shall occur _____ **Days** After Acceptance (or ☐ on _____ (date)).
2. **FINANCING:** Obtaining the loans below **is a contingency** of this Agreement unless: (i) either 2H or 2I is checked below or (ii) otherwise agreed. Buyer shall act diligently and in good faith to obtain the designated loans. Obtaining deposit, down payment and closing costs **is not a contingency**.
   A. **BUYER HAS GIVEN A DEPOSIT TO THE AGENT SUBMITTING THE OFFER** . . . .$_____
   (or to ☐ _____), made payable to _____ by Personal
   Check, or ☐_____ which shall be held uncashed until Acceptance and then
   deposited within **3 business days** after Acceptance or ☐ _____,
   ☐ with Escrow Holder, ☐ into Broker's trust account, or ☐ _____.
   Buyer represents that funds will be good when deposited with Escrow Holder.
   B. **INCREASED DEPOSIT** shall be deposited by Buyer with Escrow Holder within _____ **Days** After Acceptance, ... $_____
   or ☐ _____
   C. **FIRST LOAN IN THE AMOUNT OF** . . . .$_____
   (1) NEW First Deed of Trust in favor of LENDER, encumbering the Property, securing a note payable at maximum
   interest of _____% fixed rate, or _____% initial adjustable rate with a maximum interest rate cap of
   _____%, balance due in _____ years, amortized over _____ years. Buyer shall pay loan fees/points not to
   exceed _____. (These terms apply whether the designated loan is conventional, FHA or VA.)
   (2) ☐ FHA, ☐ VA: (The following terms only apply to the FHA or VA loan that is checked.)
   Seller shall pay (i) _____% discount points, (ii) other fees not allowed to be paid by Buyer,
   not to exceed $_____, and (iii) the cost of lender required Repairs not otherwise provided for
   in this Agreement, not to exceed $ _____
   (Actual loan amount may increase if mortgage insurance premiums, funding fees or closing costs are financed.)
   D. **ADDITIONAL FINANCING TERMS:** _____ . . . . . $_____
   _____
   ☐ Seller financing, (C.A.R. Form SFA-11); ☐ junior financing; ☐ assumed financing (C.A.R. Form PAA-11).
   E. **BALANCE OF PURCHASE PRICE** (not including costs of obtaining loans and other closing costs) to be deposited with . . . .$_____
   Escrow Holder within sufficient time to close escrow.
   F. **TOTAL PURCHASE PRICE** . . . .$_____
   G. **LOAN CONTINGENCY** shall remain in effect until the designated loans are funded (or ☐ _____ **Days** After Acceptance, by which time Buyer shall give Seller written notice of Buyer's election to cancel this Agreement if Buyer is unable to obtain the designated loans. If Buyer does not give Seller such notice, the contingency of obtaining the designated loans shall be removed by the method specified in paragraph 14).
   H. ☐ **NO LOAN CONTINGENCY:** (If checked) Obtaining any loan in paragraphs 2C, 2D or elsewhere in this Agreement is not a contingency of this Agreement. If Buyer does not obtain the loan, and as a result Buyer does not purchase the Property, Seller may be entitled to Buyer's deposit or other legal remedies.
   I. ☐ **ALL CASH OFFER:** (If checked) No loan is needed to purchase the Property. Buyer shall, within **5 (or ☐ _____) Days** After Acceptance, provide Seller written verification of sufficient funds to close this transaction. Seller may cancel this Agreement in writing within **5 Days** After (i) time to provide verification expires, if Buyer fails to provide verification or (ii) receipt of verification, if Seller reasonably disapproves it.
   J. **LOAN APPLICATIONS; PREQUALIFICATION:** Within **5 (or ☐ _____) Days** After Acceptance, Buyer shall provide Seller a letter from lender or mortgage loan broker stating that, based on a review of Buyer's written application and credit report, Buyer is prequalified for the NEW loan indicated above. If Buyer fails to provide such letter within that time, Seller may cancel this Agreement in writing.
   K. ☐ **APPRAISAL CONTINGENCY:** (If checked) This Agreement is contingent upon Property appraising at no less than the specified total purchase price. If there is a loan contingency, the appraisal contingency shall remain in effect until the loan contingency is removed. If there is no loan contingency, the appraisal contingency shall be removed within **10 (or ☐ _____) Days** After Acceptance.

Buyer and Seller acknowledge receipt of a copy of this page.
Buyer's Initials (_____)(_____)
Seller's Initials (_____)(_____)

EQUAL HOUSING OPPORTUNITY

Reviewed by _____
Broker or Designee _____ Date _____

REVISION DATE 10/2000 Print Date
RPA-11 (PAGE 1 OF 8)

RESIDENTIAL PURCHASE AGREEMENT (RPA-11 PAGE 1 OF 8)

Reprinted with permission, California Association of REALTORS®. Endorsement not implied.

FIGURE 6.3 (continued)

Residential Purchase Agreement and Joint Escrow Instructions (and receipt for deposit)

Property Address: _____   Date: _____

3. **CLOSING AND OCCUPANCY**
   A. Buyer ☐ does, ☐ does not intend to occupy Property as Buyer's primary residence.
   B. Seller occupied or vacant property: Occupancy shall be delivered to Buyer at _____ AM/PM, ☐ on the date of Close Of Escrow, ☐ on _____, or ☐ no later than _____ **Days** After Close Of Escrow. (See C.A.R. Form PAA-11, paragraph 2.) If transfer of title and occupancy do not occur at the same time, Buyer and Seller are advised to (i) enter into a written occupancy agreement, and (ii) consult with their insurance advisors.
   C. Tenant occupied property: At Close of Escrow, Property shall be vacant unless otherwise agreed in writing. **Seller has the responsibility to (i) comply with rent control and other Law necessary to deliver Property vacant, and (ii) determine whether timely vacancy is permitted under such Law.**
   D. At Close Of Escrow, Seller assigns to Buyer any assignable warranty rights for items included in the sale and shall provide any available copies of such warranties. Brokers cannot and will not determine the assignability of any warranties.
   E. At Close of Escrow, unless otherwise agreed in writing, Seller shall provide keys and/or means to operate all locks, mailboxes, security systems, alarms and garage door openers. If Property is a unit in a condominium or other common interest subdivision, Buyer may be required to pay a deposit to the Homeowners' Association ("HOA") to obtain keys to accessible HOA facilities.

4. **ALLOCATION OF COSTS** (If checked): If any of the inspections or reports in 4A, B, C and D are checked, then with regard to that item, Buyer shall have approval (including approval of alternate methods of treatment, if any, recommended by the Pest Control Report), removal and cancellation rights, and obligations as specified in paragraph 14. (The rights in paragraph 14 apply whether or not Buyer and Seller agree below who is to pay for Section 1 or Section 2 recommended work.)
   A. PEST CONTROL
      ☐ Buyer ☐ Seller shall pay for a Pest Control Report (for wood destroying pests and organisms only) ("Report"). The Report shall be prepared by _____, a registered structural pest control company, who shall separate the Report into sections for evident infestation or infection (Section 1) and for conditions likely to lead to infestation or infection (Section 2). The Report shall cover the main building and attached structures and, if checked: ☐ detached garages and carports, ☐ detached decks, ☐ the following other structures on the Property: _____. The Report shall not cover roof coverings. If Property is a unit in a condominium or other common interest subdivision, the Report shall cover only the separate interest and any exclusive-use areas being transferred, and shall not cover common areas. Water tests of shower pans on upper level units may not be performed unless the owners of property below the shower consent. If Buyer requests inspection of inaccessible areas, Buyer shall pay for the cost of entry, inspection and closing for those areas, unless otherwise agreed. A written Pest Control Certification shall be issued prior to Close Of Escrow, unless otherwise agreed, and only if no infestation or infection is found or if required corrective work is completed.
      (Section 1) ☐ Buyer ☐ Seller shall pay for work recommended to correct "Section 1" conditions described in the Report and the cost of inspection, entry and closing of those inaccessible areas where active infestation or infection is discovered.
      (Section 2) ☐ Buyer ☐ Seller shall pay for work recommended to correct "Section 2" conditions described in the Report if requested by Buyer.
      OTHER INSPECTIONS AND REPORTS
   B. ☐ Buyer ☐ Seller shall pay to have septic or private sewage disposal system inspected._____
   C. ☐ Buyer ☐ Seller shall pay to have domestic wells tested for water potability and productivity._____
   D. ☐ Buyer ☐ Seller shall pay for a natural hazard zone disclosure report prepared by _____.
      GOVERNMENT REQUIREMENTS AND RETROFIT
   E. ☐ Buyer ☐ Seller shall pay for smoke detector installation and/or water heater bracing, if required by Law. Prior to Close Of Escrow, Seller shall provide Buyer a written statement of compliance in accordance with state and local Law, unless exempt.
   F. ☐ Buyer ☐ Seller shall pay the cost of compliance with any other minimum mandatory government retrofit standards, inspections and reports if required as a condition of closing escrow under any Law.
      ESCROW, TITLE AND OTHER COSTS
   G. ☐ Buyer ☐ Seller shall pay escrow fee._____
      Escrow Holder shall be _____.
   H. ☐ Buyer ☐ Seller shall pay for **owner's** title insurance policy specified in paragraph 12.
      Owner's title policy to be issued by _____
         (Buyer shall pay for any title insurance policy insuring Buyer's **Lender**, unless otherwise agreed.)
   I. ☐ Buyer ☐ Seller shall pay County transfer tax or transfer fee._____
   J. ☐ Buyer ☐ Seller shall pay City transfer tax or transfer fee._____
   K. ☐ Buyer ☐ Seller shall pay HOA transfer fees. _____
   L. ☐ Buyer ☐ Seller shall pay HOA document preparation fees. _____
   M. ☐ Buyer ☐ Seller shall pay the cost, not to exceed $ _____, of a one-year home warranty plan, issued by _____, with the following optional coverage: _____.

REVISION DATE 10/2000   Print Date
RPA-11 (PAGE 2 OF 8)

Buyer and Seller acknowledge receipt of a copy of this page.
   Buyer's Initials (_____)(_____)
   Seller's Initials (_____)(_____)

EQUAL HOUSING OPPORTUNITY

Reviewed by _____
Broker or Designee _____ Date _____

RESIDENTIAL PURCHASE AGREEMENT (RPA-11 PAGE 2 OF 8)

FIGURE 6.3 (continued)

Residential Purchase Agreement and Joint Escrow Instructions (and receipt for deposit)

Property Address: _____ Date: _____

5. **TRANSFER DISCLOSURE STATEMENT; NATURAL HAZARD DISCLOSURE STATEMENT; LEAD-BASED PAINT HAZARD DISCLOSURES; AND OTHER DISCLOSURES WITH CANCELLATION RIGHTS:**
   A. Within the time specified in paragraph 14, if required by Law, a Real Estate Transfer Disclosure Statement ("TDS"), Natural Hazard Disclosure Statement ("NHD"), Federal Lead-Based Paint Disclosures and pamphlet ("Lead Disclosures"), disclosure regarding industrial use (Property is in or affected by a zone or district allowing manufacturing, commercial or airport use) and military ordnance disclosure shall be completed and delivered to Buyer, who shall return Signed Copies to Seller.
   B. In the event Seller, prior to Close Of Escrow, becomes aware of adverse conditions materially affecting the Property, or any material inaccuracy in disclosures, information, or representations previously provided to Buyer (including those made in a TDS) of which Buyer is otherwise unaware, Seller shall promptly provide a subsequent or amended disclosure, in writing, covering those items. **However, a subsequent or amended disclosure shall not be required for conditions and material inaccuracies disclosed in reports received by Buyer.**
   C. Seller shall (i) make a good faith effort to obtain a disclosure notice from any local agencies that levy a special tax on the Property pursuant to the Mello-Roos Community Facilities Act, and (ii) promptly deliver to Buyer any such notice made available by those agencies.
   D. If the TDS, the NHD, the Lead Disclosures, industrial use disclosure, military ordnance disclosure, the Mello-Roos disclosure notice, or a subsequent or amended disclosure is delivered to Buyer after the offer is Signed, Buyer shall have the right to cancel this Agreement within **3 Days** After delivery in person, or **5 Days** After delivery by deposit in the mail, by giving written notice of cancellation to Seller or Seller's agent. (Lead Disclosures sent by mail must be sent certified mail or better.)

6. **DISCLOSURES:** Within the time specified in paragraph 14, Seller shall: (i) disclose if Property is located in any zone identified in 6A and provide any other information required for those zones; (ii) if required by Law, provide Buyer with the disclosures and other information identified in 6B; and, (iii) if applicable, take the actions specified in 6C and 6D. Buyer, within the time specified in paragraph 14, shall then investigate the disclosures and other information provided to Buyer, and the database in 6E, and take the action specified in paragraph 14.
   A. **NATURAL HAZARD ZONE:** Special Flood Hazard Areas; Potential Flooding (Inundation) Areas; Very High Fire Hazard Zones; State Fire Responsibility Areas; Earthquake Fault Zones; Seismic Hazard Zones; or any other zone for which disclosure is required by Law.
   B. **PROPERTY DISCLOSURES AND PUBLICATIONS:** Earthquake Guides (and questionnaire) and Environmental Hazards Booklet.
   C. ☐ (If checked) **CONDOMINIUM/COMMON INTEREST SUBDIVISION:** Property is a unit in a condominium, or other common interest subdivision. Seller shall request from the HOA and, upon receipt, provide to Buyer: (i) Copies of any documents required by Law; (ii) disclosure of any pending or anticipated claims or litigation by or against the HOA; (iii) a statement containing the location and number of designated parking and storage spaces; (iv) Copies of the most recent 12 months of HOA minutes for regular and special meetings, if available; and (v) the names and contact information of all HOAs governing the Property (C.A.R. Form HOA-11).
   D. **NOTICE OF VIOLATION:** If, prior to Close Of Escrow, Seller receives notice or is made aware of any notice filed or issued against the Property for violations of any Law, Seller shall immediately notify Buyer in writing.
   E. **DATA BASE DISCLOSURE:** NOTICE: The California Department of Justice, sheriff's departments, police departments serving jurisdictions of 200,000 or more and many other local law enforcement authorities maintain for public access a data base of the locations of persons required to register pursuant to paragraph (1) of subdivision (a) of Section 290.4 of the Penal Code. The data base is updated on a quarterly basis and a source of information about the presence of these individuals in any neighborhood. The Department of Justice also maintains a Sex Offender Identification Line through which inquiries about individuals may be made. This is a "900" telephone service. Callers must have specific information about individuals they are checking. Information regarding neighborhoods is not available through the "900" telephone service.

7. **CONDITION OF PROPERTY:**
   A. Unless otherwise agreed, (i) **Property is sold (a) in its PRESENT physical condition on the date of Acceptance and (b) subject to Buyer inspection rights;** (ii) Property, including pool, spa, landscaping and grounds, is to be maintained in substantially the same condition as on the date of Acceptance, and (iii) all debris and personal property not included in the sale shall be removed by Close Of Escrow.
   B. **SELLER SHALL DISCLOSE KNOWN MATERIAL FACTS AND DEFECTS AND MAKE OTHER DISCLOSURES REQUIRED BY LAW.**
   C. Buyer has the right to inspect the Property and, based upon information discovered in those inspections, may reasonably request that Seller make Repairs, corrections or take other action as specified in paragraph 14.
   D. Note to Buyer: You are strongly advised to conduct inspections of the entire Property in order to determine its present condition since Seller may not be aware of all defects affecting the Property or other factors that you consider important. Property improvements may not be built according to codes or in compliance with current Law, or have had permits issued.
   E. Note to Seller: Buyer may request that you make certain Repairs and, in the event you refuse or are unable to make those Repairs, Buyer may cancel this Agreement as specified in paragraph 14.

8. A. **ITEMS INCLUDED IN SALE:** All EXISTING fixtures and fittings that are attached to the Property are INCLUDED IN THE PURCHASE PRICE (unless excluded in paragraph 8C below), and shall be transferred free of liens and without Seller warranty. Items to be transferred shall include, but are not limited to, existing electrical, mechanical, lighting, plumbing and heating fixtures, fireplace inserts, solar systems, built-in appliances, window and door screens, awnings, shutters, window coverings, attached floor coverings, television antennas, satellite dishes and related equipment, private integrated telephone systems, air coolers/conditioners, pool/spa equipment, garage door openers/remote controls, attached fireplace equipment, mailbox, in-ground landscaping, including trees/shrubs, and (if owned by Seller) water softeners, water purifiers and security systems/alarms.
   B. **ADDITIONAL ITEMS INCLUDED:** The following items of personal property, free of liens and without Seller warranty, are INCLUDED IN THE PURCHASE PRICE _____
   _____
   _____.
   C. **ITEMS EXCLUDED FROM SALE:** _____
   _____.

REVISION DATE 10/2000   Print Date
RPA-11 (PAGE 3 OF 8)

Buyer and Seller acknowledge receipt of a copy of this page.
Buyer's Initials (_____)(_____)
Seller's Initials (_____)(_____)

Reviewed by _____
Broker or Designee _____ Date _____

FIGURE 6.3 (continued)

Residential Purchase Agreement and Joint Escrow Instructions (and receipt for deposit)

Property Address: _____   Date: _____

9. **BUYER'S INVESTIGATION OF PROPERTY CONDITION:** Buyer's Acceptance of the condition of and any other matter affecting the Property is a contingency of this Agreement, as specified in this paragraph and paragraph 14. Buyer shall have the right at Buyer's expense, unless otherwise agreed, to conduct inspections, investigations, tests, surveys, and other studies ("Inspections"), including the right to: (i) inspect for lead-based paint and other lead-based paint hazards; (ii) inspect for wood destroying pests and organisms ("Pest Control Report"); and (iii) review the registered sex offender database. No Inspections shall be made by any governmental building or zoning inspector, or government employee, without Seller's prior written consent, unless required by Law. Buyer shall complete these Inspections and give any written notice to Seller within the time specified in paragraph 14. At Seller's request, Buyer shall give Seller, at no cost, complete Copies of all Inspection reports supporting Buyer's written requests. Seller shall make Property available for all Inspections. Seller shall have water, gas and electricity on for Buyer's Inspections and through the date possession is made available to Buyer.

10. **REPAIRS:** Repairs shall be completed prior to final verification of condition unless otherwise agreed in writing. Repairs to be performed at Seller's expense may be performed by Seller or through others, provided that work complies with applicable Law, including governmental permit, inspection and approval requirements. Repairs shall be performed in a skillful manner with materials of quality and appearance comparable to existing materials. It is understood that exact restoration of appearance or cosmetic items following all Repairs may not be possible. Seller shall: (i) obtain receipts for Repairs performed by others; (ii) prepare a written statement indicating the Repairs performed by Seller and the date of such Repairs; and (iii) provide Copies of receipts and statements to Buyer prior to final verification of condition.

11. **BUYER INDEMNITY AND SELLER PROTECTION FOR ENTRY UPON PROPERTY:** Buyer shall: (i) keep Property free and clear of liens; (ii) indemnify and hold Seller harmless from all liability, claims, demands, damages and costs; and (iii) Repair all damages arising from Inspections. Buyer shall carry, or Buyer shall require anyone acting on Buyer's behalf to carry, policies of liability, workers' compensation, and other applicable insurance, defending and protecting Seller from liability for any injuries to persons or property occurring during any inspections or work done on the Property at Buyer's direction prior to Close Of Escrow. Seller is advised that certain protections may be afforded Seller by recording a Notice of Non-responsibility for Inspections and work done on the Property at Buyer's direction.

12. **TITLE AND VESTING:**
    A. Within the time specified in paragraph 14, Buyer shall be provided a current preliminary (title) report, which is only an offer by the title insurer to issue a policy of title insurance, and may not contain every item affecting title. Buyer shall provide written notice to Seller in accordance with and within the time specified in paragraph 14.
    B. At Close Of Escrow, Buyer shall receive a grant deed conveying title (or, for stock cooperative or long-term lease, an assignment of stock certificate or of Seller's leasehold interest), including oil, mineral and water rights if currently owned by Seller. Title shall be subject to all encumbrances, easements, covenants, conditions, restrictions, rights and other matters that are of record or disclosed to Buyer prior to Close Of Escrow, unless otherwise requested in writing by Buyer and agreed to by Seller within the time specified in paragraph 14. However, title shall not be subject to any liens against the Property, except for those specified in this Agreement. Title shall vest as designated in Buyer's supplemental escrow instructions. THE MANNER OF TAKING TITLE MAY HAVE SIGNIFICANT LEGAL AND TAX CONSEQUENCES.
    C. Buyer shall receive a CLTA/ALTA Homeowner's Policy of Title Insurance, if available for the Property. If not, Buyer shall receive a standard coverage owner's policy (CLTA or ALTA-R with regional exceptions). A title company, at Buyer's request, can provide information about availability, desirability, coverage, and cost of various title insurance coverages and indorsements. If Buyer desires title coverage other than that required by this paragraph, Buyer shall instruct Escrow Holder in writing and pay any increase in costs.

13. **SALE OF BUYER'S PROPERTY:**
    A. This Agreement is NOT contingent upon the sale of any property owned by Buyer unless paragraph 13B is checked.
    OR B. ☐ (If checked) This Agreement IS CONTINGENT on the Close Of Escrow of Buyer's property, described as (address) _____ ("Buyer's Property").
    (1) Buyer's Property is:
        (a) ☐ (if checked) not yet listed for sale.
        OR (b) ☐ (if checked) listed for sale with _____ company.
        OR (c) ☐ (if checked) in escrow No. _____ with _____ escrow holder, scheduled to close escrow on _____ (date). Buyer shall deliver to Seller, within **5 Days** After Seller's request, a Copy of the contract for the sale of Buyer's Property, escrow instructions, and all amendments and modifications thereto. If Buyer fails to provide the documents within that time, Seller may cancel this Agreement in writing. If Buyer's Property does not close escrow by the date specified in this paragraph for close of escrow of Buyer's Property, then either Seller or Buyer may cancel this Agreement in writing.
    (2) After Acceptance:
        (a) **(Applies UNLESS B (2)(b) is checked):** Seller SHALL have the right to continue to offer the Property for sale. If Seller accepts another written offer, Seller shall give Buyer written notice to: (i) remove this contingency in writing; (ii) **remove the loan contingency, if any, in writing;** and (iii) comply with the following additional requirement(s): _____.
        If Buyer fails to complete these actions within **72 (or ☐___) hours** After receipt of such notice, Seller may cancel this Agreement in writing.
        OR (b) ☐ (if checked) Seller shall have the right to continue to offer the Property for sale for back-up offers only and shall not invoke the notice provisions in paragraph 13 B(2)(a) during the term of this Agreement.

Buyer and Seller acknowledge receipt of a copy of this page.
Buyer's Initials (_____)(_____)
Seller's Initials (_____)(_____)

EQUAL HOUSING OPPORTUNITY

Reviewed by _____
Broker or Designee _____ Date _____

REVISION DATE 10/2000   Print Date
RPA-11 (PAGE 4 OF 8)

RESIDENTIAL PURCHASE AGREEMENT (RPA-11 PAGE 4 OF 8)

FIGURE 6.3 (continued)

Residential Purchase Agreement and Joint Escrow Instructions (and receipt for deposit)

Property Address: _____   Date: _____

14. **TIME PERIODS;REMOVAL OF CONTINGENCIES;CANCELLATION RIGHTS: The following time periods may only be extended, altered, modified or changed by mutual written agreement.**
   A. **ORDERING, COMPLETING AND REVIEWING INSPECTIONS AND REPORTS:**
      (1) **SELLER HAS: 5 (or ☐ _____) Days** After Acceptance to order, request or complete all reports, disclosures and information for which Seller is responsible under paragraphs 4, 5, 6A, B and C, and 12. Seller has **2 Days** After receipt (or completion) of any of these items to provide it to Buyer. **Buyer** has **5** (or ☐ _____) **Days** After receipt of **(i)** each of the above items and **(ii)** notice of code and legal violation under paragraph 6D to review the report, disclosure or other information.
      (2) **BUYER HAS: 14 (or ☐ _____) Days** After Acceptance to complete all Inspections, investigations and review of reports and other applicable information, including the sex offender database (paragraph 6E), for which Buyer is responsible.
      (3) **BUYER HAS: 10 (or ☐ _____) Days** After Buyer's receipt of Lead Disclosures pursuant to paragraph 5A, to complete Inspections for and review reports on lead-based paint and lead-based paint hazards.
   B. (1) **APPROVAL OR REQUEST:** Within the times specified above (or 2G for loan contingency), Buyer shall provide Seller with either **(i)** an unconditional approval and removal of the applicable contingency, or **(ii)** a reasonable written request that Seller Repair or take other action (or for loan contingency, cancellation if Buyer is unable to obtain the designated loan).
      (2) **EFFECT OF BUYER'S REQUEST:** If, pursuant to B(1), Buyer reasonably requests that Seller Repair or take other action, Buyer and Seller have **5** (or ☐ _____) **Days** After Seller's receipt of Buyer's request to reach mutual written agreement on Buyer's request. If **(i)** Seller has agreed in writing to unconditionally and completely take the action requested by Buyer, or **(ii)** Buyer and Seller have reached a mutual written agreement with respect to those items, then the transaction shall proceed on those terms. Seller has no obligation, express or implied, to satisfy Buyer's requests.
      (3) **EFFECT OF NO WRITTEN AGREEMENT ON BUYER'S REQUESTS:** If, at the expiration of the time in B(2), neither B(2)**(i)** nor **(ii)** has occurred, Buyer has **2** (or ☐ _____) **Days** to cancel this Agreement in writing.
   C. **ACTIVE OR PASSIVE REMOVAL OF CONTINGENCIES AND CANCELLATION RIGHTS:**
      (1) ☐ **ACTIVE METHOD** (Applies only if checked):
         (a) **(No written request or removal by Buyer)** If, within the time specified in A, Buyer does not give Seller written notice pursuant to B(1), Seller may cancel this Agreement in writing. Notwithstanding the expiration of the time specified, Buyer retains the right to give Seller written notice under B1 at any time prior to receiving Seller's written cancellation. Once Seller receives Buyer's written request or removal, Seller may not cancel this Agreement pursuant to paragraph C(1)(a).
         (b) **(No written cancellation by Buyer)** If, within the time specified, Buyer does not give Seller written notice of cancellation pursuant to B(3), either Buyer or Seller may cancel this Agreement in writing at any time prior to Buyer and Seller reaching mutual written agreement with respect to any requests made pursuant to B(1).
      (2) **PASSIVE METHOD:** If, within the time specified, Buyer does not give Seller **(i)** a reasonable written request pursuant to B(1) (or for loan contingency, cancellation if Buyer is unable to obtain the designated loan) or **(ii)** written notice of cancellation pursuant to B(3) if no agreement is reached on Buyer's requests, then Buyer shall be deemed, as applicable, to have unconditionally approved and removed the contingency or withdrawn the request and waived any right to cancel associated with the requested item.
   D. **EFFECT OF REMOVAL:** If Buyer removes any contingency or cancellation right by the active or passive method, as applicable, Buyer shall conclusively be deemed to have: **(i)** completed all Inspections, investigations, and review of reports and other applicable information and disclosures pertaining to that contingency or cancellation right; **(ii)** elected to proceed with the transaction; and, **(iii)** assumed all liability, responsibility, and expense for repairs or corrections pertaining to that contingency or cancellation right, or for inability to obtain financing if the contingency pertains to financing, unless, pursuant to B(2) or elsewhere in this Agreement, Seller agrees to make Repairs or take other action.
   E. **EFFECT OF CANCELLATION ON DEPOSITS:** If Buyer or Seller gives written NOTICE OF CANCELLATION pursuant to rights duly exercised under the terms of this Agreement, Buyer and Seller agree to Sign mutual instructions to cancel the sale and escrow and release deposits, less fees and costs, to the party entitled to the funds. Fees and costs may be payable to service providers and vendors for services and products provided during escrow. **Release of funds will require mutual, Signed release instructions from Buyer and Seller, judicial decision or arbitration award. A party may be subject to a civil penalty of up to $1,000 for refusal to sign such instructions if no good faith dispute exists as to who is entitled to the deposited funds (Civil Code §1057.3).**
15. **FINAL VERIFICATION OF CONDITION:** Buyer shall have the right to make a final inspection of the Property within **5 (or _____) Days** prior to Close Of Escrow, NOT AS A CONTINGENCY OF THE SALE, but solely to confirm **(i)** Property is maintained pursuant to paragraph 7A, **(ii)** Repairs have been completed as agreed, and **(iii)** Seller has complied with Seller's other obligations.
16. **LIQUIDATED DAMAGES: If Buyer fails to complete this purchase because of Buyer's default, Seller shall retain, as liquidated damages, the deposit actually paid. If the Property is a dwelling with no more than four units, one of which Buyer intends to occupy, then the amount retained shall be no more than 3% of the purchase price. Any excess shall be returned to Buyer. Release of funds will require mutual, Signed release instructions from both Buyer and Seller, judicial decision or arbitration award.**
   BUYER AND SELLER SHALL SIGN A SEPARATE LIQUIDATED DAMAGES PROVISION FOR ANY INCREASED DEPOSIT. (C.A.R. FORM RID-11)

Buyer's Initials _____/_____	Seller's Initials _____/_____

REVISION DATE 10/2000   Print Date
RPA-11 (PAGE 5 OF 8)

Buyer and Seller acknowledge receipt of a copy of this page.

Buyer's Initials (_____)(_____)
Seller's Initials (_____)(_____)

EQUAL HOUSING OPPORTUNITY

Reviewed by
Broker or Designee _____ Date _____

RESIDENTIAL PURCHASE AGREEMENT (RPA-11 PAGE 5 OF 8)

FIGURE 6.3 (continued)

Residential Purchase Agreement and Joint Escrow Instructions (and receipt for deposit)

Property Address: _____ Date: _____

17. DISPUTE RESOLUTION:

A. MEDIATION: Buyer and Seller agree to mediate any dispute or claim arising between them out of this Agreement, or any resulting transaction, before resorting to arbitration or court action. Paragraphs 17B(2) and (3) below apply whether or not the Arbitration provision is initialed. Mediation fees, if any, shall be divided equally among the parties involved. If, for any dispute or claim to which this paragraph applies, any party commences an action without first attempting to resolve the matter through mediation, or refuses to mediate after a request has been made, then that party shall not be entitled to recover attorney fees, even if they would otherwise be available to that party in any such action. THIS MEDIATION PROVISION APPLIES WHETHER OR NOT THE ARBITRATION PROVISION IS INITIALED.

B. ARBITRATION OF DISPUTES: (1) Buyer and Seller agree that any dispute or claim in Law or equity arising between them out of this Agreement or any resulting transaction, which is not settled through mediation, shall be decided by neutral, binding arbitration, including and subject to paragraphs 17B(2) and (3) below. The arbitrator shall be a retired judge or justice, or an attorney with at least 5 years of residential real estate Law experience, unless the parties mutually agree to a different arbitrator, who shall render an award in accordance with substantive California Law. In all other respects, the arbitration shall be conducted in accordance with Part III, Title 9 of the California Code of Civil Procedure. Judgment upon the award of the arbitrator(s) may be entered in any court having jurisdiction. The parties shall have the right to discovery in accordance with Code of Civil Procedure §1283.05.

(2) EXCLUSIONS FROM MEDIATION AND ARBITRATION: The following matters are excluded from mediation and arbitration: **(i)** a judicial or non-judicial foreclosure or other action or proceeding to enforce a deed of trust, mortgage, or installment land sale contract as defined in Civil Code §2985; **(ii)** an unlawful detainer action; **(iii)** the filing or enforcement of a mechanic's lien; **(iv)** any matter that is within the jurisdiction of a probate, small claims, or bankruptcy court; and **(v)** an action for bodily injury or wrongful death, or any right of action to which Code of Civil Procedure §337.1 or §337.15 applies. The filing of a court action to enable the recording of a notice of pending action, for order of attachment, receivership, injunction, or other provisional remedies, shall not constitute a violation of the mediation and arbitration provisions.

(3) BROKERS: Buyer and Seller agree to mediate and arbitrate disputes or claims involving either or both Brokers, provided either or both Brokers shall have agreed to such mediation or arbitration prior to, or within a reasonable time after, the dispute or claim is presented to Brokers. Any election by either or both Brokers to participate in mediation or arbitration shall not result in Brokers being deemed parties to the Agreement.

"NOTICE: BY INITIALING IN THE SPACE BELOW YOU ARE AGREEING TO HAVE ANY DISPUTE ARISING OUT OF THE MATTERS INCLUDED IN THE 'ARBITRATION OF DISPUTES' PROVISION DECIDED BY NEUTRAL ARBITRATION AS PROVIDED BY CALIFORNIA LAW AND YOU ARE GIVING UP ANY RIGHTS YOU MIGHT POSSESS TO HAVE THE DISPUTE LITIGATED IN A COURT OR JURY TRIAL. BY INITIALING IN THE SPACE BELOW YOU ARE GIVING UP YOUR JUDICIAL RIGHTS TO DISCOVERY AND APPEAL, UNLESS THOSE RIGHTS ARE SPECIFICALLY INCLUDED IN THE 'ARBITRATION OF DISPUTES' PROVISION. IF YOU REFUSE TO SUBMIT TO ARBITRATION AFTER AGREEING TO THIS PROVISION, YOU MAY BE COMPELLED TO ARBITRATE UNDER THE AUTHORITY OF THE CALIFORNIA CODE OF CIVIL PROCEDURE. YOUR AGREEMENT TO THIS ARBITRATION PROVISION IS VOLUNTARY."

"WE HAVE READ AND UNDERSTAND THE FOREGOING AND AGREE TO SUBMIT DISPUTES ARISING OUT OF THE MATTERS INCLUDED IN THE 'ARBITRATION OF DISPUTES' PROVISION TO NEUTRAL ARBITRATION."

Buyer's Initials _____ / _____   Seller's Initials _____ / _____

18. PRORATIONS OF PROPERTY TAXES AND OTHER ITEMS: Unless otherwise agreed in writing, the following items shall be PAID CURRENT and prorated between Buyer and Seller as of Close Of Escrow: real property taxes and assessments, interest, rents, HOA regular, special, and emergency dues and assessments imposed prior to Close Of Escrow, premiums on insurance assumed by Buyer, payments on bonds and assessments assumed by Buyer, and payments on Mello-Roos and other Special Assessment District bonds and assessments that are now a lien. The following items shall be assumed by Buyer WITHOUT CREDIT toward the purchase price: prorated payments on Mello-Roos and other Special Assessment District bonds and assessments and HOA special assessments that are now a lien but not yet due. Property will be reassessed upon change of ownership. Any supplemental tax bills shall be paid as follows: **(i)** for periods after Close Of Escrow, by Buyer; and, **(ii)** for periods prior to Close Of Escrow, by Seller. TAX BILLS ISSUED AFTER CLOSE OF ESCROW SHALL BE HANDLED DIRECTLY BETWEEN BUYER AND SELLER. Prorations shall be made based on a 30-day month.

19. WITHHOLDING TAXES: Seller and Buyer agree to execute any instrument, affidavit, statement or instruction reasonably necessary to comply with federal (FIRPTA) and California withholding Law, if required (C.A.R. Forms AS-11 and AB-11).

20. MULTIPLE LISTING SERVICE ("MLS"): Brokers are authorized to report the terms of this transaction to any MLS, to be published and disseminated to persons and entities authorized to use the information on terms approved by the MLS.

21. EQUAL HOUSING OPPORTUNITY: The Property is sold in compliance with federal, state and local anti-discrimination Law.

22. ATTORNEY FEES: In any action, proceeding, or arbitration between Buyer and Seller arising out of this Agreement, the prevailing Buyer or Seller shall be entitled to reasonable attorney fees and costs from the non-prevailing Buyer or Seller, except as provided in paragraph 17A.

23. SELECTION OF SERVICE PROVIDERS: If Brokers give Buyer or Seller referrals to persons, vendors, or service or product providers ("Providers"), Brokers do not guarantee the performance of any of those Providers. Buyer and Seller may select ANY Providers of their own choosing.

REVISION DATE 10/2000   Print Date
RPA-11 (PAGE 6 OF 8)

Buyer and Seller acknowledge receipt of a copy of this page.
Buyer's Initials (_____)(_____)
Seller's Initials (_____)(_____)
Reviewed by
Broker or Designee _____ Date _____

RESIDENTIAL PURCHASE AGREEMENT (RPA-11 PAGE 6 OF 8)

Residential Purchase Agreement and Joint Escrow Instructions (and receipt for deposit)

Property Address: _____   Date: _____

24. TIME OF ESSENCE; ENTIRE CONTRACT; CHANGES: Time is of the essence. All understandings between the parties are incorporated in this Agreement. Its terms are intended by the parties as a final, complete and exclusive expression of their Agreement with respect to its subject matter, and may not be contradicted by evidence of any prior agreement or contemporaneous oral agreement. If any provision of this Agreement is held to be ineffective or invalid, the remaining provisions will nevertheless be given full force and effect. **Neither this Agreement nor any provision in it may be extended, amended, modified, altered or changed, except in writing Signed by Buyer and Seller.**

25. OTHER TERMS AND CONDITIONS, including ATTACHED SUPPLEMENTS:
    A. ☑ Buyer's Inspection Advisory (C.A.R. Form BIA-11)
    B. ☐ Purchase Agreement Addendum (C.A.R. Form PAA-11 paragraph numbers: _____)
    C. _____
    _____
    _____

26. DEFINITIONS: As used in this Agreement:
    A. **"Acceptance"** means the time the offer or final counter offer is accepted in writing by the other party and communicated in accordance with this Agreement or the terms of the final counter offer.
    B. **"Agreement"** means the terms and conditions of this Residential Purchase Agreement and any counter offer and addenda.
    C. **"Days"** means calendar days, unless otherwise required by Law.
    D. **"Days After"** means the specified number of calendar days after the occurrence of the event specified, not counting the calendar date on which the specified event occurs, and ending at 11:59PM on the final day.
    E. **"Close Of Escrow"** means the date the grant deed, or other evidence of transfer of title, is recorded. If scheduled close of escrow falls on a Saturday, Sunday or legal holiday, then the close of escrow date shall be the next business day after the scheduled close of escrow date.
    F. **"Copy"** means copy by any means including photocopy, NCR, facsimile and electronic.
    G. **"Law"** means any law, code, statute, ordinance, regulation, rule or order, which is adopted by a controlling city, county, state or federal legislative, judicial or executive body or agency.
    H. **"Repairs"** means any repairs (including pest control), alterations, replacements, modifications and retrofitting of the Property provided for under this Agreement.
    I. **"Signed"** means either a handwritten or electronic signature.
    J. **Singular and Plural** terms each include the other, when appropriate.
    K. **C.A.R. Form** means the specific form referenced, or another comparable form agreed to by the parties.
    L. **"Electronic Copy" or "Electronic Signature"** means, as applicable, an electronic copy or signature complying with California Law. Buyer and Seller agree that electronic means will not be used by either one to modify or alter the content or integrity of the Agreement without the knowledge and consent of the other.

27. AGENCY:
    A. **POTENTIALLY COMPETING BUYERS AND SELLERS:** Buyer understands that Broker representing Buyer may also represent other potential buyers, who may consider, make offers on or ultimately acquire this Property. Seller understands that Buyer may consider, make offers on or purchase other properties similar to the Property. Buyer and Seller acknowledge and consent to Broker(s)' representation of such potential buyers and sellers before, during and after Broker(s)' representation of Buyer and Seller.
    B. **CONFIRMATION:** The following agency relationships are hereby confirmed for this transaction:
    Listing Agent _____ (Print Firm Name) is the agent of (check one):
    ☐ the Seller exclusively; or ☐ both the Buyer and Seller.
    Selling Agent _____ (Print Firm Name) (if not same as Listing Agent) is the agent of (check one): ☐ the Buyer exclusively; or ☐ the Seller exclusively; or ☐ both the Buyer and Seller.
    Real Estate Brokers are not parties to the Agreement between Buyer and Seller.

28. JOINT ESCROW INSTRUCTIONS TO ESCROW HOLDER:
    A. **The following paragraphs, or applicable portions thereof, of this Agreement constitute the joint escrow instructions** of Buyer and Seller to Escrow Holder, which Escrow Holder is to use along with any relating counter offers and addenda, and any additional mutual instructions to close the transaction: 1, 2, 4, 12, 13B, 14E, 18, 19, 24, 25B and C, 26, 28, 30, 32A and 33. The terms and conditions of the Agreement not set forth in the specified paragraphs are additional matters for the information of Escrow Holder, but about which Escrow Holder need not be concerned. Buyer and Seller will receive Escrow Holder's general provisions directly from Escrow Holder and will execute such provisions upon Escrow Holder's request. To the extent the general provisions are inconsistent or conflict with this Agreement, the general provisions will control as to the duties and obligations of Escrow Holder only. Buyer and Seller will execute additional instructions, documents and forms provided by Escrow Holder that are reasonably necessary to complete this transaction.
    B. A Copy of this Agreement shall be delivered to Escrow Holder within 3 business days After Acceptance (or ☐ _____). **Escrow will be deemed open when Escrow Holder has Signed an acknowledgement of receipt of a Copy of this accepted Agreement.** Buyer and Seller authorize Escrow Holder to accept and rely on Copies and Signatures as defined in this Agreement as originals, to open escrow and for other purposes of escrow. The validity of this Agreement as between Buyer and Seller is not affected by whether or when Escrow Holder Signs the Agreement.
    C. Brokers are a party to the Escrow for the sole purpose of compensation pursuant to paragraphs 30 and 32A. Buyer and Seller irrevocably assign to Brokers compensation specified, respectively, in paragraphs 30 and 32A and irrevocably instruct Escrow Holder to disburse those funds to Brokers at Close Of Escrow. Compensation instructions can be amended or revoked only with the written consent of Brokers.

29. Buyer and Seller acknowledge and agree that : (a) Brokers do not decide what price Buyer should pay or Seller should accept; (b) Brokers do not guarantee the performance or Repairs of others who have provided services or products to Buyer or Seller; and (c) they will seek legal, tax, insurance, title and other desired assistance from appropriate professionals.

Buyer and Seller acknowledge receipt of a copy of this page.
    Buyer's Initials (_____)(_____)
    Seller's Initials (_____)(_____)

EQUAL HOUSING OPPORTUNITY

REVISION DATE 10/2000   **Print Date**
RPA-11 (PAGE 7 OF 8)

Reviewed by _____
Broker or Designee _____ Date _____

FIGURE 6.3 (continued)

**Residential Purchase
Agreement and Joint
Escrow Instructions (and
receipt for deposit)**

Property Address: _____ Date: _____

30. BROKER COMPENSATION FROM BUYER: Upon Close Of Escrow, **Buyer** agrees to pay compensation for services as follows:
_____ to _____, Broker.

31. TERMS AND CONDITIONS OF OFFER: This is an offer to purchase the Property on the above terms and conditions. All paragraphs with spaces for initials by Buyer and Seller are incorporated in this Agreement only if initialed by all parties. If at least one but not all parties initial, a counter offer is required until agreement is reached. Unless Acceptance of offer is Signed by Seller, and a Copy of the Signed offer is personally received by Buyer, or by _____, who is authorized to receive it, by (date) _____, at _____ AM/PM, the offer shall be deemed revoked and the deposit shall be returned. Seller has the right to continue to offer the Property for sale and to accept any other offer at any time prior to communication of Acceptance as above. Buyer has read and acknowledges receipt of a Copy of the offer and agrees to the above confirmation of agency relationships. If this offer is accepted and Buyer subsequently defaults, Buyer may be responsible for payment of Brokers' compensation. This Agreement and any supplement, addendum or modification, including any Copy, may be Signed in two or more counterparts, all of which shall constitute one and the same writing.

BUYER _____ Date_____ BUYER _____ Date_____
_____
(Print name)   **(Print name)**
_____
(Address)

32. BROKER COMPENSATION FROM SELLER:
 A. Upon Close of Escrow, **Seller** agrees to pay compensation for services as follows:
 _____, to _____, Broker, and
 _____, to _____, Broker, and
 (if checked) ☐ an administrative/transaction fee of $_____ to _____ Broker
 (or, if not completed, as per listing agreement).
 B. (1) If escrow does not close, compensation in 32A is payable: **(i)** upon Seller's default if completion of sale is prevented by default of Seller; or **(ii)** when and if Seller collects damages from Buyer, by suit or otherwise, if completion of sale is prevented by default of Buyer and then in an amount equal to one-half of the damages recovered, but not to exceed the above compensation, after first deducting title and escrow expenses and the expenses of collection, if any. **(2)** In any action, proceeding or arbitration relating to the payment of compensation in 32A or B, the prevailing party shall be entitled to reasonable attorney' fees and costs, except as provided in paragraph 17A.

33. ACCEPTANCE OF OFFER: Seller warrants that Seller is the owner of this Property, or has the authority to execute this Agreement. Seller accepts the above offer, agrees to sell the Property on the above terms and conditions, and agrees to the above confirmation of agency relationships. Seller has read and acknowledges receipt of a Copy of this Agreement, and authorizes Broker to deliver a Signed Copy to Buyer.
 ☐ (If checked) **SUBJECT TO ATTACHED COUNTER OFFER, DATED** _____.

SELLER _____ Date_____ SELLER _____ Date_____
_____
(Print name)   **(Print name)**
_____
(Address)

Agency relationships are confirmed as above. Real Estate Brokers are not parties to the Agreement between Buyer and Seller.

Agent who submitted offer for Buyer acknowledges receipt of deposit, if any, if specified in paragraph 2A:

Real Estate Broker (Selling Firm Name) _____ By _____ Date _____
Address _____ Phone/Fax/E-mail _____
Real Estate Broker (Listing Firm Name) _____ By _____ Date _____
Address _____ Phone/Fax/E-mail _____

(_____/_____) **ACKNOWLEDGMENT OF RECEIPT:** Buyer or authorized agent acknowledges receipt of Signed Acceptance on (date) _____,
 (Initials)   at _____ AM/PM.

Escrow Holder Acknowledgment:
Escrow Holder acknowledges receipt of a Copy of this Agreement, (if checked, ☐ a deposit in the amount of $_____),
counter offer numbers _____ and _____, and agrees to act as Escrow Holder subject to paragraph 28 of this Agreement, any supplemental escrow instructions and the terms of Escrow Holder's general provisions.

The date of communication of Acceptance of the Agreement as between Buyer and Seller is _____.

Escrow Holder _____ Escrow # _____
By _____ Date _____
Address _____ Phone/Fax/E-mail _____
Escrow Holder is licensed by the California Department of ☐ Corporations, ☐ Insurance, ☐ Real Estate. License # _____

THIS FORM HAS BEEN APPROVED BY THE CALIFORNIA ASSOCIATION OF REALTORS® (C.A.R.). NO REPRESENTATION IS MADE AS TO THE LEGAL VALIDITY OR ADEQUACY OF ANY PROVISION IN ANY SPECIFIC TRANSACTION. A REAL ESTATE BROKER IS THE PERSON QUALIFIED TO ADVISE ON REAL ESTATE TRANSACTIONS. IF YOU DESIRE LEGAL OR TAX ADVICE, CONSULT AN APPROPRIATE PROFESSIONAL.

This form is available for use by the entire real estate industry. It is not intended to identify the user as a REALTOR®. REALTOR® is a registered collective membership mark which may be used only by members of the NATIONAL ASSOCIATION OF REALTORS® who subscribe to its Code of Ethics.

Published and Distributed by:
REAL ESTATE BUSINESS SERVICES, INC.
a subsidiary of the CALIFORNIA ASSOCIATION OF REALTORS®
525 South Virgil Avenue, Los Angeles, California 90020

Reviewed by _____
Broker or Designee _____ Date _____

REVISION DATE 10/2000 Print Date
RPA-11 (PAGE 8 OF 8)

RESIDENTIAL PURCHASE AGREEMENT (RPA-11 PAGE 8 OF 8)

Paragraph 11: Provides that buyer shall keep property free of liens and hold seller harmless for liability from claims relating to buyer entry for inspection or work prior to close of escrow.

Paragraph 12: Provides that buyer shall receive a grant deed and homeowner policy of title insurance.

Paragraph 13: By checking the appropriate block, the offer is either contingent upon the sale of another property or there is no such contingency. If there is a contingency, seller may have right to offer property for sale and give buyer opportunity to remove the contingency if seller accepts another offer.

Paragraph 14: Provides time periods for removal of contingencies as well as cancellation rights. In the event of cancellation, release of funds requires mutual agreement. If a party refuses to release funds when there is no good-faith dispute, the party may be subject to $1,000 in civil damages.

Paragraph 15: Provides for a final inspection of property prior to close of escrow to determine if property has been maintained and that seller has completed agreed repairs and complied with other obligations.

Paragraph 16: Limits liquidated damages to three percent of purchase price in the event of buyer default. The limitation only applies where buyer intended to occupy premises as a principal residence and both parties initialed this paragraph.

Paragraph 17: The parties agree to mediate any dispute arising from this agreement. Dispute involving brokers shall be mediated if brokers agree to mediation. By initiating the arbitration clause, parties agree to give up their rights for court litigation and agree to arbitration of disputes if mediation was not successful.

Paragraph 18: Provides that taxes and assessments will be paid current and prorated.

Paragraph 19: Applies to tax withholding in some situations where seller is a foreign national (Foreign Investment in Real Property Tax Act—FIRPTA—and CAL FIRPTA) or the property was not the seller's residence.

Paragraph 20: Allows for broker reporting of sale terms to an MLS service. Without this authorization, such reporting could be a breach of agent's duty of confidentiality.

Paragraph 21: Asserts that the sale is in compliance with fair housing laws.

Paragraph 22: Provides that in the event of any legal action or arbitration, the prevailing party shall be entitled to reasonable attorney fees (this paragraph also serves to reduce the likelihood of frivolous lawsuits).

Paragraph 23: Provides that broker referral of service providers does not guarantee the performance of the service providers and parties are free to select providers of their own choosing.

Paragraph 24: Provides that time is of the essence for all performance, that this agreement is the final expression of this agreement and may not be contradicted by prior or contemporaneous oral agreement, and that if any portion is invalid, the remaining portions remain valid. Extension modifications, alterations, and changes require the signature of both buyer and seller.

Paragraph 25: Provides for other terms and conditions including Buyer's Inspection Advisory.

Paragraph 26: Provides definition of terms used.

Paragraph 27: Includes a final agency confirmation.

Paragraph 28: Provides that applicable portions of the agreement shall constitute joint escrow instructions.

Paragraph 29: Provides that buyers and sellers, not brokers, determine price to be offered or accepted and that brokers do not guarantee performance of repairs or service providers. Buyer and seller should seek legal, tax, insurance, and title information from professionals.

Paragraph 30: Provides for broker compensation from buyer (where broker represents buyer).

Paragraph 31: Reiterates that this is an offer to purchase and sets time period for acceptance. Buyer acknowledges reading and receiving copy of the agreement as well as agreeing to agency confirmation.

Paragraph 32: Provides for broker compensation from seller if the sale is completed as well as when seller fails to close.

Paragraph 33: This is the acceptance of the offer and may provide for a counteroffer.

The CAR form provides for the final agreement on the amount of the commission. If the amount stated in the purchase contract is different from that provided by the listing, the purchase agreement will govern because it was entered into at a later date.

If the listing does not provide for a commission, signing the purchase contract authorizing the commission will satisfy the statute of frauds.

If neither the listing agreement nor the purchase contract authorizes a commission, the signing of escrow instructions providing for the seller (or buyer) to pay a commission probably will satisfy the statute of frauds and entitle the agent to the commission.

If a purchase offer fails to provide a period for acceptance, the offer will terminate after the expiration of a "reasonable period of time." Because an offeror normally does not receive consideration to keep an offer open, the offer can be withdrawn by the offeror any time prior to acceptance even if the offeror agreed to keep the offer open for a stated period of time.

Additions to the Purchase Agreement

Contingencies.   Offers to purchase often are contingent on something happening, such as receiving an appraisal for a stated amount or more, obtaining a loan to stated specifications, or even selling another property. The most common contingency is an offer contingent on financing.

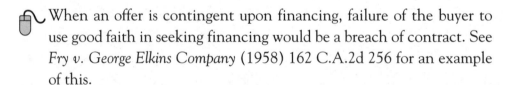 When an offer is contingent upon financing, failure of the buyer to use good faith in seeking financing would be a breach of contract. See *Fry v. George Elkins Company* (1958) 162 C.A.2d 256 for an example of this.

Contingencies can tie up a property for months. Rather than accept an offer with a contingency, the seller would be in a better position if he or she agreed to the Contingency Supplement/Addendum shown in Figure 6.4. This addendum allows the seller to continue to offer the property. A subsequent offer could be accepted conditioned on the original buyer's waiving his or her contingency within a stated period of time. If the original buyer fails to waive the contingency, his or her offer becomes null and void and the deposit is returned.

A notice should be provided to a buyer to remove and waive contingencies when a Contingency Supplement/Addendum is used. This notice provides that failure to remove the contingencies in the time authorized will result in the termination of all of the buyer's rights, and any agreement shall become null and void, but the deposit shall be returned to the buyer.

FIGURE 6.4

**Contingency Supplement/
Addendum**

CALIFORNIA
ASSOCIATION
OF REALTORS®

CONTINGENCY SUPPLEMENT/ADDENDUM
(TERMS OF CONTINGENCY, NOTICE TO REMOVE CONTINGENCY,
AND REMOVAL OF CONTINGENCY)

TERMS OF CONTINGENCY

The following terms and conditions are hereby incorporated and made a part of the: ☐ Residential Purchase Agreement and Joint Escrow Instructions, ☐ Manufactured Home Purchase Agreement and Receipt for Deposit, ☐ Business Purchase Agreement and Receipt for Deposit, ☐ Other _____ dated _____, on property known as _____ ("Property"), between _____ _____, ("Buyer"), and _____, ("Seller").

A1. Seller has the right to continue to offer the Property for sale.

A2. In the event Seller accepts another written offer, Seller shall deliver a written **NOTICE TO REMOVE** the following contingency(s):
_____
_____
_____
_____

A3. Other requirements at time of removal: _____
_____
_____

A4. **NOTICE TO REMOVE** shall be deemed delivered when personally received by Buyer or _____, who is authorized to receive it. Delivery may be in person, by mail, or facsimile. If by certified mail, delivery shall be deemed to have occurred three (3) calendar days after date of certified U.S. postal mailing receipt, even if personal receipt has not occurred.

A5. Buyer shall deliver to Seller, a written **REMOVAL OF CONTINGENCY(S)** within ☐ _____ hours or ☐ _____ calendar days from receipt of Notice to Remove. In the event Buyer fails to remove the contingency(s) and comply with the requirements in paragraph A3, within the time limit specified, the purchase contract and escrow shall terminate and the deposit shall be returned to Buyer. (Funds deposited in trust accounts or in escrow are not released automatically. Release of funds requires written agreement of the parties, judicial decision or arbitration.)

A6. The contingency(s) in paragraph A2 shall be effective until Close of Escrow, or the time specified in paragraph A5, or _____, whichever occurs first.

The undersigned acknowledge receipt of a copy of this page.

Date _____   Date _____
Buyer _____   Seller _____
Buyer _____   Seller _____

NOTICE TO REMOVE CONTINGENCY(S)

B1. Buyer is hereby notified that Seller has accepted a written offer conditioned upon Buyer's rights to remove the contingency(s) in paragraph A2.

B2. Buyer must remove all contingency(s) in paragraph A2 and meet the other requirements in paragraph A3 within the time specified in paragraph A5. In the event Buyer fails to remove the contingency(s) and comply with the requirements in paragraph A3, within the time limit specified, the purchase contract and escrow shall terminate and the deposit shall be returned to Buyer. (Funds deposited in trust accounts or in escrow are not released automatically. Release of funds requires written agreement of the parties, judicial decision or arbitration.)

Date _____   Seller _____
                                          Seller _____

Receipt of this notice on _____ (date) at _____ AM/PM by Buyer _____ or person authorized by Buyer to receive it
_____ is acknowledged.   Initials
Initials

REMOVAL OF CONTINGENCY

C1. Buyer removes all of the contingencies in paragraph A2 and has satisfied the requirements to be met by Buyer under paragraph A3.

Date _____   Buyer _____
Time _____   Buyer _____

RECEIPT BY SELLER

Receipt of a copy of the above Removal of Contingency(s) is hereby acknowledged.

Date _____   Seller _____
Time _____   Seller _____

R E B S
I N C

Published and Distributed by:
REAL ESTATE BUSINESS SERVICES, INC.
a subsidiary of the CALIFORNIA ASSOCIATION OF REALTORS®
525 South Virgil Avenue, Los Angeles, California 90020

Reviewed by _____
Broker or Designee _____ Date _____

EQUAL HOUSING
OPPORTUNITY

REVISION DATE 10/2000   Print Date
CS-11 (PAGE 1 OF 1)

CONTINGENCY SUPPLEMENT/ADDENDUM (CS-11 PAGE 1 OF 1)

A contingency can be removed by signing the removal on the Contingency Supplement/Addendum.

The person who benefits from a contingency can always waive the contingency. For example, if an offer were contingent on an appraisal of $100,000 by a lender, the offeror could waive this contingency and go ahead with the purchase if the appraisal came in for a lower amount. The refusal to waive a contingency that cannot be corrected would end the agreement.

Case Study

In *Beverly Way Associates v. Barham* (1990) 226 C.A.3d 49, a buyer of a $3,900,000 apartment building had a purchase agreement that provided the buyer with the contingency to approve specified documents. The ALTA survey showed an electrical room that reduced parking by one space from what had been shown on a tract map. The buyer wrote to the seller, "We reluctantly disapprove of the matters disclosed on the survey and relating to the property." The letter later stated, "Advise as to how you wish to proceed with this transaction." The seller did not answer. The buyer later agreed to waive the objections. When the seller refused to sell, the buyer filed a *lis pendens*, a notice of a pending lawsuit involving a claim involving an interest in a property. The court held that the buyer had a right not to consummate the purchase as long as he acted reasonably. However, once the agreement was rejected, the contract was terminated and the buyer could not later waive his objection, even though the contract lacked a "time is of the essence" clause.

Case Study

An offer provided five days for acceptance in the case of *Sabo v. Fasano* (1984) 154 C.A.3d 502. The offer was accepted on the sixth day. The buyer and seller then opened escrow. The seller later refused to sell, claiming that there was no contract because acceptance came after the five-day period. The court held that in this case the time limit for acceptance was for the benefit of the offeror, not the offeree. The offeror waived the right to object to the late acceptance by opening escrow. Upon the waiver, both buyer and seller were bound to the agreement.

"As Is" Clause

An "as is" clause in a purchase agreement can lead to problems. As discussed in Chapter 3, "as is" generally applies only to patent defects, which are obvious defects, and not to latent or hidden defects known by the seller and/or agent.

A seller who wishes to sell "as is" should make a full disclosure of all defects known to him or her and state that additional defects, which the seller is unaware of, may be found. A seller who is not familiar with the property for any reason (such as occupancy by tenants) should disclose this fact. Doing so puts the purchaser on notice that he or she cannot rely on the very limited knowledge of the seller.

The "as is" clause also should provide a right of the purchaser to inspect the property within a stated number of days and communicate any defects to the seller. The seller then should have the option to cure the defects within a stated period or return the buyer's deposit. The parties also could agree to a change in price, or the purchaser could waive the defect.

If "as is" is to be enforceable as to defects discovered later, full disclosure is important, and the buyer should be given not just the right but also the responsibility to inspect. Commercial property is treated differently from residential property regarding the effect of an "as is" clause. "As is" can protect a commercial seller who fails to disclose defects but is not guilty of fraud or concealment of the defects.

 See *Shapiro v. Hu* (1986) 188 C.A.3d 324 for an example of this.

Interim Occupancy Agreement.   At times a buyer will be given possession prior to closing. It must be fully understood that the buyer's position is as a renter and not a buyer taking early possession.

If a problem such as a defect were to be discovered by the buyer, he or she conceivably could delay closing for many months without payment of rent if he or she were not clearly a renter. Allowing even a few days' early occupancy could create enormous problems.

An **interim occupancy agreement** such as CAR form 10A makes it clear that the buyer is in possession as a renter. If the sale is not completed on its designated date, the form allows a different rental amount. By setting an amount that is fairly high, but not so high as to be regarded as a penalty, the buyer is encouraged not to delay the purchase.

Counteroffer.   As discussed in Chapter 5, an acceptance that varies from the original offer on a material term is considered a counteroffer, which is a rejection of the original offer. California Association of REALTORS® Counter Offer form (CO) can be used as a counter to an offer, an exchange agreement, or even another counteroffer.

When separate forms are signed and dated individually for each counteroffer, the sequence of negotiations can be followed from the records and the final agreement will be clear.

Release of Contract.   The parties to a purchase agreement can agree to release each other from the contract. The agreement could provide for a full return of the deposit to the offeror (a rescission) or forfeiture of the total deposit or partial forfeiture. A release agreement should provide that all further rights and obligations are null and void. California Association of REALTORS® Release of Contract form (RC) is used for this purpose.

Because brokers may have commission rights, they should be parties to release agreements.

Seller Financing Disclosure Statement.   When the seller provides carryback financing on one to four residential units, Section 2956 of the Civil Code requires that a disclosure statement be provided to both buyer and seller. While technically not a contract, it is ordinarily an attachment or addendum to a purchase agreement. California Association of REALTORS® Seller Financing Addendum and Disclosure (SFA) complies with the statutory disclosure requirements.

Estimated Buyer's Costs.   The estimated buyer's cost sheet is similar to a seller's net form and is not a contract. It is a disclosure form to show a buyer the funds needed to complete a transaction. The form can be used for purchase agreements, counteroffers, exchange agreements, or even option agreements. California Association of REALTORS® Estimated Buyer's Cost form (EBC) provides for the purchaser's signature. The agent is thus protected against later allegations that the buyer was misled about the cash requirements for purchasing the property.

Mortgage Loan Disclosure Statement.   Before a borrower is obligated to complete a nonfederally related loan agreement arranged by a real estate broker, the borrower must be given and must sign a mortgage loan disclosure statement setting forth all costs and fees, payments, liens, etc. The disclosure must be made on a form approved by the Department of Real Estate and the mortgage broker must keep a copy of the disclosure form for three years. The California Association of REALTORS® Mortgage Loan Disclosure Statement (MS) is an approved form for this purpose.

■ LEASES

Listing forms to lease or rent, such as the CAR Exclusive Authorization to Lease or Rent (Form LL), are quite similar to sale listing agreements.

When a landlord accepts a deposit on a rental from a prospective tenant, the landlord could be entering a lease agreement unless it is clear it is only an application to rent and not an agreement to rent. Most standard forms make it very clear that it is an application to rent only and must be approved by the owner.

Many types of leases and lease forms are available. Figure 6.5 provides a simple residential lease form. Agents should seek legal advice for any major modification of a simple lease form. For commercial and industrial leases, using preprinted forms is dangerous because the forms probably will not accurately reflect the needs and intent of the parties.

The cut-and-paste leases that are frequently prepared by agents from other leases could subject an agent to a charge of the unauthorized practice of law as well as liability for errors or omissions. An agent who assumes the responsibility of preparing a lease has the duty to do so properly.

■ BROKER-SALESPERSON AGREEMENT

A broker is required to have a written contract with his or her salespeople.

Figure 6.6 presents the CAR standard form for broker-salesperson contracts. Note that paragraph 3 makes it quite clear that the salesperson is intended to be an independent contractor. The broker-salesperson relationship is covered in detail in Chapter 3.

■ RETENTION OF RECORDS

A real estate broker shall retain for three years copies of all listings, deposits, receipts, canceled checks, trust records, and other documents executed by the broker or obtained in connection with any transaction for which a real estate license is required. The retention period runs from the date of closing a transaction or, if not closed, from the date of the listing.

(Note: A book of sample forms is available from the California Association of REALTORS®, 525 South Virgil Ave., Los Angeles, CA 90020. Sample forms are also available from First Tuesday and Professional Publishing Co.)

FIGURE 6.5

Residential Lease or Month-to-Month Rental Agreement

CALIFORNIA ASSOCIATION OF REALTORS®

RESIDENTIAL LEASE OR MONTH-TO-MONTH RENTAL AGREEMENT
(C.A.R. Form LR, Revised 10/01)

_____ ("Landlord") and
_____ ("Tenant") agree as follows:

1. PROPERTY:
   A. Landlord rents to Tenant and Tenant rents from Landlord, the real property and improvements described as: _____
   _____ ("Premises").
   B. The following personal property is included: _____

2. TERM: The term begins on (date) _____ ("Commencement Date"), **(Check A or B):**
   ☐ **A. Month-to-month:** and continues as a month-to-month tenancy. Either party may terminate the tenancy by giving written notice to the other at least 30 days prior to the intended termination date, subject to any applicable local laws. Such notice may be given on any date.
   ☐ **B. Lease:** and shall terminate on (date) _____ at _____ AM/PM.
   Any holding over after the term of this Agreement expires, with Landlord's consent, shall create a month-to-month tenancy which either party may terminate as specified in paragraph 2A. Rent shall be at a rate equal to the rent for the immediately preceding month, unless otherwise notified by Landlord, payable in advance. All other terms and conditions of this Agreement shall remain in full force and effect.

3. RENT:
   A. Tenant agrees to pay rent at the rate of $ _____ per month for the term of the Agreement.
   B. Rent is payable in advance on the **1st (or** ☐ **_____) day** of each calendar month, and is delinquent on the next day.
   C. If Commencement Date falls on any day other than the first day of the month, rent shall be prorated based on a 30-day period. If Tenant has paid one full month's rent in advance of Commencement Date, rent for the second calendar month shall be prorated based on a 30-day period.
   D. PAYMENT: The rent shall be paid by ☐ cash, ☐ personal check, ☐ money order, ☐ cashier check, ☐ other_____, to
   (name) _____ (phone)_____ at
   (address) _____,
   (or at any other location specified by Landlord in writing to Tenant) between the hours of _____ and _____
   on the following days_____

4. SECURITY DEPOSIT:
   A. Tenant agrees to pay $ _____ as a security deposit. Security deposit will be ☐ transferred to and held by the Owner of the Premises; or ☐ held in Owner's Broker's trust account.
   B. All or any portion of the security deposit may be used, as reasonably necessary, to: (1) cure Tenant's default in payment of rent, Late Charges, non-sufficient funds ("NSF") fees, or other sums due; (2) repair damage, excluding ordinary wear and tear, caused by Tenant or by a guest or licensee of Tenant; (3) clean Premises, if necessary, upon termination of tenancy; and (4) replace or return personal property or appurtenances. **SECURITY DEPOSIT SHALL NOT BE USED BY TENANT IN LIEU OF PAYMENT OF LAST MONTH'S RENT.** If all or any portion of the security deposit is used during tenancy, Tenant agrees to reinstate the total security deposit within five days after written notice is delivered to Tenant. Within three weeks after Tenant vacates the Premises, Landlord shall: (1) furnish Tenant an itemized statement indicating the amount of any security deposit received and the basis for its disposition; and (2) return any remaining portion of security deposit to Tenant.
   C. No interest will be paid on security deposit unless required by local ordinance.
   D. If security deposit is held by Owner, Tenant agrees not to hold Broker responsible for its return. If security deposit is held in Owner's Broker's trust account, **and** Broker's authority is terminated before expiration of this Agreement, **and** security deposits are released to someone other than Tenant, **then** Broker shall notify Tenant, in writing, where and to whom security deposit has been released. Once Tenant has been provided such notice, Tenant agrees not to hold Broker responsible for security deposit.

5. MOVE-IN COSTS RECEIVED/DUE:

Category	Total Due	Payment Received	Balance Due	Date Due
Rent from _____ to _____ (date)				
*Security Deposit				
Other _____				
Other _____				
Total				

*The maximum amount that Landlord may receive as security deposit, however designated, cannot exceed two month's rent for an unfurnished Premises, or three month's rent for a furnished premises.

6. PARKING: (Check A or B)
   ☐ **A.** Parking is permitted as follows: _____
   The right to parking ☐ is, ☐ is not, included in the rent charged pursuant to paragraph 3. If not included in the rent, the parking rental fee shall be an additional $ _____ per month. Parking space(s) are to be used for parking operable motor vehicles, except for trailers, boats, campers, buses or trucks (other than pick-up trucks). Tenant shall park in assigned space(s) only. Parking space(s) are to be kept clean. Vehicles leaking oil, gas or other motor vehicle fluids shall not be parked on the Premises. Mechanical work or storage of inoperable vehicles is not allowed in parking space(s) or elsewhere on the Premises.
   OR ☐ **B.** Parking is not permitted on the Premises.

Landlord and Tenant acknowledge receipt of copy of this page.

Landlord's Initials (_____)(_____)
Tenant's Initials (_____)(_____)

EQUAL HOUSING OPPORTUNITY

LR-11 REVISED DATE 10/01 (PAGE 1 OF 4)   Print Date

Reviewed by _____
Broker or Designee _____ Date _____

RESIDENTIAL LEASE OR MONTH-TO-MONTH RENTAL AGREEMENT (LR-11 PAGE 1 OF 4)

Reprinted with permission, California Association of REALTORS®. Endorsement not implied.

FIGURE 6.5 (continued)

Residential Lease or Month-to-Month Rental Agreement

Premises: _____   Date: _____

7. **STORAGE: (Check A or B)**
    ☐ A. Storage is permitted as follows: _____
    The right to storage space ☐ is, ☐ is not, included in the rent charged pursuant to paragraph 3. If not included in rent, storage space shall be an additional $ _____ per month. Tenant shall store only personal property that Tenant owns, and shall not store property that is claimed by another or in which another has any right, title, or interest. Tenant shall not store any improperly packaged food or perishable goods, flammable materials, explosives, or other inherently dangerous material.
    OR ☐ B. Storage is not permitted on the Premises.

8. **LATE CHARGE/NSF CHECKS:** Tenant acknowledges that either late payment of rent or issuance of a NSF check may cause Landlord to incur costs and expenses, the exact amount of which are extremely difficult and impractical to determine. These costs may include, but are not limited to, processing, enforcement and accounting expenses, and late charges imposed on Landlord. If any installment of rent due from Tenant is not received by Landlord within 5 (or ☐ _____) **calendar days** after date due, or if a check is returned NSF, Tenant shall pay to Landlord, respectively, an additional sum of $ _____ as Late Charge and $25.00 as a NSF fee, either or both of which shall be deemed additional rent. Landlord and Tenant agree that these charges represent a fair and reasonable estimate of the costs Landlord may incur by reason of Tenant's late or NSF payment. Any Late Charge or NSF fee due shall be paid with the current installment of rent. Landlord's acceptance of any Late Charge or NSF fee shall not constitute a waiver as to any default of Tenant. Landlord's right to collect a Late Charge or NSF fee shall not be deemed an extension of the date rent is due under paragraph 3, or prevent Landlord from exercising any other rights and remedies under this Agreement, and as provided by law.

9. **CONDITION OF PREMISES:** Tenant has examined Premises, all furniture, furnishings, appliances, landscaping, if any, and fixtures, including smoke detector(s).
    (Check one:)
    ☐ A. Tenant acknowledges that these items are clean and in operative condition, with the following exceptions _____ _____
    OR ☐ B. Tenant's acknowledgment of the condition of these items is contained in an attached statement of condition (such as C.A.R.'s MIMO-11).
    OR ☐ C. Tenant will provide Landlord a list of items that are damaged or not in operable condition within 3 (or ☐ _____) **days** after Commencement Date, not as a contingency of this Agreement but rather as an acknowledgment of the condition of the Premises.
    OR ☐ D. Other: _____

10. **NEIGHBORHOOD CONDITIONS:** Tenant is advised to satisfy him or herself as to neighborhood or area conditions, including schools, proximity and adequacy of law enforcement, crime statistics, registered felons or offenders, fire protection, other governmental services, proximity to commercial, industrial or agricultural activities, existing and proposed transportation, construction and development that may affect noise, view, or traffic, airport noise, noise or odor from any source, wild and domestic animals, other nuisances, hazards, or circumstances, facilities and condition of common areas, conditions and influences of significance to certain cultures and/or religions, and personal needs, requirements and preferences of Tenant.

11. **UTILITIES:** Tenant agrees to pay for all utilities and services, and the following charges: _____ except _____, which shall be paid for by Landlord. If any utilities are not separately metered, Tenant shall pay Tenant's proportional share, as reasonably determined by Landlord.

12. **OCCUPANTS:** The Premises are for the sole use as a personal residence by the following named persons **only:** _____ _____

13. **PETS:** No animal or pet shall be kept on or about the Premises without Landlord's prior written consent, except _____

14. **RULES/REGULATIONS:** Tenant agrees to comply with all rules and regulations of Landlord, which are at any time posted on the Premises or delivered to Tenant. Tenant shall not, and shall ensure that guests and licensees of Tenant shall not, disturb, annoy, endanger, or interfere with other tenants of the building or neighbors, or use the Premises for any unlawful purposes, including, but not limited to, using, manufacturing, selling, storing, or transporting illicit drugs or other contraband, or violate any law or ordinance, or commit a waste or nuisance on or about the Premises.

15. **CONDOMINIUM/PLANNED UNIT DEVELOPMENT:** ☐ (If checked) The Premises is a unit in a condominium, planned unit, or other development governed by a homeowners' association ("HOA"). The name of the HOA is _____. Tenant agrees to comply with all covenants, conditions and restrictions, bylaws, rules and regulations and decisions of HOA. Landlord shall provide Tenant copies of rules and regulations, if any. Tenant shall reimburse Landlord for any fines or charges imposed by HOA or other authorities, due to any violation by Tenant, or the guests or licensees of Tenant.

16. **MAINTENANCE:**
    A. Tenant shall properly use, operate and safeguard Premises, including if applicable, any landscaping, furniture, furnishings, and appliances, and all mechanical, electrical, gas and plumbing fixtures, and keep them clean and sanitary. Tenant shall immediately notify Landlord, in writing, of any problem, malfunction or damage. Tenant shall pay for all repairs or replacements caused by Tenant, or guests of Tenant, excluding ordinary wear and tear. Tenant shall pay for all damage to Premises as a result of failure to report a problem in a timely manner. Tenant shall pay for repair of drain blockages or stoppages, unless caused by defective plumbing parts or tree roots invading sewer lines.
    B. ☐ Landlord ☐ Tenant shall water the garden, landscaping, trees and shrubs, except _____
    _____
    C. ☐ Landlord ☐ Tenant shall maintain the garden, landscaping, trees and shrubs, except _____

17. **ALTERATIONS:** Tenant shall not make any alterations in or about the Premises without Landlord's prior written consent, including: painting, wallpapering, adding or changing locks, installing antenna or satellite dish(es), placing signs, displays or exhibits, or using screws, fastening devices, large nails or adhesive materials.

18. **KEYS/LOCKS:**
    A. Tenant acknowledges receipt of (or Tenant will receive ☐ prior to the Commencement Date, or ☐ _____):
    ☐ _____ key(s) to Premises,   ☐ _____ remote control device(s) for garage door/gate opener(s),
    ☐ _____ key(s) to mailbox,   ☐ _____,
    ☐ _____ key(s) to common area(s),   ☐ _____.
    B. Tenant acknowledges that locks to the Premises ☐ have, ☐ have not, been rekeyed.
    C. If Tenant rekeys existing locks or opening devices, Tenant shall immediately deliver copies of all keys to Landlord. Tenant shall pay all costs and charges related to loss of any keys or opening devices. Tenant may not remove locks, even if installed by Tenant.

LR-11 REVISED DATE 10/01 (PAGE 2 OF 4)   Print Date

Landlord and Tenant acknowledge receipt of copy of this page.

Landlord's Initials (_____)(_____)
Tenant's Initials (_____)(_____)

EQUAL HOUSING OPPORTUNITY

Reviewed by _____
Broker or Designee _____ Date _____

RESIDENTIAL LEASE OR MONTH-TO-MONTH RENTAL AGREEMENT   (LR-11 PAGE 2 OF 4)

FIGURE 6.5 (continued)

Residential Lease or Month-to-Month Rental Agreement

Premises: _____ Date: _____

19. **ENTRY:** Tenant shall make Premises available to Landlord or representative for the purpose of entering to make necessary or agreed repairs, decorations, alterations, or improvements, or to supply necessary or agreed services, or to show Premises to prospective or actual purchasers, tenants, mortgagees, lenders, appraisers, or contractors. Landlord and Tenant agree that twenty-four (24) hours notice (oral or written) shall be reasonable and sufficient notice. In an emergency, Landlord or representative may enter Premises at any time without prior notice.

20. **SIGNS:** Tenant authorizes Landlord to place For Sale/Lease signs on the Premises.

21. **ASSIGNMENT/SUBLETTING:** Tenant shall not sublet all or any part of Premises, or assign or transfer this Agreement or any interest in it, without prior written consent of Landlord. Unless such consent is obtained, any assignment, transfer or subletting of Premises or this Agreement or tenancy, by voluntary act of Tenant, operation of law, or otherwise, shall be null and void, and at the option of Landlord, terminate this Agreement. Any proposed assignee, transferee or sublessee shall submit to Landlord an application and credit information for Landlord's approval, and if approved, sign a separate written agreement with Landlord and Tenant. Landlord's consent to any one assignment, transfer or sublease, shall not be construed as consent to any subsequent assignment, transfer or sublease and does not release Tenant of Tenant's obligation under this Agreement.

22. ☐ **LEAD PAINT (CHECK IF APPLICABLE):** Premises was constructed prior to 1978. In accordance with federal law, Landlord gives and Tenant acknowledges receipt of the disclosures on the attached form (such as C.A.R. Form FLD-11) and a federally approved lead pamphlet.

23. **POSSESSION:** If Landlord is unable to deliver possession of Premises on Commencement Date, such Date shall be extended to date on which possession is made available to Tenant. If Landlord is unable to deliver possession within **5 (or** ☐ _____ **) calendar days** after agreed Commencement Date, Tenant may terminate this Agreement by giving written notice to Landlord, and shall be refunded all rent and security deposit paid.

24. **TENANT'S OBLIGATIONS UPON VACATING PREMISES:** Upon termination of Agreement, Tenant shall: (a) give Landlord all copies of all keys or opening devices to Premises, including any common areas; (b) vacate Premises and surrender it to Landlord empty of all persons; (c) vacate any/all parking and/or storage space; (d) deliver Premises to Landlord in the same condition as referenced in paragraph 9; (e) clean Premises, including professional cleaning of carpet and drapes; (f) give written notice to Landlord of Tenant's forwarding address; and (g) _____
_____
All improvements installed by Tenant, with or without Landlord's consent, become the property of Landlord upon termination.

25. **BREACH OF CONTRACT/EARLY TERMINATION:** In addition to any obligations established by paragraph 24, in event of termination by Tenant prior to completion of the original term of Agreement, Tenant shall also be responsible for lost rent, rental commissions, advertising expenses and painting costs necessary to ready Premises for rerental.

26. **TEMPORARY RELOCATION:** Tenant agrees, upon demand of Landlord, to temporarily vacate Premises for a reasonable period, to allow for fumigation, or other methods, to control wood destroying pests or organisms, or other repairs to Premises. Tenant agrees to comply with all instructions and requirements necessary to prepare Premises to accommodate pest control, fumigation or other work, including bagging or storage of food and medicine, and removal of perishables and valuables. Tenant shall only be entitled to a credit of rent equal to the per diem rent for the period of time Tenant is required to vacate Premises.

27. **DAMAGE TO PREMISES:** If, by no fault of Tenant, Premises are totally or partially damaged or destroyed by fire, earthquake, accident or other casualty, which render Premises uninhabitable, either Landlord or Tenant may terminate Agreement by giving the other written notice. Rent shall be abated as of date of damage. The abated amount shall be the current monthly rent prorated on a 30-day basis. If Agreement is not terminated, Landlord shall promptly repair the damage, and rent shall be reduced based on the extent to which the damage interferes with Tenant's reasonable use of Premises. If damage occurs as a result of an act of Tenant or Tenant's guests, only Landlord shall have the right of termination, and no reduction in rent shall be made.

28. **INSURANCE:** Tenant's or guest's personal property and vehicles are not insured by Landlord or, if applicable, HOA, against loss or damage due to fire, theft, vandalism, rain, water, criminal or negligent acts of others, or any other cause. Tenant is to carry Tenant's own insurance (renter's insurance) to protect Tenant from any such loss.

29. **WATERBEDS:** Tenant shall not use or have waterbeds on the Premises unless: (a) Tenant obtains a valid waterbed insurance policy; (b) Tenant increases the security deposit in an amount equal to one-half of one month's rent; and (c) the bed conforms to the floor load capacity of Premises.

30. **WAIVER:** The waiver of any breach shall not be construed as a continuing waiver of the same or any subsequent breach.

31. **NOTICE:** Notices may be served at the following address, or at any other location subsequently designated:
Landlord: _____ Tenant: _____
_____ _____
_____ _____

32. **TENANT ESTOPPEL CERTIFICATE:** Tenant shall execute and return a tenant estoppel certificate delivered to Tenant by Landlord or Landlord's agent within 3 days after its receipt. The tenant estoppel certificate acknowledges that this Agreement is unmodified and in full force, or in full force as modified, and states the modifications. Failure to comply with this requirement shall be deemed Tenant's acknowledgment that the tenant estoppel certificate is true and correct, and may be relied upon by a lender or purchaser.

33. **JOINT AND INDIVIDUAL OBLIGATIONS:** If there is more than one Tenant, each one shall be individually and completely responsible for the performance of all obligations of Tenant under this Agreement, jointly with every other Tenant, and individually, whether or not in possession.

34. ☐ **MILITARY ORDNANCE DISCLOSURE:** (If applicable and known to Landlord) Premises is located within one mile of an area once used for military training, and may contain potentially explosive munitions.

35. **TENANT REPRESENTATIONS; CREDIT:** Tenant warrants that all statements in Tenant's rental application are accurate. Tenant authorizes Landlord and Broker(s) to obtain Tenant's credit report at time of application and periodically during tenancy in connection with approval, modification, or enforcement of this Agreement. Landlord may cancel this Agreement: (a) before occupancy begins; (b) upon disapproval of the credit report(s); or (c) at any time, upon discovering that information in Tenant's application is false. A negative credit report reflecting on Tenant's record may be submitted to a credit reporting agency if Tenant fails to fulfill the terms of payment and other obligations under this Agreement.

36. If Landlord has entered into a contract for periodic pest control treatment of the Premises, Landlord shall give tenant a copy of the notice originally given to Landlord by the pest control company.

Landlord and Tenant acknowledge receipt of copy of this page.
Landlord's Initials (_____)(_____)
Tenant's Initials (_____)(_____)

LR-11 REVISED DATE 10/01 (PAGE 3 OF 4) Print Date

Reviewed by _____
Broker or Designee _____ Date _____

RESIDENTIAL LEASE OR MONTH-TO-MONTH RENTAL AGREEMENT (LR-11 PAGE 3 OF 4)

FIGURE 6.5 (continued)

Residential Lease or Month-to-Month Rental Agreement

Premises: _____ Date: _____

37. DATA BASE DISCLOSURE: NOTICE: The California Department of Justice, sheriff's departments, police departments serving jurisdictions of 200,000 or more, and many other local law enforcement authorities maintain for public access a data base of the locations of persons required to register pursuant to paragraph (1) of subdivision (a) of Section 290.4 of the Penal Code. The data base is updated on a quarterly basis and a source of information about the presence of these individuals in any neighborhood. The Department of Justice also maintains a Sex Offender Identification Line through which inquiries about individuals may be made. This is a "900" telephone service. Callers must have specific information about individuals they are checking. Information regarding neighborhoods is not available through the "900" telephone service.

38. OTHER TERMS AND CONDITIONS/SUPPLEMENTS: _____
_____

The following ATTACHED supplements are incorporated in this Agreement: _____

39. ATTORNEY FEES: In any action or proceeding arising out of this Agreement, the prevailing party between Landlord and Tenant shall be entitled to reasonable attorney fees and costs.

40. ENTIRE CONTRACT: Time is of the essence. All prior agreements between Landlord and Tenant are incorporated in this Agreement, which constitutes the entire contract. It is intended as a final expression of the parties' agreement, and may not be contradicted by evidence of any prior agreement or contemporaneous oral agreement. The parties further intend that this Agreement constitutes the complete and exclusive statement of its terms, and that no extrinsic evidence whatsoever may be introduced in any judicial or other proceeding, if any, involving this Agreement. Any provision of this Agreement that is held to be invalid shall not affect the validity or enforceability of any other provision in this Agreement.

41. AGENCY:
   A. Confirmation: The following agency relationship(s) are hereby confirmed for this transaction:
   Listing Agent: (Print firm name) _____ is the agent of
   (check one): ☐ the Landlord exclusively; or ☐ both the Landlord and Tenant.
   Leasing Agent: (Print firm name) _____ (if not same as Listing Agent) is the agent of
   (check one): ☐ the Tenant exclusively; or ☐ the Landlord exclusively; or ☐ both the Tenant and Landlord.
   B. Disclosure: ☐ (If checked): The term of this lease exceeds one year. A disclosure regarding real estate agency relationships (such as C.A.R. form AD-11), has been provided to Landlord and Tenant, who each acknowledge its receipt.

42. ☐ INTERPRETER/TRANSLATOR: The terms of this Agreement have been interpreted/translated for Tenant into the following language: _____ Interpretation/translation service has been provided by (print name) _____, who has the following Driver's License or other identification number: _____. Tenant has been advised to rely on, and has in fact solely relied on the interpretation/translation services of the above-named individual, and not on the Landlord or other person involved in negotiating the Agreement. If the Agreement has been negotiated primarily in Spanish, Tenant has been provided a Spanish language translation of this Agreement pursuant to the California Civil Code. (C.A.R. form LR-11-S fulfills this requirement.)

Signature of interpreter/translator _____ Date _____

Landlord and Tenant acknowledge and agree that Brokers: (a) do not guarantee the condition of the Premises; (b) cannot verify representations made by others; (c) cannot provide legal or tax advice; (d) will not provide other advice or information that exceeds the knowledge, education or experience required to obtain a real estate license. Furthermore, if Brokers are not also acting as Landlord in this Agreement, Brokers; (e) do not decide what rental rate a Tenant should pay or Landlord should accept; and (f) do not decide upon the length or other terms of tenancy. Landlord and Tenant agree that they will seek legal, tax, insurance and other desired assistance from appropriate professionals.

Tenant _____ Date _____
Tenant _____ Date _____
Landlord _____ Date _____
(Owner or Agent with authority to enter into this lease)
Landlord _____ Date _____
(Owner or Agent with authority to enter into this lease)
Landlord Address _____ Telephone _____

Agency relationships are confirmed as above. Real estate brokers who are not also Landlord in this Agreement are not a party to the Agreement between Landlord and Tenant.

Real Estate Broker _____ By _____ Date _____
(Leasing Firm Name)
Address _____ Telephone _____ Fax _____
Real Estate Broker _____ By _____ Date _____
(Listing Firm Name)
Address _____ Telephone _____ Fax _____

THIS FORM HAS BEEN APPROVED BY THE CALIFORNIA ASSOCIATION OF REALTORS® (C.A.R.). NO REPRESENTATION IS MADE AS TO THE LEGAL VALIDITY OR ADEQUACY OF ANY PROVISION IN ANY SPECIFIC TRANSACTION. A REAL ESTATE BROKER IS THE PERSON QUALIFIED TO ADVISE ON REAL ESTATE TRANSACTIONS. IF YOU DESIRE LEGAL OR TAX ADVICE, CONSULT AN APPROPRIATE PROFESSIONAL.

This form is available for use by the entire real estate industry. It is not intended to identify the user as a REALTOR®. REALTOR® is a registered collective membership mark which may be used only by members of the NATIONAL ASSOCIATION OF REALTORS® who subscribe to its Code of Ethics.

Published and Distributed by:
REAL ESTATE BUSINESS SERVICES, INC.
a subsidiary of the CALIFORNIA ASSOCIATION OF REALTORS®
525 South Virgil Avenue, Los Angeles, California 90020

Reviewed by _____
Broker or Designee _____ Date _____

LR-11 REVISED DATE 10/01 (PAGE 4 OF 4)   Print Date

RESIDENTIAL LEASE OR MONTH-TO-MONTH RENTAL AGREEMENT (LR-11 PAGE 4 OF 4)

FIGURE 6.6

Independent Contractor Agreement

FORM ICA-11

CALIFORNIA
ASSOCIATION
OF REALTORS®

INDEPENDENT CONTRACTOR AGREEMENT
(Between Broker and Associate-Licensee)

This Agreement, dated _____ is made between _____
_____ ("Broker") and
_____ ("Associate-Licensee").

In consideration of the covenants and representations contained in this Agreement, Broker and Associate-Licensee agree as follows:

1. **BROKER:** Broker represents that Broker is duly licensed as a real estate broker by the State of California, ☐ doing business as _____
_____ (firm name), ☐ a sole proprietorship, ☐ a partnership, ☐ a corporation.
Broker is a member of the _____
Association(s) of REALTORS ®, and a subscriber to the _____ multiple
listing service(s). Broker shall keep Broker's license current during the term of this Agreement.

2. **ASSOCIATE-LICENSEE:** Associate-Licensee represents that, (a) he/she is duly licensed by the State of California as a ☐ real estate broker,
☐ real estate salesperson, and (b) he/she has not used any other names within the past five years, except _____
_____. Associate-Licensee shall keep his/her license current during
the term of this Agreement, including satisfying all applicable continuing education and provisional license requirements.

3. **INDEPENDENT CONTRACTOR RELATIONSHIP:**
   A. Broker and Associate-Licensee intend that, to the maximum extent permissible by law: **(i)** This Agreement does not constitute an employment agreement by either party; **(ii)** Broker and Associate-Licensee are independent contracting parties with respect to all services rendered under this Agreement; **(iii)** This Agreement shall not be construed as a partnership.
   B. Broker shall not: **(i)** restrict Associate-Licensee's activities to particular geographical areas or, **(ii)** dictate Associate-Licensee's activities with regard to hours, leads, open houses, opportunity or floor time, production, prospects, sales meetings, schedule, inventory, time off, vacation, or similar activities, except to the extent required by law.
   C. Associate-Licensee shall not be required to accept an assignment by Broker to service any particular current or prospective listing or parties.
   D. Except as required by law: **(i)** Associate-Licensee retains sole and absolute discretion and judgment in the methods, techniques, and procedures to be used in soliciting and obtaining listings, sales, exchanges, leases, rentals, or other transactions, and in carrying out Associate-Licensee's selling and soliciting activities, **(ii)** Associate-Licensee is under the control of Broker as to the results of Associate-Licensee's work only, and not as to the means by which those results are accomplished, **(iii)** Associate-Licensee has no authority to bind Broker by any promise or representation and **(iv)** Broker shall not be liable for any obligation or liability incurred by Associate-Licensee.
   E. Associate-Licensee's only remuneration shall be the compensation specified in paragraph 8.
   F. Associate-Licensee shall not be treated as an employee with respect to services performed as a real estate agent, for state and federal tax purposes.
   G. The fact the Broker may carry worker compensation insurance for Broker's own benefit and for the mutual benefit of Broker and licensees associated with Broker, including Associate-Licensee, shall not create an inference of employment.

4. **LICENSED ACTIVITY:** All listings of property, and all agreements, acts or actions for performance of licensed acts, which are taken or performed in connection with this Agreement, shall be taken and performed in the name of Broker. Associate-Licensee agrees to and does hereby contribute all right and title to such listings to Broker for the benefit and use of Broker, Associate-Licensee, and other licensees associated with Broker. Broker shall make available to Associate-Licensee, equally with other licensees associated with Broker, all current listings in Broker's office, except any listing which Broker may choose to place in the exclusive servicing of Associate-Licensee or one or more other specific licensees associated with Broker. Associate-Licensee shall provide and pay for all professional licenses, supplies, services, and other items required in connection with Associate-Licensee's activities under this Agreement, or any listing or transaction, without reimbursement from Broker except as required by law. Associate-Licensee shall work diligently and with his/her best efforts: **(a)** To sell, exchange, lease, or rent properties listed with Broker or other cooperating Brokers; **(b)** To solicit additional listings, clients, and customers; and **(c)** To otherwise promote the business of serving the public in real estate transactions to the end that Broker and Associate-Licensee may derive the greatest benefit possible, in accordance with law. Associate-Licensee shall not commit any unlawful act under federal, state or local law or regulation while conducting licensed activity. Associate-Licensee shall at all times be familiar, and comply, with all applicable federal, state and local laws, including, but not limited to, anti-discrimination laws and restrictions against the giving or accepting a fee, or other thing of value, for the referral of business to title companies, escrow companies, home inspection companies, pest control companies and other settlement service providers pursuant to the California Business and Professions Code and the Real Estate Settlement Procedures Acts (RESPA). Broker shall make available for Associate-Licensee's use, along with other licensees associated with Broker, the facilities of the real estate office operated by Broker at _____
_____ and the facilities of any other office
locations made available by Broker pursuant to this Agreement.

Broker and Associate-Licensee acknowledge receipt of copy of this page, which constitutes Page 1 of _____ Pages.
Broker's Initials (_____) (_____) Associate-Licensee's Initials (_____) (_____)

REVISED 10/98

OFFICE USE ONLY
Reviewed by Broker
or Designee _____
Date _____

EQUAL HOUSING
OPPORTUNITY

INDEPENDENT CONTRACTOR AGREEMENT (ICA-11 PAGE 1 OF 3)

FIGURE 6.6 (continued)

**Independent Contractor
Agreement**

5. **PROPRIETARY INFORMATION AND FILES: (a)** All files and documents pertaining to listings, leads and transactions are the property of Broker and shall be delivered to Broker by Associate-Licensee immediately upon request or termination of their relationship under this Agreement. **(b)** Associate-Licensee acknowledges that Broker's method of conducting business is a protected trade secret. **(c)** Associate-Licensee shall not use to his/her own advantage, or the advantage of any other person, business, or entity, except as specifically agreed in writing, either during Associate-Licensee's association with Broker, or thereafter, any information gained for or from the business, or files of Broker.

6. **SUPERVISION:** Associate-Licensee, within 24 hours (or ☐ _____) after preparing, signing, or receiving same, shall submit to Broker, or Broker's designated licensee: **(a)** All documents which may have a material effect upon the rights and duties of principals in a transaction, **(b)** Any documents or other items connected with a transaction pursuant to this Agreement in the possession of or available to Associate-Licensee and, **(c)** All documents associated with any real estate transaction in which Associate-Licensee is a principal.

7. **TRUST FUNDS:** All trust funds shall be handled in compliance with the Business and Professions Code, and other applicable laws.

8. **COMPENSATION:**
   A. **TO BROKER:** Compensation shall be charged to parties who enter into listing or other agreements for services requiring a real estate license:
      ☐ as shown in "Exhibit A" attached, which is incorporated as a part of this Agreement by reference, or
      ☐ as follows: _____
      _____
      Any deviation which is not approved in writing in advance by Broker, shall be (1) deducted from Associate-Licensee's compensation, if lower than the amount or rate approved above; and, (2) subject to Broker approval, if higher than the amount approved above. Any permanent change in commission schedule shall be disseminated by Broker to Associate-Licensee.
   B. **TO ASSOCIATE-LICENSEE:** Associate-Licensee shall receive a share of compensation actually collected by Broker, on listings or other agreements for services requiring a real estate license, which are solicited and obtained by Associate-Licensee, and on transactions of which Associate-Licensee's activities are the procuring cause, as follows:
      ☐ as shown in "Exhibit B" attached, which is incorporated as a part of this Agreement by reference, or
      ☐ other: _____
      _____
   C. **PARTNERS, TEAMS, AND AGREEMENTS WITH OTHER ASSOCIATE-LICENSEES IN OFFICE:** If Associate-Licensee and one or more other Associate-Licensees affiliated with Broker participate on the same side (either listing or selling) of a transaction, the commission allocated to their combined activities shall be divided by Broker and paid to them according to their written agreement. Broker shall have the right to withhold total compensation if there is a dispute between associate-licensees, or if there is no written agreement, or if no written agreement has been provided to Broker.
   D. **EXPENSES AND OFFSETS:** If Broker elects to advance funds to pay expenses or liabilities of Associate-Licensee, or for an advance payment of, or draw upon, future compensation, Broker may deduct the full amount advanced from compensation payable to Associate-Licensee on any transaction without notice. If Associate-Licensee's compensation is subject to a lien, garnishment or other restriction on payment, Broker shall charge Associate-Licensee a fee for complying with such restriction.
   E. **PAYMENT: (1)** All compensation collected by Broker and due to Associate-Licensee shall be paid to Associate-Licensee, after deduction of expenses and offsets, immediately or as soon thereafter as practicable, except as otherwise provided in this Agreement, or a separate written agreement between Broker and Associate-Licensee. **(2)** Compensation shall not be paid to Associate-Licensee until both the transaction and file are complete. **(3)** Broker is under no obligation to pursue collection of compensation from any person or entity responsible for payment. Associate-Licensee does not have the independent right to pursue collection of compensation for activities which require a real estate license which were done in the name of Broker. **(4)** Expenses which are incurred in the attempt to collect compensation shall be paid by Broker and Associate-Licensee in the same proportion as set forth for the division of compensation (paragraph 8(B)). **(5)** If there is a known or pending claim against Broker or Associate-Licensee on transactions for which Associate-Licensee has not yet been paid, Broker may withhold from compensation due Associate-Licensee on that transaction amounts for which Associate-Licensee could be responsible under paragraph 14, until such claim is resolved. **(6)** Associate-Licensee shall not be entitled to any advance payment from Broker upon future compensation.
   F. **UPON OR AFTER TERMINATION:** If this Agreement is terminated while Associate-Licensee has listings or pending transactions that require further work normally rendered by Associate-Licensee, Broker shall make arrangements with another associate-licensee to perform the required work, or Broker shall perform the work him/herself. The licensee performing the work shall be reasonably compensated for completing work on those listings or transactions, and such reasonable compensation shall be deducted from Associate-Licensee's share of compensation. Except for such offset, Associate-Licensee shall receive the compensation due as specified above.

9. **TERMINATION OF RELATIONSHIP:** Broker or Associate-Licensee may terminate their relationship under this Agreement at any time, with or without cause. After termination, Associate-Licensee shall not solicit **(a)** prospective or existing clients or customers based upon company-generated leads obtained during the time Associate-Licensee was affiliated with Broker, or **(b)** any principal with existing contractual obligations to Broker, or **(c)** any principal with a contractual transactional obligation for which Broker is entitled to be compensated. Even after termination, this Agreement shall govern all disputes and claims between Broker and Associate-Licensee connected with their relationship under this Agreement, including obligations and liabilities arising from existing and completed listings, transactions, and services.

Broker and Associate-Licensee acknowledge receipt of copy of this page, which constitutes Page 2 of _____ Pages.
Broker's Initials (_____) (_____)   Associate-Licensee's Initials (_____) (_____)

REVISED 10/98

OFFICE USE ONLY
Reviewed by Broker
or Designee _____
Date _____

EQUAL HOUSING OPPORTUNITY

Page 2 of ___ Pages.

PRINT DATE

INDEPENDENT CONTRACTOR AGREEMENT (ICA-11 PAGE 2 OF 3)

FIGURE 6.6 (continued)

Independent Contractor Agreement

10. **DISPUTE RESOLUTION:**

    A. **Mediation:** Mediation is recommended as a method of resolving disputes arising out of this Agreement between Broker and Associate-Licensee.

    B. **Arbitration:** All disputes or claims between Associate-Licensee and other licensee(s) associated with Broker, or between Associate-Licensee and Broker, arising from or connected in any way with this Agreement, which cannot be adjusted between the parties involved, shall be submitted to the Association of REALTORS® of which all such disputing parties are members for arbitration pursuant to the provisions of its Bylaws, as may be amended from time to time, which are incorporated as a part of this Agreement by reference. If the Bylaws of the Association do not cover arbitration of the dispute, or if the Association declines jurisdiction over the dispute, then arbitration shall be pursuant to the rules of California law. The Federal Arbitration Act, Title 9, U.S. Code, Section 1, et seq., shall govern this Agreement.

11. **AUTOMOBILE:** Associate-Licensee shall maintain automobile insurance coverage for liability and property damage in the following amounts $_____/$_____. Broker shall be named as an additional insured party on Associate-Licensee's policies. A copy of the endorsement showing Broker as an additional insured shall be provided to Broker.

12. **PERSONAL ASSISTANTS:** Associate-Licensee may make use of a personal assistant, provided the following requirements are satisfied. Associate-Licensee shall have a written agreement with the personal assistant which establishes the terms and responsibilities of the parties to the employment agreement, including, but not limited to, compensation, supervision and compliance with applicable law. The agreement shall be subject to Broker's review and approval. Unless otherwise agreed, if the personal assistant has a real estate license, that license must be provided to the Broker. Both Associate-Licensee and personal assistant must sign any agreement that Broker has established for such purposes.

13. **OFFICE POLICY MANUAL:** If Broker's office policy manual, now or as modified in the future, conflicts with or differs from the terms of this Agreement, the terms of the office policy manual shall govern the relationship between Broker and Associate-Licensee.

14. **INDEMNITY AND HOLD HARMLESS:** Associate-Licensee agrees to indemnify, defend and hold Broker harmless from all claims, disputes, litigation, judgments, awards, costs and attorney's fees, arising from any action taken or omitted by Associate-Licensee, or others working through, or on behalf of Associate-Licensee in connection with services rendered. Any such claims or costs payable pursuant to this Agreement, are due as follows:

    ☐ Paid in full by Associate-Licensee, who hereby agrees to indemnify and hold harmless Broker for all such sums, or

    ☐ In the same ratio as the compensation split as it existed at the time the compensation was earned by Associate-Licensee

    ☐ Other: _____
_____

Payment from Associate-Licensee is due at the time Broker makes such payment and can be offset from any compensation due Associate-Licensee as above. Broker retains the authority to settle claims or disputes, whether or not Associate-Licensee consents to such settlement.

15. **ADDITIONAL PROVISIONS:** _____
_____
_____

16. **DEFINITIONS:** As used in this Agreement, the following terms have the meanings indicated:

    (A) "Listing" means an agreement with a property owner or other party to locate a buyer, exchange party, lessee, or other party to a transaction involving real property, a mobile home, or other property or transaction which may be brokered by a real estate licensee, or an agreement with a party to locate or negotiate for any such property or transaction.

    (B) "Compensation means compensation for acts requiring a real estate license, regardless of whether calculated as a percentage of transaction price, flat fee, hourly rate, or in any other manner.

    (C) "Transaction" means a sale, exchange, lease, or rental of real property, a business opportunity, or a manufactured home, which may lawfully be brokered by a real estate licensee.

17. **ATTORNEY FEES:** In any action, proceeding, or arbitration between Broker and Associate-Licensee arising from or related to this Agreement, the prevailing Broker or Associate-Licensee shall be entitled to reasonable attorney fees and costs.

18. **ENTIRE AGREEMENT; MODIFICATION:** All prior agreements between the parties concerning their relationship as Broker and Associate-Licensee are incorporated in this Agreement, which constitutes the entire contract. Its terms are intended by the parties as a final and complete expression of their agreement with respect to its subject matter, and may not be contradicted by evidence of any prior agreement or contemporaneous oral agreement. This Agreement may not be amended, modified, altered, or changed except by a further agreement in writing executed by Broker and Associate-Licensee.

Broker:

_____
(Brokerage firm name)

By _____
Its Broker/Office manager (circle one)

_____
(Print name)

_____
(Address)

_____
(City, State, Zip)

_____
(Telephone)   (Fax)

Associate-Licensee:

_____
(Signature)

_____
(Print name)

_____
(Address)

_____
(City, State, Zip)

_____
(Telephone)   (Fax)

This form is available for use by the entire real estate industry. It is not intended to identify the user as a REALTOR®. REALTOR® is a registered collective membership mark which may be used only by members of the NATIONAL ASSOCIATION OF REALTORS® who subscribe to its Code of Ethics.

PRINT DATE

REVISED 10/98

Page 3 of ___ Pages.

┌─ OFFICE USE ONLY ─┐
Reviewed by Broker
or Designee _____
Date _____

EQUAL HOUSING OPPORTUNITY

INDEPENDENT CONTRACTOR AGREEMENT (ICA-11 PAGE 3 OF 3)

■ SUMMARY

The real estate agency agreement is known as the *listing*. The types of listings are as follows:

- Exclusive-right-to-sell listing: This listing provides that the broker is entitled to a commission if the listing broker or any other broker or the owner sells the property.
- Exclusive-agency listing: This listing makes the broker the owner's exclusive agent. The broker is entitled to a commission if the listing broker or any other broker sells the property, but the owner can sell the property himself or herself without being obligated to pay a commission.
- Open listing: This is a nonexclusive listing whereby the broker is entitled to a commission only if he or she is successful.
- Verbal listing: Generally a verbal real estate listing is unenforceable because of the statute of frauds. An owner might waive statute of frauds protection if he or she encourages a broker to continue to work on a listing after it has expired.
- Buyer listing: Such listings can be of various types, but the agency is with the buyer, who pays the commission.
- Net listing: A net listing can be any of the preceding listing types. *Net* refers to the broker's commission, which is all monies over a net price for the owner.

In open listings and exclusive-agency listings, procuring cause is often an issue. The agent may not be entitled to a commission if the agent failed to initiate an uninterrupted series of events that led to the sale.

Besides listing contracts, other agreements that have relevance between the principal and the agent include these:

- Advance fee addendum to listing: This agreement sets forth activities for which the agent is to be compensated as well as the fee to be paid in advance.
- Advance costs addendum: This addendum covers costs to be advanced to cover expected broker outlays.
- Listing modification: This agreement allows changes to the listing without an entire new agreement.
- Loan broker listing agreement: This listing gives the loan broker the right to obtain a loan for a prospective borrower.
- Seller's net: This is a statement from the agent that shows what the owner will have after all costs, payments, and expenses.

Options are contracts to make contracts whereby the optionee has an irrevocable right to make a contract if he or she wishes to do so.

A finder's fee agreement sets forth the conduct of the finder and the compensation. It protects both the broker and the finder.

Cooperating broker agreements: While agreements between brokers to split commissions need not be in writing, this form prevents misunderstanding.

Estimated buyer's costs: By using this disclosure form, the broker is protected against later allegations that the buyer was misled regarding financial requirements for purchase.

The real estate purchase contract generally is the buyer's offer to purchase. When accepted by the seller, it becomes a binding contract. Additional forms of interest include the following:

- Contingency removal: When signed by the buyer, this simple form will remove contingencies from his or her offer.
- Interim occupancy agreement: This agreement allows the purchaser early possession of the premises as a tenant, not a buyer.
- Counteroffer: Rather than modify an offer, a party can counter an offer with a separate counteroffer form. The advantage of a counteroffer form is that it helps to reconstruct the events clearly.
- Seller financing disclosure statement: This statement, which is provided to both buyer and seller, warns parties of the effect of terms and provides a full disclosure.
- Release of contract: By signing a release agreement, the parties can agree to cancel an agreement.
- Mortgage loan disclosure statement: This form is required when the broker is arranging credit, acting as a mortgage loan broker.
- Exclusive authorization to lease or rent: This is the listing agreement for rentals.
- Residential lease: Agents should not attempt major modifications of lease forms because of their liability for errors and omissions as well as because it could be the unauthorized practice of law. The use of preprinted forms for other than simple residential leases is dangerous because they are unlikely to reflect the intent of the party.
- Broker-salesperson contracts: Often contracts specify independent contractor status rather than employee-employer relationships.

■ DISCUSSION CASES

1. An exclusive listing entered into on August 4, 1966, was revoked by the owners on November 25, 1966, prior to its expiration. It was alleged that the broker failed to advertise, show the property, and present offers. **If the allegations were correct, was the cancellation of the irrevocable exclusive listing proper?**

   Coleman v. Mora (1968) 263 C.A.2d 137

2. While a listing was in force, the broker sent a letter to the owner saying that she had obtained a $500 deposit on the purchase price of the property. She did not reveal the name of the buyer or submit the written offer. The owner never received the offer because he was taken to the hospital and died.

   The broker claimed she was entitled to her commission because she had produced a purchaser who was ready, willing, and able to buy on the listing terms. **Was she right?**

   Duin v. Security First National Bank (1955) 132 C.A.2d 904

3. In February 1955 Hunter authorized Rose, a licensed broker, to sell a motel for $197,500 (open listing). Spratt, a salesman for Rose, showed the property to Schmidt. In April 1955 Spratt sent a letter to Hunter stating, "This letter is being sent to you to put you on notice that this office was the procuring agent and that all brokerage rights are being claimed and in the event of a sale to Mr. Schmidt a five percent brokerage commission of the sales price will be due Robert Rose Realty Company."

   There was no reply to this letter, but on May 5 Hunter notified Rose that the motel was "off the market." On May 31 Hunter sent a letter to Rose saying he could show the property again. A postscript stated, "No Trades Accepted."

   In the meantime Schmidt had continued to negotiate with Hunter and purchased the motel for $165,000 and traded personal property valued at $30,000.

   Evidence was introduced to show that another agent first called Schmidt's attention to the motel in September 1954. **Is Rose entitled to a commission?**

   Rose v. Hunter (1957) 155 C.A.2d 319

4. **Is a verbal agreement of a broker to pay a finder's fee enforceable?**

   Grant v. Marinell (1980) 112 C.A.3d 617

5. A broker sued the seller for a commission. The seller's defense was the lack of a written listing. In this case the seller's attorney had advised the broker that a listing had been prepared and adopted by the seller's board of directors. **Is the broker entitled to a commission?**

   Owens v. Foundation for Ocean Research (1980) 107 C.A.3d 179

6. A broker found a buyer under a verbal listing. The deposit receipt signed by the parties provided a commission of $8,250 or one-half of the forfeited deposit.

   The escrow instructions differed from the deposit receipt and provided, "Pay at close of escrow any encumbrances necessary to place this title in the condition called for and the following: Pay commission of $8,250 to Ruth Lipton Realty Company. . . ."

   The sale was never completed. The defendant claimed the close of escrow was a condition precedent to payment of the commission. **Was the broker entitled to a commission?**

   Lipton v. Johansen (1951) 105 C.A.2d 363

7. A 20-day exclusive listing provided for $5,000 down. Within the 20 days the agent brought the owner $1,000 as a deposit. The offer provided for $5,000 in cash 20 days after execution of a contract to purchase.

   The owner refused to accept the $1,000 check offered, claiming he was entitled to $5,000, which he demanded in gold. The purchaser then said, "Give me time to step out to the bank, and I'll get the money for you." The seller replied, "You need not, because I don't want to sell the property on those terms anyway." **Is the agent entitled to a commission?**

   Merzoian v. Papazian (1921) 53 C.A. 112

8. Under an exclusive-right-to-sell listing a broker advertised a country club property and contacted members of the club about the property, which was located on a fairway. No offers were received.

   The defendant's fiancé and the broker argued prior to the expiration of the listing. The defendant's fiancé told the broker to remove his sign because his services were no longer wanted. The broker asked the defendant if she concurred, and she said that she did.

Upon request from the broker's attorney for commission, the defendant softened her position and requested that the broker continue to work on the property.

The listing provided that the broker was entitled to his commission if the owner withdrew the property from the market. Is **the broker entitled to his commission?**

Blank v. Borden (1974) 11 C.A.3d 963

9. The plaintiff's help was requested to obtain financing for a shopping center. The plaintiff asked for a 3 percent fee, which was agreed on, and then contacted various lenders.

The plaintiff located a lender and brought the parties together, but talks broke off. Some months later, after being unable to find financing, the defendant contacted the same lender, and a loan commitment was made for $7 million. The plaintiff was not notified.

The defendant claimed that the plaintiff was not a licensed real estate broker, so no fee need be paid. **Do you agree?**

Tyrone v. Kelly (1973) 9 C.A.3d 1

10. A broker had a listing on eight buildings with a commission of $1,000 on each. The broker agreed that no commission would be due if there was no sale.

Because of a cloud on the title, escrow could not close. The broker orally agreed to reduce the commission by 50 percent (to $4,000) if the sellers would clear the title. Pursuant to this agreement the title was cleared, and the broker aided in closing escrow. After receiving a $4,000 check, which the broker cashed, he changed his position and demanded the balance of his commission according to the listing. **Was the broker entitled to additional compensation?**

Fidler v. Schiller (1963) 212 C.A.2d 569

11. The broker made fraudulent representations about a well. He stated that it could provide sufficient water for a parcel and that it produced at least 60 miner's inches.

The escrow instructions stated, "Buyer has inspected well and accepts same 'as is.'" **Is the broker and/or vendor liable because of the insufficiency of the well?**

Crawford v. Nastos (1960) 182 C.A.2d 659

12. A sale was to be subject to testing the water availability. If the test was not satisfactory to the buyers, the deposit was to be returned to them.

    The buyer was not satisfied and asked for and was given the deposit without the concurrence of the owner. The seller then sued the broker for wrongfully returning the deposit. **Should the broker have returned the buyer's deposit?**

Lyon v. Giannoni (1959) 168 C.A.2d 336

13. A builder contacted a subdivider to purchase a lot for a client. The subdivider, as a condition of sale, required that the subdivider's broker be paid a commission if the lot was resold within three years. This provision was insisted on even though the builder already had a buyer. After the builder conveyed title to the buyer, he refused to pay the commission. **Was the refusal proper?**

Classen v. Weller (1983) 145 C.A.3d 27

14. A seller agreed to pay a broker's commission out of the payments received. The seller foreclosed on the property but then reconveyed the property to the original buyer on different terms. The broker actively participated in the second sale, but no new listing was entered into. **Is the broker entitled to further commission payments?**

Hughes v. Morrison (1984) 160 C.A.3d 103

15. The owner of a home had a contract with a builder. The builder would take the home in trade at $113,000 for a new home under construction if the owner was unable to sell it. The house was listed for sale, and an offer was received for $115,000. Because this was less than the $113,000 credit the builder had offered (after commissions), the owner turned down the offer. After the listing expired, the offeror was contacted, and the property was transferred to the builder and then immediately to the original offeror by the builder. The listing contained a safety clause requiring a commission if the property was sold during a stated time period to

anyone who had made an offer during the listing. **Does this safety clause apply when the sale was made by the builder and not the owner who had listed the property?**

McKay and Company v. Garland (1986) 701 S.W.2d 392

16. Chan was a buyer's broker for Tsang. Chan located a shopping center, and Tsang agreed to pay $4 million. The purchase contract provided that if the buyer defaulted the seller would retain the $20,000 deposit as liquidated damages. Tsang defaulted, on the purchase agreement, and Chan sued Tsang for the commission he would have received had the sale been completed. **Does Chan have a valid claim?**

Chan v. Tsang (1991) 1 C.A.4th 1578

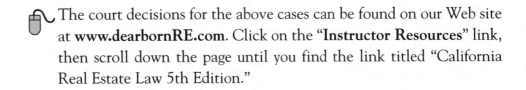 The court decisions for the above cases can be found on our Web site at **www.dearbornRE.com**. Click on the "**Instructor Resources**" link, then scroll down the page until you find the link titled "California Real Estate Law 5th Edition."

■ CHAPTER QUIZ

1. Which of the following would best describe an owner's verbal agreement to pay a real estate sales commission?

   a. Enforceable if the seller benefited by the broker's efforts
   b. Enforceable for commercial property only
   c. Unenforceable
   d. Enforceable only for sales up to $1,000

2. A broker brought an offer to an owner. While the broker did not have a listing, the offer provided for a commission. The owner crossed out the provision for a commission above the signature block and signed the acceptance. Which of the following is true regarding the broker's rights?

   a. By signing the acceptance, the owner made the broker his agent.
   b. The broker is entitled to a reasonable commission.
   c. The broker is entitled to a full commission if the sale is completed.
   d. There was no listing, so no commission need be paid.

3. A valid listing agreement must contain which of the following?

   a. The preprinted rate of commission
   b. A hold harmless clause
   c. Specific reference to the subject matter of the listing
   d. The right of either party to cancel upon notice

4. The effect of a hold harmless clause is that it

   a. warrants that the property presents no risks.
   b. indicates the property is to be sold "as is."
   c. means the owner agrees to indemnify the agent for losses suffered because of the owner's failure to disclose or the owner's incorrect disclosure.
   d. None of the above

5. An exclusive-right-to-sell listing provides for 20 percent down and owner financing at 13 percent interest. The owner received a full-price cash offer that he does not wish to accept. Which of the following is true regarding the owner's rights?

   a. He must pay the commission but can reject the offer.
   b. He must accept the offer and pay the commission.
   c. He may reject the offer without obligation regarding commission.
   d. He may accept the offer without obligation regarding commission.

6. After signing an exclusive-right-to-sell listing, an owner refuses to accept an offer that conforms exactly to the terms of the listing. In this case specific performance can be obtained by

   a. the broker.   c. Either a or b
   b. the offeror.   d. Neither a nor b

7. The rate of commission for the sale of real property is set by

   a. the real estate law.
   b. local real estate boards.
   c. the real estate commissioner.
   d. agreement between the parties.

8. A commission is ordinarily earned by a broker when

   a. escrow closes.
   b. the broker procures a ready, willing, and able buyer.
   c. escrow opens.
   d. the purchaser deposits the full purchase money or liens in escrow.

9. A broker's promise to use diligence makes a listing

   a. a bilateral contract.
   b. an illusory contract.
   c. a unilateral contract.
   d. voidable.

10. On an exclusive listing of a single-family home a broker can be disciplined for failure to

    a. include a definite termination date.
    b. indicate that the commission is negotiable.
    c. give a copy to the owner.
    d. All of the above

11. The exclusive listing that broker Jones had on the Adams farm expired at noon on December 15. At 1:00 P.M. on December 15 Adams gave broker Riley an exclusive listing on the farm. At 2:30 P.M. on December 15 broker Jones procured a buyer at the price and terms of the listing. Who is legally entitled to the commission?

    a. Broker Jones, because a buyer was procured within a reasonable period of time of the listing
    b. Broker Riley
    c. Brokers Riley and Jones, who must split the commission equally
    d. None of the above

12. Which of the following would least likely be found in a real estate purchase contract?

    a. Safety clause
    b. Occupancy intentions
    c. Financing contingency
    d. Provision for physical inspection

13. A termination date is required for all of the following except an

    a. open listing.
    b. exclusive-agency listing.
    c. exclusive-right-to-sell listing.
    d. option.

14. To be the procuring cause of a sale, the broker must have

    a. made the sale.
    b. supplied the owner with the name of the purchaser.
    c. initiated an uninterrupted chain of events that led to the sale.
    d. made first contact with the buyer.

15. Procuring cause is of greatest significance in

    a. options.
    b. verbal listings.
    c. open listings.
    d. rights of first refusal.

16. To collect a commission for a sale on an exclusive-right-to-sell listing the broker must prove all of the following *except* that

    a. there was a valid listing.
    b. the sale took place during the listing, an extension of it, or its safety period.
    c. the broker was licensed at the time the commission was earned.
    d. the broker was the procuring cause of the sale.

17. When a listing includes a purchase right and the broker informs the owner that the broker will buy the property, the broker must

    a. disclose all known facts to the seller.
    b. present any offers received.
    c. obtain the seller's written consent to exercise the option.
    d. All of the above

18. A verbal agreement most likely to be enforceable would be a(n)

    a. option to purchase.
    b. agreement between brokers to split a commission.
    c. open listing.
    d. real estate purchase contract.

19. A listing broker refuses to split a commission with a cooperating broker after agreeing verbally to do so. To collect, the cooperating broker would likely

    a. notify the real estate commissioner.
    b. file a complaint with the state labor commissioner.
    c. start legal action against the other broker.
    d. do nothing, because a verbal agreement cannot be enforced.

20. Liquidated damages can exceed 3 percent of the sales price when the subject property is

    a. five residential units.
    b. residential property that the buyer did not intend to occupy.
    c. a commercial building.
    d. All of the above

21. An offer to purchase stated that it would remain open for 48 hours. Which of the following is a true statement regarding this offer?

    a. This offer is really an option.
    b. This offer is irrevocable for 48 hours.
    c. This offer can be revoked by the offeror prior to the expiration of 48 hours without penalty.
    d. While the offer is revocable immediately, the offeror must forfeit the deposit.

22. A real estate purchase offer fails to specify a time for acceptance. The offer

    a. must be accepted immediately.
    b. can be accepted within a reasonable period of time.
    c. cannot be withdrawn prior to acceptance.
    d. is void.

23. As to contingencies in purchase offers, which of the following is true?

    a. They must be reasonable to be enforceable.
    b. The person benefiting by the contingency can waive it.
    c. They make the contract illusory.
    d. If one party can be relieved by the failure of a contingency, the other party can also be relieved from performance should the contingency fail.

24. A contract for the sale of a residence stated "as is." Which of the following is a true statement relating to this provision?

    a. It is void because a buyer has a right to a habitable dwelling.
    b. It applies to visible conditions only.
    c. It applies only to matters of title.
    d. It is a valid disclaimer as to all defects.

25. "As is" would be most likely to protect a seller from hidden defects when the sale is

    a. to a buyer who does not intend to occupy the premises.
    b. of a commercial property.
    c. a single-family residence only.
    d. of one to four residential units.

7

PROPERTY, ESTATES, AND RECORDINGS

■ KEY TERMS

acknowledgment	emblements	remainder interest
actual notice	fee simple	restraint against
appurtenance	fixture	alienation
bundle of rights	freehold estates	reversionary interest
chattels real	life estate	rule against
concurrent estates	*lis pendens*	perpetuities
condition subsequent	nonfreehold estate	successive estates
constructive notice	patent	trade fixture
defeasible estate	real property	waste

■ ORIGIN OF CALIFORNIA LAND OWNERSHIP

In 1513, Balboa crossed the Isthmus of Panama and claimed for Spain all of the land washed by the waters of the Pacific Ocean. In 1542, Cabrillo sailed up the Pacific coast and landed in California, again claiming ownership for Spain. Under Spanish domination, title to California land was held in the name of the crown. Some grants of land were made, but they were primarily grants of use (agriculture and grazing) and not of title.

A number of presidios, or military garrisons, were established, as were several *pueblos*, or towns. The pueblos received four square leagues of land (about 4,400 acres) and had the power to grant city lots.

The Mission period started in 1769 with the establishment of a string of missions along the California coast. Most of the padres returned to Spain after Mexican independence (1822) and the subsequent secularization of the missions.

Under the short period of Mexican control (1822-1848), huge tracts of land, known as *ranchos*, were granted. As mentioned in Chapter 1, the Treaty of Guadalupe Hidalgo, which ended the Mexican War (1848), provided that the U.S. government would recognize the property rights of Mexican owners, including community property rights.

Most of California was not privately owned. The United States took title to all lands not given by Spanish or Mexican grants that were not cities, towns, or tidelands. Tidelands, between high and low tide lines, belong to the state.

The United States gave tracts of land to private owners under various homestead, timber, and mining acts. The Preemption Act gave a preferential right to occupants of land to purchase it at a low price. Special congressional grants gave land to the State of California. Additional tracts of land were given to Native Americans by treaty. Railroads received sections of land in a checkerboard pattern along their rights-of-way as an inducement to build. Land also has been given to colleges by the federal government and from time to time sold or traded by government agencies. Grants of land from the government were known as **patents**. Today, approximately 50 percent of California land is owned by private citizens or corporations; the balance is owned by federal, state, and local governments.

■ PROPERTY

Property is anything capable of being owned. The two major categories of property are real property and personal property.

Real Property

Real property generally consists of

- land;
- what is affixed to land;

■ what is incidental, or an **appurtenance,** to land (appurtenances include rights, privileges, and improvements that transfer with the land); and

■ what is immovable by law except that, for the purposes of sale, emblements, industrial growing crops, and things attached to or forming part of the land that are agreed to be severed before sale or under the contract of sale are treated as goods (personal property).

Structures such as buildings, sheds, and fences are affixed to the land and are real property. Examples of incidental rights considered to be real property are riparian rights (the beneficial use of a stream or river by an adjacent landowner, covered in Chapter 12) and the right to lateral support (your neighbor cannot perform any activity such as excavation that would cause your land to settle or collapse).

Fructus naturales (naturally growing trees and crops) are considered real property until severed or constructively severed (sold).

Air rights and mineral, oil, and gas (subsurface) rights generally are considered real property. Easement rights, which are covered in Chapter 12, also are considered real property.

Case Study

In the case of *U.S. v. Causby* (1946) 328 U.S. 256, the Supreme Court held that a landowner owns at least as much space above the ground as he or she can occupy or use in conjunction with the land, even though the owner does not occupy it in a physical sense. Therefore, low-flying aircraft that interfere with the normal use of property would be interfering with the owner's rights.

Personal Property

Personal property, also known as *chattels*, is any property that is not real property. Personal property generally is considered to be movable. Title to personal property does not automatically pass with the transfer of title to the real property where it is located.

Chattels Real. **Chattels real** are personal property interests that concern real property. Examples of chattels real are leasehold interests, mortgages, trust deeds, shares in real estate syndicates, and shares in housing cooperatives. While real property oriented, they are considered personal property.

Fructus Industriales.   Also known as **emblements**, fructus industriales are crops resulting from labor. While generally regarded as personal property, in the absence of any agreement between the buyer and seller of real property, they transfer with the land.

If the crops are the fruit of the labor of a tenant, they remain the personal property of the tenant, even though the lease may expire prior to harvest. The former tenant has the right to return to the land to harvest the crops.

Mineral, Oil, and Gas Rights.   As previously stated, mineral, oil, and gas rights are real property. An oil lease for an indefinite period of time also is real property. However, an oil lease for a definite period of time is personal property.

Because oil and gas are considered fluid, no ownership of the actual oil or gas exists until it is extracted from the ground. Ownership of subsurface rights is actually the right to extract the minerals, oil, or gas. After it has been captured, or removed from the ground, it becomes personal property. The owner of rights actually can take fluid oil and gas from under the land of another to which he or she has no rights. The owner, however, cannot intrude on or under the land of the other party to do so; for example, he or she cannot slant-drill into the land of another.

An owner can sell mineral and oil and gas rights but retain a royalty interest as well as land ownership.

Case Study

In the case of *Geothermal Kinetics Inc. v. Union Oil Co.* (1977) 77 C.A.3d 56, the court held that where the specific intent of the parties cannot be ascertained, a grant of a mineral estate includes all geothermal resources located on or under the property. It held that a general grant of a mineral estate is intended to convey commercially valuable underground resources that are not necessary for the enjoyment of the surface estate.

Fixtures

Fixtures are former items of personal property that have become affixed to realty so that they are now part of the real property. For example, a household furnace is personal property before it is installed in a residence but becomes real property (a fixture) after it is installed. Title to fixtures generally transfers with the real property.

There are three basic tests for determining whether or not an item is a fixture:

1. *Intent:* This is the most important test. Did the improver intend to make a permanent improvement to the property? If so, it is likely to be a fixture.

Case Study

In the case of *Larkin v. Cowert* (1968) 263 C.A.2d 27, the court held that the fact that carpets and drapes in an apartment house could be removed without damage was of no significance. The court held that the intent was that they remain as long as they served their purpose of higher rents and rentability.

2. *Method of attachment:* Is the item attached in a permanent manner? Bolts, nails, concrete, and pipe generally are considered permanent, even though an item can be readily removed. If an item is attached by roots (a tree or plant), it generally is regarded as a fixture.

A fixture could be attached by its weight alone. An example would be a building that is not anchored to a foundation.

Personal property does not become a fixture when it has been wrongfully attached when it is attached by a person who is not the owner of the real property and who had no right or permission to make the attachment.

Case Study

The case of *Seatrain Terminal of California, Inc. v. County of Alameda* (1978) 83 C.A.3d 69 involved two cargo cranes. The cranes weighed 750 tons each and ran on rails on a wharf. They were not attached to the realty. However, the terminal had been designed for the use of cranes. The court held that even though not attached to the realty, the cranes were fixtures. They were a necessary part of the wharf and were intended to be permanent.

(Note: Alameda County sought to have the cranes declared real property so that they would be subject to real property taxes.)

3. *Adaptability:* Was the item specifically adaptable to the use of the real property? For adaptability, the item need not be custom made; it need only relate reasonably to the use.

For example, an argument could be made that a refrigerator placed in a specially built alcove is a fixture, even though its only connection to the real property is a plug in a wall socket.

Case Study

In *Allstate Ins. Co. v. County of Los Angeles* and *Security Pac. Nat'l Bank v. County of Los Angeles* (1984) 161 C.A.3d 877 (consolidated cases), the plaintiffs had elaborate computer systems placed in rooms with elevated floors (to hide the cables). They also had added supplemental air-conditioning. The County of Los Angeles took the position that the systems were real property for taxation purposes.

The buildings had not been specifically designed or substantially modified for the computer systems. There was no evidence that the systems were installed with the intention to affix them to the real estate. The court thus held that standardized general-purpose computers placed in general-purpose office buildings are personal property. The minor alterations required did not make the systems real property.

All three of the preceding tests need not be met for the courts to determine that an item is a fixture. Civil Code Section 1019 added two additional tests for fixtures:

4. *Agreement:* Parties are free to agree on whether an item is real or personal property, and their agreement will govern the nature of the property.
5. *Relationship of the parties:* When it is not clear if an item is a fixture or personal property, the issue will be determined in favor of
   - the tenant between landlord and tenant,
   - the buyer between seller and buyer, and
   - the lender between borrower and lender.

Trade Fixtures.   **Trade fixtures** are fixtures installed for the purpose of trade or business. They remain the property of the tenant and may be removed at any time prior to the expiration of the lease. In California, a tenant may remove from the premises anything the tenant has affixed thereto for the purposes of trade, manufacture, ornament, or domestic use if the removal can be effected without substantial injury to the premises and unless some agreement to the contrary has been made between the landlord and the tenant.

Case Study

In the case of *Roberts v. Mills* (1922) 56 C.A. 556, the court held that a building was a trade fixture. The building erected by the tenant was built in such a manner that it could be removed without injury to the premises.

Civil Code Section 1019 restricts tenants' rights to remove trade fixtures if the trade fixture becomes an integral part of the premises.

Case Study

In the case of *Yokohama Specie Bank Ltd. v. Higashi* (1943) 56 C.A.2d 709, a tenant installed a refrigeration plant in a building. Installation required removal of columns supporting the building and substitution of refrigerating rooms. The court held that because the refrigerating rooms had become an integral part of the building, they were not subject to removal by the tenant.

For month-to-month leases courts generally will allow a reasonable period after the end of the lease for removal of trade fixtures.

A "mistaken improver" is allowed to remove the improvements, even though they would otherwise be regarded as fixtures. He or she will, however, be liable for damages resulting from the removal.

Mobile Homes

Since July 1, 1980, mobile homes attached to a foundation have been taxable as real property. Besides placing the mobile home on a foundation, to have the home considered real property the owner must

- obtain a building permit,
- obtain a certificate of occupancy, and
- record a document reflecting that the mobile home has been affixed to a foundation.

A mobile home may not be removed from a foundation (real property) unless

- all persons who have any interest in the real property consent to its removal and
- the Department of Housing and Community Development is notified 30 days prior to removal.

Mobile homes sold new after July 1, 1980, and not attached to a foundation and mobile homes sold prior to that date whose vehicle license fees are 120 days or more delinquent are taxed as personal property. While the tax rate and procedure for personal property and real property are virtually indistinguishable, mobile homes attached to permanent foundations have certain advantages over mobile homes that are taxed as personal property. Under Proposition 13, the assessed value for mobile homes taxed as real property can increase only 2 percent each year. If taxed as personal property, the mobile home would be taxed at full market value.

Mobile homes sold new on or before June 30, 1980 continue to be taxed as vehicles. The vehicle fees are now paid to the Department of Housing and Community Development, not the Department of Motor Vehicles.

■ DEGREE OF OWNERSHIP

The degree of ownership a person has in property is known as an *estate*.

Fee Simple or Fee Simple Absolute

The **fee simple** or fee simple absolute estate is the highest degree of ownership possible. Normal home ownership would be held in fee simple. There are three characteristics of fee simple ownership:

1. There is no time limit.
2. Owners can transfer title freely.
3. The estate may be inherited.

A grant that does not indicate the extent of the interest being conveyed is presumed to be made in fee simple.

The beneficial rights of ownership are called the **bundle of rights**, and they include the right to convey, lease, use, encumber, inherit, and exclude others. Ownership rights are not, however, absolute. Under the police power of the state, land use can be regulated (see Chapter 13) and property can be taken, with compensation, for public purposes (see eminent domain, Chapter 9).

Defeasible Estates. A **defeasible estate** is an estate that can be lost. The fee interest is qualified. For example, with a fee on a **condition subsequent,** property is transferred to a grantee with a condition. If the condition is breached, the estate can revert to the grantor by court action. The grantor must bring action within five years of the breach (Civil Code Section 784). The grantor therefore retains a **reversionary interest**.

Grantors sometimes use grants with a condition subsequent to advance their personal convictions. For example, a common condition subsequent is the prohibition of the sale of alcoholic beverages. The deed could provide that the property, if ever used for the sale of alcoholic beverages, shall revert to the grantor or his or her heirs. If a grantor failed to take action within a five-year period after a condition subsequent was breached, the courts could determine that the grantor has waived the right to enforce the reversion.

Property also may be dedicated to a municipality or charity with instructions for its specific use, the condition being that abandonment of that use will result in reversion of the property to the grantor. Courts generally will interpret the specified use quite liberally to avoid forfeiture.

Case Study

In *Springmeyer v. City of South Lake Tahoe* (1982) 132 C.A.3d 375, the city acquired title with a condition subsequent that provided for automatic reversion to the grantor if "the city failed to build office buildings for municipal government use by a specified date or" the buildings no longer were used for government office purposes.

The city allowed the county to use the buildings, and the grantor demanded reversion under the second condition. The court held that because reversion is such a harsh penalty, if more than one interpretation is possible, it must fall against triggering a reversion. In this case "government office purposes" was held to include federal, state, county, and local offices, so the property did not revert to the grantor.

Case Study

The case of *Alamo School District v. Jones* (1960) 182 C.A.2d 180 involved a deed given to a school district subject to the right of the grantor to buy back the land at the same price should it ever be abandoned by the school district. The court held that this was not a defeasible estate but rather was simply a contingent option to purchase. This option was held to be personal, so it did not pass to the heirs of the grantor. It was void upon the grantor's death.

Because the law abhors forfeiture, courts often will determine that a condition is only a covenant so that the remedy for breach will be monetary damages rather than forfeiture.

Restraints Against Alienation.   A restraint in a transfer that unreasonably restricts future alienation (the ability to grant, sell, devise, lease, or encumber) is unenforceable and void because it is contrary to public policy. An example of such a **restraint against alienation** would be a conveyance on the condition that the grantee not convey to other than "heirs of my body."

Life Estates

Life estates are given to a grantee for life. The life tenant has exclusive and absolute use of the property, for his or her lifetime, is entitled to the rents and profits from the property, and can even file a homestead declaration on his or her interest.

A life estate is generally granted to a person for his or her own lifetime, although it is possible to grant a life estate for the life of another (pur autre vie). When it is based on the life of another, the death of the life tenant does not affect the estate. The heirs of the deceased will have the use of the property as long as that third party is alive. Normally, however, the life estate is based on the life of the life tenant.

When the life tenant dies, the property either reverts to the grantor or his or her heirs (a reversionary interest) or passes to a designated third party, who is said to have a **remainder interest**. Upon the death of the life tenant the reversionary or remainder interest holder customarily holds title in fee simple.

If the remainder interest requires that the third party outlive the life tenant, the third-party interest is a contingent remainder (contingent on the third party's being alive to receive the remainder interest). If, however, there are no contingencies, the remainder will, upon the death of the life tenant, pass to the remainder holder or his or her heirs. This type of estate is called a *vested remainder interest* because someday the life tenant must die, ensuring that the remainder holder will receive the property.

Life estates might be granted to give the grantors a charitable tax deduction while they are alive and allow them to keep all the benefits of ownership. They often are used to care for spouses or others during their lifetime and then go to others to fulfill the wishes of the grantor.

Farmers often give their farmland to a child but retain a life estate. Knowing that he or she will eventually get the farm, the grantee thus is more likely to stay, and the grantor retains control, along with the income, for his or her life.

Life estates also can be subject to a condition subsequent, such as a life estate that goes to a remainder interest holder should the life tenant remarry. This type of estate often is used when the grantor feels that he or she has a duty to support the life tenant only while the life tenant remains unmarried.

Life estates can be granted to more than one life tenant. The interests of the joint life tenants would be much like a joint tenancy (see Chapter 8) with the last survivor having sole possession [*Green v. Brown* (1951) 37 C.2d 391].

A life tenant cannot use the property in any way that would diminish its value. For example, if tearing down structures or clearing out timber would reduce the property's value, the life tenant would be prohibited from these acts. The life tenant may, however, cut timber as necessary for repairs and fuel. The life tenant also may mine the property but only if it was mined prior to the life estate.

A life tenant may not commit **waste**; that is, he or she must maintain the property, pay taxes, and protect the rights of reversionary or remainder interest holders. If a life tenant does commit waste, the court might appoint a receiver.

Case Study

In the case of *King v. Hawley* (1952) 113 C.A.2d 534, a testator gave a life estate in all of his property to his sister. The will provided that she could "use all of the proceeds of my estate for her comfort and support, but that whatever may be left shall go" to the remainder interest. The life tenant transferred some of the property to friends without consideration and some with inadequate consideration. The life tenant was held to have fraudulently attempted to defeat the remainder interest.

For an extraordinary expense, such as a sewer hookup, the expense will be borne proportionately by the life tenant and the remainder or reversionary rights holders, based on the life of the improvement and the age of the life tenant. Courts prorate extraordinary costs based on the benefits to be received.

The life tenant can borrow against the property but cannot encumber the property beyond his or her lifetime without the concurrence of remainder or reversionary interest holders. Lenders might lend on the life tenant's interests alone if the loan is coupled with a policy of life insurance payable to the lender.

Remainder and reversionary interest holders also can assign or encumber their interests; however, neither they nor their assignees or creditors will have any right to use the property or receive rents or profits until the life estate ends.

Unless the life tenant's use is restricted, the life tenant can lease the property, but the death of the life tenant will terminate the lease unless the reversionary or remainder interest holders also sign the lease as lessors and thus obligate their interests. Before signing a long-term lease, a prospective tenant who will be making substantial improvements should have a title search conducted to be certain of the lessor's interests.

Unless restricted, a life tenant can sell his or her interest, but the purchaser will receive no more than the life tenant possessed. Upon the death of the life tenant the purchaser's interest will cease.

A life tenant has no duty to insure the property. If the life tenant does insure and the property is destroyed, the prevailing view is that the life tenant is entitled to the insurance proceeds. Some courts have held that the insurance was taken out for the joint benefit of the life tenant and the remainder or reversionary interest holder. A remainder or reversionary interest holder who is not specifically named as an insured should obtain insurance to protect his or her interests.

If a life tenant receives a property with a mortgage or trust deed against it, the principal payments on the mortgage or trust deed will be a charge against the remainder or reversionary holder, but the interest payments will be the responsibility of the life tenant.

If a property is taken by eminent domain (see Chapter 9), which requires the payment of "just compensation" by the government, the life tenant and remainder interest owners will share the proceeds based on the benefits to which they are entitled.

A deed transferring the interest of the remainder interest holders to a life tenant will merge the two interests into a fee simple estate owned by the former life tenant.

Case Study

In the case of *Osborne v. Osborne* (1954) 42 C.2d 358, a deed granting a fee simple estate was deposited into escrow with the provision that it not be delivered to the grantee until the death of the grantor. The court held that, if the grantor intended the transaction to be irrevocable, the deed created a remainder interest in fee simple with a life estate reserved in the grantor.

Rule Against Perpetuities.   The **rule against perpetuities** states that any noncharitable interest must vest without limitations within the lives of persons in being at the time of conveyance, plus 21 years. The interest is further restricted in that it must either vest with an owner or terminate within 90 years of its creation. This rule would prohibit a perpetual trust to support the heirs of the grantor.

Freehold and Nonfreehold Estates

Nonfreehold estates are leasehold interests (personal property). **Freehold estates** (fee simple and life estates) are real property. Nonfreehold estates are tenancies and are covered in detail in Chapter 15.

Concurrent Estates

Concurrent estates—more than one ownership or estate at the same time—can exist in a property. For example, a tenant can have a leasehold estate while an owner has a fee simple interest. The fee simple owner would have a reversionary interest of possession at the expiration of the leasehold interest.

Air and mineral interests also can be conveyed, creating separate interests. Property even can be divided horizontally, with the mineral, oil, and gas rights being conveyed in layers.

Successive Estates

Estates can be established to succeed existing estates. An example of **successive estates** is a remainder or reversionary estate to follow a life estate.

■ RECORDING OF REAL PROPERTY INTERESTS

Under the Spanish and Mexican governments, California had no system for recording and safeguarding interests in real property. To prove ownership, a person physically had to possess the original grant or deed.

When California became a state in 1850, one of the first acts of the California legislature was to institute a system for recording interests in real property. The system adopted was patterned after that established by the original 13 states. By providing for evidence of title to be collected and made available at central locations, recording statutes protect buyers against secret conveyances and interests and make real property readily and freely transferable.

The basic real property recording laws are found in Civil Code Sections 1169-1220 and Government Code Sections 27201-27383. The recording statutes provide that, after being acknowledged, any instrument or judgment affecting title to, possession of, or rights in real property may be recorded. Real estate listings may not be recorded, because the agent has no rights in real property, only rights to compensation.

Prohibitions against recording contained in documents that could otherwise be recorded would be considered contrary to public policy, and the document could be recorded in spite of the attempted prohibition.

Acknowledgment

Before a document can be recorded it must be acknowledged. **Acknowledgment** is made before a notary or other designated official by the person attesting to the document. That person acknowledges that he or she is the person claimed and is the one who has signed the instrument as his or her own free act. The maker of an instrument must appear personally before the notary, and the notary has a duty to ascertain his or her identity by personal knowledge or by identification by a third person under oath. A notary can accept driver's licenses and passports as proof of identity. The notary does not verify the facts of the document.

Notary publics who verify the acknowledgment of a deed, quitclaim deed, or deed of trust must place in the notary's journal the right thumbprint of the person signing the document.

The acknowledgment must include the state and county where acknowledged and the name and capacity of the acknowledging party.

When two or more persons are executing a document requiring acknowledgment, each of their signatures must be acknowledged. Without acknowledgment, constructive notice (discussed in the next section) of that person's interest has not been given.

A person who holds an instrument that otherwise could be recorded except for the lack of acknowledgment can bring an action against the other party to prove the instrument and can then record a certified copy of the judgment (Civil Code Section 1203).

Excepted from the requirement that instruments be acknowledged to be recorded or filed are

- judgments authenticated by the clerk of the court;
- notices of mining claims;
- tax certificates of amount due;
- leases from the federal government; and
- documents required to be signed by an attorney, such as a *lis pendens*, which is a notice of a pending lawsuit involving a claim against real property.

Constructive Notice

Recording a document gives the whole world **constructive notice** of an interest in real property. If A conveyed to B and B recorded the deed, subsequent grantees of the property from A would get nothing because they would have had constructive notice that A no longer owned the property.

If a document is recorded with a defect, such as the absence of acknowledgment, the recording would not give constructive notice until one year after the recording. A defect, such as a document filed in the wrong county or with a name spelled incorrectly, so that a reasonable search of the records would not reveal the document, does not provide constructive notice.

Possession also gives constructive notice. Assume A deeded to B, who took possession but did not record. If A later conveyed the same property to C, who recorded, title would be with B. C had constructive notice by B's possession of B's interest. In failing to check with the party in possession to ascertain his or her interests, C did not act diligently. If a buyer checks with a party in possession and is not informed of an adverse claim, however, the possession does not provide constructive notice of the interests of the party in possession.

A plaintiff in an action involving real property may file a *lis pendens* with the county recorder to provide subsequent purchasers or encumbrancers with constructive notice of the plaintiff's claim of interest.

While the law is clear that recording gives constructive notice of the documents recorded, it is not clear whether recording gives constructive notice of all other documents referenced in the recorded document. The prevailing view is that a person should reasonably investigate the referenced document.

Case Study

Gates Rubber Co. v. Ulman (1989) 214 C.A.3d 356 involved a tenant under a 25-year lease who also had a separate option to purchase the property for $550,000 during the 20th year of the lease. Neither the lease nor the option was recorded, although a short-form lease was recorded that named the parties and referenced the lease. The landlord sold the property six years later for $633,000. Fourteen years later, in the 20th year of the lease, the tenant sought to exercise the purchase option (the property was now worth $2 million). The court of appeal affirmed the trial court's decision that the defendant (Ulman) should prevail if he qualifies as a bona fide purchaser without notice. While in some instances possession places a duty to inquire, the court held that this is the case only when the possession is inconsistent with record title. In this instance the

(continued on next page)

tenant's possession was consistent with a recorded lease that made no reference to an option to purchase. While Ulman had a duty to check the lease referenced in the recorded lease, there was no duty to inquire as to any other rights the tenant might have. Ulman therefore had taken title free of the option.

Actual Notice

While recording and possession give constructive notice of an interest in real property, **actual notice** is express knowledge of the prior interest. A person who has actual knowledge of a prior interest cannot claim priority of interest because he or she recorded first. Actual notice has the same effect as the constructive notice of recording.

Figure 7.1 illustrates the difference between actual notice and constructive notice.

Priority

Besides providing constructive notice of an interest, recording determines priority of interests. Recording often has been called "the race of the diligent" because priority of interest in the absence of actual knowledge is determined by time and date of recording and not time and date of execution of an instrument (Civil Code Section 1214). (The first to record is first in right.)

Assume A conveyed to B and A later conveyed the same property to C. If C arrived at the recorder's office ahead of B, then C's deed would be recorded first. As a general rule C would take title and B would have nothing (other than a claim against A). If C had diligently searched the records, C would have found no evidence of B 's interest. If anyone should suffer, it should be the one who was negligent in failing to immediately make his or her interest known as a matter of record rather than a diligent later purchaser, which would mean that C would have good title.

FIGURE 7.1

Notice

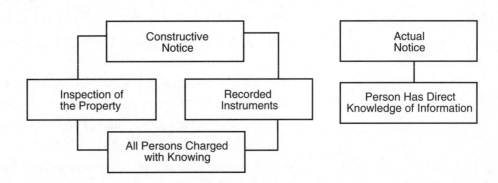

Recording does not give priority over prior unrecorded conveyances if the person recording is not acting in good faith or has not paid a valuable consideration. For example, a recorded deed given without consideration (a gift deed) would not give the grantee priority over a prior unrecorded deed or trust deed that was given for valuable consideration. Therefore, for recording to give priority it must be done by a bona fide purchaser (or lender) for value without prior notice of other interests. The courts would consider the adequacy of consideration in determining whether a party is a bona fide purchaser. A person who receives notice of a prior interest at any time prior to paying the consideration would not be a bona fide purchaser.

A purchase-money trust deed (a trust deed given to finance the purchase) would take priority over liens against the grantee, even though those liens attach as soon as title is passed.

Failure to Record

The recording act does not legally require recording; it merely permits recording. Between a grantor and a grantee of an unrecorded deed, the grantee would have title. The grantee's title, however, would not take priority over a later recorded deed or trust deed given by the original grantor, provided that the later grantee or beneficiary (lender) had no constructive or actual notice of the prior conveyance.

Recording is required for homestead declarations, mechanics' liens, and judgment liens. Without recording, these instruments have no effect.

Documents Recordable Without Owner's Consent

Recording documents in proper form with the owner's notarized signature cannot be prohibited. But the following documents can be recorded without the owner's notarized signature: judgment liens, mining claims against the federal government, tax deeds, trustee's deeds, mechanics' liens, federal and state income tax liens, child support liens, homeowners' association liens, and *lis pendens*.

Defective Recording

To provide constructive notice of an interest, a document must be recorded in the county where the real property is located. Recording in the wrong county would have the same effect as not recording at all.

A person who gave a deed of trust on property without owning it would find this lien against the property upon later acquiring title. This principle is called the *doctrine of after-acquired title*. But, because a reasonable title search by a later lender would not reveal a lien placed prior to ownership, the earlier lien would not take priority over a purchase-money lien.

If an instrument required to be acknowledged is recorded without acknowledgment or with a defective acknowledgment, the recording does not provide constructive notice to other parties until one year after the recording. A party who has actual knowledge of a defectively acknowledged instrument within one year of its recording would take subject to the interests disclosed in the defectively recorded document and could not raise the defense that the document failed to provide notice.

An instrument with the grantor's or grantee's name spelled incorrectly or with a different name given for the grantor or grantee, so that the instrument would not be discovered in a diligent search of the chain of title, does not give constructive notice.

A wild document, one outside the chain of title, gives no constructive notice because it would not be discovered by a diligent search of the records.

A recorded assignment or sublease of an unrecorded lease also would be outside the chain of title and therefore would not give constructive notice.

A forged document is void and does not give constructive notice of any interest and has no effect. Knowingly recording a forged or false document is a felony (Penal Code Section 115). Such an action would also be a tort (slander of title).

Recently there has been a rash of incidents in which unscrupulous individuals have forged deeds to themselves, using both forged owner signatures and forged notary seals. They have then borrowed on the property. Because a forged document does not transfer any interest, the lenders did not obtain a valid lien interest in the property. Filing a false deed or deed of trust can result in criminal penalties.

An improper description of land being conveyed does not give constructive notice as to the land intended to be conveyed.

The Recording Process   While it is in the best interests of a grantee to record a document as soon as possible, there is no time limit for recording (except in the case of mechanics' liens). A document is deemed recorded when it is deposited in the recorder's office and marked "filed for record." The recorder gives each document a filing number indicating the order in which the document was received and time-stamps the document.

The recorder transfers the document to the appropriate book of records. Documents are indexed alphabetically by grantor-grantee, showing the name, nature of the recording, date of recording, and reference where the document is filed. Ordinarily the document is photocopied and the original returned to the person indicated as the recipient in the heading of the document.

If the recorder improperly indexes a document, the recording does not provide constructive notice. The duty to see that a document is recorded properly falls on the person recording.

> ## Case Study
> In the case of *Hochstein v. Romero* (1990) 219 C.A.3d 447, an abstract of judgment was improperly indexed. The court held because the abstract was not locatable by search, it did not impart constructive notice. It must therefore be treated as if it were never recorded, and a bona fide purchaser for value took title free of the judgment lien.

The name of the grantor and grantee must be signed legibly or printed for the recorder.

The recorder will not accept for recording a document that is not in English unless a certified English translation is attached to it.

A document can be recorded in more than one county and would apply to the property within the counties where recorded. A certified copy can be used to record in more than one county.

The recorder will not record until the recording fee is paid. The county recorder also will require that the documentary transfer tax (tax on seller's equity being conveyed) be paid prior to recording deeds.

The county recorder will require that deeds contain the name and address to which tax statements are to be sent. Failure to comply, however, does not affect constructive notice.

Any person has the right to check the county recorder's records.

Change of Ownership   As provided in Proposition 13, real property is reassessed upon sale. Therefore, transferees of ownership interests are required to file a change of ownership statement with the county recorder or tax assessor within 45 days after receipt of a request from the assessor. Failure to comply could result in a penalty of $100 or 10 percent of the current year's taxes, whichever is greater.

■ SUMMARY

Ownership passed from government to private ownership in California under Spanish rule by the establishment of *pueblos* or towns. Under Mexican rule, large tracts of land known as *ranchos* were given out. The United States gave tracts of land to private owners under various homestead, timber, and mining acts. Additionally, large tracts were given to railroads and colleges. Government grants were known as *patents*. Only about half of the land in California is owned privately.

Real property consists of land and what goes with the land. Personal property, known as *chattels*, consists of movable property that does not automatically transfer with the conveyance of real property. Chattels real are personal property interests in real estate such as lease interests, mortgages, and trust deeds.

Fixtures are former items of personal property that have become so affixed to real property that they are part of the real estate. In the absence of an agreement, three basic tests are used to determine whether an item is a fixture. They are intent, method of attachment, and adaptability.

Trade fixtures installed for the purpose of conducting a business or trade remain personal property and may be removed by the tenant.

While mobile homes attached to a foundation are considered real property, mobile homes not permanently attached are personal property.

A person having property in fee simple, the highest degree of ownership, owns it without time limitation, can convey it freely, and can pass it by inheritance.

Defeasible estates are estates that can be defeated or lost upon the happening of some event (estate on a condition subsequent).

Life estates are given for the life of a person. Upon the death of the life tenant the life estate either reverts to the grantor or his or her heirs (a reversionary interest) or passes to a third person (a remainder interest). The life tenant cannot encumber the property beyond his or her lifetime.

Both fee simple estates and life estates are known as *freehold estates*. *Nonfreehold estates* are leasehold interests.

Recording gives constructive notice of an interest in real property. To be recorded, an instrument must be acknowledged. Possession also provides constructive notice to parties who acquire later interests of the rights of the party in possession.

Recording does not give priority notice when the party recording had actual notice of a prior unrecorded interest. Recording of a deed given without consideration would not take precedence over a prior unrecorded interest given for good and valuable consideration.

Defective recording that would not reveal an interest by a diligent search of the records does not give constructive notice.

The recording process involves depositing the document with the county recorder. It is marked "filed for record" and given a number. The document then is transferred to the appropriate book of records and the original is returned to the person recording. The recorder keeps an alphabetical grantor-grantee index.

■ DISCUSSION CASES

1. A computer system was housed in a building designed for that use. The components, which were of great weight and size, were interconnected by hundreds of cables. The floor was raised to accommodate these cables. Air-conditioning and humidity controls were installed for the system's efficiency. **For the purpose of taxation, is the computer system a fixture?**

   Bank of America v. County of Los Angeles (1964)
   224 C.A.2d 108

2. The county assessor assessed the plaintiff's leasehold interests in the *Queen Mary* as real property. The plaintiff claimed that it was attached to a floating vessel, so the interests were personal property. **Considering the manner in which the vessel is attached to its pier and its adaptability, is the *Queen Mary* real or personal property?**

   Specialty Restaurants Corp. v. County of Los Angeles (1977)
   67 C.A.3d 924

3. Two trust deeds were presented to the recorder at the same time. The trust deed intended to be recorded second was recorded first, and the trust deed intended to be recorded first was recorded second. The trust deed that was recorded second stated on its face that it was to be a first trust deed. Which trust deed has priority?

   Phelps v. American Mortgage Company (1936) 6 C.2d 604

4. A dealer negotiated a franchise with a beverage firm. A recorded mortgage showed the dealer to be a corporation. **Was the prior recorded mortgage constructive notice to the beverage firm that the dealer was a corporation?**

    Nesbitt Fruit Products Inc. v. Del Monte Beverage Co. (1966) 177 C.A.2d 353

5. A notary personally did not know the person who it was claimed had acknowledged a document, and the executing party was not present when the notary acknowledged the signature. **Does the recording give constructive notice?**

    Thomas v. Speck (1941) 47 C.A.2d 512

6. A house was built on the wrong lot. It was sold several times, and the owners believed they owned the house. The defendants, who were in possession, made improvements to the house and walks. **What are the rights of these innocent improvers?**

    Taliafero v. Colasso (1956) 139 C.A.2d 903

7. A delivered deed provided that it was not to take effect until the grantor died. **Was this a valid conveyance?**

    Lowe v. Ruhlman (1945) 67 C.A.2d 828

8. A recorded mortgage indicated one date for its execution, and the acknowledgment was dated five days later. The trustee in bankruptcy sought to set aside the instrument and make the creditors unsecured. **Does the discrepancy affect the constructive notice of recording?**

    Clements v. Snider (1969) 409 F.2d 549

The court decisions for the above cases can be found on our Web site at **www.dearbornRE.com**. Click on the **"Instructor Resources"** link, then scroll down the page until you find the link titled "California Real Estate Law 5th Edition."

■ CHAPTER QUIZ

1. Real property includes which of the following?

   a. Growing annual crops
   b. Mineral rights
   c. Leasehold interests
   d. Trust deeds

2. Examples of chattels real include all of the following *except*

   a. furniture.
   b. trust deeds.
   c. lease interests.
   d. shares in a housing cooperative.

3. Which of the following would be classified as personal property?

   a. Mineral rights
   b. An oil lease for ten years
   c. Fixtures
   d. Riparian rights

4. Which is not an important test of a fixture?

   a. Cost
   b. Intent
   c. Method of attachment
   d. Adaptability

5. Which of the following is *not* an appurtenance?

   a. A right of egress
   b. Mineral rights
   c. Water rights
   d. Trade fixtures

6. A new mobile home located in a rental park in 1999 was not attached to a foundation. It would be taxed

   a. as real property.
   b. as personal property.
   c. as a vehicle with fees to the Department of Motor Vehicles.
   d. with fees paid to the Department of Housing and Community Development.

7. Which of the following is a characteristic of an indefeasible estate?

   a. It cannot be canceled.
   b. It can be lost upon a happening.
   c. It is voidable.
   d. It is a reversionary interest.

8. Which of the following best describes a fee on a condition subsequent?

    a. Ownership interest that does not transfer to grantee until something happens
    b. A qualified interest that may be lost should something happen
    c. A recording charge that need not be paid until the property is sold
    d. A nonfreehold interest

9. The future interest of a grantor of a life estate would likely be a

    a. reversionary interest.
    b. contingent remainder interest.
    c. vested remainder interest.
    d. nonfreehold estate.

10. A future uncertain interest of possession would most likely be a

    a. personal property interest.
    b. vested remainder interest.
    c. contingent remainder interest.
    d. life estate.

11. Which of the following is a right of a life tenant?

    a. To refuse to pay taxes
    b. To lease the property
    c. To convey the interest by will
    d. To encumber the reversionary interest

12. The following is *not* a characteristic of fee simple ownership:

    a. Nonfreehold interest   c. Freely transferable by owner
    b. No time limit   d. Inheritable

13. Henry willed his property in trust with the beneficiaries to be all future heirs of his body. His action is prohibited by

    a. the statute of limitations.
    b. the rule against perpetuities.
    c. laches.
    d. the recording statutes.

14. A received a life estate in property, but the property had a mortgage against it. Which of the following statements is true regarding this situation?

    a. Mortgage payments are the responsibility of the remainder interest holder.
    b. The mortgage nullifies the life estate.
    c. The life tenant pays the interest, but the remainder interest pays the principal.
    d. The mortgage payment is split evenly between life tenant and remainder holder.

15. Which of the following is a characteristic of an estate in real property?

    a. It can exist within another estate.
    b. It will always run forever.
    c. It requires possession.
    d. It is a nonfreehold interest.

16. What is the result when the grantee records a deed that states that it cannot be recorded?

    a. The recordation does not give constructive notice.
    b. The deed has been voided.
    c. The title reverts to the grantor.
    d. The recording gives constructive notice.

17. A person who states that his or her signing is a free act would be making a(n)

    a. affirmation.
    b. acknowledgment.
    c. notarization.
    d. verification.

18. A sold property to B. B took possession but did not record his deed. A learned of this and immediately sold to C. C recorded his deed. Which of the following decisions would a court of law most likely render?

    a. C wins because he did the proper thing by recording his deed.
    b. C wins because he had no notice.
    c. B wins because he was in possession.
    d. B wins because he purchased first.

19. Which of the following is *not* true of recording?

    a. It provides constructive notice of the recorded instrument.
    b. It provides actual notice of an interest.
    c. It determines the priority of liens.
    d. It creates a presumption of delivery.

20. Priority of trust deeds can easily be ascertained by the

    a. date of recording.　　c. heading of the instrument.
    b. date of the instrument.　　d. date on the note.

21. A sold to B on January 1. B took possession on January 15 and recorded her deed on February 1. A obtained a home equity loan on the same property on January 10. The lender, C, recorded the same day. On January 20, A sold the same property to D who recorded on January 21. What are the rights of the parties?

    a. D has title subject to C's lien.
    b. B has title clear of any lien.
    c. B has title but C has a valid lien against it.
    d. None of the above

22. A recorded gift deed would *not* take priority over

    a. subsequent recorded deeds for value.
    b. a prior unrecorded deed given for valuable consideration.
    c. subsequent trust deeds.
    d. prior unrecorded gift deeds.

23. Which of the following would result when Albert deeded to Henry, but Henry inadvertently recorded in the wrong county?

    a. Albert would retain title.
    b. Between Henry and Albert, Henry would have title.
    c. The minor defect in recording would not affect the constructive notice.
    d. The deed could be voided upon return of consideration.

24. The county recorder indexes deeds by

    a. time received.
    b. location.
    c. grantor's and grantee's names.
    d. tax assessor's number.

25. Which of the following is true regarding recordation?

    a. A document can be recorded in more than one county.
    b. To be recorded, deeds must include the name and address where tax statements are to be sent.
    c. The duty to see that the instrument is properly recorded falls with the person recording the instrument.
    d. All of the above

CHAPTER EIGHT

OWNERSHIP OF REAL PROPERTY

■ KEY TERMS

attractive nuisance
  doctrine
community apartment
  project
community property
condominium
corporation
fictitious name
general partner
joint tenancy

joint venture
limited liability
limited partnership
partition action
partnership
planned unit
  development (PUD)
real estate investment
  trust (REIT)
severalty

stock cooperative
survivorship
tenancy in common
time-share
unincorporated
  association

■ OWNERSHIP IN SEVERALTY

Every property must have an owner. In Pennsylvania a 600-acre forest that was deeded to God reverted to the state for nonpayment of taxes.* Ownership in **severalty** is ownership by one individual or corporation. (A

---

*American Forests, February 1931, p. 112.

corporation is a legal entity.) It is singular ownership with no other party or parties having a common ownership interest. A city (municipal corporation) would own city property in severalty, as would an individual owning property by himself or herself.

■ TENANCY IN COMMON

A **tenancy in common** is undivided ownership—of real or personal property— by more than one party without the right of survivorship. An undivided interest means that the tenant in common has a share in the whole and not ownership of a separate portion. For example, a tenant in common having a one-half interest in ten acres of land would have a one-half interest in the entire ten acres and not one-half of the land (five acres).

The right of **survivorship** means the right of other co-owners to receive one co-owner's interest upon his or her death. Upon the death of a tenant in common his or her interest does not pass by survivorship to the other tenants in common. The interest passes by will or intestate succession to the heirs of the decedent. If the tenant in common dies intestate (without a will) and leaves no heirs, the interest will escheat (pass) to the state. (Unmarried partners who live together will often choose tenancy in common as their form of ownership when the survivorship feature is not desired.)

Interests of tenants in common do not have to be equal and can be created at different times by different instruments; however, each tenant in common has an equal right of possession. Therefore, if one tenant in common is in sole possession of the premises, that tenant in common will not be obligated to the other tenants in common for rent unless he or she agrees to it. A tenant in common cannot, in the absence of an agreement to the contrary, exclude other tenants in common from the property.

One tenant in common cannot give an exclusive lease to a third party without the agreement of all of the tenants in common, because such a lease would be inconsistent with the other tenants' equal rights of possession.

A tenant in common who farms the property does not have to share the crops with the other tenants in common. However, if a tenant in common receives rents or royalties from a third person, the other tenants in common have the right to share in the income based on their proportional ownership.

See *Black v. Black* (1949) 91 C.A.2d 328 for rights of a tenant in possession.

If one tenant in common pays reasonable and necessary property expenses or taxes, that tenant is entitled to recover proportional shares of the expenditures from the other tenant(s) in common.

While a tenant in common can get contributions for repairs, one tenant in common cannot get contributions for improvements from the others if the others have not agreed to the improvements. Otherwise it would be possible to make unauthorized improvements beyond the payment ability of another tenant in common. The result would be that the tenant in common who could not pay his or her share of the cost could end up losing his or her interest.

One tenant in common can get an injunction against another tenant in common to stop waste. One tenant in common also can force another to make an accounting for rents, royalties, expenses, and profits of a property held in common.

Under extremely unusual circumstances a tenant in common who has exclusive use may acquire title from the other tenants in common based on adverse possession. Should a tenant in common who has exclusive possession of the jointly owned property clearly indicate that his or her possession is intended to preclude the possession by the other tenants in common, that action could be considered an ouster. The tenant's use would be hostile and would enable him or her to obtain title by adverse possession by continuing the open, notorious and hostile use continuously for a five-year period and paying the taxes for that period (see Chapter 9).

No consent of the other tenants in common is required to transfer an interest or even a portion of an interest to another.

A tenant in common can encumber his or her own undivided interest. Any subsequent foreclosure by a creditor would apply only to the interest of that tenant in common.

A conveyance to two or more persons, other than spouses, that fails to indicate how title is to be held will pass title as a tenancy in common.

■ JOINT TENANCY

Joint tenancy, like tenancy in common, is an undivided interest in either real or personal property (or both). Unlike a tenancy in common, however, joint tenancy has the right of survivorship. Upon the death of a joint tenant his or her interest ceases. The interest is incapable of being transferred by will or by intestate succession. The surviving joint tenants receive the interest of the deceased joint tenant. Joint tenancy property does not need to be probated, because it could not be part of the estate of the deceased person. Because of survivorship, the property interest passes to the surviving joint tenants free of claims of the personal creditors of the deceased.

Assume A, B, and C are joint tenants. If C dies, A and B will be joint tenants. If B then dies, A will be an owner in severalty.

A _____ B _____ C   Joint tenants

Each owns an undivided ⅓ interest.

        C Dies:

A _____ B _____ χ

A and B are joint tenants; each owns an undivided ½ interest.

        B Dies:

A _____ χ _____ χ

A owns the entire property in severalty.

Because corporations can live forever, which would defeat survivorship, corporations cannot hold title as joint tenants. Also, because of potential conflicts with community property laws, an unmarried person ordinarily should not own property in joint tenancy with a married person unless the spouse of the married person signs a quitclaim deed or otherwise consents to the joint tenancy.

The legal principle that a murderer cannot inherit from the victim applies to joint tenancies. The courts will not allow the murderer to profit by survivorship. They will view the victim as being a tenant in common, and his or her interest will pass to the heirs.

In the event of the simultaneous deaths of all of the joint tenants, the Uniform Simultaneous Death Act will treat the interest of each of the joint tenants as if he or she had survived the other(s). This would result in separate probates of each of their interests.

For title purposes, when a joint tenant dies, the survivor(s) should record, in the county where the property is located, either

- a certified copy of a court decree determining the fact of death and describing the property or
- a certified copy of the death certificate (an affidavit identifying the

deceased as one of the joint tenants in described property) and an affidavit of survivorship normally would be attached.

Creation of Joint Tenancy

The conveying instrument must expressly state that ownership will be held in joint tenancy; otherwise any conveyance to two or more persons, other than spouses, will be considered a conveyance to tenants in common.

Two couples could own property as tenants in common with each couple's interest a joint tenancy. A deed could express this through language such as "Tom and Helen Smith (as joint tenants) as tenants in common with Frank and Ethyl Jones (as joint tenants)." Also required to create a joint tenancy are the four unities of

1. time,
2. title,
3. interest, and
4. possession.

Time.   Joint tenants must get their interests at the same time. Formerly, if a person who owned property in severalty wished to create a joint tenancy with another, the grantor had to convey his or her interest to a third party (a straw man), who would then convey the property back to the grantor and the other party(ies) as joint tenants. One problem with this procedure was that if any judgments against the straw man existed, they would become encumbrances on the property the instant the straw man took title. The property conveyed as the joint tenancy thereby could be subject to liens. Now Section 683 of the Civil Code makes it unnecessary to follow this procedure. A joint tenancy can be created by an owner's simply deeding the property to himself or herself and the other party(ies) as joint tenants.

Title.   Joint tenants must acquire their interests by the same document.

Interest.   Joint tenants, unlike tenants in common, must have equal interests. A grant that provides for unequal interests will create a tenancy in common even if it states that the property being conveyed will be owned in joint tenancy.

Possession.   Possession is the only one of the four unities that is also applicable to tenants in common. The joint tenants' rights as to use and contributions are identical with those of tenants in common.

Termination of Joint Tenancy

The sale or transfer by a joint tenant of his or her interest terminates the joint tenancy as it applies to that interest.

Assume A, B, and C are joint tenants. If C sells to D, then A and B will remain joint tenants, each with an undivided one-third interest, and D will have an undivided one-third interest as a tenant in common.

A _____ B _____ C   Joint tenants

A _____ B _____ C
                ↓
                D

If B dies, A will take B's interest by survivorship, and A will be a tenant in common with D. The joint tenancy cannot continue, because no two owners have the four unities of joint tenancy. A will have an undivided two-thirds interest as a tenant in common with D, who will be a tenant in common with an undivided one-third interest.

A _____ D   Tenants in common

One of the problems with a joint tenancy is that a joint tenant can convey his or her interest to another, and the other joint tenant(s) might be completely unaware that his or her survivorship rights have been defeated.

Bankruptcy of a joint tenant terminates the joint tenancy as it applies to the bankrupt party's interest.

Case Study

The case of *Riddle v. Harmon* (1980) 102 C.A.3d 524 held that one joint tenant can terminate the joint tenancy by a conveyance to himself or herself as a tenant in common.

A judgment against one joint tenant does not sever the joint tenancy, but levying execution against the property and having a sale does end the joint tenancy. If the joint tenant dies prior to the execution of the judgment against the property, the property will pass free and clear of the debt to the surviving joint tenant(s).

A joint tenant can borrow on his or her interest without destroying the joint tenancy. If the loan is foreclosed, the joint tenancy of course will be broken. However, if the borrower dies, the surviving joint tenant(s) will get the interest free and clear. In lending on a joint tenant's interests, a lender would want to couple the loan with a life insurance policy that would pay off the loan in the event of the borrower's death.

Because of changing relationships, a person might no longer wish to remain a joint tenant or tenant in common. In that case a **partition action** can be brought to break up the joint tenancy or tenancy in common. (By agreement the parties can give up their rights to a partition action.) If possible, the court will order the property divided among the co-owners.

When division is not possible or practical, the property will be sold under judicial supervision and the sale proceeds divided among the co-owners.

Case Study

In the case of *Formosa Corp. v. Rogers* (1952) 108 C.A.2d 397, the plaintiff sought a sale of a movie studio where Mary Pickford Rogers owned a 41/80 ownership. The court held that the party seeking partition by sale had the burden of proof that sale was necessary for equitable distribution. In this case the court determined that the value of the separate properties was less than the value of the whole because the property as a whole had added value resulting from its adaptation for use in making motion pictures.

■ COMMUNITY PROPERTY

Community property, originally a Spanish concept, holds that property acquired by a husband and wife during marriage is owned equally by the husband and wife. This principle differed greatly from the early English concept that the wife's property became the property of the husband.

As noted earlier, the Treaty of Guadalupe Hidalgo ending the Mexican War in 1848 called for the rights of Mexican ownership of property to be respected. The Mexicans had adopted the Spanish concept of community property. The California Constitution specifically adopted the community property concept.

Until very recently only Louisiana and a few western states had adopted the concept of community property. Because of the fundamental fairness of community property and the increased interest in women's rights, a number of states have been considering this concept. Wisconsin recently became a community property state.

Formerly, property acquired in the wife's name alone was presumed to be her separate property. Now property acquired by either spouse alone during marriage is presumed to be community property. The burden of proving it to be separate property falls on the spouse claiming separate property.

Property that is acquired with community property funds is community property.

Property that is acquired by one spouse using the credit of the other spouse is community property.

Separate property remains separate property unless it becomes commingled so as to be indistinguishable from community property, in which case it could become community property by the commingling. One spouse's use of community property to improve the separate property of the other spouse is considered a gift and is not commingling. One spouse's use of community property to improve his or her separate property could be commingling, which would convert the separate property to community property. However, the courts are more likely to give a community property interest proportionally based on the community property investment.

Exclusions   In California, excluded from the equal ownership of community property are

- property separately owned by husband or wife prior to marriage,
- rents and profits from separate property,
- property acquired by either spouse by gift or inheritance,
- property acquired with separate property funds,
- damages received for personal injuries, and
- earnings and accumulations of a spouse while living separate and apart (includes legal separation).

Case Study

The case of *Marriage of Rico* (1992) 10 C.A.4th 706 involved a couple who lived together and purchased a house as tenants in common prior to their marriage. After their marriage they refinanced their home and converted title to joint tenancy. In dividing the community property upon the couple's divorce, the court determined that each party should receive his or her separate property contribution before the appreciated value was equally divided. However, the court ruled that proper measure of reimbursement was the fair market value of each spouse's separate property at the time of conversion to community property, not the original contribution. This case shows how complicated the division of separate and community property can become upon dissolution of marriage.

Case Study

In re Marriage of Branco (1996) 47 C.A.4th 1621 involved a situation where community property funds were used to pay off a mortgage on the separate property of one spouse. The court held that the community is entitled to its share of the appreciation during the marriage.

Generally, when there is no marriage, there is no community property. When one or both spouses believe that a valid marriage existed, however, the property acquired that would have been community property had a valid marriage existed will be considered quasi-marital property and will be divided as if it were community property.

Case Study

Estate of Leslie (1984) 37 C.3d 186 involved a couple married in Mexico who lived together for nine years in California. The probate court determined that the marriage was invalid because it was not recorded as required under Mexican law. The supreme court reversed the decision and held that as a matter of fairness a putative spouse (reputed or commonly established spouse) is entitled to succeed to the property of the deceased spouse in the same manner as a legal spouse.

Case Study

Estate of Vargas (1974) 36 C.A.3d 714 involved a decedent who had led a double life. He had two separate families, neither of which knew of the other's existence. The court of appeal affirmed the trial court's finding that the second wife was a putative spouse, even though the second marriage of 24 years was void. She had married with the good-faith belief that her husband had been divorced from his first wife. The court deemed it equitable to divide the property equally between the legal and putative spouses.

Premarital and Marital Agreements

Premarital agreements about property rights generally are valid. Agreements entered into after marriage may be valid if undue influence is not a factor.

Many unmarried people living together enter into contracts concerning their property rights. These agreements may provide community-property-like rights should the relationship terminate or may otherwise specify property rights and/or division of property. California courts will enforce these nonmarital agreements unless they are based on the consideration of sexual services.

Case Study

In the case of *In re Marriage of Stitt* (1983) 147 C.A.3d 579, a couple agreed to live together and combine their earnings. During this period the woman acquired a vacant parcel of land in her name alone, and a residence was constructed with a loan in her name. Payments were made on the loan from a joint account. In a proceeding for dissolution of their subsequent marriage the court held that the property was community property upon marriage. The parties had purchased the property with the intention that it be co-owned. The court held that unmarried cohabitants may enter into express or implied contracts respecting their property rights and earnings.

Community Property Rules

Prior to January 1, 1975, the husband was by law the manager of the community property. Community property assets were subject to the premarital and postmarital debts of the husband but only the postmarital debts of the wife. Since January 1, 1975, each spouse has had coequal management and control of the community property. Community property now is liable for the debts of either spouse after marriage. The earnings of a spouse are not liable for the debts of the other spouse incurred prior to marriage. An exception to equal rights of management is that one spouse alone can have sole management of a business owned as community property.

Neither spouse can make a gift of community property to a third person without the other spouse's permission, because this could defeat community property rights. A gift of one spouse to the other of property that would otherwise qualify as community property would become the separate property of the donee spouse.

A married person cannot use community property funds to form a joint tenancy with a third person. Despite the language of the deed, a tenancy in common would be formed, with the married person and his or her spouse owning their shares as community property.

Community property transfers as well as leases for more than one year require the signatures of both spouses. Neither spouse alone can encumber or obligate community real property.

Neither spouse can partition community property by selling his or her one-half interest to another.

Neither spouse can encumber or sell the furniture or furnishings of the home without the other spouse. Neither spouse can sell the clothes of the other spouse or of the minor children without the other's approval.

Because community property actually is owned equally by both spouses, either spouse can transfer his or her one-half interest by will. If a spouse dies intestate, the community property interest will pass to the surviving spouse without probate.

Community property is divided equally upon dissolution of marriage. For the purpose of division of property or separate maintenance only, joint tenancy property is presumed to be community property. To overcome this presumption, strong and persuasive evidence to the contrary must be present (Civil Code Section 4800.1). However, a spouse is entitled to reimbursement for separate property contributions toward community property assets unless he or she has made a written waiver of that right (Civil Code Section 4800.2).

Case Study

In Re Marriage of Campbell (1999) 74 C.A.4th 1058 involved a house owned by the husband prior to marriage. Because the husband had little income during the first years of marriage, the wife contributed money from her separate property to keep the marriage afloat. She also contributed $34,000 to buy equipment for the husband's business and $66,000 to remodel her husband's house. The wife claimed that she relied on a promise to place her name on the title to the house. At marriage dissolution, she claimed an ownership interest in her husband's house, claiming fraudulent conduct. The husband claimed that Family Code 852, which requires a written agreement, does not allow oral transmutation from separate to community properties. The wife claimed equitable estoppel as an exception to the statute of frauds.

The Sonoma County Superior Court ruled that the house was the separate property of the husband. The court of appeal affirmed, explaining that a writing is required for transmutation (conversion) of separate property to community property, and extrinsic evidence could not be allowed. There must be a written agreement if separate property is to become community property.

Note: While contributions did not change separate property to community property, the wife could be entitled to her separate property contributions toward the community property.

If property acquired in other states by California residents would have been considered community property had it been in California, it will be treated as community property upon marriage dissolution or death (quasi-community property). New residents of California should understand that once they take California residency, property owned in other states by one or both spouses will be regarded as community property if that property would have been community property had it been acquired in California.

A former advantage of community property over joint tenancy was that community property acquired a new cost basis stepped up to market value upon the death of a spouse, while only the deceased spouse's half interest in joint tenancy property acquired a new cost basis. This distinction has been removed by Revenue Ruling 87–98, which allows both joint tenancy and community property to acquire a new cost basis upon the death of a spouse if the property was acknowledged as community property before the death of the spouse. For property that has appreciated in value, this reduces the taxable income upon a later sale to the difference between the new cost basis and the sales price.

Table 8.1 shows the differences and similarities among tenancy in common, joint tenancy, and community property.

Community Property with Right of Survivorship (CPRS)

This form of ownership applies only to real estate instruments created after July 2, 2001 (Civil Code 682.1). To be effective, the CPRS ownership must be expressly declared on the deed. When one spouse dies, the surviving spouse, as in joint tenancy, takes title regardless of any will. CPRS, as in joint tenancy, avoids probate costs and delays. Prior to death, either or both spouses can terminate the tenancy by executing and recording a new deed as to their interests.

The major reasons for using the CPRS form of ownership are

- avoidance of probate costs and delays;
- a tax benefit of a new stepped-up cost basis for the surviving spouse to the fair market value at the time of the other spouse's death;
- the CPRS property is not subject to the will of the deceased.

■ TENANCY IN PARTNERSHIP

Two or more persons associated to carry on a business for profit compose a **partnership**. An agreement to share in the profits would create a presumption of a partnership's existence.

A **general partner** is an active partner in the partnership who has unlimited personal liability for the debts of the partnership. A new general partner to an existing partnership would have unlimited liability for future debts of the partnership, but his or her liability for the existing partnership debts would be limited to the extent of his or her contribution to capital (partner's investment).

Under the Uniform Partnership Act (Corporation Code Sections 15001–15004) general partners

- have equal rights to use partnership property for partnership purposes;
- cannot transfer their interests to another without the consent of the other partners; and
- the death or bankruptcy of a general partner dissolves the partnership.

Creditors of the partnership have first claim on the assets of a partnership. Partnership assets are not subject to attachment or execution for the private debts of the partners. However, bankruptcy of a partner would dissolve the partnership as it applies to the bankrupt partner, which would allow the creditors to reach the bankrupt partner's share of partnership assets.

Partners' interests are undivided. The interests need not be equal, but in the absence of any agreement the partners have equal rights in the partnership.

Spouses of partners do not have a direct community property interest in partnership property. Partnership property can be conveyed by the partnership without the signatures of the spouses of the partners.

The heirs of a deceased partner have no right to the partnership business, because a partnership requires consent. The heirs are entitled only to the value of the deceased partner's share of the assets over the liabilities, or surplus, not to the continuing business.

General partnership agreements need not be in writing to be valid.

A partnership can acquire property in the name of the partnership. The recording of a statement of partnership that has been signed, acknowledged, and verified by two or more partners is proof of membership in the partnership. A bona fide purchaser for value from the partnership can rely on the statement about the identity of all of the partners and be protected against unnamed parties claiming a partnership interest.

If a partner takes title to partnership property in his or her separate name, other partners can claim their interests by showing it to be partnership property.

TABLE 8.1

Common Ownership Forms

	Tenancy in Common	Joint Tenancy	Community Property
Parties	Any number of persons (can be husband and wife)	Any number of persons (can be husband and wife)	Only husband and wife
Division	Ownership can be divided into any number of interests, equal or unequal	Ownership interests cannot be divided and must be equal	Ownership interests are equal
Title	Each co-owner has a separate legal title to his or her undivided interest	There is only one title to the whole property	Title is in the "community" (similar to title being in a partnership)
Possession	Equal right of possession	Equal right of possession	Equal right of possession
Conveyance	Each co-owner's interest may be conveyed separately by its owner	Conveyance by one co-owner without the others breaks the joint tenancy	Both co-owners must join in conveyance of real property; separate interests cannot be conveyed
Purchaser's Status	Purchaser becomes a tenant in common with the other co-owners	Purchaser becomes a tenant in common with the other co-owners	Purchaser can acquire only whole title of community, cannot acquire a part of it
Death	Upon co-owner's death his or her interest passes by will to the devisees or heirs; no survivorship right	Upon co-owner's death his or her interest ends and cannot be willed; survivor owns the property by survivorship	Upon co-owner's death half goes to survivor in severalty; up to one half goes by will or succession to others (consult attorney with specific questions)
Successor's Status	Devisees or heirs become tenants in common	Last survivor owns property in severalty	If passing by will, tenancy in common between devisee and survivor results
Creditor's Rights	Co-owner's interest may be sold upon execution sale to satisfy his or her creditor; creditor becomes a tenant in common	Co-owner's interest may be sold upon execution sale to satisfy creditor; joint tenancy is broken, and creditor becomes tenant in common	Co-owner's interests cannot be seized and sold separately; the whole property may be sold to satisfy debts of either husband or wife, depending on the debt (consult attorney with specific questions)
Presumption	Favored in doubtful cases except husband and wife (see Community Property)	Must be expressly stated and properly formed	Strong presumption that property acquired by husband and wife is community property

While a partner is entitled to an accounting of cash or property from other partners, a partner cannot sue the partnership; in so doing the partner in effect would be suing himself or herself.

A partner cannot compete with his or her partnership. See *Leff v. Gunter* (1983) 33 C.3d 508 for an example of this.

Fictitious Name

A **fictitious name** is a name that does not include the surname of every partner. If a partnership fails to comply with the fictitious name statutes, the partnership cannot sue or defend a suit in the partnership name on contracts made using the fictitious name.

To comply with the fictitious name statutes the partnership must

- file, within 40 days of beginning business, a fictitious name statement with the county clerk that identifies the principals, the business, and its fictitious name and
- publish, within 30 days of filing, the fictitious name statement in a newspaper of general circulation within the county where the principal place of business is located, once a week for four successive weeks.

All fictitious name statements expire at the end of five years from December 31 of the year filed with the county clerk. Renewal statements again must be filed but need not be advertised.

A partnership can abandon a fictitious name by filing a statement of abandonment.

Taxation of Partnerships

An advantage that partnerships have over corporations is that partnerships do not pay income tax. Taxes are paid by the individual partners, while a corporation has double taxation: corporate profit is taxed, and then the stockholders also are taxed on their dividends.

Termination of Partnerships

Partnerships may be terminated by

- agreement,
- bankruptcy of a partner or the partnership,
- court order that results when a partner petitions the court for a dissolution of the partnership, or
- death of a general partner.

Joint Ventures

Joint ventures are partnerships for a single undertaking rather than a continuing business. Because a joint venture is set up for a limited purpose, the implied authority of its members is more limited than in a general partnership.

A joint venturer does not necessarily have the power to bind the other joint venturers. A joint venture is generally considered a partnership. A joint venture is taxed in the same way as a partnership (taxes are paid by the individual joint venturers), and joint venturers also have the joint and several liability of partners as to third parties. Unlike in a partnership, one joint venturer can sue the joint venture. The death of a partner automatically terminates a partnership, but the death of a joint venturer does not necessarily dissolve the joint venture. Control of the joint venture is normally given to a managing partner.

Limited Partnerships

Limited partnerships are partnerships in which the limited partners have **limited liability** rather than the unlimited liability of a general partnership. Limited partners are liable only to the extent of their investment. However, a limited partnership must have at least one general partner who has unlimited liability.

Limited partnership names must end with "A California Limited Partnership." The agreement must be in writing, and a formal certificate of limited partnership must be filed. A limited partner cannot allow his or her name to be used in a manner that would indicate he or she is a general partner.

The 1983 Revised Limited Partnership Act (Corporation Code Sections 15611–15721) allows partners to contribute services but not a promise concerning future services (formerly, a limited partner could not provide other than money).

A limited partner can get an accounting from the general partner, and the limited partners can oust the general partner for cause.

Case Study

The case of *BT-1 v. Equitable Life Assurance Society* (1999) 75 C.A.4th 1406 involved a partnership that owned real property. Equitable was the general partner, and BT-1 was the limited partner. Equitable purchased $62.5 million in loans against the property for the discounted price of $38.5 million. Equitable then demanded payment and took sole title to the property by foreclosure. BT-1 sued Equitable for its loss of equity as well as the gain from the discharge of indebtedness.

While the trial court entered judgment for Equitable, the court of appeals reversed. It ruled that the acquisition of partnership debt by a general partner is a breach of fiduciary duty, and the duty cannot be contracted away in the partnership agreement. Equitable was B-1's partner, not its lender, and it lost sight of this basic distinction in its haste to pounce on the loan. A general partner cannot take advantage of a limited partner by self-dealing.

Syndicates. Syndicates are generally limited partnerships. Real estate syndicates fall under the jurisdiction of the Department of Corporations.

Real estate brokers are authorized by the Corporation Code to sell real estate security interests without having to obtain a broker/dealer license from the Department of Corporations.

An investor in a real estate syndicate has the advantage of the limited liability of a corporation investor. That is, the investor's liability is limited to the amount invested.

A major attraction of syndicates to investors formerly was their unlimited tax shelter aspect; losses from depreciation could be passed through to the investors. Current tax laws do not allow the unlimited use of losses on these passive investments. Consequently, interest in syndicates has diminished.

Trusts.   Property may be held in the name of a trust for a specific purpose, such as for a charitable purpose. Living trusts (revocable) are used for estate planning purposes, as probate can be avoided. Community property placed in a living trust would still entitle each spouse to community property interests.

■ REAL ESTATE INVESTMENT TRUSTS

Real estate investment trusts allow smaller investors to pool their resources for quality investments with limited liability. Under federal law a **real estate investment trust (REIT)** is an unincorporated trust or association managed by a trustee that meets the following criteria:

- ■ It cannot hold property for sale to customers in the ordinary course of business.
- ■ It must be owned by at least 100 investors.
- ■ Five persons or fewer cannot hold more than a 50 percent interest.
- ■ Interests must be in the form of transferable shares or certificates. California requires that each share carry with it an equivalent vote in determining trust policy.
- ■ Investments must account for at least 90 percent of the trust's gross income.
- ■ Up to 75 percent of the trust's gross income may result from short-term gains on sales of stocks or securities held for less than six months plus sales of real estate held for less than four years. This does not apply to involuntary conversion such as eminent domain.

If the real estate investment trust distributes 90 percent or more of its ordinary earnings to shareholders, it is taxed only on its retained earnings at the corporate rate.

The trustee in a real estate investment trust must have exclusive power to manage the trust. Trusts are either equity trusts (real estate), mortgage trusts (investments in mortgages and trust deeds), or hybrid trusts (investments in both real estate and mortgages).

Unlike syndicate interests, which are often difficult to resell, many REITs are listed on major stock exchanges so that interests are more readily salable.

■ CORPORATIONS

A **corporation** is a separate legal entity established under state law by the filing of articles of incorporation with the secretary of state. It can own property in the corporate name.

Shareholders of a corporation have limited liability and have no direct management of the corporation.

Shareholders elect the directors, who set corporate policy. The directors appoint the corporate officers, who operate the corporation. The authority of the corporate officers is set forth in the corporate bylaws, which are the rules of the corporation.

Because a corporation is a separate legal entity, shareholders can sue the corporation. Also, because it is a legal entity, corporations have an unlimited life and theoretically "live" forever.

A corporate conveyance that involves a sale of all or a majority of the corporate assets must be approved by a majority of the stockholders.

If a corporation exists in name only—that is, individual funds are commingled with corporate funds—the courts will "pierce the corporate veil" and determine that the corporation is in fact a partnership or sole proprietorship, and the limited liability protection of the corporation will be lost.

A closely held, or close, corporation is one in which the stock is held by a few persons who actively control the business. Closely held corporations often are able to avoid significant corporate taxation by not showing a profit. They accomplish this through salaries, benefits, and bonuses to the officers, who are also the stockholders.

Foreign Corporations

A domestic corporation is a corporation organized in California. A corporation organized in any other state is a foreign corporation in California. To do business in California, a foreign corporation must get permission from the secretary of state; otherwise it cannot sue in California courts. The foreign corporation also must file with the secretary of state a consent to allow legal process to be served against the corporation by service on the secretary of state; this eliminates the need to go to the state of incorporation to bring suit.

S Corporations

As mentioned earlier, corporations are subject to double taxation. To avoid this, a small corporation can elect to be taxed as a partnership by becoming an S corporation. An S corporation must meet the following criteria:

- It must have fewer than 75 shareholders.
- Only one category of stock may be issued.
- All stockholders must be individuals, not corporations.
- The business cannot receive more than 20 percent of its income from interest, rents, dividends, and royalties.
- The corporation cannot be affiliated with any other corporation. It must be independent.
- It must be incorporated in the United States.

Limited Liability Companies (LLC)

Limited liability companies provide the limited liability protection of corporations without the regulations associated with S Corporations. Limited liability companies have operating agreements that are similar to corporate bylaws, but unlike corporations, they do not have perpetual existence. Two or more members can file articles of organization with the secretary of state to engage in any lawful business activity. They must also file annual statements.

■ UNINCORPORATED ASSOCIATIONS

An **unincorporated association** is a nonprofit organization, which under common law could not hold title because it is not an entity. In California, however, unincorporated associations for religious, scientific, social, educational, recreational, or benevolent purposes may hold title to real property necessary for their purposes in the name of the organization. Property nonessential to the operation of the organization cannot be held for more than ten years.

An unincorporated association can convey property by a deed executed by the president and secretary or others as authorized by the bylaws. Recording a verified certificate listing the names of officers and other persons authorized to convey would be conclusive proof that a deed so executed was a properly executed conveyance.

In California, members of such associations are not personally liable for leases or purchases of property used by the association unless they agree to liability in writing.

■ MULTIPLE HOUSING DEVELOPMENTS

Generally, the division of property into five or more parcels for the purpose of sale, lease, or financing is considered a subdivision. Subdivision classifications include the following:

- *Standard subdivision:* A standard subdivision is a land division with no common areas.
- *Common interest:* A common interest is a division whereby owners own their unit, separate interests, and an area in common with other owners. Common interests include condominiums, planned unit developments (PUDs), stock cooperatives, community apartment projects, and time-share projects.
- *Undivided interest:* An undivided interest is a development in which owners are tenants in common with all other owners without an exclusive right of ownership of a particular lot or unit. An example would be many of the large, member-owned recreational vehicle parks. Purchasers in an undivided interest subdivision have a three-day right of rescission. (The subdivision process and the Interstate Land Sales Full Disclosure Act are covered in Chapter 13.)

There are several types of ownership forms for common-interest and undivided-interest subdivisions.

Condominiums

A **condominium** is an interest in real property consisting of an undivided interest in common in a portion of a parcel together with a separate interest in space. The property can be residential, commercial, or industrial.

A condominium is really a vertical subdivision with the unit owner having a separate deed showing ownership of the airspace in fee simple but owning the common areas, including the land, as a tenant in common with the other owners.

Each unit owner can encumber his or her interest separately without affecting the interests of the other owners. Each unit owner pays separate real property taxes that include a share of the common areas. A condominium owner may not sell his or her unit without conveying the rights to the common areas.

A homeowners' association board of directors, elected by the owners, is the governing body for the condominium. (Homeowners' associations also govern cooperatives, community apartment projects, planned unit developments, and time-shares.) Homeowners' associations can place reasonable assessments against the units, which if unpaid are liens against the individual units. Membership in a homeowners' association is generally a deed covenant that runs with the land.

Stock Cooperatives

A **stock cooperative** is a corporation formed for the purpose of holding title to an improved property. Each shareholder has the exclusive right to the occupancy of a unit through a proprietary lease with the elected governing body. The transfer of shares also transfers occupancy by a sublease.

While a condominium owner can freely transfer his or her unit, most cooperative associations have the right to approve the purchaser of stock before the stock seller can sublease to the stock purchaser.

There are two basic disadvantages of cooperatives:

1. The stockholder does not have a real property interest, so borrowing on equity is more difficult.
2. There is only one tax bill. If tax payments are not made by all owners, a lien can be placed on the entire property. If there is only one deed of trust, the failure of one or more owners to make their share of the payment also could result in the entire cooperative's being foreclosed.

Developments of five or more cooperative units fall under the jurisdiction of the real estate commissioner. Cooperatives with four or fewer units are under the jurisdiction of the corporation commissioner.

Community Apartment Projects

In a **community apartment project** the owners purchase the property together as tenants in common with the right to exclusive occupancy of their units through a lease agreement.

As in stock cooperatives, owners could have difficulty borrowing on their undivided interest. Because there is only one trust deed, the failure of one owner to pay could jeopardize all of the owners. Because of these problems, resale of an owner's interest is often very difficult.

Developments of five or more units are under the jurisdiction of the real estate commissioner.

Planned Unit Developments

A **planned unit development (PUD)** is a subdivision with the unit and the land under it owned by the individual unit owner. Areas for the use of all of the owners, such as recreational facilities or common areas, are owned by all of the owners as tenants in common. The major difference between a planned unit development and a condominium is that PUD owners actually own their own land and not just airspace.

Time-Sharing Projects

A **time-share** is an interval or fractionalized ownership whereby the owner gets the exclusive use of a unit annually for a set period of time. Time-share interests may be in perpetuity, for life, or for a stated number of years.

Twelve or more time-share estates of five years or more are considered a subdivision and fall under the jurisdiction of the real estate commissioner. A real estate license is required to sell any time-share interests in California. Because of abusive sales tactics of some time-share developers, purchasers have a rescission right of three days following their offer.

Time-shares are often marketed based on exchange privileges with other time-share developments. The buyer must be informed that the purchase does not guarantee a right to use or occupy accommodations other than the unit purchased.

A resort vacation club is similar to a time-share, except the investor does not purchase an ownership interest. The investor has the right to rent a unit and use club facilities. These developments are now under the control of the real estate commissioner and are classified as time-share projects.

Sale of Units

Prior to transfer of title, owners of condominiums, community apartment projects, cooperatives, and planned unit developments must provide purchasers with a copy of restrictions, bylaws, and articles of incorporation, plus an owners' association financial statement including any delinquent assessments and costs.

An owners' association must furnish the owner with a copy of the latest version of documents within ten days of request by an owner. A reasonable fee for doing this may be charged.

■ OWNER LIABILITY

An owner of real property is liable for injuries to other persons and/or property caused by negligence in maintaining or operating the property.

Civil Code Section 1365.9 has given individual owners in a common interest subdivision some protection from liability resulting from injuries relating to the common areas. If the association carries specified minimum liability coverage, then the individual owners will not be held liable. The coverage required is as follows:

■ At least two million dollars ($2,000,000) if the common interest development consists of 100 or fewer separate interests

■ At least three million dollars ($3,000,000) if the common interest development consists of more than 100 separate interests

If dangerous conditions are obvious, an injured party might be denied relief if he or she could be said to have assumed the risk.

The duty of care an owner of real property owes to others extends beyond tenants or invitees. An owner's liability could extend to trespassers as well as neighbors who are injured because of dangerous conditions on the property.

Case Study

The case of *Privette v. Superior Court* (1993) 5 C.4th 689 involved an employee of an independent contractor who was injured by hot tar and sought to recover damages from the property owner (in addition to workers' compensation). The California Supreme Court held that employees of independent contractors, even those performing high-risk activity, can recover only their workers' compensation benefits and cannot receive damages from the property owner.

An owner is not liable for "trivial" defects and need not maintain property in an absolutely perfect condition. See *Ursino v. Big Boy Restaurants of America* (1987) 192 C.A.3d 394.

Case Study

The case of *Brunelle v. Signore* (1989) 215 C.A.3d 122 involved a weekend houseguest who was bitten by a brown recluse spider. The guest sued the homeowner for damages. The court held that negligence exists only when there has been a breach of duty. In this case brown recluse spiders had not previously been seen on the premises, so the defendant was held not to have a duty to prevent the spider bite. The court pointed out that an owner or occupier of a property is not an insurer of the safety of persons on the premises.

Under Civil Code Section 846 an owner of an interest in real property owes no duty of care to keep the premises safe for entry by others for recreational purposes or to give warning of hazardous conditions. This does not apply to willful or malicious failure to guard or warn against a dangerous condition, use, structure, or activity.

Case Study

Shipman v. Boething Treeland Farms Inc. (2000) 77 C.A.4th 1424 involved trespassers who were injured when their all-terrain vehicle collided with a vehicle driven by a farm employee. The accident occurred at a tree-obstructed intersection on the property. The trespasser, Shipman, sued for negligent operation of a motor vehicle and premises liability. The superior court granted summary judgment for the defendant ruling that Civil Code Section 846 bars liability to recreational user trespassers.

The court of appeal affirmed, explaining that Section 846 affords broad immunity protection to property owners from liability to trespassers.

Note: Apparently the immunity would extend even if the owner's employee had been driving negligently.

Case Study

In *New v. Consolidated Rock Prods* (1985) 171 C.A.3d 681, two motor-cyclists were injured when they drove their motorcycles over a 20-foot cliff at the end of an abandoned road. The owner had posted "no trespassing" signs, but the signs had little deterrent effect on motorcyclists. The court held that the defendant had acted willfully or in conscious disregard of the duty to warn plaintiffs of a dangerous condition under Civil Code Section 846 and was thus liable for the resulting injury.

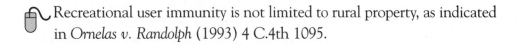 Recreational user immunity is not limited to rural property, as indicated in *Ornelas v. Randolph* (1993) 4 C.4th 1095.

Case Study

In the case of *Preston v. Goldman* (1986) 42 C.3d 108, the California Supreme Court held that a former landlord is not liable for patent defects after he or she relinquishes possession and control. In this case the Kubichans built a pond and then sold the property to the Goldmans, who leased it with an option to buy to the Reids. The two-year-old son of the visiting plaintiff fell into the pond and suffered brain damage. While the court of appeal held that a landowner who creates a dangerous condition is liable for resulting injuries after transfer, the California Supreme Court reversed, ruling that the controlling factors are possession and control as to liability for patent defects, so the previous owner was not liable.

If an owner maintains premises that are dangerous to children of tender years and the premises reasonably can be expected to attract such children, the owner has a duty to use reasonable care to protect children from injury. Failure to do so could subject the owner to resulting damages. This is known as the **attractive nuisance doctrine.**

Owner liability for injuries to tenants and invitees is covered in Chapter 15.

Hazardous Substance Disclosure

Health and Safety Code Section 25359.7(a) requires that owners of nonresidential real property, before they sell or lease, give notice to buyers or lessees of the release of hazardous substances that they know of; they also must give notice when they have reasonable cause to believe hazardous substances are located on or beneath the property.

Section 25359.7(b) requires that lessees (both nonresidential and residential) give written notice to owners regarding hazardous substances they know to have been released or believe to exist on or beneath the property. Failure to disclose constitutes a default by the tenant under the lease.

Under the Federal Comprehensive Environmental Response, Compensation, and Liability Act of 1980 (Superfund), owners, operators, and lessees of real property have cleanup liability for actual or threatened release of hazardous substances. Also liable are those who generated, transported, or disposed of the hazardous substances. Under federal law landowners may raise the defense of innocence when they conducted appropriate inquiry prior to acquiring the property. Because California law requires prior owner and lessee disclosure, the defense of innocence will likely be removed if any disclosure was made.

Case Study

The case of *Wiegmann & Rose International Corp v. NL Industries, Inc.* (1990) 735 F.Supp. 957 involved a sale of land where the seller had dumped hazardous waste. The sale provision included an "as is" clause. The court held that the "as is" provision in the deed did not absolve the seller because the purchaser of the contaminated property had no knowledge, actual or constructive, of the presence of hazardous waste. Applying federal law, the U.S. district court ruled that NL Industries was strictly liable for cleanup costs. The liability imposed by CERCLA (Comprehensive Environmental Response, Compensation, and Liability Act of 1980) is not absolved by an "as is" clause.

Purchasers (and renters) of one to four residential units built prior to 1978 must be given a "Watch Out for Lead-Based Paint" booklet, and have up to ten days after signing the sales contract to have the residence inspected for lead-based paint. While sellers cannot refuse to allow this inspection, this right can be waived by the buyer. Foreclosed residences and housing designed for the elderly or disabled where children under six years old are unlikely to reside are exempt. Penalties include fines up to $10,000, criminal prosecution, and/or treble damages to the buyer and renter.

When a landlord who receives federal subsidies or loans is confronted with deteriorating paint in a pre-1978 housing unit, the landlord must alert affected tenants to the possible health dangers and use government-certified workers and special containment practices to abate any risk of public exposure.

In several states the hazardous substance removal liens take precedence over all other liens, which could effectively wipe out a lender's interests. While both California and federal laws set forth landowner liability for removing hazardous substances, however, neither California nor federal law provides for such superliens.

Case Study

The case of *United States of America v. Maryland Bank & Trust* (1986) 632 F.Supp. 573 involved a bank that foreclosed on a mortgage it held. At the foreclosure sale the bank bid $381,500 and took title to the property. The prior owners had used the site as a dump for hazardous waste. The EPA ordered the bank to clean up the site, and when it failed to do so, the EPA removed the toxic material at a cost of $551,713.50. The bank was held liable for the cleanup costs. The court's ruling indicates that lenders must protect themselves. Before lenders foreclose, they should consider possible liability from activities of former owners and tenants.

In California, Code of Civil Procedures Section 726.5 allows a lender to waive its security interest (lien) on environmentally impaired property and to proceed directly against the borrower for the debt. In this way the lender is spared the possible liability of cleanup costs.

Disclosures are also required for natural hazards (see Chapter 6).

■ SUMMARY

Ownership of property can be held in a number of forms:

- Ownership in severalty: This is ownership by one person or corporation alone.
- Tenancy in common: This is an undivided ownership by two or more persons without the right of survivorship.
- Joint tenancy: This is an undivided interest by two or more persons with the right of survivorship. Upon the death of a joint tenant his or her interest immediately passes to the surviving joint tenant(s). To form a joint tenancy, the four unities of time, title, interest, and possession are necessary.
- Community property: Property acquired by husband and wife during marriage is, with some exceptions, considered to be owned jointly and equally by the spouses. Both spouses must agree to the transfer or encumbrance of community property.
- Tenancy in partnership: A partnership is two or more persons associated to carry on a business for profit. Property can be held in the name of the partnership.
- Joint venture: A joint venture is a partnership for a particular undertaking rather than a continuing business.
- Limited partnership: This is a partnership that has limited partners who are inactive and have limited liability. They are liable only to the extent of their investment. Limited partnerships must have at least one general partner who is active and has unlimited liability.
- Real estate investment trust (REIT): This type of trust, having 100 or more investors, issues certificates or shares to the investors. The shares are freely transferable.
- Corporation: A corporation is an artificial person created by law that can own property. Corporations pay taxes on their profits, and the dividends paid to the shareholders are taxed to the shareholders (double taxation). S corporations are small corporations that have elected to be taxed as partnerships to avoid double taxation.
- Unincorporated associations: These are nonprofit organizations. In California, unincorporated associations for specific purposes can hold title to real property.

There are a number of forms of ownership for housing developments:

- Condominium: A condominium interest is a separate interest in the airspace of a unit coupled with an undivided interest in common in the common areas.

■ Stock cooperative: A stock cooperative is a corporation in which each shareholder also has a lease interest that entitles him or her to occupancy of a unit.

■ Community apartment project: A community apartment project is an undivided tenancy-in-common interest in the real property, with each owner having the right to occupy a unit.

■ Planned unit development: A PUD is a subdivision in which some areas are owned in common. Individual unit owners own their own units and the land under the units.

■ Time-share: A time-share is a fractionalized ownership in which each owner has exclusive use of the property for a set time period.

Owners of real property are liable for injuries to other persons and/or property resulting from negligence in maintaining their property. Owners, however, are not absolute insurers regarding the safety of others.

Owners generally have no duty of care to keep their premises safe for recreational users. However, owners have a special duty regarding children. They must protect small children from injuries caused by attractions on the property likely to interest children (attractive nuisance doctrine).

Owners and lessees have duties of disclosure regarding hazardous substances, and owners can be held liable for removal of hazardous wastes even when they were not responsible for the waste being on their property.

■ DISCUSSION CASES

1. **When a property is given to two or more parties as life tenants, what is the relationship between the life tenants?**

   Green v. Brown (1951) 37 C.2d 391

2. One joint tenant used a property for 22 years, paid the taxes, and maintained the property. In a quiet title action he claimed title to the entire property by adverse possession. **Does his claim have merit?**

   Dimmick v. Dimmick (1962) 58 C.2d 417

3. A property settlement between joint tenants gave the former husband exclusive possession for life. The husband agreed not to convey his interest and to pay the taxes and maintain the property. **What is the form of ownership, and what are the rights of the former wife?**

   Cole v. Cole (1956) 139 C.A.2d 691

4. An unmarried couple lived together for six years. Upon the end of the relationship the woman claimed rights in the man's assets. **What are the woman's rights?**

Marvin v. Marvin (1976) 18 C.3d 660

5. A corporation authorized to enforce the provisions of a recorded declaration of restrictions assessed residents for expenses incurred in suing the city to abate airport noise. The restrictions covered activities within the complex but not those outside the complex. **Was the assessment proper?**

Spitzer v. Kentwood Home Guardians (1972) 24 C.A.3d 215

6. A developer fraudulently represented to plaintiffs in a class action suit that the monthly assessments for the common areas would be $12.99 per month, which the developer claimed was the actual apportioned cost for each unit. The costs were really around $40 per unit, and the developer was subsidizing the costs. In 1971, the developer gave the plaintiffs an option either to pay the actual costs of $40 or to accept reduced services and pay $20. Should the developer be assessed damages? **If so, what should the damages be?**

*Occidental Land, Inc. v. Superior Court
of Orange County* (1976) 18 C.3d 355

7. A man purchased a tenant in common's interest in an island-type property used for waterfowl hunting. He wanted the entire parcel, but the other tenant in common refused to sell. He brought a partition action and asked that the property be sold. **Should the court order a sale?**

Butte Creek Island Ranch v. Crim (1982) 136 C.A.3d 360

8. A trespasser crawled through a hole in the fence of a paint-stripping plant. He climbed on top of a vat and fell through a thin plywood cover into acid. The owner who leased the premises to the operator was unaware of the vats of acid. **Is the owner liable for the injuries to the trespasser?**

Bisetti v. United Refrigeration Corp. (1985) 174 C.A.3d 643

9. A husband whose wife was in a mental hospital acquired an interest in real property with a woman with whom he was living. He used

community property for his contribution, and she used her separate property. **Can they hold title as joint tenants?**

Yeoman v. Sawyer (1950) 99 C.A.2d 43

10. During the process of marriage dissolution a husband alone gave a trust deed to property held in joint tenancy. The court later gave the wife title to the property. **What would be the effect of foreclosure of the trust deed?**

Kane v. Huntley Financial (1983) 146 C.A.3d 1092

11. While standing outside the door of an arcade, the plaintiff was shot by a security guard who had been hired by a tenant of the landlord. The guard was a convicted felon who was unlawfully in possession of the gun. **Is the landlord liable for the plaintiff's injury?**

Leakes v. Shamoun (1986) 187 C.A.3d 772

12. A law student was assaulted after leaving the school property and walking in a public area toward his car. The student alleged the school did not properly light the area. **Assuming the area was dark and the darkness allowed the student to be assaulted, is the school liable?**

Donnell v. California Western School of Law (1988)
200 C.A.3d 715

13. After leaving a convenience store, a customer was assaulted and injured in a vacant lot adjacent to the store, where customers often parked. The defendants had a nonexclusive right to use the lot for extra parking under their lease and knew customers used the lot. On several occasions they had sought police assistance to remove loiterers from the lot. **What, if any, were the duties of the defendants?**

Southland Corp. v. Superior Court (1988) 203 C.A.3d 656

14. A husband signed a contract to sell community property. The buyer was unaware of the existence of the wife, who refused to perform. **Can the buyer obtain specific performance?**

Andrade Development Co. v. Martin (1982) 138 C.A.3d 330

15. A motorcyclist fell into a percolation test hole and sued the landowner as well as the responsible contractor and subcontractor. **Are the defendants entitled to raise the recreational use immunity?**

Jensen v. Kenneth Mullen Co. (1989) 211 C.A.3d 653

16. A wife quitclaimed her interest in a community property residence to her husband for value while separated. During subsequent reconciliations she lived in the house with her husband, and community funds were used to pay the mortgage. **In a subsequent marriage dissolution, would the wife have a community property interest in the residence?**

Marriage of Broderick (1989) 209 C.A.3d 489

17. A lessee of 40,000 acres under a U.S. Forest Service grazing permit placed a barbed wire gate across a forest service road to control his cattle. The land was also open for recreational users. The plaintiff drove his off-road motorcycle into the wire and was injured. **Is the lessee liable?**

Hubbard v. Brown (1990) 50 C.3d 189

18. A passerby slipped on dog feces on the public sidewalk in front of a store. The owner of the store did not create the hazard; however, a municipal ordinance required landlords to keep city sidewalks clean. **Is the landlord liable for the pedestrian's injuries?**

Selger v. Steven Bros. Inc. (1990) 222 C.A.3d 1585

19. A park brochure described a trail as safe for cycling and advertised its bikes. A tourist died from a cycling accident. **Does recreational immunity protect the defendant?**

Pau v. Yosemite Park (1991) 928 F.2d 880

20. Migrant farm workers built a camp without the permission or knowledge of the owner. A fire in the encampment led to personal injury. **Should the owner of the property be held liable?**

Lucas v. Pollock (1992) 7 C.A.4th 668

21. A wife used $40,000 of her separate property to extinguish a $53,000 debt against community property. (The debtor agreed to settle for $40,000.) **What were the wife's rights upon marriage dissolution?**

In re Marriage of Tallman (1994) 22 C.A.4th 1697

22. A five-year-old girl was jumping up and down on her bed in a second story apartment. She sustained injuries when she fell through a window screen, dropping 30 feet. (The window ledge was 44 inches from the floor.) The building was in compliance with

local codes, but the tenant claimed that the window should have had bars. **Is the landlord liable?**

Pineda v. Ennabe (1998) 61 C.A.4th 1403

23. Two couples owned a beachfront townhouse as partners. On default on the trust deed, one couple purchased the property at the lender's trustee's foreclosure sale. **Was this a breach of fiduciary duty?**

Jones v. Wagner (2001) 90 C.A.4th 466

The court decisions for the above cases can be found on our Web site at **www.dearbornRE.com**. Click on the **"Instructor Resources"** link, then scroll down the page until you find the link titled "California Real Estate Law 5th Edition."

■ CHAPTER QUIZ

1. What would be the ownership form for property that is solely owned by a married woman?

   a. Community property
   b. Tenancy in common
   c. Ownership in severalty
   d. Ownership in partnership

2. Which of the following ownership forms is matched with an *incorrect* characteristic?

   a. Joint tenancy/undivided interest
   b. Tenancy in common/survivorship
   c. Community property/equal ownership
   d. Severalty/alone

3. To convey your property to a son and daughter on a one-third/two-thirds basis, you would want to convey title as

   a. community property.
   b. tenancy in severalty.
   c. tenancy in common.
   d. joint tenancy.

4. Agnes and Alfred, who were recently married, want to purchase a house together. They each want their interest to pass to their individual children from previous marriages in the event of death. They should buy the house

   a. in partnership.
   b. in severalty.
   c. as tenants in common.
   d. as joint tenants.

5. A single tenant in common may *not*

   a. sell her interest without approval of the other tenants in common.
   b. will her interest to her children.
   c. use the property without compensating the other tenants in common.
   d. give exclusive possession to another.

6. Which of the following accurately describes a tenancy in common?

   a. Interests must be equal.
   b. There is an equal right of possession.
   c. Interests must be acquired at the same time.
   d. Interests must be acquired from the same documents.

7. Albert, Baker, Charlie, and David are joint tenants. What form of ownership exists when David sells to Edith and Albert then dies?

   a. Baker, Charlie, and Edith are tenants in common.
   b. Baker and Charlie are joint tenants, and Edith is a tenant in common.
   c. Albert's heirs, Baker, Charlie, and Edith are tenants in common.
   d. None of the above

8. Thomas and Andrew own property in joint tenancy. Thomas put a $50,000 mortgage on his interest. A short time later Thomas died. Who owns the property and how?

   a. Andrew owns the property clear of the mortgage.
   b. Andrew owns the property with a mortgage against it.
   c. Because the mortgage destroyed the joint tenancy, Andrew and the heirs of Thomas own the property as tenants in common.
   d. Andrew and the mortgagee own the property as tenants in common.

9. Which of the following is an example of a partition action?

   a. Dividing an apartment building into condominiums
   b. Any land subdivision
   c. A court proceeding to divide jointly owned property
   d. Breaking large apartments into smaller units

10. After Albert and Helen were married, they purchased a home. The $40,000 down payment was the separate property of Helen. Payments on the home were made with community property funds. Upon marriage dissolution, what are the rights of the parties to the sale proceeds from the house?

    a. Albert and Helen share the proceeds equally.
    b. Albert gets one-half of the payments made, but Helen gets the remainder.
    c. Helen is entitled to $40,000 plus one-half of the balance of the sale proceeds (if any).
    d. None of the above

11. Without the consent of the other spouse, one spouse can

    a. buy real estate using community property funds.
    b. sell community property.
    c. give community property away.
    d. lease community property for 18 months.

12. According to community property rules, one spouse alone may

    a. sell his or her community property interest.
    b. encumber his or her community property interest.
    c. will his or her community property interest.
    d. None of the above

13. Jim and Tom are general partners in a real estate office. Jim dies, leaving all of his property to his wife, Lois, who is also a real estate broker. What is the result?

    a. Lois and Tom are general partners.
    b. Lois has an interest in the partnership assets but not in the business.
    c. Lois becomes a limited partner.
    d. Lois has no interest in the business or the assets of the business.

14. A partnership that has not complied with the fictitious name statute

    a. would be a limited partnership.
    b. cannot sue in the partnership name.
    c. is an unincorporated association.
    d. All of the above

15. Which of the following is (are) true of a joint venture?

    a. One joint venturer can sue the joint venture.
    b. The death of a joint venturer automatically dissolves the joint venture.
    c. Joint venturers have the same power to bind other joint venturers as partners have to bind other partners.
    d. All of the above

16. A new limited partnership must

    a. end its name with "A Limited Partnership."
    b. have a written agreement.
    c. file a formal certificate of limited partnership.
    d. All of the above

17. Under federal law a real estate investment trust must have

    a. a corporate charter.
    b. fewer than 100 investors.
    c. 100 or more investors.
    d. 1,000 or more investors.

18. Two separate corporations could hold title together as

    a. tenants in severalty.
    b. joint tenants.
    c. community property.
    d. a partnership.

19. Which of the following is (are) true regarding income tax?

    a. Partnerships do not pay income tax.
    b. A disadvantage of corporations is double taxation.
    c. An S corporation does not pay taxes.
    d. All of the above

20. Rights of occupancy of owners in a cooperative are based on

    a. a proprietary lease.
    b. the articles of incorporation.
    c. the bylaws of the association.
    d. individual deeds to each unit.

21. Ownership as tenants in common with a right to occupy a unit describes a

    a. cooperative.
    b. community apartment project.
    c. planned unit development.
    d. None of the above

22. Interval exclusive occupancy coupled with a joint ownership likely refers to a(n)

    a. cooperative.
    b. community apartment project.
    c. undivided interest subdivision.
    d. time-share.

23. The seller of a condominium property must provide the purchaser with

    a. a copy of the restrictions.
    b. the association bylaws.
    c. the owners' association financial statement showing delinquent assessments.
    d. All of the above

24. An owner is likely to be liable to a recreational user of his or her property when

    a. he or she failed to post "No Trespassing" signs.
    b. he or she failed to warn against a dangerous condition.
    c. the property is urban in nature.
    d. All of the above

25. Notice of known hazardous substances on the premises must be given by

    a. owners to buyers.   c. lessees to owners.
    b. owners to lessees.   d. All of the above

CHAPTER NINE

ACQUISITIONS AND CONVEYANCES

■ KEY TERMS

ademption	escheat	quitclaim deed
adverse possession	gift deed	sheriff's deed
after-acquired title	grant deed	simultaneous death
dedication	intestate succession	tax deed
deed	inverse condemnation	warranty deed
eminent domain	probate	

■ VOLUNTARY TRANSFERS OF REAL PROPERTY

Deeds

Prior to the statute of frauds, title was passed by a voluntary ceremony known as *livery of seisin*. The parties would physically indicate transfer of title through the symbolic transfer of a clod of earth, a twig, or a key. It became common for unscrupulous individuals, using perjured testimony, to claim a transfer when in fact a livery of seisin had not taken place. The statute of frauds was really enacted to defeat this type of fraud.

The statute of frauds requires that transfers of real property interests be in writing (Civil Code Section 1624). The **deed** is the transfer instrument in a voluntary transfer. When the deed is properly executed, delivered, and accepted, it transfers title to real property from a grantor to a grantee.

Requirements of a Deed

Written.   The statute of frauds requires that every instrument dealing in rights in real estate, other than a lease for one year or less, be in writing.

Execution.   The deed must be executed—that is, signed—by the grantor. The grantee, who receives the deed, need not sign the deed.

The grantor must sign the deed with the same name in which he or she took title. If there is a material variance in the name, the recording of the deed will not provide constructive notice of the transfer. For example, a married woman who is conveying a title that she took before her marriage must identify the maiden name or different married name under which title was taken.

An attorney-in-fact may convey marketable title only if the power of attorney under which the deed is executed is acknowledged and recorded.

A deed that is executed in blank does not transfer title when a property description is inserted at a later date by another person unless that person was authorized to insert the description.

A forged deed is void and transfers no interest. A deed containing unauthorized alterations also is void.

Case Study

The case of *People v. Sanders* (1998) 67 C.A.4th 1403 involved forgery of deeds. Wesley Sanders III forged 10 deeds on 11 parcels of property in Los Angeles County. He located property from tax collector lists of property to be sold at tax collector sales. He forged the owners' signatures (owners were deceased in most cases) and used a forged notary public stamp. He then redeemed the property by paying the taxes. Because of the large number of deeds transferred to him, the tax collector became suspicious and a sheriff's investigation resulted in Sanders being arrested, charged, and convicted of grand theft. Sanders was sentenced to five years in prison.

(continued on next page)

The court of appeal reversed the decision and Sanders was released. The basis of the decision was that a forged deed is void so no transfer of real estate was possible. In addition Sanders had no contact with the owners and there was no evidence of false pretense or misrepresentation.

Note: Sanders should have been charged with forgery and possibly conspiracy to defraud, but not theft.

Description.   The property must be described sufficiently so that no doubt exists about the identity of the property being conveyed, and the boundaries must be positively located. A legal description is not required on a deed, although title insurance cannot generally be obtained in the absence of a legal description.

Delivery.   To transfer title, a deed must be delivered. The most important element of delivery is the intent of the grantor. The grantor must intend to transfer title irrevocably to the grantee or a trustee and to divest himself or herself of title immediately. The grantor's intent can be determined by words or acts before, at the time of, and after execution of the deed.

Although an agreement for a future transfer of title is not a delivery, a legal delivery is possible, even if the grantee's rights to possession and enjoyment of the property are to accrue at a future date. For example, a deed could be given in an irrevocable trust to be given to a grantee at a later date. The delivery of a deed to an escrow or a third party where the grantor cannot get the property back is considered a proper delivery. However, in an escrow situation, the title is not actually conveyed to the grantee until close of escrow.

Recording the deed creates a presumption that the deed was delivered. A deed also is presumed to have been delivered if it is in the possession of the grantee. However, if the grantor is in possession of the deed, it is presumed not to have been delivered. These presumptions can be overcome by evidence to the contrary, and legal delivery can be made even if the deed was not physically transferred.

A deed to more than one grantee need be delivered to only one of them for effective delivery. Delivery must be absolute; it cannot be conditional. For example, assume a deed is given to a third party to hold with the provision that it should be given to the grantor's son upon the grantor's death but it should be returned to the grantor upon his or her request. In that case title would not pass, because the transfer was conditioned on the grantor's not voiding it before death.

See *Stone v. Daily* (1919) 181 C.571.

Acceptance. To be valid, a deed must be accepted. The law will not force a person to take title. Acceptance generally is presumed if the grant is to the benefit of the grantee. Failure to repudiate a transfer within a reasonable period of time also will imply its acceptance. Acts, words, or conduct of the grantee could show an intent to accept. Any exercise of dominion over the property, such as repairing it, occupying it, placing a sign on it, putting the property on the market, or borrowing on the property would show acceptance of the grant.

Case Study

In the case of *Brown v. Sweet* (1928) 95 C.A. 117, when the grantee received a deed in the mail, she immediately returned it to the grantor. Because she did not accept the deed, title was held not to have passed to the grantee.

If the grantee conditionally accepts the grant, title does not pass to the grantee until the conditions set are satisfied.

Granting Clause. While particular wording is not required, the language of the deed must clearly indicate a transfer of title.

Competent Parties. The grantor must be a competent party. In the case of a gift deed, however, the grantee can be an incompetent or a minor. In this situation the legal representative of the incompetent or minor would accept the deed, or acceptance could be presumed on the basis that the grant was beneficial.

Grantee. The grantee must be identified. While a grant may be made to a real person using an assumed name, title cannot pass to a nonexistent person.

Not Required for Deeds

Acknowledgment. Acknowledgment is made by a grantor before a notary public or another authorized person. The grantor acknowledges that the signing of the deed is his or her own free act. The notary has a duty to determine the identity of the person executing the document. The notary and his or her sureties would be liable for negligence in ascertaining the identity of the person signing. A deed need not be acknowledged to be a valid transfer, but without acknowledgment the deed will not be accepted for recording. California notaries must now obtain the right thumb print of the grantor of any deed in their record book.

> ## Case Study
> In the case of *Cordano v. Wright* (1911) 159 C. 610, a deed described the grantor as John McDonald, but it was signed and acknowledged by both John and Catherine McDonald. The court held that the grantee did not get the interests of Catherine McDonald, because a deed acknowledged by a person not named in the instrument as a grantor does not transfer that person's interest.

Recording. Between the parties an unrecorded deed can convey good title. However, an unrecorded deed does not give constructive notice to the world of the grantee's interest.

Besides acknowledgment, a deed to be recorded must contain the name and address to which future tax statements are to be sent. The recorder also will require that the documentary transfer tax be paid prior to recording. The county tax assessor requires filing a "Change of Ownership" form.

Consideration. While a promise to give a deed would require consideration to be enforceable, a deed is not a contract. It is a completed transfer, and consideration generally is not required. However, consideration is required for deeds by personal representatives (executors, guardians, attorneys-in-fact, etc.).

If a deed is given without consideration or for inadequate consideration while the grantor is insolvent, creditors of the grantor or a trustee in bankruptcy might be able to reach the property because the transfer would have constituted fraud against the creditors. While the courts ordinarily are not concerned with the adequacy of consideration, inadequate consideration would be admissible to show fraud or undue influence.

The recording of a deed given without consideration would not give the grantee priority over prior unrecorded conveyances and encumbrances for value.

The conveyance of a deed given on the promise of later consideration will remain valid, even in the event of failure to give the consideration.

Manner of Taking Title. The deed need not indicate how title is being taken. If the grantee is a single individual, he or she would take title in severalty. In the case of more than one grantee, it would be presumed that they are taking title as tenants in common. An exception to this is that deeds to husbands and wives that do not indicate how title is to be taken pass title as community property.

Witnesses and Seals. In California deeds need not be witnessed (unless they are signed with an *x*), nor are seals required. As for other documents, the presence of a seal on a corporate deed creates the presumption that the person signing had corporate authority.

Dated. A deed need not be dated. The deed takes effect on delivery. A mistake in the date on the deed does not affect its validity. However, the date of a deed could be important in the case of a conflicting claim.

Types of Deeds

Grant Deed. The deed used most commonly in California to transfer title, the **grant deed**, has two implied covenants:

1. That prior to the time of execution of such conveyance the grantor has not conveyed the same estate or any right, title, or interest therein to any person other than the grantee
2. That such estate is at the time of execution of the conveyance free from encumbrances done, made, or suffered by the grantor or any person claiming under him or her (other than those declared)

If one of the grantor's implied covenants in a grant deed is breached, the grantee will be entitled to either rescission or damages.

A grant deed customarily is used along with a policy of title insurance.

Grants by grant deed are presumed to be in fee simple (Civil Code Section 1105). When a person purports to grant real property in fee simple and subsequently acquires any claim or title to the real property, the claim or title passes to the grantee or successors (Civil Code Section 1106). Grant deeds, therefore, convey **after-acquired title** as if the grant deed stated ". . . and all interest that I may at any time hereafter acquire." For example, suppose a grantor executes a grant deed to property the grantor thinks he inherited from a distant relative. However, the relative is still alive! When the relative later dies and the grantor inherits title, the grantee would thereby receive after-acquired title.

Quitclaim Deed. A grantor under a **quitclaim deed** transfers only the interest that the grantor has and makes no warranties of title. If the grantor has a fee simple title, then that is the title conveyed. If the grantor has only a life estate, then only the life estate will be conveyed.

Quitclaim deeds often are used to clear title from grantors who have a possible or disputed interest.

Warranty Deed.   The grantor under a **warranty deed** expressly guarantees that he or she has good title and agrees to defend the title and to be liable if the title is defective. Because of the use of title insurance in California, warranty deeds are not commonly used.

Sheriff's Deed.   A **sheriff's deed** is given at foreclosure of a judgment under a sheriff's sale. It transfers only the former owner's interest and contains no warranties (see Chapter 10).

Tax Deed.   A **tax deed** is given when property is sold by the tax collector to the public for nonpayment of taxes. After one year from date of purchase, the property is acceptable for title insurance. Because real estate taxes are a priority lien, a tax sale removes junior encumbrances.

Trustee's Deed.   A trustee's deed is given to the highest bidder at a nonjudicial foreclosure sale on a deed of trust (see Chapter 10).

Gift Deed.   Any deed where no valuable consideration was given is considered a **gift deed**. The deed is valid unless it was given to defraud creditors, in which case it can be voided.

Void and Voidable Deeds.   A void deed transfers no interest whatsoever, even if a purchaser paid value and acted in good faith. The following would make a deed void:

- Forgery
- Alteration
- The fact that the grantor is a minor
- The fact that the grantor has been declared insane or is entirely without understanding
- Failure of delivery

Voidable deeds are valid deeds unless or until they are voided. The following would allow a deed to be voided:

- Fraud
- Undue influence
- Duress or menace
- The grantor's not being of sound mind (but not declared insane or entirely without understanding)

The statute of limitations to challenge a void or voidable deed is 5 years, 20 years if the claimant is a minor or insane (Civil Code Sections 318, 319 and 328).

Case Study

The case of *Anderson v. Reynolds* (1984) 588 F.Supp. 814 involved a plaintiff who had befriended the defendant, an aspiring opera singer. The defendant became a trusted adviser to the plaintiff. The plaintiff wished to sell her Lake Tahoe estate, which was valued between $1 million and $1.6 million. The defendant told the plaintiff that several movie stars he knew, including Paul Newman, were interested in her property. The defendant convinced the plaintiff to deed the property to him so he could market the property for her as a principal. He indicated that the movie stars would not deal through agents because they wanted to avoid claims for real estate commissions. The plaintiff lost faith in the defendant, who had failed to procure a buyer, and asked for the return of her deed. The defendant gave excuses and subsequently recorded the deed. The defendant issued a trust deed to his attorney for $375,000 for the apparent purpose of encumbering the property. Other trust deeds were given to further cloud the title. There was no evidence that anything of value was given for the trust deeds.

In an action for cancellation of the deed and revocation of the trust deeds the court stated that the elements of fraudulent representation are

- false representation,
- knowledge or belief that the representation was false,
- intent to induce another to act or refrain from acting in reliance on the representation,
- justifiable reliance on the misrepresentation, and
- damages resulting from reliance.

The court held that the deed was induced by intentional fraud, so it should be considered null and void and of no force whatsoever and should be set aside along with the trust deeds.

Reservation in a Deed.   A reservation in a deed gives the grantor a right that did not exist separately prior to the grant. For example, a grantor could reserve an easement over the property conveyed, retain a life estate, and retain oil and mineral rights, and so on.

Exception in a Deed.   An exception withdraws part of the described property from the grant. For example, the grantor, after describing the deeded property, could except the south 20 feet from the grant. Exceptions in deeds often use the word *sans*, which means "without."

Dedication

A **dedication** is a donation of land for public use. Because it is a donation, the donor receives no consideration.

A person cannot dedicate more than he or she owns. One cotenant cannot dedicate land to public use without the consent of the other cotenants.

To obtain subdivision map act approval (local control over subdivisions), subdividers might donate land for streets, bike paths, parks, schools, etc., in fee as well as easement rights.

Dedication may be accomplished through a grant deed or by recording a subdivision map showing the publicly owned areas, which would be implied dedication. A deed dedicating property to a government body must be accepted by the government body.

If property is given for a particular purpose only, the dedication should state clearly that the property shall revert to the grantor if the use ceases or is abandoned. Otherwise, courts likely would determine it really was given for any public purpose.

Formerly, if an owner knew that a government entity was using his or her private property by spending public funds on improvements, clearing, or performing maintenance related to the public good for five years, an implied dedication of the property could result.

Case Study

The case of *Gion v. City of Santa Cruz* (1970) 2 C.3d 29 involved a parcel of oceanfront property. Since 1900, members of the public had parked their vehicles on the land and proceeded toward the sea to fish, swim, and picnic. The city posted signs on the property, built an embankment, and filled in holes. The court held that if an owner has not effectively halted public use in any significant way, it will be held as a matter of law that he or she intended to dedicate his or her property. For an owner to negate a finding of intent to dedicate, the owner either must prove affirmatively that he or she granted the public a license (gave permission) or must demonstrate that he or she made a bona fide attempt to prevent public use. Because the owner had done neither, in this case there was an implied dedication to the city.

In response, the state legislature enacted Civil Code Section 1009, which states that future public use of private property shall not ripen into public use by implied dedication.

Dedication cannot be required as a condition of obtaining a building permit where the purpose of the use of the dedicated land does not relate to the new structure.

Case Study

The case of *Dolan v. City of Tigard* (1994) 114 S.Ct. 2309 involved a property owner who wished to redevelop a property by tearing down an existing structure and erecting a new building. The proposed development conformed to zoning. The planning commission granted the permit subject to the dedication of a 15-foot pedestrian and bike path along an adjacent creek. This dedication amounted to 10 percent of the property. The city claimed that the dedication would help mitigate traffic. The U.S. Supreme Court ruled that the dedication requirement violated the Fifth Amendment as it was a taking of property. The city had failed to prove that additional traffic generated by the new building had any relationship to the dedication of a bike/pedestrian path.

■ INVOLUNTARY TRANSFERS OF REAL PROPERTY

Besides foreclosure sales, sheriff's sales, tax sales, and property that escheats to the state (discussed later in this chapter), title can be passed involuntarily—without the consent of the owner—in several ways.

Adverse Possession
A user of land can acquire title to the land of another by **adverse possession.** The rationale is that property should be used productively and taxes should be paid. Several conditions must be met:

■ The possession must be an actual occupation. A person need not actually live on the property to get title by adverse possession. The person must, however, use or fence the property. Title cannot be claimed for more than what a person exercises dominion over, except when a person claims title under a defective deed. Title to all the property described in the deed could be obtained under adverse possession, even if all of the property were not used. There also must be exclusive use. If another adverse user or the owner is also in possession, an adverse user cannot gain title by adverse possession.

A claim of occupancy can be based on the occupancy of a tenant of the person claiming the adverse interest.

- Possession must be open, notorious, and hostile to the true owner's title. If a person uses property with permission, he or she will not be able to get title by adverse possession because the use is not hostile. A tenant therefore could not obtain title by adverse possession because he or she would be in possession with permission.

- Use must be under a claim of right or color of title. A claim of right for adverse possession does not mean that a person believes he or she has title; it means only that he or she claims title against others. Any hostile use would be regarded as a claim of right. Color of title could be a claim under a defective document; for example, a forged deed or a deed that is void because of a defect.

- Possession must be continuous and uninterrupted for a period of five years. The five-year period is satisfied if an adverse user uses the property for two years and a successor in interest to him or her uses the property for an additional three years (tacking on). For tacking on there must be some sort of privity (mutual or successive relationship) between the two users. While the use does not have to occur every day, it must be of a continuous nature. If the use is interrupted, a new five-year period will start.

- The adverse user must pay all property taxes for five years. If the owner continues to pay the taxes, the adverse user cannot obtain title unless the user also paid the taxes. Use based on a mistaken boundary probably would not give the adverse user title, because no taxes would have been paid. However, a prescriptive easement might arise.

Title cannot be taken from a government entity, public utility, or railroad by adverse possession. Title also cannot be taken from a minor or an insane person. The five-year continuous use must occur when an owner is competent.

An adverse user cannot get greater rights than the true owner had. For example, the adverse possession of the surface would not include any mineral rights previously separated from the land.

A user cannot defeat future interests by obtaining an interest by adverse possession. If the true owner had a life estate, by adverse possession all the adverse user could obtain would be an estate for the life of the former life tenant.

To obtain a marketable title, an adverse user either would have to obtain a quitclaim deed from the title owner of record or would have to commence a quiet title action to have the court determine ownership. An adverse user who recorded a court's determination of title in the adverse user would have a marketable title.

Eminent Domain

The power of the government to take private property for the public good is called **eminent domain** and is set forth in the Fifth Amendment to the U.S. Constitution as well as the California Constitution. Eminent domain may be exercised at any level of government. It may be delegated to schools, hospitals, and public utilities.

The condemning entity must compensate the owner for the property taken. The power of eminent domain should not be confused with the exercise of police power. The exercise of police power, which generally cannot be delegated, does not entitle an owner to compensation. Examples of police power would be enforcement of zoning ordinances or fire, building, and health codes.

The owner is entitled to the fair market value of the property at the time it is taken. Any increase in value because of the use by the condemning entity is not considered in determining value.

An owner who is not satisfied with the compensation offered has the right to have the value determined by the court. In that event, a jury will determine market value as a question of fact. The condemnation award should be based on the highest and best use of the property, even if the property is being used for another purpose (Code of Civil Procedure Section 1250.410).

Case Study

The case of *People ex Rel. Caltrans v. Woodson* (2002) 93 C.A.4th 954 involved a condemnation offer of $1,400,000 based on the property's current use as a trailer park, rather than its highest and best use for storage rentals. The trial court awarded $1,876,750 but refused to award litigation costs.

The court of appeal explained that Civil Code Procedure Section 1250.410 requires awarding litigation costs where the final offer is unreasonable in relation to the final award. The court emphasized that to determine reasonableness, the guidelines are (1) the amount of the difference between the offer and the compensation awarded, (2) the percentage of the difference between the offer and the award, and (3) the good faith, care, and accuracy of how the amount of the offer and owner's demand were determined. In this case, there was a $476,750 difference between positions, the offer was only 74 percent of the final award, and Caltrans' offer was based on the obviously wrong current property use. Litigation costs were awarded.

Relocation expenses are allowed by statute in cases of eminent domain. Compensation also is allowed for goodwill of a business if the loss cannot be prevented by relocation.

Case Study

The case of *City of San Diego v. Sobke* (1998) 65 C.A.4th 379 involved a condemnation for street improvements. Baja-Mex Insurance and Money Exchange in San Ysidro, near the Mexican border, had to move, thus increasing operating costs. The move, which was to a less desirable and more costly location, coincided with a peso devaluation, which resulted in Baja-Mex showing an increase in monthly earnings of 400 percent.

Baja-Mex sought a condemnation award for loss of goodwill. In affirming the trial court decision, the court of appeals pointed out that while tenants are entitled to goodwill damages in cases of eminent domain, the damages must be proven by a change in pretaking and posttaking positions. Increased expenses was not the proper measurement of lost goodwill.

Note: With business up 400 percent, Baja-Mex had an impossible task to prove a loss of goodwill resulting from relocation.

Tenants are entitled to be compensated for their remaining leasehold interests unless the lease provides that it terminates upon condemnation.

Every taking of property in fee or a lesser interest (easement) means that an owner is entitled to compensation for the value of the property or interest taken. The taking for a street or a utility easement could result in a benefit to the remaining property so that the owner would not be entitled to compensation for any detriment caused to the balance of the parcel.

Even if a property is not used for the purpose for which it was taken under eminent domain, the former owner has no right to reclaim the property.

Private parties can obtain an easement for utility services over the land of others by eminent domain, provided

- there is a great necessity for the easement,
- the easement location provides the most reasonable service and is consistent with the least damage to the burdened property, and
- the hardship of the owner of the appurtenant property, if the taking is not permitted, clearly outweighs any hardship to the owner of the burdened property [Civil Code Section 1001(c)].

Inverse Condemnation.   If an owner is unable to use the property as a result of public action, an action could be brought for **inverse condemnation:** to force condemnation proceedings. For example, if the construction of a new airport caused jets to pass 500 feet over the roof of a house, the noise might destroy the owner's peaceful use of the premises, and an action for inverse condemnation would be proper.

If a public entity delays for more than six months in commencing eminent domain after announcing it will take the property, an owner can bring an action for inverse condemnation (Code of Civil Procedure Section 1245.260).

Case Study

The case of *Terminals Equipment Co. v. City and County of San Francisco* (1990) 221 C.A.3d 234 involved a firm operating from a 31,400-square-foot building in San Francisco. The city adopted a redevelopment plan calling for a park to be located on the site. TEC requested a building permit to tear down its two-story structure and erect an eight-story office building. The permit was denied. TEC asked the city to condemn the property for acquisition, but the city refused to do so. TEC then sued the city for inverse condemnation. The court of appeal held that a public agency has no liability to a property owner for announcing redevelopment plans unless all reasonable use of a property is taken away. Because TEC could continue to use the property, there was no liability for refusal to allow new construction that was inconsistent with the redevelopment plan.

Case Study

Gilbert v. State (1990) 218 C.A.3d 234 involved a moratorium on new water connections because of a water shortage. The owners of the property alleged inverse condemnation. The court held that California law does not recognize potential water use as a compensable property right. While the court indicated a regulation effects a taking if it does not substantially advance legitimate state interests, in this case the conditions imposed were in the state's interest in ensuring a potable water supply. Further, because the land was purchased without a water supply, the state did nothing to diminish the value of the land.

Case Study

The case of *City of Monterey v. Del Monte Dunes* (1999) 199 S.Ct. 1624 involved a situation where the City of Monterey denied building permits

(continued on next page)

for a housing development that conformed to the city's general land-use plan and zoning ordinance. The plaintiff sued, alleging inverse condemnation.

Severance Damage. If the taking of property results in a lower value to the remaining property that has not been taken, the owner will be entitled to severance damage (Code of Civil Procedure Section 1240.150).

Government Seizure

The government can seize property without compensation to the owners when the property was used with the owner's knowledge for unlawful acts such as the sale, manufacture, or distribution of controlled substances or was purchased with revenue derived from drug traffic.

The Financial Institutions Reform, Recovery, and Enforcement Act (FIRREA) provides for the forfeiture to the United States of any real or personal property derived from proceeds traceable to violation of 18 U.S. Code Section 1014, which prohibits "knowingly making any false statement . . . for the purpose of influencing in any way the action of . . . any institution the accounts of which are insured by the Federal Deposit Insurance Corporation upon any application for a loan." Falsifying a loan application could, therefore, result in the forfeiture of the property securing the loan.

Case Study

The case of *U.S. v. 3814 N. W. Thurman St.* (1999) 164 F.3rd 1191 involved a fraudulent loan application. Three-year income was shown as $308,106 when it was actually $27,286, and $108,356 in outstanding liabilities was not disclosed. Based on the false loan application, the U.S. Government filed an action in rem (against the property) in a forfeiture action for knowingly making false statements to a federally insured financial institution. The district court granted judgment in favor of the government and ordered the property forfeited. The trial court refused to consider if the forfeiture was excessive under the Eighth Amendment.

The Ninth Circuit U.S. Court of Appeals reversed, ruling that forfeiture was an excessive penalty because there was no loss to the bank, and the owner had not been involved in other criminal activity. If this were a criminal case, the penalty would have been six months' imprisonment and a fine of $500 to $5,000. The court held that forfeiture of 40 times the maximum fine violates the excessive fines clause of the Eighth Amendment to the U.S. Constitution.

The Fourth Amendment protects property owners against seizure without a notice and hearing.

Case Study

The case of *U.S. v. James Daniel Good* (1993) 114 S.C. 492 involved a drug seizure in which a quantity of marijuana was found in a home. Good pleaded guilty to a state drug offense. In an *ex parte* proceeding (without the defendant being present), the federal magistrate ordered the immediate seizure of the property. The tenants who were in possession were ordered to pay their rent to the government rather than to Good.

The Ninth Circuit Court of Appeal held that the civil seizure without prior notice or hearing violated the Fifth Amendment's due process clause. The U.S. Supreme Court agreed that the property interests of Good were protected by the Fifth Amendment. The Fourth Amendment also protected Good against wrongful search and seizure. While seizure could be justified to protect evidence and prevent it from being moved, this was not the situation, as real property is not movable. A *lis pendens* notice would have served to protect government interests. The court held that absent a pressing reason, seizure requires a notice and hearing.

■ TRANSFERS OF REAL PROPERTY UPON DEATH

Upon an owner's death, his or her property can be transferred voluntarily to the heirs—by will—or involuntarily by the laws of intestate succession to relatives, or by escheat to the state.

Testate Succession

A will is a testamentary declaration about the disposition of a person's property, to take effect upon the maker's death. A will is said to be an *ambulatory instrument* because it can be changed any time prior to the maker's death. The maker of a will is a testator (*trix*, formerly added as a suffix to designate a woman, is not used in this book). Anyone 18 or older and of sound mind may make a will. The testator must understand the nature of his or her property and the disposition of the property.

A later valid will that makes a complete disposition of the property of the testator in a manner different from an earlier will completely revokes the earlier will.

A codicil, an amendment to a will, requires the same formalities as a will.

A *devise* is a transfer of real property by will. A *bequest* is a transfer of personal property. *Legacy* refers to money.

Types of Wills

Formal Will. A formal will must be signed in the presence of at least two witnesses who, at the maker's request, attest to the testator's declared will. Beneficiaries under the will should not be witnesses. While a formal will need not be dated, an undated will could create a problem when more than one will is found, because the dated will is presumed to be the latest in time.

Holographic Will (Probate Code Section 6111). A holographic will is handwritten by the testator. For such a will to be valid, the material provisions must be in the handwriting of the testator, and it must be signed by him or her, but neither witnesses nor a date are required. A letter could meet the requirements of a valid holographic will if it were handwritten with testamentary intent.

Nuncupative Will. Oral, or nuncupative, wills are no longer valid in California.

Ademption

Disposition of property prior to a person's death revokes the portion of the will giving that property to a named beneficiary (**ademption**). For example, if a man's will gave a specific property to his cousin, but he sold that property prior to his death, the devise to the cousin would be revoked. The proceeds from the sale would go to residual beneficiaries and not to the cousin.

Simultaneous Death

When spouses die in a common disaster (**simultaneous death**) and there is insufficient evidence to conclude that one spouse survived the other, the estate of each spouse will be distributed as if each had survived the other (Uniform Simultaneous Death Act, California Probate Code Sections 220–230). For this reason, joint tenant property owners should each have wills.

Intestate Succession

When a deceased leaves no will, the property passes to his or her heirs by the law of **intestate succession:** All community property passes to the surviving spouse. Separate property passes as follows:

- No spouse, no children—Property passes to the parents.
- No spouse, no children, no parents—Property passes to siblings (or their heirs).
- No spouse, no children, no parents, no siblings—Property passes to blood heirs going back through a common ancestor.
- Spouse, no children—Half of the property passes to the spouse and half to the parents (or blood heirs).

- Spouse, one child—Half of the property passes to the spouse and half to the child.
- Spouse, more than one child—One-third passes to the spouse and two-thirds to the children.
- No spouse, child (or children)—All to the child (children).

Heirs take by right of representation (per stirpes). That is, children would share equally in the share their deceased parent would have received had their parent survived.

Inheritance is by blood (or adoption). In-laws do not inherit.

Escheat. If a person dies intestate and his or her representative is unable to locate an heir within two years after death, the attorney general will bring an action to declare title to be vested in the state. If heirs fail to come forward within five years of the person's death, the property will **escheat** to the state (Probate Code Sections 220–231), and it can then be sold.

Probate

Probate is the legal procedure that provides for the transfer of the real and personal property of the deceased as well as the payment of the debts of the deceased.

The person appointed under the will to serve as the personal representative of the deceased during probate is commonly referred to as the *executor*.

If the deceased died intestate (without a will), the court will appoint a personal representative (commonly referred to as an *administrator*) to represent the deceased.

Upon a person's death his or her property becomes immediately vested in the beneficiaries named in the will or the heirs if there is no will. Theoretically they immediately could encumber or transfer their interests; however, title would not be insurable, because the property would be subject to the control of the deceased's representative until probate was concluded. Heirs and beneficiaries often will transfer their interests for consideration prior to completion of probate. Some people are in the business of buying the interests of heirs and beneficiaries.

Real property is probated in the state where the property is located. Probates in the state where the deceased resided are domiciliary probates. Probates in other states are ancillary probates. In California estates are probated in superior court in the county where the real property is located or the deceased resided.

Probate starts with a petition for probate (if a will) or letters of administration (if intestate). A hearing is held, and a representative is appointed or confirmed. Creditors generally have four months from publication of notice to file their claims. An inventory and appraisal are filed with the county clerk. The representative files an accounting of all receipts and disbursements and requests court approval. Finally the representative petitions the court to distribute the remaining assets to the proper heirs and devisees.

If a deceased had a pending contract for the sale of real property, the court would have to confirm the sale.

When it is in the best interests of the estate, property may be sold in probate. Money may be needed to pay debts, taxes, or costs or simply to allow the division of assets among heirs or beneficiaries.

The representative of the estate can grant an exclusive listing for a period not to exceed 90 days. Generally, sales by the representative of the deceased are subject to court approval unless heirs waive confirmation.

Bids usually would be taken to the court for an approval hearing. Late bids from other parties will be considered. However, for a late bid to be considered, it must be at least 10 percent higher on the first $10,000 and 5 percent higher on the balance of the bid being considered. For example, if the bid being considered were for $90,000, a late bid would have to be $5,000 higher:

$$10 \text{ percent of } \$10,000 = \$1,000$$
$$5 \text{ percent of } \underline{\$80,000} = \underline{\$4,000}$$
$$\$90,000 \quad \$5,000$$

(An easy way to remember this formula is 5 percent plus $500.)

The court can set increments for further bids and then confirm the sale.

The probate code requires completion of the probate sale for the broker to earn a commission.

Case Study

At a confirmation hearing on an estate sale the person who made the successful overbid listed broker Henry Tong as the person entitled to a real estate commission.

(continued on next page)

Tong's license had expired at the time of the purchase, although it was subsequently renewed. The superior court held that Tong was not entitled to a commission because he was not licensed at the time the cause of action arose (the time of the bid).

The Court of Appeal reversed because the Probate Code states that an estate is not liable for a commission unless the sale is consummated. While the general rule is that a broker is entitled to a commission when an offer from a ready, willing, and able buyer is accepted by the property owner, that rule is superseded by Probate Code Section 10160, which requires completion of the probate sale for the broker to earn a commission. Because Tong was licensed when the commission was earned (the sale was completed), Tong was entitled to his commission [*Estate of Lopez* (1992) 8 C.A.4th 317].

Probate sales are one of the few instances where commissions are subject to court review. When the probate court confirms the bid and there is no overbid in court, the listing agent receives all of the sales commission. When there is no listing, but a real estate agent procures an acceptable offer that is confirmed by the probate court, the agent receives all the sales commission (the rate is set by the court).

If there is no agent on the original offer and there is an agent for the late bid, the agent's commission cannot exceed 50 percent of the difference between the original offer and the accepted offer.

If an agent procures a bid that is overbid in probate court by a buyer represented by an agent, the two agents split the commission on the original amount, and the agent who obtains the overbid receives all of the commission on the overbid amount, but is limited to 50 percent of the increased bid, with the court determining the commission rate.

If the original offer was made through the listing agent and the overbid is made by a buyer not represented by an agent, the listing broker earns a commission on the amount of the original bid, with the court determining the commission rate.

Living Trusts

A living trust may be used in addition to a will. Under the living trust the trustor(s) generally transfer their property to themselves as trustees for the beneficiaries, who are usually the same persons. The living trust, which is a revocable trust, avoids probate because the trustees have already conveyed their property to the trust. The trust provides for the division of the property after the death of the last trustor. The successor trustee makes the conveyance, thus avoiding probate costs and delays.

By use of more involved A-B living trusts, it is also possible to reduce the federal inheritance tax by increasing the exemption to a nonspouse from $1 million as of January 1, 2003, to $2 million. Because of this tax benefit plus avoidance of probate costs and delays, living trusts are gaining in popularity.

■ SUMMARY

Title can be transferred by both voluntary and involuntary conveyances. The most common way is by deed.

Deed requirements include

- writing (because of the statute of frauds),
- execution,
- description of the property,
- delivery,
- acceptance,
- granting clause,
- competent grantor, and
- definite grantee.

The following are *not* required for a valid deed:

- Acknowledgment (although a deed must be acknowledged to be recorded)
- Recording (although an unrecorded deed does not give constructive notice to later purchasers for value)
- Consideration (a valid deed can be given for love and affection)
- Manner of taking title (if not specified, conveyances to spouses transfer title as community property; conveyances to two or more parties who are not spouses transfer title as tenants in common; conveyances to one party transfer title in severalty)
- Witnesses and seals
- Date (deed takes effect on date of delivery)

The types of deeds include the

- grant deed, in which the grantor implies that he or she previously has not conveyed the property and that he or she has not encumbered the property other than what has been disclosed; grant deeds convey after-acquired title;

- quitclaim deed, which conveys whatever interest the grantor has but makes no warranty of title;
- warranty deed, through which the grantor expressly warrants that he or she has good title and agrees to defend the title and be liable should it be defective (not used in California);
- sheriff's deed, which is given after a sheriff's sale and transfers only the interest a former owner had;
- tax deed, which is given when property is sold for nonpayment of taxes (because taxes are a priority lien, the sale wipes out junior encumbrances); and
- gift deed, given for love and affection.

Dedication is the voluntary transfer of real property through donation for public use.

Involuntary transfers include

- adverse possession, through which a user can acquire title by open, notorious, hostile, adverse use for a period of five years, as well as paying the taxes during that period; and
- eminent domain, through which the government can take property for the public good but must pay the former owner the fair market value of the property taken.

A will is a testamentary declaration to dispose of the property of a deceased. A formal will requires the signature of the testator and two witnesses. A holographic will, a handwritten will signed by the testator, also is valid in California, but a nuncupative (oral) will is not.

If a person dies intestate with no heirs, his or her property is transferred involuntarily to the state by escheat.

Probate is the legal procedure to carry out the wishes of the deceased and pay the debts.

■ DISCUSSION QUESTIONS AND CASES

1. **Under what circumstances could a life tenant transfer his or her interests by will?**

2. Grantors conveyed title to grantees, retaining a life estate in a portion of the property conveyed. The description of the portion reserved was ambiguous. **What are the rights of the grantors?**

Lehman v. Kamp (1969) 273 C.A.2d 701

3. A cotenant conveyed the entire fee title. Subsequently the cotenant acquired the interest of his cotenant. **What are the rights of the parties?**

Emeric v. Alvarado (1891) 90 C. 444

4. A deed was given to a grantee with the request that it not be recorded until the grantor died. **Is this a valid transfer?**

McCarthy v. Security Trust & Savings Bank (1922) 188 C. 229

5. After a deed was delivered, it was placed in the grantor's deposit box. The grantor continued to collect the rents and pay expenses on the property. **Did a valid transfer occur?**

Huth v. Katz (1947) 30 C.2d 605

6. The federal government took all of the land bordering a lake by eminent domain. Condemnees had three cabin barges on the lake that were used in their business. The cost of moving the barges would have been excessive. The government refused to pay for the barges because they were personal property. **Are the condemnees entitled to the value of the barges?**

U.S. v. 967.905 acres of land (1969) 305 F.Supp. 83

7. The United States condemned three summer camps. The camps, owned by nonprofit organizations, had a fair market value of less than $1 million, but the replacement cost was approximately $6 million. **What are the owners entitled to?**

U.S. v. 564 acres of land (1979) 99 S.Ct. 1854

8. Muller owned property that he rented to his veterinary corporation. The state condemned the building. Muller built another building in the same area, which he also rented to his corporation. Because of higher costs, Muller charged the corporation a higher rent. Because of the higher rent, the corporation suffered a decrease in profits. **Is the corporation entitled to compensation for this loss?**

People ex rel. Dept. of Transportation v. Muller (1984)
36 C.3d 263

9. A deed was placed in escrow for one-half of a lot. The evidence was conclusive that the deed later was altered to convey the entire lot.

Are the sellers entitled to the value of the property they did not intend to convey?

Montgomery v. Bank of America (1948) 85 C.A.2d 559

10. A redevelopment agency acquired a junkyard by eminent domain. The owner was unable to relocate her business. She was forced to sell her inventory as scrap for far less than its value for parts. **Is this a compensable loss?**

Baldwin Park Redev. Agency v. Irving (1984) 156 C.A.3d 428

11. A foreclosure was imminent, and one joint tenant signed the name of the other joint tenant on a deed because the other joint tenant was not available. **Was the transfer valid?**

Handy v. Shiells (1987) 190 C.A.3d 512

12. When the Johnsons were purchasing their home, their son suggested he be the purchaser so they could take advantage of his GI financing. The parents supplied the down payment and treated the home as their own. Upon the father's death the son asked his widowed mother to leave so he could sell his house. **Is the son's action proper?**

Johnson v. Johnson (1987) 192 C.A.3d 551

13. A decedent's will left a valuable piece of property to you. However, before her death she sold the property. The sale did not close until three days after her death. Both you and the residual beneficiary claim the sale proceeds. **What are your rights?**

Estate of Worthy (1988) 205 C.A.3d 760

14. A dedication of property was made to the City of Palm Springs for specific use as a library. The city wished to convey a portion of the property to a developer for access to a prepared neighboring commercial development. The conveyance would require that a portion of the library be demolished. **Was the proposed conveyance to the developer proper?**

Save the Welwood Murray Memorial Library Comm.
v. City Council (1989) 215 C.A.3d 1003

15. A development plan called for B.F. Goodrich to consolidate its holdings. B.F. Goodrich was unable to reach an agreement to purchase 3.2 acres adjacent to its corporate offices. The

redevelopment agency brought an eminent domain action so they could then convey title to B.F. Goodrich. **Was this action proper?**

Redevelopment Agency of the City of Chula Vista v.
Rados Bros. (2002) 95 C.A.4th 309

The court decisions for the above cases can be found on our Web site at **www.dearbornRE.com**. Click on the **"Instructor Resources"** link, then scroll down the page until you find the link titled "California Real Estate Law 5th Edition."

■ CHAPTER QUIZ

1. After a deed was signed by the grantor, the grantee made a slight unauthorized alteration that increased the size of the property conveyed from 600 acres to 620 acres. The effect of this modification was that

   a. the entire deed became void.
   b. only 600 acres would be transferred, because the alteration cannot pass title.
   c. 620 acres were transferred, but the grantee could be liable for damages.
   d. the grantor has one year to discover the forgery and void the transfer.

2. Title transfers with a deed at the time of

   a. delivery.   c. acknowledgment.
   b. signing.   d. recording.

3. The most important factor in the delivery of a deed is

   a. the intent of the grantor.   c. possession.
   b. physical conveyance.   d. recording.

4. After a man's death a deed giving his home to a nephew is discovered in the same envelope as his will. The will, dated prior to the deed, gave the house to his church. Who gets the house?

    a. The church, because the will was dated prior to the deed
    b. The church, because the deed was never delivered
    c. The nephew, because the deed was dated later and thus modified the will
    d. The nephew, because deeds have priority over wills

5. Which of the following deeds would fail to transfer title?

    a. A deed to John Jones using his stage name "Mr. Marvelous"
    b. A deed made to Henry Schmidt and wife
    c. A deed made to Henry or Henrietta Schmidt
    d. A deed to Tom Brown, an emancipated minor

6. Acknowledgment is necessary to

    a. deliver a deed.
    b. validate a deed for recording.
    c. have a formal will.
    d. convey legal title.

7. Which of the following is (are) characteristic(s) of a recorded deed?

    a. It must be acknowledged.
    b. It is presumed to have been delivered.
    c. It provides constructive knowledge of the transfer.
    d. All of the above

8. Which of the following is a requirement of a valid deed?

    a. Acknowledgment   c. Witnesses
    b. Dated   d. None of the above

9. Which of the following is a characteristic of a quitclaim deed?

    a. It conveys after-acquired interests.
    b. It can convey a partial interest.
    c. It warrants that the grantor has not previously conveyed the property.
    d. It warrants that there is nothing against the property that the grantor knows about that has not been disclosed.

10. What type of deed is received by a purchaser after a sheriff's sale?

    a. Limited warranty deed   c. Sheriff's deed
    b. Quitclaim deed   d. Grant deed

11. When you receive and record a gift deed, which of the following could adversely affect your title?

    a. Creditors of the grantor
    b. Rights of parties in possession
    c. Prior unrecorded deeds given for valuable consideration
    d. All of the above

12. A grantor retained an easement over land previously conveyed. What is this called?

    a. A reservation   c. A codicil
    b. An exception   d. An after-acquired interest

13. In obtaining title by adverse possession it is *not* necessary to

    a. live on the property.
    b. actually pay taxes.
    c. have open and notorious use.
    d. have use that is hostile to the interests of the owner.

14. *Tacking on* refers to

    a. an additional party to an agreement.
    b. additionally acquired security.
    c. adverse use of a previous or subsequent user.
    d. None of the above

15. Able's property was taken by the city for a new civic center. Baker was Able's tenant in the property and had five years remaining on an advantageous lease. Which of the following is true of Baker's rights?

    a. Baker's only right is to 30-day notification.
    b. Baker has rights against Able for the value of his lease interest.
    c. Baker has rights against the city for the value of his lease interest.
    d. Both b and c

16. Loss of value of remaining land caused by a taking under eminent domain is known as

    a. inverse condemnation.
    b. the police power of the state.
    c. severance damage.
    d. exemplary damage.

17. An owner's property was seized because it was used for drug sales. Which of the following statements is correct?

    a. The owner is entitled to the fair market value of the property.
    b. If the owner is not found guilty of a felony, the property must be returned.
    c. Innocence of any knowledge of the use would be a defense against seizure.
    d. None of the above

18. A codicil providing for transfer of real property is a(n)

    a. type of deed.   c. original government transfer.
    b. amendment to a deed.   d. amendment to a will.

19. Alex's inheritance of a house from his uncle George would be called a

    a. bequest.   c. legacy.
    b. devise.   d. dedication.

20. Which of the following is a requirement of a holographic will?

    a. Verbal disposition   c. Witnessed
    b. Handwritten   d. Dated

21. Agnes sold her house and purchased stocks and bonds with the proceeds. Upon her death a will was found giving her house to her best friend, Mildred. What is Mildred entitled to?

    a. The stocks and bonds
    b. The value of the house at the time Agnes died
    c. The price Agnes received for the house
    d. Nothing

22. Alice and Jack, a married couple, hold all of their property as community property. When Alice dies intestate, each of the couple's five children will receive

    a. one-fifth of her property.
    b. one-fifth of two-thirds of her property.
    c. one-tenth of her property.
    d. nothing.

23. A woman died intestate, leaving one living son and two grandchildren (by a deceased daughter) as her only living relatives. The disposition of her property would be

    a. one-half to her son and one-quarter to each of the grandchildren.
    b. one-third to her son and one-third to each grandchild.
    c. to the state by escheat.
    d. None of the above

24. A will provided that all of an unmarried testator's estate would go to his only child. His child predeceased the testator, but the child left a spouse and three children. The estate would

    a. escheat to the state.
    b. pass one-third to the spouse and two-thirds to the grandchildren.
    c. pass one-half to the spouse and one-half to the grandchildren.
    d. pass one-third to each of the grandchildren.

25. The executor brought a bid of $190,000 to the probate court for approval. The court will not consider late bids less than

    a. $190,001.   c. $200,000.
    b. $191,000.   d. None of the above

CHAPTER TEN

10

REAL PROPERTY SECURITY DEVICES

■ KEY TERMS

antimerger clause
blanket encumbrance
California Housing
  Financial
  Discrimination Act
  of 1977
certificate of sale
defeasance clause
deficiency judgment
due-on-sale clause
Equal Credit
  Opportunity Act
Fair Credit Reporting
  Act

fictitious trust deed
financing statement
holder in due course
hypothecate
lock-in clause
mortgage
negotiable instrument
obligatory advances
Real Estate Settlement
  Procedures Act
  (RESPA)
real property sales
  contract

Soldiers and Sailors
  Civil Relief Act
subject to
trust deed
Truth-in-Lending Act
wraparound loan

■ PROMISSORY NOTES

A promissory note is the evidence of the debt. It is an unconditional written promise signed by the maker to pay a certain sum in money now or at a specific time in the future.

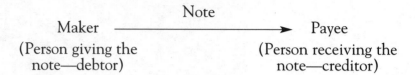

Maker ———————Note————————→ Payee
(Person giving the   (Person receiving the
note—debtor)   note—creditor)

Classification of Promissory Notes

Straight Note.   A straight note is an interest-only payment note with the principal to be paid in full when due.

Installment Note.   An installment note provides for regular payments of principal and interest.

Amortized Note.   The regular payments for a fully amortized installment loan pay off the entire principal as well as the interest during the loan term. A partially amortized note would have payments based on an amortization schedule, but it would have to be paid in full at a date prior to the end of the amortization schedule (balloon payment).

Negotiable Instruments

While not money, **negotiable instruments** are freely transferable and are used in lieu of money. They are either promises to pay (notes) or orders to another to pay (drafts).

To be a negotiable instrument, a note or draft must be

- in writing,
- signed by the maker,
- an unconditional promise or order to pay another, and
- payable on demand or at a specific time in the future, for a certain sum in money, and payable to the order of the payee or to the bearer.

Whether an instrument is negotiable is of great importance to holders. Assume A gave a note to B:

A ———————Note————————→ B

A could have valid personal defenses against paying B. These defenses could include

- lack of consideration for the promise,
- fraud on the part of B,
- prior payment or cancellation,
- setoffs from other claims A has against B, or
- the fact that the note was never delivered to the payee.

Holder in Due Course.   If the note were negotiable, A could not raise these personal defenses against a transferee from B who was a **holder in due course**, often called a *BFP*—bona fide purchaser:

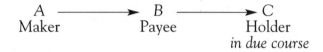

For a party to be a holder in due course,

- the instrument must be proper and complete on its face,
- the holder must have acquired the instrument prior to its due date without any notice as to previous dishonor,
- the transferee must have been a good-faith purchaser for value, and
- the transferee must have had no notice of any defenses of the maker or any defects in the title of the transferor of the paper.

Assume that the maker (A) had already paid the payee (B) but had failed to get back the note. While A would have a valid defense against any efforts by B to collect again on the note, A could not use the prior payment defense against C, a transferee from B who is a holder in due course. Because a holder in due course is not subject to the personal defenses of the maker, the holder in due course has greater rights than the payee (B).

Some defenses are valid against even a holder in due course. These are known as *real defenses* and include

- incapacity—the maker lacked legal or mental capacity;
- illegality—the note was executed for an illegal purpose;
- forgery; and
- material alteration by the holder. (If the note were raised by a prior holder, a holder in due course could collect on the original terms.)

Case Study

The case of *Wilson v. Steele* (1989) 211 C.A.3d 1053 involved a note secured by a trust deed that was given by a homeowner for remodeling work performed by an unlicensed contractor. The assignee of the note claimed to be protected as a holder in due course. Business and Professions Code Section 7031 requires that contractors be licensed. The court of appeal held that because the contractor was not licensed, the contract was illegal and unenforceable. Commercial Code Section 3305 (2) (b) provides that a holder in due course takes free from defenses, but one of the exceptions is illegality of the transaction, which renders the obligation a nullity.

Common Provisions of Notes

Balloon Payments. Often installment notes provide that the entire balance shall be due at a date prior to the note's being fully amortized. Such notes are called *partially amortized notes*, and the large payment is known as a *balloon payment*. A balloon payment is described as a payment more than twice the amount of the smallest payment (Business and Professions Code Section 10244).

Balloon payments are limited for regulated loans made or arranged by loan brokers. These restrictions do not apply to first trust deeds of $30,000 or more or to second trust deeds of $20,000 or more (Business and Professions Code Section 10245), nor do they apply to construction loans or notes given by the buyer to the seller to finance the purchaser or to loans made by institutional investors.

A loan with a term of less than three years for non-owner-occupied property may not have a balloon payment. A loan with a term under six years on an owner-occupied dwelling of fewer than three units may not have a balloon payment.

The holder of a balloon note secured by an owner-occupied dwelling of four or fewer units must give from 90 to 150 days' warning of the due date of the balloon payment (applicable to loans made after January 1, 1984). Construction loans and loans where seller financial disclosures have been made are exempt from the notification requirement.

Due-on-Sale Clause. Also known as an *alienation clause*, the **due-on-sale clause** calls for the note to be paid in full upon sale of the property. (It accelerates the payments.)

Loans with due-on-sale clauses cannot be assumed. A number of state courts determined that loans made by private individuals and state-licensed lenders were assumable loans despite the language in the notes. In California, in *Wellenkamp v. Bank of America* (1978) 21 C.3d 943, the court determined that an institutional lender could not automatically enforce a due-on-sale clause unless the sale increased the risk of default or impaired the lender's security. Based on California decisions, a huge number of loans with due-on-sale clauses were assumed.

Decisions in California and other states seemed to indicate that all loans were assumable (including those made by federally chartered lenders) unless the assumption impaired the lender's security or otherwise increased the lender's risk.

In 1982 the U.S. Supreme Court, in *Fidelity Federal Savings & Loan v. de la Questa* (1982) 458 U.S. 141, determined that due-on-sale clauses were fully enforceable by federally licensed lenders.

After the *de la Questa* decision, savings associations chartered by states were requesting federal charters to be able to enforce their due-on-sale clauses. Congress then passed the Garn Act (Garn–St. Germain Depository Institution Act). The act allowed lenders to enforce due-on-sale clauses unless the loan was made or assumed under state law that allowed loan assumptions at that time. Such loans would remain assumable until October 15, 1985 (a three-year window period for assumptions). The Garn Act really allowed loan assumptions of state-licensed lenders until the cutoff date. The due-on-sale full enforcement by federally chartered lenders was not affected by the act.

Because due-on-sale clauses are now considered to be fully enforceable by lenders, a number of methods have been devised to get around the assumption prohibitions. They are at best of questionable legality and at worst could subject the property owner to criminal liability for fraud against a lender. These methods include

- long-term unrecorded lease options,
- unrecorded land contracts,
- friendly foreclosures, in which the lender is really the buyer and the seller does not make payments, so the lender forecloses and obtains the buyer's interest,
- land trusts, and
- equity skimming.

Not all transfers trigger the due-on-sale provision of notes. Exceptions include transfers resulting from the death of one of the coborrowers and from the dissolution of a marriage as well as transfers resulting from the foreclosure of a junior lien. A lender knowing of a transfer and failing to act might waive its rights to enforce the due-on-sale clause.

Case Study

In *Rubin v. Los Angeles Federal Savings and Loan et al.* (1984) 159 C.A.3d 292, the court of appeal refused to allow enforcement of the due-on-sale clause because the lender knew of the transfer for four years before it demanded the full payment. The court stated, ". . . although waiver is frequently said to be the intentional relinquishment of a known right, waiver may also result from 'conduct' which according to its natural import, is so inconsistent with the intent to enforce the right in question as to induce a reasonable belief that such a right has been relinquished. . . ."

Due-on-Encumbrance Clause.   The due-on-encumbrance clause accelerates the payments on a loan if the owner places a further encumbrance on the property. Civil Code Section 2949, however, prohibits such acceleration for single-family owner-occupied dwellings. For other than a single-family dwelling, a lender can accelerate payments only if the encumbrance endangers the lender's security. (This would be a very unusual situation.)

Acceleration upon Default.   Even when a note states that all payments on the note become due upon default, a borrower can cure a debt that becomes accelerated because of default of payment on principal, interest, taxes, or insurance by paying the amount owed plus costs within five days before sale under a trust deed power-of-sale foreclosure or at any time prior to entry of a decree on a mortgage foreclosure by court action. Trustee's or attorney's fees are limited by statute.

Late Charges.   Late charges for a single-family dwelling loan made after January 1, 1976, cannot exceed 6 percent of the principal and interest due; however, a $5 minimum late charge is allowed. No late charge is allowed for payments less than ten days late (Business and Professions Code Section 10242.5).

However, regulated loans of first trust deeds of less than $30,000 and second trust deeds of less than $20,000, made or arranged by a loan broker, can charge 10 percent of the principal and interest as a late charge or $5, whichever is greater.

Late charges for loans not regulated must be reasonable. A late charge that is not reasonably related to the expenses incurred because of the late payment will be considered a penalty and will be unenforceable.

Prepayment Penalties.   The justification for prepayment penalties is that prepayment means an interest loss for the lender until the money has been placed in a new loan as well as the expense of placing a new loan.

The prepayment fee must be reasonable, based on when the loan was made. An unreasonably high prepayment penalty could be considered an unreasonable restraint on alienation and would not be collectible.

Prepayment penalties are not allowed on FHA-insured or VA-guaranteed loans. For Cal-Vet loans, a prepayment penalty of six months' interest on the amount pre-paid in excess of 20 percent of the original loan amount is allowed during the first five years of the loan.

On real property contract sales (land contracts) of one to four residential units entered into on or after January 1, 1969, the buyer has the right to prepay; however, the lender can prohibit prepayment for 12 months after the sale.

A clause that provides for payments of a specified amount "or more" allows prepayment without penalty.

The absence of any provision allowing prepayment would have the effect of being a **lock-in clause**, locking the borrower in to the full interest for the term of the loan even if the loan is prepaid. To avoid this harsh effect, prepayment is allowed by statute on one to four residential units.

Loans on one to four residential units that were not negotiated by a real estate broker can be prepaid at any time, but prepayment penalties can be assessed for only five years. Twenty percent of the loan can be prepaid in any 12-month period without penalty. Prepayment penalties can be for only the amount prepaid in excess of 20 percent of the original loan amount, and the penalty cannot exceed six months' advance interest on that amount (Civil Code Section 2954.9).

When the loan is for other than one to four residential units, a prepayment fee can be collected only if the borrower expressly waived the right to prepay or agreed in writing to a penalty for prepayment. For a loan made after January 1, 1984, the borrower must sign this waiver separately.

If the lender does not elect to accelerate the loan upon sale, but the buyer wanted to prepay, a prepayment penalty would appear to be proper (even for one to four residential units), because the lender has not accelerated the payments.

A lender may not collect a prepayment penalty when the lender accelerates the payments upon default for one to four residential units (Civil Code Section 2954.10).

Business and Professions Code Section 10242.6 and Civil Code Section 2954.9 prohibit prepayment penalties for residences that have been damaged by a natural disaster for which the governor has declared a state of emergency and that cannot be occupied when the prepayment is causally related to the disaster.

For loans negotiated by a real estate broker on single-family owner-occupied dwellings, prepayment may be made at any time, but prepayment within seven years of the date of execution could be subject to a prepayment charge. The charge can be imposed only on that portion of the prepayment in excess of 20 percent of the unpaid balance paid in any 12-month period, and the prepayment charge is limited to six months' advance interest on that amount (Business and Professions Code Section 10242.6).

Under the Civil Code, 20 percent of the original amount can be repaid in any 12-month period, but under the Business and Professions Code it is 20 percent on the unpaid balance.

Usury Interest Rate. Usury is charging a rate of interest greater than allowed by law. The rate of interest individuals (not exempt from usury limitations) can charge for loans to purchase, construct, or improve real estate cannot exceed 10 percent, or 5 percent greater than the rate designated by the Federal Reserve Bank of San Francisco to member banks for advances as of the 25th day of the month preceding the loan.

This usury rate does not apply to individuals who sell their property and carry back paper (purchase-money loans).

The usury rate also does not apply to loans made or arranged by real estate brokers. The broker is exempt from usury restrictions, even though a loan made by a broker is outside the scope of activity requiring a real estate license (Civil Code Section 1916.1).

Case Study

The case of *Stickel v. Harris* (1987) 196 C.A.3d 575 involved a real estate broker who borrowed money at 30 percent interest for himself and his partners to buy property. The lender sued to recover principal and interest after foreclosure by a prior lienholder. The borrowers argued that the loan rate exceeded the 10 percent usury limit and was not within the usury exemption because the borrower was not acting as a real estate broker. The court of appeal upheld the trial court's award to the lender. In this case the broker acted for both himself and his partners and expected compensation in the form of profit. Therefore the loan was exempt from the usury limitation.

The broker's usury exemption does not extend to real estate salespeople. See *People v. Asuncion* (1984) 152 C.A.3d 422 for an example where a 288 percent interest rate was held to be usurious.

The usury rate applies to cash loans or forbearance (agreements granting additional time after a loan is due).

Points charged by nonlicensed lenders are considered to be interest in determining whether a loan is usurious.

If a contract is usurious, that portion of the contract calling for interest is void (interest cannot be collected). If a borrower has paid usurious interest, the borrower is entitled to recover the entire amount of the interest paid in the last two years plus treble damages (three times the interest paid) for the last year of the loan.

Impound Accounts.   Impound accounts are trust account reserves kept by the lender for advance payments made by the borrower for property taxes and insurance. The impound account protects the lender in that funds will be available for the taxes and insurance when they are due.

Impound accounts cannot be required for single-family residences unless

- they are required by state or federal law (such as FHA and VA loans) or
- the trustor has failed to pay two consecutive tax payments or
- the loan is 90 percent or more of the property value or sales price, and the lender requires impounds.

Civil Code Section 2954.1 prohibits excessively large impound accounts. The borrower cannot be required to deposit more than would be required in a federally related loan under the Real Estate Settlement Procedures Act (RESPA; discussed in detail later in this chapter). The section also requires that any sum in excess of monies reasonably necessary to pay obligations must be refunded to the borrower within 30 days unless agreed otherwise. The lender also must make payments in such a manner that insurance is not canceled or property taxes are not allowed to become delinquent.

RESPA (12 U.S. Code §2609) limits the amount of impound accounts for federally related lenders [lenders with Federal Deposit Insurance Corporation (FDIC) insurance]. The accounts, when established, can be no more than the prorated taxes and insurance plus an estimated two months' advance charges.

Impound accounts are required for FHA loans. Lenders on FHA loans can require a tax reserve of six months and an insurance reserve of one year.

Impound accounts are not required on VA-guaranteed loans, although the lenders customarily require them.

For impound accounts for one to four residential units, state-licensed lenders must pay interest of at least 2 percent.

Attorney's Fees.   Notes frequently provide that the maker agrees to pay reasonable attorney's fees if legal action becomes necessary for collection.

■ MORTGAGES AND TRUST DEEDS

While a promissory note is the evidence of the debt, a security device such as a mortgage or a trust deed provides security for the note. Mortgages and trust deeds **hypothecate**, or pledge, the property (the borrower keeps possession but gives a security interest).

Mortgages

A **mortgage** is a two-party security instrument in which the mortgagor is the owner or buyer who gives a lien to the mortgagee. The mortgagee is the lender in cases of a hard-money loan (where money actually is advanced) or the seller in cases of a purchase-money loan (where the seller finances the buyer).

Note
(Evidence of debt)

Mortgagor   ——————————▶   Mortgagee
(Owner or buyer)   (Lender or seller)

Mortgage
(Lien as security for note)
——————————▶

Mortgages are the most common real estate financing instrument in the United States. California, however, favors trust deeds, and mortgages are seldom encountered.

In California, Civil Code Section 2924 provides that a transfer of title given for security purposes is considered a mortgage (a sale with an option of the seller to repurchase). Parties will enter agreements such as this in an attempt to evade the mortgagor's legal rights.

When a mortgage is recorded, it becomes a lien on the property. When the note is paid, the mortgagee gives the mortgagor a "satisfaction of mortgage." The satisfaction, when recorded, removes the lien. The **defeasance clause** in the mortgage provides for the cancellation of the lien upon full payment.

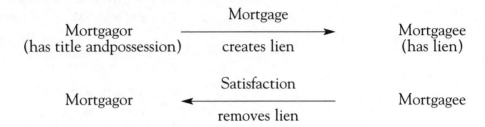

After payment of the note, if the mortgagee fails to record a satisfaction of mortgage within 21 days of a written request by the mortgagor, the mortgagee is liable for all damages as well as the sum of $500.

Mortgage Foreclosure.   Under common law, the mortgagee received the property without a sale upon the mortgagor's default. This so-called strict foreclosure is not permitted in California.

In the event of nonpayment by the mortgagor, the mortgagee can enforce the lien and foreclose by court action. Because foreclosure is considered an equitable action, it must be brought in superior court.

The property is sold at a public sale conducted by the county sheriff. The mortgagee can bid the amount of the mortgage lien. Other bidders have to bid cash. Because a foreclosure sale would wipe out all liens junior to the foreclosing mortgage, a junior lienholder who wanted to protect his or her interest would have to bid against the foreclosing mortgagee.

Case Study

In the case of *Webber v. Inland Investments Inc.* (1999) 74 C.A.4th 884, Hyatt Land Development sold four properties to Forecast Mortgage Corporation, carrying back a $754,000 second deed of trust that was later sold to Webber. Sanwa Bank made a $3,653,650 first trust deed loan. Title was transferred to All Cities Mini-Storage. Inland Empire Investments bought the Sanwa Bank note and first trust deed. After default, Inland Empire Investments foreclosed, wiping out Webber's second trust deed. Forecast Mortgage Corporation, All Cities Mini-Storage, and Inland were all owned or controlled by James Previti.

(continued on next page)

Webber sued all of the companies and Previti for declaratory relief and conspiracy to intentionally interfere with a contractual relationship.
The Riverside County Superior Court awarded Webber $1,254,946 in compensatory damages and $50,000 punitive damages.

The court of appeal affirmed as to interference with contract.

Note: This case holds that it is an intentional interference with a contractual relationship for a borrower to use a corporate entity to acquire a senior lien, default on that lien, and foreclose in order to wipe out a junior lien. Because Priviti owned or controlled all the corporations, the court had little difficulty in finding this to be a sham foreclosure with the intent of eliminating a junior lien.

When a junior lienholder forecloses, the foreclosure does not affect prior liens, but liens junior to the foreclosing lien are eliminated (the priority of liens, as discussed in Chapter 7, is based on time of recording).

In the event the proceeds of the sale exceed the costs of the sale and the foreclosing mortgagee's lien, the excess goes to pay off junior lienholders in the order of their priority. If any money is left after paying off all of the lienholders, it goes to the mortgagor.

The foreclosure sale is made by sheriff's sale in the same manner as a sale when execution is obtained on a judgment. The property is sold to the highest bidder. Notice of the sale must be posted on the property for 20 days and published once a week for three weeks in a newspaper of general circulation.

The mortgagor can stop the foreclosure anytime prior to the sale by paying past delinquencies plus costs and fees. Even if the note has an acceleration clause making the entire balance due if a payment is late, the mortgagor need only make the payments current.

The title that is given to the successful bidder is said to *relate back* to the date of the foreclosing lien. The result of this relating-back doctrine is that all subsequent liens other than liens for taxes or special assessments are eliminated by the foreclosure.

Right of Redemption.   California statutes allow a mortgagor to reinstate the mortgage after a judicial foreclosure sale. This is called the *right of redemption*. If the sale proceeds are less than the foreclosing mortgage debt, the mortgagor has a one-year period of redemption. If the sale proceeds satisfy the foreclosing mortgagee's debt, the period of redemption is three months. By paying the purchaser at foreclosure the sale costs plus interest within the redemption period, the mortgagor can regain title. The mortgagor cannot waive this right of redemption.

Purchasers at mortgage foreclosure sales will have difficulty disposing of property while the mortgagor can still redeem.

The mortgagor has the right to occupy the property during the redemption period, although the mortgagee is entitled to reasonable rent during this period. In reality the mortgagee might have difficulty collecting the rent, and courts tend to be reluctant to evict a mortgagor during the redemption period.

Mortgages and trust deeds for income property often provide for an *assignment of rent,* which allows the mortgagee to take over the property during the redemption period and apply the rents received to the debt. Without this provision, the mortgagor would keep possession and would be collecting the rents.

Only the mortgagor or successors in interest (heirs or assignees) can redeem after the foreclosure sale.

After the sale the sheriff provides the high bidder a **certificate of sale** stating that the property is subject to redemption rights. This certificate of sale is recorded. Within one week of the sale the sheriff must inform the debtor of his or her redemption rights.

If the property is not redeemed during the redemption period, the sheriff issues a *sheriff's deed.* The grantee receives all of the rights of the foreclosed mortgagor without the foreclosing lien and liens junior to it. Liens senior to the foreclosing lien will still be in force against the property. At this point the grantee can evict the mortgagor or tenant in possession.

Deficiency Judgments.   Should the judicial foreclosure sale bring less than the amount owed on the mortgage, the foreclosing lienholder can apply for a **deficiency judgment** for the difference, but must do so within three months of the sale. Only after the judicial foreclosure sale can the mortgagee sue the mortgagor for any deficiency amount. Very few deficiency judgments are granted, however, because they are not possible in the following situations:

1. **Foreclosure is under a power-of-sale clause.** (No deficiency judgments for mortgages or trust deeds foreclosed under power of nonjudicial sale are allowed.) However, a lender on a VA-guaranteed home loan can seek a deficiency judgment after a trustee's sale [*Jones v. Turnage* (1989) 699 F.Supp. 795]. This exception may also apply to FHA home loans.

2. **The foreclosing lien is a purchase-money loan.** There can be no deficiency judgment when the seller provided credit. The seller started out owning the property and ends up owning it, called a *purchase-money mortgage.*

   Money advanced by a third-party lender for purchase purposes is also a purchase-money loan. A mortgagee who provides funds to purchase one to four residential units for occupancy by the mortgagor cannot obtain a deficiency judgment. Purchase-money third-party lenders can obtain deficiency judgments for five or more residential units, non-owner-occupied residential property, or nonresidential property.

3. **The fair market value of the property is equal to or greater than the amount of the lien.** A deficiency judgment is possible only for the difference between the fair market value of the property and the amount of the lien. This prohibits a mortgagee from bidding much less than is owed to manufacture a deficiency.

Anti-deficiency-judgment protection does not extend to debtors when the loan was procured by fraud.

A borrower cannot waive his or her anti-deficiency-judgment protection in advance or at the time of the loan or loan renewal when the buyer is likely to be under the coercion of the lender.

Case Study

The case of *First Commercial Mortgage Co. v. Reece* (2001) 89 C.A.4th 731 involved a purchase-money loan of $207,593 that was allegedly made based on an inflated $215,000 appraisal. The lender, First Commercial, sold the loan to First Nationwide Mortgage Co. with the agreement that First Commercial would repurchase any bad loans.

After default of the buyer, First Nationwide foreclosed and purchased the property with a full-credit bid. As agreed, First Commercial then repurchased the property, which it subsequently sold for $79,252. First Commercial sued the mortgage broker, alleging fraud and negligent representation as well as breach of contract.

The superior court ruled that the full-credit bid at foreclosure satisfied the loan debt; therefore, this plaintiff could not prove damages. The court of appeal reversed, ruling that the full-credit bid rule does not bar a repurchasing lender who suffers damages by misrepresentation, fraud in the inducement, or breach of contract.

(continued on next page)

Note: If First Commercial had been the one making the full-credit bid, then it would have been an admission of property value so damages could not be shown.

A sold-out junior lienholder whose rights were lost by the foreclosure may sue the mortgagor directly for his or her note. However, if the junior lien-holder had made a purchase-money loan, which would have been precluded from a deficiency judgment, no further collection would be possible.

Even though a deficiency judgment is not possible, it could be a mistake for a creditor to bid the full amount owed under the foreclosing lien.

Case Study

The case of *Altus Bank v. State Farm Fire and Cas. Co.* (1991) 758 F.Supp. 567 involved a fire loss. After the loss, there was a foreclosure sale and the lender bid its full credit amount owed. The lender then brought action against the insurance carrier for acting in bad faith by refusing to pay the insurance loss.

The court held that the mortgagees' full-credit bid at foreclosure extinguished the mortgagee's right to make a claim against the homeowner's insurer for the fire loss. In this case, the loss exceeded the debt. By bidding the full amount of the debt owed, the bank cut off any chance of other offers relating to true value. By a full-credit bid, the bank was stating that the property was worth what it paid. The court also pointed out that the insurer had no duty to tell the mortgagee the effect of a full-credit bid.

During the early 1980s some purchasers were buying property without down payments and renting the property. They were pocketing the rent receipts and not making payments on the mortgages. Because the seller financing constituted purchase-money loans, they felt immune from deficiency judgments.

Civil Code Sections 890–895 were enacted to provide criminal penalties for using rental income during the first year after purchase without first applying it to payments on debts secured by the property (rent skimming).

Deed in Lieu of Foreclosure.   Often a mortgagee, instead of foreclosing, will have the mortgagor deed the property to the mortgagee. The mortgagee benefits by saving time and foreclosure costs as well as by avoiding the mortgagor's rights of redemption. The mortgagor benefits by avoiding having his or her credit report show a foreclosure. Deeds in lieu of foreclosure often are given in exchange for cash or several months' free rent.

A foreclosure of a prior lien will wipe out tenant leases entered into after the lien was created. When rents may have declined on commercial property, creditors have been negotiating deeds in lieu of foreclosure to hold the tenant to leases that are advantageous to the lessor. While a foreclosure wipes out the tenancy, a deed merely transfers the lessor's interest.

A deed in lieu of foreclosure should not be used without a title search. The mortgagee could end up getting the property back subject to a number of liens such as recorded judgments against the mortgagor. These junior liens would have been eliminated by a foreclosure but now could be in a priority position and able to foreclose on the property. A grantee of a deed in lieu of foreclosure could be buying litigation.

An **antimerger clause** in a mortgage provides that the senior lienholder will retain priority over junior liens in the event of merger. Normally a lien is extinguished by merger when the lienholder acquires title. If there is an antimerger clause, a foreclosing junior lienholder will be paid only after the sale proceeds have satisfied the senior encumbrances.

A deed in lieu of foreclosure that really was intended as a security device, giving the creditor greater security, rather than as a title transfer will be considered invalid because it attempted to defeat the debtor's statutory redemption rights.

Some mortgages have sale provisions that provide for a nonjudicial sale in the event of default. These sales would be similar to the sale provision of trust deeds.

Trust Deeds

Because of the lengthy and costly foreclosure associated with mortgages as well as the redemption rights that accrue after the foreclosure sale, the trust deed is the most common real estate financing instrument in California.

While a mortgage is a two-party instrument, a **trust deed** is a three-party transaction. Naked legal title is transferred by the buyer or borrower (the *trustor*) to a third person (a *trustee*) as security for a note that is given to the lender or seller (the *beneficiary*).

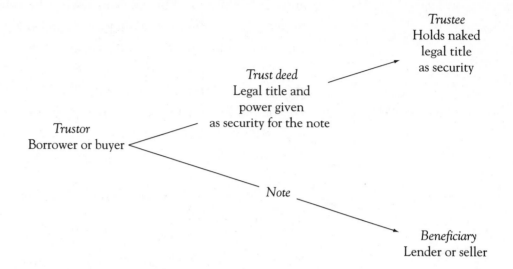

When the trustor finishes paying on the note, the beneficiary delivers the note and trust deed to the trustee with a request for a full reconveyance. Failure to provide the deed of reconveyance within 21 to 30 days of demand can subject the trustee to damages plus a $500 penalty (the same penalty as for failure to provide satisfaction of a mortgage). Failure to provide the deed of reconveyance could, however, result in more than a $500 penalty.

Case Study

The case of *Pintor v. Ong* (1989) 211 C.A.3d 837 involved a lender who refused to deliver a deed of reconveyance after the note had been paid. The failure to remove the lien made it impossible for the plaintiffs to refinance a first trust deed, which would have allowed them a lower interest rate. They sued for damages for emotional distress and were awarded $15,000, which was upheld upon appeal.

Trust Deed Foreclosure.   In the event the trustor defaults on his or her obligations, foreclosure is made by private sale and is relatively quick and inexpensive, because the trustee—not the trustor—has the legal title. Default can occur for a number of reasons, such as failure to make loan payments, to pay taxes, to keep the property insured, or to maintain the property.

Upon the direction of the beneficiary, the trustee forecloses by taking the following actions:

Three-Month Notification of Default.   Within 10 days of recording the notice of default, a copy must be sent by registered mail to all persons who recorded a request for notice, and at least 20 days prior to sale the person authorized to make the sale must send, by registered mail, a copy of the notice (often called *special notice*) of the time and place of sale to all those who recorded requests for notification.

According to Civil Code Section 2924b(3), within one month of recording the notice of default, notice must be sent by registered or certified mail to parties whose recorded interests provide constructive notice to the trustee.

The notice of default must advise the trustor of his or her right to sell prior to the trustee's sale.

Notice of Sale.   The trustor can stop the sale up to five business days prior to the sale by curing any deficiency and paying costs. To cure the default, in addition to the amount shown in the notice of default the debtor must also cure all "recurring obligations"—current payments, property taxes, insurance, senior lien payments, etc.—not shown in the notice. If the sale is extended for more than five business days, the reinstatement period is revived.

Notice of sale must be published once a week (three times) for 20 days and not more than 7 days apart. Notice also must be recorded and posted in a public place such as city hall or the courthouse and on the property.

Trustee's Sale.   A trustee's sale is a public sale in which title is given in the form of a trustee's deed to the highest bidder.

Because deficiency judgments are not possible when foreclosure is made under the sale provisions of a trust deed, the beneficiary generally bids only the amount of his or her lien. However, when a suit for waste is contemplated, the bidder can bid less than the amount of his or her lien. Other bidders are required to bid cash or by certified check.

Trustee's sales, like mortgage sales, wipe out all junior encumbrances except a mechanic's lien where work commenced prior to the trust deed or mortgage's being recorded (in which case the mechanic's lien would have priority; see Chapter 11).

The trustee may postpone the sale three times at his or her discretion without published notice and announce a new sale at the same location. After three postponements, unless excused by statute, a new notice of sale must be published, recorded, mailed, and posted.

The sale must be on a business day between 9:00 A.M. and 5:00 P.M. in a public place within the county where the property is located.

A trustee may reject all bids if he or she believes they are inadequate.

Criminal penalties can be imposed for bid-fixing or offering or accepting consideration for not bidding.

Case Study

The case of *Lo v. Jensen* (2001) 88 C.A.4th 1093 involved a foreclosure sale by a condominium association for $5,412 in unpaid assessments. The day before the sale, one defendant called the other defendant to ascertain interest in the sale. Both defendants regularly competed at sales for similar property. They decided to bid together, sharing expenses and profits. Both had been considering bids around $100,000. They estimated the fair market value of the condominium between $150,000 and $160,000. The partners were able to buy the property for $5,412. There were no other liens against the property.

After the sale, the foreclosed owners sued the buyers for violation of the Civil Code Section 2924h(g), which states, "It shall be unlawful for any person, acting alone or in concert with others, (1) to offer to accept from another, any consideration of any type not to bid, or (2) to fix or restrain bidding in any manner, at a sale of property conducted pursuant to a power of sale in a deed of trust or mortgage."

The trial court vacated the sale, ruling that the defendants violated Civil Code 2924h(g) by restraining bidding. The court of appeals affirmed, noting that there was unfairness and inadequate price. The plaintiffs were denied the benefit of competition to which they were entitled.

After the trustee's sale, the trustor has no redemption rights and the purchaser is entitled to immediate possession. (Reinstatement rights are rights of the debtor prior to the foreclosure sale, while redemption rights are rights to regain the property after the sale, such as in a mortgage foreclosure by court action.)

Foreclosure by Court Action.   If a trust deed failed to include the power of sale, foreclosure would have to be made by judicial sale, the same as for a mortgage.

Any trust deed can be foreclosed by court action rather than by sale under its sale provisions. The reason for foreclosing a trust deed by court action would be to obtain a deficiency judgment. If the trust deed is foreclosed as a mortgage, the trustor has the same redemption rights as a mortgagor.

A creditor can sue directly on the note for the full amount due; however, a creditor who does so gives up the right to foreclose on any security interest.

Case Study

In *Walker v. Community Bank* (1984) 10 C.3d 729, the California Supreme Court held that a creditor can use only one form of action to collect a debt.

Case Study

In the case of *Bank of America v. Daily* (1984) 152 C.A.3d 767, a borrower defaulted on a loan secured by real property. The Bank of America seized the amount in the borrower's checking account as a setoff against the loan. The bank then attempted to foreclose on the property. The borrower raised the defense that the bank had waived its security interest. The court held that a creditor is entitled to only one form of action. In this case the bank elected to forgo its right to the security in taking the defendant's bank account. The Bank of America lost its substantial security in a valuable property by seizing a relatively small checking account.

Junior Lienholders. Because beneficiaries of second trust deeds would be wiped out by senior lien foreclosing, the second trust deed beneficiary would want to know of the senior lien foreclosure to protect his or her interests.

By recording a Request for Notice of Default, the junior lienholder will be notified of any "Notice of Default" by the trustee. The junior lienholder can then stop foreclosure and cure the trustor's deficiency by making the trustor's payments. The junior lienholder can then start his or her own foreclosure (based on the monies advanced) and give his or her own three-month notice of default and notice of sale and have a trustee's sale. By buying at the sale, the second trust deed beneficiary owns the property subject to senior encumbrances but wipes out all encumbrances that were junior to it.

Delay by the senior lienholder in foreclosing could result in the junior lienholder's having to cure a significant delinquency. However, with the borrower's written consent, the junior lienholder can request notice from the senior lienholder when the trustor becomes more than four months delinquent (notice of delinquency). For a $40 fee the right to notice is good for five years. Five-year renewals can be obtained by paying a $15 fee.

Liens by Nonowners. Persons who give a mortgage or trust deed on property they do not own will have created a valid lien if they later acquire title. As an example, if a son gives a mortgage or trust deed on a property owned by his father, the lienholder will have no right against the property because the lien was not given by the owner. If the son later acquires title to the property from the father, the lienholder will be able to make a claim against the property to satisfy the lien.

Fictitious Trust Deed. Recording costs are charged per page. To reduce such costs, lenders record what is known as a master **fictitious trust deed** that includes all of their special provisions (boilerplate). Each trust deed then can be a simple one-page document that incorporates by reference all of the provisions of the fictitious trust deed.

Repossession of Mobile Homes. Mobile homes that have become real property are foreclosed in accordance with the trust deed. Mobile homes that are not real property are foreclosed in accordance with the Commercial Code.

If the creditor repossesses a mobile home, any person liable under the contract can reinstate the contract by paying the amount in default plus costs and expenses. This right continues until the mobile home is sold in foreclosure. This right of reinstatement may be exercised only once in any 12-month period and only twice during the period of the contract.

The buyer may be precluded from reinstatement if

- the buyer provided false credit information to obtain the loan,
- the buyer moved the mobile home to avoid repossession, or
- waste has been committed on the mobile home.

In these cases the buyer must pay the entire balance due plus costs.

Any sale proceeds in excess of liens and repossession and sale costs are paid to the former owner.

Case Study

A deficiency judgment from the sale is possible only if substantial damage to the mobile home has occurred [*Cornelison v. Kornbluth* (1975) 15 C.3d 590].

Real Property Sales Contract

A **real property sales contract**, contract of sale, or land contract is a two-party instrument whereby the seller (vendor) retains legal title and transfers possession to the buyer (vendee).

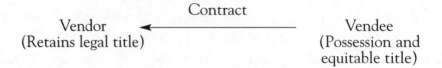

The vendee does not get a grant deed until the vendor has been fully paid. A real property sales contract can prohibit prepayment for one year. Therefore, the grantor would not be required to convey legal title for one year.

The danger for the vendee in a real property sales contract is that the vendor might be unable to transfer marketable title to the vendee when the contract is paid. Vendees can, however, protect themselves by ensuring that the contract is recorded (the vendor must acknowledge the contract for it to be recorded) and obtaining title insurance. (Title insurance is now available for buyers under land contracts.) If a contract were not recorded, the vendor could encumber the property beyond the amount due by the vendee.

A land contract must state the number of years required to pay it off. If taxes are included with the payments, the land contract must include the basis for the tax payment, and the taxes must be kept in a separate escrow account. Land contracts also must include a legal description of the property and must indicate all existing encumbrances.

The buyer on a land contract for one to four residential units has the right to prepay a land contract without penalty after 12 months.

The risk of loss in a land contract sale is with the buyer, even though the seller retains the legal title. Without the written permission of the buyer, a seller under a land contract cannot encumber the property in an amount exceeding the amount owed on the contract. The seller must apply payments received from the buyer to the encumbrances so that the encumbrances will be paid up when the purchaser has finished paying.

If the seller sells his or her interest in the contract to another party, the seller also must convey title so that the buyer can get title when he or she finishes paying off the contract.

The case of *Tucker v. Lassen Savings and Loan Association* (1974) 12 C.3d 629 held that a sale by a land contract was not an alienation because title did not pass. Therefore a land contract sale would not automatically trigger the due-on-sale clause. This decision created a revival of interest in land contracts. Since the passage of the Garn Act, land contracts are no longer a means to avoid due-on-sale provisions, although unrecorded land contracts are still used for this purpose. The benefits probably are outweighed by the dangers to the buyer. As an example, if a land contract were not recorded, an unscrupulous vendor could borrow against the property.

When the vendee finished paying on the land contract, the vendee could find that there was still a substantial lien against the property.

A former advantage land contracts had over trust deeds was quick foreclosure. Because of this feature, they often were used when the purchaser had a very low down payment. Courts no longer allow the automatic forfeiture provisions of land contracts, which means that sellers require a quiet title action.

Case Study

The California Supreme Court held in *MacFadden v. Walker* (1971) 5 C.3d 809 that a buyer's default could not be used by a seller to terminate a land contract automatically, even though the default was intentional.

Case Study

In 1968 the California Supreme Court, in *Smith v. Allen* (1968) 68 C.2d 93, allowed a land contract purchaser to get back payments that exceeded the fair rental because the payments unjustly enriched the seller.

Case Study

In the case of *Petersen v. Hartell* (1985) 40 C.3d 102, the California Supreme Court held that a purchaser who willfully defaulted but had made substantial payments or improvements could redeem prior to a judgment in a quiet title action and within a reasonable period after such judgment as set by the court.

The time and expense of a quiet title action plus the fact that the purchaser may be entitled to a refund or redemption has made the land contract disadvantageous to California sellers.

If the vendor under a land contract violates the law in impairing the rights of the vendee, the vendor could be subject to a fine of up to $10,000 and/or up to one year in county jail or state prison.

Sales in Foreclosure

It is illegal for any person to take unconscionable advantage of a property owner in default. An unconscionable sale of a residence may be voided by the owner-occupant trustor within two years of the date of transaction (Civil Code Section 2945 et seq.), unless the owner-occupant was given a five-day written right to rescind.

A great number of so-called mortgage consultants or mortgage saviors literally will steal homes through deceit. Mortgage consultant agreements now must be in writing. Real estate agents must take particular care when dealing with owner-occupants who have received notification of default. As a special precaution for the agent, the property owner should have legal representation.

Civil Code Sections 1695.15 et seq. and 2945.95 et seq. require that buyer's agents of property in foreclosure and representatives of foreclosure consultants who will not be occupying the one- to four-unit property as their residence must provide written proof to the seller that

- they have a real estate sales license and
- there is a surety bond for twice the fair market value of the property being purchased (such bonds are not widely available in California).

An equity purchaser or foreclosure consultant is liable for all damages from statements made by the equity purchaser's or foreclosure consultant's agent. Violations of the law make the sales contract void and may require damage payments to the seller (no time limit is set).

The effect of these statutes is that buyers' agents for investors/buyers should avoid property in foreclosure unless the parties will agree to an agent's representing the seller only, as a surety bond is then not required.

Case Study

In re Wallace Reed Phelps (2001) 93 C.A.4th 451 involved an owner who moved out of her residence while it was in foreclosure. She was subsequently contacted by criminal defendant Wallace Reed Phelps, and induced to sell the home to him. On the advice of his attorney, the defendant pled guilty of violating the Home Equity Contracts Act. The defendant was not allowed to withdraw his guilty plea and he was sentenced for a felony violation.

(continued on next page)

The court of appeals reversed, ruling that Phelps could not have violated the Home Equity Sales Contract Act or the Mortgage Foreclosure Consultants Act because at the time he contacted the homeowner; she was not living in her home. The statutes apply only to owner-occupants, and the court held that Phelps was wrongfully convicted.

■ LOAN TYPES, CONDITIONS, AND REGULATIONS

Construction Loans

Construction loans are normally short-term loans for a term of from one to three years, depending on the type of building. Loan payments ordinarily are released based on performance of construction tasks. The final payment usually is not made until the mechanic's lien period has expired.

If the builder has not protected the lender through a bond, the lender will insist on lien waivers from all material suppliers and subcontractors. Otherwise the money might not be sufficient to finish construction.

The payments under construction loans are known as **obligatory advances** because the lender is obligated to make the payments.

The advances made under the loan are covered in a "dragnet" clause that includes the future advances and prevents a subsequent lien from taking priority over the loan advances.

Obligatory advances take precedence over intervening liens, but an optional advance (not required by the original loan agreement) would be junior to intervening liens if the lender had actual notice of the intervening liens.

Seller Financing

Besides mortgages, trust deeds, and real property purchase contracts, several additional financing methods are available exclusively to sellers.

Wraparound Trust Deed.   When a property has an assumable below-market-interest-rate loan, the seller could be better off using a wraparound loan than letting a buyer assume the loan and taking back a second trust deed.

A **wraparound loan** (all-inclusive trust deed) is written for the amount of the existing loan as well as for any seller financing. For example, assume a home is to be sold for $70,000, the seller has an existing $30,000 FHA-insured loan at 6 percent, and the buyer has $10,000 down. The wraparound loan would be written for $60,000 at 12 percent interest. The seller would then get 12 percent over the entire $60,000.

$60,000
at
$\left\{\begin{array}{l}\text{\$30,000 first trust deed on which seller pays} \\ \text{6 percent} \\ \text{12 percent\$30,000 seller's equity}\end{array}\right.$

The seller, by getting a 6 percent interest differential on the first trust deed, is getting the equivalent of 18 percent interest on his or her equity.

Because wraparound loans involve seller financing, usury limitations do not apply.

If the buyer assumed the first trust deed and gave a second at 12 percent, this situation would exist:

> First trust deed, $30,000—buyer assuming at 6 percent
> Second trust deed, $30,000—buyer paying seller 12 percent

If the first trust deed had a balloon payment and the seller failed to include one in the wraparound loan, the seller could find that costly refinancing was necessary, and the interest rate being paid might end up exceeding the interest rate being received.

Besides interest differentiation, another advantage that a wraparound loan offers to a seller is that the seller actually makes the payment on the priority loan so he or she knows it is not in default. Because the buyer is not making the payments on the first trust deed, some buyers require lender verification that payments are being made.

Lease Options. Lease options are often subterfuges to avoid the due-on-sale clause as well as keep the property from being reassessed for property taxes.

These leases might have a large down payment (fee for the option), high rent, and an option to buy at a very low purchase price at a particular time when the existing loan is almost paid off. The courts could be expected to regard such an arrangement as a sale that triggers the due-on-sale clause.

In determining whether a lease option is really a sale, the courts will consider the option cost, purchase price, and rental arrangements.

A disadvantage to the buyer on a lease option agreement is that rent for a residence is not a deductible expense, but interest on a loan as well as property taxes is deductible on personal income tax returns. Because a normal loan payment is mostly interest, the purchaser on an option could be giving up a great deal more than he or she supposes the benefits to be.

Seller Financing Disclosure. When the seller provides carryback financing for a sale involving one to four residential units, the arranger of credit (broker) must comply with special disclosure requirements set forth in Civil Code Sections 2956–2967. (See Chapter 6.)

The disclosure requirements include

- identification of the note or other credit documents and of the property securing the transaction;
- description of the terms of the note or other credit document or a copy thereof;
- disclosure of the principal terms and conditions of each recorded lien that is or will be senior to the financing being arranged;
- a warning that if refinancing is required because of less than full amortization, such refinancing might be difficult or impossible to obtain in the conventional mortgage marketplace;
- clear disclosure of the fact, when applicable, that a negative amortization is possible as a result of a variable or adjustable interest rate and an explanation of its potential effect;
- an indication, when financing involves an all-inclusive trust deed, of who is liable for payments or responsible for defense in the event of attempted acceleration of a prior encumbrance and what the rights of the parties are in the event of a loan prepayment that results in refinancing, prepayment penalties, or a prepayment discount;
- disclosure of the date and amount of the balloon payment, when involved, and a statement that there is no assurance that new financing or loan extensions will be available at the time of occurrence;
- a disclosure, when the financing involves an all-inclusive trust deed or real property sales contract, of the party to whom payments will be made and who will be responsible for remitting these funds to payees under prior encumbrances and that if that person is not a neutral third party, the parties may wish to have a neutral third party designated for these purposes;
- a statement that no representation of the creditworthiness of the prospective purchaser is made by the arranger and a warning that Section 580b of the Code of Civil Procedure may limit any recovering by the vendor of the net proceeds of the sale of the security in event of foreclosure (no deficiency judgment);
- a statement that loss payee clauses have been added to property insurance to protect the seller or that instructions have or will be given to the escrow or appropriate insurance carrier or a statement that if such provisions have not been made the vendor should consider protecting himself or herself by securing such clauses;

- a statement that a Request for Notification of Default has been recorded or that, if it has not, the vendor should consider recording one;

- a statement that a policy of title insurance has been or will be obtained and furnished to the vendor and purchaser insuring their respective interests or that the vendor and purchaser should consider individually obtaining a policy of title insurance;

- a statement that a tax service has been arranged to report to the vendor whether property taxes have been paid on the property and who will be responsible for the continued retention and compensation of the tax service or that the vendor should assure himself or herself that all taxes have been paid;

- a statement about whether the security documents on the financing have been or will be recorded or a statement that the security of the vendor may be subject to intervening liens if the documents are not recorded; and

- a statement, when applicable, that the purchaser is to receive cash from the proceeds of the transaction (a cash-out buyer), and disclosure of the amount and source of the funds and the purpose of disbursement as represented by the purchaser.

Subordination Agreements. When a seller agrees to subordinate his or her interests, the purchaser can put a later loan on the property that has priority over the seller's lien.

Builders often have sellers agree to a subordinate loan. The builder then can obtain a construction loan that takes precedence over the purchase loan. In effect the builder is using the seller's equity as collateral for the construction loan. If a loan simply states that it will be subordinate, it will always be last in line. If it says it will be subordinate to a particular loan, then when that particular loan is paid off, it will regain priority.

Subordination clauses have been used in many fraud situations in the past few years. For example, suppose a person owned a home worth $250,000 free and clear. A purchaser would offer the full price with $100,000 down and the balance to be carried by the seller on a subordinate trust deed at 14 percent interest, all due and payable in six months. The seller might think it was an offer too good to be true and accept it. The buyer could then get a first trust deed for $175,000, pay the seller $100,000, and be a cash-out buyer with $75,000. The buyer would not make any payments on the loan and would let the lender foreclose. To protect his or her interest, the seller would have to make the payments and foreclose on the second trust deed (subordinate). The seller would now have a house he or she owes $175,000 on. Because it was a purchase-money loan, the buyer would not be liable for a deficiency judgment.

Courts are determining in these cases that the buyer is guilty of fraud and has both civil and criminal liability.

One small protection for sellers who subordinate their interest is to include limitations on the amount and the terms of any loan to which they agree to be subordinate.

A licensee who fails to explain the effects of a subordination agreement fully to a seller could be liable for resulting damages.

Security Agreements—Personal Property

Under the Uniform Commercial Code, a security agreement (often called a *chattel lien* or *chattel mortgage*) creates a security interest in personal property. The security interest is then perfected when a **financing statement** has been filed with the secretary of state. Security agreements for consumer goods, growing crops, and growing timber are filed with the county recorder.

A financing statement, after filing, becomes a lien on the personal property for five years. Continuation statements can be filed for additional five-year periods. A termination statement, when filed, would remove the lien.

Personal property liens are extremely important in the sale of business opportunities and real property containing personal property, such as furnished motels and apartments. Besides a normal title search, a purchaser would want to check for possible liens against the personal property.

Taking Title with a Loan

Subject To.   When a property is sold **subject to** a mortgage or a trust deed, the purchaser takes title with the encumbrance but assumes no personal obligation to pay. While the purchaser must make the payments if he or she is to keep the property, failure to do so would not subject the purchaser to any deficiency judgment. The seller is the individual personally liable on the loan.

Loan Assumption.   When a purchaser assumes an existing loan, the purchaser agrees to be primarily liable on the loan and could therefore be subject to a deficiency judgment in the event of default. The seller remains secondarily liable on the loan.

If a deficiency judgment is possible, it is in the best interest of a buyer to take a "subject to" loan, but it is in the best interest of a seller to insist that a buyer "assume" the loan.

Older FHA and VA loans are assumable. Cal-Vet loans can be assumed with the approval of the California Department of Veterans Affairs if the assuming party is eligible for a Cal-Vet loan.

By obtaining a substitution of liability from the lender, the seller can be relieved of all liability in the event of default. As a practical matter a substitution of liability is important to a seller only in cases where a deficiency judgment is possible.

VA-guaranteed lenders may be barred from obtaining a deficiency judgment against a defaulting borrower, but the Department of Veterans Affairs has a separate right against the defaulting borrower. Therefore, sellers who allow assumptions of VA loans should be aware that they are liable unless they obtain a release of liability from the VA lender.

Blanket Encumbrances

A **blanket encumbrance** is a lien (mortgage, trust deed, or real property sales contract) that covers more than one property. In the absence of a release clause, which provides for the release of properties from the blanket encumbrance upon the payment of agreed sums, the debtor would have to pay off the entire blanket encumbrance to convey a property free of the lien.

Lenders often insist on blanket encumbrances to provide themselves with greater security.

Condition of Debt

Borrowers are entitled to know the amount owed (beneficiary statement). Beneficiaries and mortgagees must provide this information within 21 days of request. Failure to do so can result in a $300 penalty. There can be a charge for this information (up to $60), but the borrower must be given an annual statement without cost.

Statute of Limitations

The statute of limitations of four years on written agreements is applicable to mortgages. If a mortgagor has not made any payment within four years of a payment being due, the debt will be outlawed (not legally collectible) because of the statute of limitations.

Civil Code Sections 882.020–882.040 established a statute of limitations on trust deed powers of sale of 10 years from the due date of the obligation (last payment) or 60 years from creation of the obligation if the due date cannot be ascertained.

■ CONSUMER PROTECTION ACTS

Bankruptcy

Debtors frequently use bankruptcy to delay foreclosure. Filing of a bankruptcy petition stops the enforcement of any lien against the bankrupt's property [11 U.S.C. 362a(4)]. In a Chapter 7 bankruptcy the title to the bankrupt's nonexempt property would pass to a trustee. The creditor would have to either get the trustee to release the property (if the debtor had no equity) or bring a motion for release of the property from the automatic stay.

Real Estate Settlement Procedures Act (RESPA)

The **Real Estate Settlement Procedures Act (RESPA)** is a federal loan disclosure act (12 U.S.C. 2601 et seq.) applicable to federally related first mortgage loans (loans made by lenders insured by FDIC or regulated by the Federal Home Loan Bank Board or any other federal agency).

The purpose of the act is to provide consumers with information on settlement costs in a timely fashion. The act applies to mortgage loans on one to four residential units, including mobile homes.

The lender is required to supply a good-faith estimate of loan costs as well as a Department of Housing and Urban Development (HUD) loan information booklet to the borrower within three business days of loan application.

The RESPA disclosure requirements do not apply to

1. loans for 25 or more acres;
2. refinance loans;
3. loans to finance vacant land;
4. loan assumptions, novations, or purchases subject to existing loans;
5. construction loans, unless the construction loan is also the permanent loan;
6. permanent loans for construction when the borrower already owns the land;
7. loans where the purpose of the purchaser is resale (dealer loans);
8. home improvement loans;
9. land contracts; or
10. second mortgages or trust deeds.

The lender cannot charge for compliance with the act. The act prohibits kickbacks and referral fees from service providers. Persons giving or receiving kickbacks or referral fees are liable for civil damages and criminal prosecution, with penalties of up to one year's imprisonment and/or up to a $10,000 fine.

A justifiable service must be provided for every fee charged, and the lender cannot require that the borrower purchase insurance from any particular firm.

The reserve for taxes and insurance (impound account) at closing cannot exceed a prorated estimate plus two months' impound payments.

Upon request, the borrower shall have the right to inspect the settlement statement during the business day preceding settlement. The Uniform

Settlement Statement must be mailed or delivered to the borrower and the seller (or their agents) at or before settlement.

RESPA allows a controlled business arrangement. A broker can refer business to service providers that the broker has a financial interest in. However, a disclosure must be made as to charges and relationships. The broker may only receive compensation based on profit sharing of the controlled business arrangement, not based on referrals. The controlled business arrangement must function as a separate business.

Equal Credit Opportunity Act

The **Equal Credit Opportunity Act** (15 U.S.C. 1691 et seq.) prohibits credit discrimination because of sex, marital status, age, race, religion, or national origin or because the credit applicant is receiving public assistance.

Fair Credit Reporting Act

The **Fair Credit Reporting Act** (15 U.S.C. 1681 et seq.) restricts credit reports to those with a legitimate need. It also provides that

■ an investigative report cannot be made unless it is disclosed to the consumer;
■ the consumer has a right to know the substance of the material in his or her file as well as the names of the recipients of reports;
■ the consumer has the right to have disputed material investigated;
■ the consumer can place a statement of explanation of a dispute in his or her file; and
■ the consumer is entitled to a statement of the reasons for adverse action regarding his or her credit.

California Housing Financial Discrimination Act of 1977

The **California Housing Financial Discrimination Act of 1977**, also called the *Holden Act*, states that a lender cannot deny a loan or change loan terms for reasons unrelated to the credit of the loan applicant. Thus redlining is prohibited, as it is under the Civil Rights Act of 1968. All other discrimination also is prohibited (Health and Safety Code Sections 35800 et seq.). The Business and Transportation Agency enforces the act and can require compliance as well as a $1,000 payment to persons discriminated against. The act applies to owner-occupied residences of one to four units.

Truth-in-Lending Act (Regulation Z)

Part of the federal Consumer Protection Act of 1968, the **Truth-in-Lending Act** (15 U.S.C. 1601 et seq.) aims to let consumers know what they are paying for credit in a percentage term (annual percentage rate) as well as the total finance charges.

The act's application to real estate is to ads for residential property that is to be owner-occupied. The disclosures of the act do not apply if there are to be fewer than four payments. Use of the following terms (*trigger terms*) in the ad requires full disclosure:

- Monthly payment
- Term of loan
- Dollar amount of any finance charges
- Down payment (if the seller is the creditor)

The full disclosure includes the interest rate at an annual percentage rate (APR), the down payment, the monthly payment, and the term of the loan.

The law makes bait-and-switch advertising (advertising property that is not available or that the advertiser will not sell, in an attempt to switch prospects to other property) a federal offense.

While all of the facts must be disclosed in a disclosure statement, the total dollar amount of finance charges need not be included for first mortgages or trust deeds or purchase-money loans. The lender cannot charge for preparation of the disclosure statement.

When a loan is for consumer credit secured by a borrower's residence, a rescission right applies until midnight of the third business day following the completion of the loan. The borrower can waive rescission rights if the loan is needed for a bona fide emergency.

Case Study

In *Jackson v. Grant* (1989) 876 F.2d 764, Union Home Loan gave borrower Jackson the Truth-in-Lending Disclosure Statement and three-day Notice of Right to Cancel on February 18. However, Union was not able to fund the loan until April 29. Almost three years later Jackson elected to rescind the loan because of the lender's failure to comply with the three-day right of rescission and improper truth-in-lending disclosure. The Ninth U.S. Circuit Court of Appeals allowed Jackson to rescind and not to pay any interest on the use of the money for three years.

Willful violation of the Truth-in-Lending Act is punishable by a fine of not more than $10,000 or imprisonment for not more than one year or both. It is enforced by the Federal Trade Commission.

Soldiers and Sailors Civil Relief Act

If a debt was incurred before a person entered military service, no foreclosure for nonpayment will be allowed within three months of leaving service except by court order. These are the provisions of the **Soldiers and Sailors Civil Relief Act** (50 U.S.C. appendix, 520). Normally the trustee or mortgagee files an affidavit indicating that the borrower has not been in military service.

■ SUMMARY

A promissory note is the evidence of a debt. It is an unconditional written promise to pay a certain sum in money now or at a definite date in the future.

Some common provisions of notes are

- balloon payments, whereby the balance is due in full at a set date;
- due-on-sale clause, whereby the loan must be paid should the property be sold;
- due-on-encumbrance clause, which requires the loan to be paid if an additional loan is placed against the property;
- prepayment penalties for early payment;
- interest provisions—interest rates that are usurious cannot be collected;
- impound accounts, accounts for taxes and insurance that are kept by the lender; and
- attorney-fee clauses, which provide that the borrower pay legal fees necessary for collection.

A mortgage is a two-party security instrument whereby a mortgagor (borrower) gives a lien (the mortgage) to a mortgagee (lender). The mortgage lien is given as security for a note.

Deficiency judgments are judgments for any deficiency between the amount of the foreclosing lien and the foreclosure sale price. Deficiency judgments will not be granted when

- foreclosure is under a power of sale (thus trust deeds foreclosed under the sale provisions cannot result in deficiency judgments, except for VA-guaranteed home loans);
- the foreclosing lien is a purchase-money loan; or
- the fair value of the property exceeds the foreclosing lien.

Trust deeds are three-party instruments in which the trustor (borrower) gives a note to a beneficiary (lender) and, to secure the note, gives a trust deed (naked legal title) to a third party (trustee). When the trustor pays the note in full, the trustee gives the trustor a deed of reconveyance, which, when recorded, removes the lien.

If the trustor defaults on payments, the trustee gives a three-month notification of default, which is followed by a 20-day notice of sale. At the end of this period the trustee has a sale and gives the purchaser a trustee's deed. After this sale no redemption by the trustor is possible. However, the trustor can stop the foreclosure by catching up on payments and paying costs anytime within five business days of the sale.

Junior lienholders would be wiped out by a trustee's sale. To protect their interests, they could record a request for notification of default. Upon being notified of default they could stop foreclosure by making the trustor's payments and then foreclosing on their junior lien. They then could end up owning the property subject to the prior trust deed.

A real property sales contract is a two-party instrument whereby the vendor (seller) keeps the title as security and gives the vendee (buyer) possession. The vendee does not get a deed until the contract is paid up. Real property sales contracts must include a legal description, state the number of years required to pay it up, indicate all encumbrances against the property, and if the payments include taxes, state the basis for the tax payment.

When a seller provides buyer financing, disclosure is required.

Subordination agreements are agreements that seller financing will be secondary to later-acquired liens. They place the seller's interest at risk.

Personal property is secured by a security agreement. A financing statement is filed with the secretary of state and becomes a lien on property for five years. Continuation statements can be filed for additional five-year periods. A termination statement, when filed, releases the lien.

When property is sold subject to a loan, the buyer is under no obligation to pay the loan; but when the loan is assumed, the buyer agrees to be obligated for the loan, making a deficiency judgment possible.

There are a number of consumer protection acts, including the

- Bankruptcy laws,
- Real Estate Settlement Procedures Act (RESPA),
- Fair Credit Reporting Act,
- Truth-in-Lending Act,
- Soldiers and Sailors Civil Relief Act, and
- Seller financing disclosure laws.

The Equal Credit Opportunity Act and California Financial Discrimination Act of 1977 prohibit discrimination against borrowers, and the Soldiers and Sailors Civil Relief Act prohibits foreclosure within three months after a person leaves military service.

■ DISCUSSION CASES

1. A mortgagee paid less than the amount owed on the mortgage at a foreclosure sale. The mortgagor subsequently assigned his rights to his wife, who redeemed the property by paying the amount bid. **What are the rights, if any, of the mortgagee?**

   Fry v. Bihr (1970) 6 C.A.3d 248

2. A plaintiff gave a first trust deed to her brother. On the same date she gave a second trust deed. The second trust deed beneficiary did not know of the first trust deed. The brother foreclosed on the plaintiff, and the plaintiff subsequently filed for bankruptcy. The plaintiff later purchased the property from her brother. The beneficiary of the original second trust deed then foreclosed. **Was the foreclosure proper?**

   Barberi v. Rothchild (1939) 7 C.2d 537

3. The mortgagee assigned the note and mortgage to the mortgagor. The mortgagor then sold the note and mortgage to the plaintiff. **What defenses does the mortgagor have against the foreclosing plaintiff?**

   O'Meara v. De La Mater (1942) 52 C.A.2d 665

4. A judicial sale was conducted in accordance with state law. After the expiration of the statutory redemption period, a sheriff's deed was issued to the purchaser. Fifteen days after the sheriff's deed was issued, the mortgagors filed for bankruptcy. They claimed that the lender had purchased the property for less than its real value. **Is the purchaser at the sheriff's sale protected?**

   First Federal Savings v. Hulm (1984) 738 F.2d 323

5. The beneficiary of a purchase-money trust deed gave an additional loan to the trustor. Prior to this additional loan the trustor had given a second trust deed to another beneficiary. The trustor defaulted, and the purchase-money loan beneficiary foreclosed. **What are the rights of the parties?**

   Pike v. Tuttle (1971) 18 C.A.3d 746

6. The defendant helped owners in default. He agreed to stop foreclosure actions against their homes. Houses were deeded to the defendant, who then deeded them to straw men who refinanced the property with larger loans. The property then was deeded back to the original owners clear of their default. The defendant kept the

difference in the loans as his fee. **Has the defendant done anything wrong?**

United States v. Miller (1982) 676 F.2d 359

7. **Instead of a definite dollar amount, may a late charge be a percentage of the unpaid principal?**

Garrett v. Coast & Southern Federal Savings & Loan Ass'n. (1973) 9 C.3d 731

8. A vendor did not wish to go through with a contract of sale. The contract called for the contract of sale to be subordinate and imposed no limitations on subsequent loans. The vendees were not to make their first payment for three years. **Can the vendee get specific performance for this agreement?**

Handy v. Gordon (1967) 65 C.2d 578

9. The mortgagor was deceased. During foreclosure the court appointed a receiver, who harvested the crops and applied the proceeds toward the mortgage deficiency judgment. The mortgage decree was not entered into until after the crops had been harvested. **Was the action of the receiver proper?**

Locke v. Klunker (1898) 123 C. 231

10. In a sale with an option to repurchase, the substantial disparity between the sales price and the option price provided the buyer with an adequate return on his money. **Does the usury law apply to this transaction?**

Orlando v. Berns (1957) 154 C.A.2d 753

11. **Would the fact that the broker is the borrower exempt a loan from usury limits?**

Winet v. Roberts (1986) 179 C.A.3d 909

12. **If a trustee's sale results in a sale for far less than the property's value, should the sale be set aside?**

Moller v. Lien (1994) 25 C.A.4th 822

13. The defendant borrowed $7,060,000 from California Federal Bank (Cal Fed). The note provided for a prepayment clause. Cal Fed sold the loan to the Federal National Mortgage Association (Fannie Mae) at origination, but retained the loan servicing. The defendant

inquired if a prepayment penalty would be charged for paying the loan off early. Cal Fed said there would be none. The defendant refinanced without penalty, paying off the Cal Fed loan and receiving the canceled note and deed of reconveyance. Subsequently Cal Fed had to pay Fannie Mae a prepayment penalty of $653,998.74, which Fannie Mae refused to waive. **Is the defendant liable to Cal Fed for the prepayment penalty?**

California Federal Bank v. Matreyek (1992) 8 C.A.4th 125

14. A buyer gave a broker a promissory note as a finder's fee. The note was secured by property other than the property purchased. After the security property was foreclosed, the holder of the note sought a deficiency judgment. **Is the note holder entitled to a deficiency judgment?**

Kurtz v. Calvo (1999) 75 C.A.4th 191

15. A borrower on a $73 million loan defaulted on loan payments and failed to pay property taxes. The owner continued to collect rent during the default period. After the lender foreclosed, the lender sued the borrower for bad-faith waste in failure to pay the property taxes as well as for punitive damages. **Should the lender be entitled to these damages?**

Nippon Credit Bank v. 1333 N. California Blvd. (2001)
86 C.A.4th 486

16. A mortgage servicing firm mistakenly notified a default service that the minimum bid for the trustee's sale should be $10,000. This was a clerical error since $100,000 was intended (the loan balance was $144,656.17). The trustee opened bidding at $10,000 and the high purchasing bid was $10,000.01. **Should the sale be set aside?**

6 Angels, Inc. v. Stuart-Wright Mortgage, Inc. (2001)

85 C.A.4th 1279

The court decisions for the above cases can be found on our Web site at **www.dearbornRE.com**. Click on the "**Instructor Resources**" link, then scroll down the page until you find the link titled "California Real Estate Law 5th Edition."

■ CHAPTER QUIZ

1. To be a negotiable instrument a note or draft need not be

   a. a sum certain.
   b. signed by the payee.
   c. an unconditional promise or order.
   d. in writing.

2. Angie signed a negotiable note to Baxter. Baxter knows she cannot legally collect on the note so she transfers the note to Clarence for consideration. Clarence can collect from Angie because he is

   a. the payee.   c. a holder in due course.
   b. the maker.   d. the negotiator.

3. A maker could *not* use which of the following as a defense against a holder in due course?

   a. A raised note
   b. Prior payment of the maker to a previous holder
   c. A note given for an illegal purpose
   d. Legal incapacity of the maker

4. The usury law interest regulations do *not* apply to

   a. seller purchase-money financing.
   b. cash loans.
   c. loans made or arranged by mortgage loan brokers.
   d. Both a and c

5. For loans on one to four residential units not made or arranged by a real estate broker, prepayment charges can

   a. be charged only for five years.
   b. not be charged on payments up to 20 percent of the original loan in one year.
   c. not exceed six months' interest.
   d. All of the above

6. The maximum period after a judicial foreclosure sale during which a mortgagor has the right to possession is

   a. 30 days.   c. 6 months.
   b. 90 days.   d. 1 year.

7. Which of the following is more closely related to trust deeds than to mortgages?

    a. Redemption rights after sale
    b. Nonjudicial sale
    c. Deficiency judgments
    d. Legal title with borrower

8. Which of the following constitutes default by a mortgagor?

    a. Failure to pay taxes
    b. Failure to make monthly payments
    c. Failure to pay insurance
    d. All of the above

9. Which of the following is a true statement regarding trust deeds?

    a. A trust deed is a two-party instrument.
    b. Legal title is held by the beneficiary.
    c. Trustor can reinstate up to five business days prior to sale.
    d. Foreclosure would wipe out all other encumbrances.

10. The total required foreclosure time under a trust deed (power of sale) is most nearly

    a. 4 months.   c. 1 year.
    b. 9 months.   d. 18 months.

11. The beneficiary of a second trust deed would be most likely to insist on a

    a. subordination clause.
    b. request for notification of default.
    c. subrogation clause.
    d. financing statement.

12. A junior lienholder was worried that a prior lienholder would delay foreclosure until the amount owed was so great that redemption by the junior lienholder would be difficult. To protect against this situation, the junior lienholder should record a

    a. request for notice of default.
    b. request for notice of delinquency.
    c. notice of nonresponsibility.
    d. lis pendens.

13. A financing instrument whereby the seller retains the legal title is a

    a. trust deed.   c. real property sales contract.
    b. mortgage.   d. None of the above.

14. Which of the following need *not* be included in a real property sales contract?

    a. The number of years required to pay it off
    b. A legal description
    c. A subordination agreement
    d. The basis for tax payments when taxes are included

15. A dragnet clause in a trust deed covers

    a. any contingency.
    b. future advances.
    c. additional parties.
    d. increases in the interest rate.

16. A subordinate loan that includes the amount of other loans is known as a(n)

    a. purchase-money loan.   c. open-end loan.
    b. wraparound loan.   d. usurious loan.

17. Seller financing disclosure requires that the broker disclose

    a. whether the purchaser will receive cash from the transaction.
    b. the date and amount of any balloon payment.
    c. Both a and b
    d. Neither a nor b

18. A subordination clause in a trust deed is of greatest benefit to the

    a. trustor.   c. trustee.
    b. beneficiary.   d. tenant.

19. Chattel liens would be located in the records of the

    a. Franchise Tax Board.   c. secretary of state.
    b. Board of Equalization.   d. Department of Real Estate.

20. A financing statement is removed from the records by

    a. final payment of the debt.
    b. a reconveyance deed.
    c. a notice of abandonment.
    d. the filing of a termination statement.

21. Which of the following is (are) true of beneficiary statements?

    a. There can be a $60 charge by the beneficiary.
    b. Failure to provide a statement within 21 days of request could result in a $300 penalty.
    c. Both a and b
    d. Neither a nor b

22. RESPA disclosure is the responsibility of the

    a. lender.   c. escrow holder.
    b. broker.   d. title insurer.

23. A lender can properly refuse to grant a loan to a borrower based on

    a. the high rate of loan defaults in the area.
    b. the borrower's public assistance income.
    c. the fact that the borrower is a single person.
    d. None of the above

24. The Truth-in-Lending Act (Regulation Z) requires that the lender provide the borrower with the

    a. annual percentage rate.   c. taxes.
    b. finance charges.   d. Both a and b

25. The Truth-in-Lending Act (Regulation Z) provides that a borrower under a contract that places a lien on his or her residence has a period of rescission of

    a. 24 hours.   c. 48 hours.
    b. three business days.   d. 30 days.

11

INVOLUNTARY LIENS AND HOMESTEADS

■ KEY TERMS

abstract of judgment	homestead	preliminary notice
affirmation	homestead exemption	specific lien
attachment	judgment lien	stop notice
certificate of sale	mechanics' liens	tax lien
cessation of work	notice of cessation	verification
declaration of	notice of completion	writ of execution
homestead	notice of	
general lien	nonresponsibility	

■ INVOLUNTARY LIENS

Involuntary liens are liens against real property that are imposed by the law, as opposed to voluntary liens, such as trust deeds, which are the result of agreement. Liens are a charge against real property, and real property can be foreclosed to satisfy liens.

Judgment Liens

A judgment is a final order of a court. A court's declaration that money is owed does not in itself create a **judgment lien** against the debtor's property. Recording a certified abstract of the court's judgment with the county recorder creates a **general lien** on all of the debtor's nonexempt real property within the county where the judgment is recorded. Certified copies of the **abstract of judgment** might be recorded in additional counties where the debtor has property. An unrecorded judgment or a judgment filed in the wrong county does not create a lien on the debtor's property.

Recording an instrument generally gives it priority over prior unrecorded conveyances and liens. Civil Code Section 1214, which gives this priority, requires that the later conveyance be made in good faith (without notice of the prior conveyance) and for valuable consideration. Judgment creditors are not considered to be bona fide purchasers or encumbrance holders [*Wells Fargo Bank v. PAL Investments Inc.* (1979) 96 C.A.3d 431]. Therefore, a recorded judgment lien would not take priority over a prior unrecorded deed or trust deed given for value.

Judgment liens are good for ten years from the entry of the judgment. Judgment liens based on alimony or child support are good for ten years from the date of recording.

Judgment liens apply to property owned by the debtor at the time the judgment is recorded as well as to postjudgment property acquisitions. While the priority of judgments ordinarily is based on the time of recording, all existing judgments have equal priority as to after-acquired property. A judgment lien applying to after-acquired property is secondary to any purchase-money liens against the property.

Termination of Judgment Liens

Judgment liens can be terminated by the following events:

- Expiration of ten years: The statute of limitations would preclude any action for collection after that period. However, a judgment can be extended for an additional ten years by again recording the abstract of judgment.
- Discharge of the debt in bankruptcy.
- Payment and satisfaction: When the debtor has paid, the judgment creditor must give a satisfaction of the judgment within 15 days of demand or be subject to a $100 penalty as well as actual damages. When recorded, the satisfaction releases the lien. Because a judgment is a general lien against all of the debtor's property, a creditor might agree to release a particular property from the general lien in consideration of a partial payment. Because a judgment can be appealed to a higher court, judgment creditors often will agree to

accept a lesser sum to satisfy a judgment so as to avoid the risk, time, and expense of an appeal. The judgment creditor also could give a satisfaction without consideration. This would be a gift.

When a debtor has no property, the lien's only value would be against possible future acquisitions. Before commencing a costly lawsuit, creditors ordinarily seek to ascertain whether a resulting judgment will likely be collectible at present or in the future.

Writ of Execution.   A judgment creditor, after locating and identifying property of the debtor, can obtain a writ from the court directing the sheriff to seize and sell the debtor's property to satisfy the judgment. This **writ of execution** is a separate lien on the debtor's property for a period of one year.

The judgment creditor who levies execution is given priority over other judgment creditors.

Prior to any sale, the court will hold a hearing at which the debtor will have an opportunity to show why an execution sale should not take place.

When the execution applies to a homesteaded dwelling (discussed later in this chapter), the court will determine the value of the property. The executing creditor can force a sale only if the homeowner's equity exceeds the statutory homeowner's exemption. The property will not be sold unless the bid received is at least equal to an amount that will pay off all liens plus the amount of the homestead exemption and the lien of the judgment creditor enforcing the execution sale. If the highest bid is insufficient, the sale will not be approved, and the judgment creditor will not be able to subject the property to another sale for at least one year.

Case Study

The case of *Little v. Community Bank* (1992) 234 C.A.3d 355 involved a sheriff's sale of homesteaded property. After the sale the purchaser discovered three IRS liens against the property that had not been listed on the title report relied on by Community Bank in obtaining court approval for the sale. The purchaser, Little, paid the IRS $125,882.94 and sued Community Bank for negligence. The court of appeal noted that a sheriff's sale to satisfy a judgment debt can be approved only if (1) the sale proceeds are 90 percent or more of the property value and (2) the sum exceeds the homestead exemption plus any extra amount needed to satisfy all liens. The court ruled that Community Bank was negligent in not discovering the IRS liens before the sale and was liable to Little, who was entitled to a clear title.

The validity of a homestead can be attacked by the judgment creditor. If the homestead declarant did not actually reside on the property or had no actual interest in the property at the time of filing, the homestead will not be valid.

A judgment by itself is not a lien on a homesteaded property. The lien does not attach until levy of execution takes place (Code of Civil Procedure Section 704.950).

Notice of Execution Sale.   Notice of an execution sale must be given by

- posting notice of the sale on the property for 20 days prior to the sale,
- publishing notice of the sale once a week for 20 days in a newspaper of general circulation within the county where the property is located, and
- mailing notice to anyone who requests notification from the clerk of the court.

The Execution Sale.   The sale must be made at public auction by sheriff's sale in the county where the property is located on a business day between 9:00 A.M. and 5:00 P.M.

The purchaser at the sale receives a **certificate of sale.**

Redemption Rights.   The debtor is allowed to redeem the property from an execution sale within 12 months of the sale (3 months if the indebtedness was paid in full by the sale proceeds). The debtor can assign his or her redemption rights to a third party.

To redeem, the debtor (or assignee) must pay the sales price plus statutory interest, plus taxes, insurance, repairs, and maintenance that were reasonably necessary for the property.

Another judgment creditor also can redeem, but his or her redemption still will be subject to the redemption rights of the debtor.

A sheriff's deed will be issued to the purchaser if a redemption does not occur within the 12-month period. The purchaser will get no greater interest than the debtor had, so the property could be subject to trust deeds, tax liens, easements, etc.

Section 701.680 of the Code of Civil Procedures provides that an action to set aside the sale must be made within 90 days (if the purchaser is a judgment creditor).

Attachment

Attachment is a process by which real or personal property of a defendant in a lawsuit is seized and kept in the custody of the law to satisfy a judgment that the plaintiff hopes to obtain. The attachment is a prejudgment lien while a case is pending that ensures the availability of property for execution after a judgment is rendered. One effect of an attachment action is that it can expedite the settlement of claims.

Attachment is now limited to claims arising from the conduct of a business, trade, or profession. Because attachment is based on the theory that only the amount of the debt, not its existence, is in dispute, attachments are limited to actions rising out of express or implied contracts requiring the payment of money.

The attachment lien is in force for three years from the date of levy. The court can extend an attachment lien for an additional two years. The lien can be released by court order, by order of the plaintiff, or by the levying officer.

There is no right of sale with an attachment lien. A sale must be made under an execution after a judgment has been rendered.

Prior to an attachment a hearing must be held. Property cannot be taken without due process [*Randone v. Appellate Dept.* (1971) 5 C.3d 536]. Before a hearing the court can issue a temporary restraining order to prohibit the sale of the property.

To obtain an attachment the plaintiff will have to convince the court that it is needed to protect his or her interests and that the claims of the plaintiff are likely to be valid.

The court will allow the defendant to post a bond or make a deposit rather than have the property attached; similarly, the court might require the plaintiff to post a bond as a condition to obtain a prejudgment writ of attachment.

The attachment lien will be lost if the defendant prevails in the lawsuit. If the plaintiff obtains a judgment, the attachment lien merges with the judgment lien as of the date of attachment for priority purposes, which would give the creditor priority over liens that otherwise could have priority.

Real Property Taxes and Assessments

As opposed to general liens, which apply to all of a debtor's property in the county where recorded, liens for property taxes and special assessments are **specific liens** attaching to the particular property on which they are due. Special assessments are for public improvements benefiting the property, such as water, sewers, streets, curbs and gutters, etc.

Property **tax liens** and assessment liens have equal priority and take priority over all other liens, regardless of purpose or when recorded. Because they are priority liens, a tax sale would wipe out not only junior encumbrances but even purchase-money first trust deeds and mechanics' liens.

Taxes on personal property also can be liens against real property if assessed on the secured assessment roll. The personal property tax assessment must be against the owner of the real property.

Real property tax rates are determined on or before September 1. One-half of the tax is due on November 1 and delinquent at 5:00 P.M. on December 10. The other half is due on February 1 and delinquent at 5:00 P.M. on April 10.

Real property on which taxes are delinquent is sold to the state each June, at which time a five-year redemption begins. If the property is not redeemed within the five-year period, it is deeded to the state, and the tax collector can sell the property to taxing agencies, revenue districts, certain nonprofit organizations, or anyone at public auction. The tax collector must attempt to sell the property within two years after it is deeded to the state. However, as long as the state retains title, the former owner's redemption rights continue. The property may not be sold for less than 50 percent of its market value. The minimum bid must be approved by the board of supervisors. The purchaser at a tax sale receives a tax deed.

Senior citizens (62 years of age and older) can defer payment of taxes on their residence, in which case the state takes a lien on the property and recovers the taxes plus interest when the owners die or sell the residence.

Federal and State Tax Liens

Liens for federal income tax are general liens and arise when the taxpayer refuses to pay a tax assessment. To have any effect against purchasers or other lienholders, the lien must be recorded.

Liens for state taxes are general liens on all property within the state. Recording is required to establish priority over subsequent liens.

Mechanics' Liens

Mechanics' liens are statutory liens, but they are provided on the basis of equity. That is, improvers of property should have a charge against the property for the value of their improvements; otherwise owners could receive undeserved enrichment. Mechanics' lien rights are set forth in the California State Constitution (Article XIV, Section 3).

Mechanics' liens are specific liens; they apply only to the property for which labor, material, or services were provided. They play an important role in both construction law and consumer law.

Persons of every class who perform labor, bestow services, or furnish material or equipment that contributes to the construction of, alteration of, addition to, or repair of any building or other structure or work of improvement can file mechanics' liens against the real property. Grading, landscaping, and demolition are included in this definition. Mechanics' liens may not, however, be filed against work contracted for by a public entity (a public work).

Generally, mechanics' liens result when the owner has contracted for services directly or through an architect, general contractor, or subcontractor (regarded as agents of the owner for the purpose of the lien law). A direct privity of contract or even knowledge by the owner of the specific mechanic is not necessary for a mechanic to have lien rights. In California a worker can file a lien even when his or her own employer does not file a lien. An unlicensed contractor, however, cannot file a mechanic's lien.

There is an exception in cases where an unlicensed worker performs contracting work where the total price is less than $500 and the owner was made aware that the contractor was not licensed.

Even when an unlicensed contractor performs the work because of fraudulent representations of the owner, the unlicensed contractor cannot sue in California courts for money owed.

Case Study

In the case of *Asdourian v. Araj* (1985) 38 C.3d 276, the plaintiff held a contractor's license in the name Artko, a sole proprietorship. He entered into a contract with the defendant, signing his own name. The defendant claimed that the Business and Professions Code precluded an unlicensed contractor from maintaining an action for which a contractor's license was required.

The California Supreme Court invoked the doctrine of substantial performance to avoid the harsh consequences from the strict application of the law. The court noted that the plaintiff's license under the name Artko listed him as the responsible party and provided evidence of his qualifications.

Case Study

Hydrotech Systems v. Oasis Waterpark (1991) 52 C.3d 988 involved a New York corporation hired as a subcontractor to install surfing pool equipment for a price of $850,000. The waterpark knew that Hydrotech Systems was not a licensed California contractor. Hydrotech sued for the $110,000 balance owed, and the defense raised was that Hydrotech was not a licensed contractor. Hydrotech amended its complaint alleging fraud. The California Supreme Court pointed out that an unlicensed contractor cannot sue in California courts for any act requiring a contractor's license (Business and Professions Code Section 7031). The court refused to allow any exceptions for fraud or any other reason.

Not only is the unlicensed contractor unable to sue for the contract price, a person who paid an unlicensed contractor may sue for recovery of amounts paid (Business and Professions Code Section 7031).

While a contractor must be licensed to file a lien, an employee need not be. The person claiming to be an employee would have the burden to prove that he or she was not an unlicensed contractor.

To avoid workers' compensation, Social Security contributions, and tax withholding, contracts will sometimes state that a person is an independent contractor and not an employee. Such a contract, by itself, would not disqualify an unlicensed employee from filing a mechanic's lien.

Notice of Nonresponsibility

A mechanic's lien also can arise if a property owner discovers unauthorized work being done on his or her property and fails to give notice that he or she will not be responsible for the work. The most common situations would be work authorized by tenants or vendees under real property sales contracts.

Within ten days of obtaining knowledge of an actual commencement of work, the owner must post a **notice of nonresponsibility** on the property in a conspicuous place and record a verified copy. Failure to verify has been held not to be a fatal defect [*Baker v. Hubbard* (1980) 101 C.A.3d 226]. Even if a notice is recorded properly, it is ineffective unless it also is posted. If the notice is posted and recorded properly, the owner's interest cannot be liened.

The notice of nonresponsibility must contain

- a property description,
- the name of the person giving notice and the nature of his or her interest,
- the name of the vendee under the contract or tenant, and
- a statement that the person signing will not be obligated.

While a vendor under a real property sales contract must file a notice of nonresponsibility to be protected against mechanics' liens, the beneficiary under a trust deed need not post or record notice, because any mechanics' liens would be subject to his or her prior interest.

If a vendor under a real property sales contract or a lessor under a lease requires the vendee or lessee to make repairs, improvements, or alterations as a condition of the contract or lease, a notice of nonresponsibility will not offer protection from mechanics' liens.

Case Study

In the case of *Los Banos Gravel Company v. Freeman* (1976) 58 C.A.3d 785, a lease required that the lessee construct a service station and restaurant. Rent was to be based on the gross receipts. The lessor posted a notice of nonresponsibility. The court held that because the property owners were participating with the lessee in the construction of the premises, they were precluded from exempting the property from mechanics' liens by the filing and posting of a notice of nonresponsibility.

Preliminary Notice. To prevent secret liens or lien claimants, a **preliminary notice** must be given prior to the recording of a mechanic's lien. To fully protect his or her lien rights, the mechanic should file a preliminary notice that the work is subject to his or her lien rights within 20 days of starting work. If the notice is given later, any subsequent liens will cover only the work starting 20 days prior to filing.

The preliminary notice may be served in person or by first class, registered, or certified mail. It must be sent to the owner, the construction lender, and the prime contractor. If the owner contracted directly with the party filing, no notice need be served on the owner. The lender's copy must contain an estimate of the total price of labor, services, and/or material to be furnished.

The preliminary notice must contain

- a general description of the labor, service, equipment, or material to be furnished;

- the name and address of the potential claimant and the name and address of the person who contracted for the purchase of labor, service, equipment, or material;
- a description of the job site; and
- a statement that if the bills are not paid in full, the improved property may be subject to a mechanic's lien.

Period To File a Lien. A recorded notice filed by an owner that work has been completed (**notice of completion**) sets the exact time of completion. Completion can also be either occupation by the owner or the owner's agent coupled with cessation of labor or acceptance of the work by the owner or the owner's agent. If no notice of completion is filed, any lien claimant can file his or her lien within 90 days of the actual completion of work.

If a notice of completion has been filed, all claimants other than the original contractor have 30 days to file their liens. The original contractor (prime contractor) has 60 days after the recording of the notice of completion to file his or her lien. The notice of completion must be filed within ten days of completion of work.

Cessation of Work. If work is stopped and no **notice of cessation** is filed, all lien claimants have 90 days from **cessation of work** to file their liens. Cessation is defined as 60 continuous days without any work being conducted.

If a notice of cessation is filed, all contractors other than the prime contractor have 30 days to file their liens, and the prime contractor has 60 days (the same as for notice of completion).

Recording Mechanics' Liens. Liens must be verified to be recorded. **Verification** is provided by the mechanic, who swears to the truthfulness of the facts stated. If for religious reasons a mechanic cannot make a public oath, the mechanic will make an **affirmation**, which is a formal declaration that a statement is true. The lien also must

- describe the work of the claimant,
- describe the property covered by the lien,
- state who hired the claimant,
- list the name of the owner or person claiming ownership,
- include the balance due (an intentional overstatement can invalidate the lien), and
- allege that the claimant was licensed at all times during his or her performance.

Enforcing Mechanics' Liens. Mechanics' liens are enforced through a foreclosure action brought by the lien holder. If they are not satisfied, the property will be sold. The redemption rights from the sale are similar to those in a mortgage foreclosure.

Priority of Mechanics' Liens. All mechanics' liens have equal priority and relate as a whole back to the date on which work actually commenced. When each mechanic started or completed his or her work makes no difference. For the starting time some work must be apparent to anyone who checks the property. In *Simons Brick Company v. Hitzel* (1925) 72 C.A. 1, the court held that starting time was indicated by "some work and labor on the ground, the effects of which are apparent, easily seen by everyone, such as beginning to dig the foundation, or work of like description that everyone readily can see and recognize as the commencement of a building."

Mechanics' liens, after filing, have priority over other liens attached subsequent to the time of commencement of work. Mechanics' liens also have priority over prior liens that were unrecorded at the time of commencement of work.

The holder of a subsequent mortgage or trust deed can obtain priority over mechanics' liens by posting a bond of not less than 75 percent of the amount of the mortgage or trust deed. The purpose of the bond is to pay judgments in suits to foreclose on mechanics' liens.

Termination of Mechanics' Liens. Mechanics' liens are lost if no action is taken to enforce them within 90 days of filing. The failure to start action or to file a lien extinguishes only lien rights, not the debt.

Mechanics' liens could be wiped out by a priority lien foreclosing; for example, a trust deed that was recorded prior to the commencement of work.

An owner can get a mechanic's lien released by filing a surety bond of 1½ times the amount of the lien claimed. This is common when an amount due is in dispute.

A tender of full and proper payment that is refused by the mechanic will serve to release the lien. (The debt will still exist.)

Voluntary release of a lien terminates the lien (usually after payment of the debt). A judicial sale also terminates the lien.

Stop Notice. This is a notice to a lender or an owner that a mechanic claimant has not been paid. It is served on the parties (not recorded). To serve a stop notice, the mechanic first must have filed a preliminary notice.

A **stop notice** is a lien on the balance of the funds the lender is holding. It has priority over the lender's using the funds remaining for completion. While a mechanic's lien could be wiped out by a lender's foreclosing, a stop notice protects the mechanic with a lien on the unexpended funds.

Upon receipt of a stop notice the lender must withhold monies due or to become due in the amount of the claim. If the owner, lender, or prime contractor disputes the validity of the stop notice, a bond in the amount of 125 percent of the amount claimed can be posted; the funds then would be released from the lien.

Lis Pendens

As previously stated, a *lis pendens* is a notice of a pending lawsuit involving rights concerning real property. When recorded, it is notice to anyone to examine the proceedings because title is in litigation. Any purchaser after the filing takes subject to the adverse claims; however, a *lis pendens* has no effect on any prior interests.

A *lis pendens*, while not a lien, protects claimants from a transfer of property that could affect their interests. Wrongfully recording a *lis pendens* could subject the recording party to damages for slander of title.

Before a *lis pendens* can be recorded, it must be signed by an attorney or approved by a judge, and all adverse parties must be served with notice. A *lis pendens* can be expunged (removed from the record) if a court finds that the claimant has not established by a preponderance of evidence the probable validity of the claim.

■ DECLARATION OF HOMESTEAD

Article XX, Section 1.5, of the California Constitution provides for homestead rights. The purpose of a **homestead** is to provide a home free from the fear and anxiety that it will be lost to creditors. A **declaration of homestead** may be recorded by an owner (or lessee under a lease for 30 years or more) to protect the homesteaded property from execution by subsequent judgment creditors.

A homestead declaration does not protect an owner from voluntary liens such as trust deeds or from tax liens, mechanics' liens, or homeowners' association assessments. It also does not protect the homesteaded property against judgment creditors whose liens were perfected by recording of the abstract of judgment prior to the recording of the homestead.

To file a homestead declaration the person recording must reside on the property homesteaded. Actual title is not necessary. Besides a lessee on a lease for 30 years or more, a buyer on a real property sales contract also can file a homestead declaration. A homestead can be filed on any property used as a residence (single-family dwelling, apartment building, farm, condominium, cooperative, mobile home, boat, etc.).

The **homestead exemption** is $50,000 for a single person and $75,000 for a family unit. A $125,000 exemption is available for persons 65 or older, persons who are physically or mentally handicapped, and low-income persons over the age of 55 ($15,000 or less annual income for a single person and $20,000 or less if married).

The homestead exemption is available in bankruptcy even though a homestead declaration was not filed.

Case Study

In re Howell (1980) 638 F.2d 81 held that a father who lived with his 23-year-old unemployed son, who was dependent on the father for support, qualified as a family unit for the homestead exemption.

The homestead exemption applies to an owner's equity. If a home had a fair market value of $80,000 and a $10,000 trust deed against it, the homeowner's equity would be $70,000. If the owner filed as a family unit, the homestead exemption would be $75,000. Subsequent judgment creditors could not force the sale of the property, because the homestead exemption exceeds the owner's equity.

Assume that the same homeowner was single and under the age of 65. The homestead exemption then would be $50,000. Because the owner's equity of $70,000 exceeds the $50,000 homestead exemption, subsequent judgment creditors could force the sale.

The proceeds from a creditor's sale of homesteaded property first go to pay off the secured liens ($10,000 first trust deed). Next the owner receives the amount of his or her exemption ($50,000) in cash, and the balance, after deducting sale costs, goes to the creditors. The owner has six months to change the cash proceeds into another homesteaded property (the cash cannot be reached by creditors during this period). The homestead exemption does not, however, extend to loan proceeds from refinancing homesteads.

Proceeds from the sale of homesteaded property are protected from creditors for six months. Similarly, if the homestead is destroyed by fire, the proceeds of the insurance are exempt from creditors' claims for six months. In either case the money can be reinvested in a new dwelling and a new homestead declaration can be filed.

When the owner's equity would allow a sale, the court could partition the property to create a smaller protected homestead. For example, a farm home and a few acres could be partitioned from the balance of the property.

If a husband and wife own separate interests as their separate property, each spouse can file a separate homestead declaration, but their combined exemption cannot exceed that of a family unit.

Either spouse can file a valid homestead on property jointly owned by both spouses. While one spouse formerly could file a declaration of homestead on property separately owned by the other spouse, after July 1, 1983, this was no longer possible. Code of Civil Procedure Section 704.910(b)(1) requires an ownership interest to file a homestead declaration.

Unmarried parties who have an ownership in the same dwelling can file separate homestead exemptions.

Section 6520 of the Probate Code provides that, if no homestead property is selected during life, a court can select a probate homestead for the spouse and minor children. This homestead would be effective against the creditors in probate. This homestead protection is limited to the lifetime of the spouse.

When a homesteaded property is sold and a new one is purchased immediately, the new homestead rights take priority as of the date of the prior homestead declaration.

To be valid, a declaration of homestead must be recorded in the county where the property is located. A homestead is not valid unless it is acknowledged. However, Civil Code Section 1207 provides that a recorded instrument that is otherwise valid gives constructive notice after it has been recorded for one year, notwithstanding any defect in or omission of an acknowledgment.

A declaration of homestead must include the following:

- The name of the declared homestead owner (can be both husband and wife if each owns an interest)
- A description of the declared homestead

- A statement that the property is the principal dwelling of the homestead owner and that the homestead owner is residing in the declared homestead at the time the homestead is recorded.

Case Study

In the case of *Skinner v. Hall* (1886) 69 C. 195, an owner had rented out his house. He leased one room back from his tenant, where he slept for one night. (His family did not join him.) He then filed his declaration of homestead. The court in this case held that one may file a homestead after residing for one day, a month, or a year. It held that one can have a residency even when one's family resides elsewhere and even in property partially rented out.

A person may have more than one homestead but only one at a time. To terminate a homestead, the owner must either sell the property or file a declaration of abandonment. Moving from the property does not end the homestead.

If a person files a homestead when he or she is heavily in debt, creditors may become very nervous. Filing a homestead at the time of purchase generally would not have a negative effect on credit.

■ SUMMARY

Involuntary liens are imposed by law, as opposed to voluntary liens, which are created by agreement. Involuntary liens include judgment liens, attachment liens, tax liens, and mechanics' liens.

Judgment liens are general liens against all of the property of the debtor in the county where the abstract of judgment is recorded. A judgment creditor can obtain execution on the judgment, in which case the sheriff seizes and sells the property. The purchaser at the sale receives a certificate of sale. If the debtor fails to redeem the property within 12 months of the sale, the purchaser will receive a sheriff's deed.

An attachment is a prejudgment lien to ensure the availability of property for execution if a judgment is rendered. The attachment is a lien against real property for three years from the date of levy. A hearing must be held, and the court will grant an attachment only if it believes it is necessary to protect the creditor and that the creditor's claim is valid. The defendant can post a bond in lieu of the attachment; an attachment would tie up the property.

Liens for real property taxes and special assessments are specific priority liens. A tax sale will wipe out trust deeds and mechanics' liens.

Federal and state tax liens are general liens, and recording determines their priority.

Mechanics' liens are statutory liens for the value of improvements by a contractor, subcontractor, equipment and material supplier, or laborer. An unlicensed contractor cannot file a mechanic's lien.

Prior to filing a lien a mechanic must provide a preliminary notice that the work is subject to a lien. The notice covers work subsequent to the notice and up to 20 days prior to the notice.

If no notice of completion is filed, all mechanics have 90 days to file their liens. If a notice of completion is filed, subcontractors have 30 days to file and the prime contractor has 60 days. Within 90 days of filing a mechanic's lien, action must be brought under the lien to foreclose the property, or the lien will be lost. A homeowner, or a lessor on a lease for 30 years or more, can record a declaration of homestead, which provides protection against subsequent judgment creditors in the following amounts:

- Single person: $50,000
- Family unit: $75,000
- 65 or older (or unable to work because of physical or mental disability): $125,000

To file a homestead declaration, the person must live there at the time of filing. To terminate a homestead, the owner must either file a declaration of abandonment or sell the property.

■ DISCUSSION CASES

1. A building corporation also owned a lumberyard. The building corporation sought to foreclose on its own property because the lumber had not been paid for. Why would a company want to foreclose on its own property? **What was the court's probable reaction to this action?**

Superior Lumber Co. v. Sutro (1979) 92 C.A.3d 954

2. An owner leased property to a convalescent hospital. After the lease was entered into, it was discovered that a great deal of work would be required if the property were to be approved and used for a convalescent home. The owner refused to pay for the work. The tenant authorized the work. The owner filed a notice of nonresponsibility. **Should the property be subject to a mechanic's lien?**

Baker v. Hubbard (1980) 101 C.A.3d 226

3. A broker furnished trucks, drivers, and equipment for excavating and grading. The broker was not the owner of the equipment provided. **Is the broker entitled to a mechanic's lien?**

Contractors Dump Truck Service Inc. v. Gregg Construction Co. (1965) 237 C.A.2d 1

4. **Should a mechanic be allowed to foreclose on valuable property when the lien is for a relatively insignificant amount?**

Robinett v. Brown (1914) 167 C. 735

5. A spouse contracted for work on the separate property of the other spouse. **Is the other spouse liable for the work?**

Loviet v. Seyfarth (1972) 22 C.A.3d 841

6. After an attachment lien but before a judgment was recorded, a property owner filed a declaration of homestead. **Does the declaration of homestead take priority over the attachment and judgment liens?**

Becker v. Lindsay (1976) 16 C.3d 188

7. A contractor abandoned a job before the work was substantially completed in accordance with the plans and specifications. The contractor filed a mechanic's lien for the value of material and services he had rendered. **Was the lien proper?**

Marchant v. Hayes (1897) 117 C. 669

8. Prior to filing voluntary bankruptcy, a bankrupt conveyed her homesteaded property to her daughter for no consideration. **What are the rights of the creditors?**

Gardner v. Johnson (1952) 195 F.2d 717

9. A judgment was entered for child support. After the judgment the father was absent from the state for most of the time. Twenty-two years later the wife sought execution of the judgment. **Was she entitled to execution?**

Nutt v. Nutt (1966) 247 C.A.2d 166

10. An engineering firm made aerial topographic maps and studies of a property for a proposed subdivision. It placed engineering stakes and aerial markers on the property. While they could be seen from the air or by walking the property, they could not be seen from the street because of weeds. The engineering firm claimed priority over a loan because of a priority in staking the property and placing the markers. **Does the engineering work constitute commencement of work in terms of the priority of mechanics' liens?**

*South Bay Engineering Corp. v. Citizens Sav.
& Loan Assn.* (1975) 51 C.A.3d 453

The court decisions for the above cases can be found on our Web site at **www.dearbornRE.com**. Click on the "**Instructor Resources**" link and then scroll down the page until you find the link titled "California Real Estate Law 5th Edition."

■ CHAPTER QUIZ

1. Involuntary liens include all of the following *except*

   a. judgment liens.
   b. tax liens.
   c. attachment.
   d. trust deeds.

2. Which of the following is *not* a specific lien?

   a. Property tax lien
   b. Judgment lien
   c. Special assessment lien
   d. Mechanic's lien

3. Henry was injured while swimming in the pool of his neighbor Tom. Henry obtained a $100,000 judgment against Tom. As applied to Tom's house, this would be a(n)

   a. unenforceable lien.
   b. general lien.
   c. specific lien.
   d. priority lien.

4. To create a lien after judgment the creditor would file a(n)

    a. writ of attachment.
    b. execution of judgment.
    c. abstract of judgment.
    d. None of the above

5. A judgment lien is effective

    a. only in the county where rendered.
    b. only in the county where the debtor resides.
    c. in every county where it is recorded.
    d. for 25 years from recordation.

6. Which of the following is true about a judgment that has been enforced by an execution sale?

    a. The buyer receives a certificate of sale.
    b. The former owner has a 12-month period of redemption.
    c. The sale need not be held at the property being sold.
    d. All of the above

7. Which of the following is an example of a prejudgment lien?

    a. Mechanic's lien
    b. Attachment
    c. Homestead declaration
    d. *lis pendens*

8. An attachment is a lien for

    a. three years from the date of levy.
    b. four years from the date of levy.
    c. ten years from the date of levy.
    d. ten years from recordation.

9. Which of the following shows the proper legal order for these events?

    a. Execution, attachment, judgment
    b. Judgment, execution, attachment
    c. Attachment, execution, judgment
    d. Attachment, judgment, execution

10. The following is true of priority of liens:

    a. Tax liens take priority over prior liens for special assessments.
    b. Tax liens take priority over prior trust deeds.
    c. Judgment liens take priority over prior mechanics' liens.
    d. None of the above

11. Unpaid real estate taxes have a lien priority superior to

    a. prior judgment liens.
    b. prior trust deeds.
    c. Both a and b
    d. Neither a nor b

12. An unpaid contractor would file which type of lien?

    a. General
    b. Specific
    c. Voluntary
    d. Attachment

13. An unlicensed person who has mechanic's lien rights would be a(n)

    a. general contractor.
    b. subcontractor.
    c. independent contractor.
    d. employee of the contractor.

14. A notice of nonresponsibility would not be filed by a

    a. vendor under a real property sales contract.
    b. lessor.
    c. beneficiary of a prior recorded trust deed.
    d. None of the above

15. A preliminary notice was filed by a contractor 40 days after work started. The period covered by a subsequent lien would start

    a. with the notice.
    b. 20 days prior to notice.
    c. 20 days after notice.
    d. None of the above

16. If there is no notice of completion, subcontractors have how many days to file their liens after completion?

    a. 30
    b. 60
    c. 90
    d. 180

17. A contractor started a foundation for a new dwelling, but the owner was not satisfied with his work and paid him off. Three weeks later the owner got a construction loan secured by a trust deed, which was recorded. The owner proceeded to hire another contractor to build his home, and when the building was finally completed, a painting subcontractor filed a mechanic's lien against the property. What is the result in this case?

    a. The trust deed takes priority over the mechanic's lien.
    b. The mechanic's lien will take priority, because a mechanic's lien always takes priority over a trust deed.
    c. The subcontractor will not be able to file against the property but will be able to file a lien against the contractor's property.
    d. The mechanic's lien will take priority over the trust deed because some work was done before the trust deed was recorded.

18. A stop notice

    a. requires that a contractor stop work.
    b. is a lien on construction funds held by a lender.
    c. is equivalent to a *lis pendens* notice.
    d. None of the above

19. A notice of a pending lawsuit involving rights in a property is known as a(n)

    a. attachment.   c. execution.
    b. *lis pendens.*   d. judgment.

20. By filing a valid homestead declaration the homeowner receives protection against

    a. subsequent mechanics' liens.
    b. prior judgments.
    c. tax liens.
    d. subsequent unsecured claims by creditors.

21. A purchaser of a condominium unit filed a declaration of homestead. The purchaser refused to pay his assessment fees, and the owners' association filed a lien. The lien would be

    a. void, because homesteaded property is protected against liens.
    b. enforceable only if the owner's equity exceeds his homestead exemption.
    c. collectible as if there were no homestead.
    d. valid but collectible only when the homestead is sold.

22. A recorded abstract of judgment has priority over a homestead declaration when

    a. it was recorded prior to the homestead.
    b. the homestead is invalid.
    c. the homestead is abandoned.
    d. Any of the above

23. A declaration of homestead would not be valid if filed by

    a. a spouse without the other spouse's permission on community property.
    b. a tenant on a 35-year lease.
    c. an owner of a 60-unit apartment complex.
    d. a husband and wife at the start of construction of their future residence.

24. A search of the county records would always show a valid recorded

a. judgment lien.
b. mechanics' lien.
c. homestead.
d. All of the above

25. To give up a valid homestead the owner would

a. change residency.
b. rent the premises.
c. change marital status.
d. None of the above.

CHAPTER TWELVE

12

ADJACENT PROPERTY RIGHTS

■ KEY TERMS

abatement	easement in gross	right of correlative
accretion	encroachment	user
affirmative easement	implied easement	right of prior
avulsion	lateral support	appropriation
dominant tenement	license	riparian rights
easement	littoral rights	servient tenement
easement by estoppel	merger	subjacent support
easement by necessity	negative easement	trespass
easement by	nuisance	
prescription	reliction	

■ BOUNDARY DISPUTES

When exact property boundaries are uncertain or in dispute, the parties involved can mutually agree to set a fixed line that is clear to both parties. According to the doctrine of agreed boundaries, agreed-on boundaries are binding on successors in interest after the boundary has been accepted by the parties for five years. An agreement about the placement of a wall or fence is, however, not necessarily an agreement setting the boundary lines.

In the event of an ambiguity, a boundary reference to a natural monument will prevail over angles or distances.

> ## Case Study
>
> In the case of *Armitage v. Decker* (1990) 218 C.A.3d 887, a property owner argued on the basis of the doctrine of agreed boundaries that the boundary should be set along a fence. The neighbors successfully argued that the neighbors had not agreed that the boundary should be the fence and that the true boundary was not uncertain but could be proved by legal descriptions and surveys.

When a boundary is clear, an oral agreement setting a different boundary will not bind the parties because it is a grant, which is required to be in writing under the statute of frauds.

The following are additional boundary rules:

- If a boundary is a road, the boundary line ordinarily will be the center of the road.
- If a boundary is a nonnavigable river, the boundary will be the center of the river.
- If a boundary is a navigable nontidal river, the boundary will be the average low-water mark.
- If a boundary is tidelands, the boundary will be the average high-tide line.

Division Fences and Party Walls

Division fences are fences on the boundary line. A fence that rests entirely on the land of one owner is not a division fence. A long-standing fence implies an agreed division.

Party walls can be either on the boundary line or entirely on the land of one owner. Generally they are the support walls of row-type housing. Party walls are established by express or implied agreement.

For division fences and party walls on the boundary line, each owner owns that portion of the wall or fence on his or her property and also has the right of support of the rest of the wall or fence. Either owner can alter his or her part of the wall or fence but cannot weaken it.

Parties can reach express agreements on the costs of maintaining party walls and division fences, and these agreements will govern. In the absence of any agreement, costs for a division fence will be borne equally by the parties unless one party decides to leave his or her land unfenced. However, if that party fences the land in the future, he or she could be liable for the share of the original cost of the division fence.

It is a misdemeanor to leave a gate open willfully or tear down the fence of another [Penal Code Section 602(h)] that is on the boundary line, because part of the fence is owned by another.

Spite fences—fences more than ten feet high that are erected or maintained for the purpose of annoying an adjoining owner—are a private nuisance and can be abated (nuisances and abatement are explained later in the chapter).

Case Study

The case of *Wilson v. Handley* (2002) 97 C.A.4th 1301 involved a row of cypress trees that were planted by the Handleys parallel to a property line. The trees were within two to ten feet of the property line and were a hybrid variety designed as a screening barrier or windbreak. Their neighbors, the Wilsons, sued the Handleys, relying on Civil Code 841.4 that "any fence or other structure in the nature of a fence" that unnecessarily exceeds ten feet in height and is maliciously erected or maintained for the purpose of annoying a neighbor is a private nuisance.

While the superior court ruled that a naturally growing row of trees is not within the scope of the spite fence nuisance law, the court of appeal reversed, ruling that the trees could be regarded as a spite fence. The case was remanded for trial on the issue of whether the fence was maliciously erected or maintained for the purpose of annoying the Wilsons. Note: The court pointed out that California has no recognized property right to a view. The court also pointed out that a fence over ten feet may be justified if it serves some additional purpose.

Trees

Trees or shrubs whose trunks are on a boundary line are known as *line trees* and belong to both owners. While either owner can remove branches that overhang his or her property (this rule applies to all trees), both owners are liable for the maintenance of and both must agree to the removal of line trees.

Case Study

The case of *Booska v. Patel* (1994) 24 C.A.4th 1786 involved a defendant who had a contractor sever the roots of a neighbor's tree at the lot line, causing the tree to die. The trial court held for the defendant. But the court of appeal reversed. While the owner has the right to the surface and everything beneath it (Civil Code Section 829), "one must so use his own rights as not to infringe on the rights of others" (Civil Code Section 3514). The court ruled that Patel did not have an absolute right to sever the roots of Booska's tree if he could have protected his own property interest by taking less severe action. A rule of reasonableness applies, the court explained.

■ ENCROACHMENT

An **encroachment** is an intrusion into, under, or over the land of another. Unless the encroacher has taken title by adverse possession or obtained use by a prescriptive easement, a property owner can go to the courts for relief in the form of an injunction prohibiting the continued encroachment or an ejectment, which is an action for ouster and/or damages.

The courts will consider the degree of encroachment, the intent of the parties, the value of the encroaching structure, and the effect on the parties in determining appropriate relief.

An encroaching party might have to remove the encroaching structure as well as pay damages caused by its removal.

When an encroachment is unintentional and the value of the structure is great compared with the value of the land encroached, the courts and statutes will allow the encroachment to remain but will have the encroacher pay appropriate damages. While the courts in some instances will allow a good-faith improver of the property of another to retain the use as a matter of equity, such relief will not be available if the encroachment was intentional (Code of Civil Procedure Section 871.1 et seq.).

Case Study

The case of *Raab v. Casper* (1975) 51 C.A.3d 866 involved improvers who were warned by the plaintiff that they were building a cabin on the plaintiff's land. The defendant disregarded the warning and completed the cabin without a survey. Code of Civil Procedure Section 871.3 requires

(continued on next page)

that the improver's degree of negligence be taken into account in determining his or her good faith and in formulating the relief. The court held in this case that the law should not allow an improver to worsen an owner's position after being warned of a possible trespass. Because of failure to heed the warning, the improver failed to act in good faith.

California courts have applied a relative hardship rule in determining whether to grant an injunction to enjoin a trespass encroachment on another's land.

Case Study

The case of *Hirshfield v. Schwartz* (2001) 91 C.A.4th 749 involved an unclear boundary line. The defendants built waterfalls, a Koi fishpond, stone decking, a putting green, etc., over an area later determined to encroach on the plaintiff's property in three places. The trial court refused to order the encroachment removed and set monetary damages in lieu of removal. The court of appeals determined that the cost of removal of the improvements would be substantial, but the benefits of removal to the plaintiff would be minimal. The court therefore upheld the superior court's decision.

While the courts in some instances will allow a good-faith improver of the property of another to retain the use as a matter of equity, such relief will not be available if the encroachment was intentional (Code of Civil Procedure Section 871.1 et seq.).

Under the common law the improvements of the improver, even though made in good faith, belong to the landowner. Under California law a good-faith improver who under mistake of fact or law made improvements believing he or she had the right to do so can remove the improvements; however, the improver will be liable to the owner for any damages to the property.

If an owner knew of the improvements and allowed the innocent improver to continue adding on the improvements, the improver could be allowed the value of his or her labor and materials.

An action to remove a permanent **trespass** (encroachment) such as a building must be taken within three years of the encroachment, or the encroachment will be allowed to remain. The encroacher will have no right to expand his or her use, nor will the encroacher have the right to rebuild should the encroachment be destroyed.

While a permanent trespass involves taking possession of the land of another with the intent to remain, a continuing trespass is use only. An example of a continuing trespass would be using the land of another for ingress and egress. In the continuing trespass each repetition is considered a separate wrong. Therefore the statute of limitations cannot be raised as a defense by a user whose use is continuing. The landowner could sue for an injunction to force the user to cease his or her trespass as well as for damages for the wrongful use.

■ NUISANCE

Ownership does not carry with it the right to use property in any manner the owner wishes. A person cannot use property in such a manner as to interfere with the reasonable use and enjoyment of others. Such unreasonable use would be considered a nuisance.

A **nuisance** is normally a nonphysical invasion that affects the use or enjoyment of others. It could be smell, dust, light, vibrations, radio interference, dangerous activity, indecent acts, or hours of operation.

In California the difference between a public and a private nuisance is based on degree. Civil Code Section 3480 states, "A public nuisance is one which affects at the same time an entire community or neighborhood, or any considerable number of persons, although the extent of the annoyance or damage inflicted upon individuals may be unequal."

Any nuisance not a public nuisance is considered a private nuisance. While there is no statute of limitations on public nuisances, there is a three-year statute of limitations on private nuisances. Laches is not a defense against the party bringing an action to abate a nuisance.

Courts consider reasonableness in determining whether a use is a nuisance. Livestock noises in an area of farms probably would not be considered a nuisance merely because several suburban residents were disturbed by the noise. Similarly, noise during construction is reasonable and nonpermanent and would not be considered a nuisance, although the noise could constitute a nuisance if the work was done at unreasonable hours.

Case Study

The case of *Lew v. Superior Court* (1993) 20 C.A.4th 866 involved a nuisance.

The Lews were the owners of a 36-unit HUD-insured Section 8 apartment complex. Seventy-five small claims actions were filed by neighbors, each requesting $5,000 damages for allowing illegal drug activity to occur on the premises, causing the neighbors emotional and mental distress.

The small claims court awarded each complainant $5,000 plus costs. The superior court set total damages at $218,325, finding that the Lews knew or should have known of the problems generated by their building and failed to remedy the situation. The award was based on the theory of both public and private nuisance.

The court of appeal affirmed, holding that by California Statute, a drug house is a nuisance and small claims court damages by private parties is a proper remedy. The fact that a nuisance is public does not deprive an individual of his action because, as to him, it is private and obstructs free use and enjoyment of private property.

Note: The above case provides a strong private remedy for neighbors to fight a neighborhood problem.

The fact that zoning permits a use does not mean the use is not a nuisance; it will be considered a nuisance if it unreasonably interferes with the rights of others. It also is not a defense in California that the nuisance was present before the plaintiff moved in.

Action involving a nuisance could be money damages, injunction or **abatement** (removal) of the nuisance.

A public nuisance that affects the entire community or neighborhood must be abated by a public body or an officer authorized by law. An individual may not abate a public nuisance unless it materially deprives use of private property.

If the roots of a line tree or neighboring tree cause problems, an owner can abate the nuisance. Civil Code Section 3502 provides that "A person injured by a private nuisance may abate it by removing, or, if necessary, destroying the thing which constitutes the nuisance without committing a breach of the peace or doing unnecessary injury."

This "self help" remedy can be extremely risky, however, because a party whose actions are not justified or reasonable could be liable for damages.

An owner cannot abate the nuisance if it is weeds that are on neighboring land.

Courts will consider the economic effects of the nuisance abatement or injunction compared with the damages caused by the nuisance. Courts also will consider the motives of the parties, such as a personal feud. If an interference is not substantial, courts are unlikely to enjoin a use.

■ WATER RIGHTS

Water is an extremely valuable resource in California, and water rights frequently are subject to litigation. The courts are authorized to refer all water litigation to the state Water Resources Control Board for either investigation and report or hearing and preliminary determination, subject to final court decision.

Surface water rights depend on whether water is flowing in a defined channel. A property owner generally cannot obstruct the flow of surface water not in a defined channel. An owner can dike against overflow water from a defined channel, which is floodwater, even when such actions cause flooding to land of another.

To dam or divert water in a defined channel requires approval of the local flood control district.

Runoff Damage

Under common law an owner who changed natural surface water runoff was liable for resulting damages. However, because the development of buildings and paved areas has dramatically increased the amount of runoff, California has modified this liability. While an upper-land owner may be liable if he or she fails to exercise reasonable care, the lower owner also must take reasonable precautions to avoid or reduce potential damage.

The rule of reasonableness applies to the use of the upper-land owner. The fact that runoff from use causes some damage to a lower-land owner's land does not in itself make the upper-land owner liable.

 See *Keys v. Romley* (1966) 64 C.2d 396.

Water-Related Terms

- **Riparian rights** are rights of owners to the reasonable use of water flowing adjacent to, under, or through the property (rivers or streams). Riparian rights are held in common with other riparian owners, even though an owner might never use them.

- **Littoral rights** are rights of owners of property bordering lakes, seas, or oceans (nonflowing water) to a reasonable use of the water.

- An owner does not have absolute use of the water under his or her property. When water is scarce, an owner must share the water table with other owners. The use of underground percolating water in relation to the other owners must be reasonable according to the **right of correlative user**.

- The **right of prior appropriation** is a concept in several western states that whoever takes water first gets a priority right to future use. While California courts have followed this concept, it has not been followed by the federal courts. One who does not own riparian rights can get rights of prior appropriation through either an easement by grant or an easement by prescription (discussed later in the chapter). An easement by prescription would require the open, notorious, and hostile taking of water under some claim of right for five years without interruption.

- **Accretion** is the gradual and imperceptible buildup of soil by natural causes such as by action of water. The addition to the land belongs to the property to which it is joined.

- **Avulsion** is the sudden loss of land by action of water such as a change in a river's course. A property owner has one year to reclaim his or her property. (The river could be diverted back to its original course.)

- When a lake, sea, or river permanently recedes, the adjoining property owners take title to the adjacent land created by the withdrawal of the water through the right of **reliction**.

■ SUPPORT

Lateral Support

An owner has a right to have his or her land supported in its natural state by the land of neighbors. This support by adjoining property is known as **lateral support**. However, an owner cannot prohibit excavation on a neighbor's property.

A person who is negligent in excavating his or her property will be liable in tort for the resulting damages. In the absence of negligence an owner does not have absolute liability for damages caused to the property of others by excavations.

Civil Code Section 832 requires that an owner give reasonable notice to neighboring owners of the date of excavation and the depth intended. An excavator who fails to notify adjoining owners of the excavations will have absolute liability for any resulting damages. If the depth is below the neighbors' foundations, the owner must allow the neighbors 30 days to protect their property. An owner has the right to enter the land to be excavated to extend his or her foundations.

If an excavation is to be deeper than nine feet from the curb, the excavator will be liable for damages to neighboring structures. The excavator can enter the neighboring property to protect the structures.

The excavator will not be liable for minor settlement cracks. Heavy rains will not excuse an excavator, because rains can be anticipated.

Because damage might appear later, there is a three-year statute of limitations for damages caused by excavations.

Subjacent Support

Subjacent support is support from below. An underground excavator has an absolute duty to support the surface regardless of any negligence. Cases generally involve owners of mining rights and tunnels for utilities or subways.

■ EASEMENTS

An **easement** is a legal interest in the land of another that entitles the owner of the easement to a limited use or enjoyment in the land of another. It is a nonpossessory interest of one who does not control possession as an owner or tenant. Most residential properties are subject to easements, with utility easements being the most common.

An easement right is for a specific purpose such as ingress or egress. The easement right could be for continuous use or for intermittent use at specific times. The owner of the property may not interfere with the reasonable exercise of the easement right by the easement holder. Unless the easement specifies exclusive use, it can be used as well by the owner.

Servient Tenement

The land being used by another is in servitude, or serves the needs of another. The land being used therefore is known as the **servient tenement**. Because the use by another necessarily places restrictions on an owner's use, a servient tenement is an encumbrance on the land. If the location of an easement is not specified, the servient tenement holder can reasonably designate the easement area.

Dominant Tenement

Normally an easement benefits other land. For example, ownership of a parcel of land could carry with it the right to cross another parcel. The land being benefited by the easement dominates the servient tenement and is known as the **dominant tenement**. Because a dominant tenement carries benefits with it in the use of the land of another, the easement is considered an appurtenance to the land. Easement rights run with the land, so transfer of title also transfers the rights and/or obligations. The rights of the dominant tenement cannot be separated or conveyed without the land, nor can the dominant tenement holder extend the easement benefit to additional property.

The dominant tenement need not be adjacent to the servient tenement.

Maintenance of Easement

In the absence of any agreement on the maintenance of a right-of-way, the responsibility rests on the dominant tenement. The dominant tenement holder has the right to enter the servient tenement for the purpose of repair and maintenance.

If an easement is jointly used with the landowner and/or with other easement users, the costs of maintaining and repairing the easement will be based on the percentage of use of each user.

Easement in Gross

An **easement in gross** is an easement right that is not joined to any dominant tenement. It is considered personal in nature. Examples of easements in gross would be a right to erect a sign on the land of another or a utility company's right to run lines over a property.

While an easement in gross is personal in that it does not go with the land, it is considered an assignable right unless the right is expressly or impliedly made personal to an individual. An easement in gross must be expressly transferred to be assigned.

Case Study

Pacific Telephone had an easement "for the stringing of telephone and electric light and power wires" over the property of Salvaty. A cable television company obtained a license from Pacific Telephone to use its poles. In *Salvaty v. Falcon Television* (1985) 165 C.A.3d 798, Salvaty brought an action for trespass, inverse condemnation, and unfair business practice against the cable company and Pacific Telephone. The court held that inclusion of cable television fell within the scope of the original easement. It was part of the natural evolution of communication and did not increase the burden on the servient tenement.

Affirmative and Negative Easements

An **affirmative easement** gives the owner of the dominant tenement the right to do something, normally the right to enter and cross the land of the servient tenement.

A **negative easement** gives the owner of the dominant tenement the right to prohibit the owner of the servient tenement from some action. For example, the owner of the dominant tenement could impose a height limitation so that the servient tenement owner does not block a view.

Private and Public Easements

Most easements are given to specific property or persons and so are said to be private easements. An easement given to the general public to cross the property is a public easement.

Creation of Easements

Easement by Grant.   An easement can be created by an actual grant, such as when a person purchases an easement right. Sometimes easements are needed to obtain map act approval of a subdivision; these easements by dedication also are really easements by grant. Owners might agree to grant easements to each other for a common good such as a private road serving their properties.

Easement by Reservation.   An easement can be created by a grant whereby the grantor retains an easement right over the property granted.

Easement by Prescription.   An **easement by prescription** is an easement obtained by use. For the user to obtain the easement the use must be open, notorious, hostile, under some claim of right, and continuous for five years. Courts hold that a claim of right does not mean any actual right but only that the user is claiming a right. An easement by prescription cannot be obtained against a state, federal, or local governmental unit.

The principal difference in establishing an easement by prescription and title by adverse possession is that to establish title the user in California also must pay the taxes for five years.

An easement established by prescription is the only easement that is lost by nonuse. Five years of nonuse will end the easement right. The five-year use need not, however, be by the same user but could be by successors in interest. Tacking on—where, for example, one user uses property for two years and a successor uses it, based on a privity relationship, for three years—will constitute the five years necessary for a prescriptive easement.

Any interference in the use by the legal owner of the property will cause a new five-year period to begin, because the five-year use must be continuous.

An easement by prescription obtained against a tenant-occupied property applies only to the tenant's interest.

Case Study

In the case of *Dieterich International Truck Sales v. J.S. & J. Services, Inc.* (1992) 3 C.A.4th 1601, a truck sales and repair business had used part of an adjoining property for trucks entering service bays for 22 years. The adjoining truck stop property lessee fenced off the property to install underground tanks for its service station. The truck sales business claimed a prescriptive easement. The court held that while the truck sales and service business had a prescriptive easement against the tenant, who was on a 49-year lease, there was no prescriptive easement against the owner, who would not get possession until 2005.

An easement by prescription applies to the use established during the prescriptive period and may not be expanded for greater use. If the nature of the use changes, a new five-year prescriptive use period will be required to obtain easement rights. In other easements (by grant or reservation) the courts take a liberal view of use.

 See *Connolly v. McDermott* (1984) 162 C.A.3d 973.

Civil Code 1009 bars a recreational user from acquiring a prescriptive easement over private land. Therefore, the use would have to be for other than recreational purposes.

The fact that others also are using the property does not defeat an easement by prescription, because multiple easements are possible. However, permission defeats an easement by prescription because the use is not hostile.

A prescriptive easement could be an exclusive easement if the use of others would not be compatible with the prescriptive easement.

Case Study

The case of *Otay Water District v. Beckwith* (1991) 1 C.A.4th 1041 involved a water district that sought quiet title to a prescriptive easement. The water district had purchased property for a reservoir. A grant deed that it received included property that the grantor did not own. The water district then built a reservoir.

(continued on next page)

The court held that the district's use was hostile and under a claim of right. Its use created a prescriptive easement. The easement was held to be exclusive use because the owner's planned recreational use would have interfered with the use of the reservoir.

Note: While the water district could not obtain title by adverse possession because it did not pay the taxes, an easement of exclusive use gives it all the benefits of ownership.

An implied dedication of an easement to the public is possible if the public, with the owner's knowledge and without consent, uses the right-of-way for five years.

An owner can protect against unauthorized user interests by recording: "The right of the public or any person to make any use whatsoever of the above-described land or any portion thereof (other than use expressly allowed by a written or recorded map, agreement, deed or dedication) is by permission and subject to control of owner" (Civil Code Section 813). This recording would be conclusive proof that the use was permissive in any lawsuit claiming dedication to public use. For use by other than the general public, the notice must be served by registered mail on the user to be effective.

An owner also can protect himself or herself from prescriptive easements by posting, at intervals of 200 feet or less, "Right to pass by permission and subject to control of owner, Section 1008, Civil Code."

A servient tenement owner can get title by adverse use against a dominant tenement's easement. Assume a servient owner builds across an easement so that use will be impossible; after five years this adverse use by the servient tenement holder could defeat the prior easement.

Case Study

In the case of *Masin v. LaMarche* (1982) 136 C.A.3d 687, a servient tenement owner used a road for the storage of material and equipment so that access was denied to the dominant tenement. After seven years' nonuse the dominant tenement holder wished to have the road cleared so it could be used. The court held that the easement had been lost because of the adverse possession by the servient tenement.

Easement by Implication

Besides being expressly created, an easement can be created by implication. An **implied easement** is one that was probably intended but not expressed. The following are necessary to create an easement by an implied grant:

- There must be a separation of title (prior to separation the dominant and servient tenements were under the same or common ownership).
- Prior to separation of title there must have been a use that was obvious and of such duration to indicate it was intended to be permanent.
- The use must have been reasonably necessary for the beneficial enjoyment of the land conveyed.

Case Study

Dubin v. Robert Newhall Chesebrough Trust (2001) 96 C.A.4th 465 involved a landowner who blocked an access driveway to the plaintiff's property, which was over other land owned by the defendant. The access over the driveway was not mentioned in the lease. After the death of the lessor, the successor owner asked Dubin not to use the driveway. When Dubin did not comply, the new owners erected crash posts to block the driveway, which had been used by heavy trucks and trailers. Dubin sued the landlord, alleging an implied easement appurtenant, an easement by necessity and a prescriptive easement. While the superior court granted the landlord's demurrer, the court of appeal reversed.

Although other access precluded an easement by necessity and a prescriptive easement was not available because the use was for less than five years, the court ruled Dubin did state a claim for implied easement appurtenant. The court indicated the easement use was reasonably necessary for use of the premises.

Note: The court seemed to be saying that if the landlord and tenant had thought about it, they would have included the easement in the lease. Because they did not, an implied easement appurtenant was created.

If an owner sells a lot that in the past has been reached through land retained by the grantor, the courts could say that an easement right was implied. The courts would consider whether the use was reasonably necessary for proper use, whether it was apparent at the time of sale, and whether the parties intended an easement to exist.

For an implied easement by reservation the use must have been necessary (not reasonably necessary) for the reasonable enjoyment of the property retained by the grantor.

To defeat the possibility of an easement by implication, the parties can specify that no easement by grant or reservation will arise by implication.

Oil and mineral rights carry with them an implied easement to enter and drill or mine unless the right is clearly excluded (in which case entry would have to be made outside the property).

A former tenant has an implied easement to enter and harvest the crops that were the fruit of his or her labor (emblements).

California generally does not recognize the common-law-implied easement of light and air. An exception is the Solar Shade Act (California Public Resources Code Sections 25980–25986), which provides an implied easement of light in special cases. After a party has installed a solar collector in compliance with the act, a neighbor cannot permit trees to shade more than 10 percent of the solar collector between the hours of 10:00 A.M. and 2:00 P.M.

Easement by Necessity

California courts will in some instances create an **easement by necessity** when an easement is required to allow reasonable use of a property. The dominant and servient tenements must have been under common ownership at some time. There also can be no other way to get to the property, no matter how inconvenient or difficult. It is a strict necessity concept. Once granted, an easement by necessity runs with the land but will be lost if another access becomes available.

No payment is required when an easement by necessity is created, under the theory that the prior common owner just forgot about creating an easement.

Easement by Eminent Domain

Easements can be obtained by condemnation for any public purpose. This right has been given to utilities for rights-of-way. As for other condemnation, the landowner is entitled to be compensated for any loss in value caused by the taking of the easement.

It is possible for a property owner to use condemnation to obtain an easement for utility services over the land of another. It does not have to be the only way to obtain utilities, just the most practical.

Easement by Estoppel

An **easement by estoppel** can be created when an owner, by words or acts, causes another party to act to his or her detriment. For example, if an owner told a prospective purchaser of a neighboring parcel that there was an easement to it over his road, the owner could be estopped (prevented) from denying the existence of the easement after the other party purchased the land.

Termination of Easements

Easements are lost upon the following events:

- Destruction of the servient tenement: If there is no longer a servient tenement, there can be no easement.
- Merger: If the dominant and servient tenements become owned by the same person, the easement can be lost. A person would not have an easement over his or her own property. When a lesser interest and a greater interest are joined, the lesser interest is lost by **merger**.
- Nonuse: Nonuse terminates only an easement by prescription (five years' nonuse).
- Deed: A quitclaim deed from the holder of the dominant tenement to the holder of the servient tenement ends the easement. This would be an express release of the easement.
- Prior lien foreclosure: If a prior lien against the property exists at the time an easement is granted, the subsequent foreclosure of that lien will wipe out the easement. The dominant tenement holder could have obtained an agreement with the lienholder to subordinate his or her interest to the easement.
- Estoppel: If a dominant tenement holder indicates to the servient tenement holder that the easement will not be used or has been abandoned and the servient lienholder relies on this statement to his or her detriment, the dominant tenement holder will be estopped from claiming an easement right.
- End of purpose: An easement ends when the stated purpose of the easement ends. An easement to enter so as to hunt game will end with the urbanization of the area.
- End of necessity: An easement granted because of necessity ends when the necessity no longer exists.
- Eminent domain: The taking of the property for a public purpose ends the easement. The dominant tenement holder will, however, have a claim for his or her interest based on just compensation for the fair market value.
- Misuse: An easement can end by misuse, although an injunction and/or monetary damages, not forfeiture, would be the normal remedy granted by the courts.

■ LICENSE

Unlike an easement, a **license** is not an interest in land; it is a permissive use. What would otherwise be a wrongful trespass would be permissible with a license. Unauthorized use or trespass does not create a license. A license always requires permission and is revocable.

While a license can be an exclusive privilege, in the absence of any agreement it will be nonexclusive.

A license is personal to the licensee. It does not transfer with real property, cannot be assigned by the licensee, and cannot be inherited. Transfer of ownership of the property over which the licensee has permission will revoke the license.

A licensee is not a tenant. A tenant has possession and can assign his or her interests. A licensee does not have possession but merely a revocable privilege to use.

Because a license is not an interest in real property, the statute of frauds does not prohibit the creation of oral licenses.

An owner has a duty to keep the property in a safe condition for the licensee. The licensee should be warned of any danger.

While a license generally can be revoked, courts have held that where the licensee has expended capital and labor in reliance on the license, it would not be equitable to allow the owner to revoke the license. The principle of estoppel will apply.

 See *Stoner v. Zucker* (1906) 148 C. 516.

Case Study

In the case of *Cooke v. Ramponi* (1952) 38 C.2d 282, a license was granted to use a road. The licensee expended a great deal of money and energy improving the road and building culverts. The court held that the license was irrevocable. Using the doctrine of equitable estoppel, the court determined that to decide otherwise would allow the licensor to perpetrate fraud against the licensee.

■ SUMMARY

Parties can agree on fixed boundaries when exact boundaries are in dispute. Such agreements bind successors in interest to the parties (doctrine of agreed boundaries).

In the event of an ambiguity in a boundary, reference to a natural monument will take precedence over angles or distances.

An encroachment is an intrusion into, under, or over the land of another. An action to remove a permanent encroachment must be taken within three years of the encroachment, or it will be allowed to remain. A good-faith improver of the property of another will be allowed to remove his or her improvements but will be liable for damages to the property of another. If the improvement is costly, however, the court might allow the unintentional encroachment to remain intact.

A nuisance is a use that interferes with the use or enjoyment of the land of another. An abatement action would be taken to remove a nuisance, and an injunction would require a use to cease.

An upper-land owner may be liable if he or she fails to exercise reasonable care and runoff consequently causes damage to a lower property. The courts will consider the utility of the upper-land owner's use compared to the harm caused.

Riparian rights are the rights of an owner to reasonable use of water flowing through, under, or adjacent to a property. Littoral rights refers to reasonable use of nonflowing water (lakes or seas).

The right of correlative user is the reasonable right to use, in conjunction with others, the underground percolating water.

California follows the doctrine of prior appropriation. The first user of water has priority over later users.

Owners have duties toward others, which include lateral and subjacent support of other lands.

An easement is an interest in the land of another (normally for ingress and egress). The property using the land of another is the dominant tenement, and the property being used is considered the servient tenement. If there is no dominant tenement—that is, no other property is being benefited—it is an easement in gross. An easement in gross specifically must be transferred by the easement holder, while a normal easement runs with the land.

Easements allowing use of the land of another are affirmative easements, and easements that prohibit the owner of the servient tenement from a use are negative easements.

Easements may be created by grant or reservation in a deed, prescription (adverse use), implication, necessity, eminent domain, or estoppel.

Easements may be lost by destruction of the servient tenement, merger, nonuse (easements by prescription), deed, foreclosure of a prior lien, estoppel, end of purpose, end of necessity, eminent domain, or forfeiture for misuse.

■ DISCUSSION CASES

1. A general right-of-way was granted, but its location was not specified. **Who would decide where the easement would be located?**

   Collier v. Oelke (1962) 202 C.A.2d 843

2. A tenant leased 2,400 acres. The landlord plaintiff claimed that the defendant failed to remove millions of pounds of waste rocket fuel material and other hazardous substances from the property. The complaint alleged causes of action for nuisance and trespass. **Were these proper causes for relief?**

   Mangini v. Aerojet General Corp. (1991) 230 C.A.3d 1125

3. A lessee of property in a quiet rural area invited others to use the oil dump on the property for wastes. One hundred fifty to 200 heavy trucks would use the easement in a ten-hour period. The owners of the servient tenements objected. **Was their objection valid?**

   Wall v. Rudolph (1961) 198 C.A.2d 684

4. An easement to use a common stairway for two buildings stated that the stairway "shall be perpetually kept open." The building with the stairway was destroyed. **Must the owner rebuild?**

   Muzio v. Erickson (1919) 41 C.A. 413

5. An owner cut down trees on the boundary line to use them for firewood. **Was this action proper?**

   Scarborough v. Woodill (1907) 7 C.A. 39

6. Weeds were growing on the banks of a drainage ditch. Seeds from the weeds invaded the neighboring property. An action was brought to abate a nuisance. **Must an owner remove his or her weeds?**

   Boarts v. Imperial Irrigation District (1947) 80 C.A.2d 574

7. A home slid into a neighbor's home. This loss was caused by natural conditions. **Should the upper-land owner be liable for the loss?**

   Sprecher v. Adamson Cos. (1981) 30 C.3d 358

8. A shopping center's drainage runoff went through a concrete drainage ditch and eventually led to a 15-foot-wide natural stream. The natural stream crossed the plaintiff's land, and some of the water flowed across the land, leaving mud and debris. **Assuming that the volume of water from the shopping center caused the stream to overflow, is the shopping center liable for resulting damages?**

   Deckert v. County of Riverside (1981) 115 C.A.3d 885

9. Bel Air Country Club used a strip of land adjacent to the sixth fairway as a rough for 40 years. The plaintiff had actual knowledge that balls were hit and retrieved from the area daily but had never erected permissive use signs or taken steps to halt the use. **What are the rights of the Bel Air Country Club?**

   MacDonald Properties Inc. v. Bel Air Country Club (1977) 72 C.A.3d 693

10. Drivers to the plaintiff's warehouse would trespass on adjacent property to turn around and back into loading docks. Depending on individual drivers' habits and skills, drivers utilized different portions of the adjacent property. **After use for the statutory period, does the plaintiff have a prescriptive easement?**

    Warsaw v. Chicago Metallic Ceilings Inc. (1984) 35 C.3d 564

11. Lots were sold by a subdivider from a subdivision plat map that showed an area adjacent to a lake as being a park. The developers later wished to build condominiums in the area designated as a park. **What are the rights of the lot purchasers?**

Walker v. Duncan (1976) 223 S.E.2d 675

12. An easement holder lined a ditch with Gunite to stop the water seepage. The result was that vegetation that had flourished in the soil from water percolating through the walls of the ditch died from lack of water. Was the easement holder's action proper?

Krieger v. Pacific Gas & Electric Co. (1981) 119 C.A.3d 137

13. A property owner brought an action against a neighbor to prevent the neighbor from cutting out his light. **Does a property owner have a right to light?**

Ingwersen v. Barry (1897) 118 C. 342

14. Underground telephone lines were installed outside the easement area. These lines were intended to remain in place for 100 years. After 25 years the landowner wants their removal because they are a continuing nuisance/trespass. Must the lines be moved?

Spar v. Pacific Bell (1991) 235 C.A.3d 1480

15. The San Diego Gas and Electric Company added power lines on an easement adjacent to plaintiff's home, resulting in increased levels of electromagnetic radiation. Should the San Diego Gas and Electric Company have any liability to the homeowner?

San Diego Gas and Electric Co. v. Superior Court (1996)
13 C. 4th 893

16. An oral agreement was made between two property owners where one owner would build a wall on the top of a slope rather than on the property line at the bottom. The party building the wall would do so at his own expense but it would be on the neighbor's property. The reason for the agreement was that a wall on the bottom of the slope would not afford either property owner any privacy. Can a later owner of the upper property require the removal of the wall?

Noronha v. Stewart (1988) 199 C.A.3d 485

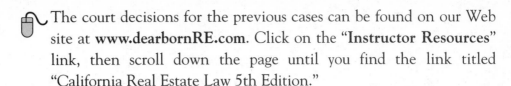 The court decisions for the previous cases can be found on our Web site at **www.dearbornRE.com**. Click on the **"Instructor Resources"** link, then scroll down the page until you find the link titled "California Real Estate Law 5th Edition."

■ CHAPTER QUIZ

1. Which of the following correctly matches the boundary with its boundary line?

    a. Road/center of the road
    b. Nonnavigable river/center of the river
    c. Navigable river/average low-water mark
    d. All of the above

2. When a tree trunk is on the boundary line

    a. both owners must agree to its removal.
    b. it belongs to both owners.
    c. either owner can trim branches over his or her property.
    d. All of the above

3. An action for the removal of a permanent encroachment must be commenced within

    a. three years of the encroachment.
    b. four years of the encroachment.
    c. ten years of the encroachment.
    d. a reasonable period of time.

4. A nonphysical invasion of the property of another would likely be a(n)

    a. encroachment.   c. nuisance.
    b. trespass.   d. easement.

5. Which of the following statements is(are) true regarding nuisances?

    a. There is a three-year statute of limitations on a private nuisance.
    b. A public nuisance cannot be abated by the action of a private citizen.
    c. Nuisances that are not private nuisances are considered public nuisances.
    d. All of the above

6. A dispute between riparian rights holders would likely be heard by the

   a. federal district court.
   b. local water agency.
   c. Water Resources Control Board.
   d. None of the above

7. After an owner developed his property, water runoff from it damaged a lower property. Which of the following is a true statement about liability for this damage?

   a. The upper-land owner is strictly liable.
   b. The upper-land owner is liable for only the percentage of damage based on the percentage of increase in runoff.
   c. If the development was reasonable use of the land with reasonable care, the upper-land owner is not liable.
   d. None of the above

8. Riparian rights can best be described as which of the following?

   a. The absolute right to adjacent water
   b. Reasonable use of flowing water
   c. Reasonable use of nonadjacent water
   d. Reasonable use of nonflowing water

9. Littoral rights refer to

   a. the underground water table.
   b. water within a defined flowing channel.
   c. nonflowing water.
   d. the right of ingress and egress.

10. Which of the following would be rights in nonflowing surface water?

    a. Right of correlative user   c. Riparian rights
    b. Avulsion rights   d. Littoral rights

11. "Acquired by accession" most likely refers to

    a. a prescriptive easement.   c. an encroachment.
    b. accretion.   d. an easement in gross.

12. A boundary stream suddenly changed course, resulting in removal of land from one owner to another. This is an example of

    a. accretion.   c. erosion
    b. avulsion.   d. reliction.

13. An owner who excavates on her property below the level of a neighbor's foundation

    a. is always responsible for damages to her neighbor's structure.
    b. must give notice to the neighbor of the proposed excavation.
    c. Both a and b
    d. Neither a nor b

14. "It goes with the land" best describes a(n)

    a. homestead right.
    b. license right.
    c. appurtenant easement.
    d. easement in gross.

15. A sign company that has a *right* to place a billboard on the land of another would most likely hold a(n)

    a. license.   c. appurtenant easement.
    b. easement in gross.   d. fee simple.

16. John had all of the elements of an easement by prescription for four years. The owner then gave permission to others for similar use of the property. What are John's rights?

    a. A new five-year period would start.
    b. Multiple use defeats the user's rights to an easement by prescription.
    c. The permission granted to others defeats John's chances of obtaining an easement right.
    d. With one more year of open, notorious, and hostile use John can obtain an easement.

17. Owners may *not* protect themselves against users obtaining prescriptive easements by

    a. recording a permissible use statement.
    b. posting "right to pass by permission and subject to control of owner."
    c. ordering wrongful users to cease their trespass.
    d. None of the above

18. A grant of mineral rights made no mention of an easement to enter the property. What are the rights of the mineral rights holder?

    a. The holder must make a subterranean entrance from outside the property.
    b. The holder has no right of entrance.
    c. The holder has an implied easement to enter and mine.
    d. The holder can obtain an easement by necessity but must pay the fee owner for all resulting damages and loss of use.

19. A landlocked property owner would likely ask the court for

    a. an easement by prescription.
    b. an easement in gross.
    c. an easement by necessity.
    d. adverse possession.

20. An easement by necessity requires

    a. payment for the easement right.
    b. former common ownership of the dominant and servient tenements.
    c. Both a and b
    d. Neither a nor b

21. In the course of a sale the seller told the buyer there was an easement to the property over other land the seller owned. The seller cannot deny the easement, because of

    a. prescriptive use.   c. the statute of frauds.
    b. estoppel.   d. necessity.

22. An easement by grant will be lost through

    a. nonuse.
    b. foreclosure of a prior lien.
    c. merger of the dominant and servient estates.
    d. Both b and c

23. Which of the following would not terminate an easement created by grant?

    a. The destruction of the servient tenement
    b. A merger
    c. Nonuse
    d. A quitclaim deed to the encumbered property from the dominant tenement to the servient tenement

24. For six years Alfred, with Smith's permission, used a shortcut over Smith's land to get to his home. Alfred likely now has a(n)

    a. easement by necessity.   c. easement by prescription.
    b. easement in gross.   d. license.

25. Which of the following is(are) false regarding a license?

    a. It goes with the land.
    b. It is an interest in real estate.
    c. It can be inherited.
    d. All of the above.

13

LAND USE CONTROLS

■ KEY TERMS

aesthetic zoning
Alquist-Priolo Special
  Studies Zone Act
bulk zoning
California
  Environmental
  Quality Act
Coastal Zone
  Conservation Act
comprehensive zoning
conditional public
  report
conditional-use permit
covenants, conditions,
  and restrictions
  (CC&Rs)
cumulative zoning

declaration of
  restrictions
downzoning
Endangered Species
  Act
environmental impact
  report (EIR)
exclusionary zoning
general plan
historical designations
incentive zoning
Interstate Land Sales
  Full Disclosure Act
National
  Environmental
  Policy Act
negative declaration

nonconforming use
noncumulative zoning
partial zoning
preliminary public
  report
public report
rezoning
spot zoning
Subdivided Lands Law
Subdivision Map Act
variance
zoning

■ ZONING

Zoning is public control of land use and is permitted under the constitutional doctrine of police power. Police power allows government units to enact legislation for the health, safety, morals, and general welfare of the community. Besides covering use, zoning sets standards for height, open space, setbacks, parking, lot size, building size, and similar issues. Zoning can even cover aesthetics and serve to limit growth.

California has no uniform requirement for zoning symbols. For example, uses allowable under the designation M-3 could vary greatly from area to area. Therefore one who wants to determine how land in a particular area is zoned must first determine the meaning of the zoning symbols in that city or county.

Every city and county in California is required to develop a **general plan**. This plan, when approved by the local legislative body, becomes the comprehensive zoning for the area. Enabling legislation gave cities and counties the right to control land use through zoning. Adoption of zoning and changes in zoning require public hearings. Cities are required to bring their zoning into conformance with their general plan.

Zoning can be appealed to the courts, but the plaintiffs first must exhaust all administrative appeals. Zoning must be a reasonable exercise of the police power of the state. The courts therefore will not uphold arbitrary zoning or restrictions that tend to create a monopoly.

Case Study

The Pennsylvania case of *National Land and Investment Co. v. Kohn* (1965) 215 A.2d 597 involved a zoning ordinance that required four-acre lots. The developer wanted to reduce the lot size to one acre. The court conceded that there is a presumtion of validity to a zoning ordinance and that the burden of proving it invalid falls on the one challenging it. It further indicated that the fact that a developer will suffer an economic loss is not a reason to declare zoning unconstitutional. Nevertheless, the court held that the zoning in this case was invalid because zoning must bear a substantial relationship to police power purposes and must not be unreasonable, arbitrary, or confiscatory. Keeping the area exclusive was not a proper exercise of police power. The court indicated that evidence of protection from pollution could have supported the reasonableness of four-acre sites, but such evidence was not introduced.

Case Study

Zoning can have the effect of keeping the poor and minorities out of an area. The federal case of *Hope v. County of DuPage* (1983) 717 F.2d 1061 concerned zoning regulations of DuPage County, Illinois. This wealthy county regulated lot size, set backs, and parking, which effectively precluded housing for the poor and minorities. The court determined that the regulations were discriminatory and enjoined the enforcement of the ordinances. The county was ordered to develop a plan that would provide more housing for the poor.

Case Study

In *Southern Burlington County NAACP v. Township of Mount Laurel* (1975) 336 A.2d 713, the New Jersey Supreme Court required that a township redo zoning to provide a fair share of housing for the poor. A similar California case was *Associated Homebuilders Inc. v. City of Livermore* (1976) 18 C.3d 582, in which the court held that zoning must respond to regional welfare.

California courts will not award owners damages when a change in zoning reduces property value. California courts treat zoning as a police power regulation, not eminent domain, which is a taking of property. Several federal courts have taken a contrary position and have awarded damages when zoning change adversely affected value. Indications are that the U.S. Supreme Court might rule that zoning can be a taking of property for which damages must be paid. If it does, cities and counties will be reluctant to change zoning after it has been established.

Case Study

The case of *Lucas v. South Carolina Coastal Council* (1992) 112 S.Ct. 2886 involved a real estate developer, Lucas, who paid $975,000 for two residential lots 300 feet from the beach. While Lucas was developing plans, the legislature enacted the Beachfront Management Act that created the South Carolina Coastal Council. The council prohibited development on the Lucas lots, which were within a "baseline critical area." There were homes on the adjoining lots.

The trial court found that the new law rendered the lots valueless and ordered compensation to Lucas. The South Carolina Supreme Court reversed, holding that payment to Lucas was not required because the primary purpose of the law was to prevent the nuisance of public harm from

(continued on next page)

storm or water damage. The U.S. Supreme Court reversed, holding that this was a total regulatory taking and it must be compensated. This ruling requires payments when government regulations prohibit all economically beneficial use of land. It does not, however, allow an owner to use his or her land for activities that will harm adjacent landowners, nor will it stop regulations that prohibit specific uses as long as some other economic use

Case Study

The case of *Lake Nacimiento Ranch v. San Luis Obispo County* (1987) 830 F.2d 977 involved 1,500 acres of land bordering a lake that had been zoned for recreational use. In 1980 the county rezoned the property as "rural lands," which limited the use. The ranch claimed the rezoning was a taking.

The court pointed out that rezoning is invalid if it does not advance legitimate state interests or if it denies an owner economically viable use of the land. The fact that the restriction does not allow an owner to recover the initial investment does not mean the restriction is constitutionally defective. "Disappointed expectations in that regard cannot be turned into a taking. . . ." Because the ranch failed to show there was no other beneficial use for the land, it was not proved that there had been a taking of property without compensation.

Case Study

Palazzolo v. Rhode Island (2001) 121 S.Ct. 2448 involved a claim for inverse condemnation. After Rhode Island created a coastal resources management council to regulate and protect coastal properties, Palazzolo acquired a coastal property. He asked the council to allow him to fill 11 wetland acres in order to build a private beach club. After denial of his application, he filed an inverse condemnation action alleging that the state had taken his property without compensation. The Rhode Island Supreme Court upheld lower court rulings that Palazzolo had no right to challenge regulations that predated his ownership and all economic use of the property was not denied because the upland portion could be developed.

While the U.S. Supreme Court reversed the Rhode Island court as to Palazzolo's right to challenge rules enacted prior to his ownership, it upheld the ruling Palazzolo had not lost all economic use of his property because he could still build a residence on the upland nonmarsh portion.

Because Palazzolo could not build on the marshland portion, the case was remanded to determine the amount of Palazzolo's damages for a partial taking.

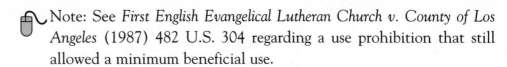 Note: See *First English Evangelical Lutheran Church v. County of Los Angeles* (1987) 482 U.S. 304 regarding a use prohibition that still allowed a minimum beneficial use.

Types of Zoning

Besides zoning categories such as residential, commercial, and industrial, there are a number of types of zoning.

Cumulative zoning allows all more restrictive uses. For example, an area zoned for multiple-family use would allow single-family homes as well if the zoning were cumulative.

Noncumulative zoning allows only the use specified. Most zoning today is noncumulative.

Exclusionary zoning prohibits specified uses. Restrictions on condominium conversions are exclusionary zoning.

Cities and counties cannot prohibit mobile homes on foundations on lots that are zoned for single-family dwellings.

Restrictions that prohibit an owner or his or her agent from erecting a For Sale sign of reasonable dimensions are void as unreasonable restraints on alienation.

Case Study

In *City of Cleburne v. Cleburne Living Center, Inc.* (1985) 473 U.S. 432, a city ordinance required special-use permits for hospitals for the mentally disabled. Cleburne Living Center wished to operate a group home for 13 retarded men and women. The center was required to apply for a special-use permit. The city denied the application.

The U.S. Supreme Court rejected the argument that the retarded were a "quasi-suspect classification." The city did not require conditional-use permits for other types of group housing such as boarding houses, fraternity houses, and apartment houses. The Supreme Court held that requiring a special permit was unconstitutional in that it violated the equal protection clause of the Constitution by discriminating against the mentally retarded.

The dissenting opinion indicated that the case could require a city to justify distinctions in its zoning.

Bulk zoning is zoning for density through height restrictions, open-space requirements, parking requirements, ratios of floor space to total area, etc.

Comprehensive zoning is zoning of a large area. A broad plan of zoning such as a general plan would be included in this category.

Partial zoning is zoning one area without considering its effect on the rest of the community.

Aesthetic zoning is zoning for beauty through regulations governing signs, architectural styles, and even colors.

Incentive zoning can be a boost to building by allowing a use such as commercial stores on the first floor of a multistory office or residential structure or a greater height if a public plaza is included.

Spot zoning allows the zoning of individual parcels that are not in conformance with the general-area zoning. Spot zoning is often the result of political influence. Spot zoning that is arbitrary and discriminatory will not be upheld by California courts.

Case Study

Ross v. City of Yorba Linda (1991) 1 C.A.4th 954 involved a family that owned a 1.117-acre lot and home with zoning for one house per acre. The family wished to divide the property into two lots and build an additional home. Its request for rezoning was denied despite the fact that most of the surrounding property was zoned for one house per one-half acre. The court held that the restriction requiring one acre was arbitrary and discriminatory and therefore unconstitutional. The court of appeal affirmed the trial court, pointing out that spot zoning is one of the zoning categories that California courts typically hold as invalid and unreasonable.

Downzoning is a change in zoning to a more restrictive use.

Rezoning is an actual change in the zoning category.

Variance

A **variance** is a special exception to the zoning, although the zoning is not changed. It usually is granted to prevent hardship, where strict application of the zoning would deprive an owner of benefits available to other, similar property owners. For example, a preexisting lot that does not meet the size requirements to build a home under the zoning might be granted a variance.

Conditional-Use Permit   Unlike a variance, which is simply an exception to the zoning, a **conditional-use permit**, or special-use permit, allows a use not permitted to every parcel. It is not granted because of owner hardship but because allowing the use in the area is considered to be in the best interest of the community. An example would be to allow warehouses in an area that was designated for dock use and ship repair.

Case Study

In *Griffin Dev. Co. v. City of Oxnard* (1985) 39 C.3d 256, an Oxnard city ordinance required every condominium to contain at least 1,000 square feet, have two separate bedrooms, have space for a washer and a dryer and two garage spaces plus one visitor parking space, and have a private storage area.

Griffin wished to convert his 72 apartment units into condominiums and was denied a special-use permit.

The California Supreme Court rejected Griffin's argument that denial of a permit denied him due process because it was not a change in use. The court held that the city had legitimate objectives in preserving rental houses as well as justification for different standards for condominiums and apartments. Because condominiums were expected to be a major source of housing for low-income and moderate-income buyers, the city could impose standards for condominiums different from those for apartments. The court held the regulations to be the proper exercise of police power and not confiscatory.

Nonconforming Use   Zoning generally is not retroactive. Uses that exist prior to zoning are not automatically excluded by the zoning. These **nonconforming uses** generally are allowed to continue if they were legal when started. They are said to be covered by the laws of that time (grandfather clause).

Case Study

The case of *Jones v. City of Los Angeles* (1930) 211 C. 304 involved a city ordinance that excluded sanitariums within a designated district. The City of Los Angeles sought to enforce the removal of a sanitarium erected prior to the ordinance. The court held that a properly conducted sanitarium for the care and treatment of persons affected with mental or nervous diseases cannot be held to constitute a nuisance. Where a retroactive zoning ordinance causes substantial injury and the prohibited business is not a nuisance, zoning that is retroactive was determined to be an unreasonable and unjustifiable exercise of police power.

The owner of a nonconforming use does not have the right to expand the use. Generally, if the use is abandoned, it cannot be resurrected later. If a nonconforming structure is destroyed, it generally cannot be rebuilt. Courts will uphold zoning that allows nonconforming uses to continue for a stated amount of time (amortization period).

Case Study

In the case of *City of Stanton v. Cox* (1989) 207 C.A.3d 1557, a municipal zoning ordinance prohibited adult bookstores within 1,000 feet of another similar use or within 500 feet of a school, park, playground, or residence. This left only six available sites in the city. The court held that the ordinance was invalid because it did not provide the owner of an adult bookstore a reasonable opportunity to operate a business in the city. The number of available sites would rapidly decrease if any site were occupied by an adult business.

Case Study

In the case of *Ebel v. City of Corona* (1985) 767 F.2d 635, the city passed an ordinance prohibiting adult bookstores and requiring that existing adult bookstores be closed down within 60 days. Ebel, the owner of an adult bookstore, brought this action. The Ninth Circuit Court of Appeals held that the ordinance left Ebel no alternative relocation site and therefore restricted free speech. The court also indicated that 60 days was too short because it did not consider the length of Ebel's lease or her investments.

While zoning does not immediately eliminate a previously existing use, a use that is also a nuisance can be eliminated by an abatement action.

Insuring Zoning

Title insurance is not available to protect owners from changes in zoning. Endorsements are available that ensure that a present use is not in violation of the then-current zoning or that the current zoning is as stated.

In an action for declaratory relief an owner can ask the courts to determine the extent of his or her rights regarding the zoning.

■ COVENANTS, CONDITIONS, AND RESTRICTIONS

Covenants are private, voluntary restrictions that run with the land. They are promises among landowners that are mutually enforceable. The remedy for a breach of a covenant will be damages or an injunction.

Conditions differ from covenants in that they create a defeasible estate. A breach of a condition subsequent means that title will be lost (usually it will revert to the original grantor or his or her heirs). Because of the harsh penalty of forfeiture, courts will construe conditions narrowly and if at all possible will determine that a covenant rather than a condition was intended.

Covenants, conditions, and restrictions (CC&Rs), also known as *restrictive covenants*, can cover setbacks, lot size, height, building size, outbuildings, materials, colors, landscaping, signs, pets, antennae, etc. CC&Rs can go beyond zoning because they are private agreements not limited to health, safety, morals, and the general welfare. CC&Rs might set up architectural review committees for approval of plans. The committees' actions must be in good faith to prevail if they are challenged in court. CC&Rs are generally beneficial restrictions in that they tend to keep up property values.

CC&Rs usually are negative covenants, where parties promise not to do something. They are like negative easements because others who are subject to the covenant can get an injunction to make a party cease violating a covenant.

Case Study

In *Edmond's of Fresno v. McDonald Group, Ltd.* (1985) 171 C.A.3d 598, the lease on a jewelry store in a shopping mall provided that the lessor would not permit more than one more jewelry store at the Fresno Fashion Fair. The lessor built an addition to the mall and intended to lease to other jewelry stores.

The restriction on additional jewelry stores was a bargained-for-restrictive covenant, and allowing additional competitors would reduce the benefits bargained for. The court held that the covenant of good faith and fair dealing required that the restrictive covenant apply to the addition. If an ambiguity in what constituted "Fresno Fashion Fair" were present, the court held it should be resolved against the lessor, who drafted the instrument. A permanent injunction prohibiting the lessor from entering into additional jewelry store leases was granted.

CC&Rs also can be affirmative covenants, where a party is required to do something such as build a structure or construct a fence within a stated period of time.

When CC&Rs and the zoning are at variance, whichever is more restrictive generally will prevail.

Creation of CC&Rs

CC&Rs involve rights in real property, so the statute of frauds requires that they be in writing.

Normally CC&Rs are created by subdividers, who record the CC&Rs as a **declaration of restrictions** and then incorporate them by reference into every deed. After they are made a matter of record, the CC&Rs run with the land. Unless stated otherwise, CC&Rs have no time limitation.

To be enforceable, CC&Rs must be reasonable.

Case Study

The case of *Cunningham v. Superior Court* (1998) 67 C.A.4th 743 involved a homeowners' association that was displeased with the house-keeping of a homeowner, although a city inspection found no building or fire code violations. Under threat of litigation, Cunningham allowed home-owners' association representatives to inspect the interior of his unit. Association lawyers wrote to Cunningham demanding he clear his bed of all papers and books, remove paper and cardboard boxes from the floor around the bed and dresser, remove unused boxes and paper in the living and dining rooms, clear boxes and objects from the interior stairs, cease using the downstairs bathroom for storage, and maintain a functioning electrical light in the downstairs bathroom. The letter also suggested that Cunningham remove clothing which had not been used for five years and donate it to the Salvation Army.

A lawsuit resulted in a jury verdict in favor of Cunningham because the association had acted unreasonably. The association moved for a new trial and a judgment notwithstanding the verdict. The trial judge granted a new trial stating that the association had acted "totally reasonably."

The court of appeal set aside the new trial and remanded the case to trial as to the amount of damages. The association had clearly gone beyond any legitimate interest it may have had. The homeowners' association cannot tell the homeowner how to maintain the interior of his or her unit.

The CC&Rs might provide for new restrictions or changes in the restrictions by agreement of a stated percentage of the property owners. In the absence of any such agreement any change would require unanimous agreement. Owners of parcels also can agree among themselves to restrictions on use.

To become a matter of record and binding on future owners, the CC&Rs must be recorded in the county where the property is located. Thus CC&Rs can be discovered through the county recorder's office or through a title company. Buyers of condominiums must be given a copy of the CC&Rs as well as the bylaws of the condominium association and the articles of incorporation. An owners' association must furnish an owner with a copy of the CC&Rs within ten days of the owner's request.

Unenforceable Restrictions

Courts will not enforce some restrictive covenants, as follows:

- A restriction against public policy will not be enforced. For example, a restriction whose purpose is to give one party a monopoly will not be upheld.
- Racial restrictions are void and unenforceable. They have been held to violate the equal protection clause of the Fourteenth Amendment [*Shelley v. Kraemer* (1948) 334 U.S. 1, 68 S.C. 836]. (When providing CC&Rs containing racial restrictions, the real estate agent must stamp in 20-point, boldface, red type that such restrictions are void. Homeowners' associations are also required to remove racial restrictions from their CC&Rs.)
- Unreasonable restraints on alienation will not be upheld. In addition, the rule against perpetuities prohibits restrictions on alienation beyond the life of a living person plus 21 years. The interest must also vest (become definite) or terminate within 90 years of its creation. Therefore, a grantor may not require that a property remain with his or her blood heirs forever.
- Restrictions that require an illegal use are invalid.
- If a person seeking to require another to comply with the restrictive covenants is also in violation of the restrictive covenants, the courts will not grant relief. The person must be in compliance to enforce CC&Rs on others. This equitable principle is known as the "clean hands doctrine."
- Failing to enforce other violations in a timely manner may waive the right to enforce a violation of the CC&Rs later.
- Laches can prevent enforcement. If, because of a failure to enforce, a party acts to his or her detriment, the court might consider that allowing enforcement would not be equitable. An example of laches would be allowing another to build a structure, with your knowledge, that is not in compliance with the CC&Rs. Waiting until the building was completed before objecting could be considered laches, as the delay allowed another to act to his or her detriment.
- The statute of limitations for bringing action against a restriction is five years from the time of discovery (or when it should have been discovered using reasonable diligence). (Civil Code Section 784).
- Courts will not allow enforcement of CC&Rs when conditions have changed. For example, what was previously a rural area with CC&Rs allowing only residential use could now be in the center of a commercial area where taxes would make residential use impractical. A zoning change by itself would not be enough to prove changed conditions, but a change in zoning is evidence of changed conditions.

Case Study

The case of *Liebler v. Point Loma Tennis Club* (1995) 40 C.A.4th 1600, involved the plaintiff, Liebler, who owned a condo unit.

Liebler leased the unit. The lease provided that Liebler was a cotenant even though Liebler did not live in the unit. Based on this lease, Liebler used the tennis courts. The CC&Rs provided that the tennis courts were only for residents and their guests.

The association fined Liebler in accordance with its rules.

The Superior Court found that the rules were reasonable and that the association acted properly in fining Liebler. The court of appeals pointed out that when CC&Rs are uniformly enforced, they are presumed to be reasonable. The nonresident-use restriction was therefore reasonable and fairly enforced against all owners.

Note: The cotenancy in the lease was an obvious attempt to avoid the restriction on use.

Ending Restrictions

Restrictive covenants automatically cease with

- time, if they were set up for a particular number of years;
- merger, when all of the parcels are brought together under one ownership;
- agreement, when the owners, subject to the restrictions, agree to end them;
- foreclosure of a prior encumbrance; a trust deed against the property prior to the CC&Rs would remove them by its subsequent foreclosure; and
- condemnation by government authority; taking by eminent domain would remove all private restrictions.

■ REGULATION OF SUBDIVISIONS

The Subdivision Map Act

The **Subdivision Map Act** provides for local control of subdivisions. Every city and county is required to adopt an ordinance to regulate subdivisions. According to the Subdivision Map Act, a subdivision is any division of contiguous land for the purpose of sale, lease, or financing. The map act is concerned with the physical aspects of a subdivision, such as access, streets, drainage, sewage, water, electricity, phones, gas, and schools. Dedication of land for streets, parks, and school sites can be a requirement for map act approval. For school sites the subdivider may be paid his or her actual site costs for the land dedicated.

If a subdivision contains 50 or fewer parcels, the subdivider can be required to pay a dollar amount per parcel for recreational areas rather than dedicate land.

For subdivisions of fewer than five parcels the local control is limited to the dedication of rights-of-way, easements, and the construction of reasonable off-site and on-site improvements.

Condominiums and community apartment projects as well as conversions to these uses are covered by the map act.

Exceptions.   A tentative and a final map must be prepared for all subdivisions creating five or more parcels. Excepted are

- original parcels of fewer than five acres where each parcel to be created will abut a publicly maintained road and no dedications or improvements are required,
- subdivisions in which each parcel created has a gross area of 20 acres or more and has an improved access to a publicly maintained road,
- commercial or industrial developments that have approval of streets and access, and
- parcels of 40 acres or more.

These exceptions apply only to the filing of a map, not to obtaining local approval. In cases where a tentative and a final map are not required, a parcel map is required.

Conveyances to a government body are not considered conveyances of land for the purpose of the map act.

Tentative Map.   The tentative map will contain

- a legal description sufficient to ascertain the boundaries;
- the location, names, and widths of all adjoining streets;
- the width and proposed grades of all streets within the proposed subdivision;
- the width and location of all existing and proposed easements for roads, drainage, sewers, and other public utilities;
- tentative lot layout and dimensions of each lot;
- the approximate locations of all areas subject to inundations or storm water overflow and the locations, widths, and direction of flow of all watercourses;
- the source of water supply;
- the proposed method of sewage disposal;
- the proposed use of the property;

- the proposed public areas, if any; and
- the approximate contours when the topography controls street layout.

After the tentative map is submitted, the planning agency investigates and reports on the proposed tract. Copies are submitted to the health department, road department, flood control district, recreation department, school authority, and other governmental bodies, as well as to any adjacent communities so they can make recommendations. The department reports are studied, and the subdivider may be required to meet with representatives of interested departments.

The planning commission (a local advisory agency) makes a written report to the local legislative body within 50 days of the filing of the tentative map. It may approve, conditionally approve, or disapprove the map. If no action is taken by the local advisory agency, the tentative map is considered approved.

The subdivider may appeal actions of the advisory agency to any appeal agency or, if none, to the city council or county board of supervisors. Before going to the courts, a subdivider must have exhausted his or her administrative remedies. Courts generally will overrule administrative determinations only if they were arbitrary or capricious.

Final Map.   After approval or conditional approval a final map is prepared under the direction of a registered civil engineer. Prior to approval of the final map, the subdivider may be required to make improvements, provide bonds, or provide some other security so that improvements will be made.

The final map, along with all required signed certificates, is filed, and the governing body approves it at the meeting following filing. The final map is then recorded. By filing the final map, the local agency certifies that its requirements have been met.

Conveyances that do not comply with the map act are voidable, at the option of the grantee, within one year of the date of discovery of the violation. The grantee can recover damages.

Local agencies will not issue any permit to develop real estate that was divided without approval unless the local agency determines that the division complies with all requirements.

Government Code Section 66499.30 (e) allows property to be sold or leased prior to the issuance of the final map as long as the final closing is conditioned on the filing of the final subdivision or parcel map.

Subdivided Lands Law

Subdivided land sales fall under the jurisdiction of the Department of Real Estate. The primary purpose of the **Subdivided Lands Law** (Business and Professions Code Section 11000 et seq.) is to protect purchasers in new subdivisions from fraud, misrepresentation, or deceit in the marketing of subdivided lots, parcels, units, and undivided interests. The disclosures provide the buying public with knowledge of essential facts so that an informed decision to purchase can be made.

A subdivision under the Subdivided Lands Law is a division of five or more parcels for the purpose of sale, lease, or financing. The law applies to subdivisions located within the State of California as well as subdivisions located outside California that are sold within the state. For out-of-state subdividers the real estate commissioner must make a determination that the offering is fair, just, and equitable.

The differences and similarities between the Subdivided Lands Law and the Subdivision Map Act are shown in Table 13.1.

"Four-by-fouring" is an attempt to evade the subdivision laws by breaking a parcel into four parcels and selling them to separate people or entities who again break them into four parcels, and so on. This is regarded as a viola-

TABLE 13.1

Subdivision Map Act and Subdivided Lands Law

Subdivision Map Act	Subdivided Lands Law
• Local control	• Department of Real Estate control
• Improved residential subdivisions within city limits (lots sold with residencies) included	• Excluded
• Two or more lots or parcels	• Five or more lots or parcels
• "Proposed division" excluded	• "Proposed division" included
• Parcels must be contiguous	• Parcels need not be contiguous
• No exemptions for 160 acres and larger	• Parcels of 160 acres or more exempt
• Community apartments included	• Included
• Condominiums included	• Included
• Stock cooperatives not included unless a conversion of five or more existing dwelling units	• Stock cooperatives included
• Leasing of apartments, offices, stores, or similar space in apartment buildings not included; industrial and commercial buildings are not included	• Leasing of apartments, offices, stores, or similar space in apartment buildings included; industrial and commercial buildings not included
• Long-term leasing of space in mobile home parks or trailer parks exempted	• Included
• Undivided interests exempt	• Included
• Expressly zoned industrial and commercial subdivisions included	• Exempt
• Agricultural leases exempt	• Included
• Time-shares exempt	• Included
• Limited-equity housing cooperatives exempt	• Included
• Out-of-state subdivisions sold in California exempt	• Included

tion of the subdivision laws and will subject the violator to both civil and criminal penalties.

Case Study

The case of *People v. Byers* (1979) 90 C.A.3d 140 involved a father who attempted to avoid the subdivision requirements by transferring portions of his property to his son and others. The grantees then broke each parcel into four parcels, and they were sold, with the father receiving the proceeds. The father fled to avoid prosecution, but the son and two others were tried. The court indicated that the object of the subdivision law was to prevent sharp practices and fraud. The court refused to excuse the acts on the grounds that the parties believed that their actions were lawful. The defendants were found guilty of aiding and abetting a criminal act.

Public Report

Generally no subdivision can be offered for sale in California until the real estate commissioner has issued a **public report**. While subdivisions in other states that are sold in California require public reports, foreign subdivisions sold in California are exempt. The public report will not be issued until the commissioner is satisfied that the subdivider has met all statutory requirements, with particular emphasis on the financial arrangements to ensure completion and maintenance of improvements and facilities included in the offering, and shown that the parcel can be used for the purpose offered. Map act requirements also must be met prior to the issuance of the public report.

Public reports are disclosure statements. They include information on location, the size of the offering, the identity of the subdivider, and the interest to be conveyed to the purchaser or lessee, as well as provisions for handling deposits, purchase money, taxes, assessments, etc. Also included are use restrictions, unusual costs that a buyer will have to bear at the time of purchase or in the future, hazards or adverse environmental findings, special permits required, and utilities availability. The report is intended to provide information to aid a potential buyer in making a purchase decision.

Prior to being obligated, the purchaser must sign a receipt that he or she has received and read a copy of the public report. Public reports also must be given to any member of the public upon request. A copy and notice of its availability must be posted in the subdivision sales office.

A public report is good for five years from the date of issuance. Material changes that would cause the public report no longer to reflect the true facts must be reported to the commissioner. Material changes also would include changes in sales contracts or instruments of conveyance. The commissioner would revise the public report to reflect the true conditions.

Business and Professions Code Sections 11018.1 and 11016.6 provide that at the same time as a public report is provided a specified statement entitled "Common Interest Development General Information" must be given to the purchaser. Note that the term *common interest development* is now being used for subdivisions having areas in common, such as condominiums.

Preliminary Public Report.   A **preliminary public report** (known as the "pink slip"), which allows the subdivider to take refundable deposits or reservations for sales, may be issued by the commissioner.

A preliminary public report is good until the final report is issued, but not for more than one year.

Conditional Public Report.   Section 11018.12 was added to the Business and Professions Code to provide for a new category of public report. In the past the subdivider could not enter into any binding contract until the public report ("white slip") was issued. Now, however, the **conditional public report** allows a subdivider to enter into a binding contract with a buyer, but an escrow must be opened, and the funds are not to be released to the subdivider or escrow closed until the final public report is issued. The requirements for the conditional public report are more stringent than for the preliminary public report. The term for the conditional public report cannot exceed six months and may be renewed for one additional six-month period if the commissioner determines that the conditions for issuance of the public report are likely to be satisfied during the renewal term.

If the final public report is not issued within the term of the conditional public report or if the purchaser is dissatisfied with the final public report because of a material change in the setup of the offering, the entire sum of money paid or advanced by the purchaser must be returned to the purchaser.

Interstate Land Sales Full Disclosure Act

The federal **Interstate Land Sales Full Disclosure Act** is administered by the Office of Interstate Land Sale Registration (OILSR) of HUD. A disclosure statement known as the *property report* is required for subdivisions of 25 or more unimproved residential lots offered for sale in interstate commerce. Exempt from the act are parcels of five acres or more, cemetery lots, and sales to builders. The disclosure statement sets forth material facts about the development that must be provided to the purchaser prior to sale. The California public report satisfies this disclosure requirement.

Purchasers have a seven-day right of rescission after signing the purchase agreement.

The act provides civil and criminal remedies for its willful violation. Purchasers have three years after discovery of violations to bring actions for fraud.

■ ENVIRONMENTAL LAW

National Environmental Policy Act (NEPA)

The federal *National Environmental Policy Act* (42 U.S.C. 4321 et seq.) applies to federal agencies and legislation "significantly affecting the quality of human environment."

Federal action requires an environmental impact statement (EIS) if the action significantly affects the quality of life. The EIS gathers relevant data along with an analysis of its effects.

Case Study

In *No GWEN Alliance v. Aldridge* (1988) 855 F.2d 1380, the Ninth Circuit Court of Appeals held that an environmental impact statement prepared by the U.S. Air Force for the installation of a communications system need not address the environmental impact of nuclear war. (The communications system was intended to transmit messages during and after a nuclear attack.)

California Environmental Quality Act (CEQA)

California's law, the **California Environmental Quality Act** (Public Resources Code 21000 et seq.), allows local government agencies to require environmental impact reports for private and government projects that may have a significant effect on the environment (Public Resources Code Section 21151).

The city or county authorities are responsible for determining whether an **environmental impact report (EIR)**, which analyzes any adverse impact of development, how it can be reduced, and alternatives, is needed.

A **negative declaration** is a declaration by the city or county that the development will not have a significant adverse effect on the environment. When such a declaration is filed, an environmental impact report is not required.

An important feature of the California act is that private citizens can challenge a project in court if they feel that proper procedures were not followed or the report was incomplete.

Alquist-Priolo Special Studies Zone Act

A special studies zone is a geological hazard zone on a potentially active earthquake fault line. Zones customarily are one-quarter of a mile or more wide, centering on the fault. The **Alquist-Priolo Special Studies Zone Act** (Public Resources Code Section 2621 et seq.) requires that geological reports be obtained for project approvals within the zones and that prospective purchasers of property in the zones be made aware of the facts.

Coastal Zone Conservation Act

To develop land within a designated coastal zone, either a coastal development permit or an exemption from the provisions of the **Coastal Zone Conservation Act** (Public Resources Code Section 27000 et seq.) is required. The coastal zone includes about 1,800 square miles. It averages approximately 1,000 yards in width, with wider spots in coastal estuaries, marine habitat, and recreational areas. The purpose of the act is to protect the coastal zone and the marine environment and to ensure public access to the coast.

Case Study

In *Grupe v. California Coastal Comm'n* (1985) 166 C.A.3d 148, Grupe wanted to build a single-family home on coastal land. The coastal commission issued a permit conditioned on Grupe's offering to dedicate an access easement to the coast over two-thirds of his land.

Grupe argued that requiring the dedication would be valid only if it related to a public need. The court held that, while Grupe's house alone did not create a need for public access, the house was but one of several projects that collectively would create a need for public access.

The local government agency must issue a permit prior to development within the coastal zone. A person can appeal local rulings to the state coastal commission.

Case Study

In the case of *Nollan v. California Coastal Commission* (1987) 107 S.Ct. 3141, Nollan wished to demolish an oceanfront cottage to build a new residence. The California Coastal Commission conditioned its approval on Nollan's granting a public easement along the beach area. The U.S. Supreme Court held that in this case the requiring of the easement was a taking of property, which requires consideration, because there was no connection between the building permit and the easement.

(continued on next page)

This case differs from the *Grupe* case because *Grupe* involved access to the ocean. In *Nollan* the public had access to the beach, but the coastal commission wished to establish public use of beach area belonging to Nollan.

Case Study

The case of *AVCO Community Developers Inc. v. South Coast Regional Commission* (1976) 17 C.3d 785 concerned a developer who spent more than $2 million for storm drains, culverts, streets, utilities, etc., based on county zoning and map act approval. The developer also had sold 11 acres of prime sand beach to the county at a price below market value and had dedicated additional land for access. When the coastal commission act became effective, the developer was denied the right to develop the property. The California Supreme Court held that a developer is not considered to have a vested right to develop unless a building permit has been issued, which was not the case.

The legislature apparently considered the AVCO decision inequitable. It enacted Sections 65864–65869.5 of the Government Code, which provides for development agreements where the developer and the city agree to use, density, height, size, dedications, etc. These agreements are to be enforceable notwithstanding subsequent changes to the specific plan, zoning, subdivision, or building regulations.

Endangered Species

The federal **Endangered Species Act** can result in a family of owls stopping logging, a rare bird prohibiting development, and even an obscure minnow prohibiting the construction of a dam. Once a plant or animal is placed on the endangered list, it can place onerous restrictions on the owner of the property.

Historical Designations

Federal law and local ordinances provide for **historical designations**—the designation of structures having historical significance could prohibit redevelopment. In some cases, redevelopment is allowed if the structure is relocated to an approved site.

■ DEVELOPER LIABILITY

A developer who manufactures a lot has strict liability in tort for damages that are the proximate cause of any defect in design or manufacture. The manufacturer (subdivider) will be liable even in the absence of any fault on his or her own part [*AVNER v. Longridge Estates* (1982) 272 C.A.2d 607].

Because product liability law applies to the manufacture of lots, neither precautions nor care nor warnings to a purchaser will protect the manufacturer from resultant damages.

Suits for latent defects in the development of lots can be brought for up to ten years after the completion of improvements (but within three years of discovery of damage) (Code of Civil Procedure Section 338).

For builder liability there is a four-year statute of limitations for patent defects (Code of Civil Procedure Section 337.1) and a ten-year statute for latent defects (Code of Civil Procedure Section 337.15).

Builder liability would not apply for speculative losses where risks of harm are not foreseeable.

Case Study

The case of *Aas v. Superior Court* (2000) 24 C.4th 627 involved a housing project that allegedly suffered from a variety of construction defects that violated building codes but did not result in property damages or personal injury. Among other items, tile did not have the overlap required by the manufacturers, flashing was not properly lapped, and the nailing pattern failed to comply with the Uniform Building Code. Plaintiffs sued for damages including diminution in value of their property. The trial court granted defendant's motion to exclude evidence of defects that did not cause personal injury or property damage. The court of appeal denied plaintiff's petition for a writ of mandate, and the California Supreme Court affirmed. The Supreme Court stated that construction defects that have not ripened into property damage or at least into involuntary out-of-pocket losses do not comfortably fit the definition of "appreciable harm." Breaches of duty causing only speculative harm or the threat of future harm do not normally create a cause of action.

Case Study

In the case of *La Jolla Village Homeowners' Ass'n. Inc. v. Superior Court* (1989) 212 C.A.3d 1131, the court refused to extend strict liability to the subcontractors. The court pointed out that while mass producers, developers, and sellers or lessors of real estate developments may be subject to strict liability, this liability has never extended to subcontractors. The

(continued on next page)

subcontractor follows set plans provided by the general contractor and has no control over work before or after his work or over the entire project. The subcontractor also has no privity of contract with the homeowners.

■ SUMMARY

Zoning is public control of land use enacted under the police power of the state for the health, safety, morals, and general welfare of the population. Zoning can be appealed to the courts but will be overturned only if found to be arbitrary or capricious.

When zoning is changed to a more restrictive use, California courts will not award the owner damages; they do not consider it a taking of property.

Types of zoning include

- cumulative zoning (zoning that allows more restrictive uses),
- noncumulative zoning (zoning that allows only the uses provided by the zoning category),
- exclusionary zoning (zoning that prohibits specified uses),
- bulk zoning (zoning for density),
- comprehensive zoning (zoning of a large area),
- partial zoning (zoning of an area without considering its effect on other areas),
- aesthetic zoning (zoning for beauty),
- incentive zoning (zoning that allows a greater use as an incentive to build or to provide some desired feature),
- spot zoning (zoning a parcel so it is not in conformance with surrounding property),
- downzoning (a zoning change to a more restrictive use such as from R-4 to R-2), and
- rezoning (a change in the zoning category).

A conditional-use permit allows an exception to the zoning in the best interests of the community.

Zoning will not be retroactive. A nonconforming use will be allowed to continue, although the zoning could provide an amortization period, after which the use must cease.

Covenants, conditions, and restrictions are private restrictions that run with the land. Normally they are created by subdividers, who record a declaration of restrictions and then incorporate the declaration by reference in every deed. They also could be created by a recorded agreement of a group of owners.

The Subdivision Map Act allows local control of subdivisions. A tentative map is prepared by the subdivider. Local recommendations may be made for modifications. After all approvals a final map is prepared and recorded.

The Subdivided Lands Law, a disclosure law intended to protect the public, provides for Department of Real Estate approval of subdivisions having five or more parcels. A person is not required to go through with a transaction until he or she has read (and signed that he or she has received) a copy of the public report (disclosure report). Purchase reservations may be taken with a preliminary report, which is good for one year or until the public report is issued. Binding contracts can be made with buyers after a conditional public report is issued, but funds will not be released and escrow closed until the final public report is filed.

The Interstate Land Sales Full Disclosure Act is a federal law for 25 or more unimproved residential lots offered for sale in interstate commerce. The California public report satisfies the disclosure requirement. Purchasers have a seven-day right of rescission after signing a purchase agreement.

Federal projects significantly affecting the environment require an environmental impact statement that includes an analysis of the project's effect.

California provides that local agencies can require an environmental impact report on projects that will have a significant effect on the environment. Private citizens can challenge the failure to require a report as well as the completeness of the report.

Purchasers in geological hazard zones must be notified of the proximity of a fault line. Developments within special study zones require special approval.

The Coastal Zone Conservation Act requires approval for coastal zone projects to protect the coastline and environment and provide public access.

A developer who manufactures lots has strict liability for defects in design or manufacture. Also subject to strict liability are mass producers of homes.

■ DISCUSSION CASES

1. A community rezoned a parcel as "high flood danger," which prohibited all development. A purpose of the rezoning was to make the property available for public use. **What, if any, are the owners' rights?**

   Annicelli v. Town of South Kingston, R.I. (1983) 463 A.2d 133

2. Landowners attacked the validity of a zoning ordinance that rezoned their property as agricultural. They claimed the zoning was arbitrary and inconsistent with the general plan and represented the taking of their property without just compensation. **Considering that the new zoning significantly lowered property values, was this a taking without compensation?**

   Pan Pacific Properties Inc. v. Santa Cruz (1978) 81 C.A.3d 244

3. A zoning ordinance prohibited outdoor advertising other than those signs related to the businesses conducted on the site. An outdoor advertising company brought an action claiming that the zoning was unreasonable. **Is the zoning reasonable? If it is not, should it be set aside?**

   United Advertising Corp. v. Borough of Metuchen (1964) 198 A.2d 447

4. A zoning ordinance required the discontinuance of a plumbing business after five years. At the time the business was established, the zoning was proper. The owner claimed that the property was suited for this type of business and requiring its removal would be a taking of property. **Do you agree?**

   City of Los Angeles v. Gage (1954) 127 C.A.2d 442

5. A deed executed in 1917 contained a covenant that the land was to be used for residential purposes. The restriction was for a period of 50 years. Due to the growth of the area, the property became part of a business district. **Can the restriction on use be enforced?**

   Norris v. Williams (1947) 54 A.2d 331

6. The plaintiff wished to operate a rock and gravel operation on land contiguous to an operation that had become substantially depleted. The adjacent property was zoned for agricultural and residential use, which did not permit a gravel operation.

The trial court determined that the property had great value for rock, gravel, and sand excavation but very little value for any other purpose. The plaintiff maintained that the zoning was a taking of property without compensation, was discriminatory, was a denial of equal protection, and made the plaintiff's property worthless. **Was the zoning a proper exercise of police power?**

Consolidated Rock Products v. City of
Los Angeles (1962) 57 C.2d 515

7. The city denied the plaintiff a building permit on the basis of the plaintiff's refusal to dedicate land for a street extension that would go through the plaintiff's property. The plaintiff wanted to build over some of this land. **Was the action of the city proper?**

Selby Realty v. City of San Buenaventura (1973) 10 C.3d 110

8. To obtain a landowner's approval to annexation in 1965, the city agreed that the county zoning would remain in effect. In 1971 the city rezoned the property so that a shopping center would not be allowed. **Was the city's action proper?**

Carty v. Ojai (1978) 77 C.A.3d 329

9. A Los Angeles city ordinance provided that approval would not be granted for a condominium conversion if more than 50 percent of the units were occupied by the elderly, the disabled, or minors, and no reasonable relocation assistance plan was provided.

   The plan submitted by the plaintiff allowed continued occupancy by the special tenants until they could be relocated. The city disapproved the conversion because the plan's implementation was prevented by a scarcity of comparable units. **Was the city's action proper?**

Krater v. City of Los Angeles (1982) 130 C.A.3d 839

10. The City of Oakland passed a zoning ordinance that prohibited adult entertainment facilities within 1,000 feet of a residential zone. Existing uses would be allowed to continue for one year, after which they would have to obtain a conditional-use permit. The zoning also provided for an additional two-year period for hardship situations (the lessee was tied to a long lease or the user had a substantial investment in the structure). **Was the zoning reasonable?**

Castner v. City of Oakland (1982) 129 C.A.3d 94

11. Ten unrelated adults lived in a 24-room house that had ten bedrooms and six baths plus ample parking. The city sought an injunction for violating a zoning ordinance. The area provided for single-family use and defined a family as either two or more persons related by blood, marriage, or adoption living as a housekeeping unit or up to five unrelated persons. **Is this zoning valid?**

    City of Santa Barbara v. Adamson (1980) 27 C.3d 123

12. A subdivision's CC&Rs restricted occupancy to single-family residential use. It sought to exclude a residential care facility. (Section 1566.5 of the Health and Safety Code provides that a residential care facility serving six or fewer people should be considered single-family use.) **Can the subdivision exclude this use under its restrictions?**

    Welsch v. Goswick (1982) 130 C.A.3d 398

13. The City of Camarillo and Pardee Construction Co. entered into a stipulated judgment that Pardee had vested rights to develop a 1,150-acre tract in accordance with approved zoning and the master plan. The city agreed not to adopt any zoning inconsistent with that previously approved.

    In reliance on this agreement Pardee Construction Co. spent approximately $13.5 million for development costs. In June 1981 a voters' initiative limited the number of building permits for the entire city to 400 per year and provided a detailed plan for allocation of permits. **Was Pardee Construction limited in its development by the initiative?**

    Pardee Construction Co. v. City of Camarillo
    (1984) 37 C.3d 465

14. A condominium restriction prohibited the parking of any truck, camper, trailer, or boat of any kind. The carports were restricted to passenger automobiles. The defendant owned a clean noncommercial pickup truck. The condominium association sued to enjoin the defendant from parking his truck in the carport. **Will the restrictive covenant be enforced?**

    Bernardo Vilas Mgmt. Corp. v. Black (1987) 190 C.A.3d 153

15. A homeowners' association knew of lighting problems and that crimes had been committed, including a burglary, at the plaintiff's unit. The plaintiff installed her own lighting but was not permitted to use it

because it violated the CC&Rs. The plaintiff was subsequently robbed and raped. **Is the homeowners' association liable?**

Francis T. v. Village Green Owners Ass'n. (1986) 42 C.3d 490

16. The CC&Rs of a condominium prohibited renting units to tenants (with the exception of roommates). **Is this restriction enforceable by the association?**

City of Oceanside v. McKenna (1989) 215 C.A.3d 1420

17. Carmel-by-the-Sea enacted an ordinance prohibiting residential rentals of less than 30 days. **Was this ordinance a proper exercise of police power?**

Ewing v. City of Carmel-by-the-Sea (1991) 234 C.A.3d 1579

18. A San Diego ordinance limited the maximum number of renters that can occupy a residence. It was based on square footage, bedroom, and bathroom requirements, as well as off-street parking. **Were the restrictions proper?**

College Area Renters and Landlord Association v. City of San Diego (1994) 43 C.A. 4th 677

19. A San Francisco ordinance required that owners of residential hotels could not convert them to another type of hotel use. A hotel owners' association brought action claiming that the ordinance violated their Fifth Amendment rights in that it was taking without compensation. **Do you agree?**

Golden Gate Hotel v. San Francisco City and County (1993) 836 F.Supp. 707

20. A homeowners' association brought action for an injunction against the operation of a residential care facility for nonambulatory adults based on CC&Rs that prohibit commercial use. **Should an injunction be granted?**

Broadmoor San Clemente Homeowners Assn. v. Nelson (1994) 25 C.A.4th 1

21. A hotel was substantially destroyed by fire in November 1988. The owner applied for a demolition permit. The city withheld the permit because it claimed the hotel was an SRO building (Single Room Occupancy permanent housing). A city ordinance prohibited SRO demolition unless repair was not feasible and the

owner agreed to replace the SRO with similar housing. The demolition permit was finally issued in August 1990, when the city determined the hotel was not an SRO.

During the period prior to issuance of the permit, the hotel experienced a series of fires. The city determined that the owner was not providing proper security and therefore the city contracted for 24-hour security. The owner was assessed the costs of $399,000. The owner sued for refund of the security costs as well as lost income. **Should the owner be entitled to this reimbursement?**

Ali v. City of Los Angeles (1999) 77 C.A.4th 246

22. A homeowner's trees blocked an uphill homeowner's view of the Pacific Ocean. The city issued an order compelling the owner to trim the trees and restore the view under a view restoration act. (Under the act, the upper property owner was required to pay for the trimming.) **Is this an uncompensated taking of private property?**

Echevarrieta v. City of Rancho Palos Verdes (2001) 86 C.A.4th 472

23. **Because of the social and economic effects, may a city use its design review ordinance to exclude nationwide retail chains from shopping malls?**

Friends of Davis v. City of Davis (2000) 83 C.A.4th 1004

The court decisions for the above cases can be found on our Web site at **www.dearbornRE.com**. Click on the "**Instructor Resources**" link, and then scroll down the page until you find the link titled "California Real Estate Law 5th Edition."

■ CHAPTER QUIZ

1. The power to zone was given to cities and counties by

   a. the U.S. Constitution.
   b. the Thirteenth Amendment.
   c. enabling acts.
   d. the U.S. Supreme Court.

2. Least likely to be upheld by the courts is rezoning that would

   a. eliminate any beneficial use of the land.
   b. result in a reduction of value.
   c. reduce the use density.
   d. be downzoning.

3. Zoning that allows a single-family home to be built in an area zoned for apartments is an example of

   a. downzoning.   c. spot zoning.
   b. cumulative zoning.   d. bulk zoning.

4. Zoning that allows more restrictive uses would likely be

   a. cumulative zoning.   c. exclusionary zoning.
   b. noncumulative zoning. d. bulk zoning.

5. Zoning that prohibits adult entertainment within an area is

   a. inclusionary zoning. c. illegal.
   b. exclusionary zoning. d. downzoning.

6. Zoning for density is known as

   a. incentive zoning.   c. exclusionary zoning.
   b. bulk zoning.   d. inclusionary zoning.

7. Which of the following is true of a nonconforming use?

   a. It can be retroactive.
   b. It refers to private restrictions.
   c. It was a legal use prior to zoning.
   d. The use must be allowed to continue for the owner's lifetime.

8. New zoning that prohibits an existing use would *not* provide for

   a. immediate closure.
   b. the time period for closure.
   c. prohibition of expansion.
   d. continuation of use by a nonconforming user.

9. The most likely action for violation of a deed covenant would be

   a. action for injunction.
   b. forfeiture.
   c. action for specific performance.
   d. liquidated damages.

10. Which of the following is(are) true of restrictive covenants?

    a. They run with the land.
    b. If not recorded, they are not binding on a subsequent purchaser without notice.
    c. They are usually negative covenants.
    d. All of the above

11. Deed restrictions are created by

    a. the local building commission.
    b. the planning commission.
    c. action of law.
    d. the grantors.

12. A copy of the CC&Rs requested by an owner in a condominium, cooperative, or community apartment project must be furnished within

    a. 10 days.   c. 30 days.
    b. 20 days.   d. 45 days.

13. Which of the following CC&Rs would most likely be enforceable?

    a. One that prohibits resale
    b. One that prohibits resale for more than a stated price
    c. One that prohibits resale to a minority buyer
    d. One that requires property to be used only for religious purposes

14. The Subdivision Map Act is concerned with

    a. physical aspects of the subdivision.
    b. protection of the title in the purchaser.
    c. .prevention of seller fraud.
    d. All of the above

15. The Subdivided Lands Law is concerned primarily with

    a. preventing objectionable uses.
    b. providing adequate space.
    c. protecting purchasers.
    d. protecting brokers.

16. The Subdivided Lands Law does *not* apply to

    a. California subdivisions.
    b. Nevada subdivisions sold in California.
    c. division into four parcels for the purpose of sale.
    d. condominiums.

17. When three one-acre parcels are to be sold from a nine-acre parcel each year for three years, the sellers must comply with

    a. the map act.
    b. the Subdivided Lands Law.
    c. Both a and b
    d. Neither a nor b

18. The Subdivided Lands Law covers

    a. undivided interests.
    b. out-of-state subdivisions sold in California.
    c. time-shares.
    d. All of the above

19. The Subdivision Map Act applies to

    a. agricultural leases.
    b. two or more parcels.
    c. out-of-state subdivisions.
    d. time-shares.

20. Public reports expire

    a. five years from the date of the first sale.
    b. five years from the date of the last sale.
    c. five years from the date of issuance.
    d. one year after issuance.

21. A subdivider who has not received a final public report but is able to enter into binding contracts with purchasers has a

    a. preliminary public report.
    b. conditional public report.
    c. variance.
    d. conditional-use permit.

22. Seven parcels of land were subject to a restrictive covenant limiting use for residential purposes. A woman acquired all seven parcels and intends to build a commercial property in conformance with zoning. Which of the following describes her rights?

    a. She will not be issued a building permit because the use would violate the restrictions.
    b. The restrictive covenant terminated by merger.
    c. Any former owner can obtain an injunction to stop the project.
    d. Anyone can enforce the restrictions.

23. Which of the following is(are) true of the Interstate Land Sales Full Disclosure Act?

   a. There is a 14-day right of rescission.
   b. It applies to 50 or more parcels.
   c. The California public report can be used to satisfy the disclosure requirements.
   d. All of the above

24. The statute of limitations for builder liability is

   a. four years for patent defects and ten years for latent defects.
   b. one year.
   c. three years.
   d. ten years for patent defects and four years for latent defects.

25. Excluded from strict liability for defects are

   a. latent defects.   c. builders.
   b. developers of lots.   d. subcontractors.

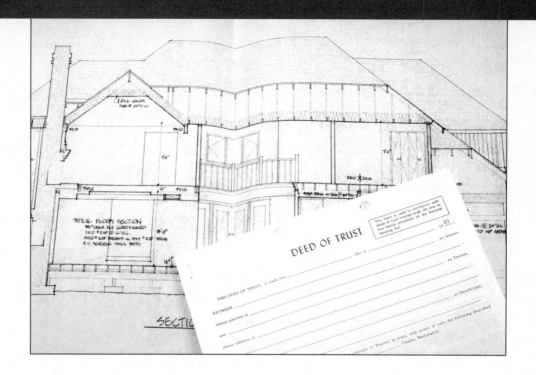

14

DEED OF TRUST

ESCROW AND TITLE INSURANCE

■ KEY TERMS

abstract of title
amendment to the
  escrow instructions
American Land Title
  Association (ALTA)
closing
elder abuse law

escrow
escrow instructions
extended-coverage
  policy of title
  insurance
interpleader action
opinion of title

preliminary title report
rebate law
relation-back doctrine
standard policy of title
  insurance
title insurance

■ ESCROWS

In many states real estate settlements are conferences attended by buyers and sellers, their attorneys, the real estate agent, and sometimes the agent's attorney. At this **closing** all documents are signed and monies are paid.

In California the closing process is simplified by using an independent depository to handle the closing process. **Escrows** are neutral third-party depositories that are limited in authority to the instructions given by the principals.

FIGURE 14.1

Escrow Function

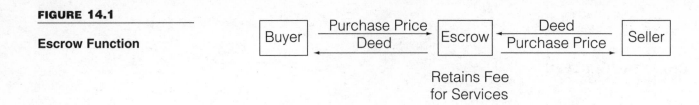

Section 1057 of the Civil Code defines an escrow as follows: "A grant deed may be deposited by the grantor with a third person to be delivered on the performance of a condition, and on delivery by the depository, it will take effect. While in the possession of the third person, and subject to condition, it is called an escrow."

Figure 14.1 illustrates the primary function of the escrow.

While the escrow is the process, the escrow agent is the individual holder of the funds (usually an employee of the escrow company). An escrow agent is not an arbitrator or a mediator of disputes. Prior to the fulfillment of the escrow conditions, the escrow dual agent is the agent of the buyer and the seller. After the fulfillment of the conditions, the escrow agent is the agent of each of the parties, with separate obligations to deliver the deed to the buyer and to deliver the consideration paid to the seller.

Because an escrow is an agency, the escrow agent should not have any discretionary powers. An essential element of an escrow is the irrevocability of the deposit of both the deed and the purchase money. An escrow never acquires title; the escrow is always an agency.

Within one month of closing, brokers must inform the buyer and the seller of the final selling price. In actual practice the broker does not do so, because the escrow provides this information in the closing statement.

Escrows are required by law in cases of court-ordered sales, bulk sales, and sales involving the transfer of a liquor license.

Escrow Instructions

In southern California, both the buyer and the seller customarily sign the escrow instructions. In northern California, the escrow instructions often are separate documents separately signed by the buyer and the seller. The separate documents cannot contain any difference regarding the escrow's duties. The escrow is not effective until both the buyer and the seller have signed identical or conforming escrow instructions.

In southern California, the escrow instructions are customarily signed upon opening of the escrow. In some areas of northern California the escrow instructions, while given at the opening of escrow, are not signed until escrow closes.

Because the real estate broker is not a party to the escrow, the escrow agent cannot change the escrow instructions at the direction of the broker.

For a valid escrow, the signed instructions must be returned to the escrow holder.

Escrow instructions include

- names of purchasers and sellers;
- how title is to be taken;
- terms;
- any contingencies;
- date of closing;
- date of possession (if not specified, possession will be given on the date of closing);
- prorations;
- what documents are to be delivered to escrow;
- the authority to accept documents and funds;
- disbursements to be made;
- costs and charges;
- designation of the title insurance company; and
- items of personal property to be included.

When new financing is involved, the lender will submit its own escrow instructions, so the lender becomes an additional party to the escrow.

The escrow instructions should be clear and unambiguous. It is possible for the escrow instructions to be the only agreement between the parties. The signed escrow instructions could meet the requirements of the statute of frauds and form the contract for sale. In fact, escrows frequently are opened without a prior buy-sell agreement. Escrow instructions often are prepared based on the oral instructions of the real estate agent.

Any changes in the escrow instructions (**amendments to the escrow instructions**) should be signed by both buyer and seller.

Escrow agents that violate their instructions are liable to their principal for losses suffered, but the escrow agent is not liable if the principal does not suffer a loss [*Mains v. City Title Insurance Company* (1949) 34 C.2d 580].

Conflict Between Purchase Agreements and Escrow Instruction.
Escrow instructions are actually independent of any purchase agreement
between the parties. If a difference exists between the instructions and the
purchase agreement, the escrow instructions generally will prevail because,
signed at a later date, they more clearly show the final agreement of the parties. However, escrow instructions might state that the purchase contract
will govern in the event of an ambiguity. In such a case, the purchase contract would prevail. If the escrow instructions and a later amendment by the
parties are in conflict, the later amendment will govern.

Escrow Duties

Escrow duties might include

- ordering preliminary title reports;
- accepting structural pest control reports and other reports as
  required by escrow for delivery to the buyer;
- obtaining beneficiary statements on existing loans so balances can
  be ascertained;
- accepting instructions for new loans and obtaining the buyer's signature to satisfy the lender;
- ascertaining amounts in impound accounts;
- determining payoff penalties;
- arranging for the transfer of insurance;
- obtaining deeds of reconveyance;
- drafting grant deeds, trust deeds, notes, etc.;
- preparing closing statements showing all receipts, expenditures,
  costs, and prorations;
- requesting necessary funds for closing;
- recording all documents, disbursing funds, and issuing closing statements; and
- reporting sale to IRS on form 1099-S.

Escrow Agents

Designating the Escrow Holder.   The designation of the escrow holder
is the responsibility of the buyer and seller. Normally the buyer designates
the escrow holder in the offer; the seller, by his or her acceptance, has agreed
to the escrow.

Real estate brokers cannot nominate an escrow holder as a condition precedent to the transaction but may recommend an escrow holder to the parties.

Licensing.   Escrows must be licensed by the commissioner of corporations. Exempt from the licensing requirements of the escrow law are

- banks and savings associations;
- title insurance companies;

- attorneys (attorneys essentially are unregulated unless they operate an escrow company); however, they must have had a bona fide client relationship with one of the parties; and
- real estate brokers. (This exemption applies only to transactions where the broker was either a principal or the listing or selling agent.)

Individuals cannot be licensed as escrows. Escrows must be corporations. Applicants for escrow licenses must furnish a $10,000 surety bond, and all directors, trustees, and employees of an escrow who have access to money or valuable securities must be bonded. All money deposited in escrow must be placed in a trust account that is exempt from execution or attachment for any claim against the escrow agent.

Prohibitions.   Licensed escrows are prohibited from

- paying referral fees to anyone except for the normal compensation of their employees;
- accepting escrow instructions or amendments containing any blanks to be filled in after signing or initialing of the instructions;
- turning over buyer funds to the seller without buyer authorization or until the seller has conveyed title (some of the creative financing arrangements with extremely long escrows providing for funds to be turned over to the seller prior to the close of escrow can be dangerous because intervening liens could attach to the property); and
- permitting any party to unilaterally change or amend signed instructions.

Prohibitions on Broker/Escrow.   While a real estate broker can act as an escrow agent in transactions where he or she represented the buyer, represented the seller, or acted as a principal to the transaction, Section 2950 of the real estate commissioner's regulations prohibits the following acts by a broker/escrow. These acts are considered to be grounds for disciplinary action:

- Soliciting or accepting an escrow instruction or amendment containing blanks to be filled in after signing or initialing
- Permitting any person to make an addition, a deletion, or an alteration to escrow instructions or amendments unless signed or initialed by all the parties to the escrow instructions
- Failing to provide a copy, at the time of signing, to persons executing escrow instructions or amendments
- Failing to maintain books, records, and accounts in accordance with accepted principles of accounting and good business practice
- Failing to maintain all records relating to escrows freely accessible for audits, inspections, and examination by the commissioner

- Failing to deposit all money received, as an escrow agent and as part of an escrow transaction, in a bank trust account or escrow account on or before the close of the next full working day after receipt thereof
- Withdrawing or paying out any money deposited in such trustee account or escrow account without the written instructions of the party(ies) paying the money into escrow
- Failing to advise all parties, in writing, that any licensee, acting as such in the transaction, has any interest in the escrow agency— stockholder, partner, officer, owner, etc. (prohibits a broker from having any undisclosed interest in the escrow)
- Failing to provide a written closing statement to the principals showing all receipts and disbursements and to whom they were made

Section 2995 of the Civil Code prohibits a real estate developer from requiring, as a condition precedent for a sale of a single-family dwelling, that escrow be provided by an escrow entity in which the developer has a financial interest. (A financial interest is defined as 5 percent or more.) The penalty for a violation is the greater of $250 or three times the escrow charge, plus attorney's fees and costs. This provision cannot be waived by the purchaser.

The Department of Corporations has interpreted Section 17006(d) of the Financial Code (broker's exemption) as follows:

- The exemption is available only to the real estate broker.
- The exemption is personal to the broker and cannot be delegated to others (other than ministerial functions).
- In a purchase and sale agreement the broker must be either a party to the transaction or the listing or selling broker.
- The exemption is not available for any association of brokers for the purpose of conducting escrows.
- When the broker's escrow business is a substantial factor in the utilization of the broker's services, the broker may not delegate or contract out any services that may be provided pursuant to the exemption. (This apparently covers the ministerial functions.)

A broker cannot advertise that he or she conducts escrows without specifying in the advertisement that such services are only in connection with the real estate brokerage business.

The broker may not use a fictitious name or a corporate name containing the word *escrow* or advertise in any other manner that would tend to be misleading to the public.

A broker who acts as an escrow agent must put aside any agency relationship with the seller as well as any special interests. The broker must maintain the position of a neutral depository as would any other escrow agent.

Disclosure.   The escrow agent has a duty to both parties to keep the escrow matters confidential. There is some disagreement among the courts, however, as to an escrow agent's duty to warn the parties of possible fraud or to advise them to take actions to protect their interests. At present the majority of the cases indicate that an escrow holder need not warn a seller of exceptional risk or likely fraud. A broker acting as escrow agent still, however, has the duty to protect the parties through full disclosure of any detrimental fact or risk involved in the transaction.

Case Study

In *Lee v. Escrow Consultants, Inc.* (1989) 210 C.A.3d 915, an escrow paid out $100,000 to a seller upon a forged amendment to the escrow instructions authorizing the release of the funds. The court held that the plaintiff had stated a valid cause of action and indicated the escrow agent had a duty to verify the signatures when the escrow instructions require that amendments be in writing.

Case Study

In *Christenson v. Commonwealth Land Title Insurance Company* (1983) 666 P.2d 302, a party to an escrow requested that the escrow agent provide information to a creditor. The escrow agent provided the wrong information, with the result that the creditor suffered a loss. The court held that while the escrow agent had no duty to supply information to third parties, after it did so it had a duty of reasonable care. The escrow agent was therefore liable for the loss suffered by its negligence.

While an escrow has duties to parties to the escrow, it has no duties to other parties.

Case Study

The case of *Summit Financial Holdings Ltd. v. Continental Lawyers Title Co.* (2002) 27 C.4th 705 involved a loan that was assigned and subsequently paid off with the monies going to the original lender, not the assignee.

(continued on next page)

Dr. Furnish borrowed $425,000 from Talbert Financial secured by a note and deed of trust. Talbert assigned the note and deed of trust to Summit Financial Holdings. Dr. Furnish was never notified of the recorded assignment and Talbert apparently continued to service the loan.

Dr. Furnish obtained a new loan from Dundee Securities that was to pay off the existing loan. Continental Lawyers Title Co. (CLTC) acted as escrow. Neither Talbert nor Summit was a party to the escrow. Although the preliminary title report showed an assignment to Summit, CLTC paid the loan off to Talbert. But Talbert failed to remit the proceeds to Summit.

Dr. Furnish filed Chapter 11 bankruptcy and ordered the property sold to pay off Dundee and another secured creditor. The bankruptcy court rejected Summit's claim because Dr. Furnish did not receive a notice of the assignment and he had paid off Talbert. Summit sued CLTC, contending that the escrow was negligent in paying Talbert rather than Summit.

While the superior court awarded judgment to Summit, the court of appeals reversed. On appeal, the California Supreme Court upheld the court of appeals. It ruled that an escrow holder has a fiduciary duty only to the parties to the escrow and that CLTC could not foresee any harm in paying off Talbert as directed because there was no evidence that Talbert would not remit the funds to Summit.

Case Study

In the case of *In re Marriage of Cloney* (2001) 91 C.A.4th 429, the court ruled that an escrow agent had a duty to disclose to its principal, First American Title, and the purchaser that the seller had used alternative names and that the agent's knowledge can be imputed to the principal. (First American Title failed to check records as to liens for other names used by the seller.)

The Elder Abuse Law. Welfare and Institutions Code Section 15610.30 (the elder abuse law) requires that escrow holders, realty agents, and others report elder financial abuse, fraud, or undue influence. The county public guardian is authorized to take control of the elder's assets to prevent such abuse.

Possession and Risk of Loss

Unless agreed otherwise, the seller retains possession until the close of escrow. The seller generally bears the risk of loss of the property. Any expenses incurred for the property are the seller's responsibility until the close of escrow. Rents and other income also accrue to the seller until the close of escrow. However, rents paid in advance normally are prorated at closing.

During the escrow period the legal title remains with the seller, even though the escrow holder has the deed. The buyer has an equitable title when all monies and documents have been deposited into escrow.

The parties normally agree that title passes when the deed is recorded or on a particular date. In the absence of such agreement the title could pass when all conditions are met. The risk of loss therefore could be on a buyer before he or she realizes title has transferred. The buyer's insurance usually will not take effect until the close of escrow, so a buyer who takes possession or title prior to the close of escrow will need to obtain earlier insurance coverage.

If possession is given to the buyer prior to close of escrow, the risk of loss normally will transfer to the buyer unless it is clear that the buyer has possession as a tenant rather than as a buyer in possession.

Termination of Escrow Full performance, by completion of the escrow, terminates the escrow. Escrows also can be terminated by the mutual agreement of both the buyer and the seller. In addition, impossibility of performance will terminate an escrow.

If only one party has signed the escrow instructions, that party can terminate the escrow prior to the other party's signing and forming a bilateral agreement. However, the person terminating the escrow still could be liable under the purchase contract.

Escrows customarily provide for time being "of the essence," so failure to complete an escrow on time will terminate the escrow. The parties then will have to agree to amend the escrow instructions if they want it to continue.

In practice, however, the majority of escrow instructions provide that they will continue unless canceled by either party. Nevertheless, a person whose failure to perform was the reason for a delay cannot use the delay as the basis for terminating the escrow.

Court decisions have shown some inconsistency relating to "time is of the essence" clauses. Several courts have allowed a reasonable period beyond the date specified.

Case Study

In the case of *First National Bank of La Habra v. Caldwell* (1927) 84 C.A. 438, no time limit was placed on an escrow. The court held that where no time is specified in an escrow it must be performed within a reasonable period of time. A delay from June 7 to September 21 was considered an unreasonable delay and allowed the purchaser to rescind.

Unless the purchase contract is terminated along with an escrow, unilateral cancellation of escrow will not cancel the rights and obligations of the parties. Specific performance or damages still might be possible based on the purchase contract.

A breach of a material provision of an escrow by one party will allow the other party to cancel. A breach can be waived by the party it was intended to benefit.

If the escrow agent dies, the parties select a substitute agent. After escrow instructions have been signed, escrow will not be terminated by the death of either the buyer or the seller. The escrow, unless agreed otherwise, will be binding on the estate of the deceased principal.

Buyer's Deposit. When an escrow is terminated, the escrow agent ordinarily requests that the parties sign a termination or cancellation agreement that specifies how to dispose of funds being held. Returning funds to the buyer or paying funds to the seller as liquidated damages could subject the escrow holder to liability should the court later determine the action to have been improper.

For an escrow involving one to four residential units where the buyer indicated an intention to occupy a unit, Civil Code Section 1057.3 provides for a penalty for the wrongful refusal of a party to execute documents required by the escrow holder to release funds. The aggrieved party is entitled to

- the amount of the funds deposited in escrow,
- treble the amount of escrow funds (but not less than $100 or more than $1,000), and
- reasonable attorney's fees.

When the buyer of one to four residential units indicates an intention to occupy a unit and then defaults, the liquidated damages cannot exceed 3 percent of the sales price.

If both buyer and seller claim a deposit when an escrow has terminated, the escrow agent should file an **interpleader action** asking the courts to determine who has valid claim to the funds held.

Money deposited by the buyer into escrow is given conditionally because it is to be paid to the seller only when title is transferred. The deposit ordinarily remains the property of the buyer until the closing, even though the buyer has given up control of the deposit.

The buyer generally assumes the risk of loss of the deposit through embezzlement by the escrow or bank failure. If, however, the loss results from a delay in closing caused by the seller's act or negligence, the seller bears the risk of loss.

If a buyer's deposit is a personal check rather than cash, a cashier's check, or a certified check, the escrow agent should wait until the check clears before conveying title. The escrow agent could be liable if the buyer's check fails to clear the bank.

Escrow Charges and Prorating.   Who pays for the escrow services is determined by the parties to the escrow. Normally, escrow charges are split between the parties. Title insurance costs are paid by the buyer or the seller according to their agreement. Taxes, insurance, interest, rents, etc., are prorated, with the seller responsible up to and including the day of closing and the buyer responsible after the date of closing. Proration is based on a 360-day year and a 30-day month. Parties may, however, make other payment or prorating agreements.

If no provision is made for who is to pay for escrow charges, title insurance, etc., local custom and usage generally prevail. Custom and usage among the counties in California vary. For example, in most areas of southern California the seller pays for the standard policy of title insurance, while in a number of northern areas the buyer pays.

Doctrine of Relation Back.   Title does not pass until escrow conditions have been performed. Prior to title being passed, the property could acquire liens. If a lien is acquired during this period by a party who had knowledge or notice of the escrow or of the rights of the grantee, the buyer's rights relate back to the delivery of the deed to the escrow, to defeat these intervening liens.

If the grantor dies after the deed is given to escrow, the delivery date of the deed relates back to the date it was given to escrow. Because that date preceded the grantor's death, there is no need for probate court approval. If the deed were not delivered to escrow, the grantee could bring an action for specific performance against the seller's heirs.

Because the **relation-back doctrine** is equitable, it does not apply to third parties who obtain interest without the knowledge of the escrow agent or of the grantee's interest.

■ TITLE INSURANCE

An **abstract of title** is a history of title showing every recorded document. Lawyers give opinions of the marketability of titles based on the abstracts. This method is still used in many states.

The problem with **opinions of title** based on abstracts is that abstracts do not show hidden items such as the contractual capacity of a grantor, a forged or altered document in the chain of title, an unknown spousal interest, failure of delivery, or unrecorded documents. The abstractor is liable only for negligence in failing to report a recorded document, and the attorney is liable only for failing to discover problems that were evident in the abstract.

The need for greater protection led to title insurance. In California, title insurance is used to prove marketable title. For a single premium, title insurance companies insure a purchaser as to the marketability of title. **Title insurance** is a contract to indemnify the insured against loss through defects in the title or against liens and encumbrances that may affect the title at the time the policy is issued.

Case Study

In the case of *Southwest Title Ins. Co. v. Northland Bldg. Corp.* (1976) 542 S.W.2d 436, the title policy failed to indicate that a first trust deed included a dragnet clause. (A dragnet clause allows for later advances that take priority as of the date the original trust deed was recorded.) A lender gave a second trust deed based on the seller's equity revealed by the title policy. Subsequent advances on the first trust deed took precedence over the second trust deed. The title insurance company was held liable for the loss suffered. The court held that the policy should have revealed not only the prior liens but also the existence of dragnet clauses.

While title insurance also covers the executor, administrator, and heirs of the insured, it does not directly cover other successors in interest. A new buyer must obtain his or her own insurance protection.

Case Study

In the case of *Harrison v. Commonwealth Land Title Ins. Co.* (1979) 97 C.A.3d 973, at a sheriff's sale the sheriff read from a title policy that had been issued to an attorney for the judgment creditor. The purchaser at the sheriff's sale discovered that the title policy failed to indicate a trust deed. The court held that the insurance company had no liability to the purchaser. The report was not issued to the purchaser as an insured, and the purchaser was held not justified in relying on it.

Title insurance could, however, indirectly cover subsequent purchasers who successfully sue an insured grantor because of a title defect included in the grantor's coverage.

Title insurance offers indemnification against loss up to the amount of coverage purchased. Some policies have an inflation endorsement that provides increases in coverage. The title insurance company is obligated to defend the title in legal action, cure the defects, or pay for the loss up to the policy limits.

Prior to issuing a title insurance policy, the title company will search the records to determine if it will write a policy. Title insurance companies use a title plant that is a microfilm or computer system showing every document that has been recorded within the county.

The title insurer has no actual duty to ascertain if the title is good. Any records search it performs is for its own protection in deciding if it wants to take the risk of insuring title.

California title insurance companies are regulated by the California insurance commissioner.

For escrows in which no policy of title insurance is to be issued to the buyer, the following statement must be signed and acknowledged by all parties to the escrow:

Important: In a purchase or exchange of real property, it may be advisable to obtain title insurance in connection with the close of escrow since there may be prior recorded liens and encumbrances which affect your interest in the property being acquired. A new policy of title insurance should be obtained in order to ensure your interest in the property that you are acquiring.

Preliminary Title Report

After deciding that it will issue title insurance, the title company issues a **preliminary title report**, which indicates exceptions to its coverage. The preliminary title report is not insurance. A separate fee is charged for the title insurance policy, which is usually issued at close of escrow.

According to Section 12340.11 of the Insurance Code, preliminary title reports are offers to issue a title policy subject to stated conditions. The reports are not abstracts, nor are there any rights, duties, or responsibilities applicable to the issuance of the preliminary report. The report will not be construed as or constitute a representation of the condition of title but will constitute a statement of the terms and conditions on which the issuer is willing to issue its title policy, if such offer is accepted.

Case Study

Southland Title Corporation v. Superior Court (1991) 231 C.A.3d 530 involved a preliminary title report that did not mention a flood control easement. The court held that the title insurer is not liable for its negligence in preparing the preliminary title report. It held that the report was merely an offer to issue a title policy. The home purchasers were able to collect only up to the limits of their title insurance policy. (They had sought to collect beyond their policy limits based on the negligence of the insurance carrier.)

Homeowner Standard Policy Coverage (California Land Title Association—CLTA)

The **homeowner standard policy of title insurance** covers matters of record not specifically excluded from coverage as well as matters not of record, such as

- forgery,
- lack of capacity of a grantor,
- undisclosed spousal interest (a grantor who claimed to have been single could have a spouse with community property interests),
- failure of delivery of a prior deed,
- federal estate tax liens,
- deeds of a corporation whose charter has expired, and
- deeds of an agent whose capacity has terminated.

Standard Policy Exclusions. Not covered by a homeowner standard policy of title insurance are

- defects known by the insured and not disclosed to the title insurer,
- zoning (a special endorsement is available stating that property currently is zoned properly or that a current use is authorized by the zoning),

- mining claims (these are filed in mining districts, and legal descriptions are not required),
- taxes and assessments that are not yet liens,
- easements and liens not a matter of public record (such as mechanic's lien rights),
- rights of parties in possession (unrecorded deeds, options, leases, etc.) and matters that would be disclosed by making inquiry of persons on the property,
- matters not of record that would be disclosed by checking the property (such as encroachment),
- matters that would be revealed by a correct survey,
- water rights, and
- reservations in government patents.

Homeowner Extended-Coverage Policies

Both the California Land Title Association (CLTA) and the American Land Title Association (ALTA) now offer extended coverage title policies for homeowners. These nearly identical policies offer limited extended coverage for a higher premium. In addition to the standard coverage, these policies offer coverage, with limitations, for

- building permit violations,
- restrictive covenant violations,
- postpolicy forgery,
- postpolicy adverse possession,
- access,
- postpolicy encroachment,
- postpolicy prescriptive rights,
- map inconsistencies,
- living trust coverage (homeowner deeds to living trust), and
- structure damage from mineral extraction by others.

Lender Extended-Coverage Policy

Because many lenders are from other areas, the physical inspection necessary to protect their interests under a standard policy has not been feasible. Therefore, the **American Land Title Association (ALTA)** policy was developed to meet lender needs. Besides offering greater protection to the lenders, the **extended-coverage policy of title insurance** allowed assignment, because loans frequently are transferred between lenders. The lender's policy provides coverage only until the loan is paid. It actually offers decreasing coverage each year.

Owners also wanted increased coverage, so an owner's policy, which provides the same extended coverage to owners, was developed.

Case Study

In the case of *Walters v. Marler* (1978) 83 C.A.3d 1, a house was constructed on the wrong lot. While the lender had an extended-coverage policy of title insurance, the owner had only a standard policy. The court held that while the lender was insured for the risk, the owner was not. The owner cannot benefit from the extended-coverage policy without having paid the additional premium.

The physical condition of the property is not guaranteed by extended-coverage policies.

Case Study

Lick Mill Creek Apartments v. Chicago Title Co. (1991) 231 C.A.3d 1654 involved a case where land with hazardous waste was purchased. The buyer sought reimbursement of removal costs from the title insurer. The court held that while an ALTA title policy offers more complete off-record coverage than a CLTA policy, it does not cover physical defects such as contamination. The court noted that encumbrances are defined (Civil Code Section 1114) as "taxes, assessments, and all liens upon real property." An order to clean up property is not a lien unless recorded. (Marketability of title and market value are not the same thing.)

In addition to the coverage offered by the standard policy, an ALTA extended-coverage policy of title insurance includes

- unrecorded liens,
- off-record easements,
- rights of parties in physical possession, including tenants and buyers under unrecorded instruments,
- rights and claims that a correct survey or physical inspection of the land would show,
- mining claims,
- reservations in patents,
- water rights, and
- lack of access.

Lender Extended-Coverage Exclusions

Extended-coverage policies do not cover

- matters known by the insured but not conveyed to the insurer,
- government regulations such as zoning,

■ liens placed by the insured,
■ eminent domain, or
■ violations of the map act.

Table 14.2 shows what is covered by title insurance.

Special Policies

A number of special policies are available, including construction lender policies (with endorsements protecting against prior mechanics' liens), vendee policies for purchasers under real property sales contracts, leasehold loan policies, leasehold owners' policies, and oil and gas interest policies.

Endorsements can be obtained for special additional coverage or exclusion from coverage.

Policy Interpretation

Title policies should be interpreted in accordance with the reasonable expectations of the insured. Any questions about ambiguities in a policy normally will be resolved against the insurer.

Title Insurance Companies

Every title insurance company in California must have at least $500,000 paid-in capital and must deposit with the insurance commissioner a guarantee fund of $100,000 in cash or approved securities.

Title insurance companies must set apart annually, as a title insurance surplus fund, a sum equal to 10 percent of premiums collected during the year until this fund equals the lesser of 25 percent of the paid-in capital of the company or $1 million. This fund offers further security to the holders and beneficiaries of title insurance policies.

Rebate Law.   Title insurance companies in California must charge for services and make a sincere effort to collect such charges.

The **rebate law** extends the anticommission provisions of the Insurance Code to prohibit direct or indirect payments by a title insurer to principals

	Standard Coverage	Lender Extended Coverage	Not Covered by Either Policy
TABLE 14.2 **Owner's Title Insurance Policy**	1. Defects found in public records 2. Forged documents 3. Incompetent grantors 4. Incorrect marital statements 5. Improperly delivered deeds	Standard coverage plus defects discoverable through 1. property inspection including unrecorded rights of persons in possession 2. examination of survey 3. unrecorded liens not known of by policyholder	1. Defects and liens listed in policy 2. Defects known to buyer 3. Changes in land use brought about by zoning ordinances

in a transaction as a consideration for business. The rebate prohibition extends to any title business, including escrows.

It is a criminal offense for an employee of a title company or controlled escrow company to pay a commission (directly or indirectly) to a real estate licensee as an inducement for placement or referral of title business. The criminal penalties apply to both giving and receiving the kickback. The penalty is up to one year in jail and a fine up to $10,000 for each offense (Penal Code 641.4).

The title insurance company may, however, furnish the names of owners of record and the legal description of parcels of real estate without charge.

The California Department of Insurance has indicated that providing a broker with a "Comparative Market Analysis" is a prohibited inducement. Some title companies had given free computer software to real estate licensees. This practice violates the law unless the software relates "exclusively" to the ordering and delivery of title products and services.

■ SUMMARY

Escrows are neutral depositories that handle the functions of real estate closings. The escrow is not effective until both the buyer and the seller sign identical or conforming escrow instructions. The escrow agent represents the buyer and seller and must obey their instructions.

Generally escrow instructions that are signed after the purchase agreement will prevail if an ambiguity between the two develops.

Escrow instructions would include the names of the parties, how title is to be taken, special terms, contingencies, and transfer instructions, as well as the payment of costs and charges.

The escrow agent handles all of the paperwork of closing, such as drafting documents, obtaining signatures, paying off existing liens, dispersing funds, and issuing closing statements.

Escrows must be licensed by the commissioner of corporations, with the exception of banks and savings associations, title insurance companies, attorneys, and real estate brokers. Real estate brokers can serve as escrows on transactions in which they represented either the buyer or the seller or were a principal. A real estate broker cannot delegate other than ministeri-

al functions to others and cannot use the word **escrow** in his or her fictitious or corporate name.

An escrow will be terminated by

- full performance,
- mutual agreement of the parties,
- failure to fulfill a condition necessary for closing, or
- a breach of a material provision by one party (which allows the other party to cancel).

Title insurance protects purchasers and/or lenders by insuring the marketability of title. A title insurance company agrees to indemnify against
losses that are not excluded, up to the amount of coverage purchased. Title
insurance protects only the named insured and his or her estate or heirs.

A title insurer will issue a preliminary title report, which indicates that the
insurer will insure with named exceptions. The preliminary title report
provides no insurance protection if a policy of insurance is not issued.

A standard policy of title insurance (California Land Title Association—
CLTA) covers matters of record as well as matters not of record, including

- forgery,
- lack of capacity of a grantor,
- undisclosed spousal interest,
- failure of delivery of a prior deed,
- federal estate tax liens,
- deeds of a corporation whose charter has expired, and
- deeds of an agent whose capacity has terminated.

The need for greater protection for lenders who were not in an area led to
the development of the American Land Title Association (ALTA) policy,
which offers extended coverage to lenders. The same protection also can
be obtained by buyers.

Extended coverage includes

- unrecorded liens,
- off-record easements,
- rights of parties in possession,
- rights and claims a correct survey would have revealed,
- reservations in patents,
- water rights, and
- lack of access.

Special title insurance policies are available for construction lenders, purchasers on real property sales contracts, lessees, leasehold lenders, oil and gas interests, etc.

Ambiguities in title policies generally are resolved against the insurance carrier.

Title insurers and escrows are prohibited from providing rebates to brokers for referral of business. This prohibition extends to special rates and not making a sincere effort to collect for services.

■ DISCUSSION CASES

1. An escrow delivered title to a buyer before the conditions of the escrow were met. **What are the rights of the parties?**

   Kish v. Bay Counties Title Guaranty Co. (1967) 254 C.A.2d 725

2. The sellers signed escrow instructions directing that the broker's commission be paid out of the sale proceeds. The sales agreement authorizing the commission was not deposited into escrow. On the day prior to closing the seller instructed the escrow holder not to pay the commission. **In not paying the broker, was the escrow liable for the broker's loss?**

   Contemporary Invs., Inc. v. Safeco Title Ins. Co. (1983) 145 C.A.3d 999

3. An escrow received a check unaccompanied by any instructions. (The purchaser had not signed the escrow instructions.) The check was for $880 more than was required as an increased deposit in a transaction. The title company put the undeposited check in the file. The purchaser subsequently notified the seller that the transaction would not be completed. The seller's attorney demanded that the $5,000 be turned over to the seller. The purchaser had emptied the account, so the check could not be cashed. **Was the escrow liable to the seller?**

   Riando v. San Benito Title Guarantee Co. (1950) 35 C.2d 170

4. It was alleged that the escrow knew that the plaintiffs were being defrauded by others. **Does the escrow have a duty to warn the purchaser?**

   Lee v. Title Insurance & Trust Co. (1968) 264 C.A.2d 160

5. An amendment to escrow instructions called for security to be a fourth trust deed rather than a second trust deed as originally called for. A prior lienholder subsequently foreclosed on the property. The plaintiff claimed that the escrow was negligent and breached a fiduciary duty in that it failed to call the substituted consideration specifically to the attention of the plaintiff. **Was the plaintiff's claim valid?**

    Axley v. Transamerica Title Ins. Co. (1978) 88 C.A.3d 1

6. The plaintiff was to loan a property owner enough money to pay off an existing first trust deed and was to take back a new first trust deed as security. The plaintiff paid off the existing first trust deed outside of escrow. The escrow, contrary to verbal instructions, recorded the deed of reconveyance. This allowed the owner to place another first trust deed on the property. **Is the escrow liable?**

    Zang v. Northwestern Title Co. (1982) 135 C.A.3d 159

7. Warrington agreed to assume the mortgages of record. A preliminary title report issued to the seller in a different transaction failed to disclose a second mortgage. **Is the insurance company liable for its negligence?**

    Warrington v. Transamerica Title Ins. Co. (1979) 546 P.2d 627

8. An insurance company failed to defend an attack on a title because it believed that the claim was not covered. **If the claim actually was covered by the policy, what would be the limits of the insurer's liability?**

    Samson v. Transamerica Ins. Co. (1981) 30 C.3d 220

9. The buyers, the sellers, and the buyers' agent went to an escrow agent to draw up instructions on the sale of a chicken ranch. The escrow instructions included a bill of sale for all of the equipment that turned all of the fixtures into personal property and a trust deed for the ranch. The purchaser promptly removed all of the equipment and defaulted on the purchase price. Because it was a purchase-money trust deed, a deficiency judgment was not possible. **Was the escrow agent negligent?**

    Cunningham v. Security Title Ins. Co. (1966) 241 C.A.2d 626

10. An escrow agent agreed to withhold funds to cover a debt due the plaintiff for material. The escrow agent failed to withhold the funds

as agreed. The plaintiff was not a party to the escrow. **Is the escrow agent liable to the plaintiff?**

Warrington Lumber Co. v. Fullerton Mtg. & Escrow Co. (1963)
222 C.A.2d 706

11. A title insurer's policy had an exclusion for "water rights, claims or title to water." The title insurance failed to discover a recorded easement given by the previous owner to a water company for drilling and running a pipeline. **Is the insurer liable?**

White v. Western Title Ins. Co. (1985) 40 C.3d 870

12. The buyer's deposit into escrow was a check that remained uncashed. The seller did not know that the check was not deposited. The buyer defaulted. **What, if any, is the escrow agent's liability to the seller?**

Wade v. Lake County Title Co. (1970) 6 C.A.3d 824

The court decisions for the above cases can be found on our Web site at **www.dearbornRE.com**. Click on the **"Instructor Resources"** link, then scroll down the page until you find the link titled "California Real Estate Law 5th Edition."

■ CHAPTER QUIZ

1. After escrow instructions have been signed, the escrow agent may

    a. fill in blanks left by the parties.
    b. return the deposit to the buyer if the escrow fails to close on time.
    c. refuse to obey instructions received from the broker.
    d. None of the above

2. If escrow instructions fail to provide for the date of possession, possession will be given

    a. within 30 days of close of escrow.
    b. within a reasonable time.
    c. at close of escrow.
    d. prior to close of escrow.

3. An amendment to the escrow instructions requires the agreement of

   a. the buyer and the escrow.
   b. the agent and the escrow.
   c. the buyer, seller, agent, and escrow.
   d. None of the above

4. When the signed escrow instructions differ from the purchase agreement

   a. the escrow takes precedence.
   b. the purchase agreement takes precedence.
   c. the contract becomes void for lack of certainty.
   d. the escrow is required to commence an interpleader action.

5. Duties of an escrow do *not* include

   a. ordering preliminary title reports.
   b. mediating buyer-seller disputes.
   c. drafting deeds.
   d. issuing closing statements.

6. Exempt from the licensing requirements are escrows conducted by

   a. a real estate broker in transactions in which the broker represents either the buyer or seller.
   b. title insurance companies.
   c. banks.
   d. All of the above

7. A real estate broker, not licensed as an escrow, can conduct an escrow when he or she

   a. represents the seller.
   b. represents the buyer.
   c. is a principal to the transaction.
   d. Any of the above

8. Which of the following actions of an escrow would be improper?

   a. Accepting fees from both buyer and seller
   b. Refusing to pay a commission for referral to the escrow
   c. Refusing to handle an escrow
   d. Accepting escrow instructions with blanks to be filled in by the escrow after the instructions are signed

9. Which of the following is proper for a broker who, while not licensed as an escrow, conducts escrows on his or her sales?

   a. Delegating the escrow function to another
   b. Using the name "Jones Realty and Escrow Company"
   c. Charging for the escrow services
   d. None of the above

10. A buyer given possession by the seller one week prior to close of escrow should be most concerned about

    a. the impound account.
    b. risk of loss.
    c. extended title coverage.
    d. designation of the escrow holder.

11. Which statement is true of the rights and obligations during escrow?

    a. The seller retains risk of property loss.
    b. Rents belong to the seller.
    c. Property expenses are the responsibility of the seller.
    d. All of the above

12. Which of the following would not terminate an escrow?

    a. Full performance of escrow duties
    b. Mutual agreement of the parties
    c. The broker's order to terminate
    d. Impossibility of performance

13. When both buyer and seller make demands on escrow for the buyer's deposit after the escrow failed to close, the escrow holder should

    a. deduct its fees and return the deposit to the person who made it.
    b. deduct its fees and return the deposit to the seller.
    c. file an interpleader action.
    d. give the deposit to the first party making a claim to it.

14. Which of the following best describes an abstract of title?

    a. The complete legal description
    b. An abbreviated description such as a street address
    c. A recorded history of title
    d. An opinion of title

15. Which of the following is(are) true regarding title insurance?

    a. Executors and heirs are protected by the title insurance of the deceased insured.
    b. A buyer obtains greater title protection if the lender is issued an extended-coverage policy.
    c. Both a and b
    d. Neither a nor b

16. A title insurer will not be liable for a loss if

    a. its negligence was not the cause of the loss.
    b. the person suffering the loss was not the insured or his or her estate or heirs.
    c. Either a or b
    d. Neither a nor b

17. To issue a standard title policy, the insurer must

    a. have a survey.
    b. determine whether title is good.
    c. provide an abstract.
    d. None of the above

18. Which of the following is true of the preliminary title report?

    a. It provides interim coverage.
    b. It shows the condition of title.
    c. It provides no insurance.
    d. Both b and c

19. A standard policy of title insurance protects against

    a. rights of parties in possession.
    b. unrecorded easements.
    c. zoning restrictions.
    d. forgery in the chain of title.

20. A standard policy of title insurance does *not* cover

    a. unknown spousal interests.
    b. rights of parties in possession.
    c. forgery.
    d. lack of capacity of the grantor.

21. A standard policy of title insurance covers

    a. unrecorded mechanics' liens.
    b. instruments outside the chain of title.
    c. easements that are not a matter of public record.
    d. None of the above

22. *After* buying a home and receiving a standard policy of title insurance, you determine that the "tenant" claims to be an owner under an unrecorded grant deed. Which of the following statements is true?

    a. You are protected by your insurance.
    b. If you record first, you will be protected.
    c. You are not insured for this loss.
    d. An abstract would have given you greater protection.

23. Extended-coverage title insurance adds which of the following to the coverage of the standard policy?

    a. Forgery
    b. Unknown spousal interests
    c. Lack of capacity
    d. Off-record easements

24. Extended-coverage policies of title insurance do not generally cover

    a. claims of a party in possession.
    b. building and zoning regulations.
    c. prescriptive easements.
    d. water rights.

25. The rebate law prohibits

    a. escrows from giving rebates to brokers.
    b. title companies from giving rebates to brokers.
    c. brokers from rebating commissions to buyers.
    d. Both a and b

15

LANDLORD-TENANT LAW

■ KEY TERMS

assignment	periodic tenancy	tenancy at sufferance
constructive eviction	quiet enjoyment	tenancy at will
exculpatory clause	rent control	tenancy for years
habitability	retaliatory eviction	30-day notice
implied warranty	security deposit	three-day notice
lease	sublease	unlawful detainer action
nondisturbance clause	surrender	writ of possession

■ TYPES OF TENANCIES

A leasehold interest (also known as a *demise*) is a nonfreehold estate in real property.

Tenancy for Years

A **tenancy for years**, or estate for years, is a leasehold interest with a definite termination date. The tenancy does not renew itself, and no notice is required to end it. A tenancy for years could be a rental of a summer cabin for a weekend or a multiyear lease.

Agricultural land in California cannot be leased for more than 51 years. Other property leases and mineral leases cannot exceed 99 years. (Mineral leases differ from mineral rights, which are grants or reservations of a fee interest and can go on forever.) Leases that provide for renewal options that could exceed these statutory limits are unenforceable.

Periodic Tenancy

A **periodic tenancy** renews itself automatically from period to period unless notice of termination is given. Customarily the period would be the rent-paying period, and the most common periodic tenancy is a month-to-month tenancy.

Either the lessor (landlord) or the lessee (tenant) can give notice to terminate. Notice of up to the length of the rent-paying period is required to terminate, but in no event must it be more than 30 days. The parties to a periodic tenancy can agree to a notice period of less than 30 days, but notice always must be given at least 7 days before termination. Effective January 1, 2003, if the tenant has lived in the property at least 12 months, then the landlord must give a 60-day notice to terminate.

In California, the notice to terminate does not have to coincide with the rent-paying period. For example, on a month-to-month tenancy that ends on the first of the month, notice could be given to end the tenancy on the tenth of a month if the notice were given at least 30 days prior to the termination (**30-day notice**).

Rent increases and changes in the terms of a periodic tenancy also require notice for the length of the rent-paying period, but generally, notice need not be given more than 30 days in advance. However, if a rent increase is greater than a 10 percent increase over rent charged within the prior 12 months, then a 60-day notice of the rent increase is required.

In the absence of any agreement, housing units and nonresidential properties are presumed to be rented on a month-to-month basis when no local custom to the contrary exists. However, agricultural rentals are presumed to be for one year unless another period was indicated.

Tenancy at Will

A **tenancy at will** is held at the pleasure of the lessor for an unspecified period of time. Under a tenancy at will, there is possession without an agreement on the rent payment. If rent were paid or rent were agreed on, the tenancy would convert to a periodic tenancy. An example of a tenancy at will might be a tenant given possession while a lease was still being negotiated, before any agreement on rent has been reached. Under common law no notice was required to terminate a tenancy at will, and it could be terminated by the lessor or lessee. Because California requires, by statute, a notice for the length of the rent-paying period (but in no event more than 30 days), California does not have a true tenancy at will.

Tenancy at Sufferance

In a **tenancy at sufferance** the lessee is a holdover tenant. For example, one who retains possession beyond the expiration of a tenancy for years or a home seller who fails to vacate by the agreed move-out date is a holdover tenant.

California regards a tenant at sufferance as a trespasser rather than a tenant and considers an ejectment action or an unlawful detainer action (discussed later in this chapter) to oust the trespasser a proper remedy.

When a lessor consents to the holdover or accepts rent from the tenant at sufferance, a periodic tenancy, which would require statutory notice to terminate, results.

■ THE LEASE

A **lease** is an agreement that transfers a right of exclusive possession for a stated term from a landlord (lessor) to a tenant (lessee). The lessor under the lease subordinates his or her rights of occupancy to the rights of the tenant. The lessor retains a reversionary interest; the lessor is entitled to possession when the tenancy has ended.

Leasehold interests are considered personal property (chattels real) rather than real property. The laws of personal property therefore apply.

Because a lease is a contract, all the requirements of a valid contract are required for a valid lease.

Leases can be oral or written agreements. However, an oral lease is enforceable only if it can be fully performed within one year of being agreed on. For example, a one-year oral lease beginning on the date of agreement is enforceable, but a one-year lease starting one month after the agreement must be in writing to be enforceable.

Leases may be recorded, but recordation is not necessary between the parties. Recording does give constructive notice of a tenant's interest, and this could be important in defining priority of interests when there is a subsequent trust deed or purchaser. A subsequent purchaser is not required to honor a lease for more than one year unless a memorandum of the lease is recorded or the purchaser has constructive notice. Possession is deemed constructive notice, so a tenant's rights could be challenged by a subsequent purchaser only if the tenant had vacated the premises at the time of transfer and also had failed to record the lease.

To be recorded, a lease must be acknowledged by the lessor.

Form and Provisions of Lease

No particular language is required to create a tenancy as long as the intent is clear. However, the language must include the names of the parties and clearly describe the premises, the amount of rent and the term of the lease.

Commercial leases can be complex documents of dozens of pages, while residential leases are normally simpler contracts, as is the lease in Chapter 6.

If the lease is in writing, the lessor must sign the lease. A tenant who moves in or pays rent after receiving a copy of the lease will be viewed as having accepted the lease even when the tenant has not signed it.

If jointly owned property is leased by a husband and wife for more than one year, both spouses must sign the lease.

Unless use is restricted by the lease, the tenant can use the premises for any lawful purpose.

In the absence of any agreement or practice to the contrary, for leases of one year or less rent is due at the end of each rent-paying period. The parties to a lease generally agree, however, that rent will be paid in advance.

Lease provisions that call for forfeiture of the premises upon some default must be stated clearly. The courts generally will construe agreements to avoid forfeiture if the result will be inequitable. For forfeiture, a demand must be made for performance unless such demand would be futile. Failure to pay rent does not justify a forfeiture.

If a tenant breaches a provision of the lease that calls for forfeiture and the landlord accepts rent knowing of the breach, the landlord could be said to have waived his or her right to declare forfeiture. This would not be the case if the lease specifies that acceptance of rent will not waive the landlord's rights to declare a forfeiture in the event of a continuing or subsequent breach.

Civil Code Section 1670.5, which prohibits the enforcement of unconscionable contracts, also applies to leases. Clauses that are so harsh as to be considered unconscionable will not be enforced by the courts. For example, courts will not enforce acceleration clauses in leases where the entire rent for the term of the lease becomes due if the lessee fails to make a payment by a specified date.

Leases often provide that they are renewed automatically if either party fails to give notice. An automatic renewal under such a lease would be voidable by the lessee if the lessee did not prepare the lease, or if the automatic renewal clause was not printed in at least eight-point type and a reference to the automatic renewal was not placed in at least eight-point type just above where the lessee signs.

Notices and Management

The owner or agent of every multiunit dwelling of more than two units must disclose and keep current the name and address of each person authorized to manage the premises and to receive notices and demands on behalf of the owner.

Every residential property containing 16 or more units must have a resident manager.

Fair Housing

The Civil Rights Acts of 1866 and 1968 and the California Rumford and Unruh Acts apply to discrimination in rentals. For a detailed discussion of these rights, see Chapter 4.

Fixtures

The lease may provide the tenant with rights to remove improvements. In the absence of such an agreement, fixtures stay with the property.

Because forfeiture is a harsh penalty, courts often will find tenant improvements to be personal property when they clearly would be justified in declaring the items fixtures. When there is doubt about whether an improvement can be defined as a fixture, courts generally will find in favor of the tenant.

As mentioned in Chapter 7, a tenant has the right to remove the annual crops that are the fruit of his or her labor, even after the tenancy has ended.

Trade Fixtures.   Trade fixtures, also discussed in Chapter 7, generally must be removed prior to the expiration of the lease. In the case of a month-to-month lease the courts usually allow a reasonable period for removal of the fixtures; this period could extend beyond the termination date.

As discussed in Chapter 11, the lessor should record and file a notice of nonresponsibility to be protected from mechanics' liens when a tenant makes improvements or repairs. If the lease obligates the tenant to make alterations, improvements, or repairs, a lien could be placed against the property even when the notice of nonresponsibility was filed. The tenant may become an agent of the owner in authorizing the work required by the lessor.

Options

Leases frequently contain options to purchase or options to renew. Part of the rent is generally regarded as consideration for the option. Ordinarily time is considered to be of the essence for options; that is, they must be exercised within the period provided.

Exculpatory Clauses

Leases frequently contain **exculpatory clauses**, which purport to relieve the landlord of all liability for injury to the tenant and others as well as damage to the tenant's property. Despite the language of these clauses, a lease cannot excuse the landlord for acts, fraud, or violations of the law that are either willful or negligent. The tenant cannot waive the landlord's duty. Civil Code Section 1953 declares that exculpatory clauses in residential leases executed after January 1, 1976, are invalid.

Security Deposits

A **security deposit** is any payment, fee, deposit, or charge (not limited to the advance payment of rent) required by the lessor to secure the performance of a rental agreement. The maximum allowable security deposit for unfurnished units is two months' rent. For furnished units it cannot exceed three months' rent [Civil Code Section 1950.5(c)].

The lessor may appropriate necessary amounts from the deposit to remedy rent default, to repair damage done by the tenant, or to clean the premises upon termination of the tenancy if the deposit was made for those purposes [Civil Code Section 1950.5(e)].

Security deposits do not apply to normal wear and tear. They apply to negligence and failure to maintain the premises in a reasonable manner.

When the landlord transfers the property, the security deposit must be either transferred to the new owner with notice given to the tenant or returned to the tenant. In either case, the landlord can deduct sums due for rent, repairs, or cleaning. If the security deposits are not transferred to the new owner, the new owner and the former owner are jointly liable for the repayment of security deposits to the tenants [Civil Code Section 1950.5(i)].

An amendment to Civil Code Section 1950.5 makes the landlord liable for interest on unreturned security deposits at 2 percent per month. Any successor in interest of the landlord also will be liable.

No later than three weeks after the tenant has vacated the premises, the landlord must furnish the tenant an itemized written statement of the basis for and the amount of any security deposit retained, as well as the disposition of such security, and must return any remaining portion of such security [Civil Code Section 1950.5(e)].

The bad-faith retention by the landlord (or transferee in interest) of any portion of the deposit may subject the landlord to $600 in damages in addition to actual damages [Civil Code Section 1950.5(h)].

The tenant's right to the return of the security deposit is a priority claim above those of any creditor of the landlord other than a trustee in bankruptcy.

In the absence of any agreement to pay interest or a local statute requiring interest, a landlord need not pay interest on security deposits. (Berkeley and San Francisco have statutes requiring such interest.)

Case Study

The case of *Korens v. Zukin Corp.* (1989) 212 C.A.3d 1054 was a $1.5 million class-action suit for interest on security deposits. In dismissing the lawsuit the court pointed out there was no state law requiring landlords to pay interest on security deposits. "Any requirement that interest be paid should be enacted explicitly by the legislature, not developed through doctrinal manipulation by the courts."

If a lessor takes a security deposit in the form of the last month's rent, it is taxable to the lessor as regular income in the year received. If, however, the deposit is intended strictly to secure the payment of rent, cleaning, and possible damages, the deposit will be taxable only if and when it is forfeited.

Case Study

In the case of *People v. Parkmerced Co.* (1988) 198 C.A.3d 683, the district attorney sued the owner and management company of a 3,400-unit apartment complex. Tenants were charged $65 more for the first month's rent on a one-year lease than for the other 11 months and were also charged a $50 transfer fee if they wished to change apartments.

The court of appeal affirmed the trial court's decision that these fees were security deposits within the meaning of Civil Code Section 1950.5. Because the fees were not intended to cover repairs or tenant defaults, the defendants were not allowed to keep them. Defendants were ordered to reimburse past tenants for fees charged, notify current tenants of their right to receive a refund, and pay $222,000 in civil penalties and $40,000 in attorney's fees.

A landlord can require a nonrefundable applicant screening fee for tenants (up to $30). Upon request the landlord must supply the rental applicant a copy of a credit report paid for by the applicant. (Civil Code 1950.6.)

■ ASSIGNMENTS AND SUBLEASES

An **assignment** of a lease transfers the entire leasehold interest. The assignee becomes the tenant of the original lessor. The assignee is primarily liable on the lease, while the assignor retains secondary liability. (The assignor remains as a surety on the lease.)

Instead of assigning, the lessee would be better off surrendering the premises to the lessor and letting the assignee become a tenant on a new lease. If the lessor agrees to this, the original lessee will be free from any liability on the lease.

In a **sublease** the lessee becomes a lessor (sublessor) and the sublessee is the tenant of the original lessee, not the tenant of the original lessor.

Figure 15.1 illustrates the differences between an assignment and a sublease.

Under a sublease the lessee remains primarily liable on the lease. A sublease can be for the same term or less than the term of the original lease and can be for all or part of the leased premises.

No privity of contract between the sublessee and the lessor exists. If the original lessee is evicted or the lease otherwise terminates, the rights of the sublessee also terminate.

The sublessee cannot have any greater rights than the original lessee had, because the sublessee's rights were granted by the sublessor.

FIGURE 15.1

Assignment versus Subletting

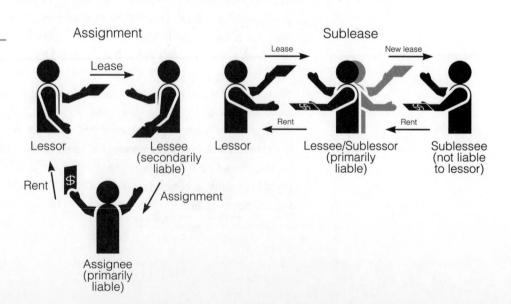

Besides the ability to sublet only part of the premises, an important advantage of subleasing is that a rent differential is possible.

An option to purchase in a lease would go with an assignment, or it even can be separated from the lease unless the transfer of the option is prohibited by its terms. An option to purchase does not go with a sublease.

If a lease fails to restrict assignment or subleases, the lessee can freely transfer the lease interest. A lease may prohibit transfer of a tenant's rights (Civil Code Section 1995.230), but if transfer is allowed with the lessor's consent, consent cannot be refused unreasonably. The lease can require that the landlord share in some or all of the profits from an assignment or sublease (Civil Code Sections 1995.240 and 1995.250).

See *Kendall v. Ernest Pestana Inc.* (1985) 40 C.3d 488 and *Pay 'N' Pak Stores v. Superior Court* (1989) 210 C.A.3d 1404.

Case Study

The case of *Girard v. Delta Towers* (1994) 20 C.A.4th 1741 involved a Delta Towers lease of office space to Mediacom.
The President of Mediacom guaranteed the lease. Mediacom encountered financial difficulties and subleased the space to WFI, Inc., at a $2,676.83 monthly profit.

WFI, Inc., then encountered financial difficulties and subleased space across the hall, breaking its lease with Mediacom. The building owner approved this sublease. Because Mediacom's space was now vacant, they could not pay the rent. The building owner sued Mediacom and the President, Girard, who had guaranteed the lease. Girard counter sued Delta Towers for the tort of intentionally inflicting damages on Mediacom by approving the WFI, Inc., move.

The superior court ruled for Girard but the appellate court reversed, holding that a landlord has no fiduciary duty to a tenant. The appellate court clarified that California landlords cannot refuse to approve subleases without a commercially reasonable objection. Delta Towers had no choice but to approve the new WFI, Inc., sublease.

An assignment or sublease made when prohibited by the lease may be voidable but is not void. A lessor who accepts rent after having knowledge of the assignment or sublease, however, has consented to it.

■ TERMINATION OF LEASES

A lease can be terminated by or for the following reasons:

- Destruction of the premises—some leases, however, provide that the rent is merely tolled and the landlord has a period of time to rebuild.
- Action of a public body (eminent domain)—the tenant is released if the entire property is taken, but in cases of partial condemnation, where the portion remaining continues to meet the needs of the lessee, the lessee could be required to continue to pay rent (or a reduced rent). For example, the taking of several feet to widen a road probably would not allow the tenant to terminate the lease. A tenant could have a claim of loss against the public body for condemnation. In some cases commercial tenants have received as much compensation in condemnation cases as the owners of the structures.
- Commercial frustration—this applies to unforeseen events, the nonoccurrence of which was a condition precedent of the contract (see Chapter 5).
- Merger—where the same party acquires both the lessee's interests and the lessor's interests, the lesser interest is lost by merger. For example, when a tenant under a long-term lease purchases the premises from his or her landlord and later sells the property, the former tenant will have lost the rights under the lease. When the tenant purchased the property, he or she became the owner and no longer was a tenant.
- Bankruptcy of the tenant—the bankruptcy court could, however, determine that the lease was an asset of the bankrupt and assign it to another.
- Expiration or notice—estates for years terminate automatically by their terms. Notice ends a periodic tenancy.
- Foreclosure—the foreclosure of a trust deed recorded prior to the lease terminates the lease. (The cancellation is not automatic, as the new owner can elect to accept the existing lease.) A tenant who is entering a lease that requires a great expenditure of labor and/or capital on the premises should consider obtaining the agreement of any prior trust deed beneficiary to recognize the lease in the event of foreclosure (**nondisturbance clause**).
- Failure to pay rent.
- Failure to give possession.
- Violation of any material condition of the lease.
- Use of the premises for an illegal or unauthorized purpose.
- Abandonment of the premises by the lessee.

- Surrender of the premises by the lessee (accepted by the lessor).
- The landlord's violation of the implied warranties of quiet enjoyment and habitability.
- The landlord's failure to make needed or agreed-on repairs.

In the absence of an agreement to the contrary the death of neither the lessor nor the lessee will terminate a lease.

■ RIGHTS AND RESPONSIBILITIES OF LANDLORDS

Right of Entry

In the absence of any agreement, the landlord can enter leased premises only when

- an emergency requires entry;
- the tenant consents to an entry;
- the entry is during normal business hours after reasonable notice (24 hours is considered reasonable) to make necessary or agreed repairs, alterations, or improvements or to show the premises to prospective or actual purchasers, mortgagees, tenants, workers, or contractors (Civil Code Section 1954);
- the tenant has abandoned or surrendered the premises; or
- the landlord has obtained a court order to enter.

The tenant cannot waive or modify his or her rights to privacy (Civil Code Section 1953).

Habitability

A residential lease has an implied warranty of **habitability.** The landlord must put a building intended for human habitation in a condition fit for occupancy and repair subsequent dilapidation. The landlord does not have this duty when the problem relates to a tenant's cleanliness, willful damage, or use in a manner other than intended. Under English common law the landlord had no responsibility for any repairs, and the tenant had a duty to make only minor repairs.

The landlord must ensure at least that

- the plumbing is in proper working order,
- the heat, lights, and wiring work and are safe,
- the floors, stairways, and railings are in good condition,
- when rented the premises are clean, with no pests,
- areas under lessor control will be maintained, and
- the roof does not leak and no doors or windows are broken.

The landlord is required to notify residential tenants in advance of pest control treatment, including repeat treatment.

A tenant cannot waive his or her rights under the landlord's implied warranty of habitability; however, the landlord and tenant can agree that the tenant will make the required repairs based on a rent reduction.

A landlord who demands or collects rent for an untenable dwelling as defined in Civil Code Section 1942.4 is liable for actual damages sustained by the tenant and special damages of not less than $100 or more than $1,000.

Landlords of substandard uninhabitable properties can be required to pay relocation costs for displaced tenants.

Civil Code Section 1174.2 provides that where a tenant prevails in an unlawful detainer action due to the landlord's breach of the warranty of habitability, the court will set the rent. The tenant must pay the rent set by the court within five days.

Case Study

In the case of *Hyatt v. Tedesco* (2002) 96 C.A.4th Supp. 62, a tenant raised the affirmative defense of breach of the warranty of habitability to an unlawful detainer action. The superior court appellate division in reversing the trial court held that the trial court is required to determine if a substantial breach has occurred. (Substantial breach is a failure of the landlord to comply with applicable building and housing standards, which materially affect health and safety.) If so, the trial court should reduce the rent to reflect the breach, give the tenant right to possession conditioned upon paying the reduced rent, order the rent reduced until repairs are made, and award costs and attorney fees to the tenant. The landlord can also be ordered to make the repairs.

Case Study

The case of *City and County of San Francisco v. Sainez* (2000) 77 C.A.4th 1302 involved landlords who failed to maintain their premises. Building inspection found no or inadequate heat; deterioration of walls, ceilings, and windows; lack of fire extinguishers; hazardous wiring; hazardous plumbing; lack of smoke detectors; etc. The superior court imposed fines of $767,000. The court of appeals ruled the fines were proper but reduced them to $663,000 because of a miscalculation. The

(continued on next page)

court of appeals ruled the fines were not excessive because the landlords owned at least 12 properties with net equity of $2,300,000. While the landlords had the ability to do so, they had refused to bring the building up to a safe standard.

Note: This case shows court frustration with landlords who refuse to correct serious health and safety problems.

Liability for Injuries

If a landlord is negligent and that negligence results in injury to another, the landlord is liable for those resulting injuries.

For a period of time, California courts were following a rule of strict liability, holding landlords liable for injuries to others, even when there was no negligence by the owner. The following case illustrates the present view as to landlord liability; now proof of negligence is required.

Case Study

The case of *Peterson v. Superior Court* (1995) 10 C.4th 1185 involved a hotel that was sued by a guest for an injury caused by a slippery bathtub. The court pointed out that because the innkeeper did not build the structure or its components, strict liability should not be imposed without proof of negligence. The court decided it was in error when it previously held landlords strictly liable in tort for personal injuries caused by defective components. The court pointed out that landlords still are liable under general tort principles for injuries caused by defects in their premises if the landlord is negligent.

Case Study

The case of *Penner v. Falk* (1984) 153 C.A.3d 858 indicated that punitive damages would be proper if the landlord knew of an existing dangerous condition and failed to correct it.

Commercial leases customarily require that tenants carry liability insurance coverage, which also protects the landlords from claims resulting from the condition of the premises.

A landlord who knows of a dangerous situation has, at the very least, a duty to warn a tenant.

See *Lundy v. California Realty* (1985) 170 C.A.3d 813.

Case Study

A child was bitten by a pit bull owned by a tenant in a neighboring property not owned by the plaintiff's landlord. In *Wylie v. Gresch* (1987) 191 C.A.3d 412, the parents sued the landlord because they had not been warned of the dog's dangerous propensities. The court held the landlord was not liable because the duty of disclosure applied to the landlord's own property but should not extend to the neighborhood.

A landlord, in some instances, could be liable for injuries occurring off the premises.

Case Study

The case of *Barnes v. Black* (1999) 71 C.A.4th 1473 involved a child who died from injuries received when his big wheel veered off the sidewalk to the play area, down a steep driveway, and into a busy street where he was hit by an automobile. The parents sued the apartment owners for negligence, premises liability, and negligent and intentional infliction of emotional distress.

Because the injury occurred in the street, not on the premises, the superior court granted summary judgment for the landlord.

Several residents had complained to the apartment manager, who informed the owner of dangers to children passing the steep driveway.

The court of appeal pointed out that the fact that the injury was on a public street was not controlling.

The scope of the landlord's duty of care related to the foreseeability of harm and the closeness of connection between the defendant's conduct and the injury. The court of appeal reversed.

Case Study

The case of *McDaniel v. Sunset Manor Co.* (1990) 220 C.A.3d 1 indicates any landlord who undertakes to protect a tenant can be liable if he or she does so negligently. The plaintiffs resided in a large, federally subsidized

(continued on next page)

complex having approximately 300 children. The defendant had constructed a wood fence 857 feet on one side and 400 feet on the other. Evidence was given that holes in the fence would develop, and sometimes a week would pass before a hole was repaired. The plaintiff's two-year-old child was found floating in the creek on the other side of the fence. She suffered brain damage and quadriplegia, having apparently crawled through a large hole in the fence. The court of appeal noted that simply because the injuries occurred on adjacent property did not automatically bar recovery. In constructing the fence, Sunset Manor Company affirmatively assumed a duty.

Note: This case sends a message to landlords that they shouldn't build a fence, because if they do so and the fence is not kept in good repair, they could be liable for injuries on adjacent property.

Case Study

The case of *Davis v. Gomez* (1989) 207 C.A.3d 1401 involved Ms. Townsend, a tenant in the defendant's building, who began to "deteriorate." Besides being observed talking to herself, she allegedly attempted to cast spells on other tenants. Other tenants alleged they had seen a gun in her apartment. Tenants complained to the manager about her behavior. Subsequently she shot and killed another tenant. The parents of the victim sued the landlord for damages.

The court held that the landlord had no duty to check Townsend's background before renting. The landlord was also not qualified to judge whether she was psychotic. If the landlord had evicted Townsend, the landlord might have been subject to liability. While her conduct was bizarre, it had not been violent. Townsend was more of a nuisance than a danger. A landlord's failure to eliminate a nuisance is not the same as a failure to prevent a serious criminal act. In this case it was not foreseeable that she would shoot another tenant.

Security

A landlord who represents a building to be secure or indicates it is protected by a security service or device and then fails to maintain security could subject the landlord to liability.

Failure of a landlord to take reasonable measures to correct a security problem after the landlord has become aware of the problem also could subject the landlord to liability. Civil Code 1941.3 requires that landlords install and maintain security devices in residential structures, which include deadbolt door locks, security or locking devices on windows and sliding doors, and specified locks on doors to common areas.

■ RIGHTS AND RESPONSIBILITIES OF TENANTS

Quiet Enjoyment

There is an **implied warranty** in a lease that the landlord will not interfere with the tenant's quiet enjoyment of the premises. Civil Code Section 1927 requires that the lessor secure **quiet enjoyment** of the lessee against all persons lawfully claiming the premises. A landlord who harasses a tenant by making unnecessary repairs or encourages other tenants to disturb the tenant has breached the tenant's right to quiet enjoyment.

Tenant Repairs

If, after a reasonable period of receiving written or oral notice, the landlord fails to make needed repairs, the tenant can make the repairs necessary to make the premises habitable, spending up to one month's rent. The tenant then can deduct the expenditures from rent payments. The tenant can use this remedy no more than twice during any 12-month period (Civil Code Section 1942). As an alternative, the tenant may consider the landlord's failure to make the premises habitable a breach of the lease and vacate the premises, relieved of all further lease obligations.

A tenant who acts to make repairs after the 30th day following a notice to repair is presumed to have acted after a reasonable notice. California courts have allowed another remedy: they will allow a tenant to remain in possession and pay a reduced rent, based on the reduction of usefulness of the premises, when the landlord fails to maintain a habitable dwelling [Hinson v. Delis (1972) 26 C.A.3d 62].

Case Study

In the case of *Schulman v. Vera* (1980) 108 C.A.3d 552, a commercial tenant raised as a defense in an unlawful detainer action that the owner had breached a covenant to repair. The court held that the tenant could not remain without paying rent. The court refused to extend the breach of an implied warranty of habitability as a defense available to commercial tenants.

Tenants, as well as homeowners subject to restrictive covenants, may not be prohibited from installing satellite dishes within the area of the homeowner's or tenant's control.

Case Study

The case of *Sachs v. Exxon Co.*, U.S.A. (1992) 9 C.A.4th 1491 involved refusal by the tenants to allow the landlord to conduct soil-contamination tests.

The landlord contended that leakage from tanks could damage the soil, for which the landlord could be liable under state and federal laws. The trial court determined in favor of the lessee but the decision was reversed by the court of appeal.

The lease required that the tenants comply with all laws and ordinances. The court pointed out that there is an implied covenant of good faith and fair dealing in the lease that provides a reasonable means for the landlord to get assurance of protection as to environmental hazards.

Duties of Tenants

The tenant's duties include

- paying rents and other charges as agreed;
- keeping the premises under control in a clean and sanitary manner and disposing of garbage and trash properly (unless the lessor by agreement has taken this responsibility);
- exercising reasonable care in the use of plumbing, electrical, and gas fixtures and appliances;
- not permitting others to damage or deface the premises and not doing so himself or herself;
- using the premises for the purpose for which they were intended to be used; and
- using the leased premises for a lawful purpose.

Case Study

The case of *Brown v. Green* (1994) 8 C.4th 812 involved a dispute between a landlord and a tenant as to responsibility for compliance with an order for asbestos abatement in a commercial building.

The trial court determined that the language of the lease required the tenant to remove and clean up the asbestos, and the Supreme Court affirmed. The 15-year lease was a net lease for an entire warehouse building. The tenants were sophisticated business partners with substantial experience in leasing commercial property. Prior to the execution of the lease, they were on written notice of a potential for asbestos contamination; however, they failed to conduct any investigation. The court pointed out that the

(continued on next page)

cost of the asbestos removal only amounted to five percent of the total rent due on the lease.

Note: The court's consideration of the term of the lease, cost of repair, and sophistication of the tenant leaves the impression that if the tenant were less sophisticated, the lease were for a shorter term, and the cost to comply was great, then a different decision might have been made.

■ THE EVICTION PROCESS

"Self-help" evictions such as removing doors, changing locks, seizing tenants' property, and engaging in extreme harassment could subject the landlord to damages as well as require the landlord to return the premises to the tenant (Code of Civil Procedure Section 1174).

Case Study

The case of *Camacho v. Shaefer* (1987) 193 C.A.3d 718 involved a self-help eviction action. The tenant had withheld rent because only one electrical outlet functioned, there were holes in the bathroom ceiling, there was no hot water or gas, and the apartment was infested with roaches and rats. The owner came to the apartment and removed the sofa, beds, table, and chairs. The tenant then obtained a restraining order against the landlord, but the landlord returned, forced the door open, breaking the chain, and removed the refrigerator. The court of appeal upheld compensation and punitive damages as well as attorney's fees totaling $32,600 for the defendant's failure to follow unlawful detainer procedures.

Evictions usually start with a **three-day notice** to quit, to quit or cure, or to quit or pay rent.

Notice to quit must be served in the following manner:

1. A copy of the notice must be delivered to the tenant personally.
2. If the tenant is absent, a copy must be left with a resident over the age of 18, and a copy must be sent through the mail to the tenant's place of residence.
3. If the tenant's place of residence or business cannot be found or if a person of suitable age or discretion cannot be found, a copy of the notice may be affixed in a conspicuous place on the property; a

copy should be given to a person residing on the property, if applicable; and a copy must be mailed to the property address by first-class mail. This process is informally called "nail and mail."

If the tenant does not quit, cure, or pay rent, the lessor may initiate an **unlawful detainer action** to evict the lessee. An unlawful detainer action can be used not only against a tenant who fails to pay rent or to perform conditions or covenants of the lease but also against a tenant at sufferance.

For an unlawful detainer action the landlord must allege that

- proper three-day notice was given and the tenant is still in possession, and
- rent is due or a condition of the lease has been breached.

The summons issued requires that the defendant (tenant) appear and answer the charges within five days after service.

If the tenant fails to respond within five days, a default hearing is set, and the court can issue a **writ of possession**. After service of the writ on the tenant, the tenant has five days to vacate, or the tenant can be evicted physically by the sheriff.

A tenant who does respond can appear and claim a defense such as a denial or that the landlord breached a condition or covenant, that the rent has been paid as agreed, that the tenant made an appropriate deduction from the rent, and so forth. The court then will decide on the facts and enter either a judgment for the landlord, entitling him or her to a writ of possession, or a finding for the tenant, in which case the eviction will fail.

If the tenant delivers possession prior to trial or before judgment, the unlawful detainer action can be allowed to continue as a civil claim for damages.

Because of drug-related crime in Los Angeles County, the legislature has authorized a pilot program allowing several city attorney and prosecutor offices to bring unlawful detainer actions to abate drug-related nuisances if the landlord does not act. The landlord will be charged fees and costs.

Because the landlord is an unsecured creditor of the tenant, the landlord has no lien against the personal property of the tenant for rent.

Inventory of property left on the premises must be taken and verified by an enforcing officer. A tenant's personal property remaining on the premises after they are restored must be stored by the owner for 30 days and may be reclaimed by the tenant during that period upon payment of reasonable storage costs.

Any property not redeemed by the tenant within 30 days may be sold at a public sale, and the proceeds may be used by the owner to pay the costs of storage and sale. Any balance remaining after payment must be returned to the tenant.

A landlord can sue on each rent installment as it becomes due. Usually, however, the landlord retakes possession through eviction proceedings and sues the tenant at the end of the term for damages in the amount of the difference between the lease rental and any lesser amount obtained by reletting.

A landlord has a duty to mitigate damages after retaking possession. The landlord must use reasonable efforts to rerent to keep the damages as low as possible.

Unlawful Detainer Assistants

A number of persons have gone into business offering assistance to persons being evicted. They would help tenants file questionable counterclaims and come up with, in some cases, defenses based on other than fact. Because of these abuses, Business and Professions Code 6400 et seq. requires that such assistants be registered and post a $25,000 bond. The advertisements of these assistants require disclosures, and if landlords or managers are awarded damages for acts of a registered assistant, they can recover their damages from the bond.

Retaliatory Eviction

A landlord cannot decrease services, increase rent, or evict within 180 days after a tenant exercises a protected right, including

- complaining to the landlord about the habitability of the premises,
- complaining to a public agency about defects, and
- lawfully organizing a tenant association.

A tenant cannot waive his or her rights of defending against such **retaliatory evictions**. If a landlord can be shown to have acted maliciously, the tenant will be entitled to from $100 to $1,000 in punitive damages.

Case Study

The case of *Vargas v. Municipal Court* (1978) 22 C.3d 902 concerned farm workers who received free housing as part of their compensation. The workers were fired for organizing a union and given notice to vacate their premises. The tenants raised the defense that their employment had been wrongfully terminated. The California Supreme Court held that, even though the employees had redress through labor legislation, wrongful discharge was a valid defense against eviction. The employees were not deprived of the defense of retaliatory eviction.

Constructive Eviction

An act of the lessor that is inconsistent with the quiet enjoyment of the lessee or the implied covenant of habitability can be treated by the lessee as being **constructive eviction**, that is, equivalent to eviction. The tenant may vacate and will be released of all further obligations under the lease. If a tenant fails to vacate within a reasonable period after a noncontinuous act by the lessor, the tenant may waive his or her rights to declare the act to be constructive eviction.

Examples of acts, or failure to act, that could constitute constructive eviction include

- failing to make required repairs,
- failing to maintain the premises in a habitable condition,
- making needless or unnecessary repairs that interfere with the tenant's peaceful possession,
- interfering with the tenant's access to the premises,
- harassing the tenant,
- leasing the premises to another party,
- wrongfully entering the premises by the landlord, and
- cutting off utilities to the tenant.

A landlord who cuts off utilities, removes doors, removes tenant property, or prevents access to the premises will be subject to a penalty of $100 per day but in no event less than $250 for each cause of action (Civil Code Section 789.3).

Case Study

The case of *Segalas v. Moriarty* (1989) 211 C.A.3d 1583 involved a landlord who sued for unpaid rent. The tenant cross-complained, alleging constructive eviction because remodeling in another part of the building had produced disruptive noise and inconvenience. The court held that a tenant who fails to vacate within a reasonable time after the breach waives the right to claim constructive eviction, with the exception of a tenant who commits to leasing other space before the breach is cured. In this case Moriarty did not commit for other space until three months after the remodeling was finished, so the court held that he had no valid claim for constructive eviction.

Surrender

A surrender terminates all further obligations under the lease. **Surrender** is the turning over of possession by the tenant with the understanding that all future obligations are canceled. A new lease is considered a surrender of the obligations of the old lease.

When a tenant moves out and the landlord retakes possession, the landlord should inform the tenant that he or she is still liable under the lease, that the landlord will attempt to rerent the premises to mitigate damages, and that taking possession is not an agreement to surrender of the premises.

■ MOBILE HOME TENANCIES

While the sale or lease of five or more lots in a mobile home park falls under the jurisdiction of the real estate commissioner under the Subdivided Lands Law, the rental of two or more lots in a mobile home park falls under the jurisdiction of the state Department of Housing and Community Development.

Mobile homes are not really mobile. Double-wide and triple-wide units generally are not intended to be moved after they are set in place. The addition of awnings, porches, and even permanent foundations makes removal extremely costly. Because of the special nature of mobile homes, the rights of landlords and tenants differ from those in other tenancy situations.

Tenants in mobile home parks are entitled to a 60-day notice to terminate. This 60-day notice also applies to rental increases and tenants who wish to terminate their leases.

Tenants in a mobile home park are entitled to a 12-month lease upon request at the prevailing month-to-month charge. A copy of the Mobile Home Residency Law must be attached to all rental agreements.

Park management must provide a written disclosure form that discloses any park defects in common facilities or utilities to lessees at least three days prior to signing the park's rental agreement.

Leases entered into after January 1, 2001, cannot prohibit a homeowner from keeping at least one pet subject to reasonable park rules.

A mobile home park can require that a single-wide mobile home 17 years old or older or a double-wide 20 years old or older be removed from the park when sold. Mobile homes built after September 1971 must be 25 years old or older to require removal upon sale. (Mobile home park management is limited in requirements as to exterior repairs upon a sale or transfer of a mobile home.)

Eviction

Tenants can be evicted from mobile home parks only under the following circumstances:

- A tenant who fails to comply with a local or state law within a reasonable time after being notified of his or her violation can be evicted.
- A tenant who fails to comply with reasonable park rules and regulations that were either in the rental agreement or agreed to later by the tenant can be evicted. If, however, the rules were established without tenant permission, the tenant is entitled to a six-month notice to terminate. To change park rules, other than for recreational facilities, the park owner first must give six months' notice. Any rule violation must be spelled out, and the tenant must be given seven days to comply prior to notice to terminate tenancy.
- When the tenant's use interferes with the quiet enjoyment of (causes substantial annoyance to) other tenants, the tenant can be evicted.
- A tenant who fails to pay rent or other reasonable charges can be evicted.
- A park owner can evict the tenant from a mobile home park with a 60-day notice if the tenant has received more than three 3-day notices. However, the legal owner as well as junior lienholders, have a 30-day window to cure (this applies to individual lienholders, not financial institutions or mobile home dealers).
- A tenant convicted of prostitution or of a felony controlled substance offense, if the offense was committed on the mobile home park premises, can be evicted.
- If the park is condemned, its tenants can be evicted.
- When the use of the park is changed by the owner, tenants can be evicted. For changes in park use the tenant is, however, entitled to 15 days' notice for appearances before local governing boards and 6 months' notice of termination after approval of the changes. If no local approvals are needed, the park owner must give tenants 12 months' notice.

Other Rules

The lessor cannot terminate a tenancy to accommodate other mobile homes sold by the park owners.

Mobile home parks cannot require a cleaning deposit or liability insurance from tenants for use of the clubhouse or recreational facilities for meetings of residents and invited guests.

If a tenant in a mobile home park has made timely payments of rent, utilities, and other charges for a period of 12 months, the security deposit must be returned to the tenant within 60 days of request.

Mobile home parks cannot unreasonably refuse to approve a new purchaser for lease assignment or a new lease. The park may reject a new purchaser who has financial ability only on the basis of prior tenancy problems or failure to obey park rules.

Parks may not charge a fee for the sale or transfer of a mobile home if no services are performed.

Mobile home parks cannot charge a move-in fee unless a service is rendered for the fee (Civil Code Section 798.72).

Mobile home parks cannot require that sale listings be given to the park management or prohibit outside agents from listing for sale a mobile home in a park (Civil Code Section 798.71).

Parks cannot charge any fee for a lessee's guests who stay for 14 days or less (annually, not consecutively).

Mobile home parks cannot require submission of an applicant's income tax returns; however, an applicant can be required to document gross monthly income (Civil Code Section 798.74).

Parks cannot charge extra for larger families or discriminate based on family size.

Tenants in mobile home parks cannot waive any of their rights under the law. Any tenant in a mobile home park is entitled to a 12-month lease on request. The park cannot charge more for the lease than is charged for a month-to-month tenancy.

Park owners cannot enter mobile homes without the written permission of the owner, except in emergency situations.

A park owner who enters into a listing agreement to sell the park must provide written notice to the residents' association not less than 30 days or more than one year before entering into the agreement or making an offer to sell.

Homeowners' groups must be permitted to hold meetings in recreation halls during reasonable hours.

■ CONDOMINIUM CONVERSIONS

For conversion of existing residential units to a condominium project, a community apartment project, or a stock cooperative, certain actions are required of the subdivider:

- ■ At least 60 days prior to the filing of a tentative map, written notification of this intention must be provided to the tenants.

- Tenants also must receive at least ten days' notice of application for a public report.
- Each tenant must be notified within ten days of approval of the final map for the proposed conversion.
- Each tenant must be given 180 days' written notice of intent to convert prior to termination of tenancy.
- Each of the tenants must be given at least 90 days' notice from the date of issuance of the public report of an exclusive right to purchase the unit the tenant occupies, on the same terms and conditions under which the unit initially will be offered to the public.

A subdivider who wishes to convert a mobile home park to another use must file a report about the impact of the conversion on the displaced residents of the mobile home park. The report must address the availability of adequate replacement space in mobile home parks. The subdivider must make a copy of the report available to each resident of the park at least 15 days prior to the hearing on the map by the advisory agency (planning commission).

■ RENT CONTROL

Rent control has been held to be a legitimate government purpose. The argument that rent control violates an owner's due process rights because tenants are in the majority and always will vote in favor of rent control was rejected by the court in *Birkenfield v. City of Berkeley* (1976) 17 C.3d 129. In the same case, a prohibition on evicting a tenant in good standing at the end of the lease unless the property is withdrawn from the rental market or the tenant refuses a new lease was considered a reasonable means to enforce rent control.

The Ellis Act, Government Code Section 7060.7, allows a landlord to go out of business and withdraw property from the rental market.

Case Study

The case of *Channing Properties v. City of Berkeley* (1993) 11 C.A.4th 88 involved a landlord who wanted to remove 33 apartments from the rental market. Berkeley's Municipal Code requires that (1) tenants be given 180-day notice to move, (2) the landlord pay $4,500 per unit for relocation costs, and (3) the city be notified at least 60 days prior to terminating the rentals. Section 7060 of the Government Code (the Ellis Act) requires only 60-day advance notice to tenants and requires relocation payments

(continued on next page)

only to low-income hotel residents. The court of appeal held that the Ellis Act preempts local action with respect to landlords who wish to withdraw accommodations from the rental market. The court noted that the Berkeley ordinance would create insurmountable obstacles for removal of rental units, and that was contrary to the intent of the Ellis Act, which allows rental removal regardless of local laws.

Because of fixed rents, landlords under rent control often reduce maintenance and defer repairs. In the case of *Sterling v. Santa Monica Rent Control Board* (1984) 162 C.A.3d 1021, the court held that the rent control board could reduce rents for Health and Safety Code violations.

Civil Code 1954.53 provides that landlords who are subject to rent control are free to establish new base rents for new tenants as well as for subleasees and assignees where the landlord's consent is necessary for the sublease or assignment.

Case Study

In *Gross v. Superior Court* (1985) 171 C.A.3d 265, a purchaser of a San Francisco condominium rented the units and subsequently defaulted on his trust deed. The beneficiary foreclosed and then filed an unlawful detainer action against the tenant. While the court conceded that a foreclosure wipes out junior liens, this is subject to modification by legislative action under police power. The court compared rent control to zoning. While the trust deed was given before rent control, the parties could not agree that future rent control would not apply. Nor could they agree that future zoning would not apply. The fact that the value of the premises for resale was diminished by having a tenant does not make the ordinance unconstitutional. The court held that a foreclosure purchaser should be regarded as a successor in interest.

Rent control can result in tenants getting the advantage of appreciation in value at the expense of the property owner.

Case Study

In *Yee v. City of Escondido* (1992) 112 S.Ct. 1522, the Supreme Court ruled unanimously that local rent control laws apply even when mobile home tenants sell their units. The Yees, represented by Robert Bork, cited *Hall v. City of Santa Barbara* (1987) 833 F.2d 1270, where Judge Kozinski

(continued on next page)

held that a similar ordinance constituted a taking of property by requiring the landlord to accept the tenant's transferee, thus increasing the value of mobile home lots for existing tenants and transferring wealth from landlords to tenants. The U.S. Supreme Court rejected this argument, pointing out that for decades the court has given government wide latitude in regulating business arrangements, from setting minimum wages to regulating apartment rents.

■ SUMMARY

Leasehold interests include

- ■ tenancies for years (leases for a definite period of time),
- ■ periodic tenancies (leases that automatically renew themselves unless a notice to terminate is given),
- ■ tenancies at will (tenancies at the pleasure of the lessor), and
- ■ tenancies at sufferance (tenancies in which the lessee holds over, which also are not true tenancies in California because the lessor can treat the holdover tenant as a trespasser).

Leases are personal property (chattels real). Leases for one year or less need not be in writing. For written leases the lessor must sign to be bound. The lessee can be bound without signing by moving in or paying rent after receiving a copy of the lease.

When a lease contains an option, part of the rent will be considered consideration for the option.

Nonrefundable security deposits are not allowed. The total security deposit cannot exceed three months' rent for furnished rentals or two months' for unfurnished units.

An assignment of a lease is a transfer of all interests by the lessee to a third party, who becomes a tenant of the original lessor. The assignee becomes primarily liable under the lease, while the assignor (original lessee) remains secondarily liable.

Under a sublease the original lessee becomes a sublessor and leases the premises to a sublessee. The sublessee is the tenant of the sublessor (original lessee) and not the tenant of the original lessor (owner).

A lease can be terminated by or for destruction of premises, eminent domain, commercial frustration, merger, bankruptcy of tenant, expiration of term, notice, foreclosure of a prior encumbrance, failure to pay rent, failure to give possession, violation of a material lease provision, illegal use of the premises, abandonment, surrender, violation of implied warranty, or failure to make needed or agreed-on repairs.

The landlord has the right of entry in an emergency, when the tenant consents, after reasonable notice to make repairs or show the premises, when the tenant has abandoned or surrendered the premises, and under court order.

A residential lease has an implied warranty of quiet enjoyment and habitability. As a minimum the landlord must ensure that

- plumbing is in proper working order,
- heat, lights, and wiring work and are safe,
- floors, stairways, and railings are in good condition,
- the premises are clean and free of pests when rented,
- areas under lessor control will be maintained, and
- the roof will not leak, and no doors or windows are broken.

Landlords are liable for injury to others because of the landlords' negligence. Landlords also have been held liable for injuries to the tenant because of the condition of the premises, even when the lessor was unaware of the problem. Exculpatory clauses in residential leases do not protect the landlord.

Tenant duties include

- paying rent and other charges as agreed,
- keeping the premises in a clean and sanitary condition,
- exercising reasonable care in the use,
- not permitting others to damage or deface the premises, and
- using the premises for the purpose intended.

If a tenant fails to pay rent or violates a lease condition, the lessor can give a three-day notice to quit, quit or cure, or quit or pay rent. If the tenant does not vacate, cure, or pay rent, the lessor serves an unlawful detainer action on the tenant. The tenant must appear and answer the charges within five days, or the court will issue a writ of possession that after service gives the tenant five days to vacate.

An eviction within 180 days of the tenant's complaining about habitability of the premises to the landlord or a public agency or lawfully organizing a tenant organization will be considered a retaliatory eviction. The tenant can defend against an eviction action by claiming that it is retaliatory.

An act of the lessor that is inconsistent with the quiet enjoyment of the lessee or the implied covenant of habitability can be treated by the tenant as being equivalent to eviction (constructive eviction).

Because of the immobility of mobile homes, tenants can be evicted only for limited reasons. Special notices of any change in the use of the park must be provided to tenants. Tenants are entitled to a 12-month lease upon request. Mobile home parks cannot unreasonably refuse to approve a new purchaser for lease assignment or a new lease.

Tenants in apartments being converted to condominiums must be given statutory notices. They also must be given a 90-day exclusive right to buy their unit at the price, terms, and conditions at which it initially will be offered to the public.

Rent control has been held by the courts to be a legitimate government purpose. Rent control also can control the right to evict or to change property use.

■ DISCUSSION CASES

1. A tenant complained to the police that the landlord had molested her minor daughter. The landlord later pleaded guilty to the charge. After the complaint was made, the landlord started eviction proceedings. The landlord claimed that the charge made it impossible to live together peacefully. **Was the landlord's action a retaliatory eviction?**

   Barela v. Superior Court (1981) 30 C.3d 244

2. An exculpatory clause in a miniwarehouse lease stated that the warehouse operators would be free from all liability for damage to the property stored and that it was the customer's obligation to obtain insurance coverage. **Does this clause protect the lessor from damage caused by the lessor's negligence?**

   Cregg v. Ministor Ventures (1983) 148 C.A.3d 110

3. A tenant defended an unlawful detainer action by claiming that the lessor breached the implied warranty of habitability. **Is this a valid defense? What is habitability?**

   Green v. Superior Court (1974) 10 C.3d 616

4. The plaintiff was raped in her apartment. It was alleged that the owners and manager of the apartment complex (the defendants) knew of three previous rapes in the complex. The defendants had been given a composite drawing as well as a description of the suspect by the police.

   The defendants did not disclose the information about the assaults to the plaintiff. It was alleged that the premises were represented as being safe and patrolled at all times by professional guards. The plaintiff alleged she was intentionally misled by the defendants to advance their own interests by renting the apartment. If the plaintiff's allegations are correct, are the defendants liable? **If they are liable, what is their liability?**

   O'Hara v. Western Seven Trees Corp. (1977) 75 C.A.3d 798

5. An owner had not raised rents on some units for 15 to 20 years. After she finally raised rents, a rent control ordinance rolled back the rents to a time when she was charging below-market rents. The owner filed for a rent increase and was denied. The owner filed for a writ of mandate challenging the base-year rent. **Is the owner subject to the base-year rent?**

   Vega v. City of West Hollywood (1990) 223 C.A.3d 1343

6. A lease provided for a renewal option at fair market rental value. The property was used as a movie theater. Appraisals indicated that at the highest and best use (retail stores) the property would have its highest rental value. **For renewal purposes, what should be the basis of the rent?**

   Wu v. Interstate Consol. Indus. (1991) 226 C.A.3d 1511

7. In leasing her condominium an owner told the tenant that the premises were safe and security precautions for tenants had been taken. The condominium association also represented the safety of the complex. After being assaulted, the tenant sued, claiming that security precautions had not been taken. **If the tenant was correct, are the owner and condominium association liable?**

   Olar v. Schroit (1984) 155 C.A.3d 861

8. A tenant leased garage space for the purpose of replacing a truck engine. While the defendant made a down payment on the rent and was given possession, the defendant failed to pay the balance. The owner went into the garage and found auto parts strewn about the garage. The owner contacted law enforcement authorities to

ascertain whether illegal activity was taking place. A government investigator found stolen truck parts. The garage was placed under surveillance, and the defendant was arrested when he returned several days later. **Did the landlord act properly?**

People v. Roman (1991) 227 C.A.3d 674

9. In checking a building prior to purchase a buyer found several rooms were locked. After purchase the buyer discovered these rooms were held by a lodge under an unrecorded ten-year lease that the purchaser had not been informed of. **Is the lease valid?**

Scheerer v. Cuddy (1890) 85 C. 270

10. A party injured in an auto accident claimed that a property owner was negligent in maintaining shrubs that obscured the view of motorists. The property had been rented for several years, and the lease required the tenant to maintain the landscaping. **If the tenant was negligent in failing to trim the shrubs, is the owner liable?**

Swanberg v. O'Mectin (1984) 157 C.A.3d 325

11. Prior to the Santa Monica rent control ordinance, which also limited removal of units from the rental market, a developer expended $1,700 for condominium conversion approval, and the final subdivision map was approved. **Is the developer subject to the rent control ordinance?**

Santa Monica Pines Ltd. v. Rent Control Board (1984) 35 C.3d 858

12. The defendants owned six cabins rented to 16 persons. The defendants deliberately failed to pay the gas bill, knowing the gas would be cut off and the renters would be forced to leave.

The trial court awarded the plaintiffs compensatory damages of $7,901 plus $6,000 per cabin ($100 per day for 60 days), or a total of $36,000 in penalties. **Was the trial court's action proper?**

Kinney v. Vaccari (1980) 27 C.3d 348

13. A lessor leased part of the premises that had been previously leased to another. The original tenant claimed partial eviction and stopped paying rent. **Was the tenant's action proper?**

Dussin Inv. Co. v. Bloxham (1979) 96 C.A.3d 308

14. The City of Berkeley passed a tax relief ordinance that required a one-year reduction on commercial leases of 80 percent of the property tax savings resulting from the passage of Proposition 13. A landlord alleged the ordinance was unconstitutional because it violated the contract clauses of the state and federal constitutions. **Was the ordinance proper?**

    Rue-Ell Enterprises Inc. v. City of Berkeley
    (1983) 147 C.A.3d 81

15. A tenant parked on the street because she was afraid to use her poorly lighted garage space. She was robbed and shot on the street outside her apartment. She sued the landlord alleging negligence for failure to install adequate garage lighting. **Should the landlord be held liable?**

    Rosenbaum v. Security Pacific Corp. (1996) 43 C.A.4th 1084

16. A housing-authority lease had a zero tolerance drug clause. During a lawful search, a tenant's son who lived on the premises was found to have 4 packets of narcotics on the premises. Even though the parents required their son to move out, the parents were evicted. **Was the eviction justified?**

    City of South San Francisco Housing Authority v. Guillory
    (1996) 41 C.A.4th 13

17. Islay Investments managed many apartment complexes. Instead of charging new tenants a security deposit, Islay charged a higher rent for the first month than for the following months. **Did Islay charge an illegal nonrefundable security deposit?**

    Granberry v. Islay Investments (1993) 18 C.A.4th 885

18. A commercial lessor conditioned consent to a lease assignment upon a $30,000 payment plus 75 percent of the profit from the sale of a business. **Was the requirement enforceable?**

    Ilkhchooyi v. Best (1995) 37 C.A.4th 395

19. A mobile home park imposed a new rule requiring occupancy of the registered owner of the mobile home. **Is this rule enforceable?**

    Rancho Santa Paula Mobile Home Park Ltd. v. Evans
    (1994) 26 C.A.4th 1139

20. A two-year-old child was injured after falling through a hall window in an apartment building. The window was 28 inches above the floor. While it had a screen, tenants would remove the screen to throw garbage into a dumpster. The lease stated, "Children are not allowed to play in hallways, stairways, or other common areas in the project." **Did the landlord have a duty to ensure that a child would not fall through the window?**

    Amos v. Alpha Property Management (1999) 73 C.A.4th 895

21. Tenants were 12 months behind in rent. A fire broke out in the garage and the tenants' personal property was destroyed. **If the fire was the result of the landlord's breach of warranty of habitability, should the landlord be responsible for the tenants' loss?**

    Fairchild v. Park (2001) 90 C.A.4th 919

The court decisions for these cases can be found on our Web site at **www.dearbornRE.com**. Click on the **"Instructor Resources"** link, then scroll down the page until you find the link titled "California Real Estate Law 5th Edition."

■ CHAPTER QUIZ

1. Which of the following estates is of definite duration?

    a. An estate at will
    b. An estate for years
    c. A freehold interest
    d. A periodic tenancy

2. A tenancy for years must be created by

    a. express agreement.
    b. adverse possession.
    c. written agreement.
    d. None of the above

3. Which of the following is the maximum term for which a home in a rural area may be leased?

    a. 51 years
    b. 99 years
    c. 100 years
    d. None of the above

4. A tenant who remains in possession after giving notice that she would vacate the premises becomes

    a. a tenant at will.
    b. a tenant at sufferance.
    c. an indefeasible tenant.
    d. None of the above

5. To be enforceable, a written lease must

   a. describe the premises.   c. Both a and b
   b. be signed by the lessor.   d. Neither a nor b

6. For a furnished apartment the total security deposit cannot exceed

   a. one-half month's rent.   c. two months' rent.
   b. one month's rent.   d. three months' rent.

7. The landlord must return the security deposit to the residential tenant within what time frame after regaining possession if there is no damage other than normal wear and tear?

   a. Seven days   c. Thirty days
   b. Three weeks   d. None of the above

8. Which of the following statements is true regarding the assignment of a lease?

   a. The original lessee is the sole party liable for the payment of rent.
   b. It is the same as a sublease.
   c. The original lessee would retain a right to use the property for a limited time.
   d. The entire leasehold is transferred.

9. A tenant on a long-term lease at $500 per month wishes to go out of business. The premises are currently worth $1,000 per month. You would likely advise the tenant to consider

   a. surrendering the premises.   c. assigning the lease.
   b. subleasing.   d. None of the above

10. An assignee of a lessee has a relationship to the lessor of

    a. sublessee.   c. grantor.
    b. tenant.   d. None of the above

11. A tenant on a long-term lease purchased the premises from the lessor. Later, to raise cash, he sold the property to an investor, who gave the tenant a 30-day notice to vacate. What are the rights of the parties?

    a. The lease preceded the sale; therefore, the tenant prevails.
    b. Occupancy was constructive notice to the investor of the lease.
    c. The purchase by the tenant ended the lease.
    d. Tenant rights were lost by accord and satisfaction.

12. In the absence of a lease provision, when would a landlord have the right of entry?

    a. During normal business hours after reasonable notice to show to a prospective buyer
    b. In the event of an emergency
    c. Either a or b
    d. Neither a nor b

13. A landlord must ensure all of the following *except* that the

    a. premises are air-conditioned.
    b. premises are clean and clear of pests at the time of rental.
    c. plumbing is in proper working order.
    d. roof does not leak and windows are not broken.

14. Under a residential rental the tenant must do all of the following *except*

    a. use the premises for a lawful purpose.
    b. keep the plumbing in proper working order.
    c. pay rent as agreed.
    d. keep the portion of the premises under the tenant's control clean and sanitary.

15. Which of the following accurately describes the liability of the landlord of a residential building?

    a. The landlord is liable for injury only if he or she knows of a dangerous situation and fails to act.
    b. The landlord is not liable for any injury to a tenant if the lease has an exculpatory clause.
    c. The landlord is liable only for risks that could be foreseen.
    d. The landlord is liable for injury caused by a dangerous condition if the landlord was negligent in acting or failed to act.

16. Strict liability of the landlord for dangerous conditions not known to the landlord

    a. applies to single-family homes.
    b. applies to one to four residential units.
    c. applies to nonresidential property.
    d. no longer applies.

17. When one residential tenant attacks another tenant, is the landlord liable?

    a. Yes, the landlord is strictly liable for the injury.
    b. Yes, if a check on the tenant's background would have shown aggressive behavior.
    c. Probably, if the attack was foreseeable.
    d. Yes, if the premises were represented as being safe.

18. A three-day notice to quit or pay rent could be used against a tenant who

    a. violated a lease provision.
    b. was delinquent in rent.
    c. used the premises for an illegal purpose.
    d. All of the above

19. After a landlord has served an unlawful detainer action, the tenant

    a. is given three days to quit or pay rent.
    b. has five days to answer the charges.
    c. must vacate within five days.
    d. must vacate within 30 days.

20. When a tenant abandons the premises with three years remaining on the lease, the landlord *cannot*

    a. sue for the balance due on the lease.
    b. consider the abandonment a surrender.
    c. rerent the premises.
    d. sue for the rent as it becomes due.

21. Which of the following would constitute constructive eviction?

    a. Expiration of a tenancy for years
    b. A notice to quit
    c. An unlawful detainer action
    d. The lessor's leasing the premises to a third party

22. A landlord cut off a tenant's electricity because the tenant was delinquent in rent. What would be the likely result of this action?

    a. The landlord could be subject to a $100-per-day penalty.
    b. The landlord could be subject to a $1,000 penalty.
    c. No penalty will be assessed if a proper three-day notice was served.
    d. There will be no penalty if there was a 24-hour notice of service cutoff.

23. When a lessor and lessee agree to terminate a lease three years prior to its termination, the lessee's turning over possession to the lessor is known as

    a. accord and satisfaction.
    b. surrender.
    c. reformation.
    d. novation.

24. A tenant of a mobile home park *cannot* be evicted because of

    a. failure to comply with a reasonable park rule.
    b. use that interferes with the quiet enjoyment of other tenants.
    c. forming a tenant organization.
    d. failure to comply with local or state laws.

25. In a condominium conversion of an apartment building the residents must be given an option to purchase their units for

    a. 90 days from issuance of the final public report.
    b. 30 days from the sale announcement.
    c. 180 days from public hearing.
    d. None of the above

GLOSSARY

THE LANGUAGE OF REAL ESTATE LAW

abatement An action to remove a nuisance.

abstract of judgment A statement from the court of the judgment. When recorded it becomes a general lien on all of the debtor's property in the county where recorded.

abstract of title A copy of all recorded documents dealing with a property. Attorneys give title opinions based on abstracts.

acceleration upon default All payments become due upon default of any payment. For trust deeds and mortgages in California the debtor still can cure the default prior to foreclosure or sale by getting payments caught up and paying the costs.

accord and satisfaction An agreement to accept a lesser consideration than bargained for based on disagreement over performance.

accretion The gradual buildup of land by natural causes (generally by action of water).

acknowledgment A statement made before a notary or court officer that the signing of a document was the signer's own free act.

actual notice Notice that has been expressly given and is known to a party.

ademption The revocation of a specific property grant in a will by disposing of said property prior to death.

administrative agency A government agency that makes rules and regulations to carry out the law.

Administrative Procedure Act A procedural act that must be complied with prior to revocation, suspension, or denial of a real estate license.

administrator A person appointed by the court to administer the estate of a deceased person.

advance costs Advance payments made to an agent to cover expected cash outlays in carrying out the agency.

advance fee A fee for rental information accepted in advance or a promotional fee for a sale listing.

advance fee addendum An agreement specifying activities for which the agent is to be compensated. It would include a provision for an advance payment of fees.

adverse possession A method to acquire title. It requires five-year, open, notorious, uninterrupted use under some claim of right and the payment of taxes.

aesthetic zoning Zoning for beauty. (It can require architectural styles and colors and regulate signs, etc.)

affirmation A formal declaration of the truthfulness of a statement, given in lieu of a verification.

affirmative covenant A covenant under which an owner is required to do something such as build within a stated period of time.

affirmative easement An easement that gives the dominant tenement owner the right to use the servient tenement.

after-acquired title Title or interest acquired by the grantor after property has been conveyed.

agency Legal relationship under which an agent represents another (a principal) in dealings with third parties.

agency by estoppel An agency created when a principal's conduct led another to believe in the existence of the agency and thereby to act to his or her detriment.

agency by ratification An agency created by a principal's approving an unauthorized act of another.

agency coupled with an interest An agency in which the agent has a financial interest in the subject matter of the agency.

agent One who represents another in an agency relationship.

Alquist-Priolo Special Studies Zone Act Provides for project approval in close proximity to earthquake faults as well as disclosures to buyers.

alteration A change made to a note or contract by one of the parties without the consent of the other.

amendment to the escrow instructions A change in the escrow instructions, which requires the agreement of both the buyer and the seller.

American Land Title Association (ALTA) The association that developed an extended-coverage policy of title insurance for lenders. (The same coverage is available to buyers.)

amortized note A note that will liquidate itself over its term in equal installments.

antimerger clause A clause in a mortgage or trust deed that the senior lienholder will retain lien priority in the event of a merger (title given to the senior lienholder).

appurtenance Something that belongs to and goes with property (examples are a structure and easement rights).

arbitration Nonjudicial process for resolution of disputes either by agreement or mandated by law.

Article 5 Part of the Business and Professions Code governing transactions in trust deeds and real property sales contracts.

Article 7 Part of the Business and Professions Code covering loan costs, commissions, and payment requirements relating to loan brokerage activity.

"as is" A phrase used in sale contracts by sellers as an attempt to limit liability for the condition of the premises (not generally valid when applied to latent defects known by the seller but not disclosed to the buyer).

assignment Transfer of all interest in a contract or lease.

assignment of lease The transfer of all rights under a lease by a lessee to a third party, who becomes a tenant of the lessor. The assignee is primarily liable under the lease, while the assignor has secondary liability.

assumable loan A loan that can be taken over (assumed) by a purchaser. Such a loan would not have a due-on-sale clause.

assuming a loan The buyer's agreeing to be primarily liable on the loan while the seller has secondary liability.

attachment A prejudgment lien that can be obtained to ensure the availability of property for execution after a judgment is obtained.

attorney-in-fact A person appointed as an agent under a power of attorney.

attractive nuisance doctrine An owner has a duty to reasonably protect children from injury when the premises are likely to attract children.

avulsion The sudden removal of land by action of water such as a river changing its course.

balloon payment A final payment that is more than twice the amount of the lowest payment.

bankruptcy Federal proceedings to declare a debtor bankrupt. The debtor is relieved of unsecured obligations (secured obligations when security is given up).

beneficiary Lender (or seller) in a trust deed loan situation.

bequest Personal property transferred by will.

bilateral contract A mutual exchange of promises; a promise given for a promise.

blanket encumbrance A mortgage or trust deed covering more than one property.

blind ad An advertisement that fails to reveal that the advertiser is an agent and not a principal.

blockbusting Inducing panic selling based on fear of the entry of persons of another race, color, religion, or ancestry into the area.

breach of contract Failure to comply with a material term or provision of a contract.

broker A licensed real estate agent who can deal directly with principals and employ licensed real estate salespersons.

broker's loan statement A disclosure statement given to borrowers by mortgage loan brokers that provides information on all costs, fees, and loan terms.

Bulk Sales Act An act that requires recording and publication of a sale not in the normal course of business.

bulk zoning Zoning for density with open-space requirements as well as setback, parking, and height restrictions.

bundle of rights All beneficial rights that go with ownership of real property.

burden of proof The party required to prove a fact when an issue is in dispute.

business opportunity A business including fixtures, stock in trade, and goodwill.

buyer listing An agreement whereby a buyer agrees to pay a commission if the broker locates a property the buyer purchases.

California Environmental Quality Act Law that allows local government to require environmental impact reports and allows private citizens to challenge a project if they feel proper procedures were not taken or a report is not complete.

California Housing Financial Discrimination Act of 1977 (Holden Act) California act prohibiting lender discrimination for any reason unrelated to the credit of the loan applicant.

carryback financing Financing where the seller is financing the buyer.

certificate of sale Certificate issued to purchaser at sheriff's sale. (The sheriff's deed is given at the expiration of the redemption period.)

cessation of work A period of 60 days without any work being conducted.

chattels Items of personal property.

chattels real A personal property interest in real property, such as a leasehold interest, trust deed, or mortgage.

civil law System of law codified by statutes.

Civil Rights Act of 1866 An act providing that every citizen shall have the same rights as white citizens to inherit, purchase, lease, sell, or hold real and personal property.

Civil Rights Act of 1968 Title VIII of this act is known as the federal Fair Housing Act. The act prohibits discrimination in housing with few exceptions.

clean hands doctrine A person who is in violation of an agreement will not be able to enforce compliance on another (applies to covenants, conditions, and restrictions).

closing The final performance of a real estate transaction where title is transferred and consideration is given.

Coastal Zone Conservation Act Law that requires a permit or an exemption to develop land within a coastal zone.

commercial frustration Performance that is not impossible but is impractical because of an unforeseen occurrence. The nonoccurrence of the act or event was considered an implied condition for the contract, which allows relief from the contractual obligations.

commingling Failure to properly separate property of the agent from property of the principal.

common law Law that has evolved based on precedent rather than statutes.

community apartment project An apartment building owned by the tenants in tenancy in common, with each owner having the right to occupy a unit.

community property Property acquired during marriage that is considered, as a matter of law, to be owned equally by the spouses.

ompensatory damages Monetary damages to reimburse an injured party for a sustained loss.

competent parties Parties having the legal and mental capacity to contract.

comprehensive zoning A broad plan of zoning over a large area.

concurrent estates More than one estate interest in a property at the same time (such as a leasehold estate in a fee simple ownership).

conditional public report An interim report that allows a subdivider to enter a binding contract prior to issuance of a public report.

conditional-use permit A change in the zoning granted for the best interest of the community, where the zoning contemplated the use based on approval.

condition subsequent A condition that, if it occurs, results in the reversion of an estate to another.

condominium Separate ownership of the airspace of a unit and common ownership of the land and common areas.

condominium conversion The conversion of a property (generally an apartment building) to condominiums.

consideration Value that is given for the promise of another.

constitutional law Law set forth in federal and state constitutions.

constructive eviction An act of the landlord that would be inconsistent with the quiet enjoyment of the tenant or the implied covenant of habitability. The tenant can treat the action of the landlord as being equivalent to eviction and may vacate the premises and be relieved of all future obligations.

constructive notice Notice imputed by law although not necessarily actually known (recording as well as possession by another provides constructive notice to a purchaser of other interests).

continuation statement A statement that, when filed, continues a financing statement for an additional five years.

contract An enforceable agreement.

contract of adhesion "take it or leave it" contract that takes unreasonable advantage of the party who did not prepare the instrument.

cooperating broker fee agreement An agreement between brokers as to the commission split should the cooperating broker sell a property listed by the listing broker.

corporation A separate legal entity established under state law. An artificial person.

corporation license A real estate license held by a broker in a corporate capacity as an officer of the corporation.

court of appeal (California) Primarily appellate jurisdiction from superior court.

court of appeals (federal) Appellate jurisdiction from the district courts.

covenants, conditions and restrictions (CC&Rs) Private restrictions created by grantors that run with the land.

cumulative zoning Zoning that allows more restrictive uses. For example, a lot zoned for a duplex would allow a single-family residence if the zoning were cumulative.

customary authority Authority implied by virtue of an agent's position.

declaration of homestead When recorded, this declaration provides the homeowner a statutory exemption from execution by unsecured creditors.

declaration of restrictions Declaration recorded by a subdivider and incorporated by reference in every deed.

declaratory relief action An action to have a court determine the rights of parties.

dedication The transfer of real property to a public entity without consideration.

deed The transfer instrument for real property.

deed in lieu of foreclosure A deed given by the debtor to his or her creditor to avoid foreclosure.

deed of reconveyance The deed from the trustee to the trustor that is given when the note is paid in full. It returns the title to the trustor.

defeasance clause A clause that cancels the lien on payment of the note.

defeasible estate An estate that can be defeated by some future happening (condition subsequent).

deficiency judgment A judgment given to a creditor when a foreclosure sale is for less than the amount owed (judgment is for deficiency amount).

delivery The actual transfer of an interest. Delivery requires the intent to make an irrevocable transfer.

demise A transfer of a leasehold interest.

Department of Real Estate Administers the California real estate law (part of the Business, Transportation and Housing Agency).

divisible contract A contract consisting of separate agreements that are not dependent on each other.

devise The transfer of real property by will.

district court Federal court of original jurisdiction.

division fence A fence on a boundary line.

domestic corporation A corporation organized in California under California law.

dominant tenement The estate having an easement right over land of another.

double taxation Corporate taxation whereby first corporate profits and then stockholders' dividends are taxed.

downzoning A change in zoning to a more restrictive use.

dual agency An agency situation in which the agent

represents more than one party to the transaction.

due care Reasonable (nonnegligent) care.

due-on-encumbrance clause A clause that makes the loan balance all due and payable should the owner put another encumbrance on the property.

due-on-sale clause (alienation clause) A clause that makes the entire loan balance due when the property is sold. A loan having a due-on-sale clause cannot be assumed.

duress Force or confinement that makes a contract voidable.

easement A right the owner of one property has to the land of another.

easement by eminent domain An easement that is taken for a public purpose under the power of eminent domain.

easement by estoppel An easement created when a person's words or actions led another to believe in the existence of the easement. If, in relying on those words or actions, the easement user acts to his or her detriment, the party will be estopped from denying the existence of the easement.

easement by necessity An easement that may be granted by the court when no other access to property exists and the easement is necessary for reasonable use of the property.

easement by prescription An easement obtained through five years' continuous, open, notorious, and hostile use of the property of another under a claim of right.

easement in gross An easement that is not appurtenant to land. It is personal in nature, and there is no dominant tenement.

Education, Research and Recovery Allocation A fund maintained by 20 percent of license fees; 12 percent of the fund goes into a Recovery Account, and 8 percent goes into the Education and Research Account.

elder abuse law Requires that realty agents and escrow holders report elder financial abuse, fraud, or undue influence.

emancipated minor A minor who is allowed to contract (in military service, declared emancipated by a court, married, or formerly married).

emblements The right of a tenant to harvest the annual crops that were the fruit of his or her labor. This right extends beyond the expiration of a lease.

eminent domain The power of the government to take private property for the public good. Consideration must be given for the property taken.

employee One who works under the direction and supervision of an employer.

enabling legislation Legislation that gives cities and counties the right to enact zoning.

encroachment An intrusion into, over, or under the land of another.

endangered species Federal legislation limiting development when it will have a negative effect on an endangered species.

Endangered Species Act (ESA) Federal act that can limit or prohibit development when a development adversely effects a species designated as endangered.

environmental impact report (EIR) A report that can be required under the California Environmental Quality Act when projects may have a significant effect on the environment.

environmental impact statement A statement required under the National Environmental Policy Act when a federal project will affect the environment significantly.

Equal Credit Opportunity Act A federal act prohibiting credit discrimination because of sex, marital status, age, race, religion, national origin, or because the credit applicant is receiving welfare.

equal dignities rule If an agency act must be in writing, the agency authority to perform the act also must be in writing.

escheat A reversion of property to the state when a person dies without a will or heirs.

escrow A neutral depository to carry out the closing function of a real estate transaction.

escrow instructions The instructions given to the escrow agent by the buyer and seller.

estate Any interest in property.

estoppel The legal doctrine that a person cannot raise a right or defense after their words or actions to the contrary led another party to act to their detriment.

ethics Morals. The golden rule is considered to be the test of whether an act is ethical.

eviction Removal of a tenant by action of law.

exception in a deed An exclusion of part of the property from a grant.

exclusionary zoning Zoning that excludes stated uses such as adult entertainment.

exclusive-agency listing A listing whereby the owner can sell the property personally without paying a commission, but if it is sold by any agent the listing agent is entitled to a commission.

exclusive authorization and right-to-sell listing A listing whereby the agent is entitled to a commission no matter who sells the property, including the owner.

exculpatory clause A clause in an agreement that purports to relieve a party of all obligation for his or her acts or failure to act.

executed contract A contract that has been fully performed.

execution The signing of an instrument.

executory contract A contract that has yet to be performed fully.

exemplary damages (punitive damages) Monetary damages to punish or make an example of a wrongdoer for willful, wrongful conduct.

express agency An agency agreement that is stated either verbally or in writing.

express authority The stated authority of an agent (written or verbal).

express contract A contract in which the terms have been stated either verbally or in writing.

extended-coverage policy of title insurance A policy

that includes coverage for rights of parties in possession and claims that a survey would have revealed, as well as other risks.

Fair Credit Reporting Act Provides consumer rights as to knowledge of and correction to credit reports.

Fair Housing Amendment Act of 1988 Extends the Civil Rights Act of 1968 to handicapped persons and families with children.

fee simple The highest possible degree of ownership in real property.

fictitious name A name that does not include the surname of every principal in an enterprise.

fictitious name statute Provides procedure for filing and advertising a fictitious name. When the statute is complied with, the firm can sue and defend a suit under the fictitious name.

fictitious trust deed A trust deed that is recorded for the sole purpose of being referenced in other trust deeds to incorporate its terms.

fiduciary duty The duty of trust and confidence.

final map Under the Subdivision Map Act the final map is recorded when local approval has been obtained.

financing statement A statement that when filed with the secretary of state, becomes a lien on personal property for five years.

finder's fee A fee paid to a nonlicensee for introducing a party.

fixture An item of personal property that has become so attached to realty as to become real property.

foreclosure Procedure to bar all rights of a debtor in property.

foreign corporation A corporation organized in a state other than California.

forfeiture Loss of a right as punishment for an act or nonperformance of an act.

four-by-fouring The illegal attempt to avoid the Subdivided Lands Law by breaking a parcel into four parcels and having the grantees again break each parcel into four parcels.

franchise The right to engage in a business under a common marketing plan.

Franchise Investment Law A disclosure law administered by the corporation commissioner to protect prospective purchasers of franchises.

fraud An act or omission for the purpose of deceiving another.

freehold estate A fee simple or a life estate.

fructus industriales Crops produced by labor and industry.

fructus naturales Products of the land produced by nature alone.

general agent An agent with broad powers for the purpose of conducting a business.

general lien A lien against all of the property of the debtor rather than specific property.

general partner A partner with management responsibility and unlimited liability.

general plan Every city and county is required to develop a general plan of comprehensive zoning for the area.

gift deed A deed given for love and affection.

good faith Conscientious and honest behavior.

good-faith improver An improver acting honestly under a mistake of fact or law who makes improvements to the land of another.

grandfather clause A provision that exempts present users from a requirement such as zoning and allows existing nonconforming uses.

grant deed The most common deed used in California to convey title. The grant deed warrants that the seller has not conveyed title previously and that the grantor knows of nothing against the property that has not been disclosed.

granting clause The words of conveyance in a deed.

grantor-grantee index The index of a county recorder that is kept by grantor and grantee names alphabetically.

habitability Reasonably fit for human habitation.

historical designation Buildings that have federal or state historical designations; could be limited as to alterations and/or removal.

hold harmless clause A clause that purports to relieve a person of liability for his or her actions.

holder Person having legal possession of a negotiable instrument.

holder in due course A purchaser of a negotiable instrument for value before its due date when the instrument appears proper on its face and the purchaser has no notice of any prior dishonor, defenses of the maker, or defects in title of the transferor.

holdover tenant A tenant who remains in possession after the end of a tenancy for years or after having given notice to vacate.

holographic will A will that is handwritten and signed by the testator.

homestead The residential property for which an owner has recorded a declaration of homestead.

homestead exemption The amount of homestead protection from unsecured creditors. It is $50,000 for single persons, $75,000 for family units, and $100,000 for persons over 65 years of age and persons with physical or mental disabilities unable to work.

hypothecate To use property as security for a loan without giving up possession.

illusory contract An apparent contract that is no contract at all because the parties have not agreed to be bound.

implied agency An agency created by the conduct of the parties rather than express agreement.

implied authority Understood (not express) authority that is reasonably necessary to carry out the agency.

implied contract A contract not expressly agreed to but understood by the parties.

implied dedication An implied donation of the property to the government that could result from allowing open government use of private property for five years.

implied easement An easement intended but not expressly provided for.

implied warranty Warranty understood but not stated. For residential leases the implied warranties are of quiet possession and habitability.

impossibility of performance When required performance is impossible, the contract will be considered void.

impound account An account kept by a lender for taxes and insurance (included in borrower's payments).

incentive zoning Zoning that offers an incentive to developers, such as allowing retail stores on the street level in an area zoned for offices.

independent contractor A contractor employed for the completion of a task who is not under the supervision or control of his or her employer.

injunction A court order to desist from some activity.

installment note A note that is paid off according to an installment payment schedule.

interim occupancy agreement An agreement that allows the buyer to take possession as a tenant prior to the close of escrow.

intermediate theory (mortgage) A mortgage in which the title remains with the mortgagor but automatically transfers to the mortgagee in the event the mortgagor defaults.

interpleader action An action brought by a third party (escrow or broker) when two or more parties claim property or money held by the third party. The action forces the parties to litigate their rights.

Interstate Land Sales Full Disclosure Act A disclosure act for subdivisions of 25 or more unimproved residential lots offered for sale in interstate commerce.

intestate succession The succession of property to the heirs when the deceased died without a will.

inverse condemnation An owner's forcing a governmental unit to take property by eminent domain when the government's actions resulted in the owner's inability to use the property.

involuntary liens Liens placed against property by creditors, such as judgments, as opposed to those voluntarily placed against the property by owners.

joint tenancy Undivided ownership by two or more persons with the right of survivorship.

joint venture A partnership for one particular venture rather than a continuing business.

judgment lien A general lien against all property of the debtor in the county where the abstract of judgment is recorded.

junior lien A lien recorded later in time than another lien (senior lien).

laches Loss of rights because the delay in enforcing them now makes enforcement inequitable.

land projects California unimproved subdivisions of 50 or more parcels in sparsely populated areas, which are subject to state regulations; purchasers have a 14-day rescission period. (Repealed)

late charge A lender charge for a late payment.

latent defect Defects that are not apparent by visually checking the property.

lateral support Right of a property owner to have his or her property supported by the adjacent properties.

law Enforceable rules that govern conduct.

lease A tenancy agreement between a landlord (lessor) and a tenant (lessee).

leasehold A lease estate in realty.

lease option A lease whereby the lessee has an option to purchase (or extend the lease).

legacy Money that is transferred by will.

legal capacity Being of legal age.

license A revocable privilege to use the land of another.

lien An encumbrance against real property that can be foreclosed.

lien theory (mortgage) The theory in California that a mortgage conveys lien rights and not title to the mortgagee.

life estate An estate conveyed for the life span of a particular person.

limited liability Liability limited to the extent of a person's investment.

limited partnership A partnership having partners who are not active and whose liability is limited to the extent of their investment (limited partners).

Limited Partnership Act That part of the corporation code that provides for limited partnerships.

liquidated damages Damages agreed to, prior to a contractual breach, as the remedy in the event of a default.

lis pendens A notice of a pending lawsuit in which an interest in real property is involved.

littoral rights Rights of a landowner to reasonable use of water from lakes, seas, or oceans (nonflowing water) bordering his or her property.

livery of seisin Early English ceremony of transfer of title by delivery of a symbol of title such as a key or clod of earth.

loan broker (mortgage loan broker) A broker who solicits borrowers and investors for loans secured by real estate.

loan broker listing A loan broker's contract with a buyer to obtain a loan.

lockbox authorization An owner's authorization that allows the broker to install a lockbox. It includes a warning of danger and recommends that valuables be removed and insurance coverage be considered.

lock-in clause A loan prohibiting prepayment so that the borrower is locked in to all of the interest should he or she wish to repay.

marketable title A defensible title that a reasonably prudent purchaser would accept.

master lease The original lease between the lessor and lessee when the lessee subleases the premises.

maxims of jurisprudence Rules of common law that have been codified into the California Civil Code.

mechanics' liens Statutory liens by improvers of property for labor, material, and equipment.

mediation A nonjudicial process for resolving disputes in which the third-party mediator works with the parties to reach an agreement.

Megan's Law A law requiring public availability of location of sex offenders.

menace The threat of confinement of a person, detention of property, or injury to a person or property. Menace makes a contract voidable at the option of the injured party.

mental capacity Being of sound mind.

merger The joining of a lesser right with a greater right so that the lesser right is lost. When a dominant tenement owner purchases the servient tenement, the easement is lost by merger. An owner would not have an easement over his or her own land.

mineral lease Lease of the right to extract minerals for the lease period (also oil and gas leases).

mineral, oil, and gas broker A broker authorized to engage in transactions involving mineral, oil, and gas rights; options; leases; exchanges; and properties.

mineral, oil, and gas (MOG) permit A permit formerly issued to a broker who did not have a mineral, oil and gas license to engage in a mineral, oil, and gas transaction.

misrepresentation A false statement to induce another to act. Unlike fraud, misrepresentation does not require intent. It makes a contract voidable at the option of the injured party.

mobile home A factory-built housing unit that is transported on its own chassis.

mortgage A two-party instrument that creates a lien on real estate. The mortgagor (the borrower) gives a lien to the mortgagee (the lender).

mortgagee The lender under a mortgage.

mortgagor The borrower under a mortgage. The mortgagor gives the lien to the mortgagee.

municipal court (California) Court of original jurisdiction limited to matters involving $25,000 or less. (Being phased out)

mutual consent The meeting of the minds required for a binding contract.

mutual mistake A mistake by both parties to an agreement. A mutual mistake as to fact allows a mistaken party to void the contract.

National Environmental Policy Act This act requires an environmental impact statement on federal projects that could significantly affect the environment.

natural monument A point or boundary in a metes-and-bounds description that is natural, such as a rock, tree, or river, as opposed to an artificial monument, such as a road, iron stake, wall, etc.

navigable Waters capable of being used for commerce.

negative covenants Promises not to do something, such as a prohibition against any detached garages or sheds.

negative declaration A declaration by the developer that a project will not have an adverse effect on the environment.

negative easement An easement that prohibits the servient tenement owner from a use. An example would be a building height restriction so the dominant tenement owner retains a view.

negotiable instrument A written, signed, unconditional promise or order to pay to bearer or a payee a sum certain in money now or at a definite time in the future.

net listing A listing whereby the agent receives all money received over a net price as his or her commission.

no deal–no commission A listing requiring that escrow actually be closed and title transferred before the agent is entitled to a commission.

nominal damages Damages awarded in a token dollar amount for a wrongful act where no actual loss occurred.

nonconforming use An existing use that is not in conformance with the zoning.

noncumulative zoning Zoning that allows only the stated use and not more restrictive uses as well.

nondisturbance clause An agreement where the mortgagee agrees to honor the tenant's lease in the event that the prior mortgage (trust deed) is foreclosed.

nonfreehold estate A less-than-freehold interest; a leasehold estate.

nonresident licensee A licensee who is a resident of a state other than California.

notice of cessation A notice that, when recorded, gives subcontractors 30 days to file their liens and the prime contractor 60 days.

notice of completion A notice that, when recorded, gives subcontractors 30 days to file their liens and the prime contractor 60 days.

notice of default Notice given to interested parties of the default of the trustor.

notice of nonresponsibility A notice by an owner, or a vendor under a real property sales contract, that the owner will not be liable for work on the property authorized by a tenant or vendee under a real property sales contract. The notice must be recorded and posted in a timely manner to protect the property from mechanics' liens.

novation A substitution of a party to a contract or the substitution of one agreement for another.

nuisance An act that disturbs the use or enjoyment of the property of another.

obligatory advances Advances that the lender is obligated to make to the borrower; e.g., progress payments on a construction loan.

open listing A nonexclusive-right-to-sell listing.

opinion of title An opinion of the marketability of a title given by an attorney based on the abstract of title.

option An irrevocable right given to one party to bind another party to an agreement if the party wishes to do so.

optional advances Advances on a loan that the lender is not obligated to make.

option listing A listing combined with an option of the agent to purchase the property.

order paper A negotiable instrument payable to the order of a named party.

ostensible agency An agency created by implication when the principal intentionally, or by want of ordinary care, causes a third person to believe another person is the agent of the principal, although no actual agency exists.

parol evidence rule The general rule that verbal evidence cannot be used to modify a clearly written contract.

partial zoning Zoning that does not take into consideration its effect on other areas.

partition action A legal action to break up a joint ownership.

partnership Two or more persons associated to carry on a business and to share in the profits.

party wall A wall established by agreement for the common benefit of adjacent owners.

patent Original conveyance of land from the government.

patent defect A defect that would be obvious from a reasonable inspection of the property.

per stirpes Inheritance by right of representation. Children share equally in the share their deceased parent would have taken.

periodic tenancy A leasehold interest from period to period that automatically renews itself unless a notice to terminate is given.

permanent trespass A continuing trespass such as an encroachment.

personal defenses Defenses the maker of an instrument would have against the payee.

personal property Chattels.

planned unit development (PUD) Ownership of the individual unit and land under it by the unit owner plus common areas owned in common with others.

police power The power of the government to regulate use for health, safety, morals, and general welfare.

power of attorney A written agency agreement whereby a principal appoints an attorney-in-fact as an agent.

Preemption Act A federal act that gave purchase preference to occupants of land.

preliminary notice A notice must be given by a lien claimant that the work is subject to a mechanic's lien if a lien is to be obtained. The notice covers work subsequent to the notice and up to 20 days prior to the notice.

preliminary public report Under the Subdivided Lands Law the preliminary public report can be issued prior to the public report. The preliminary public report allows the subdivider to take reservations but not to sell parcels.

preliminary title report A report of the condition of title given by a title insurer prior to issuance of a title policy. The preliminary title report does not provide any insurance of title.

prepayment penalty Payment penalty for paying an obligation before it is due.

presumption A legal inference, which can be overcome by evidence to the contrary.

principal The employer of an agent for whom the agent acts.

private easement An easement given to specific property or persons.

private nuisance A nuisance that is limited in scope. A private nuisance does not affect the entire community or neighborhood.

privity of contract The relationship between contracting parties.

probate The legal procedure to carry out the wishes of the deceased and pay his or her debts.

procuring cause That cause that initiated an uninterrupted chain of events that led to a sale.

promissory note A two-party instrument whereby a maker unconditionally promises to pay a payee a certain sum of money now or at a definite time in the future.

promotional note A subordinate promissory note on real estate for a term of three years or less issued to finance improvements prior to the first sale (subdivision).

publication period The 20-day period prior to a trustee's sale during which the notice of the sale is published.

public easement An easement given to the general public.

public nuisance A use that disturbs the use and enjoyment of an entire neighborhood or community.

public report A disclosure statement required under the Subdivided Lands Law. A purchaser is not obligated until he or she has read the report and signed a receipt.

puffing Statements of opinion (not fact) made to induce a party to contract.

qualified endorsement An endorsement on a note "without recourse." The endorser will not be liable if the maker dishonors the note.

quasi contract A contract implied by law, as a matter of equity, when no actual contractual agreement took place.

quiet enjoyment An implied warranty that the landlord will not interfere with the tenant's reasonable use and enjoyment of the premises.

quiet title Legal action to determine ownership or rights in real property.

quitclaim deed A deed that conveys whatever interest the grantor has without claiming any specific interest.

race of the diligent Recording priority based on date and time of recording.

ratification Approval of an agreement to which the approving party was not legally bound. By ratification the party agrees to be bound by the agreement.

real defenses Defenses that could be raised against a holder in due course.

Real Estate Advisory Commission An advisory group consisting of six brokers and four public members that advises the real estate commissioner.

real estate commissioner The executive officer of the Department of Real Estate, who is appointed by the governor.

real estate investment trust (REIT) A trust organized under federal law having at least 100 investors. Ownership interest is in the form of certificates or shares that are freely transferable.

Real Estate Settlement Procedures Act (RESPA) A federal loan disclosure act applicable to federally related first mortgages and trust deeds.

real property Land and those appurtenances that go with the land.

real property sales contract (land contract) A contract whereby the seller retains title and the buyer is given possession.

real property securities Securities with guaranteed yields, promotional notes, and designated by Article 6 of the real estate law to be real property securities. (Repealed)

real property securities dealer A broker whose license has been endorsed to sell real property securities.

real property securities dealer statement A disclosure statement issued to purchasers of real property securities.

Realtist A member of the National Association of Real Estate Brokers (NAREB).

REALTOR® A member of the National Association of REALTORS® (NAR).

rebate law Law that prohibits escrows and title insurers from giving rebates or favorable treatment as consideration for the referral of business.

recording Making an interest public knowledge by recording the interest with a county recorder. Recording provides constructive notice of the interest.

redlining Refusal to loan (or insure) within an area.

reformation action To reform a contract to read as it was intended to read.

relation-back doctrine The doctrine that a buyer's rights relate back to the delivery of the deed into escrow regarding intervening liens of a party who had knowledge or notice of the escrow.

reliction Rights of property owners bordering on lakes or seas to the land increase when the water recedes.

remainder interest An interest that goes to other than the original grantor upon some event, generally the death of a life tenant.

rent control Ordinances that limit the rent a lessor can charge for premises, as well as other lessor rights.

rent skimming Collecting rent and not using it to make mortgage payments or collecting rent on property not owned or controlled by the renter.

request for notification of default A recorded request by a junior lienholder to be informed if the trustor is given a notice of default.

rescission Setting a contract aside and returning the consideration given.

reservation in a deed The retention of a right, such as an easement, in the grantor.

respondeat superior The doctrine that the master is liable for the acts of his or her servants (applies to agency and employment relationships).

restraint against alienation A restriction on the power to convey property.

restricted license Probationary real estate license granted after a license was revoked, suspended or denied.

retaliatory eviction An eviction because of a tenant's complaints to the landlord or a public agency about defects or for lawfully organizing a tenant association. A landlord cannot decrease services, increase rent, or evict within 180 days of a tenant's exercising any of these rights.

reversionary interest An interest that returns to the grantor or his or her heirs upon some event, such as the death of a life tenant.

rezoning A change in the zoning.

right of correlative user The right of a landowner to the reasonable use of the underground percolating water.

right of first refusal The right given to a party to meet the price and terms of a third party if the owner decides to sell.

right of prior appropriation A concept in California and other states that the first user of riparian water obtains priority over later users.

right of redemption The redemption right of the mortgagor after a foreclosure sale.

riparian rights Right of a landowner to water flowing through, under, or adjacent to his or her property.

rule against perpetuities The rule that an estate must vest in an owner within the life of a person in being plus 21 years and a gestation period.

Rumford Act California's fair housing law.

safety clause A clause in a listing that provides that, should the seller sell to a person the agent negotiated with within a set period of time after the listing expires, and whose name the agent submitted to the owner in writing prior to expiration, the broker shall be entitled to the sale commission.

salesperson A real estate licensee who must be employed by a licensed broker.

satisfaction of mortgage Instrument given by the mortgagee to the mortgagor that releases the mortgage lien when recorded.

S corporation A small corporation whose earnings are taxed as a partnership rather than as a corporation.

secret profit A profit of the agent that was not fully disclosed to the principal.

security agreement An instrument that creates a security interest in personal property.

security deposit A deposit for the last month's rent or to secure against tenant damage that must be refundable.

self-help eviction A nonlegal act by the lessor to force the tenant to vacate.

send-out slip An agreement that if a property is disclosed, the prospective buyer will negotiate for it only through the broker who made the disclosure.

separate property Property owned by a spouse in severalty rather than jointly with the other spouse.

servient tenement The land being used by another under an easement.

severalty Ownership in severalty is ownership by one individual or corporation alone.

severance damage Damage to the remainder of the property resulting from the taking of a portion by eminent domain.

sexual harassment Offensive, sexually, related actions or language that could constitute a tort and/or discriminatory act.

sheriff's deed A deed given after a sheriff's sale.

simultaneous death When parties die in the same accident and it is unclear which one died first, they are presumed to have died at the same time. Therefore each estate will be probated as if that person had survived the other.

small claims court (California) A division of the municipal court. Jurisdiction is limited to $5,000 or less.

Solar Shade Act An act providing an easement of light after a person has installed a solar collector.

Soldiers and Sailors Civil Relief Act An act that prohibits foreclosures while a person is in military service and within three months thereafter except by court order.

special agent An agent whose authority is limited to specified duties.

special assessments Tax assessments for improvements such as streets and sewers. Liens for special assessments are priority liens.

special endorsement An endorsement on a negotiable instrument to a named party.

specific lien A lien against particular property only, such as a trust deed, mechanic's lien, or tax lien.

specific performance Requiring a person to perform as he or she agreed to perform.

spite fence A fence over ten feet in height maliciously erected or maintained to annoy a neighbor; considered a nuisance.

spot zoning Zoning of parcels not in conformance with the general area zoning.

standard policy of title insurance A policy of title insurance that covers matters of record not specifically excluded, as well as forgery, lack of capacity of a grantor, undisclosed spousal interests, failure of delivery, federal estate tax liens, corporation deeds when a charter has expired, and deeds of agents whose capacity has ended.

stare decisis The principle that previous decisions should be used to determine present rights and obligations.

statute of frauds The requirement that certain agreements must be in writing to be enforceable (adopted from the common law).

statute of limitations The period in which legal action must be started or the right to bring action is lost.

statutory law Law that is based on enacted statutes rather than precedent; civil law.

steering Directing prospective buyers to areas based on race, religion, national origin, etc.

stock cooperative Corporate ownership of real property with each shareholder entitled to occupancy of a unit under a lease.

stop notice A notice to a lender that a mechanic has not been paid. Unless a bond is posted, the lender must withhold monies due to the prime contractor.

straight note A note whereby interest only is paid and the entire balance is due on the due date.

strict foreclosure Common law foreclosure whereby the mortgagee receives the property without a sale upon the mortgagor's default.

strict liability Liable for injury occurring without regard to negligence or fault.

subagent Agent appointed by an agent. Subagents have agency duties to the principal.

Subdivided Lands Law A disclosure law to protect purchasers of subdivided parcels. A public report is required for subdivisions of five or more parcels.

Subdivision Map Act An act providing local control of the physical aspects of land divisions.

subjacent support Support from below that an excavator must provide.

subject to Purchasing a property without agreeing to pay encumbrances. If there is a default, no deficiency judgment is possible.

sublease A lease given by the original lessee (sublessor) to a sublessee. The sublessee is the tenant of the sublessor and not the original lessor.

subordination clause A clause that makes a mortgage or trust deed secondary to a later recorded mortgage or trust deed.

subrogation Substitution of one person's rights for another's. When an insurer pays a claim of the insured, the insurer can sue the party who caused the damage. The insurer has the insured's rights by subrogation.

substantial performance Inadvertent, minor variance from the required performance.

successive estates states established to succeed other estates, such as a remainder estate to follow a life estate.

superior court (California) Court of original jurisdiction for matters over $25,000 as well as appellate jurisdiction from the municipal court.

supreme court (California) Appellate jurisdiction over all California courts.

Supreme Court (U.S.) Discretionary appellate jurisdiction from federal courts as well as state courts if a federal issue is involved.

surrender The giving up of leasehold rights by a tenant in exchange for being released from future obligations under the lease.

survivorship Right of the surviving joint tenant(s) to the interests of another joint tenant upon the latter's death.

syndicate A limited partnership.

tacking on Allowing successors in interest to add on their adverse use in obtaining the five years necessary for an easement by prescription or title by adverse possession.

tax deed A deed given at a tax sale.

tax lien A lien for property taxes is a specific priority lien against the property assessed. Liens for state and federal income tax are general liens against the property of the taxpayer.

tenancy at sufferance The tenancy of a holdover tenant. The lessor can treat such a tenant as a trespasser.

tenancy at will A tenancy at the pleasure of the lessor.

tenancy for years A tenancy for a definite period of time. The tenancy does not renew automatically, and the tenant must give up possession at the end of the lease unless an extension to the lease or a new lease is agreed on.

tenancy in common Undivided interest in property without the right of survivorship.

tender An offer of money or full performance of an agreement without any conditions.

tentative map Initial map filed by a subdivider under the Subdivision Map Act. When all approvals and changes are made, the final map is recorded.

termination statement A statement that, when filed, releases the lien of the financing statement.

testator A person who died having a will.

30-day notice A notice to vacate under a periodic tenancy. Notice must be for the length of the rent-paying period but need not be for more than 30 days.

three-day notice A notice to quit, quit or pay rent, or quit or cure that must be given prior to an unlawful detainer action.

tidelands Land between ordinary high and low tides.

time is of the essence A statement in a contract that requires performance within the stated time period if the other party is to be bound by the agreement.

time-share Fractionalized ownership whereby each owner has exclusive right of occupancy for an agreed-on period of time.

title insurance A policy that insures the marketability of title. The insurance contract indemnifies the insured against losses not excluded by the policy, up to the policy amount.

title theory (mortgage) The theory in some states that a mortgage transfers title to the mortgagee as security for the loan.

trade fixture A fixture installed by a tenant for the purpose of conducting a business or trade. The trade fixture remains personal property and can be removed by the tenant.

transfer disclosure statement Requires seller disclosures for residential sales.

Treaty of Guadalupe Hidalgo Treaty ending the Mexican War whereby the United States agreed to honor property rights of Mexican citizens, which included the community property concept.

trespass Unlawful entry of or injury to the property of another.

trust deed A three-party security transaction in which the trustor (borrower) gives a note to the beneficiary (lender) and a title (trust deed) to a trustee as security for the note.

trustee The third party holding naked legal title for security purposes under a trust deed.

trustee sale Sale by the trustee when the trustor defaults. A trustee's deed is given to the purchaser.

trustor The buyer or borrower under a trust deed.

Truth-in-Lending Act A disclosure law to let borrowers know what they are paying for credit. It provides a right of rescission when credit is secured by a borrower's residence.

undue influence Improper influence so that a person really is not acting under his or her own free will. Such influence makes a contract voidable.

uniform laws Laws drafted by the National Conference of Commissioners on Uniform State Laws to provide uniformity for commercial purposes.

unilateral contract An offer that is accepted through performance rather than a mutual promise.

unilateral mistake A mistake by only one party to a contract. It does not void the agreement.

unincorporated association Nonprofit association.

unlawful detainer action A legal eviction action. The tenant must appear and answer charges within five days of service.

Unruh Civil Rights Act The act that prohibits businesses from discriminating.

usury An illegally high rate of interest.

valid Good and enforceable.

variance A special exception to the zoning generally granted to avoid hardship.

vendee Buyer on a real property purchase contract.

vendor Seller on a real property purchase contract.

verification Swearing under oath as to the truthfulness of a statement.

voidable contract A contract whereby one party only can declare the contract void.

void contract A contract that has no effect.

waiver Voluntary relinquishment of a right. A person can waive rights that are for his or her sole benefit. Failure to insist on proper performance could be a waiver of the right to the required performance.

warranty deed A deed in which the grantor warrants good title.

waste Unreasonable and destructive use of property.

will A testamentary instrument.

wraparound loan A loan written for the amount of an existing loan as well as an additional amount usually used by sellers to take advantage of a low interest existing loan.

wraparound trust deed (all-inclusive deed of trust) A trust deed written for the amount of the existing encumbrances plus the seller's equity.

writ of execution A court writ directing the sheriff to seize and sell property of a debtor to satisfy the claim of the judgment creditor.

writ of possession A court order for the tenant to vacate.

zoning Public control of land use enacted under police power for the health, safety, morals, and general welfare of the community.

INDEX OF CASES*

*Cross–Indexed Plaintiff-Defendant

564 acres of land, *See* U.S. v. 564 acres of land

6 Angels, Inc. v. Stuart-Wright Mortgage, Inc. (2001) 85 C.A.4th 1279 **346**

967.905 acres of land, *See* U.S. v. 967.905 acres of land

1333 N CA. Blvd., *See* Nippon Credit Bank v. 1333 N. CA Blvd.

A

Aas v. Superior Court (2000) 24 C.4th 627 **419**

Ach v. Finkelstein (1968) 264 C.A.2d 667 **39**

Adamson Cos., *See* Sprecker v. Adamson Cos.

Adamson, *See* City of Santa Barbara v. Adamson

Adams v. Herman (1951) 106 C.A.2d 92 **44**

Aerojet General Corp., *See* Mangini v. Aerojet General Corp.

Alamo School District v. Jones (1960) 182 C.A.2d 180 **226**

Aldridge, *See* No GWEN Alliance v. Aldridge

Alexander v. McKnight (1992) 7 C.A.4th 973 **78**

Allen, *See* Smith v. Allen

Ali v. City of Los Angeles (1999) 77 C.A.4th 246 **425–426**

Allred v. Harris (1993) 14 C.A.4th 1386 **19**

Allstate Ins. Co. v. County of Los Angeles and Security Nat'l Bank v. County of Los Angeles (1984) 161 C.A.3d 877 **223**

Alpha Property Management, *See* Amos v. Alpha Property Management

Altus Bank v. State Farm Fire and Gas Co. (1991) 758 F.Supp. 567 **323**

Alvarado, *See* Emeric v. Alvarado

American Mortgage Company, *See* Phelps v. American Mortgage Company

American Savings, *See* Gibbs v. American Savings

Amos v. Alpha Property Management (1999) 73 C.A.4th 895 **488**

Anderson v. Reynolds (1984) 588 F.Supp. 814 **287**

Andrade Development Co. V. Martin (1982) 188 C.A.3d 330 **273**

Andreson, *See* People ex rel Department of Water Resources v. Andreson

Annicelli v. Town of South Kingston, R.I. (1983) 463 A.2d 133 **422**

Anthony v. Enzler (1976) 61 C.A.3d 872 **190**

Appellate Dept., *See* Randone v. Appellate Dept.

Araj, *See* Asdourian v. Araj

Armenta v. Edmonds (1988) 201 C.A.3d 464 **122**

Armitage v. Decker (1990) 218 C.A.3d 887 **374**

Arrospide, *See* Carboni v. Arrospide

ARYA Group, Inc. v. Cher (2000) **77** C.A.4th 610 **153–154**

Asdourian v. Araj (1985) 38 C.3d 276 **357**

Assilzadeh v. California Federal Bank (2000) 82 C.A.4th 399 **79–80**

Associatead Homebuilders, Inc. v. Township of Mount Laurel (1975) 18 C.3d 582 **401**

Asuncion, *See* People v. Asuncion

AVCO Community Developers, Inc. v. South Coast Regional Commission (1976)17 C.3d 785 **418**

AVNER v. Longridge Estates (1982) 272 C.A.2d 607 **419**

Axley v. Transamerica Title Ins. Co. (1978) 88 C.A.3d 1 **451**

Ayres, *See* Fair Housing Council of Orange County, Inc., v. Ayres

B

B D Inns v. Pooley (1990) 218 C.A.3d 289 **149**

Baker v. Hubbard (1980) 101 C.A.3d 226 **335, 358, 366–367**

Baldwin Park Redev. Agency v. Irving (1984) 156 C.A.3d 428 **303**

Balistreri v. Nevada Livestock Prod. Credit Association (1989) 214 C.A.3d 635 **161**

Ballou v. Masters Props. No 6 (1987) 189 C.A.3d 65 **78**

Baltimore County, *See* Greater Baltimore Board of REALTORS® v. Baltimore County

Bank of America v. County of Los Angeles (1964) 224 C.A.2d 108 **238**

Bank of America v. Daily (1984) 152 C.A.3d 767 **328**

Bank of America, *See* Montgomery v. Bank of America

Bank of America, *See* Wellenkamp v. Bank of America

Bank of Stockton v. Church of Soldiers of the Cross of Christ (1996) 44 C.A.4th 1623 **5–6**

Banville v. Schmidt (1974) 37 C.A.3d 92 **45**

Barberi v. Rothchild (1939) 7 C.2d 537 **344**

Barela v. Superior Court (1981) 30 C.3d 244 **485**

Barham, *See* Beverly Way Associates v. Barham

Barnes v. Black (1999) 71 C.A.4th 1473 **470**

Barry, *See* Ingwersen v. Barry

Barry v. Raskov (1991) 232 C.A.3d 447 **53**

Bate v. Marsteler (1959) 175 C.A.2d 573 **44**

Bay Counties Title Guaranty Co., *See* Kish v. Bay Counties Title Guaranty Co.

Beach "N" Bay Realty, Inc, *See* Jorgensen v. Beach "N" Bay Realty, Inc.

Becker v. Lindsay (1976) 16 C.3d 188 **367**

Beckwith, *See* Otay Water District v. Beckwith

Bel Air Country Club, *See* McDonald Properties, Inc. v. Bel Air Country Club

SUBJECT INDEX
OF CASES

GENERAL INDEX